THE FORGOTT

A History of the Later Empero

(1707-185

THE FORGOTTEN MUGHALS

A History of the Later Emperors of the House of Babar
(1707-1857)

G. S. CHEEMA

MANOHAR
2017

First published 2002
First paperback edition 2005
Reprinted 2012, 2017

ISBN 81-7304-416-3 (Hb)
ISBN 81-7304-601-8 (Pb)

Published by
Ajay Kumar Jain *for*
Manohar Publishers & Distributors
4753/23 Ansari Road, Daryaganj
New Delhi 110 002

Printed at
Salasar Imaging Systems
New Delhi 110 033

To
PUSHP

Contents

Preface

History has been singularly unkind to the later Mughals. While every schoolboy is familiar with the names of the first six emperors of this illustrious house, few would be able to name more than one or two of the padishahs that followed the 'Ornament of the Throne, the World Conqueror', Aurangzeb Alamgir. For the average Indian, Jahandar, Rafi ud-Darjat, or Alamgir *Sani*, are mere names, and unfamiliar ones at that.

Even the school history books do not talk of them. Only Muhammad Shah, Shah Alam II, and Bahadur Shah II receive a passing mention; the first because Nadir Shah's incursion occurred during his reign, the second on account of the battle of Buxar and the treaty of Allahabad, and the last on account of the 'Great Mutiny', his verses, and simply by virtue of being the last of his house. The others are known only to numismatists.

But the period deserves deeper study. The great lessons of history are derived (if at all) from its darker periods. The 'golden age' of Akbar and Shah Jahan are of scant relevance to the fragmented politics and confusion of the present age. On the other hand it may be easier for us to empathise with the *wazirs* of the 'Great Anarchy' who had to contend with vicious court intrigues, recalcitrant and increasingly independent provincial governors, and a ruling class which had become utterly amoral, corrupt, and unscrupulous.

It makes for a gripping story and fascinating parallels can be drawn with the political scene of today. That is the principal justification for this book which has been written primarily with the general reader in mind.

I have relied mainly on secondary sources or records already well known to historians, and my debt to the early writers on the subject, particularly, William Irvine and Sir Jadunath Sarkar is immense. Almost as great is my debt to Syed Mir Ghulam Hussain Khan Tabatabai, and to his translator, M. Raymond, or Haji Mustapha. My thanks too to Low Price Publications, Delhi, who have made available so many old historical texts at reasonable prices. A large number of other books and records have also been consulted and I am grateful to the staff of the Panjab University, the Central State, and Dwarka Das libraries at Chandigarh, the Punjab State Archives library at Patiala, and the Khalsa College library at Amritsar, who made the material available to me.

My thanks too to my late mother (now lodged in Paradise) from whom I acquired my interest in history, to my wife for her patience and support during a difficult period. Bringing forth a book is a painful process and not conducive to good humour or amiability. My thanks too to Glenda Nunes, Satnam Singh and Jasbir who helped me out with the first typescripts, and to Sabino D'Souza and Constantino D'Abreu of the Christian Brothers, former principals of St. John's, my old *alma mater*, who allowed me to use the school computer and printer, at a time when these were not as commonplace as they have since become. My son, Prabhjot, too must not be forgotten as it was he who provided the technical support for my own computer, when I finally acquired one. Whenever it caught a virus, or otherwise crashed—as all computers do occasionally—it was he who debugged and nursed it back to health.

My thanks too, to Mr. Ramesh Jain, who notwithstanding the bulk of the work, and my inexperience as a writer, accepted this book for publication. The task of Mr. B.N. Varma and his team was probably the most laborious. Their editorial suggestions were invaluable and the final book is consequently a considerable improvement on the earlier drafts, besides being of more manageable length.

Last, but not least, I must also express my gratitude to the Punjab *sarkar*, whose salt I have been eating for close on three decades. This *fidwi* still depends on it for his subsistence, and he is grateful to his government's indulgence in not over-burdening him with official duties. But for its forbearance this book would have taken so much longer to complete.

G.S. CHEEMA

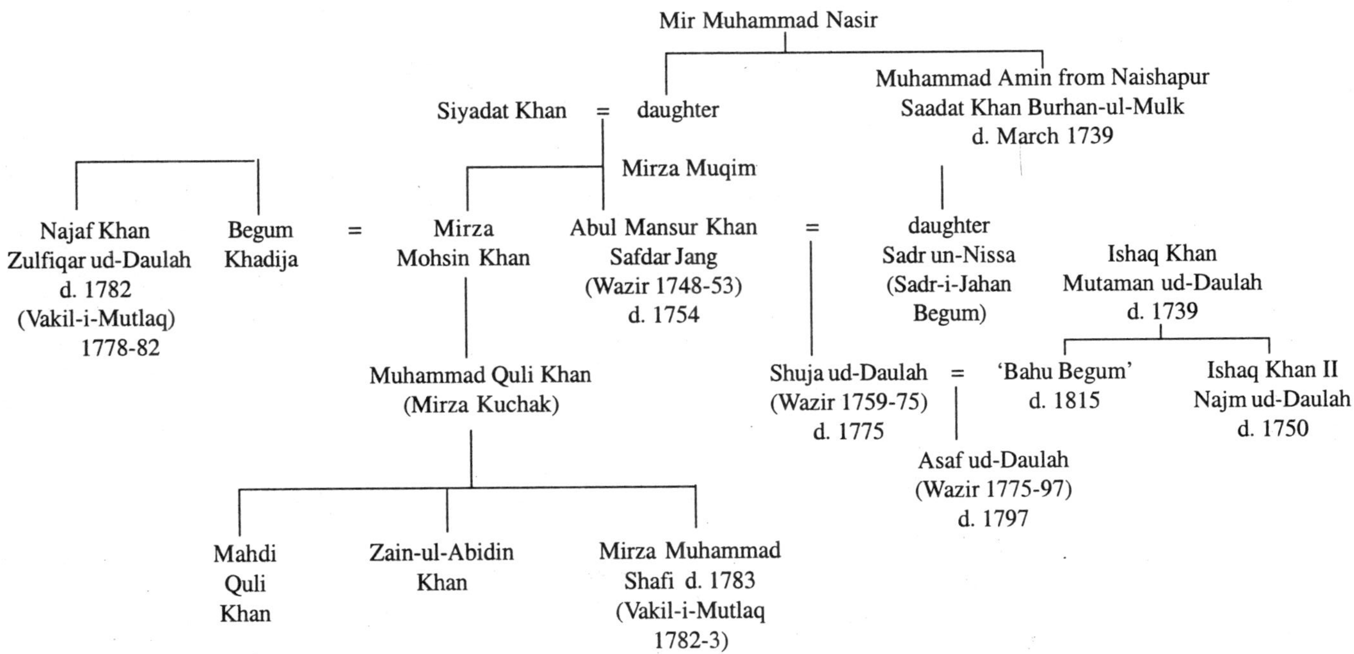

THE IRANI NOBLES

CHAPTER 1

The End of an Era

It was March 1707 and Aurangzeb Alamgir[1] lay dying in his camp at Ahmadnagar. He was now 88 and for the past two years his death had been more or less expected. Anxious and apprehensive, the court awaited the denouement. For 51 long years this old man had held together the Indian subcontinent with its teeming multitudes. He had ascended the Peacock Throne when the empire's wealth and prestige was at its zenith. But now the future seemed dark and uncertain.

He was dying, broken and disillusioned, a man who had lived too long, whom too many people wanted to see dead. The confident and self-righteous Aurangzeb of the early years was now a distant memory. His presence could still galvanize his troops and generals to win victories but they were barren, meaningless triumphs; the fort gained today would be lost on the morrow, as soon as the old emperor moved on to fresh 'victories'.

Inspite of the long hours spent in prayer and fasting he felt he had been abandoned by God. 'The Leader of this caravan has deserted me', he confided to his youngest son Kam Bakhsh.[2] He had come, 'a stranger to this world', and it was as a stranger that he was leaving, conscious of his insignificance, and weighed down by the burden of his sins. The terror of impending punishment cries out from his letters to his sons, Azam and Kam Bakhsh, written on his deathbed. 'Though I have a firm belief in the mercy and bounty of God, yet I cannot get rid of this fear', he confesses. His entire life, his tenancy of this earth, had been an utter waste. Though his destiny had raised him to the highest pinnacle of power, he had nothing to show for it. His time had been spent in vain and he had failed to even guard and protect the empire. He had ignored the dictates of his conscience, closed his eyes to its light, and now he felt overwhelmed by the sense of the transience of existence, the finality of the past and despair for the future. What was done, could not be undone.

There are few documents in Indian history as moving as these two letters, happily preserved for posterity. 'The foolish thoughts of women produce nothing but disappointment. Farewell, farewell, farewell.'

Thus ends his letter to Azam. The last lines of that addressed to the 'nearest to my heart' are even more pathetic. 'I am going,' he writes, 'Whatever good or evil I have done, it was for you. Take it not amiss, nor remember what offences I have done unto yourself, that account might not be asked of me hereafter. No one has seen the departure of his own soul, but I see that mine is going.'[3]

He had in some ways tried to be an exemplary monarch. Deeply conscious that his exalted office was a trust conferred by God, he had sought to live by the labour of his own two hands. His court was indeed as magnificent as that of his late father but he sought to meet his own personal expenses by the sale of caps, sewn by himself, and copies of the Holy Koran, beautifully self-transcribed.[4]

When he finally died, his personal treasury was found to contain Rs. 3.5 which were the proceeds from the sale of the caps, and another sum of Rs. 350 which were the earnings from the Korans. In accordance with his wish the expenses of the funeral were defrayed from the first sum while the rest of the money was spent on the ritual feeding of faqirs and mendicants.[5]

His uncovered grave is to be found in the courtyard of the tomb of the saint Zain ul-Haq near Aurangabad, at the place now named after him as Raoza Khuldabad.[6] He is the only one of the great Mughals who does not enjoy the luxury of a tomb or a garden all to himself.

There is something symbolic in the stark simplicity and poverty of the humble grave of the man who called himself the 'World Grasper' and who indeed pushed the frontiers of his empire to the limits of the peninsula. The age of grandeur passed with him. Most of his successors were condemned to the ignominy of anonymous and unmarked graves in the grim dark vaults of Humayun's mausoleum. The modern tourist today has no means of knowing which is whose. The poverty of his personal legacy seemed to symbolize the poverty of the empire he was leaving behind, in stark contrast to the opulence and splendour of the preceding reign.

Ravaged by decades of incessant warfare, large tracts of the Deccan had been reduced to waste. The depopulation was dreadful. Mannucci the Venetian traveller has painted a vivid, if perhaps slightly exaggerated, picture of the devastation wrought by the Deccan war.[7] The yearly cost is estimated to be at a hundred thousand human lives and about three hundred thousand animals—horses, mules, camels, draught cattle and elephants. Increasing difficulties were experienced in sustaining the troops and Aurangzeb's ambulant court, which, inspite of his personal austerity, he never once thought of cutting down. The hardships of the officers were aggravated by the fact that most of them depended on the receipts from their jagirs by way of pay, and because of the disturbed state of the country, these were often difficult to collect. In the interim they subsisted on loans drawn from their bankers whose agents moved with the army. The common soldiers and petty officers who had no jagirs to bank upon were at the mercy of usurers; their pay was in arrears by at least two years in 1707.

All over the country one came across widows and daughters of deceased soldiers and officers who eked out a miserable subsistence by begging. To make matters worse, there was no rain in the Deccan provinces from 1702 to 1704. Drought and famine added to the miseries of the population over two million people expired; parents were offering their children for sale for as little as a quarter or half a rupee and yet there was no one to buy them, even at that absurd 'price'.

The one besetting obsession of the aged emperor was succession. He had no doubt about what would happen after his death. Like Louis XV he observed, 'After me there will be chaos'. He had himself ascended the Peacock Throne after a civil war which had lasted nearly two years. The failure to establish any firm rule of succession was directly responsible for the exhausting series of armed struggles that the empire was now about to embark upon. This failure was not peculiar to the Indian branch of the Timurids; it was a failing common to all the Islamic world. The Ottomans were ultimately to find a solution but it was the result of a soul-destroying *tour de force*. Something like that was to be attempted by the Indian Mughals also but the effort was half-hearted and the conditions entirely different.

Given time, the Mughals might have evolved a more orderly mode of succession but at this period they seemed to be stumbling from one suicidal struggle to another. Their troubles appear to have commenced with the usurpation by Aurangzeb, and after his death the process seemed to have accelerated.

Aurangzeb has been painted worse than he actually was. The bloody nature of the civil war, the attractive, mystical nature of the heterodox but unfortunate Dara Shukoh, and the romance of the Taj, have all tempted historians to exaggerate the darker aspects of Aurangzeb who is depicted as the bigoted villain who destroyed the golden heritage of Akbar. His long heroic struggle to impose orderly central rule in the chaotic Deccan has been casually dismissed as ill-advised and the forces against which he had to contend have since been elevated to the rank of national heroes.

This tendency to denigrate 'the Ornament of the Throne' has also obscured in the popular mind the instances of fratricidal strife prior to Aurangzeb. Even in his case it is important to remember that the contest was not begun by him; Shuja and Murad had both preceded him in proclaiming their accession. He was only the most capable of them all. And it should be remembered, Shah Jahan died a natural death after a confinement of eight years. If he had wished, he could easily have had him killed, but the 'World Grasper' did not believe in unnecessary bloodshed.

Every Mughal padishah had problems with his brothers. Humayun who had three, had serious problems with two, Kamran and Askari. Askari was forced to go on a pilgrimage to Mecca, but died on the way. With Kamran, who had struck coins, proclaiming his sovereignty at Kabul, it was necessary to proceed to extremes. He was blinded, the eye being pierced repeatedly, with a lemon squeezed over it followed by sprinkling of salt. Thereafter, he was allowed to proceed on haj to Mecca, where he died some years later.

Akbar had no brothers but he had a cousin by the name of Abul Kasim, son of Kamran. The Mughal throne was not yet strong, the Afghan adherents of the late dynasty that had expelled his royal father, the unfortunate Humayun (so inaptly named)[10] had been barely put down. And he had just got rid of his over-bearing regent Bairam Khan. The young Akbar was not a man to take chances. Abul Kasim was imprisoned in Gwalior fort and put to death by his orders in 1565.

Jahangir had two siblings, but fortunately for him, they both drank themselves to death in their father's life-time. Jahangir himself had no mean capacity for hard liquor but his constitution was stronger. But inspite of the fact that he was the sole heir, he lived in the constant dread of being superseded by his own son, the young and talented Khusro, on whom the ageing emperor doted. Shortly after his accession, the son indeed rose against his father, but the rising was soon suppressed and the prince neutralized by blinding.[11]

Of all the Great Mughals it is the next emperor, Shah Jahan who is truly remarkable for his cruelty. His first victim was the unfortunate, almost sightless Khusro, whose custody was obtained by him from his father while the latter was in his cups. He was strangled to death on his orders, though the reason given for public consumption was colic.

After his father's death he had to contend with the intrigues of his stepmother, Nur Jahan, who had held the reins of power from behind the curtain during her husband's life and was determined to remain in control for as long as possible. In Shahryar, another of Shah Jahan's half-brothers, she thought she had found a suitable tool. Although the man was notorious as a playboy and riddled with syphilis she married him to her daughter Laadli Begum[12] and proclaimed him emperor.

But her own brother, the wazir, Asaf Khan deserted her. He also happened to be the father-in-law of Shah Jahan, so having sent an urgent message to his son-in-law, then in the Deccan, he placed another puppet on the throne, the young Dawar Bakhsh, son of the late unfortunate Khusro, to checkmate his sister. This was necessary because in the absence of any recognized principle which conferred the stamp of legitimacy on a particular heir it was impossible for Asaf Khan to keep the nobles and other officers of the state from rendering homage to Shahryar, however incompetent he might be.

Even before he had reached the capital Shah Jahan had issued secret orders to his father-in-law to clear the palace of all the male descendants of former emperors. Four were undoubtedly disposed of in this purge: Shahryar, Gurshasp (a younger brother of Dawar Bakhsh) and two sons of Daniyal—another of Akbar's sons. According to some accounts Dawar Bakhsh was also strangled along with these, while others say he was permitted to go into exile to Iran.

Thus five—perhaps six—possible claimants to the throne were murdered by Shah Jahan at the time of his accession. This is probably the worst of such massacres in Mughal history but the glory of the Taj has blotted out its memories from the public mind.

Shah Jahan seems to have been inspired by the traditions and practices prevalent at the court of Constantinople. The Ottomans had faced a similar problem but they had tackled it in their own peculiarly ruthless manner. Muhammad the Great, conqueror of Constantinople, had in the fifteenth century ordained that in order to ensure the 'peace of the world' his sons and grandsons who ascended the throne would have the right to execute their brothers. Fearful massacres took place. At the accession of one sultan as many as nineteen princes were executed—the usual mode was by strangulation with a silken bowstring. In the seventeenth century this barbaric custom had been replaced by the scarcely more humane institution of the *kafis* or cage.

From the seventeenth century onwards the princes would be kept confined in an isolated palace in the seraglio complex. Some of the princes entered this prison as children and left it only to answer a call to the throne—or to the grave.

Another Ottoman innovation was the substitution of wives by slave-concubines. This was intended to secure the dynasty from the destabilizing intrigues of women. For nearly two centuries none of the Ottoman padishahs had entered into a lawful marriage. All of them had been the sons of slave girls who, inspite of the honorific of 'sultan' suffixed to their names, enjoyed no legal rights. The rule was breached by Suleiman the Magnificent who was persuaded to perform the nikah by the beautiful Roxelana, a Russian slave girl with whom he was besotted. For the first time in many centuries, certainly the first time since the capture of Constantinople, a padishah of Rum honoured a woman by making her his lawfully wedded wife.

It was a strange world of the padishahs of Rum at the court of Kastantuniya.[13] In contrast, the Timurids of the house of Babar were almost normal. There were indeed enough slave-girls in the harem of the Grand Mughal, but the emperors were, for the most part, family men, and their brides were the daughters of their umara.[14] From Akbar onwards, the daughters of the native Indian princes whose ancestors had been reigning princes for centuries were also accepted as brides by the Mughals.

Shah Jahan had indeed ordered the removal by murder of all possible rivals to the throne but it never became a standard practise as was the case with the court of Stamboul. In the dark years that would follow the death of Aurangzeb, many gory scenes would be witnessed, but as many princes would 'drink the cup of martyrdom' on the field of battle, as perish by the dagger or the bowstring.

Something like the Ottoman *kafis* began with the reign of Jahandar Shah. Upto this time the shahzadas had lived in style, enjoying huge revenues and maintaining large retinues. Some of them had even lived outside the Qila-i-Mualla[15] in great mansions in the city like Prince Dara Shukoh and Jahan Ara Begum; and till the time of Aurangzeb they had been governors of the most important provinces. But after Jahandar Shah most of them lived lives of seclusion in the palace-fort and had few opportunities to gain experience in administration or military leadership.

The debilitating effect of this restricted life soon became apparent. Only Ali Gauhar the unfortunate Shah Alam II was to show some spirit, but by his time the rot had gone too far. The Persian and the Afghan shahs had by turns looted the imperial capital, leaving the treasury empty. The

Maratha light horse ranged over the entire country at will. The provincial governors were independent in all but name; the only time they referred to the faineant emperor in the Qila-i-Mualla was when they felt the need to regularize their accession to their provincial *masnads*[16] with the imperial letters-patent.

Even the offer of the once coveted office of prime minister could not tempt Shuja, the nawab-subedar of Awadh, to leave his provincial seat and take up residence at Delhi. For a while the situation of the country approached the absurd. The seat of the empire was without the sovereign or his wazir. The Amir-ul-Umara, himself an agent of the Afghan Shah, a foreign ruler, did his best to fill the vacuum. The emperor would eventually return after a twelve year exile but there would never again be a Wazir-ul-Mulk[17] at Delhi. The title became hereditary in the house of the nawabs of Awadh and the emperor's chancellors would henceforth be his nominal deputies bearing the title of Amir-ul-Umara[18] along with its attached office of paymaster general of the army, i.e. Bakhshi-ul-Mumalik, or first bakhshi, as there were several of them.

During this period of decay the descendants of former emperors, known as 'salatin'[19] were housed in a neglected portion of the palace-fort known as the salatin khana. Another similar complex was dedicated to the widows and concubines of deceased emperors and ironically called 'suhagpura'.[20]

While the immediate family of the monarch, his wives, sons and daughters lived in comfort and dignity and received a good education, living conditions for the salatin, their families and widows would deteriorate as the revenues dried up. Major George Cunningham described thus the *salatin's* quarter in an official report in 1820:

> The Salatin quarter consists of an immense high wall so that nothing can overlook it. Within this are numerous mat huts in which these wretched objects live. When the gates were opened there was a rush of miserable, half-naked, starved beings who surrounded us. Some men apparently eighty years old almost in a state of nature, who from the earliest infancy had been shut up, others young men, some sons of kings whose mothers had died or not been in favour . . . others young children who had the space within these walls to look forward to as their world. . . . The utmost allowed was a few blankets during the cold weather, distributed as if by the king, but in fact a private charity of Seton's.[21]

This was during the Golden Calm when the Pax Britannica had been established and the revenues of His Majesty were regular and assured. In the last decades of the previous century when Najaf Khan and the Marathas were the keepers of the emperor, conditions were much worse.

At times there was not enough money to keep the kitchen fires burning and even the shopkeepers of Delhi would refuse credit to the inmates of that special place in Hell, the Qila-i-Mualla or the Exalted Fort.

His women, his children the Salatin . . . are in want of Food and Clothing: it is needless after this to describe the situation of his Dependents and servants—the whole scene is absolutely a disgrace to humanity and such as has scarcely ever been exhibited even by deposed princes much less by the Monarch of a Great though broken state to which all the Component parts acknowledge Allegiance.[22]

Sic transit Gloria Mundi

NOTES

1. Aurangzeb signifies the 'Ornament of the Throne' and Alamgir, the 'World Grasper'.
2. Kam Bakhsh or the 'Gift of Desire'.
3. The quotations from the deathbed letters are from Scott's translation of the *Tarikh-i-Iradat Shahi* as contained in Elliot and Dowson's *The History of India as told by its own Historians*, vii, pp. 562-4.
4. A similar story is told of another and earlier sultan of Delhi, Nasiruddin Mahmud (1246-66) of the Slave dynasty.
5. Sarkar, *History of Aurangzeb*, v, pp. 266-7.
6. 'Raoza' means a shrine. 'Khuldabad' is after 'Khuld Makan', the posthumous title of Aurangzeb, meaning 'lodged in Paradise'. After their death the emperors were formally referred to by their posthumous titles, which while differing in form, all mean very much the same thing.
7. Manucci, *Storio do Mogor*, iv, pp. 96-7.
8. *Az ma hast fasad baqi*. Edwards and Garret, *Mughal Rule in India*, p. 155.
9. The khutba is the litany which follows the Friday prayers in which God's blessings are invoked for the ruler of a Muslim state.
10. Humayun: from Huma, a mythical bird of Persian legend. If the huma blesses a person by circling his head, that man shall be king. Humayun was indeed a king, but of all the Great Mughals, the most unfortunate.
11. It appears that his eyelids wee merely stitched to gether. Ultimately the stitches were cut, and he was never truly blinded, some vision survived.
12. Laadli means excessively loved, over-indulged, spoilt. The unfortunate girl was sacrificed to her mother's political ambition.
13. An Arabic rendition of Constantinople. 'Rum' or Rome was another name for it, for the Byzantines considered themselves to be Romans.
14. Umara: the plural of amir or nobleman. Since in elevated speech the plural form is preferred, the plural umara or 'omrah' was often used, even when the singular was intended. Hence in English we have 'omrahs'.
15. Qila-i-Mualla: The Exalted Fort, the term used for the Red Fort or Lal Qila when it was a royal residence. While on the march, the imperial camp was called the Urdu-i-Mualla.
16. Masnad: a throne in its simplest form, comprising a carpet with cushions and bolsters arranged on an elevated platform.

17. Prime Minister; commonly the plural form, Wazir-ul-Mamalik, was used.
18. The Lord of Lords. One of the premier nobles. This dignity was attached to the office of the first bakhshi (Mir Bakhshi or Bakhshi-ul-Mamalik), the Chief Paymaster of the Army. Sometimes translated as Commander-in-Chief.
19. Grammatically the plural of sultan. Ordinarily signifying monarch or ruler, it was the distinctive title used by the earlier Turkish and Pathan rulers of Delhi. Among the later Mughals it was commonly suffixed to the names of all princes (and princesses) of the blood, and applied collectively to all the descendants of former emperors.
20. *Suhag*: the state of being married. Suhagpura means the abode of the *suhagins* or the married women. In this case the ladies were of course widows, and the word was used in an ironic sense.
21. Seton: Resident at the court of Delhi. Later member of the Supreme Council of the government of India.
22. *Browne Correspondence*, letter no. 78, p. 160

CHAPTER 2

The Breakdown of Empire

Aurangzeb's last day on earth could not have been an ordinary one. Manucci records that a sudden whirlwind blew down all the tents in the imperial camp and a number of people and animals were killed, choked by the dust. Trees were uprooted and whole villages destroyed. The dust obscured the sun and day was transformed into night.[1]

Even allowing for Italian exaggeration it was unusual weather for the month of March in the Deccan where one seldom has duststorms even at the height of summer. More marvels are narrated by the unknown author of the fragment going by the name of the *Tarikh-i-Bahadur Shahi*:

> On the third day after it became known in Delhi, after sunset and before the cry to evening prayer, such a noise arose on the west as may be taken as a sample of the noise there will be at the day of judgement. If hundreds of thousands of men were to collect together and simultaneously raise the most dreadful shouts, there would be no resemblance to that noise. It exceeds all my powers to describe it. Forty years have passed up to this time, but that strange noise is still in my ears and whoever heard it must certainly remember it. The noise lasted for about half an hour, and then subsiding, nothing was heard of it after the lapse of two hours.[2]

Whatever be the explanation for the unearthly din it was natural for people to expect and look for apocalyptic signs for the passing of the aged autocrat seemed to mark the end of an age. But the peaceful manner of his death was by itself remarkable. Obsessed as he was with religion he had often expressed the desire to die on a Friday and the wish was granted, sinner though he may have been. After his morning ablutions and prayers he settled down on his bed, rosary in hand. He kept repeating the *kalima* compulsively while his fingers turned the beads. After some time the murmuring faded and the clicking of the beads ceased. When the attendants who were sitting behind the screens came forward they saw that his hand had dropped and the old emperor was no more.

It was twenty-six years since he had left his capital and plunged into a seemingly endless war. Bijapur and Golconda had been conquered and annexed. Theoretically the whole peninsula, down to the tip of Kanyakumari acknowledge the Mughal as the padishah. The whole subcontinent was divided into subas and sarkars with appointed subedars and faujdars. But the reality was different. Even before Bijapur fell the Maratha power had been spreading its wings. This hardy race had been one of the main props of the fallen states of Ahmadnagar and Bijapur, supplying soldiers for their armies and filling the lower ranks of the civil and revenue administration. Attempts had been made in the past to draw them into the Mughal system. Shahaji Bhonsle, father of the great Shivaji, in the time of Shah Jahan had, on the occasion of his defection from the Ahmadnagar service, been granted a mansab[3] in the Mughal peerage with the rank of 6,000 *zat* and 5,000 *sowar*. After some time he returned to the old allegiance but he remained in touch with the Mughals and it was on their advice that he transferred his allegiance to the Adilshahis of Bijapur when Ahmadnagar was finally annexed to the empire.

On the persuasion of his officers Aurangzeb in turn made an attempt to coopt Shivaji into the Mughal system. Mirza Raja Jai Singh, zamindar[4] of Amber and the greatest of the Rajput chiefs of Rajasthan, was sent to the Deccan command with the express purpose of winning over the Maratha chief. He was able to persuade him to accept the idea of imperial service and the Maratha left for Agra to present himself at court. But the attempt failed; Aurangzeb was determined to put this 'mountain rat', as he described him, in place. The proffered rank, that of 5,000 was too low for Shivaji. His father had been given a comparable mansab in the previous reign, his own son, still a mere child had been given this rank while still in the Deccan, another of his dependents had also been given the same mansab. *Panj hazaaris* seemed aplenty at the Mughal court. What made it worse, Raja Jai Singh had held out hopes of his being made a *haft hazaari*, i.e. a nobleman with a rank of 7,000. Shivaji left protesting loudly, without waiting for the presentation of the robes of honour and the elephant which had been prepared for him.[5]

Slipping away to the Deccan he returned to his old predatory life, seizing hill forts, plundering the rich cities of the Konkan, Khandesh and Bijapur, while the Mughals still persisted in their struggles with the Deccan sultans.

In 1680 he died. He appears to have effected a reconciliation with the emperor at some stage, who bestowed on him the title of Raja and confirmed the mansab given to his son. But these were little more than tactical moves. The Deccan states were on the verge of collapse and everywhere local chiefs and predatory bandits were endeavouring to carve out individual areas of control. If the two citadels resisted so long against the Mughals, it was on account of the strength of their walls, the distance of the Mughal armies from their base, and their distraction by Marathas and other bandits who were always on the look out for easy pickings by preying on their baggage and supply trains.

Bijapur fell in 1685, and Golconda, which had become synonymous with vice and corruption, two years later. The final dissolution of these states only added to the prevailing chaos in the Deccan. Innumerable ruffians who had hitherto been honestly employed in the armies of these states were now let loose.

Shambhaji, proved an unworthy successor to his illustrious father to whose chivalry even the Mughal historians paid tribute. The son was a lecherous drunkard, and had been placed under restraint in his father's lifetime for attempting to violate the honour of the wife of one of his father's Brahmin officers. Totally dominated by a Brahmin known as Kavi Kulesh, his guide and mentor in vice and debauchery, he was detested and hated by all. In 1689 he was captured, almost by chance, in the company of his evil counsellor, in the midst of a drinking bout.

But even this debauched scoundrel met his end with courage and fortitude. He was produced before Aurangzeb in ridiculous clothes, with a dunce's cap on his head. The old emperor asked him if he was willing to embrace Islam. He replied saucily in the affirmative, adding the proviso that the emperor must, in that case, give him his daughter as bride. This was a stinging insult in a land where even to enquire after the health of a man's female relatives was considered unmannerly. Enraged, the emperor ordered his tongue to be torn out. Then his limbs were chopped off, one by one, joint by joint, to prolong the agony. Kavi Kulesh died a similar death. Finally their heads were cut off, and after being stuffed, displayed in all the principal towns, where hordes turned out to see them.[6]

As in the case of Shivaji, Shambhaji's death made no difference to the prevailing strife. The Maratha state was well-established and personalities no longer mattered. After Shambhaji his son Shahu, then a child of six, was proclaimed ruler, and a regency established under his uncle Raja Ram. Then shortly afterwards Shahu himself was taken. After Raja Ram's death, his son was raised to the *gaddi*[7] of the Marathas with his mother as regent.

The great umara and mansabdars were all completely fed up. Most of them had not seen their homes and families for years. Even the members of the emperor's family, his sister and his wives, longed to return to a settled life in the palace at Delhi.

Inspite of the luxuries of the Urdu-i-Mualla life in the ambulant court could not have been very comfortable. Although they were by no means constantly on the move and often remained on the same site for months, conditions would soon become insanitary. The camp with all its hangers-on and bazaars was like a city of canvas, housing more than a hundred thousand souls. Careri, the Italian doctor who called on the emperor in his Deccan camp, has written that it was 30 miles in circuit with 250 bazaars![8] The imperial compound, marked by wooden palings painted red and known as the gulal bar was 3 miles in circumference while the innermost circle of cavas screens or *qanats* is given as 2,000 yards. Another source estimates the circuit of the gulal bar at a mile and quarter, and the number of tents in the imperial enclosure at 120—some so large they could contain several thousand people. There were two sets of all the tents, so that one could be sent ahead to be pitched in advance. Thus the imperial progress, even on campaign, was slow and stately. Inspite of the personal austerity of the emperor it never occurred to him to cut down the expenses by maintaining a smaller and less ostentatious equipage.

The constant movement of armies left the countryside denuded and desolate. For miles around the camp, the country had become a desert, with trees and shrubs cut down for firewood and fodder. The campsites themselves would, in a short time, become infested with flies and the unmistakable stink of urine and ordure hung thick.

After the successful conclusion of the siege of Wakinkhera which was held by a free-booter by the name of Pema Naik the emperor yielded to the importunities of his family and decided to return to the northern capital. Ahmadnagar was intended to be just a stage in the march but here his fever returned and his stay was extended. He had been on the decline for some time and soon it became evident that this was going to be his last camp.

His principal anxiety was how to avert the outbreak of a murderous civil war among his sons, like the one which had broken out on his father's illness and had brought him to the throne. He was particularly anxious on account of his youngest and favourite, Kam Bakhsh.

His eldest, Muazzam who enjoyed the regal title of Shah Alam was governor of distant Kabul, while the second, Muhammad Azam, whom we shall call by his later title of Azam Shah, was governor at Ahmedabad in the nearby province of Gujarat. Azam was ambitious and it was evident that the contest for the throne would ultimately be between these two brothers, even though Shah Alam had let it be known that he had no ambitions, and that if his brother should stake a claim he would retire to Iran, where another brother Akbar had fled after the failure of his rebellion in 1681. The shadow of suspicion had also fallen on Shah Alam. During the war with Golconda he had been arrested on suspicion of treason, stripped of his rank and kept under restraint for seven years. During this period he had learnt to keep his discretion and could dissimulate so well that he was widely believed to be a coward, and Azam was wont to dismiss him as a miser, a cattle-trader or a baniya, even though his greatest fault was excessive liberality.

Notwithstanding the well-known quotation from Hafiz about ten dervishes being able to share a blanket while a kingdom was too small to contain more than one ruler, Aurangzeb left behind a will, dividing the empire into three parts. The lion's share including the city of Delhi was to go to the eldest Muazzam who would remain titular emperor of Hind, while to Azam's share fell six provinces, including Agra, the second city of the empire, and the old capital. Kam Bakhsh, the youngest, was assigned two provinces in the Deccan, Bijapur and Hyderabad. He hoped that his brothers would allow him to reign in quiet obscurity in his Deccan appanage.

But Aurangzeb was not so naive as to expect that his will would be accepted as a matter of course. Muazzam was already far away in Kabul. Azam, on learning of his father's illness, had come down from Ahmedabad, inspite of Aurangzeb's plaintive protest that his coming at this time reminded him of his own advance to Agra at the time of Shah Jahan's illness. The prince had, with a grotesque sense of humour, used the very words which Aurangzeb had then employed.

He was most anxious on account of the youngest since he and Azam did not get along. On 16 February, Kam Bakhsh was given leave to depart for his suba of Bijapur. Placed in charge of a faithful and courageous soldier, Mir Mallang who was now given the title of Hasan Khan and appointed as his bakhshi, the young prince set out for Bijapur with all the signs and honours of sovereignty and the drums of the imperial naubat khana[9] were ordered to play as he left. The sight of all this, writes Khafi Khan, made Azam 'writhe like a poisonous serpent' with barely suppressed fury.

But during his stay in the royal camp Azam had persuaded the emperor to recall Muhammad Azim, the son of Muazzam, from his government at Patna. Azim, Muazzam's most capable son had for many years been subedar of Bengal with his seat at Patna. It was part of Aurangzeb's policy to keep his sons in check by appointing his grandsons to important positions. Thus, one son of Muazzam Muiz ud-Din was appointed as governor of Multan and Sind, while another, Azim, was subedar of Bengal. While at Patna, Azim was reported to have stashed away a large fortune, and in any contest for the throne Azim's huge treasure hoards, besides the vast resources of Bengal—the richest province of the empire—could prove decisive. Thus by recalling Muhammad Azim from Patna Azam hoped thereby to strengthen his position and weaken Muazzam.

Azim was posted to Ahmedabad, Gujarat, and Azam was designated as the subedar of Malwa with his seat at Ujjain. On receiving his orders Azim set off obediently for Ahmadnagar en route to his new charge, as his instructions were to first report at the Exalted Camp. Ironically this move, though calculated by Azam to increase his own strength and weaken his rival, was the single most important factor contributing to his ruin.

NOTES

1. Manucci, *Storio do Mogor*, iv, p. 398.
2. Elliot and Dowson, *The History of India as told by its own Historians*, vii, p. 565.
3. In brief, mansab signifies rank, expressed in terms of numbers of horse (cavalry) the officer (i.e. nobleman) was at least notionally expected to maintain. The ranks started from 100 and went up to 7,000 or 8,000, ranks above that being reserved for members of the ruling house or their close relatives. Ranks were, firstly, *zat* or personal, but often the officer had an additional *sowar* rank, which could be lower or higher than the *zat* rank. The *sowar* rank could also be *duaspa* or *seh-aspa*, signifying a rider with two horses and three horses respectively. But it does not necessarily follow that every umara was actually required to maintain that many cavalry. The basic salary depended on the *zat* rank, while the *sowar* rank appears to have signified additional allowances. For a fuller discussion on the subject, the reader is referred to Ishtiaq Husain Qureshi's *The Administration of the Mughal Empire*.
4. Zamindar, or landowner. The Mughal Emperors refused to recognise the Rajput princes as independent or autonomous rulers. They were regarded as mere landowners; the subedar of Ajmer was the governor of Rajasthan, with subordinate faujdars under him, as in any other province or *suba*.
5. Khafi Khan, *Muntakhab ul-Lubab*; Elliot and Dowson, vii, p. 276.
6. Ibid., Elliot and Dowson, vii, p. 341. Shah Nawaz Khan, *Maathir ul-Umara*, ii, 1, p. 295.
7. Gaddi, i.e. cushion. The word has the same significance as masnad, and being a pure Indian word was used in British times exclusively for Hindu states.
8. Surendra Nath Sen, *Indian Travels of Thevenot and Careri*, p. 217.
9. The naubat khana or naggar khana was the musical gallery where the imperial band played. They played at fixed times during the day and announced the entry and departure of the emperor. This band, of which the naggaras or the great kettledrums were the most striking feature, was an imperial prerogative. Senior umara were also allowed the privelege, but in the capital and in the Urdu-i-Mualla only the emperor's band could play.

CHAPTER 3

The War of Succession

Six days after the departure of Kam Bakhsh, Azam was granted leave to proceed to his new charge at Malwa. After his departure the emperor's health deteriorated rapidly. Azam had arranged to be kept informed of his father's condition. So expecting that the end was near he made no attempt to hurry. When on 3 March the emperor finally breathed his last, Azam was only about 40 miles away.

Azam enjoyed the support of the wazir, Asad Khan, as well as that of Zinat un-Nissa, his real sister—the emperor's only surviving daughter—both of them being the offspring of Dilras Banu Begum, the daughter of Shah Nawaz Khan, a wazir of Shah Jahan. Muazzam's mother on the other hand was Nawab Bai, the daughter of Raja Raju of Rajauri, a chieftain from the Jammu hills. Kam Bakhsh's mother was however of humble origin. Although she bore the decidedly Indian name of Udaipuri Bai she has been described variously as a Kashmiri, a Circassian, and a Georgian. At one time she had been a dancing girl and it was as such that she came to the harem of Dara Shukoh. After the latter's defeat and execution she entered the zenana of Aurangzeb. She was his only surviving consort but she too died a few months later at Gwalior shortly after the battle of Jajau.

Azam arrived at Ahmadnagar late the following night. His father's body had already been prepared for burial and the subsequent morning it was taken to the shrine of Sheikh Zain ul-Haq for burial. It is said that Azam showed considerable emotion and carried the bier part of the way.

After a few days of mourning a brief enthronement ceremony was held in which Azam was proclaimed the sovereign and Asad Khan confirmed as wazir. Other offices and titles were also distributed. Asad Khan had maintained order following the death of the old emperor, hence there was none of the confusion and looting which usually marked an interregnum, and all the treasures passed into the hands of Azam Shah.

Bidar Bakht was still at Ahmedabad when he got the news of his grand-father's demise. Immediately grasping that the key to success was the possession of the palace-fort at Agra, which contained the hoarded treasures of previous reigns, he proposed to his father that he should head for that city by rapid marches to forestall Muazzam. The road was clear, there were no obstacles, and to facilitate matters, the governor of the suba of Agra, Mukhtar Khan, was his father-in-law. In anticipation of his father's assent he commenced recruitment.

At first Azam assented but old suspicions rekindled by jealousy led him to revoke his orders. Fresh directives were issued asking him to discharge the soldiers he had already raised, to march upto Ujjain and there await his arrival with the main army. Full of dark premonitions, Bidar complied.

His younger brother Wala Jah had questioned whether it was wise to permit Bidar to go ahead and take possession of Agra before him. What was there to prevent Bidar from proclaiming himself emperor with the support of his father-in-law Mukhtar Khan? And with the hoarded millions of the Agra treasure at his disposal, his position would be unassailable.

The logic was irrefutable and to make matters worse, relations between Azam and Bidar had not always been cordial. As in the case of Muazzam, Aurangzeb had used Bidar as a foil to neutralize Azam. And from Iradat Khan, who served on the personal staff of this prince, we know that Azam's fears were not unfounded and Bidar contemplated rebellion several times against his father's authority during this campaign. Iradat Khan was a close confidant of the prince and he has recorded his conversations on the subject in his history.[1]

It is, therefore, not surprising that Azam was more apprehensive on his son's account than on his brother's. The greater danger lay within. As for the miserly 'bania',[2] Muazzam, defeating him would be a cakewalk. When Zulfiqar Khan, son of the wazir, and experienced general and commander of the artillery, suggested that it would be better if Azam left his family and dependents behind in a strong fort, the latter laughed scornfully. Nor did he make any worthwhile efforts to conciliate the old officers of Aurangzeb. When Zulfiqar again suggested that they take the slightly longer route via the Dewal Ghat so that they could take Ghazi ud-Din Khan with them, he declared rudely that there was no need to deviate from the direct road to seek the help of a blind man.[3] Ghazi ud-Din Khan, who is also known by his later title of Firoz Jang, was indeed blind—and had been so for twenty years—but he was one of the late emperor's most trusted officers and enjoyed great respect among the nobles, particularly the Mughal or Turanian umara.

This contemptuous dismissal of the worth of a loyal and worthy officer of the dynasty sent ripples down the ranks of the army and the nobles. His son Chin Qilich Khan who had been recently appointed to the government of Khandesh begged to be excused from the expedition on the pretext of setting his new suba in order. His cousin Muhammad Amin Khan accompanied the prince in the march to the north, but he showed little enthusiasm and it was brought to the notice of the prince that during the passage of the Tumri defile near Nimawar his men had looted the stragglers. But apart from an angry outburst no attempt was made to chastise the culprits. He was in charge of the rearguard and so it was easy for him to withdraw and the next day he made off with his troops towards Burhanpur, looting the imperial supply train as he left.

Even Asad Khan the wazir-designate and Zulfiqar had expressed their desire to be left behind in the Deccan, but their absence would have robbed the expedition of credibility, and Azam insisted on their attendance with their full complement of troops. Asad Khan was now an old man and had come to regard himself as indispensable. Zulfiqar was extremely ambitious and had shown remarkable dash and courage in the Deccan wars, but throughout this expedition his advice was on the side of caution and he has been accused of treachery and cowardice.

And so the army plodded on northwards, encumbered with all the impedimenta of an imperial Mughal army on the march, complete with the curtained elephants and purdah carts of the harem ladies, the huge and luxurious tents, with their thousands of servants, slavegirls, merchants, bankers, agents artisans and prostitutes that were normal to every imperial excursion, be it a campaign in the Deccan or Rajputana, or a leisurely progress to the pleasure resort of Kashmir. The restless Bidar who was leading the van had to repeatedly stop to enable the rest of the army to catch up.

Muazzam's progress, on the other hand, was much more business-like. Munim Khan, the diwan of the Lahore suba, was an old adherent and he had made preparations for this contingency. The crossing of the mighty Indus and the five rivers of the Punjab could have presented formidable problems but Munim had collected boats at every ford[4] that lay on the route. Thus it was not surprising that the race to Agra was won by him. However at the time his chances were not rated very highly. At sixty-three he was ten years older than Azam who, however, gave a false impression of greater activity.

Another chance incident worked in his favour. His second son Muhammad Azim (later to be known as Azim ush-Shan) subedar of Bengal, the richest province of India, had been recalled by Aurangzeb shortly before his death. His recall and posting to Gujarat had been the result of the machinations of Azam who feared that the control of the resources of Bengal and Bihar would give Muazzam an added advantage in the impending struggle.

The time had not yet come when the orders of a Mughal padishah—be he on his deathbed—could be ignored. Obediently, Azim ush-Shan set off for Ahmadnagar, bringing with him the Bengal tribute which amounted to the sizeable sum of Rs. 17 crore.

He was near Allahabad when he received the news of his grandfather's death. Concluding that it was pointless to head towards the imperial camp, now in the possession of his father's arch rival, he decided that the best course would be to go straight to Agra where he knew his father would also be heading. Like Bidar Bakht he had immediately realized the strategic advantage which the possession of Agra would give him. He paused at Allahabad just long enough to recruit more soldiers. With the Bengal treasure at his disposal and his own personal hoard this was simple.

When Azam reached Gwalior he was informed that Muhammad Azim had already reached Agra. The Governor Mukhtar Khan was surprised and the city easily occupied, but the fort under the command of Baqi Khan qiladar held out. The commandant pointed out that the prince himself was not a claimant to the throne, as for himself he was neutral in the struggle, but he would surrender the fort to whichever of the two shahzadas that arrived first.[5] He himself was a humble servitor of the throne and would not differentiate between Azam and Muazzam. Both were princes of the blood and infinitely superior to him in rank, and equally qualified to become emperor.

Satisfied with his answer, Azim settled down to await his father's arrival but not before taking the precaution of sending soldiers to guard the fords on the Chambal river which lay between Gwalior and Agra. As it happened, Bidar Bakht was able to find an unguarded ford and, despite the opposition of Zulfiqar, managed to cross over. He would have continued on to Agra and challenged Azim but a message was now received from his father ordering him to halt at Dholpur and await his arrival. Frustrated again, the prince was obliged to obey. The advantage of the surprise crossing was thus lost.

Meantime Muazzam had arrived at Agra, and negotiations were opened afresh with Baqi Khan. True to his word the commandant surrendered the fort to him. That very day Azam entered Gwalior. To his dismay the governor was not there to receive him. Having heard of Muazzam's near approach he had left for Agra to pay his respects. Azam's star was on the decline and the imperial bureaucrats were rushing to align themselves with the rising star. Ironically, one of Azam's nicknames was Azam Tara, meaning 'super-star'.

With the fall of Agra and its fort the scales were tilting in favour of Muazzam. The Bengal tribute brought by Azim was a sizeable accretion, besides, Muazzam had himself brought a substantial amount from Kabul and Lahore, and the subedar of the Delhi suba had placed whatever money that was lying in the Delhi treasury at his disposal. But now with Baqi Khan's adhesion, the great treasure of Agra, which has been variously estimated at between Rs. 13 and 24 crore, was in his possession. About Rs. 4 crore were drawn and distributed among the generals so that they could distribute it among their soldiers to encourage them on the eve of battle.

Even at this late stage Muazzam made an offer to Azam. He stood by his father's will, he said, and was willing to increase Azam's portion from four to six provinces, if that would satisfy him. If, inspite of this offer, Azam was still determined on war he suggested that the two should meet and decide the issue by single combat.

Azam laughed scornfully at his brother's offer which was conveyed to him through Mir Karim, a revered and respected faqir. The offer, he declared, was such as only a bania could make; only he could think that the sovereignty of an empire could be decided by trading subas. His elder brother had forgotten his Saadi; even a schoolboy knew that two kings could not coexist in one kingdom. And he quoted to the effect that his share was from the floor to the roof , while to Muazzam he conceded the rest, from the roof up to the firmament.[6] As for the offer of single combat, after the manner of the heroes of ancient Iran, he did not touch upon it, though considering their age difference Muazzam would have been at a decided disadvantage.

So war it was going to be, and Azam had decided that the field of choice should be Samugarh, a field judged to be auspicious as it was here that Aurangzeb had routed Dara Shukoh. Aurangzeb too, like Azam, had come up from the Deccan, determined to seize the sovereignty of Hind.

Khafi Khan, the author of the *Muntakhab ul-Lubab*, says that Azam attacked boldly without heeding the superior force of his brother, or deciding upon any clear plan of battle. He went boldly forth, 'as a fierce lion falls on a flock of sheep'. But such impetuous and improvised attacks could have only one outcome. The first clash took place quite by accident as Azam's army was lumbering towards Samugarh, near the village of

Jajau. They were fated never to reach the auspicious field they were seeking.

Neither army was quite sure of the movements of the other and Muazzam had ordered his advance tents to be pitched in a grove 4 miles to the north of Jajau. Rustam Dil Khan, Mir Tuzak, who was in charge of the imperial camp and equipage was overseeing their erection when Azam's vanguard, commanded by Bidar Bakht, stumbled upon them.

The tents were set on fire and Rustam Dil Khan's small force scattered while the Mir Tuzak himself surrendered and was permitted to ride in the train of Azam. But Muazzam's van commanded by Azim was close at hand and while Bidar Bakht's band struck up the drums in honour of the supposed victory, it closed to engage them. For a time confusion reigned and the Jat auxiliaries of Muazzam started plundering what was left of the camp. Azim found himself hardpressed.

Both sides called for reinforcements. Neither was prepared for battle. Muazzam was engaged in shikar near Jajau sarai and had planned to give battle two days later. Zulfiqar, who was with Bidar Bakht, was not in favour of an immediate contest. The troops, he reasoned, were tired, scattered and disorganized. It was the middle of June, the hottest time of the year, and they were suffering from heat and thirst. He opined that they should camp where they were and dig in, instead of grappling immediately with the main body of Muazzam's force. The disheartened soldiers of Muazzam, he pointed out, would desert in large numbers under cover of darkness, and many of the officers could also be counted upon to defect. The umara rarely had any personal commitment to any particular prince. Anxious to secure their future in the new reign they would rally under the banners of whichever seemed the more likely to win. And with the first clash having gone in his favour, the advantage lay definitely with Azam.

But Bidar, thrilled by his first success, denounced his advice as the 'counsel of women' and declared that it stank of cowardice. But it was already too late. Stung by the insult to the *pesh-khaima* of the prince, Azim Khan's main body was moving up. Iradat Khan tried to explain to the excited prince that ther was no occasion for beating the victory drums, that the riderless elephant that his flunkies had sighted fleeing towards Agra could not possibly have been Muazzam's but was most probably that of Rustam Dil Khan:

> Accidents will happen to the baggage of armies and this boasted victory is no more than that. Your troops have looted his advance tents, but they had better

look out now! If they should be attacked now they will be useless, confused as they are, and encumbered with spoil.

The prince declared angrily that he had always been a pessimist, and as he stubbornly refused to convey the news of his ridiculous victory of Azam he ordered another officer, Asim, to do so.

Within an hour, records Iradat Khan, a great dust cloud could be seen. 'There you see the consequences of our victory,' he addressed the prince, 'and of the flight of Shah Alam! The cloud signifies probably not less than 50,000 horse.' And soon behind that cloud another dusty mass could be seen. Then on the orders of the prince he set off to inform Azam Shah while the prince prepared himself for the real battle.

Iradat Khan found Azam seated on an open palki, the type called a *takht-i-rawan*. Alighting from his horse he addressed him: 'The Prince informs Your Majesty of the enemy's near approach. What orders shall I convey?' Azam, starting as if stung by a scorpion, with furious looks, eyes rolling, and as was his custom when angry, pulling up his sleeve, exclaimed, 'Comes an enemy towards me?' 'So it appears,' replied the patient but disapproving Iradat Khan.

Azam stood up in his *takht-i-rawan*, called aloud for his war elephant, whirling a crooked staff in his hand. Then in a contemptuous and taunting tone he spoke to Iradat, 'Be not alarmed, I coming to my son.'

Hurt at these taunting words, Iradat replied: 'His Highness is son to yourself, Asylum of the World, and knows not fear. He only informs of the enemy's approach, that your Majesty may advance with the troops and take the post ususal for the Emperor on the day of battle.'

Having made this little speech he rode off to join his embattled prince. Because of his suspicions with respect to his energetic and popular son, Azam lost no opportunity to run down Bidar Bakht in public and cast aspersions on his valour and ability. And his fears, as we have already observed were not unfounded.

The prince had discussed with Iradat Khan how the imminent battle could provide several opportunities for dispatching his unnatural father to the nether world. Happily for the reputation of the prince the situation did not materialize. Father and son were alike fated to drink 'the cup of martyrdum' on the field of Jajau.

The sun was high and the troops suffered severely from thirst. There were the usual displays of valour and cowardice, and rank opportunism. Khan-i-Alam Dakhini, one of Azam Shah's leading officers, was killed early leading a cavalry charge against Azim. Ram Singh Hara of Bundi and Rao Dalpat Bundela of Datia-Orchha, two Rajput chiefs serving under Zulfiqar, were other notable casualties. The first was killed by a cannon ball and the latter by a swivel shot. In his contempt for the 'bania', Azam had not bothered to bring up his artillery while Muazzam was well supplied with cannon, swivels and rockets, and soon the effects of this weakness began to tell.

The Rajputs, disheartened by the deaths of their chiefs withdrew, taking with them their chiefs' bodies. Zulfiqar was also slightly wounded, hit, it was said, by a blunt arrow which broke a tooth. He advised Azam that he should withdraw with what remained of his army, as the day was well nigh lost, and try his fortune another time. Stung to fury the prince lashed out at his general: 'Go with your bravery and save your life wherever you can! It is impossible for me to leave this field. For princes there can only be the throne or the scaffold; there is no third choice.'[7]

The 'brave' Zulfiqar then withdrew to the rear, changed his war elephant for a swifter horse, and rode off, not stopping, it is said, till he reached Gwalior. His flight was the signal for other wavering spirits to pull out or switch sides. Raja Jai Singh of Amber was the most distinguished among them. When the battle was at its fiercest, throwing his shawl over his head, he made his way to Muhammad Azim who conducted him to Muazzam where he was received coolly.

Meantime a dust storm began and added to the confusion. In the usual hyperbolic style the historian records that the wind was so strong that the very arrows shot by Azam's soldiers were deflected and rendered ineffective. Many distinguished officers had been killed. Bidar Bakht had been hit several times and his young son, Bidar Dil, who was seated behind him in the howdah received a flesh wound. He had just been handed over to a eunuch to be carried to the relative safety of the women's elephants when a musket ball killed the father.

Wala Jah, the younger brother, was also out on the field. It was his first experience of battle but he fought stoutly, wounded several times, until he fainted from loss of blood. Then his mahout withdrew towards the spot from where Azam Shah was directing the battle.

By this time there were only a few hundred horsemen left around Azam. The wind had died down and the day was drowning in a crimson sunset. But with the sinking sun, Azam's life was also drawing to an end. Wounded repeatedly and surrounded by a sea of hostile troops with only his faithful band around him he exclaimed despairingly: 'It is not Shah Alam who fights against me; God himself has abandoned me and fortune has turned against me!'[8]

He had a young son Ali Tabar with him in his howdah whom he tried to shield from the balls and arrows. That brave young prince, records Khafi Khan, desired to show the valour of his race, but his father forbade him and tried still more to protect him. Two mahouts fell wounded from the elephant, and the animal itself, severely injured, became uncontrollable. Death seemed imminent and Azam felt that his foot was in the stirrup for his last journey, but he climbed out of the howdah onto the neck of the animal in an effort to control it. It was then that a musket ball struck him in the forehead and put an end to his struggles.

Night was falling fast and the army breaking up, the vanquished soldiers fleeing south towards Gwalior. Many would be slaughtered and robbed on the way by the Jat peasantry. When word was brought to Muazzam about the death of his rival, men were dispatched to bring in the bodies. But the remnant of Azam's bodyguard continued to resist, barring the way to the royal elephant. Finally when night fell, Rustam Dil Khan, Muazzam's Mir Tuzak, who had submitted to Azam earlier in the day, saw an opportunity for performing what he thought would be appreciated as a signal service for Muazzam. He fought his way towards Azam's elephant, climbed up to the howdah and cut off his head, and then made his way towards Muazzam's tent.

It must have been a sombre spectacle, Rustam Dil Khan bearing his grisly trophy, followed first by Azam's elephant with the headless trunk of the dead prince in the howdah and behind him another elephant bearing the corpse of Bidar Bakht. Night had fallen and the scene was lit by flaming torches.

The list of officers who had 'drunk to the dregs the cup of martyrdom', to borrow the picturesque phrase of the Mughal historians, is long. Kokaltash Khan was one particularly distinguished officer who continued fighting till the end around the elephant of Azam. It is only after he was struck down that Rustam was able to reach the royal elephant. The commander of artillery, Sher Afghan Khan, Tari Khan, Janbaz Khan, Shah Nawaz Khan Safavid—the list of 'martyred' Khans is long.

On the victorious side, notable among the wounded were two brothers destined to play a crucial role in subsequent history. These were two Syeds from Barha, Hasan and Hussain Ali Khan. Both were severely wounded and left for dead on the field. Munim Khan too was wounded, and so exhausted that he had to be carried in a litter upto Muazzam to deliver his congratulations. His son Naim Khan was also among the wounded.

The third elephant bearing the corpse of Wala Jah had wandered away during the night and was found the next morning near the fort of Agra besides the Yamuna river, the body of the prince still in the howdah.

The bodies of the princes were laid out in biers and sent to Delhi for burial. The corpses of the Bundi and Orchha chiefs had already been taken by their kinsmen to their homes for cremation. The rank and file were cremated on the spot and buried in mass graves called *shahidganjs*, i.e. storehouses of martyrs.

The total number of the dead is generally given as 12,000 horsemen. Whether this means that only the cavalry were worth enumerating or whether it was the grand total is not clear, but the figure is low when compared to the numbers involved, Azam Shah's army numbered about 65,000 cavalry and 45,000 matchlockmen, while the figures for Muazzam's forces are much higher. According to a Dutch source his army numbered 1,52,000 horse and 1,78,000 foot besides 4,414 canon—which would include swivels of all types, gajnals,[9] shutarnals, etc. Then there were 62 elephants, 1,500 camels and 3,000 oxen.[10] When the numbers of the two sides are compared it is difficult to see how Azam Shah could have even hoped for a victory. Not only were his opponents' men three times as numerous but their artillery was far superior. But numbers meant little in Indian warfare and, as the English would show a few decade later, a small, trained and disciplined force could put to flight an army ten times their number. Had Zulfiqar Khan lived upto his title[11] and shown the expected zeal in the cause of his prince, and had Raja Jai Singh Kachhwaha of Amber shown equal resolve, the outcome might well have been different. At that time in Indian warfare much depended upon chance and a bold front could make up for lack of numbers.

The next day at the Bagh Dahar Ara near Agra, Muazzam—whom we shall now call by his new title of Bahadur Shah—held a formal durbar, and received congratulatory *nazars* and the homage of his officers. The four princes received new titles. The eldest Muiz ud-Din received the honorific of Jahandar Shah and the governorship of Tattah and Multan—his former charges, while Muhammad Azim, now transformed into Azim ush-Shan Bahadur, was given his old charge of Bengal and Bihar. Rafi ul-Qadr was exalted to Rafi ush-Shan Bahadur and received the charge of Kabul while Khujista Akhtar became Jahan Shah and received the province of Malwa.

Munim Khan could not attend the durbar on account of his wounds, but as promised, he was formally proclaimed as the Wazir-ul-Mulk with the rank of 7,000 and the titles of Khan-i-Khanan Bahadur Zafar Jang. The emperor honoured him by visiting his tent to enquire after his condition. His two sons also received high mansabs.

A few days later Asad Khan and the other officers of the fallen prince came to tender their submission. Asad Khan had brought with him the emperor's sister Zinat un-Nissa Begum and the other ladies and family members of Aurangzeb's and Azam Shah's families.

The sight of his late father's wazir standing with his hands tied so moved the emperor that he rose from the throne and personally untied the scarf that bound his hands while asking his son to untie that of Zulfiqar. Instead of the usual *saropas* he called for one of his own gowns to be brought from his personal wardrobe and insisted on Asad Khan putting it on there and then.

After all these extraordinary honours the question arose as to what post should be given to him. He himself laid claim to the wazarat but that had already been conferred on Munim Khan whose services to Bahadur Shah were beyond measure. Asad Khan and Zulfiqar, on the other hand, had been on the opposing side and the respect with which the emperor had now received the former wazir and bakhshi were more on account of his venerable age and his services in the previous reign. Nevertheless, Bahadur Shah, anxious to conciliate as many of the nobles as possible and to surmount the problem, revived the post of regent or Vakil-i-Mutlaq. The last time this office had been occupied was during the reign of Shah Jahan and the incumbent had been Asaf Khan Yamin ud-Daulah, the emperor's father-in-law.

In keeping with the exalted dignity of the post Asad Khan was conferred a mansab of 8,000 horse *duaspa* with the honorifics of Nizam-ul-Mulk and Asaf-ud-Daulah. His son, Zulfiqar was given a rank of 7,000 and was allowed to deputize for his father and was confirmed in his old offices of Amir-ul-Umara and Bakhshi-ul-Mumalik, that is, paymaster general of the army.

Asad Khan was not very happy with the arrangement, but the emperor had no doubt as to who should be the chief executive of his administration. When Asad Khan tried to lay claim to all the prerogatives of Yamin ud-Daulah the emperor gently reminded him that the latter's special position was due to his relationship with the emperor and the signal services rendered at the time of the succession. After some time Asad Khan gave up the attempt to assert himself and withdrew into virtual retirement, only occasionally visiting the court. His old age (he was then 76) was also a convenient excuse.

His son Zulfiqar was however a powerful and influential noble, not only by virtue of being his father's deputy but in his own right as the first bakhshi, the office being after the wazir's, the next most important at court. In additon, he was given the viceroyalty of the Deccan provinces with Daud Khan Panni as his deputy.

Zinat un-Nissa, the only surviving sister of Bahadur Shah was among the ladies brought in from Gwalior. She was Azam Shah's real sister and on the plea of being in mourning for her late brother she did not deign to congratulate Muazzam on his accession. None the less, he conferred on her the title of Padishah Begum and the rank of First Lady of the court and settled a handsome allowance on her.

The generous treatment accorded to Asad Khan and Zulfiqar was commented upon by some of the nobles. After all, whaat service had they done that they should be appointed to such exalted offices? Bahadur Shah's reply was that they could not have done otherwise. Had his own sons been in the Deccan at the time, he observed, they would have had no option but to espouse their uncle's cause, even against their own father.

Here it is interesting to note the completely apolitical nature of the Indian umara. The readiness with which great nobles switched sides, often in the midst of battle—as in the case of Raja Jai Singh at Jajau—was not solely the outcome of unashamed cupidity, ambition or self-interest—even though all these might play a part. The key factor was the absence of a political theory comparable to that of Divine Right in seventeenth century Europe. Inspite of the exaggerated titles assumed by the Mughals and earlier Turkish monarchs like Amir-ul-Mominin, Zil-il'llah, Zil-i-Subhani, al-Hami ul-Din, etc., the theory of monarchy was entirely secular. None of these epithets conferred any sanctity to the person of the monarch. All ruling monarchs were 'legitimate' and the exercise of de facto power was sufficient to legitimize the usurpation of the most outrageous upstart. The high passions excited by the Hanoverian succession in Britain and the consequent split in the British ruling class into Whigs, Tories and Jacobites, and similar factions in France after the Restoration of 1815, would have been incomprehensible to an Indian nobleman. The world of Islam is disdainful of earthly kings. They are at best a necessary evil. Hence no moral questions or elevated principales were involved in his eyes. In the case of certain individuals personal obligations and loyalties might transcend political calculations but ordinarily, the ruler of the day could demand and expect the allegiance of all.

In the event of a civil war among the princes, the usual practice was to offer one's allegiance to the one who first approached. Hence Baqi Khan's refusal to surrender the fort to Azim ush-Shan, but readiness to submit to whichever of the two principals that arrived first on the scene was perfectly correct.

In the absence of any principle more elevated than the reality of power, the key was self-interest. The official class was interested in preserving their dominant position in society which could best be done by remaining close to the ruler of the day. Hence the political principles of the Mughal monarchy, such as they were, happily coincided with the personal interest of the nobility. It must also be remembered that by and large there was no such thing as a hereditary nobility in the core area of the empire. Grants of land or assignments of revenue were at the pleasure of the monarch. Grants in perpetuity or *al tamgha*, as they were called, were usually modest.

It is fashionable to condemn the Mir Jafars and Mir Kassims of later Indian history as traitors who sold their *patria* to the foreign invaders, but the extraordinary complaisance with which the Indian umara switched sides to join what they recognized as the stronger side was the direct result of this enlightened attitude. And this extended all the way down the line. When a new state like Awadh or the Punjab was annexed neither the subordinate bureaucracy nor the higher umara experienced any notable *crise de conscience* in transferring their allegiance to the new rulers, and continuing to serve them in whichever capacity they were ready to take them on. What was more important was retaining a 'say' in the new set-up. It was virtually the dharma of the Indian gentry. The sons and grandsons of generals and governors felt no embarassment in serving the new masters as tahsildars and munsifs or common troopers and jamadars in the army, subordinate to youthful captains. The realization was only gradual that the new imperialism of the *Sahiban-i-Inglishia* was quite different from that of their predecessors.

The key difference was the racial exclusiveness of the English. The Mughal administration, on the other hand, since the time of Akbar had been open to all the talents. Except for the highest posts like wazir or bakhshi any talented man, Indian or Turanian, Muslim or Hindu, could aspire to be the governor of a province, leave alone the faujdar of a sarkar. The Indianization of the British Indian administration, on the other hand, was a painfully slow process,

NOTES

1. Elliot and Dowson, *The History of India as told by its own Historians*, vii, pp. 540-1.
2. Irvine, *Later Mughals*, i, p. 22. Elliot and Dowson, vii, p. 544. Baniya or trader was Azam's favourite epithet for his brother.
3. Irvine, i, pp. 8-9.

4. Elliot and Dowson, vii, p. 392.
5. Ibid., p. 389.
6. Ibid., pp. 396-7. Manucci, *Storio do Mogor*, iv, p. 402.
7. Elliot and Dowson, vii, p. 399.
8. Ibid.
9. Gajnal: a gun mounted on an elephant. Shutarnal: a gun mounted on a camel.
10. Valentyn, *Oud en Niew Oost-Indien*, p. 276.
11. 'There is so man like Ali, and no sword like Zulfiqar.' Zulfiqar was the name of the sword of Ali, the son-in-law of the Prophet, famed for his strength and valour. The title was eagerly sought by the Shi'ite umara.

CHAPTER 4

The End of Kam Bakhsh

The civil war was not yet over. There remained Kam Bakhsh, the favourite of his father, holding independent court at Hyderabad. But Bahadur Shah was in no hurry to deal with him. Kam Bakhsh could never be a threat to him, and had he acted with ordinary prudence his half-brother might well have left him in undisturbed possession of his southern appanage. But Kam Bakhsh was neither a man of ordinary good sense nor of common prudence. The account of his 'rule', if such it could be called, is like a horror story. But for the moment Bahadur Shah had more pressing matters to deal with in Rajasthan, where, since the time of Aurangzeb the Rajputs had been in a state of simmering rebellion. So Kam Bakhsh had to be suffered for another one and a half years.

Aurangzeb had appointed Kam Bakhsh to the government of Bijapur and he had gone to assume charge a few weeks prior to his father's death, the news of which reached him while he was still on the march. On receiving the tidings, most of the Turanian amirs in his army led by Muhammad Amin Khan deserted him *en bloc*. They realized that there was no future with a prince like Kam Bakhsh and that the great contest for the sovereignty of Hind would be between Azam and Muazzam. Furthermore, they had no desirc to stagnate in provincial Bijapur where 'Mir Mallang' Ahsan Khan, already held the premier position. As a consequence of this desertion the strength of his army was greatly depleted and much of his baggage was looted.

In this weakened state Kam Bakhsh reached Bijapur where the qiladar, to his acute embarrassment, closed the gates and refused to admit him. The subedar was Chin Qilich Khan, the son of Ghazi ud-Din Khan Firoz Jang, the blind governor of Berar. Chin Qilich Khan was away to Ahmadnagar but his nephew Syed Niyaz Khan was holding the fort and raised difficulties about handing over charge. Ahsan Khan opened negotiations and after several days Niyaz yielded and opened the gates.

Quite unaware, the prince had narrowly escaped being captured by Zulfiqar Khan. The latter was in the neighbourhood and having come to know of the weakened state of the prince's forces, toyed with the idea of taking him prisoner and making a present of him to Azam. There was ill-feeling between him and the prince dating back to the siege of Gingee in the reign of Aurangzeb. But Rao Dalpat Bundela of Orchha, his faithful lieutenant, advised him against uncalled for interference in the quarrels of princes. Zulfiqar thus continued his march towards Ahmadnagar to join Azam, while Kam Bakhsh entered Bijapur and set about establishing a court.

Ahsan Khan who had proved his usefulness in the negotiations with Niyaz Khan was appointed bakhshi while one Hakim Mohsin was named wazir with the title of Taqarrub Khan. The prince assumed all the attributes of a sovereign monarch and ordered coins to be struck, and the *khutba* was read in his name. A formal enthronement ceremony took place and he assumed the style of Din Panah or 'Protector of the faith'.[1]

About two months were spent putting the affairs of the country in order and raising an army. Thereafter his first expedition was against Wakinkhera which was again in the hands of Pema Naik who had been ejected from there only a few months earlier by Aurangzeb in person.

En route Syed Niyaz Khan slipped away one night with a small party to join Azam, abandoning his tents and baggage. But thanks to the exertions of Ahsan Khan, Gulbarga, was taken, and finally so was Wakinkhera, after a short siege of twenty days.

About this time differences arose between the wazir and the bakhshi; differences which were ultimately to have disastrous consequences. Taqarrub Khan started intriguing against Ahsan and filled the ears of Kam Bakhsh against him.

But Ahsan Khan paid no heed and did not slacken his efforts on behalf of his royal master. He next directed his army towards Hyderabad, of which the subedar was another Rustam Dil Khan, son of Jan Sipar Khan. Rustam surrendered but the commandant of Golconda, pleading that he had received the orders of Bahadur Shah, shut himself up in the citadel and refused to recognize the authority of Kam Bakhsh. The prince also transferred his court from Bijapur to Hyderabad which was a much bigger and far more imposing city.

It was here that Taqarrub Khan conspired to encompass the ruin of Ahsan Khan, while the latter, blissfully unaware of all that was afoot, went on to Arkat and Kurnool and forced the local faujdars to submit to Kam Bakhsh 'Din Panah'.

Taqarrub Khan appears to have been motivated by sheer jealousy and spite. With very limited resources Ahsan Khan had brought the entire

Hyderabad suba, besides Bijapur, under his control. But Taqarrub Khan had nothing to show and he probably felt uneasy at the success of the bakhshi. He, therefore, sought to control Kam Bakhsh by feeding his sense of insecurity by confiding to him imaginary rumours of conspiracies, and then pretending to unmask them. From the conduct of the bakhshi himself it is clear that he posed no threat to the wazir and his very nickname of Mir Mallang indicates that he was of a carefree disposition and totally free from guile. The prince, on the other hand, had long been noted for his violent disposition. He was rumoured to have personally killed several of his harem who had provoked his insane fury.[2] And in the hands of his wazir he was like putty.

Rustam Dil Khan had an intimate knowledge of the country. His father Jan Sipar Khan was from an old Deccani family and had been governor of Hyderabad in the days of the Qutb Shahs. He himself had served as faujdar in Bijapur and the Carnatic before being appointed as subedar of Hyderabad, and now after the takeover by the prince he was retained as deputy governor by Ahsan Khan. A deep bond developed between the two noblemen and the two would meet privately in the evening to discuss state affairs informally with other confidants, among whom were Saif Khan, Arshad Khan, Nazir Khan and Ahmad Khan. These harmless nocturnal get-togethers were given a conspirational colour by Taqarrub and his coterie. The plan, as they alleged, was to attack and seize Kam Bakhsh while proceeding to the Friday mosque for prayers, and if he did not act soon to counter them, they would doubtless succeed.

It was decided to first tackle Rustam Dil Khan. On the pretext that the prince wanted to consult him for drafting a reply to the letter received from Bahadur Shah, he was asked to repair immediately to the presence.

It was still dark and the sun had not yet risen, but notwithstanding the unusual hour Rustam dressed, and accompanied by his son and a small escort, hurried to the royal apartments with his pen-case and writing materials. On his arrival he was asked to wait in the tasbih khana where he was told the prince would join him immediately after breakfast. As was the normal practice Rustam removed his sword and dagger and handed them to an attendant. His son likewise removed his sidearms. They had barely sat down when armed men rushed in with drawn swords and seized them. The pen-case was searched and a letter from Saif Khan found. It was an innocuous letter in response to an enquiry of his and advised that the best way of approaching the prince was through Ahsan Khan. After his confidence had been won he should approach Ahmad Khan. Ignoring the poor man's protests that this in no way incriminated him, and only showed how anxious he was to obtain the prince's favour, he was sentenced to death, and, with a macabre twist, it was ordered that he should be crushed under the foot of his own elephant.

Three days later, bound hand and foot he was thrown before his mount but the faithful animal, in spite of the goading by the mahout, refused to be the executioner. Eventually he had to be led away and another beast was pressed for the job. Thereafter the corpse was tied to the elephant's hind foot and dragged through the streets to put the fear of God in all conspirators, and to impress the public with the awful justice of His Majesty.[3]

Bailiffs were sent by the prince to seize the property of the deceased. It is said that the nobleman's wife, who was a lady of spirit, resisted and several men were killed in the clash that followed, but ultimately she was persuaded to yield.

Rustam Dil Khan was buried in the family enclosure in Imli Bagh and his property and estates were seized. But after the reign of blood was over the family was rehabilitated and one of the sons was destined to hold positions of great trust and honour under Asaf Jah.

After Rustam Dil Khan the next victim was Saif, the author of the supposedly incriminating letter found in Rustam's possession. His protestations were in vain; for him the manic imagination of the prince ordained the amputation of the right hand, the one that had indited the traitorous letter. As the executioner set about his grisly work the despairing officer cursed the prince and swore that the manifest injustice of the prince was proof of his mother's low origins. Only a base and low born character like him could order the amputation of the hand that had taught him how to string and draw the bow.

Enraged by this allusion to his mother's professional past the prince roared that his tongue be torn out. Then horses were driven over him, again and again, until he finally expired. His mistress, who had been dragged to the site of execution and forced to watch the proceedings, died of shock.[4]

Arshad Khan's tongue was also removed. This nobleman's grandfather had been a diwan of the Deccan. Nazir Khan and Ahmad Khan were also executed, happily, for them, in a more summary manner. Their bodies were then placed on donkeys and paraded in the streets.

People had warned Ahsan Khan that he should take steps to protect himself, or else he would certainly suffer the fate of his friends. But Ahsan was incredulous. How could the prince, who owed all that he was to his exertions, ever suspect him of treachery? But he was soon undeceived when the mace-bearers arrived with constables to arrest him.

He was kept in irons in the open, exposed to the elements, alternately starved and then force-fed with heavily salted food, until he finally breathed his last.

But the prince's madness had not yet run its full course. Bahadur Shah followed up his letter with an envoy, Matabar Khan. The prince's feeble-minded advisers put the idea in his head that the escort of Matabar Khan were desperadoes sent with the express purpose of assassinating him. Kam Bakhsh was not a man to take half-measures to ensure his security. A plan was accordingly hatched to forestall the supposed assassins.

An entertainment was arranged for the envoy and his retinue. As they entered the hall one by one, they were overpowered by the prince's thugs. Among those taken prisoner were a number of citizens who had somehow contrived to wangle invitations for the dinner. The total thus seized were seventy-five. The same night scaffolds were erected in different wards of the city, and the prisoners taken out in batches of ten and executed by torchlight.[5] The honest citizens were shocked to discover the corpses of the murdered men in the morning. Matabar Khan himself was arrested and imprisoned in violation of all accepted norms.

After this it was just a matter of time. Bahadur's letter had been kind and gently admonitory:

> Our father entrusted you with the government of the two subas of Bijapur and Hyderabad with all their subjects and belongings upon the condition, according to the old rule of the Deccan, that the coins shall be struck and the khutba read in our name. The tribute which has hitherto been paid by the governors of these two provinces we remit.[6]

It was a friendly and personal letter in which he condoled the prince on the death of his mother, Udaipuri Bai, and told him about the arrangements made for her funeral and the disposal of her personal possessions which had been done, according to her wishes and under his superintendence. He gave a brief account of the battle and lamented the deaths of his brother and nephews and hoped that he would not be misled by foolish advisers. He described too his joy when he came to know of the survival of the little Ali Tabar.

By Bahadur Shah's waiver of the tribute, Kam Bakhsh was left independent in all but name. But some kind of death wish seemed to be driving Kam Bakhsh to his doom. Instead of seizing this generous offer he gave an evasive reply. A letter from the wazir Munim Khan, also urging him to arrive at an understanding, was not even acknowledged. In the meantime reports of the atrocious acts of his brother were also being received by Bahadur Shah. The news of the savage executions of Rustam Dil Khan, Saif Khan, Ahsan Khan and others were received with horror at the imperial court, and the emperor condoled with the relatives of the deceased and presented them with *khillats* of mourning, as was customary on such occasions.

The emperor now advanced into his brother's territory and pitched camp at Zafarabad-Bidar. He had been at Aurangabad for some time for, immediately after the battle of Jajau and his formal enthronement he had to leave for Rajasthan. After receiving the submission of the Rajput princes he had proceeded to the Deccan, ostensibly to offer prayers at his father's grave, and the letter to Kam Bakhsh had been dispatched from his camp near Aurangabad. This city was a convenient listening post for Hyderabad, and on failing to receive a proper and satisfactory response from his brother it was a simple matter to resume the march.

As the news of the emperor's advance spread through Kam Bakhsh's wretched kingdom his troops and officers started melting away, many turning up to pay their respects and offer their services to the emperor. With the execution of Ahsan Khan there seemed no possibility of any effective resistance, and the prince himself seemed to be living in a fool's paradise. When his new bakhshi reported that his soldiers were deserting in droves for want of pay he replied, 'What need have I of soldiers? My trust is in God and what is best will happen.'[7] The bakhshi took this to mean that there was little need for him either, and also abandoned the camp.

If soldiers and armies seemed unnecessary to the prince it was because astrologers and soothsayers had assured him of a miraculous victory. Inspite of the gross disparity of the forces, and the daily desertions, these charlatans maintained to the end that the triumph of the prince was certain.

The battle took place on 13 January 1709 near Hyderabad. The strength of the imperial army, according to the muster taken on the eve of battle was 1,40,000 horse and 1,80,000 matchlockmen.

In the prince's camp, slaves, servants and camp followers far outnumbered the soldiers. When the final clash took place it is said that there were only five or six hundred cavalry besides matchlockmen. There was practically no artillery but there was a large stock of rockets, always popular in Deccan warfare. Besides Taqarrub Khan, the incompetent wazir, the only notable officer was Abdul Razaq Khan Lari and his brother. Abdul Razaq was the son of an old Hyderabadi noble who had seen service under the Qutab Shahs and exhibited a degree of bravery and loyalty to the old dynasty which was extreme to the point of being foolhardy. His sons were apparently cast in the same inflexible mould.

Bahadur Shah hoped to avoid a battle and unnecessary bloodshed. The troops were ordered to advance closer. Zulfiqar Khan commanded one wing, while the other wing was commanded by Daud Khan Pani and Jahan Khan, while Munim Khan was at the centre with the emperor.

The movement having been completed the commanders waited for further orders but none were forthcoming. It was reported that the emperor was having a nap and could not be disturbed. Zulfiqar Khan was impatient and, having old scores to settle with Kam Bakhsh, chafed at the delay. Finally, after privately informing Munim Khan, he attacked, after which the wazir was forced to give the order for battle.

Considering the disparity of the forces a real fight was scarcely to be expected, but Kam Bakhsh used his rockets to good effect. Daud Khan Panni's column was checked and pushed back in confusion under the rain of rocket fire. The prince took up his bow and let fly the arrows, emptying quiver after quiver, inspite of several wounds. The lessons of Saif Khan his late tutor had not been lost on him. Eventually however, weakened by loss of blood, he was captured by Daud Khan's Afghans. Along with him was taken his youngest son Bariqullah, also wounded in several places.

His eldest son Muhi us-Sunnat also fought fearlessly. His elephant's mahout was killed and so was his companion in the rear seat of the howdah. Then he came out of the howdah and took over the control of the animal himself and kept up the struggle until he lost consciousness and fell down from his perch riddled with musket balls and arrows. The elephant wandered off the field and was seized by the Maratha auxiliaries who hung on the flanks of the imperial army.

After the fighting was over Kam Bakhsh and the three young princes, Muhi us-Sunnat, Firozmand and Bariqullah were brought in and placed in a tent in the royal enclosure. Bariqullah died almost immediately, but the wounds of the other two proved superficial and they recovered. But not Kam Bakhsh who had been consciously seeking death. As Azam Shah had remarked to Zulfikar at Jajau, for princes there could only be the throne or the scaffold. So Kam Bakhsh seemed to have decided that since he could not be *de jure* sovereign it was better to die with honour than live in shame. Having failed to find death in the field he rejected all treatment and refused the soup that was offered to him.

Bahadur Shah had directed his son Rafi ush-Shan to attend to his uncle, and his young cousins. The best physicians and surgeons available in the camp, European and Indian, were directed to spare no effort to save him. He went himself to the tent and sat by his bedside, comforting him and assisting in washing and dressing his wounds. Removing his own shawl he placed it around his brother's shoulders, saying: 'I had no wish to see you reduced to this state.'[8]

According to the *Seir Mutaqherin* the prince is said to have retorted that neither had he wished to see *him* in the condition that he was—of a victorious emperor—but this reply seems too saucy for a dying man. According to another version, he simply returned his greetings and murmured, 'In all things praise be to the Lord'. Khafi Khan says that he added, 'I did not wish that one of the race of Timur should be made prisoner lest people should say that I was coward and lacked spirit.'[9] This determination to defend their honour in the field of battle and the horror of the possible imputation of cowardice is the most endearing quality of the princes of this dynasty.

As was his wish, Kam Bakhsh did not long survive his wounds and died the same night. Nothing in his life—and certainly nothing in his short reign—became him like his leaving it. He died like a brave man, fighting recklessly against incredible odds, and notwithstanding his puny force put up a remarkably tough fight. Perhaps he was really mad, but we see the same ferocious courage in Azam Shah at Jajau and in many much younger princes like Bidar Bakhṭ, Wala Jah, Muhi us-Sunnat and others. On occasions they display their incompetence or stupidity but they are rarely found wanting in courage. But this blind and dogged determination to live up to their vaunted ancestry was one of the reasons for the exhaustion of the empire. The peculiar nature of Indian warfare meant that in each major battle some of the bravest of the umara would inevitably sip the cup of martyrdom. This frequent blood-letting of the cream of the Indian nobility was more than the country could afford.

Kam Bakhsh was 42 at the time of his death. On his sons—all of whom have been mentioned in the histories as having distinguished themselves on the field of battle—the eldest was Muhi us-Sunnat and he could not have been above twelve years of age at the time! He was to live upto the age 50, dying in confinement in the Qila-i-Mualla. Half a century later one of his sons, Muhi ul-Millat would briefly grace the throne as Shah Jahan III, a phantom king whose coins are almost the only proof that he ever existed.

About the same time, half way across the world on the throne of England sat Queen Anne while in France the Sun King was dazzling all Europe with his brilliance. The War of the Spanish Succession was under way but what a different war that was, compared to the wars in India, where notwithstanding the introduction of gunpowder and artillery two centuries earlier, bows, arrows and armoured elephants were still important factors in battle!

As in the case of Azam Shah due provision was made for the ladies of the prince's household and for the two little princes who were sent to Delhi.

NOTES

1. Elliot and Dowson, *The History of India as told by its own Historians*, vii, p. 390.
2. Ibid., p. 553.
3. Shah Nawaz Khan and Muhammad Haiyy, *Maathir ul-Umara*, ii, 2, p. 623.
4. Irvine, *Later Mughals*, i, p. 54.
5. Yahya Khan, *Tazkirat ul-Mulk*, p. 114a.
6. Elliot and Dowson, vii, pp. 405-6.
7. Irvine, i, p. 60.
8. Ibid., p. 64.
9. Elliot and Dowson, vii, p. 407.

CHAPTER 5

The Reign of Shah Alam Bahadur Shah: Turmoil in Rajasthan

Events in Rajasthan had been responsible for the delay on the part of Bahadur Shah in attending to the challenge posed by Kam Bakhsh. The Agra suba adjoined that of Ajmer, in the jurisdiction of which fell the principalities of Rajasthan, hence soon after Jajau he had felt compelled to march on to Ajmer and Jaipur. The troubles in the latter principality, one of the three front-ranking states of that region, were the result of the ill-advised determination of the late emperor to reduce the territories of these proud princes to the status of sarkars, squarely subordinate to the subedar of Ajmer.

Here it is necessary to describe in some detail the peculiar character of the suba of Ajmer which was quite different, geographically and politically, from the rest of north India.

The territory which is known as Rajasthan, is a vast territory of over 1,17,000 square miles, stretching from the desert of Sind to the Chambal river, and divided in two by the Aravalli range. To the west of the range the country is arid and mainly desert but the east is somewhat elevated and fertile. It was to this relatively inhospitable region that the Rajput chivalry of northern India had retreated after the Turkish conquest.

For nearly three centuries the states remained independent and the Turkish and Afghan sultans held only a few outposts like Ajmer and Ranthambor. Occasionally war would break out and after a long siege the capital would be stormed and pillaged, the warriors fighting to the death, clad in their saffron robes as a token of their determination, with the maidens immolating themselves in the dreadful rite of jauhar to escape dishonour.

That a nation of such ferocious warriors should ever be defeated seems incredible but the caste-ridden nature of Hindu society ensured that the masses were never involved in the struggle. The Rajputs, in reality, were only the thin upper crust of the warrior aristocracy which held the land in feudal tenure from their chief who was usually the head of their clan and, at least theoretically, of common descent. The mass of the population, consisting of the innumerable different castes and sub-castes of Indian society were seldom involved, and rarely felt the need to lift the sword in defence of their king, and indeed were not expected to do so. Thus the Rajput armies, even with their semi-barbaric tribal auxiliaries, were never able to match the armies of the Turkish, 'Mughal' or Pathan rulers of Delhi in manpower, even though the foreign invaders constituted but a tiny fraction of the teeming multitudes of Hind.

Politically thus, the subedar of Ajmer controlled little more than the city and its immediate neighbourhood and a few isolated strongholds. His position was comparable more to that of the British Agent in the days of the Raj—whose seat was again for the same historical reasons—Ajmer. At the time of the Turkish conquest in the thirteenth century Ajmer was part of the Chauhan state of Delhi. With the fall of that state and the extinction of the main line of the ruling house, Ajmer bowed before Turkish arms.

Until the reign of Akbar it remained thus; the Rajput states were quite independent and any signs of weakness in the dominant power would invite a Rajput attack on Ajmer and the other strongholds. But Akbar was able at last to win over the chiefs of these proud clans, the Kachhwahas, the Rathors and ultimately even the Sisodias, and build them up as one of the main pillars of his empire. For the first time in their history these paladins of western India willingly gave their daughters in marriage to the emperors at Delhi, even though the latter were 'untouchable', in the opinion of their priests. The emperors, on their side, admitted them to the higher ranks of the imperial peerage and they distinguished themselves in military commands from Balkh on the Oxus to the deep south, and as governors of provinces far more extensive than their frequently petty principalities.

But the majesty of the Great Mughal would not permit their formal recognition as tributary princes governing autonomous states. Throughout the officials records they are described by the colourless appellation of zamindar which is now used for any landowner. Their hereditary titles of Raja, Rao or Maharaja were treated as mere titles comparable to the more expressive titles or *alqab* bestowed on the other manasabdars and amirs, like Khan, Bahadur, and the infinite varieties of titles ending as Daulah and Mulk. The succession to their hereditary lands was regulated by the emperor, and no succession was considered complete until a sanad of recognition had been issued from the office of the imperial wazir, like the sanad to a subedari.

On the outbreak of the civil war in 1658 Maharaja Jaswant Singh of Jodhpur was confronted by the embarrassing problem of stopping Aurangzeb in his march northwards. A half-hearted battle took place in which the Rajputs distinguished themselves in bravery but the triumph was Aurangzeb's. An interesting anecdote is narrated as a post-script to this battle. When Jaswant Singh found his way back to Jodhpur with the remnants of his defeated army his maharani refused to open the gates of the palace. 'Surely that man must be an impostor', she declared indignantly. 'My lord could not have fled from the field of battle, he would surely have chosen to die.'[1]

Such indeed was the Rajput tradition, but notwithstanding the taunts of his scornful consort this Rajput had seemingly made his peace with Aurangzeb, and when that prince set out on his campaign against Shuja he accompanied him. But deep inside he had determined to wipe out the stain on his honour by avenging his defeat. On the night before the battle of Khajua, after sending a secret message to Shuja he made a treacherous attack on the division of Muhammad Sultan, Aurangzeb's eldest son, scattering his troops and throwing the whole camp into confusion. Unfortunately Shuja failed to attack. He had taken the message to be a ruse of Aurangzeb's and Jaswant's essay came to nought. He once again returned to Jodhpur while Aurangzeb went on to destroy Shuja's army.

Even after this treacherous attack Aurangzeb pardoned him in order to detach him from Dara and sent him to the Deccan at the head of a Rajput army against the Marathas, but again suspecting him of being in league with Shivaji he posted him as governor of Gujarat. Then an Afghan rising in the province of Kabul came handy and the restless intriguer was packed off to this frontier province from which he was destined never to return.

He died at Jamrud at the head of the Khyber Pass in December 1678. His three sons had predeceased him but two of his ranis gave birth to two posthumous male children. The emperor ordered that the infants be brought to Delhi. One of the two died; Aurangzeb demanded the other, who was named Ajit Singh—his object being to have him brought up at the court.

But the Rathors were not prepared for this. Led by the gallant Durga Das whose name was to become a byword for courage, they prepared to resist. In order to delay the imperial soldiers another infant was left behind with one of the maids dressed as the royal mother while the real prince was carried away. To ensure that the warriors could concentrate on the fight without any added worries for the safety and honour for their women, all the women were 'sent to heaven' being blown up by gunpowder.[2] The little band of warriors fought a running battle through the streets of Delhi all the way to the Aravallis where they finally shook off their pursuers. The infant prince was entrusted to the abbot of a religious establishment to be brought up in seclusion, ignorant of his birth and heritage, to be revealed to his nation at an appropriate time.

Although the masquerade was discovered soon enough Aurangzeb affected to believe that the changeling was the true Ajit and the rumoured infant in the Aravallis a pretender. So, acting in the name of his protegé the emperor tried to assume control of Marwar by establishing a regency, but the proud Rathors refused to surrender. A savage but desultory war broke out, a war which would periodically draw in the other Rajput states in a struggle that went on for thirty years. It was a brutal contest marked by massacres and the desecration of temples and mosques. Muhammad Akbar, sent by his father to lead the campaign was so moved by the devotion of the Rathors to their infant prince that he espoused their cause and revolted against his father. However a loyal imperialist general succeeded in dispersing the threatening coalition by a stratagem and the prince was forced to flee to the Deccan, and ultimately, Iran.

Aurangzeb had placed a faujdar in Jodhpur with a strong garrison but as soon as the news of his death reached Rajasthan, Ajit Singh, now a young man of 29, came forth from his hideout and ejected him along with the other imperial garrisons in Marwar. He felt his hour had come, and embittered by the long struggle against the imperialists, he failed to send the customary congratulations to the new Emperor Bahadur Shah.

Rana Amar Singh was more prudent and he sent his brother Bakht Singh with a congratulatory letter and a *nazar* of 100 gold mohurs, Rs. 1,000 in silver, an elephant, two fine horses, nine swords and other products of the country. Relations between Mewar and the late emperor had long been strained for a number of reasons, beginning with the Rana's romantic marriage to a princess of Roopnagarh for whose hand the emperor had also been a suitor. The reimposition of *jaziya*, the hated poll-tax which was levied only non-Muslims, also drew a spirited remonstrance from the Rana who was the most respected of the ruling princes of Rajasthan. However the unwonted imperial interference in the internal affairs of Marwar forced him to take up arms. Here his honour was also involved as the mother of Ajit Singh was a princess of Mewar and the *Gurukul* where the infant prince was being brought up, was located in Mewar territory. But now that the tyrant was dead he lost no time in making his peace with the new padishah.

Since 1699 the throne of Amber had been occupied by Raja Jai Singh Sawai, in contradistinction to his predecessor, the Mirza Raja of the same name. He was a savant and the most outstanding intellect of his time. The city of Jaipur was founded by him; the first Indian city to be laid out on a rectangular grid. While all Indians were interested in astrology, he went much further and was a keen astronomer, and was responsible for the construction of the great observatories of Ujjain, Jaipur, Delhi, Mathura and Banaras. The instruments erected there were superior to any in existence at the time, and certainly far superior to those of Ulugh Beg at Samarkand. The Emperor Muhammad Shah commissioned him to reform the calendar, and he had Euclid's *Elements*, Napier's *Logarithms* and other treatises on plain and spherical trignometry translated into Sanskrit.[3]

But unhappily for this scholar, the death of Aurangzeb found him in the Deccan with the army of Azam Shah, under orders to accompany him to Malwa. Thus he had no option but to fight on his side. There was of course the example of the Turani chiefs like Muhammad Amin Khan who deserted at the first possible opportunity, but that was not the Rajput way. During the battle however when there raja perceived that things were going badly for his prince he adroitly switched sides, but his reception by Bahadur Shah was cold and formal.

The reason for the indifferent attitude of Bahadur Shah was soon revealed. Jai Singh had a younger brother named Bijai Singh who was also aspiring to the seat of Amber, and he had already espoused the cause of Bahadur Shah. Thus when the emperor reached Amber, it was Bijai Singh who was installed on the throne and Raja Jai Singh's property was confiscated. This was done only *pro forma* and it was almost immediately restored but the loss of his hereditary principality in violation of the principle of primogeniture, so dear to the Rajputs, shook him.[4] It was an unforgettable degradation and it was obvious that the business was far from settled.

The emperor continued his march towards the Rathor capital. Eventually, after protracted negotiations between the Urdu-i-Mualla, the raja and Durga Das, Ajit was persuaded to come in and pay his respects to the emperor. A special durbar was held for the purpose on 26 February when the raja presented his *nazar*. *Khillats* were presented in return and over the next two months he was granted the title of Maharaja, a mansab of 3,500 *zat* and 3,000 *aspa* (of which 1,000 was *duaspa*), a standard and kettledrums. Suitable mansabs were also conferred on his sons.

After settling the affairs of Jodhpur the emperor turned towards Ajmer. As Udaipur lay in the same direction, Rana Amar Singh for some reason took fright and fled to the hills, but the deputation he sent to wait on the emperor at Ajmer was received graciously and reassuring letters were handed to them to be conveyed to the Rana. But the Rana was not convinced and nothing could persuade him to perform his duty. The imperial march was therefore resumed in the direction of Chittor, the old capital of Mewar.

But feeling that too much time was being wasted and the matter of Kam Bakhsh more pressing, the emperor decided to leave the affair of Rana Amar Singh to be settled at a more convenient time and turned towards the Deccan. While they were passing through Malwa, Ajit, Jai Singh and Durga Das slipped away from the imperial camp and returned to their homes without obtaining the Emperor's formal leave. Evidently more trouble was to be expected from them. Jai Singh could not rest until he had won back his ancestral throne while Ajit had discovered that a cruel trick had been played on him. While he was in the imperial camp with titles and mansabs being showered upon him, the imperialists retained full control over his principality. The imperial faujdar was not withdrawn and the raja's administration was little more than a puppet regime.

The three malcontents headed for Udaipur where they entered into a compact with Rana Amar Singh. Some of the clauses of the agreement signed by the three front-ranking chiefs of Rajasthan were to be the cause of much misery for their people, but the immediate effect of the alliance was a repudiation of imperial authority and the assertion of a determination to recover their lost independence. The compact entered between Akbar and the Rajputs, which was one of the fundamental bases of the Mughal empire, seemed to be falling apart.

Mihrab Khan, faujdar of Jodhpur was attacked by a vastly superior force of 30,000 Rathors. Seeing that his position was hopeless he opened negotiations and was allowed to march out with full military honours. Then Amber was cleared of the imperial garrisons and the faujdars of Mewat, Narnaul and Mairtha were killed by a freak volley in a battle at Sambhar.

Having succeeded in regaining control of their ancestral principalities and clearing virtually the whole of Rajasthan (save for the garrison at Ajmer), the three princes sent their emissaries to the camp of the emperor, who was still in the Deccan, to 'explain' their actions and effect a patch-up.

Azim ush-Shan, who was married to Raja Jai Singh's sister, was sympathetic to their cause and with his intervention a reconciliation was effected, the three rajas being restored to their former ranks and mansabs.

This was in October 1708. In the following January Kam Bakhsh's reign came to an end. It took sometime to settle the Deccan but subsequently the emperor turned again to the north. It was a slow leisurely progress and it was not until the end of December that the Narmada was crossed. The emperor had determined to return through Rajasthan to settle the unfinished business there. On 22 May 1709, the representatives of the three confederate princes were received by the emperor at Toda. The usual *nazars* were proffered and *khillats* exchanged, but on that very day trouble broke in the Punjab which again compelled the emperor to curtail his sojourn in Rajasthan.

While the *nazars* and *khillats* were being exchanged at Toda, Wazir Khan faujdar of Sirhind in the Delhi suba, came forth to give battle to a rag-tag army of Sikhs led by an unknown leader known as Banda, and, was killed, his army routed, and the city sacked with a ferocity not witnessed since centuries.

Refugees from the Punjab, including pirzadas from Sadhaura and Sirhind, who had been witnesses to the horrors of the Sikh rebellion turned up at the emperor's camp near Ajmer and narrated their experiences and sufferings. It was imperative that the emperor move up-country as fast as possible to meet this new fast developing threat.

On 21 June Raja Ajit Singh of Jodhpur and Jai Singh of Amber came in person to pay their respects to the emperor. The customary formalities were observed, *nazars* and *khillats* exchanged, and the rajas were permitted to return home.

Rana Amar Singh of Mewar had again managed to avoid a personal appearance. And notwithstanding the *nazars* and bows of the other two rajas, it was evident that the imperial authority was at that moment nonexistent in Rajasthan with the subedar and garrison at Ajmer reduced to a symbol.

NOTES

1. Tod, *Annals and Antiquities of Rajasthan*, i, pp. 494-5. On the authority of Bernier.
2. Ibid., p. 45.
3. Ibid., ii, pp. 289-90.
4. Irvine, *Later Mughals*, i, p. 47. Danishmand Khan, *Bahadur Shah Nama*, pp. 62-4.

CHAPTER 6

The Sikh Rebellion and the Death of Bahadur Shah

The Sikhs who made such a sudden and startling appearance on the stage of history represent the youngest of the major religions of India. Tracing their origins to their first guru, Nanak, who was active in the first half of the sixteenth century they acquired their distinctive identity only towards the latter part of the seventeenth, under the tenth and last guru, Gobind. But for him they would probably have remained one among the many reformist cults and sects which have periodically revolted against Brahminical domination. But Guru Gobind Singh, as he now styled himself, gave them a distinctive militant character. The core of the new faith was the Khalsa a kind of military brotherhood sworn to resist injustice and tyranny, in some ways comparable to the orders of European chivalry which personified the militant aspect of the Christian church.

Guru Gobind passed away in the Deccan in November 1708. His father Guru Tegh Bahadur had been executed in Delhi in 1675 and much of his life had been spent in arms against the imperial power, represented by the Faujdar Wazir Khan of Sirhind, in whose jurisdiction fell Anandpur, the seat of his authority. Two young sons were killed in battle, two others, still children fell into his hands and were sealed alive in the vaults of the citadel, which became thus the visible symbol of oppression and tyranny.

That the Guru himself had no ambition of attacking or challenging the imperial authority *per se* is clear from the manner in which, after the death of Aurangzeb, he complimented Bahadur Shah on his accession, and according to the Sikh traditions he is credited with having fought at Jajau with a band of his followers on his side. His object appears to have been to raise his followers from the status of servile subjects of a despotic monarchy to the level of free men who would not brook any man's tyranny and could look any badshah in his eyes, be he Turk or Indian. He had no objection to giving Caesar his due, but it was Caesar's duty to give his subjects a just and righteous government, and a responsive administration.

After his military contribution to the enthronement of Bahadur Shah the Guru for some unexplained reason retired to the Deccan, where on the banks of the sacred Godavari he ran into a *bairagi* by the name of Madhav Das, a Rajput by birth, who dabbled in sorcery and lived the life of a recluse.[1] Somehow this dubious character became the Guru's *chela*, and as he lay dying following a murderous assault by an Afghan horse trader, the Guru designated him heir to his temporal inheritance, the spiritual *gur-gaddi* having ceased with himself.

This Rajput adventurer then made his way to Delhi where he called on the Guru's widows who were living in peace in the capital. He narrated to them the circumstances of their lord's demise and showed the relics he had brought with him. They in turn introduced him to the Sikh *sangat* of Delhi which accepted him as its leader. He was now ready to embark on a career of conquest, to found a state in the name of the *Khalsa ji*, the Sikh Commonwealth.

Adventurous and lawless, both by background and disposition, he judged that the times were ripe for such an attempt. The long absence of the late emperor and the financial burden of the Deccan wars had resulted in conditions becoming increasingly oppressive for the peasantry. The faujdars and subedars exercised virtually unlimited powers with little imperial interference. As is usual in such cases, particularly in Mughal India which lacked a strong hereditary nobility and where the rules of escheat ensured that every official was always trying to make some secret provision for his dependents, the rapacity of the imperial officials seemed to know no bounds.

Banda's first clash with the imperial authorities was at Sonepat near Delhi where the faujdar came out with a small force to disperse what he thought were mere rabble. But he was unpleasantly surprised and had to beat a hasty retreat and shut himself up in his fort. Thus emboldened, Banda turned towards Sirhind where Wazir Khan, now in his eightieth year, was still the faujdar. Sirhind, of accursed memory, and its faujdar were held up to execration by the Sikhs, so they enthusiastically rallied round their new-found leader, thirsting for revenge.

As a prelude to the attack on the seat of the sarkar, Sadhaura was first sacked. Wazir Khan hurriedly mustered what trcops he could and attacked Banda's force with about 4,000 cavalry about 14 miles from Sirhind. At first the imperialists seemed to be gaining but a sudden attack in the rear, a clever flanking move on the part of Banda, turned the tables. Wazir Khan did not flinch but continued fighting till he was killed.

His body was strung up from a tree, his baggage plundered, and then the Sikhs, flushed with victory fell upon the defenceless town. For four days it was looted, its mosques defiled, and houses pillaged and burnt. All Muslims who could not get away, men, women or children, were slaughtered, the bellies of pregnant women being ripped open and infants tossed into the air and cut in two as they fell to the ground. The Mughal authorities had never been squeamish about shedding blood while suppressing rebellion but this was probably the first time since the invasions of Timur and Babar that a town had been so thoroughly sacked. Not only do the Mughal historians dwell on the horrors of the first sack of Sirhind but even the Sikh chronicler of the *Sri Gur Partap Suraj* exultantly records the terrible scenes. The worm had at last turned and was determined to avenge with interest all its ancient wrongs.[2]

Banda established himself in a small fortalice in the Shivalik foothills not far from Sadhaura and adjoining the territories of the raja of Sirmoor, or the 'Barfi' Raja (the Snow King) as he was called by the Mughals. He named it Lohgarh and assumed the style and manner of an independent ruler.

The emperor marched rapidly in his direction. It is said that he was highly gratified at this opportunity of waging a religious war against the infidel, for the savagery of the Sikh leader seemed directed specifically against Muslims. On the way near Karnal he felt elated at receiving a cartload of 300 severed heads, the fruits of an engagement between the Sikhs and a zealous imperial officer.[3]

It was in December 1710 that the emperor at last reached Lohgarh—'the Refuge of the World, the Walled city, Ornament of the Fortunate Throne', as it was described on the coins reportedly struck by Banda.[4]

The place was invested and it seemed that Banda had reached the end of his road.

It was not as if the activities of the Sikh bands had been limited to the Cis-Sutluj region of the Delhi suba. The news of the fall and sack of Sirhind had an electrifying effect on the Sikhs of the Punjab, Sikh bands had ravaged the Batala and Kalanaur parganas of the Bari Doab, right up to the environs of Lahore. Banda had crossed the Sutluj and clashed with Shams Khan, faujdar of Jalandhar. The entire central Punjab was in ferment. The rising had sent a call to all the oppressed and the down-trodden, not merely the Sikhs, the peasants and others, but also the untouchables—tanners and scavengers—the victims of Brahminical oppression as much as of Mughal tyranny. It partook in part some of the character of a revolution.

But now the man who had lit the fuse and set the two provinces of

Delhi and Lahore on fire appeared to have been caught in a trap. The emperor and his wazir were both present in person for the *coup de grace*. A special cage had been prepared for the demon. The stronghold had been surrounded and Munim Khan had assured the emperor that the ogre would not be allowed to give them the slip.

But unknown to the imperialists there was one secret path that was left unguarded and it was this that Banda used for his escape. He left behind one of his followers, a tobacconist named Gulabu who resembled him, dressed in royal finery. Gulabu was captured and the news was brought to Munim who passed it to the emperor, and at the same time asked the band to strike up the triumphal music.

But soon it was discovered that 'the hawk had flown and only the owl had been netted'.[5] Gulabu's true identity was soon exposed and the emperor flew into a rage and publicly upbraided his wazir for incompetence. The rebel had effected his escape into, or through, Sirmoor territory so the 'Barfi' Raja was summoned and an army dispatched to force his attendance. The raja of Garhwal whose territory adjoined Sirmoor was also supposed to be sympathetic to Banda and so was also sent for, but his capital was relatively distant and he ignored the summons. Nahan the capital of Sirmoor was however close by and the army soon returned with Bhup Prakash, the son of the ruler, who had fled at the approach of the imperialists. The prince was thrown into the cage that had been prepared for Banda. The Sirmoor rani had sent about 30 notables to intercede on his behalf, but Bahadur Shah was past all pleading and he ordered them to be summarily executed. The emperor had never been known to display such violence before.

Bhup Prakash was sent to Delhi and kept in confinement in the Salimgarh prison attached to the Qila-i-Mualla. He remained here for two years at the end of which period he was released in the general confusion which followed the overthrow of Jahandar Shah.

Munim Khan was so affected by the firing he had received from his royal master that he fell into a deep depression. His mind was unhinged and he died soon after. Zulfiqar Khan, the Amir-ul-Umara and bakhshi, had always been his rival and coveted his post. He had been chiefly instrumental in spreading the news about the capture of Banda even though he knew it to be false, and the violence of the emperor's reaction on the deception being discovered, was largely due to his insinuations and snide remarks about the wazir's incompetence.

But Zulifqar was not fated to attain his ambition of becoming wazir. At least not yet. Besides the paymastership of the army he also held the viceroyalty of the six subas of the Deccan which he was unwilling to relinquish, and the emperor rightly felt that combining these two offices with that of wazir would make him much too powerful, and possibly even a danger to the Crown. Therefore when the offer was made it was made with the understanding that Zulfiqar would have to give up at least one of the other two offices which he held. As a direct refusal would have been impolitic, Zulfiqar took the excuse of his father. While Asad Khan was still alive he could not dream of becoming wazir; between the two of them, his father who had been wazir under Aurangzeb had surely the prior claim.[6]

Mahabat Khan, the son of the late wazir was another claimant for the office and his cause was warmly espoused by Azim us-Shan but he was notorious for his quick temper so he was never seriously considered. Another name that came up was that of Muhammad Hashim Safavi, a scion of the royal house of Persia, recently arrived as a refugee in India—the decay of the Safavid monarchy being much further advanced that of the Indian Timurids. But this prince so offended everyone by his arrogance that he was also ruled out.

The net result was that no one was appointed. De facto control remained largely with Azim us-Shan and with one Hidayatullah Khan, diwan of the Khalsa and Tan[7] who was appointed chief diwan with orders to assist the prince. He was granted the fresh title of Wazarat Khan. Soon after he petitioned for the grant of Sadullah Khan—the title of one of the most famous of Shah Jahan's wazirs. When his petition was put upto the emperor for orders he observed, 'It is not easy to be a Sadullah Khan; let him be called Saidullah Khan.' But he was generally known as Sadullah.

After the storming of Lohgarh desultory clashes continued between the Sikh bands and the imperialists mainly in the Jalandhar and Bari Doabs. In one battle Shams Khan Khweshgi the faujdar of the Jalandhar Doab was killed. In the campaign in the Bari Doab, Muhammad Amin Khan and Rustam Dil Khan, Mir Tuzak, achieved fame but the latter soon became enmeshed in controversies which ultimately led to his disgrace and downfall. It was rumoured that he had taken a large number of ordinary people prisoner under the pretext of their being Sikhs and distributed them among his soldiers in lieu of pay. They in turn sold them in the *nakhas* or horse market at Lahore, which, on occasion, also doubled as a mart for human cattle.

Rustam had many enemies. Besides the allegations regarding this affair there were others of a more serious character as far as the government was concerned. It was alleged that he had been lax in his pursuit of the Sikhs and on more than one occasion allowed the Sikh leader to slip from his grasp after accepting large offerings of cash and valuables from him.

Whatever the precise reason he was arrested and led through the streets of Lahore in fetters. On the way some of the bystanders who bore him grudges abused and cursed him, pelting him with dirt and odure. But true to his reckless character he kept cracking jokes with his guards who were seated on the same elephant. He was stripped of rank and titles and all his property confiscated. However, after some months he was released and restored to favour with the title of Ghazanfar Khan.[8]

The emperor took no further part in the campaign and after the capture of Banda's stronghold in December 1710 he marched leisurely by slow stages towards Lahore, reaching the city in August 1711.

It was a peculiarity of this emperor that he never slept in a room if he could help it. So at Lahore instead of occupying the imperial apartments in the fort he preferred to remain in tents outside the city. He seemed a throwback to his remote ancestors who had once been nomads in Central Asia, or maybe it was merely on account of the long years spent campaigning in the Deccan with his late father. Whatever the explanation there is no mention of his ever having spent a night in the imperial suites in his palaces, whether at Delhi, Agra or Lahore.

He pitched his tents near the village of Anwala, not far from the banks of the Ravi. The princes pitched their's closed by.

Bahadur Shah seemed to have had some premonition of his approaching end. When the proposal was made that he should go to Kangra or Kashmir for the summer and return again to Lahore in the winter, he shook his head in reply. His travels were now over, he said, and there was only one last journey to be made, that to his Maker. He remained in his tents but the draught cattle were dismissed. He took some interest in embellishing the Shalamar Gardens which lay nearby. About this time he also showed some inclinations towards the Shi'ite sect and held learned discussions on the subject with the ulema and holy men. A proposal was put forward to insert some words in the litany invoking the first four caliphs which was recited before the daily prayers which would have the effect of describing Ali as the *wasih* or heir of Muhammad, but in the end he desisted. But the mere rumour that this was being contemplated was sufficient to cause a riot in Lahore. In January preparations were made to celebrate the anniversary of his accession to the throne but he was too ill to make a public appearance.

He was troubled by delusions and his reason was affected. One day he issued orders that all the dogs in the camp and the city should be destroyed. Hundreds were killed. A contemporary records how the dogs abandoned the city, but each night they would swim across the river to visit the houses where they habitually ate, and before the sun rose they would all leave.[9]

He died finally on the night of 27 February 1712 at the age of 68. Except for rare outbursts of anger, he was a kindly, easy-going ruler, ever anxious to oblige. He found it very difficult to refuse a request and his detractors have described him as the *Shah be-khabar*, i.e. the unheeding king, with reference to the reckless profusion with which he distributed titles and favours. Upto the time of Aurangzeb the grant of mansabs and alqabs had been strictly regulated, but now there were often two or more officers with the same title, something hitherto inconceivable. Danishmand Khan records that at one time there were three men bearing the title of Fazil Khan.

Except for the last six months spent in the camp outside Lahore he had passed almost his entire reign on the march. First was the march from Kabul to Agra to secure the throne. Then from Agra to Rajasthan where the Rathors and Sisodias were in rebellion, then to the south to sort out Kam Bakhsh. After that it was back again to Rajasthan and finally to the Punjab against the Sikhs.

There was however one enemy against whom he did not have to contend and this was the Maratha power. For this he had Zulfiqar Khan to thank. While on the northward march Azam Shah had, on the latter's advice, released Raja Shahu who had been in the imperial camp ever since his capture in 1689. At that time he was a child and he attracted the notice of the emperor's daughter Zinat un-Nissa. On her request she was entrusted with his upbringing. Consequently he received a good education and was brought up like a prince. Though nominally a state prisoner, he was given the rank of a *haft hazaari* (7000)—the mansab to which his grandfather had aspired.[10] Thus he lacked nothing but his freedom and had little reason to hate the Mughals. On his release, his first act was to visit Khuldabad to offer prayers at the grave of the late emperor whom he regarded in the light of a father.

During his long captivity the Maratha nation had been led by Raja Ram his uncle who administered in his name as regent. But after his death in 1700 his son Shiva was proclaimed Chhatrapati with Tara Bai his mother as regent. Tara Bai was by no means eager to surrender her power to Shahu and so, for the next decade or so, the Marathas were embroiled in an internal struggle between the two branches of the house of Shivaji and the Mughals enjoyed a respite.

NOTES

1. Ganda Singh, *Banda Singh Bahadur*, p. 1. His original name was Lachhman Dev or Lachhmi Das. He was given the name of Madhav Das upon his initiation into the bairagi order.
2. Santokh Singh, *Sri Gur Pratap Suraj*, 14, pp. 6267-71 (ed. Bhai Vir Singh). Tabatabai, *Seir Mutaqherin*, i, pp. 86-8. Elliot and Dowson, vii, p. 415. The modern view is that the horrors of the first sack have been grossly exaggerated. It was only in the third and final sack that the town was truly destroyed.
3. Kamwar Khan, *Tazkirat us Salatin-i-Chaghatai*, pp. 75-6.
4. *Aman ud dahr, Mussarat shahr, Zinat ul takht-i-mubarak bakht*.
5. Shah Nawaz Khan, *Maathir ul-Umara*, ii, 2, pp. 297-8.
6. Ibid., p. 1038.
7. The diwan of the Khalsa and Tan was incharge of the Privy Purse, the Khalsa lands being the Crown lands and the Tan being a reference to the emperor's person.
8. Irvine, *Later Mughals*, i, p. 120. Warid, *Mirat-i-Waridat*, p. 125b.
9. Tabatabai, i, p. 21.
10. Shah Nawaz Khan, ii, 2, p. 790.

CHAPTER 7

Brother against Brother again

Barely four years had passed since the last fratricidal war and now the stage was set for another similar trial. And with all four brothers at one place it promised to be even more bloody and bitter.

Bahadur Shah I had four sons, the eldest being Muizz ud-Din, known as Jahandar Shah since his father's accession. He had been governor of the two subas of Multan and Sind since the time of his grandfather but since his father's accession he had been in attendance at court, the provinces being administered through deputies. Muhammad Azim, known as Azim ush-Shan, was the second and he had since long held the triple charge of Bengal, Bihar and Orissa. He had been recalled by Aurangzeb at the instance of Azam, but after the battle of Jajau he was restored to his original post. Like Muizz ud-Din he too exercised his duties through deputies. His viceroyalty was the richest and most important, and he was reputed to have amassed a fabulous treasure. During the last phase of Bahadur Shah's reign he was all-powerful, and de facto prime minister.

Then came Rafi ul-Qadr and Khujista Akhtar. They had not held any independent charge in Aurangzeb's time but after the accession of Bahadur Rafi ul-Qadr had been given the title of Rafi ush-Shan with the nominal charge of the suba of Kabul, while Khujista Akhtar was transformed into Jahan Shah and appointed subedar of Malwa. But like all the others, he too remained at court.

Muizz ud-Din had lost his father's favour on account of his dissipated habits and indifference to public affairs. Since he and Azim ush-Shan lived apart from their father the younger princes had come closer to him. But by his proud and haughty demeanour Jahan Shah antagonized most of the court and a coolness developed between him and the wazir. Long bouts of illness and consequent absence from court let to a decline in his influence. Meantime Azim was cultivating the wazir, Munim Khan, who resented Jahan Shah's haughty airs, and his influence became paramount. So after the death of Munim it seemed but natural that Azim should become the virtual wazir.

There was a singular lack of affection between the brothers. Each looked upon the other with suspicion and during the last days of the emperor's illness the tension was palpable. The story is narrated of how one day, when both Jahandar and Azim were seated by the bedside of their dying father, the latter picked up the dagger which lay besides Bahadur Shah's pillow and started playing with it idly. He seemed to admire its craftsmanship, then unsheathing it, glanced at the shimmering steel. But Jahandar seeing these actions took fright; he stood up, agitated, and rushed out with such precipitation that he forgot to put on his slippers. His turban struck the door, and tripping over the tent pegs he fell and had to be helped up by his servants. Such was the terror and apprehension that Azim ush-Shan inspired in his brothers.[1]

He was well connected on his mother's side with the Rajput aristocracy. That lady was the daughter of Raja Rup Singh Rathor of Kishangarh, a small state in Rajasthan whose chief was the scion of a younger branch of the great house of Marwar. One of Azim's wives, Bai Jas Kaur, was the daughter of Raja Kirat Singh of Amber, the son of the famous Mirza Raja. Thus Raja Jai Singh the astronomer-savant was his brother-in-law and he could count on the support of both Amber and Marwar, two of the most important states in Rajasthan.

He had everything going for him but his overweaning self-confidence destroyed him. As Bahadur Shah lay dying, all the leading nobles of the court were calling on him to assure him of their support. Zulfiqar Khan, the Amir-ul-Umara and first bakhshi was just as anxious to secure his future in the next reign as the others. He was not overly fond of Azim and was already in touch with the other princes, but no prudent man placed all his eggs in one basket, least of all a person as ambitious as Zulfiqar.

He sought out Iradat Khan (the historian) and requested him to send Iradat's grandson to Azim ush-Shan to ask him how best he could serve him on the present occasion. The grandfather records:

> I sent him, but he returned with a reply laconic and slight as if from a nobleman of high rank to the commander of a hundred, written in the hand of his confidant as follows: 'As the imperial servants can know no place of support but this Court and have already repaired to it, the Amir-ul-Umara must also do his duty, with assurance of a gracious reception in the Presence'. When the Amir-ul-Umara read this, he shed tears and said to me, with much emotion, 'You see the manners of the Prince and his advisors. Alas! the errors of a favourite unacquainted with government often endanger the very existence of his master.'[2]

Zulfiqar had been resentful of Azim ush-Shan's preference for the late wazir and his sons. Now this cool, formal note convinced him that there was no future for him in Azim's camp. He decided to throw in his lot with the eldest, Muizz ud-Din Jahandar Shah, and accordingly moved his tents and troops closer to Jahandar.

It was not the cold formality of Azim ush-Shan's reply which was responsible for Zulfiqar championing the cause of Jahandar, but all authorities agree that the prince and his witless counseller who actually wrote the note were guilty of an unpardonable discourtesy. He was an amir of the rank of 7,000 and held the most po werful office of the empire after the wazir's and with the additional charge of the six subas of the Deccan he was easily the most formidable nobleman at the imperial court.

Zulfiqar's father Asad Khan was the Vakil-i-Mutlaq and had been wazir under Aurangzeb. Zulfiqar's marriage connections were equally impressive. He was married to Mihr un-Nissa, the daughter of Asaf Khan Yamin ud-Daulah, wazir and brother-in-law to the Emperor Shah Jahan. Zulfiqar considered the wazarat as his, virtually by right, and the failure of Azim ush-Shan to conciliate him was a cardinal blunder.

Zulfiqar had met Jahandar and inquired about his plans for the future. This happy-go-lucky prince had only a few hundred soldiers and virtually no money. He replied that it was pointless for him to fight. As soon as his father's death was announced he intended to flee to Multan where he was known and had friends, and from there, perhaps, he might make a bid for the throne, depending on how the situation developed. The Amir-ul-Umara disapproved of such a casual attitude. He offered money, troops and artillery from his own stores and proposed an alliance with the two younger princes.[3] Collectively it was possible to challenge Azim ush-Shan while individually they were hopelessly outclassed.

The idea of sharing the sovereignty with his brothers did not appeal to Jahandar but he authorized Zulfiqar to negotiate with them. The latter soon hammered out a plan that was acceptable to all. The treasure of Azim would be divided equally between them and while Jahandar, being the eldest, would be the nominal badshah, the other two brothers would share in the government with independent charge of their respective provinces. Zulfiqar would be the common wazir for all, exercising the office through deputies at the courts of the other princes.

The plan was highly impractical and probably none of the contracting parties expected it to last. But for the moment it provided a convenient fig-leaf for covering up their irreconcilable ambitions and check-mating Azim us-Shan.

Bahadur Shah died on the night of 27 February 1712. Amin ud-Daulah conveyed the news to Azim ush-Shan and after condoling him and wiping his tears he urged him to proclaim the new reign, as not a moment was to be lost. The *naggaras* of the imperial band were ordered to be beaten to announce the accession of the new emperor and all the courtiers who were present in the vicinity rushed to pay their respects to the new monarch.

About this time it was suggested to Azim that as Zulfiqar and Hamid ud-Din Khan, who were both hostile to the prince, were busy preparing the body for burial, it was a good opportunity to seize them. Azim ush-Shan, however observed, that the imperial dignity would suffer from so hasty and indecent a proceeding, and that for his part he trusted solely to his own right and to the assistance of God Almighty. If the Lord was on his side, Zulfiqar could do little.

The officers who heard him make these fatuous remarks were disturbed by his complacency. The prince's underestimation of Zulfiqar's capacity for mischief bode ill for the future. Disregarding the admonition, Niamat Ullah Khan headed for the imperial enclosure at the head of a small body of horse, but when he got there he found that the bird had flown.[4] The imperial enclosure, along with its tents and treasure, however, fell into the hands of Azim ush-Shan.

The next day was one of confusion as the non-combatants, merchants and tradesmen, dancing girls, artisans and assorted camp followers tried to get out of harm's way and sought safety in the city. Many were unlucky and were set upon and plundered by ruffians who smelling loot had suddenly become active. The soldiers, learning of the emperor's death, forced their commanders to disburse their arrears.

The next morning there were reports that Azim's host was moving and he would strike at his brothers before they had time to organize themselves. There was panic in their camp, but Zulfiqar kept his cool and rode over personally to stiffen the resolution of the younger princes and to prepare their camp for defence.

The expected clash did not take place and by evening it was confirmed that the reported movement was only to enable the sons of Munim Khan and some other nobles who were not yet within the prince's camp to come in. In the morning Zulfiqar had sent some officers to Mahabat, one of the sons of the late Munim Khan, to request him to mediate between Azim ush-Shan and the other princes. The purpose was only to gain time but the visit was reported to Azim and he interpreted it as an attempt to tamper with his allegiance, hence his anxiety to bring Mahabat Khan and his followers within his camp's perimeter. Zulfiqar had also been informed that Azim was digging in and an early attack seemed unlikely.

This was reassuring news and gave Zulfiqar the required time to secure himself. So far no one had rated the chances of the three princes very highly, but when it became known that they were acting in concert and had the backing of Zulfiqar, unemployed soldiers started flocking to their standards for enlistment. Notwithstanding the poor show put up at Jajau, Zulfiqar's reputation for military prowess acquired in the Deccan wars was still intact. It was there that he had acquired the additional title of Nusrat Jang, i.e. victorious in battle.

Azim was depending on the power of his gold. Knowing that his brothers' resources were but slight he expected that their forces would soon melt away, either deserting or crossing over to join the stronger side. Hence whenever his officers urged action he would ask them to be patient. 'Wait a little more'—*andak bashid*—was his constant refrain, while his commanders seethed in desperation.

But more important than the fact of possession was the willingness to spend, and in this quality Azim was lamentably deficient. Ghulam Hussain the historian observed that 'it seemed he would carry his treasure with him to the other world as well'. The coldest place in the imperial camp, the wits would joke, was Azim ush-Shan's kitchen. But at such a time parsimony was a liability. He hoped to avoid a battle, because battle would inevitably mean plunder and loss—and much of the loot on such occasions fell to the share of the common soldiers. Hoping to win on the cheap he ultimately lost everything.

Zulfiqar, on the other hand, displayed a vigorous and offensive spirit at the outset. Three big guns were removed from the citadel and dragged to the camp, each gun drawn by 150 oxen and 5 or 6 elephants. The old campsites were abandoned and a new site selected in a relatively cleaner place, on an open plain. Bahadur Shah had been camping outside Lahore for over six months and the huge tented city numbering hundreds of thousands of men and animals that comprised the Urdu-i-Mualla was by now in anything but an exalted state. Fortunately there was a river nearby to carry off the dead animals and at least some of the refuse, but even so the exalted camp was infested with flies and vermin, besides the all-pervading stench of human and animal wastes.

The three princes drew their forces close together on a new campsite facing Azim, and each night they would draw a little closer to their opponent. By 9 March they had come close enough to engage in artillery duels.

It was now ten days since the old emperor had breathed his last and his body still lay in its bier unburied and almost forgotten. Azim's adherents like Shah Nawaz Khan Safavid, Raj Singh Rathor and others, urged him to take the offensive but the prince seemed to be paralysed by a strange lethargy. '*Andak bashid*'—wait a little more, was still his refrain. He was convinced that misery prevailed in the opposing camp. Churaman Jat had promised that he would not let any grain and supplies reach the allied princes, while he himself would suffer no want. It was only a matter of time, he reasoned, before they would be forced to sue for terms, or fight in desperation with depleted strength.

Small chashes and skirmishes began to take place between the soldiers of the opposing sides. On 14 March there was a major engagement close to Azim's entrenchments and at night the defences were penetrated but because of the watchfulness of Suleiman Khan Panni (brother of Daud Khan of the Deccan) the alarm was raised and the men repulsed.

The next day the fighting was resumed. The princes, led by Zulfiqar, gave a good account of themselves and though Azim's officers like Nawaz Khan, Suleiman Khan Panni and Daya Bahadur gave as well as they received, the day's fighting ended with the advantage on the side of the allies. Abdus Samad Khan who commanded their artillery, had placed his batteries on the mounds of old brick kilns from where they played havoc in the cramped entrenchments of Azim ush-Shan.

Demoralization set in, and Azim's soldiers began to doubt their prince's ability to win. Under cover of night they started deserting, but the prince still refused to give the orders to break out from their positions and fall upon the allies. On the third day, tired of the constant waiting and the murderous rain of shot, Raja Mohkam Singh Khatri and Raja Daya Bahadur went up to Azim ush-Shan and declared that they could no longer bear the taunts of their men, and, whether supported or not they would take their chance and attack. But to their shock the prince still tried to soothe them with his old advice of '*andak bashid*'.

Disgusted with his attitude the two rajas set forth with their followers and cutting through the enemy ranks they seized one of the batteries that were making their lives in the entrenchments so miserable. But instead of supporting them, Azim sent an officer to reprimand them for their impulsiveness and order them to return. Unsupported, the two rajas were overwhelmed by the inevitable counter-attack and mortally wounded; and their followers who survived sought refuge in the city. Too late, Suleiman Khan Panni came with a large force to follow up their initial success, but he was hit by a musket ball and killed.

By nightfall Azim ush-Shan's force had shrunk to a third of its original strength. During the night more troops deserted and the following day the exodus continued till the numbers were down to only 2,000 or 3,000. Many of the officers also left, among the notables being the sons of the late Munim Khan, Mahabat and Khan Zaman.

The end came on the fifth day. There was no reason for waiting any longer as the army had virtually disappeared. What he had so confidently predicted as the fate of the allied princes, had actually befallen him.

When the prince's war elephant was brought it ominously refused to let him mount. It had to be led away and another elephant was brought. The important chiefs still loyal to him were Raja Jai Singh of Amber, Raja Raj Singh of Kishangarh—both his relatives—Amin ud-Daulah and Niamatullah Khan.

A musket ball set one of the cushions in the royal howdah on fire. Seeing the smoke Amin ud-Daulah shouted to enquire if the prince was hurt.

'Not at all', he answered, throwing down the burning cushion. 'Be firm and do not lose heart.'

'Firm!' shouted the general despairingly. 'What is the use of firmness now when practically all is lost and our hopes are about to be dashed on the ground? In vain have your loyal servants been begging you to act, but whenever we urged you to attack you would only reply with those inauspicious words—"andak bashid".'

The prince remonstrated but the general cut him short. 'There is just one chance left now. Get off the elephant and take a swift horse. Let us head for Bengal where you can recoup your losses and then chance your luck again.'

The prince, who was remarkably calm and composed, observed that Dara Shukoh had sought safety in flight in the hope of a second attempt after the disaster of Samugarh. But it did him no good. So was it with Shah Shuja. But even today they might prove the truth of the scriptural saying: 'Many a time did a small number prevail over a multitude'. 'Victory and success may yet be ours!' he asserted, trying to put on a brave face.

But Amin ud-Daulah was labouring under no such delusion. Disaster was staring them in the face. He looked about him and observed that he had only about twenty horsemen left.

'Very well,' said the prince nonchalantly, 'Let me have one half of these twenty that I may charge Muiz ud-Din, while with the other ten you take on that luckless Khujista Akhtar.'

It was a weird conversation in the midst of a dust storm with the sand particles stinging their faces, while musket balls and arrows whistled by Muhammad Asim called out to Amin ud-Daulah and urged him to come with him so that they could get away while it was still possible. But Amin refused, saying that while his lord lived he could not abandon him.

Just then the prince's elephant was hit by a ball from a swivel on the base of its trunk. Maddened by pain the animal turned about and thundered away towards the river. The mahout lost his seat and fell. Amin tried to intercept him but the elephant was going too fast, and before anyone could reach he jumped from the high bank into the Ravi. When Amin ud-Daulah and the others reached the bank there was nothing to be seen. There was an extraordinary churning in the waters with mud flying up, but no trace of either the elephant or its rider.[5]

Apparently both had been swallowed up by quicksand and the prince's body was never found. Khwaja Muhammad Asim managed to escape and ultimately reached Patna, from where Azim's son Farrukhsiyar would set off on his adventure to win the throne. Raja Raj Singh also survived and managed to make his way to his native Kishangarh. Amin ud-Daulah was however taken and sent to Delhi under escort. He remained a prisoner in the Salimgarh until the accession of Farrukhsiyar.

The allies had triumphed, thanks to the leadership of Zulfiqar Khan. Now remained the division of the spoil and the even more delicate division of the empire according to the fantastic plan proposed by the king-maker and agreed by the three princes.

But neither Zulfiqar nor Jahandar had any intention of implementing the agreement. The latter had placed his destiny entirely in the hands of the wily Amir-ul-Umara and the understanding was that he should ultimately be the sole sovereign as per the traditions of the Timurids in India, with Zulfiqar as the wazir.

How much treasure Azim ush-Shan had left behind is not stated precisely. Historians talk only of cart loads or camel loads. Incredible though it may seem, there were about eighty cartloads of gold *asharfis* and about a hundred filled with silver rupees. Jahan Shah the youngest of the three confederate princes wanted the cash to be divided into three equal parts but Zulfiqar tried to delay the division and ultimately three-fifths was taken by Jahandar, the others being left with one-fifth each.

Rustam Dil Khan alias Ghazanfar Khan, the Mir Tuzak of the previous reign was one of the principal confidants of Jahan Shah. From the start he had suspected the intentions of Zulfiqar and had proposed to his prince that he be killed and desired his permission. Once he was removed from the scene, he assured, all could be implemented as per the original plan. But Jahan Shah, still euphoric after the victory over Azim ush-Shan refused to believe that Zulfiqar could play dirty, and did not permit the assassination.

Ultimately when things could not be spun out any further Zulfiqar asked Jahan Shah to send an officer with him to take his share of the treasure. As he was leaving he drew aside Rustam and Mukhlis Khan both of whom he knew suspected him, and spoke to them bluntly: 'You have done your best for your master but if he does not accept, it is not your fault but his fate.'

Meantime dissensions had broken out between Rafi ush-Shan and his principal adviser Hakim-ul-Mulk. The prince had promised that he would be his prime minister, but now he discovered that the latter was in league with Zulfiqar and sending daily reports of all that transpired in the camp. He called him to his tent and ordered his servants to give him a severe flogging so that he was removed half-dead from his tent.

Thus within a few days of their common victory the allies had fallen apart and were again feverishly recruiting soldiers. On 26 March, eight days after the death of Azim ush-Shan, Jahan Shah and Jahandar clashed. Rafi ush-Shan stayed aloof. He had been neutralized by the timely dispatch of a sizeable *peshkash* sent by Zulfiqar with the promise of more after the dispute with Jahan Shah had been sorted out.

It was the latter who made the first move. He manoeuvered his troops and took position facing Jahandar, and his artillery directed by Rustam Dil did great damage. There was some skirmishing but on the first day the fighting was mainly confined to artillery exchanges.

The next day the battle was resumed. In the morning there was some indecisive skirmishing but in the afternoon when Jahandar's cavalry had withdrawn to rest and feed their horses, Jahan Shah ordered his cavalry forward.

The leaders were Rustam Dil, Mukhlis, and Ghani Khan, and their charge was remarkable successful. The vanguard was broken up and Aziz ud-Din, the eldest son of Jahandar was taken prisoner. Then they reached a small field tent where Jahandar had passed the night with his concubine, Lal Kunwar, and was even then resting within. Surprised, he at once mounted his mistress's curtained elephant and made his way to Zulfiqar. Lal Kunwar fell into the hands of Rustam Dil and our swashbuckling hero was in the process of loosening the bejewelled *azarband*[6] of her pyjamas when the lady was saved by a counter-attack.

Zulfiqar was taken aback by the sudden turn of events. He saw that the battle was practically lost and only a bold move could save the situation. He called his personal guard, and tossing handfuls of gold among them, declared that the time had come for rendering him a signal service. If they were successful in their mission he would enrich them generously. Fired by greed, and enthused by the gold he had already given, they declared that he had only to give them his orders.

The plan was simple. They were to mingle with the soldiers who were now crowding around their prince and, pushing their way upto him kill him. Audacious as the plan was, it was not as reckless as it seemed, as the soldiers did not wear distinctive uniforms, and it was easy to mix with them.

The stratagem was successful. Several hundred musketeers mingled with the crowd of cheering soldiers and one group pushing upto Jahan Shah suddenly opened fire, killing both the prince and his son Farkhunda Akhtar.

Rustam and his companions who had got separated from the main battle, hearing the news of the death of their prince, hurried back towards his camp. They fought their way upto the royal elephant but finding only the body in the howdah, they fled.

It is said that the news of the 'victory' of Jahan Shah had been immediately conveyed to the city of Lahore and from there the rich Marwari bankers had immediately passed it on to their agents all over the country, so much so that in some towns the *khutba* was actually read in the name of the 'martyred' prince.

Zulfiqar soon presented Jahandar with his brother's head. The body of Farkhunda was also brought in and two other brothers were made prisoner. The drums again announced the second victory; salutations and cheers again rent the air, and the officers stumbled over each other to acclaim their sovereign and present their *nazars*.

Rafi ush-Shan on the other hand spent a tense and sleepless night. He and his army remained on the alert about 2 miles from the battlefield. He remained seated on his armoured elephant, his ears tuned to the sound of the cannonade, trying to divine which way the struggle was going. A *peshkash* of Rs. 25 lakh from Zulfiqar had ensured that he would remain neutral. His astrologer too had assured him that he should stay aloof from the struggle; ultimately the situation would change in his favour. The astrologers may well have been in the pay of Zulfiqar.

It was late in the night before definite information about the disaster that had befallen Jahan Shah was obtained. A driverless elephant was captured wandering distractedly. In the howdah was found a child of Jahan Shah with its nurse. The child was received kindly by the uncle, food and refreshment were brought, and from the boy's lips was learnt the outcome of the battle.

The prince then sent one of his trusted eunuchs to convey his congratulations to Jahandar, to remind him that he had kept his part of the bargain and to learn what were his brother's plans with respect to him.

The eunuch went first to the tent of Jahandar whence the sound of revelry could still be heard, but the guards denied him entry saying that the prince was tired on account of the exertions of the day and could not be disturbed. Then he sought out Zulfiqar's enclosure but that amir too was disinclined to meet him. The attendants told him that their lord had retired for the night and would not see anyone till morning.

Then the faithful slave sought out the tent of Kokaltash Khan. This noble was the foster brother of Jahandar, and had been intimate with the prince since his days as the governor of Multan during the reign of Aurangzeb. But Kamwar Khan has described him as a 'block head', and he seldom thought twice before opening his mouth. 'There they lie: the corpses of both father and son. Tell Rafi if he fights he too will meet the same fate.'[7] With his arm he indicated an adjoining tent where the bodies lay.

According to Ghulam Hussain the eunuchs of Jahandar had also addressed him in the same mocking vein. He had heard and seen enough and he hurried back to inform his master how matters stood.

Whatever else the princes of the house of Timur may have lacked, courage certainly was one quality which they had in abundance. It is said that Rafi ush-Shan was all for attacking Jahandar's camp then and there. With the soldiers and officers resting after the battle they stood a good chance of success, he argued. But his officers were against a night attack. So the prince resumed his vigil, waiting for daylight.

It must have been a very long night for the prince for it was also fated to be his last. As the sun rose above the horizon the drums were beaten and the attack launched.

Zulfiqar was alerted by the sound of the drums. The prince was woken up, still in a drunken stupor and could scarcely stand up. But he was dragged out and placed in the howdah as he was, bare-headed and dishevelled, to galvanize the army to stand and resist.

Fateh Ullah Khan who commanded Rafi's right wing had been bribed by Zulfiqar so instead of fighting he wheeled away to join Jahandar. Troops sent to reinforce his charge were repulsed by musket fire from their erstwhile comrades. Then Jahandar's army advanced against the prince's centre. Most of Rafi's remaining soldiers were raw novices lacking battle experience but his officers put up a good resistance with their personal troops and many of them were killed. Finally when all seemed to be lost the prince himself decended from his elephant to fight with sword and buckler only to be struck down by a bullet. His camp, along with all his treasure and goods, was plundered, and his women and three sons, led away in litters to Jahandar's camp.

For three days the bodies of Jahan Shah, his son Farkhunda, and Rafi ush-Shan were exposed to public view on the river bank before being prepared and laid out in biers for interment. And all this while, for a full month, the body of the late emperor had been lying untended in a tent.

The house of Babar seemed to have lapsed into the barbarism of the times of Timur and Genghiz.

NOTES

1. Elliot and Dowson, *The History of India as told by its own Historians*, vii, p. 556.
2. Ibid., p. 557.
3. Tabatabai, *Seir Mutaqherin*, i, p. 24.
4. Ibid., p. 23.
5. Ibid., p. 29.
6. Ibid., p. 31. The *azarband* is the cord of loosely woven silk which holds up the pyjamas. Often it was highly decorated with tassels of gold and jewels. Ladies of the class to which Lal Kunwar belonged would secure their *azarbands* with highly complex knots, to guard against anyone forcing his entry into the perfumed garden too easily. The account of the fighting at Lahore is based on Irvine and the *Seir*.
7. Irvine, *Later Mughals*, i, p. 184.

CHAPTER 8

The Reign of Jahandar

The installation of a new emperor was a simple affair. All that it entailed was the erection of a 'throne'—often no more than a wooden platform covered with carpets and silken bolsters on which the sovereign sat while receiving the congratulations and homage of his umara. For the Turks and Mongols, descended from the nomadic wanderers of the steppes of Central Asia, any place was good enough. Akbar's coronation or *takht poshi* took place on an earthen stage in an open field near Kalanaur. Bahadur Shah's ceremony was performed in the Bagh Dahr Ara in Agra while Jahandar Shah thought the battle-field good enough for his enthronement.

Tents and screens were set up and the ceremony performed the very next day, 29 March. Three battles had been fought on that plain over the past three weeks and even if the dead had been removed, the carcasses of the animals, the horses and oxen must have been still lying around. As Jahandar Shah was receiving the homage of his umara and handing out titles, offices and *khillats*, vultures lazily circled high above.

It was to be a singularly gory accession marked by savage retribution. Neither the new emperor nor the king maker were of the forgiving type. Not for them the understanding pragmatism of Bahadur Shah who recognized that the umara would always be loyal to the ruler of the day, but in the event of a disputed succession there was bound to be confusion with the nobles having to choose between different pretenders. But once the contest was over, all would be anxious to regain favour, and could be relied upon to serve the new monarch loyally.

Asad Khan, retained his former dignities and office of Vakil-i-Mutlaq, while Zulfiqar, as was to be expected, achieved his ambition of becoming prime minister, with the rank of 8,000 and a large monetary gift. Kokaltash Khan, the emperor's foster-brother was made first bakhshi with the title of Khan-i-Jahan. His wife's sister's husband, Khwaja Hussain was made second bakhshi with the title of Khan-i-Dauran, while his brother Azam received the governorship of Agra. Kokaltash was not too happy. In his childhood days when they used to play together, Jahandar had promised

Kokaltash that he would be his wazir, should he ever be fortunate enough to become emperor. But Zulfiqar was unquestionably the man who had made that possible and promises made to his foster-brother had to put aside. Throughout the short reign there was friction between him and Zulfiqar, and unfortunately his brother-in-law Khan-i-Dauran was to prove a disaster.

After rewarding the friends who had assisted him, Jahandar and Zulfiqar were anxious to punish the others who had been conspicuous in the opposition. Some had managed to escape. Mir Ishaq, afterwards famous as Amir Khan, Khwaja Muzaffar, Khwaja Zafrullah and Fakhr ud-Din with some of the disbanded soldiers of the deceased princes managed to reach Bihar and Bengal. But others were not so fortunate. Mahabat Khan, son of Munim Khan, Hamid ud-Din Khan Alamgiri, Sarfaraz Khan Bahadur Shahi and others—in all twenty umara—were arrested, placed in irons and confined in the prison of the Exalted Fort. Their houses and properties were seized and many were tortured.

But there were others who paid with their lives. Rustam Dil Khan, Mukhlis Khan and Jani Khan were sentenced to death. All of them were notable partisans of Jahan Shah. It is said that when in the course of the battle news was brought of the death of Jahan Shah, Rustam Dil Khan had exclaimed. 'What was destined has happened. Let us kill Azzuddin and avenge the blood of Jahan Shah [Khujista Akhtar]!' Azz ud-Din had been taken prisoner earlier in the battle and was in their custody. But Jani Khan had objected that it would be more sensible for them to take steps for their own safety, and on his advice Azz ud-Din was released.

This conversation was reported to Azz ud-Din who therefore interceded on behalf of Jani Khan for the latter's life to be spared. But Rustam Dil's was a foregone case. He had urged Jahan Shah to seize and kill Zulfiqar, and in the battlefield had hurled abuse at Jahandar and personally done his best to kill him.

Of what offence or indiscretion Mukhlis Khan was guilty is not clear, but, according to some sources, both Rustam and Mukhlis were accused of having entered the late emperor's harem after his death, violating some of the women, and stealing valuables.

Rustam Dil Khan did not loose his nerve even till the end. He had been sentenced to death by slow degrees, being cut to pieces, limb by limb. Brought before Zulfiqar the latter taunted him; how inspite of his cleverness he had been reduced to nought. It is said that the nobleman—so apt was his title, 'the lord with the heart of a Rustam'—laughed nonchalantly and retorted. 'Both of us have eaten from the same plate (i.e. of ambition). The diet agreed with you but not with me.'

Zulfiqar was nonplussed and had no reply. As the executioner began his grisly work, the hero kept up a running commentary of invective against Jahandar, Zulfiqar and Kokaltash, heaping on them the strongest epithets, until at last he lost consciousness.

Mukhlis Khan's execution was more merciful, being a simple beheading. Thereafter his mangled limbs and the trunk were strung up from wayside trees.[1]

The nobles having been dealt with, Jahandar turned his attention to the surviving members of the imperial house.

Hidayat Kesh, the chief of the Intelligence Bureau, *waqia-nigar-i-kul*, reported to the emperor that Prince Muhammad Karim the eldest son of Azim ush-Shan was in hiding in Lahore. After the battle, which had killed his father, he had taken refuge in the house of a poor weaver in the city. His cash being exhausted he gave his ring to his host with instructions to pawn it for funds. The possession, in the hands of a poor weaver, of such a valuable ring was commented upon and the matter came to the notice of Hidayat Kesh through his network of informers. The poor weaver was questioned and the truth revealed. The prince was arrested and produced before Jahandar who handed him over to the custody of Zulfiqar. It is said that the poor prince, with tears of humiliation, requested his uncle for some food and refreshment as he had not eaten for three days, but his tears were ignored and Zulfiqar had him beheaded two days later in his tents.[2]

The body of the wretched prince was interred in the garden of Jahangir's tomb at Lahore. The other princes, the three sons of Rafi ush-Shan, the two surviving sons of Jahan Shah, and another son of Azim ush-Shan, were confined in the prison cells of Salimgarh. So too the young Ali Tabar, the only surviving son of Azam Shah, and the two sons of Kam Bakhsh.

That Zulfiqar was as much to blame as the dissipated and unbalanced Jahandar is evident from the fact that the murder of Muhammad Karim actually took place in his tents and he took a personal interest in the torture and execution of Rustam Dil Khan. The pointless executions and unnecessary cruelty contrast strongly with the politic moderation of Aurangzeb who even forgave Maharaja Jaswant Singh for his treacherous attack at Khajuha. The contrast with the genial Bahadur Shah is even more striking. A striking picture has been drawn by Iradat Khan of how the old emperor would sit in full durbar surrounded by his sons, grandsons and nephews. Even the sons of the deposed Adil Shahi and Qutb Shahi sultans sat with them. The new ruler, on the other hand, preferred to keep all his kinsmen immured in the cells of the Salimgarh.

Jahandar was 51 when he ascended the throne and was already known for his dissipated habits and indifference to public affairs. His infatuation with Lal Kunwar could be traced to his days as a prince but that by itself was not remarkable. But from the guarded hints of historians it is clear that he went to extraordinary lengths to indulge himself. He is described as being effeminately careful of his person and possessing 'blemishes and vices unworthy of royalty and unknown among his illustrious ancestors'.

Lal Kunwar was the daughter of Khasusiyat Khan, reputedly a descendant of the legendary Tansen. He used to sing in the court of Akbar and it is said that when on a cloudy day he sang *Raga Malkauns*, it started raining. Some traces of his genius had filtered down, over the generations to Lal Kunwar, who was besides, a very beautiful woman.

But she belonged to the caste of hereditary singing and dancing girls, and prior to being taken up by Muizz ud-Din Jahandar Shah she had lived the life of a common courtesan. Such women frequently entered royal harems—an example being Udaipuri Bai, the mother of Kam Bakhsh—but they were expected to know their place and stay there.

For instance the first lady of the emperor's harem was not usually the current favourite or even the senior consort. By right this place belonged to the emperor's mother, if she happened to be alive, or to one of his aunts or sisters. Since the death of Aurangzeb this position had been held by Zinat un-Nissa Begum, the only surviving daughter of Aurangzeb—his last surviving consort Udaipuri having died shortly after the battle of Jajau. Notwithstanding her partiality for Azam, Bahadur Shah had conferred on her the honorific of Padishah Begum; and further increased the jagirs and allowances settled on her since Aurangzeb's time.

But while the nobly-born and well-brought up daughters of the umara might have been expected to defer to the authority of a seventy-year old it was too much to expect of Lal Kunwar, the former dancing girl in the full flower of her youth and beauty.

The favourite was dignified with the title of Imtiyaz Manal (Chosen of the Palace) and jagirs of the value of Rs. 2 crore were settled on her, besides allowances for her wardrobe and jewels. Much of the huge treasure of the late Azim ush-Shan was made over to her, and she also began to affect the crimson umbrella and kettledrums—hitherto exclusive imperial prerogatives. Moreover all her brothers and relatives were made amirs with mansabs of 4,000 or 5,000 and granted the right of playing the naubat outside their houses and kettledrums while on the march.

The old lady of the haram sarai, the Padishah Begum ignored the pretensions of this hetaira and she in turn insulted her using various kinds of abusive epithets while referring to her in public. When the begum invited the emperor to an entertainment he did not attend because his favourite had not been asked and she would not let him attend without her. Thus the emperor and his aunt stopped speaking to each other.

The emperor seemed to have no consideration for his own dignity. Ignoring the established etiquette of the court, he would set off with his beloved in a carriage drawn by bullocks, drinking and picnicking from one pleasure garden to the other. At night they would visit taverns and *kothas* of courtesans. On one such occasion they returned to the palace late at night after visiting her lowly friends. Both had fallen asleep. Lal Kunwar was carried to her bedchamber by her ladies and the cart driver who had also probably had a drop too many, toodled off with the cart to his humble quarters outside the gate without checking out the carriage. As a result the emperor of Hind was left in the cart outside the hovel of the driver and was located with difficulty in the morning when a search was instituted by the alarmed Lal Kunwar.[3]

When they were not exploring the night life of Delhi there would be drunken revels in the Qila-i-Mualla. The drinking companions of his majesty were not his amirs but the friends and relatives of his favourite: former musicians, pimps and publicans, who had been transformed into amirs thanks to Lal Kunwar and her infatuated lover. No decorum was observed in these gatherings and the emperor had lost all sense of shame, his infatuation rendering him powerless to assert himself and bring the low scum with whom he was surrounded to order.

But nothing scandalized the great umara so much as the sudden elevation of the family and relatives of Lal Kunwar. 'All the customs of ancient times were changed,' laments Iradat Khan, 'He made the vast empire of Hindustan an offering to the foolish whims of a courtesan.' Her brother was given the title of Khushal Khan and the rank of 7,000, her uncle was transformed into Niamat Khan with the rank of 5,000. The entire family, including the father, brothers and brothers-in-law were ennobled, and the finest of the escheated mansions in the city were given to them. Hence, as Kamwar Khan philosophically observes, 'the owl came to dwell in the eagle's nest, and the crow took the place of the nightingale'.

An interesting story is narrated about this period. According to the *Seir Mutaqherin* orders were passed appointing Khushal Khan, governor of Agra. (According to some historians the person concerned was Niamat Khan and the subedari offered was that of Multan, but the story is substantially the same.) But when the upstart applied to the wazir, for the authentication of the royal order, Zulfiqar decided to bring him down a peg or two.

Reading the imperial order he observed that before the formal appointment order could be issued it was obligatory for certain fees to be paid. Khushal Khan expressed his willingness and enquired about the value of the required sum. Without batting an eyelid the wazir replied that he would require 5,000 *tanpuras* and 7,000 *tablas*. The former *kalawant*[4] stung by the minister's sarcasm, complained to his sister who spoke to the emperor about it. A few days later Jahandar remarked on this strange demand of the wazir and added that he must have meant it in jest. The minister however replied with a perfectly straight face that it was no joke at all.

Your amirs have for generations been serving your Majesty as governors and army commanders. Rulers have always, even in the past, amused themselves with singers and dancers and it has been customary for kings to honour them with pensions and gifts. But now that your Majesty has started appointing them and their dependents to the great offices of the State like that of provincial governors, your faithful amirs who shall be rendered jobless will have to seek some other profession. That is why I asked for the *tanpuras* and *tablas* so that the umara may train themselves for a profession and yet still be able to compete for the great offices for the State.

The story may be apocryphal but at any rate the letters patent were never issued and the emperor let the matter drop.[5]

Another incident involving a close intimate of Lal Kunwar and one of the umara shows the wazir in the light of a protector of his class. The incident involved Zohra, an 'adopted' sister of the royal favourite and Chin Qilich Khan. Since the commencement of the new reign he had been without a post like many other amirs of the former regime and was leading a retired life in Delhi. He seldom left his house and when he did venture forth it was usually to meet some scholar or person known for his piety. He had an exceeding good opinion of himself and scorned to call on the great men of the day, and had not even bothered to pay his respects to Zulfiqar.

Zohra had been a vegetable seller prior to the elevation of her friend. The friendship between the two women went back many years to the time when Lal Kunwar had been a commonplace entertainer, one among many, before she caught the eye of the middle-aged Prince Muizz ud-Din. One day while munching almonds, one of the nuts they had cracked open was found to contain a double kernel. Each took one and swore that she would regard the other as her sister for life. Now with Lal Kunwar elevated to Imtiyaz Mahal, Zohra also acquired wealth and position and she went forth on an elephant with an extensive retinue whenever she went to the Qila-i-Mualla to meet her 'sister'. In the palace this vulgar former vendor of vegetables enjoyed privileges hitherto permitted only to princesses. As a consequence of her sudden elevation she became exceedingly insolent and her retinue even more so.

One day in one of the narrower lanes of Delhi her *sowarry* and that of Chin Qilich Khan came face to face. She was atop an elephant with a numerous and noisy retinue who were shouting to the passers-by to get to the side. The amir's *sowarry* was more modest, in keeping with the status of a retired official, and his retainers few in number. Seeing the boisterous and swaggering retainers of Zohra and the elephant behind, Chin Qilich Khan who had no desire to provoke a confrontation motioned to his followers to give way and let her pass.

But inevitably there ensued some commotion between the grooms of the two parties, and Zohra enquired whose *sowarry* it was that had obstructed her passage. On being told she leaned out of her howdah, pulling aside its curtains as if to have a closer look at the famous amir, and then tauntingly called out loud and clear making sure that it was heard by all: 'Thou Chin Qilich Khan, surely thou art the son of a blind man.'

The insolent allusion to his distinguished father stung the nawab and he made a threatening gesture. Taking the hint his attendants fell upon those of Zohra and climbing up to the elephant, forced it to sit down, dragged her out, and roughed her up.

It didn't take more than a minute, but honour satisfied, Chin ordered his men to take him to the wazir. Sensible of the danger he was in, he was anxious to explain what had happened and secure his sympathy and support before the emperor ordered his arrest or worse.

He was immediately received by the minister who gave him a sympathetic hearing, and assured him that no harm would befall him. As soon as he had left he sent a brief note to the emperor: 'The honour of any one of the umara, your faithful servants, belongs to them all, and your devoted slave joins issue with Chin Qilich Khan.'

He was none too soon for Zohra too had reached the palace but seating herself in the gateway she started creating a spectacle, raising a *dohai*, for the insults suffered by her, rolling on the ground and throwing dust over her head. Lal Kunwar was informed of what had happened by her attendants and was already demanding exemplary punishment for the 'insolent' amir when the wazir's note reached the emperor. The note served its purpose and the insistent tone of the minister drove home to the emperor that any attempt to chastise the amir would have serious repercussions. The matter was ignored; nothing happened to Chin Qilich Khan, and Zohra and her 'adoptive' sister were left to wring their hands in frustration.[6]

Another outrageous incident involving Khushal Khan Kalawant is recorded by Syed Ghulam Hussain Khan. This upstart had the opportunity to catch a glimpse of a beautiful lady who was married to a gentleman living in the wazir's neighbourhood. Messages and gifts were sent through intermediaries to corrupt the lady but she was virtuous and the *kalawant's* stratagems were in vain. Then he attempted to attain his object by main force and tried to abduct her. The husband called for help and appealed to the wazir, who was infuriated at the upstart's presumption and ordered his men to bring him in, dead or alive. The order was promptly executed and his soldiers and grooms dragged in the offender who was flogged on the minister's orders and eventually sent a prisoner to the Salimgarh, inspite of the protests of the sister. It appears that the kalawant had become notorious for many similar outrageous acts.[7]

Notwithstanding these reported incidents that do credit to the minister, Zulfiqar was not a successful wazir. Perhaps Ghulam Hussain Khan who was a Shia is naturally more sympathetic to a co-religionist, but Iradat Khan gives a different view of his performance. The incidents recorded by Ghulam Hussain may well be true but they do not tell the whole story.

According to him Zulfiqar's vanity become insufferable following the success of the intrigues which had placed Jahandar on the throne. He became proud and avaricious, and plotted to achieve the disgrace and ruin of the most ancient and wealthy families, inventing causes to put great men to death or to disgrace them so that their goods and estates might be confiscated. He was corrupt and always on the lookout for ingenious ways to extract money and came to be hated by the rich and poor alike. His secretary Diwan Sabha Chand was even more grasping and unscrupulous.

Sabha Chand was insulting and obscene in his language and gave great offence to all with whom he came in contact in the course of official work. Even his subordinates were not loyal to Zulfiqar. Not only did he fail to make friends, he alienated even those who had aligned themselves with him. It is said that he had become so greedy that he was loath to part with money even to his personal staff whose pay was always in arrears.[8]

His authority was also eroded by the rivalry of Kokaltash Khan who, as mentioned earlier, was severely disappointed at being passed over by his foster-brother for the wazarat. One Sarbuland Khan was presented to the emperor through Kokaltash and appointed governor inspite of the wazir's opposition. And when the next crisis developed Khan-i-Dauran would be sent to tackle the menace posed by Farukhsiyar, inspite of the wazir's advice that he was totally unfit for the task assigned.

While the armies that would eventually topple him were already on the march the monarch and his paramour continued their revels as if there was no tomorrow. The Qila-i-Mualla was lit up three nights in a month. The whole fort would be illuminated as on Diwali. Consequently oil became scarce and prices rose. Then, say the historians, Begum Imtiyaz Mahal ordered them to use ghee instead of oil. Probably the story is apocryphal, comparable to Marie Antoinette's oft repeated 'Let them eat cake', but it aptly captures the spirit of the times.

Another day, it is said, while watching a boat crossing the Yamuna from the walls of the palace the favourite idly remarked that she had never seen a boat go down. Promptly, on the orders of the emperor, another boat set forth and on his orders the crew removed the plugs midstream so that Imtiyaz Mahal could have the pleasure of watching people struggle in the water and drown.[9]

The great desire of the favourite was for a child, a son who could be his father's heir and succeed to the empire—and through whom she could continue to reign as the First Lady of the palace. Perhaps she had been rendered infertile in preparation for her life as a courtesan by surgical intervention, or may be it was just chance, but she could not conceive and was desperate for a remedy, clutching at every straw that offered hope.

At the shrine of a saint, Sheikh Nasir ud-Din Avadhi known popularly as Chiragh-i-Delhi, there was a tank where it was said a couple desirous of having children should bathe in the nude for forty consecutive Sundays. So, religiously, every Sunday, the emperor and Lal Kunwar would set forth, for their dip while the court and indeed the city of Delhi sniggered. But long before the cycle of forty weeks could be completed the reign of this Lord of Misrule was terminated.

All the great umara, all the lords from Turan and Iran, were disgusted by the antics of the ridiculous emperor. His partiality for low men and women had disgusted everyone and all looked eastward from which direction Farrukhsiyar was advancing. His name had become a beacon of hope for every man in the army, great and small.

The tragedy was that Farrukhsiyar's reign would be just as disappointing. There would be no Lal Kunwar to lend spice to its annals, but it was no less of a disaster.

NOTES

1. Irvine, *Later Mughals*, i, pp. 188-9.
2. Ibid., p. 190.
3. Elliot and Dowson, *The History of India as told by its own Historians*, vii, p. 433.
4. *Kalawant*: a professional musician who provides the accompaniment to a singing girl.

5. Elliot and Dowson, vii, pp. 432-43. Tabatabai, *Seir Mutaqherin*, i, pp. 36-7.
6. Tabatabai, i, pp. 37-9.
7. Ibid., pp. 39-40.
8. Elliot and Dowson, vii, pp. 433, 558-9.
9. Irvine, i, p. 192. Khushal Chand, *Tarikh-i-Muhammad Shahi*, p. 390a.

CHAPTER 9

Badshah Gardi or King Making

When Azim ush-Shan set off in 1707 from Patna on the summons of his grandfather he left behind his son Farrukhsiyar. He does not appear to have ever again visited Bengal or Bihar of which he was still the nominal governor, nor did he ever send for his son, even though he was a very important person enjoying the confidence of his father, the Emperor Bahadur Shah. Probably, as is often the case in great families, relations between the father and son were cool. More likely, the mother had fallen out of favour, for years later, on the occasion of the death of Bahadur Shah we still find both mother and son miles away from Lahore.

At this point it will be necessary to describe in some detail the administrative arrangements for the viceroyalty of Bengal, which because of its extent, extraordinary wealth, and importance from the point of view of the imperial revenues was quite different from the usual pattern.

The nominal governor was of course Azim ush-Shan since the days of Aurangzeb, but he was only the nazim or military governor exercising magisterial authority. The revenue administration was with the diwan, Murshid Quli Khan, also known as Jafar Khan. In order to lighten his burden Azim ush-Shan had been able to secure the nomination of congenial deputies or naib nazims at Patna, Cuttack and Allahabad, which had been attached to Bengal since the reign of Bahadur Shah.

At Patna (officially known as Azimabad) his deputy was Hussain Ali Khan, Allahabad was with Abdullah Khan, while in Bengal proper the diwan vested himself with police and magisterial authority. Orissa was bestowed on one Khan Jahan Bahadur, an insufferable character on whom Azim ush-Shan had taken pity.

When the news came that Bahadur Shah had died and Azim ush-Shan had staked his claim for the throne Farrukhsiyar, who was then at Patna, ordered the *khutba* read in his name in the mosques of the province, the naib nazim Hussain Ali Khan being away on tour. But when the evil tidings of his death were received everyone started to cold-shoulder the prince.

Jahandar summoned Farrukhsiyar to Delhi but the news of Prince Muhammad Karim's murder had also reached Bengal. Murshid Quli Khan had also received a directive to convey the prince to Delhi. Relations between the diwan and Azim ush-Shan had been cool ever since the latter's appointment to the nizamat, but the diwan was reluctant to proceed to extremes against the son. It was evident that prison—at the very least—awaited him at Delhi. There still lingered in the provinces some traces of the old etiquette according to which a prince of the blood was infinitely superior to a nobleman, however powerful the latter, and thus it was inconceivable for a mere diwan or nazim to lay hands on him. So a message was sent to the prince who was at the time at Rajmahal that he should quit Bengal.

With a heavy heart, Farrukhsiyar packed up his goods, collected his family and moved up to Patna in Bihar. Here he decided to wait and try winning over the provincial officers to his cause. After all, the naib nazims at Patna, and in neighbouring Allahabad and Orissa, were all heavily in his late father's debt. They had all been raised to their present dignities by him, and an appeal to their sentiments, he reasoned, might prove effective in rallying support for the son. His mother and family were of the same mind and astrologers and soothsayers also suggested that he should go no further. Patna was an auspicious place for him and it was here that he should proclaim his reign, and the empire of Hind would be his.

It seemed highly unlikely. His resources were slight and he had no executive authority. All that he was banking on was the sense of honour of the officers of the province, which in the case of civil servants, with their eyes on their careers, could be very elastic.

But Hussain Ali Khan the naib nazim of Bihar was a Syed from Barah—a tract in the modern district of Muzaffarnagar in U.P.—and the Syeds of Barah, were renowned for their pugnacity and thick-headedness. When one spoke of a Syed from Barah people smiled. It was equivalent to 'a blockhead from Barah'. Many are the jokes still current in the region about them. Their's was a large fraternity. Originally descended from twelve brothers, they had been settled in that region for many generations, and had served many emperors in honourable positions, but never in the highest echelons. Perhaps their reputation as blockheads came in the way. Their genealogy was a little suspect, and it is primarily as fighters and soldiers that we known them.

Farrukhsiyar recognized these qualities of the Syed and was aware of the respect he commanded in the province. He entered into correspondence with him. At first the Syed was reluctant to even meet him. He was wary of the prince and the first unauthorized reading of the *khutba* in

Azim's name, and the act of striking coins, had made him nervous.

The prince had not entered the city but was camping in a sarai outside and the messages which he sent were humble and designed to appeal to the Syed's better nature. He stressed his present hopeless condition and the fears he had for the reception that awaited him in Delhi. The Syed's reply was respectful but formal and stressed the delicacy of his position. The orders which he had received from the court enjoined a different line of conduct and though he could not bear the thought of arresting his royal person it would be advisable for him to retire from his jurisdiction.

But ultimately the Syed was persuaded to call on him. Elaborate arrangements were made by the prince for this was to be a crucial meeting. The ladies of the family were also fully involved in the planned 'seduction' and were seated behind a curtain.

The prince received the Syed standing and bade him be seated. By way of a *khillat* he ordered him to be dressed in one of his own robes. The Syed was overwhelmed by his courtesy and graciousness. The words he spoke were sad and resigned. Unless he found some protector there was no hope and certain death awaited him at the Qila-i-Mualla. Then the curtain parted and his youngest daughter who was then about six or seven came in. She had been well-tutored and sat down, it is said, in the Syed's lap, and implored him to give shelter and protection to a friendless prince and his family, alluding delicately to the glorious ancestry of the nazim—his supposed descent from the Prophet—and how succour could be hoped only from persons of his distinguished lineage. The Syed was moved by the child's simple and direct appeal which was reinforced by that of the other ladies behind the curtain. The prince then fastened his own sabre on to the Syed's sword belt. Hussain now cast aside all his earlier apprehensions and declaring that his head and fortune were at his service desired that they should immediately proceed to raise troops.[1]

There is another version of how the governor was won over. While no less dramatic it is sounds more probable for several contacts must have preceded the final formal declaration by Syed Hussain. According to this the first move was made by the prince's mother, Sahiba Niswan, who together with her granddaughter, went to call on the Syed's mother who was also staying with him at Patna.

The two ladies had a frank talk. The princess reminded the Syeda of all that her late husband had done for her two sons. Inspite of the great services rendered to Bahadur Shah at the battle of Jajau, and the fact that they had been severely wounded, Jahandar had thought a mere expression of thanks sufficient recompense. It was only the intervention of her husband that had secured Abdullah and Hussain the charges of Allahabad and Patna, two governments that formed part of his viceroyalty. Whatever the family was today, was entirely on account of her late Lord's bounty. Therefore it was their incumbent duty to aid and protect his son, specially as the latter had lost his father, a brother and two uncles. The future of his son and his family was now entirely in his hands. And at this point the ladies commenced weeping and lamenting.

The old lady was moved by the words of the widowed princess and she called her son into the room. The little girl fell at his feet, imploring his assistance, while the Syeda told him in no uncertain terms where his duty lay. Whatever the ultimate result he would be the gainer. If he failed and death ensued, he would be remembered as one who had been faithful and loyal to his benefactor's family. If successful, he and his brother would be the first nobles of the empire, with none between them and the emperor. But if he remained with Jahandar he would have to answer God for having repudiated his mother's claims upon him.

Indian sons are powerless before their mother's appeals and Syed Hussain Ali Khan was no exception. He raised the little girl to her feet and replaced the discarded veils on the heads of the royal princesses and swore that the prince's cause was now his. The next day the prince visited the governor. He appeared with his hands tied in a loose scarf and declared that he had come prepared either to be sent a prisoner to Delhi or to make a pact with him for an attempt to gain the throne. The Syed untied the scarf and declared that he had decided to fight and, if need be, die in his Highness's cause.[2] The scene described by Ghulam Hussain in the *Seir* must have been the last formal visit by the governor to the prince's camp in which he intended to make public his adhesion to his cause. Round about this time it was decided that the two most important posts, that of wazir and first bakhshi would go to Abdullah and Hussain Ali Khan.

Then coins were struck and the *khutba* ordered to be read in Farrukhsiyar's name and letters dispatched to the elder brother by both the prince and Syed Hussain.

Abdullah Khan was at first horrified by Hussain's rashness in committing himself to an apparently hopeless enterprise, but events happened in such a manner that he found that he had little choice but to join them.

He was himself facing some embarrassment. His soldiers' pay was in arrears and in the course of a punitive expedition they had mutinied, and he was compelled to retreat to Allahabad where he shut himself in the fort. About this time Shuja-ud-Din Khan, son-in-law of Murshid Quli Khan was passing through Allahabad with the Bengal tribute. Abdullah Khan saw in this a possible means of escape from his predicament. A little while earlier, the news of the death of Bahadur Shah had also been received and no one knew which prince would finally succeed. So he sent officers to the camp of Shuja Khan advising him that in view of the disturbed situation obtaining in Allahabad (mainly because of the presence of the large number of deserters from his unpaid troops) it was not safe to camp in the open and that it would be desirable to bring the treasure into the fort where it would be secure from marauders. It would also be advisable for Shuja Khan to await the outcome of the ongoing fratricidal struggle at Lahore before proceeding further. Shuja found the advice sensible and complied, thus placing himself and his treasure at the mercy of Syed Abdullah.[3]

Shortly after, news of the success of Jahandar Shah was received. Abdullah dispatched a congratulatory letter to the victorious prince declaring his loyalty and desiring to know how he could be of service to him. He must have been nervous; the question was, would he, a known protegé of the late Azim ush-Shan be allowed to continue at Allahabad, or would he be replaced by some officer closer at hand and better able to plead his case with Jahandar and Zulfiqar?

Soon news came that he had been replaced by one Raji Muhammad Khan whose family was based in nearby Manakpur. He in turn nominated a relative of his, one Syed Abdul Ghaffar, as his deputy who raised a force of about 7,000 men and marched towards Allahabad to assume charge. On being apprised of his supersession Abdullah Khan decided to throw in his lot with Farrukhsiyar. With the Bengal treasure in the fort he was on strong ground and had the means of raising an army. A letter from the prince authorizing him to appropriate funds for this purpose from the tribute came handy, and he started preparations to resist the advancing amir.

Abdullah Khan dispatched a force of hurriedly raised levies to oppose him. Three of his younger brothers, his diwan, and bakhshi went with the force and they gave battle to Abdul Ghaffar near Sarai Alam Chand, about 15 miles from Allahabad. Most of the troops of the Syeds, being fresh recruits, were scattered by Abdul Ghaffar but the three Syeds and the hard core of their followers from Barah made a very determined attack in which Abdul Ghaffar's brother was killed along with Nur ud-Din one of the Syed brothers. A rumour spread in the imperial force that Abdul Ghaffar himself had been killed and despite the best efforts of the latter to convince the troops that this was not so, panic spread. A dust storm added to the confusion and the Syeds carried the day, Abdul Ghaffar's army soon ceasing to exist. He retreated with the remnants to Shahzadpur.

When the news of the disaster reached Delhi the emperor tried to retrace his steps and conciliate Abdullah. Fresh patents were sent from Delhi appointing him governor of Allahabad (he had earlier been a deputy under Azim ush-Shan) and raising his rank from 4,000 to 6,000 *sowar*. Compliments and titles were showered upon him, while the letter to Abdul Ghaffar was so worded that it might well have been written to a rebel rather than to an officer who had been faithfully, if unsuccessfully, trying to execute his mandate.[4] The letter highlights the peculiar methodology of imperial diplomacy which would become more and more marked in its declining years. The underlying principle was, 'if you can't fight them, join them!' We shall see many examples of the emperor and his wazirs co-opting rebel and defiant governors by conferring on them provinces and parganas previously seized, with additional titles and offices to legitimize and conciliate them, to the extent that they should not at least openly disavow their allegiance to the emperor. The final and most monstrous imposture of this nature would be the appointment of the Peshwa as the Vakil-i-Mutlaq of the empire—now but a phantom—with Mahadji Scindia as his deputy, as well as of the nominal wazir. But it was too late. Abdullah Khan had unequivocally thrown in his lot with Farrukhsiyar and his victory over the emperor's nominee had emboldened him.

Meantime Farrukhsiyar had been able to attract some other notables to his cause. Chief among them were Ahmad Beg, a man long attached to the family and bearing the titles of Ghazi ud-Din Khan Ghalib Jang, and Sidisht Narain, chief of the Ujjainya rajas of Bhojpur. It was Ahmed Beg's persuasion which was responsible for bringing over Sidisht Narayan and his adhesion was a very notable coup for he brought with him 10,000 cavalry and 3,000 musketeers. Khwaja Asim and some other fugitives from the wreck of Azim ush-Shan's army also joined the prince and finally Saif Shikan Khan, the naib nazim of Orissa, also came over, as did various other disgruntled officers from Awadh and Rohilkhand.

Money remained a problem inspite of the Bengal treasure. With the help of Hussain Ali a forced loan was raised from the merchants and bankers of Patna. More strong arm methods were used and the goods of the Dutch Company which had a factory at Patna were also seized, the factor having recently died. One Surat Singh Khatri a revenue official under the governor of Kabul, Nasir Khan, who had accumulated great wealth happened unfortunately to be in Patna at the time with a large caravan of coined bullion which he was transporting under heavy guard. The treasure was loaded in 50 or 60 carts and was escorted by 500 musketeers. Taking advantage of their slackness, the carts were seized by Farrukhsiyar's officers and the money distributed among the soldiers.[5]

Finally the army was ready and on 22 September the march began. On 5 November contact was made with Syed Abdullah at Jhusi, opposite Allahabad, where a formal engagement was signed by which the wazarat was promised to Abdullah while Hussain was designated as the first bakhshi.

When the tidings of Abdul Ghaffar's defeat reached Delhi the emperor directed Azz ud-Din, his first born, to march east to check the advance of his cousin. Azz ud-Din was only twenty and inexperienced; he had never held independent command before, hence the actual commander was Khan i-Dauran, the relative of Kokaltash Khan. Inspite of his impressive titles he was quite unqualified to lead a military expedition. Zulfiqar had advised against both the prince and Khan-i-Dauran, but the Khan had the backing not only of his brother-in-law but also of Lal Kunwar, the 'chosen of the Palace'. Reason was therefore powerless and a pair of tyros were sent to combat forces led by such redoubtable soldiers like Syed Abdullah and Hussain Ali Khan.

The army was riven with dissensions. Letters were intercepted which proved that some officers were negotiating with Farrukhsiyar. The conspirators were arrested and imprisoned but the soldiers were also dissatisfied as they had not been given the usual *nalbandi* advance, customarily disbursed before starting on a campaign. At Etawah, which fell on the way, a demand was made on the faujdar, Ali Asghar Khan, for arrears of revenue—a rather inopportune occasion. Ali Asghar predictably made excuses but he was forced to accompany the imperial army with what forces he could muster. The dispute regarding arrears of revenue had however put him off and he was but a reluctant partisan.

At Kara, a similar demand was made on Mehta Chabela Ram the faujdar of Kara-Manakpur and a known protégé of Farrukhsiyar. Some of the Bengal tribute was suspected to be lodged in his treasury but neither the lure of promotion nor that of titles could persuade him to surrender it. A few days later he was presented with his posting orders for Awadh and given the option of proceeding immediately to that place for the imperialists knew that he would desert at the first opportunity.

The option was accepted and he left, but learning that Farrukhsiyar was nearby he joined him by a detour. He brought a sizeable treasure chest so his coming was doubly welcome.[6] A few days later Ali Asghar also succeeded in giving Azz ud-Din the slip. He had Rs. 5 lakh with him which he presented to the prince and in return received the resounding title of Khan Zaman. These accretions were very timely, as Farrukhsiyar was strapped for cash. Chabela Ram was able to provide Rs. 15,000 a day, and another loan was raised at exorbitant interest from the bankers and merchants accompanying the army.

Azz ud-Din decided to fight at Khajuha, which was considered auspicious as it was the scene of Aurangzeb's victory over Shah Shuja, another pretender who had set out from Bengal. On 25 November Farrukhsiyar's artillery started a desultory cannonade directed against the imperial entrenchments. The distance was considerable and the shelling did little damage but it unnerved Khan-i-Dauran and his companions. They urged the prince to order a retreat. Azz ud-Din was also shaken by the continous shelling but he resisted. He is reported to have protested, 'O Nawab, you are like an uncle to me, so much my senior in age, and yet you advise me to flee! None of my ancestors had ever retreated before the enemy without a battle. The enemy is before us and we should not retreat without a fight.'

Abashed, Khan-i-Dauran withdrew, but he and his friends had been completely unhinged by terror. They forged a letter bearing the seals of Lal Kunwar and Kokaltash Khan informing the prince that the emperor had died, but the news had been kept a secret, and if he hurried back the throne would be his.[7]

This was all the excuse that the timid Azz ud-Din needed. A little past midnight of 28-9 November, collecting what jewels and gold they could carry, they fled with a small escort to the west. Azz ud-Din's wife Saeeda Begum and some of her ladies also accompanied them, but the rest of the camp with the bulk of the women and the treasure chests had to be abandoned. They did not stop until Agra was reached, five days later.

The next morning when the flight of the prince and Khan-i-Dauran became public, the leaderless army was seized with consternation and each man grabbed what he could and fled. It was some time before the rebels discovered that the opposing army had bolted without a fight. Immense booty was taken. The soldiers were allowed to retain what they had seized, which must have been a big morale booster. Farrukhsiyar halted two days at Khajuha during which period some more notables crossed over from the imperialist side, some of them kinsmen of the Syeds from Barha.

The flight of Azz ud-Din was stopped at Agra by Chin Qilich Khan. This nobleman had been called out of retirement by Jahandar in response to Farrukhsiyar's challenge. His instructions were to follow fast behind Azz ud-Din and join him, but instead of hurrying he found excuses to tarry. He was a very cautious man and having no particular affection for Jahandar wanted to know which way the wind was blowing before committing himself. At any rate he stopped the headlong flight of the hapless prince and brought him to his senses.[8]

A new army had to be raised but the treasury was empty. Not only had the money been squandered on Lal Kunwar and her parasitical hangers-on, but seeing the state of affairs at the capital, coupled with Farrukhsiyar's bid for the throne, the provincial governors were holding back the revenues.

The imperial plate and the golden ceilings of the state chambers were melted and coined. The store rooms were opened and jewels and precious stones taken out to raise cash for equipping the army and paying the arrears of the soldiers. Khushal Chand the historian records that in one week jewels of the value of Rs. 3.5 crore were distributed. Golden vessels which had been in use since the time of Akbar were melted down, then jewelled articles, followed by jewellery, carpets and hangings, all were removed.[9]

Nothing like this had happened since the founding of the dynasty. Even the long and wasteful wars of Aurangzeb had not reduced the state to this extremity. Three armed struggles for the succession, coupled with the extravagance of a dancing girl had brought the empire to this sorry pass!

Even with the palace denuded of its treasures the claims of the soldiery could not be satisfied, and they had to be appeased with the promise of the treasure stored at Agra. But nothing was found there. Vault after vault was opened but they were all empty, and only in one strong room were some ingots of copper found. The mystery has not been explained to this day, and stories of the Great Agra Treasure are still current in that city.

The emperor and wazir also accompanied the army for it was evident that the fate of the throne hung in the balance. Muhammad Amin Khan Chin, a cousin of Chin Qilich Khan, and a prominent member of the Turanian faction, was also recalled from the Punjab where he had been campaigning against the Sikhs.

The atmosphere in which the emperor set out to save his tottering throne was anything but reassuring. The time of departure was the midnight of 9-10 December. The astrologers had determined that this was the most auspicious time, but just as the elephant bearing the kettledrums came out of the Delhi Gate the fastenings snapped, the drums fell down and were smashed. Later the imperial umbrella got entangled in the branches of a tree and its fringe of pearls was lost. The cold too was intense. There were clouds and rain almost everyday, with icy winds and thick mists. In short the weather was as miserable as it could possibly be. And to cap it all, one day, inspite of the rain and damp, some of the tents caught fire.[10]

In numbers the army was considerable. Churaman the Jat had also been persuaded to join, the inducement of plunder being too tempting to decline. But its fighting quality was doubtful. Zulfiqar could not get along with Kokaltash and the Turki soldiers were disgusted with the emperor and his habits. The Turanian chiefs were distrusted, and, as the subsequent behaviour of Chin Qilich Khan would show, the distrust was well-founded.

On reaching Agra Zulfiqar had all the boats rounded up. The question was debated whether the imperial army should cross the Yamuna to give battle to Farrukhsiyar or await his attack on this side. In the end it was felt it would be better to wait for him to cross and then annihilate him, for with the river at his back his escape would be cut off. As it was, because of the recent rain the river had risen, and in the absence of boats it was difficult to ford the river and the crossing was delayed. This too, Zulfiqar calculated, would operate in his favour. The prince had reached Agra after a long march and his resources were meagre. The wazir expected that in a few days many of his soldiers would desert and the army would gradually melt away. As it happened it actually worked to the disadvantage of Jahandar, for during this time Farrukhsiyar was able to contact the Turanian sardars, Chin Qilich, and Muhammad Amin, who agreed to remain neutral on the day of battle.

On 7 January Abdullah Khan was able to find a ford and the next day the whole army crossed taking Jahandar by surprise. The imperialists, relying on the magic of historic associations, had chosen Samugarh as the battlefield, but as in the case of Azam Shah who had similarly hoped to crush Muazzam on that historic ground, it was not to be. The sudden crossing of Farrukhsiyar near Sikandra had upset his well-laid plans. The enemy had appeared in their rear and their camp was thrown into confusion as they regrouped to meet him.

The battle of Agra took place on 10 January immediately to the west of the city. It had rained in the morning so the armies could not engage till the afternoon. The battle was a confused melee in which the only notable who distinguished himself on the imperialist side was Kokaltash. Hussain Ali Khan was wounded early in a charge led by Abdus Samad Khan. Abdullah Khan was also at one point isolated with only a few hundred supporters, and Farrukhsiyar's men seemed to be losing heart. If Zulfiqar had thrown in his full weight at that moment Jahandar would have won the battle, but for some strange reason with 25,000 fresh troops he desisted, and not until the tables were turned against the brave Kokaltash did he throw his men into the struggle. And as for the Turanian sardars, Chin Qilich and Muhammad Amin, true to their given word, they remained spectators.

The sun was setting and rumours of the death of Hussain Ali had dispirited the broken remnants of Farrukhsiyar's army. At one stage Zulfiqar even ordered the imperial band to beat the drums of victory. Roused by the enemy's triumphal music and fearing the worst, Abdullah Khan launched his men in one last desperate charge against Jahandar's centre, resolved to sell his life as dearly as possible. The charge was successful; the imperial centre was broken and the emperor finding himself separated from his elephant was forced to mount a horse. At this point he had the misfortune of running into Lal Kunwar who was fleeing from the scene. In typical Mughal style, notwithstanding the fact that the battle was being fought just outside Agra, the emperor just had to have his beloved concubine on the field of battle—and this inspite of the indignities she had had to suffer at Lahore at the hands of the late lamented Rustam Dil Khan!

Convinced that all was lost she forced Jahandar to enter her curtained howdah and together they headed for Agra. Meantime Zulfiqar still stood firm with the bulk of his force intact. Seeing the dissolution of Jahandar's phalanx he sent out officers to look for either Azz ud-Din or the emperor. If any of them could be located he would make one last desperate attempt to retrieve the day, but he needed their presence to enthuse his troops. On the other hand, had they been killed or captured his exertions would be pointless for he was not fighting on his own account.

But neither Jahandar nor Azz ud-Din could be found. Night had fallen and the fighting was dying with the plunderers taking over. But Zulfiqar still stood his ground until Farrukhsiyar sent an officer to ascertain his intentions. If he himself, the prince observed, was a claimant for the throne his attitude was understandable. If he was not, then one prince of the imperial house was as good as another, and his duty lay in submitting to the decrees of fate. Slowly and reluctantly the wazir withdrew in good order.[11] He still hoped to find his prince and then return to fight the pretender.

But Zulfiqar's brief ministry was over. He hung around Shahganj, a suburb of Agra till past midnight but finding no trace of either Jahandar or Azz ud-Din he at last set off towards Delhi with his army.

NOTES

1. Tabatabai, *Seir Mutaqherin*, i, pp. 43-4.
2. Irvine, *Later Mughals*, i, pp. 205-6.
3. Warid, *Mirat-i-Waridat*, p. 138b. Irvine, i, p. 207.
4. Irvine, i, p. 209.
5. Ibid., pp. 210-12.
6. Ibid., p. 214.
7. Ibid., p. 218. However, Khafi Khan and Tabatabai do not mention this forgery. They simply state that the prince and his ataliq took fright and fled secretly at night.
8. Tabatabai, i, p. 51.
9. Khushal Chand, *Tarikh-i-Muhammad Shahi*, p. 392a.
10. Irvine, i, p. 222. Nuruddin, *Jahandar Nama*, p. 97.
11. Tabatabai, i, p. 56.

CHAPTER 10

The Fall of Zulfiqar

Zulfiqar reached Delhi at the head of what was still a formidable force on 14 January. He proceeded first to his father's house to consult him on the future course of action. The alternatives, as he saw, were three. If Jahandar could be located he could proceed with him to Multan where he was still popular and enjoyed support. Another was to withdraw into the Deccan of which he was the viceroy. His deputy was Daud Khan Panni on whose loyalty and devotion he could count. Prince, or no prince, he was confident he could carve out an independent principality for himself. The third course was the obvious: to fight before Delhi.

Asad Khan rejected all three propositions. If he had failed at Agra with far greater resources, there would be even less chance of success at Delhi. More troops could be raised but they would be from the scum of the bazaars on whom no faith could be reposed. Moreover he was confident that Farrukhsiyar would be anxious to retain in his service, men like him and Zulfiqar. Few of the prince's partisans had held high office before and he would be needing tried and experienced officers. With the smug complacency of the old he had come to believe in his indispensability.

Still perplexed and undecided Zulfiqar retired to bed. He did not share his father's confidence and had misgivings. But the situation soon took a new turn by the sudden appearance of Jahandar, compelling an immediate decision.

The fallen emperor had turned up alone at his *deohri*,[1] dishevelled and in disguise. The guards did not recognized him, so far had the mighty fallen! When the grooms informed the regent about the sudden appearance of the emperor the wily old man asked him to detain him in the *deohri* till further instructions. Then he woke his son to consult how this development could be turned to their advantage.[2]

Closing his eyes to the infamy of the act he decided to present him as a peace offering to Farrukhsiyar. By surrendering Jahandar to his nephew he hoped to ensure the continuation of his family's dominance in the new regime. But Zulfiqar remained uneasy. His own instinct was to leave with the emperor for Multan, Kabul or the Deccan, and to continue the struggle from there. And in the last place be felt quite sure of his ability to maintain himself, even without Jahandar to give him legitimacy.

Against his better judgement he allowed himself to be guided by his father. The wretched Jahandar was led to an isolated pavilion in the garden round which armed guards were placed. Then a letter of congratulations was despatched to Farrukhsiyar in which he assured him of his own and Zulfiqar's loyalty besides informing him of the signal service they had performed by detaining the fallen emperor.

History does not record what words, if any were exchanged between the poor duped Jahandar and the two nobles whom he had mistakenly regarded as his most dependable amirs. For all we know the wilyman may have sent him off to the fort without subjecting himself to the embarassment of a personal meeting but the betrayal would, soon be punished.

Before we proceed further with the narrative, it would be appropriate to go back a little in time and follow the adventures of Jahandar Shah after he had been persuaded by his paramour to quit the battlefield to the point when he so suddenly appeared at the *deohri* of Asad Khan.

Lal Kunwar and Azam Khan (also known as Muhammad Mah, a brother of Kokaltash Khan) took the emperor to a house in Agra where he shaved off his beard and moustache and changed his royal robes for more modest apparel. The elephant was also discarded and a lady's *rath*[3] was procured and then they set off, just the three of them with the loyal Muhammad Mah as cart driver.

They were four nights on the road. At times they slept on the ground and ate dry bread or whatever could be procured from the villages on the highway. On the third day they reached Tilpat, about 14 miles from Delhi, an estate held *al tamgah*, i.e. in perpetuity, by Muhammad Mah. Here he had a pleasant garden with a house where they spent the night in comfort.

They entered Delhi late as Jahandar did not wish to run the risk of recognition. Mah advised him to head for Multan where he had friends but the doomed emperor insisted that he must first meet and confer with Zulfiqar. He told his foster-brother to conduct Lal Kunwar to her house while he himself walked upto the *deohri* of Asad Khan Asaf ud-Daulah.

As the news spread that the defeated emperor was at the mansion of Asad Khan, a crowd assembled, and some of them being hostile to Jahandar started shouting abusive epithets. Asad felt it would be prudent to rid himself of the emperor's presence and so he sent him to the Qila-i-Mualla under escort after ensuring that arrangements had been made for his safe custody. Farrukhsiyar was informed and the *khutba* read in his name on 19 January,[4] on the orders of Asad Khan.

Meanwhile at Agra, the morning after the battle, the formal enthronement durbar took place. In the night's confusion the Jats and other looters had indiscriminately looted the baggage of both armies and it was with difficulty that a few dirty and smoky screens could be found and set up. A masnad was arranged and the ceremony gone through. Three days later the *pesh khaima* of Jahandar was located and a more becoming durbar held. The tents had been erected in a walled garden and thus escaped the notice of the looters.

Hussain Ali Khan had been severely wounded in the battle and his body was found in the morning, stark naked, stripped of all his clothes and jewels. But under the ministrations of the physicians he revived, and in the evening the emperor visited him in his tent. This reckless Syed could always be relied upon to be in the thick of every fight.

The same day Azz ud-Din was also found in the cellars of the mansion known as Dara Shukoh's haveli.

The next day the *khutba* was read in Agra's Friday Mosque in the name of the new emperor. To conciliate the native Hindu population of the empire the *jaziya* or the hated poll tax was also declared abolished after it had been levied for 34 years. This tax had been exacted by all the Muslim rulers of India upto the reign of the Emperor Akbar. Although it was by no means a heavy burden on the taxpayer it was bitterly resented and its abolition had endeared Akbar to his Hindu subjects. It is still cited in text books today as an illustration of his secular outlook while its revival by Aurangzeb is taken as proof of his bigoted attitude. But the second repeal by Farrukhsiyar brought no particular benefit, either to the emperor personally, or to the dynasty. The Marathas who had been involved in their own internal struggles resumed their depredations during his reign. The processes of decay are irreversible. Once begun they carry on to their natural conclusions. The repeal of the *jaziya* was a cosmetic measure, designed to win popularity, but the emperor himself was devoid of character and it remained an isolated gesture, instead of being part of a carefully orchestrated series of measures designed to revive the decaying empire.

Abdullah Khan, who had been appointed wazir with the title of Qutb-ul-Mulk, left for Delhi in advance of the emperor to arrest Jahandar, and to seize the mansions of the principal adherents of the former emperor. A letter conveying the imperial directives was also addressed to Asad Khan.

On the arrival of Abdullah Khan, Asad and Zulfiqar called on him at

Barahpulla on the southern outskirts of the city. They were well-received by the new wazir who assured them that they had nothing to fear and that he would personally present them to the emperor. The wazir was probably quite sincere in his assurances. He expected that even under the new regime the two noblemen would continue to hold important positions, and he hoped to win them over to his side by this minor favour. The readiness of the Indian umara to switch sides and their determination to attach themselves to the sovereign of the moment had given them an apolitical character and it mattered little if—in the event of a civil war—a noble had the bad luck to choose the wrong side. Aurangzeb had scrupulously followed this principle and so had Bahadur Shah. Jahandar Shah deviated from it somewhat but there was no reason to think that this exception would become the rule. Furthermore, Zulfiqar and Asad Khan were far too important to be compared to the likes of Rustam Dil and Mukhlis Khan.

The nobles incarcerated in the fort by Jahandar were now released and some of them set off for Agra to pay their respects to Farrukhsiyar. In the meantime the wazir's confirmation of the arrest and detention of Jahandar had also been received and preparations were made for the march to Delhi.

On 10 February, one month after the battle of Agra, Farrukhsiyar reached Khizrabad. During this brief period, with Abdullah Khan absent in Delhi and Hussain Ali confined to his tents by his wounds, the emperor's intimates had ample opportunity to work on his impressionable mind. The pernicious influence of these mediocrities would soon be felt.

The most important among these cronies was Shariat Ullah Khan, a Turk, who as qazi of Dacca had acquired great influence over Farrukhsiyar. He was soon to be anointed with the title of Mir Jumla. Another was Khwaja Asim who had been present at the battle of Lahore on the side of Azim ush-Shan. He was a native Indian and a smooth talker, his defective Persian notwithstanding. He would soon be transformed into Khan-i-Dauran and though both he and Mir Jumla held comparatively minor offices their influence was important because they had the emperor's confidence. The two Syeds often found their authority completely undermined.

They were both 'new men', without name or family, and hence antagonistic to the old aristocracy, some of whom, like Zulfiqar, had served the imperial house with distinction for many generations. Both were accused by historians of plotting the ruin of the old families for the purpose[5] of aggrandizing themselves with their confiscated properties. Their first victim was fated to be no less than Zulfiqar himself.

News had reached this coterie about Qutb-ul-Mulk's meeting with Zulfiqar and they were determined to prevent the alliance of these two families. Taqarrub Khan, Khan-i-Saman[6] was sent by them to inveigle Zulfiqar into the trap. Taqarrub was a Persian and it was felt that it would be easier for him to win the confidence of the ex-wazir. He cautioned Zulfiqar that the emperor was already unhappy with Abdullah and it would not be prudent to depend on him for gaining the favour of Farrukhsiyar. On the other hand, he swore with his hand on a Koran, if Asad and Zulfiqar would permit him to intercede on their behalf, he would ensure that their interests did not suffer.

Zulfiqar suggested that Asad Khan should be the first to be presented and he would decide only after he had seen how matters stood would he decide. But Asad was completely taken in, and laughing at his son's fears declared that they would both come together.

They presented themselves at the emperor's tents at Khizrabad on the morning of 10 February. It was the emperor's first morning and in order to create a favourable impression Taqarrub had suggested that they should be the first to be presented. Meanwhile Mir Jumla and his cronies had met the emperor and obtained his consent for the planned assassination.

Asad and Zulfiqar had spent the previous night in Taqarrub's tents; so they were the first to be presented. It is said that as they entered the imperial enclosure, Zulfiqar had a premonition of doom and again tried to suggest that he should come on the following day. But the fatuous Asad Khan pulled him up for being afraid. Zulfiqar, abashed, fell silent and followed his father into the antechamber. Here however Asad Khan also felt that perhaps it would be better if he met the emperor first.

Asad Khan went in and sat down in the tent of the Hall of Justice while his arrival was announced to the emperor who was stated to be praying in the adjoining tasbih khana.[7] As the emperor entered the old man rose and made the deep ceremonial bow prescribed by court etiquette. The emperor walked upto him, embraced him cordially, and holding both his hands in his, bade him be seated and gave directions that the old regent be invested with robes of honour and jewels. The audience seemed to be going very well when there was a pause in the conversation. Asad ventured to broach the subject of his son. 'Sire,' he began, 'I have brought with me a culprit whom I hope will be pardoned for his sins.' Still all graciousness, the emperor replied, 'Brother, let him be brought in.'

Zulfiqar was then led in, his hands tied loosely in a scarf, and looking down at his feet, the characteristic pose of a felon craving forgiveness. Farrukhsiyar made a gesture of shock and asked the attendants to untie his hands. When the scarf had been removed he bade him come forward. As he approached the throne Zulfiqar prostrated himself but the emperor raised and embraced him, speaking kind words and assuring him that he had been forgiven. A robe of honour and jewels were brought for him and after he had been invested with them Farrukhsiyar excused himself saying that he had to leave early as he planned to visit the shrine of Sheikh Nizam ud-Din. Asad, he said, should leave, but Zulfiqar, whom he deferentially described as 'my brother', should remain behind as he wanted to speak to him further.

With a sinking heart Asad took leave. Then the emperor smiled at Zulfiqar whose face showed his disquiet, and bade him be seated as he would have some refreshments sent to him.

Khwaja Asim (Khan-i-Dauran) sat down with him. When the food arrived Zulfiqar was still uneasy, and noticing his discomfort, as if to allay his suspicion that the food might be poisoned, Khan-i-Dauran addressed him in the usual style of a courtier: 'If your lordship permits, this slave will have a bite too'. Thus reassured, Zulfiqar began to eat.

After a minute or so Khan-i-Dauran remarked that the Hall of Justice was not the most appropriate place for eating and he proposed that they repair to the adjoining tents. Zulfiqar agreed humbly, got up and walked to one of the tents which was also surrounded by *qanats*. He had barely taken his seat and Khan-i-Dauran was still outside when suddenly the screens fell and he found himself surrounded by armed men, pikes and swords ready. Escape was impossible, and what he had feared had come to pass.

His situation made known to him the screens were re-erected, and his 'trial' began with the emperor himself judge and inquisitor. He was seated in the tasbih khana and posed questions which were conveyed to him by Mir Jumla, the superintendent of the pages, and his answers were conveyed back in the same manner.

In the first question the emperor desired to know why he had arrested and imprisoned Kam Bakhsh, a reference to an incident which had taken place years ago in the reign of Aurangzeb during the siege of Ginjee.

'The imprisonment of Kam Bakhsh was by his father's order', he answered. 'I was Alamgir's servant, and Kam Bakhsh his son. If he had ordered me to make my father a prisoner I would have done so.'

Having started with an event which had taken place more than twenty years ago, more questions were put, gradually coming to recent events. His conduct at the battle of Jajau was questioned, was it proper for a general to flee, abandoning his prince? What was his quarrel with the martyred prince Azim ush-Shan, the emperor's father? What wrong had he done him? Why had he caused Rustam Dil Khan, and Mukhlis Khan to be executed?

At first he tried to defend himself manfully replying boldly to the emperor's questions but when the subject of the murder of Muhammad Karim, Farrukhsiyar's brother was pressed he gave up. That his death was pre-determined was evident so he dropped his stance of meekness and declared. 'No more of this; if you want to kill me, be done with it whichever way you like.'

As if on a signal a number of Kalmuck slaves then fell upon him and one of them, Lachin Beg, entitled Bahadur Dil Khan threw a leather thong round his neck and strangled him. Then they kicked him, stamped on his chest, and just to make sure, stabbed him repeatedly. The body was then dragged out by the heels and exposed to the public outside.[8]

That day was also the last for the prince whom he had raised to the throne. The same team of Kalmucks led by Lachin Beg was sent to the small room above the Tripolia, one of the few land marks still standing in the Fort, to despatch Jahandar to the nether world. Again the mode was the same, the *tasma* or the Turkish bow string.

The governor, Muhammed Yar Khan read the warrant and sorrowfully admitted the executioners. While they were about their work he remained downstairs pacing nervously, having declined to be a witness to their proceedings.

Lal Kunwar was with Jahandar and had to be forcibly torn from his arms. She was carried out screaming hysterically. The emperor struggled with his assailants and was some time a-dying, but was finally finished off by one of the Kalmucks who kicked him repeatedly in a vulnerable spot with his heavy Turkish boots.

Then Lachin Beg asked Muhammed Yar Khan for an executioner to cut off the head. Apparently chopping heads was not his job, his speciality being the bowstring. But the jailor who was sweating profusely expressed his inability and after looking at the corpse muttered, 'What is left for an executioner to do?' So the head had to be cut off, however inexpertly, by the Kalmucks themselves.

It was carried in a silver tray to be shown to Farrukhsiyar while the rest of the body was taken in an open litter to the imperial camp after nightfall. There it was dumped outside the royal enclosure besides that of Zulfiqar, the man who had made him king.

The next day Farrukhsiyar made his entry through the Delhi Gate. Behind the emperor's howdah sat Mir Jumla, weaving a peacock fan over his head. After him came a trooper, carrying the head of the murdered Jahandar held aloft on the tip of a bamboo pole. On the following elephant, thrown across the back, was his headless body. And tied by its feet to the elephant's tail, bumping over the cobbles, was the corpse of Zulfiqar. The aged father, the former regent, was also forced to join the procession in an open palki to complete the triumph of Farrukhsiyar. Behind him came the women of his zenana, some of them in palkis, the rest on foot.[9]

As was usual on such occasions, largesse of gold and silver was thrown at the crowds lining the street. The chronicler Khushal Chand who was watching from a balcony recalls how a filigree rose was caught by him. And how many among the spectators were moved to tears by this spectacular illustration of the fickleness of fortune.

More was to follow. The previous reign had set a precedent but Farrukhsiyar's rule became notorious for its arbitrary assassinations. The high officers of the state left their homes with fear in their hearts. When they had to go to court they would solemnly bid farewell to their wives and children, as if that was their last leave taking. Lachin Beg became so notorious for his dexterity with the bow string that he was given the epithet of *tasma-kash* (thong-puller). This mode of execution, so common in the annals of the Ottoman sultans was an innovation in Indian, where *naqqals* and performers would demonstrate the novel method on the stage in public, in fairs and street shows.[10]

The first notable executions after the emperor's installation in the Qila-i-Mualla were those of Sadullah Khan, Hidayat Kesh Khan and Sidi Kasim Habshi, all of whom were despatched by Lachin Beg's Kalmuck squad. Sadullah Khan had been deputy wazir in the last year of Bahadur Shah, after the death of Munim Khan, with the little of Wazarat Khan. He was imprisoned immediately after Farrukhsiyar's meeting with his great aunt, Zinat un-Nissa, known as the Padishah Begum.

The reasons are obscure. One story, the most likely, links his execution with that of Zulfiqar. It is said that soon after his victory Farrukhsiyar wrote a letter to his great-aunt seeking her advice as to what should be done about Zulfiqar and Asad Khan. Her reply was that they should not be harmed and ought to be retained in service. Sadullah was her steward and was charged with the delivery of the reply to Farrukhsiyar. But he was hostile to Zulfiqar on account of the latter's opposition to his appointment as wazir on the death of Munim Khan, and he cleverly contrived to alter one word so that the letter now read that Zulfiqar should be killed. When the emperor met the old lady, she reproached him for the murder of Zulfiqar. Farrukhsiyar was surprised by her reproaches and protested that he had only followed her advice and produced her letter as proof. Thus Sadullah's interpolation was discovered and the man exposed, resulting in his execution.

The second victim, Hidayat Kesh Khan had been chief of the secret police in the reign of Bahadur Shah and it was he who had informed Jahandar of the hiding place of Prince Muhammad Karim, resulting in his arrest and execution. Thus his execution seemed to be a retribution for the prince's betrayal.

The reason for the execution of the kotwal is obscure. He was of Abyssinian origin and the police chief of the capital. It was rumoured that his death was an act of private revenge by some persons in the city who were inimical to him. These enemies had access to Mir Jumla who accepted a large sum of money from them for the purpose of fixing the poor kotwal.

Then occurred the incident of Sheikh Qudrat Ullah of Allahabad. This gentleman had become acquainted with Prince Azim ush-Shan, won his confidence and achieved a complete ascendency over him even though he did not hold any official position. After the prince's death the Sheikh retired to his native city of Allahabad thinking it prudent to maintain a low profile. He made no attempt to meet Farrukhsiyar even when the latter passed through Allahabad. When news came of his triumph over Jahandar the Sheikh still made no effort to meet him, being uncertain as to his reception.

But then he chanced to meet another learned man, Mulla Shadman of Patna who was passing through Allahabad on his way to Delhi. He was reputed to have prophesied the victory and accession of Farrukhsiyar and was consequently held in great regard by him. He urged the Sheikh to accompany him to Delhi and offered to introduce him to the emperor. The Sheikh considered him a reliable person and was persuaded to try his fortune once again.

They travelled together and the Mulla was cordially received by the emperor. He had arranged with Qudrat that he would take him to court on his second visit. First he would speak to the emperor about him and then with his permission introduce him.

Mir Jumla was present when the Mulla spoke to the emperor about the Sheikh. He was greatly perturbed. He had seen the Sheikh in his heyday and recognized in him a potential rival should he have the same luck with the son, as he had had with the father. After excusing himself he hurried to the Sheikh who was in the antechamber and after greeting him effusively he confided that the day was not suitable for meeting the emperor, that the Sheikh should leave his affairs in his hands and he would arrange a meeting the following day.

Knowing the great influence which Mir Jumla exercised over the emperor the poor Sheikh readily agreed, and so dazed was he by the nobleman's solicitude that he forgot all about Mulla Shadman, and agreeing to accept the hospitality of Mir Jumla, left for his house in the latter's palki. He took his chance meeting with Mir Jumla and his friendly reception as a happy augury for the future.

After the durbar was over Mir Jumla set to work on the emperor. He convinced him that Sheikh Qudrat Ullah was a dangerous necromancer who had been the root of great mischief in the circle of Azim and it would not be prudent to encourage him. He had not cared to pay his respects earlier, even though His Majesty had passed through Allahabad, but now seeing that the ground was safe and His Majesty firmly established on the throne he had come to try his luck. In short he was a rank opportunist. The emperor nodded in agreement, he trusted Mir Jumla implicitly and gave his assent to whatever he proposed.

That very night Mir Jumla had the Sheikh strangled by having him hanged from a *maulsri* tree that stood in his courtyard. The next morning the body was handed over to his servants. When Mulla Shadman came to know the facts he protested. The emperor felt sheepish and mumbled some excuses that as the man was dead, there was nothing that could be done. In protest the Mulla left his court and returned to Patna.

Another victim of the royal favourite was a woman, a Kalmuck slave by the name of Raiman. This woman who was a stout and well-built Amazon had had the honour of saving the life of the late emperor during the fighting at Lahore. Azim ush-Shan had sent some assassins to murder Jahandar one night. They had eluded the guards but Raiman who was a light sleeper awoke and hearing their stealthy approach, came out of her tent and raised the alarm. More, she actually grappled with them and killed one with her dagger, receiving a small wound herself. For this service Jahandar had honoured her with the titles of Raza Bahadur, Rustam-i-Hind and the rank of 5,000 *zat*.

The reasons for her execution are obscure and there are some vague rumours that she or one of her male relatives had at some time or the other offended or insulted Mir Jumla. Whatever be the reason, she was stripped of rank and title and beheaded by the orders of the kotwal at the chabutra in front of the kotwali like a common felon.[11]

There were many other unfortunate victims of the caprice of Mir Jumla and the weak emperor, like the poet Zattali who had the impertinence to parody the verse that appeared on the coinage of Farrukhsiyar and Hakim Salim, a personal attendant of Azim ush-Shan. But the worst atrocity was the blinding of the princes.

Azz ud-Din the hapless prince who had fled in panic from Khajuha and was captured cowering in the cellars of Dara Shukoh's mansion was probably that exception in Mughal history, a prince who was a coward. He could never have been a threat to anyone but Farrukhsiyar's executioner pierced his eyes with a needle. Ali Tabar, the sole surviving son of Azam Shah also had the light extinguished from his eyes. And finally there was little Humayun Bakht, Farrukhsiyar's own little brother aged not more than nine or ten. The little boy was doomed to live the remainder of his life in darkness. And he had to wait more than thirty years before death relieved him of his misery.

NOTES

1. The *deohri* is the principal entrance of a mansion, often substituted for the mansion itself.
2. Irvine, *Later Mughals*, i, pp. 237-9. According to Khafi Khan and Tabatabai the emperor was the first to reach Asad Khan's house and Zulfiqar followed shortly after.
3. *Rath*: a curtained bullock-cart, used by ladies.
4. Warid, *Mirat-i-Waridat*, p. 143b. Irvine, i, p. 240.
5. Tabatabai, *Seir Mutaqherin*, i, p. 267.
6. The Khan-i-Saman was the superintendant of the Household, or butler.
7. Tasbih khana: private chapel where prayers are said. Tasbih means prayer beads or rosary.
8. Shah Nawaz Khan, *Maathir ul-Umara*, ii, 2, p. 1042. Mirza Muhammad, *Tarikh-i-Muhammadi*, pp. 61-2. Irvine, i, pp. 250-2. Tabatabai, i, pp. 61-2.
9. Tabatabai, i, p. 62. Elliot and Dowson, vii, p. 445.
10. Tabatabai, i, p. 63.
11. Irvine, i, pp. 277-81.

CHAPTER 11

The King and his Makers

One would have expected the venture of Farrukhsiyar to have had a happier ending. There was a touch of romance about it. Inspite of the apparently hopeless nature of the enterprise, luck favoured him from the beginning. The dauntless spirit of his mother and the reckless courage of Syed Hussain surely deserved a more satisfactory conclusion. But his luck sufficed only to place the prince on the Peacock Throne and to secure for the brothers the first two offices of the empire. Thereafter everything went awry.

Hussain is said to have described Farrukhsiyar to his brother as an utterly faithless, ungrateful and shameless prince. He is said to have written thus in a letter to Abdullah when the latter had gone to Delhi ahead of the emperor. It was only the superior character of the Validah Sultan,[1] Sahiba Niswan, the emperor's mother that kept the partnership going as long as it did.

At Allahabad the prince had entered into a solemn compact with the two brothers, promising Abdullah the office of Wazir-ul-Mulk (Prime Minister) and Hussain the Bakhshi-ul-Mumalik (Paymastership) of the army. But the dust of battle had not yet settled when he tried to renege. Another aspirant had come forward in the person of Ahmad Beg Khan known as the *Khosa* or Goat-Beard, another or Jahandar's foster brothers. He had become intimate with Farrukhsiyar during his days in Bengal where he had retired on account of his disappointment with Jahandar who showered all his favours on Kokaltash Khan. At that time, before the prince had entered into an understanding with the Syeds, he promised Ahmad that, should he ever become padishah, he would be his wazir.

To avoid embarrassment the emperor suggested that Abdullah should accept the more dignified but honorary post of Vakil-i-Mutlaq while Ahmad Beg became wazir. But Abdullah stood firm. His case was very different from that of Asad Khan, the last incumbent. Therefore, the emperor had to give way and the *Khosa* had to be content with the minor offices of Mir Tuzak, Mir Atish and superintendent of the Jalau, and the resonant titles of Ghazi ud-Din Khan Ghalib Jang.

While at Delhi Abdullah had promised the diwani of the Khalsa (or Crown lands) to Lutfullah Khan Sadiq and the post of Sadr-us-Sadur to Syed Amjad Khan. But at Agra, Farrukhsiyar, unknown to the wazir had nominated Chabela Ram to the diwani and Afzal Khan as Sadr-us-Sadur. When the emperor and wazir met at Delhi there was another confrontation.

'What is the point of being wazir', stormed Abdullah, 'if I cannot make appointments?' Ultimately there was a compromise: Lutfullah retained the diwani while Afzal Khan remained Sadr-us-Sadur. Chabela Ram was compensated with the subedari of Agra.

There were other occasions for friction which the emperor's cronies did nothing to alleviate. On the contrary they considered it their duty to keep insinuating that Qutb-ul-Mulk was exceeding his authority and was careless of imperial dignity. Abdullah had taken the mansion known as Mir Jafar's which had earlier been occupied by Kokaltash, while Hussain occupied Shaista Khan's, whose previous occupant had been Zulfiqar. The emperor's friends insinuated that they had become dangerously rich for these mansions contained not only the hoarded wealth of their late occupants but also, according to rumour, a good part of Jahandar's treasure as well. The emperor, on the other hand, was quite poor, the treasury being empty.[2]

To aggravate matters there was a prophecy current in the bazaars of Delhi that one day a Syed would sit on the throne of the Mughals.[3] This could only have added to the credulous emperor's sense of insecurity. As a result the court was soon divided into two parties—the emperor's and the wazir's. The former was larger. Its core consisted of men like Mir Jumla and Khan-i-Dauran while others came and went, falling out in disgust with the emperor's shiftiness and the pusillanimity of the core members.

But first order had to be restored. In the vast tracts of the Ajmer suba, imperial authority had touched a new low. By his military demonstrations and conciliatory gestures Bahadur Shah had restored peace and forced the rajas to submit to imperial authority. But Jahandar had frittered away the gains of the pervious reign. Maharaja Ajit Singh of Marwar was again in revolt; the imperial officers were again expelled and other symbols of the empire destroyed.

Ajit was the chief of a dynasty that had enjoyed sovereign status long before the coming of Babar in 1526 and his state had been in rebellion almost since his birth in 1678. But now he was being courted with promises of forgiveness, if only he would destroy Hussain Ali Khan, the Bakhshi-ul-Mumalik, paymaster-general of the imperial armies and the sword arm of the padishah. But Hussain was a redoubtable warrior and he tenaciously pursued the wily Rajput and ultimately forced him to negotiate. It was agreed that he would send his son and heir, Abhai Singh, to wait on the emperor and give his daughter, Bai Inder Kunwar in marriage to the emperor. The maharaja also bound himself to serve whenever called upon to do so. He returned in July and was received, to all appearances, with honour in a special durbar but his return had been hastened by urgent messages from his brother Abdullah who was finding his position more and more vulnerable.

The latter was an unfortunate choice as prime minister. He was a soldier by temperament, and would have made a good general, but as wazir he was incompetent. He left most of the official business to his diwan, Rattan Chand, who was by caste a baniya, and conformed fully to the popular image of that fraternity by his venality. What Sabha Chand was to Zulfiqar, Rattan Chand was in much greater measure to Qutb-ul-Mulk.

Sabha Chand had been hated for his arrogance and insolence but Rattan Chand's besetting sin was avarice. In addition to the customary fees charged from those receiving appointments Rattan Chand demanded huge sums which people were unable to raise. Consequently they sought an alternative conduit in the much more accessible person of Mir Jumla. The 'rates' of his staff were also appreciably lower and consequently the wazir and his factotum Rattan Chand found themselves increasingly isolated and bypassed.[3]

The champions on whom Farrukhsiyar was counting were anything but men of action. The historian Mirza Muhammad calls them *sher-i-kalin*, or lions of the carpet, while the occasion demanded warriors or *mard-i-maidan.* But relying on their bluster the emperor had promoted both these nobles to the rank of 7,000 each. Khan-i-Dauran was also given the command of 5,000 Wala Shahi troops while Mir Jumla was given 5,000 crack Mughal troopers with a commission to raise another 6,000.

Qutb-ul-Mulk and Hussain Ali Khan were completely eclipsed and their fall seemed imminent. But they were even more irresolute than the emperor. The Syeds stopped attending the durbar and stayed at home, their mansions closely guarded.

The emperor was fond of shikar and it was rumoured that the shikar expeditions were actually intended to be demonstrations against the Syeds and that they might be seized on some such occasion. But nothing happened. Mir Jumla and Khan-i-Dauran found excuses for not taking any action. The Wala Shahis, for instance, they grumbled, were no longer what they once were, and the Mughal troopers of Khan-i-Dauran were Mughal only in name. Their ranks had been infiltrated by lowbred townsmen and artisans who had joined for the sake of the high salaries and had no stomach for battle.[4]

An attempt was made to interest Muhammad Amin Khan Chin in the matter. He suggested that the emperor appoint a new wazir and leave the Syeds alone. As power begets friends, in due course the Syeds' following would melt away and they would have no option but to beg forgiveness and leave to retire to their homeland. The advice was sound but Muhammad Amin had given it in the expectation that he would be the natural choice as the leader of the Mughal or Turani party; however the king's friends were wary of him. They knew that Muhammad Amin would be a much harder nut to crack than Qutb-ul-Mulk and they would be rendered powerless under him.

On one occasion after the failure of a rumoured attempt to seize them the Syeds demanded an audience with the emperor. If he did not trust them, Syed Abdullah thundered, they were ready to resign and quit. They were real Syeds and honour was more important to them than power. All they wanted was respectable jagir in their own country. 'Or', added Hussain, 'give us an army and leave to cross the Hindukush and we shall reconquer Balkh and Badakhshan, and rule those provinces in your behlaf, to your greater glory.' Those provinces had been lost to the empire since the reign of Shah Jahan!

But the king's friends advised against accepting this request. If they were allowed to leave for their own country they were certain to revolt. Unable to tackle the problem head on, their cowardly minds could only think in terms of surprise seizures which never materialized.

Official business was at a standstill, the wazir and the bakhshi would not attend court for weeks and on the rare occasions when they did, they went heavily armed. The whole city bristled with armed men and occasionally clashes took place between the retainers of rival lords.

The emperor suggested to one Islam Khan Mashhadi, a former artilleryman, that he should train one of the fort's guns on Hussain Ali Khan's house and try to kill him. A hare-brained scheme, indeed, considering the highly uncertain trajectory of the cannons of the times. Islam Khan was more sensible than his master. He declined the suggestion on account of the danger to neighbouring houses, but offered his services as mediator between the emperor and his two amirs.[5]

There were others working towards the same end. The suggestion was made that one brother should be sent to Bengal and the other to the Deccan, but this was rejected. As Qutb-ul-Mulk pointed out, their enemies would say they contemplated independence. Then it was proposed that the Amir ul-Umara and Mir Jumla should leave Court.

As chance would have it, the viceroyalty of the Deccan had only recently been taken over by Syed Hussain, the Nizam-ul-Mulk, Chin Qilich Khan, having been recalled and posted as faujdar of Moradabad. At the time Syed Hussain had no intention of going there himself; he hoped to govern through a deputy, preferably Daud Khan Panni who had had long experience in the Deccan, having deputized earlier under Zulfiqar.

A personal visit by the emperor's mother to the house of Qutb-ul-Mulk put the seal of finality on the proposed arrangements. This lady had never forgotten the debt she owed the Syeds and had always felt a certain responsibility towards them, not hesitating to warn them of those plots which came to her knowledge.

The Queen Mother's visit took place on 28 November 1714, and the following day the prime minister, accompanied by his entire retinue, attended the durbar at the Qila-i-Mualla.

Qutb-ul-Mulk entered the Diwan-i-Am with fifty trusted veterans. The emperor embraced him, and there was a display of emotion. Tears, probably hypocritical welled up in their eyes as the emperor gave excuses for the misunderstandings of the past and the minister recounted all his past services and protested his undying devotion and unshaken loyalty. It was decided that Mir Jumla would be sent to Bihar as governor, and Lutfullah Khan Sadiq, his closest adviser was deprived of his offices.

Even on this day, just before the audience, Lutfullah had tried to sow fresh suspicions between the emperor and the minister. First he whispered in a lowered voice that His Majesty's mood had changed and they should be wary of treachery. Then he hurried back to the emperor and confided to him that he feared mischief on the part of Qutb-ul-Mulk, which angered him and he ordered the number of guards to be doubled.

But unluckily for Lutfullah the minister decided to confront the emperor after the durbar with what he had heard, under the pretext that slanderers and mischief mongers should be discouraged. The emperor then disclosed what he had been told and the knave was exposed.[6]

Syed Hussain came to the court on 20 December after Mir Jumla had left Delhi. The usual polite speeches and protestations of loyalty were made and it was agreed that the Amir-ul-Umara would take over the Deccan command in person. However he made it known that if in his absence Mir Jumla was recalled, or his brother subjected to harassment, his return should be expected within twenty days.

After things had settled down arrangements were made for the emperor's marriage. Shaista Khan, the emperor's maternal uncle, left Delhi in May to bring the bride from her home in Jodhpur. The bridal party reached Delhi in September and the princess was housed in the mansion of Hussain Ali.

Maharaja Ajit Singh did not attend, and as the Amir-ul-Umara had left for the Deccan, the honours were performed by Qutb-ul-Mulk. Since the bridegroom was the emperor himself the marriage was a lavish affair, a public celebration in which the people of Delhi joined.

The intrigues, however, continued. The target once more was the old favourite Syed Hussain, and, as on the occasion of the earlier expedition against Ajit Singh, every effort of the coterie was directed at ensuring that he never returned to plague them. This time there was no obvious enemy who could be incited as Shahu was still at peace with the empire, but this was a minor problem.

The chosen instrument was Daud Khan Panni, and the bait offered, the viceroyalty of the six subas of the Deccan. He was, at the time, governor of Ahmedabad-Gujarat, as mentioned earlier, holding independent charge, while earlier under Zulfiqar he had only been his deputy for the Deccan. Now he was given, in addition to Ahmedabad, the charge of Burhanpur as well. Burhanpur was one of the six subas which fell to the responsibility of the Deccan viceroy; hence, here he would have been under the superintendence and control of Hussain Ali Khan.

But not for long. For according to the secret instructions communicated by Khan-i-Dauran he was to oppose the advance of the Amir-ul-Umara, and if he succeeded in destroying him, the charge of the entire viceroyalty would be his.[7]

This, thought Daud, was his great opportunity, the kind that comes once in a lifetime. He at once collected all his troops, and marched to Burhanpur where he assumed all the state of the Deccan viceroy. Several Maratha chiefs who were well-known to him, because of his long service in the Deccan, were also summoned with all their troops to assist in the struggle.

The Amir-ul-Umara had set out from Delhi in April 1715, and it was in May that Daud was appointed to Burhanpur. The unfolding conspiracy became clear.

The bakhshi invited Daud for talks but the latter had set his eyes on the viceroyalty and nothing could sway him from the chosen goal. On 6 September the battle was joined outside Burhanpur. It was a bloody and hard-fought battle, both commanders being brave and celebrated soldiers. Daud was famous for his reckless courage. He never wore protective armour, a light muslin robe being his usual dress in peace as well as war. The issue was finally decided through the death of Daud who was struck by a musket-ball on the forehead.

The Marathas, as usual, observes Ghulam Hussain, contributed nothing to the outcome. Nima, the Maratha commander, just kept scampering about the field without coming to grips, and when Daud Khan was killed and he saw that victory lay with the Amir-ul-Umara, he galloped over with all his officers to present his congratulatory *nazar*. His men commenced plundering their former allies.

Among the spoils which fell into the hands of Hussain were the letters received by Daud from the Qila-i-Mualla explaining his behaviour. At this stage he did not make their contents public but conveyed the news of the discovery to his brother, urging him to remain alert.

In Punjab meanwhile the Sikh rebellion was in its final phase. After the fall of Lohgarh in December 1710 the Sikhs had been dispersed and for some time a low level conflict continued in the Bist and Bari Doabs. But with the death of Bahadur Shah and the resulting confusion and civil wars they were able to regroup and reoccupy Sadhaura and rebuild their old stronghold. In 1713 Abdus Samad Khan was appointed subedar of Lahore and his son Zakariya posted as faujdar at Jammu. The new subedar's mandate was to crush the Sikhs and so he made preparations to set out for Sadhaura where the faujdar of Sirhind was not making much of an impression.

In October 1713 Sadhaura fell, but again Banda managed to elude the imperial forces. Thereafter several clashes took place with the Sikh bands, or *jathas* as they were called, but no major encounter occurred.

By April 1715 Banda had established another stronghold at Gurdas Nangal in the Bari Doab which was invested by the imperialists, fresh reinforcements being sent from Delhi for the purpose. The investment was complete, no supplies were able to get in, but there was no thought of surrender inspite of the fact that they were starving. All the animals—asses, horses and even oxen—were eaten, with the bones ground and consumed as flour. Only when disease and dysentry started claiming large numbers did the garisson sue for terms. Ultimately on 17 December they surrendered unconditionally.

A pair of flags were set up on an eminence and they were instructed to leave their weapons behind and come down to the camp. About three hundred were beheaded by the riverbank, the heads being loaded into carts for display as trophies. Since it was rumoured that the Sikhs had swallowed their gold to prevent its plunder their bodies were torn up by the soldiers and camp followers who were thus able to recover a substantial amount of treasure. The remains were then thrown into the river.

Apart from this, the official spoils were pitiful. They have been listed by Kamwar Khan[8] and comprised 1,000 swords, 278 shields, 173 bows and quivers, 180 matchlocks, 114 daggers, 217 long knives, a few gold ornaments, 23 gold coins and only about 6,000 silver rupees. Inspite of his contemptible military strength Banda had been able to keep the imperialists at bay for eight months. The honorific of 'Bahadur' which is generally suffixed to his name by the Sikhs today is certainly well-deserved.[9]

The heads were stuffed and mounted on pikes. Banda and his principal officers were fettered and mounted on mangy asses and camels, each with a paper cap on his head to make him look ridiculous. A few hundred prisoners were spared to be slaughtered later after they had been exhibited in the great cities of the empire like Lahore and Delhi, to grace the triumph of Abdus Samad.

In Lahore they were saved with difficulty from the fury of the mob and Abdus Samad had to rush them out early in the morning; otherwise it seemed quite unlikely that he would have any prisoners left to show to his grateful monarch at Delhi.

The governor had requested permission to come to Delhi with his prisoners but he was asked to stay in his province and Zakariya and Qamr ud-Din Khan (son of Muhammad Amin Khan, who had later joined the besiegers at Gurdas Nangal) were asked to bring them to Delhi.

When they reached the suburbs they were asked to stop and Muhammad Amin Khan Chin was sent ahead to make arrangements. The ceremonial to be followed was the some as observed at the time of the capture of Shambhaji in 1689.

The road up to the Lahori Gate of the palace was lined with troops. Banda sat in an iron cage placed on the back of an elephant, his face blackened with a wooden cap on his head. He wore a long, heavy skirted court dress of brocade and a gold embroidered turban of fine red muslin. Behind him stood an officer in chain mail, with drawn sword. In front of the elephant were carried, stuck on bamboo pikes, the heads of the Sikh prisoners who had been executed, their long hair streaming over their heads like a veil. Along with these, a cat was carried stuck at the end of a long lance, to signify that everything living, even down to four-footed animals had been destroyed. Behind Banda came the rest of the prisoners, 740 in number. They were seated four to a camel without saddles. One hand of each man was attached to his neck by two pieces of wood. On their heads were high sheepskin caps adorned with glass beads. A few officers nearest to the elephant were clad in sheepskins, the woolly side turned out, so that the common people compared them to bears. Behind them rode Nawab Muhammad Amin Khan Chin, and then the victorious generals, his son Qamr ud-Din, and son-in-law Zakariya Khan.

The date of the entry was 10 March 1716. Considerable effort and ingenuity had been expended to make it spectacular. The route was packed with spectators who jeered at the prisoners. But the Sikhs maintained their dignity and no sign of dejection and humility could be seen. Many indeed, seemed happy and cheerful, and gave sharp retorts to the jeering crowds.

About twenty or thirty of the chief officers were sent with Banda to Salimgarh while Banda's wife, his three year old infant and the child's nurse were kept in the harem. The rest were made over to the kotwal for execution.

The bloody operation began on 15 March. Every day for about a week a hundred men were beheaded at the *chabutra* in Chandni Chowk. All spectators, Indian and European, are united in their observations about the patience and fortitude with which the Sikhs met their end. Although life was promised to those who embraced Islam not one took advantage of the offer. A widow interceded successfully for the life of her only son through Rattan Chand, diwan to Qutb-ul-Mulk, who ordered his release, but the youth refused to recognise her and insisted on meeting his fate with the rest of his comrades.

The execution of Banda and his officers took place on 19 June; the venue was different. Banda was again decked out in his ridiculous finery, placed in his iron cage and led in procession to the shrine of Khwaja Qutb ud-Din Bakhtiyar Kaki at Mehrauli. After being led around the tomb of Bahadur Shah—in whose reign he had begun his career—he mounted the scaffold where he was beheaded.

His son was placed in his lap and he was asked to slit his throat. He refused. Then the executioner killed the child with a long knife and extracting its liver thrust it into Banda's mouth. Then his limbs were lopped off, joint by joint, and finally he was beheaded. Thereafter his companions were executed, though their tortures were less elaborate. As for his wife she is said to have been converted and handed over to Dakhini Begum, the emperor's maternal aunt.

The story, probably apocryphal, is that Muhammad Amin Khan came up close to Banda and after studying his face was struck by the nobility of his features and could not help commenting, 'It is surprising that you who show so much acuteness in your features and nobility in your carriage should have committed so many horrid crimes that will assuredly ruin you, not only in this world but in the next as well.'

'I will tell you my Lord,' Banda replied, 'whenever men become so corrupt and wicked as to cross all limits, then—it happens in all countries and in all religions—God sends such a scourge like me whose only office is to punish a race become totally criminal. But when the measure of punishment has been filled then the butcher's job is finished and his mission is over, and then God sends a mighty man like you whose mission is to slay him in turn.'[9]

The executions of the Sikhs must have provided an exciting diversion for the Delhi *vulgus* which was quite fed up with the constant gossip and rumours regarding the differences between the padishah and the wazir. But after the blood had dried on the *chabutra* it was back to the same old games. The disastrous effect which these factional intrigues had on administration is well-illustrated by the story of Jai Singh's expedition against Churaman Jat.

Braj, the region between Mathura and Agra was the home of a sturdy peasant community known as the Jats. With their villages close to the highway linking Delhi with Agra they had preserved a robust independence, refusing to be cowed down by rajas or emperors. When the imperial authority became too oppressive they did not hesitate to revolt. On the other hand when it appeared to be weakening they would take to banditry, preying on the traffic between the two premier cities of the empire.

The principal personality in the region at this time was a freebooter named Chura (or Churaman), son of Bhajja—who had in his time been a menace to public order and faced chastisement on that account. At the time when the struggle for the throne was on between Bahadur Shah and Azam, Churaman was also in the field, hanging on the skirts of the two armies, on the look-out for loot.

As a result of the battle of Jajau so much plunder fell into his hands that he became a formidable force in the area. He paid homage to Bahadur

Shah after the battle and was given a mansab of 1,500 *zat* and 500 *aspa* and on various occasions assisted the imperial authorities. He was present in Lahore at the time of the death of Bahadur Shah and Azim ush-Shan, and in Agra when Jahandar and Farrukhsiyar met in battle, on which occasion he is said to have looted the baggage of both armies with strict impartiality.

Chabela Ram, subedar of Agra, tried to curb the upstart without success. The next governor was Samsam ud-Daulah Khan-i-Dauran who tried to make a deal with him. Through his good offices he was presented at Court and given charge of the highway from Delhi to the Chambal but he used his authority to aggrandize himself further and build more strongholds. Complaints increased, and finally Raja Jai Singh of Amber offered to lead operations against him.

Sawai Jai Singh set out on 25 September 1716, which happened to be the day of Dussehra, a festival considered particularly auspicious for military operations. A substantial sum was advanced to him, and his troops which consisted of Rajputs, under the command of the minor chiefs of Kota, Bundi and Narwar. But the wazir was annoyed with the raja. The latter had direct access to the emperor and did not care too much for the wazir. And now that Jai Singh had taken up the challenge of humbling Churaman, the last thing the wazir desired was his success.

The siege of Thun, stronghold of the Jat, which had been invested by Jai Singh, dragged on, month after month, while the roads remained unsafe as predatory Jat bands took advantage of the concentration around Thun. The rains failed in 1717 and grain had to be brought at great expense by Jai Singh from his own country. The imperialists defeated many Jat bands but because of the minister's support Churaman continued to hold out. Khan Jahan, maternal uncle of the wazir and subedar of Ajmer, was also with the imperialists having been sent to reinforce Jai Singh but the divided command had its own problems. It is quite likely that Churaman's prolonged resistance was possible only because supplies were still reaching him thanks to the good offices of Khan Jahan. Meanwhile Churaman opened negotiations directly with the wazir through his agent in Delhi. A tribute of Rs. 30 lakh was promised to the government, with a personal douceur of Rs. 20 lakh for Qutb-ul-Mulk. Finally the minister persuaded Farrukhsiyar to agree to the proposal. After all, nearly twenty months had passed and Raja Jai Singh had not been able to accomplish anything. Reluctantly imperial assent was given, and letters sent to Khan Jahan to bring Churaman to court along with his sons and nephews, after making arrangements for the protection of his property from pillage. As for Jai Singh, the nominal commander, a letter was sent thanking him for his exertions and informing him that Churaman had offered terms which had been accepted and hostilities must therefore cease.[10]

Before Sawai Jai Singh set off on his ill-starred campaign against Churaman, and even before the executions of the Sikhs, Mir Jumla had abandoned his post in Patna and returned without orders to Delhi. He had been unable to pay the large and unruly body of Mughals he had recruited. In order to escape their demands he abandoned his post, and travelling incognito in a curtained palki, suddenly turned up at Delhi in January 1716.

The emperor was panic-stricken and Qutb-ul-Mulk warned him that the return of Hussain Ali Khan was now only a matter of time. But the hapless Mir Jumla had been followed by his mercenaries, who surrounded his house, loudly demanding their arrears. The nobleman had to sneak out of his mansion and go into hiding in another house which he owned in the city. For sometime the city was in a very disturbed situation with mailed troops rushing up and down the streets. The emperor called out his personal guard, the *haft chowki*, and the Qila-i-Mualla was under heavy guard. Qutb-ul-Mulk also summoned his nephew and son-in-law, Ghairat Khan, recently appointed faujdar of nearby Narnaul. For all he knew the whole drama might be only a ploy on the part of the emperor and Mir Jumla to seize him.

But at the end of February it was decided to pay off the Mughal mercenaries, Rs. 10 lakh being given by the emperor to clear their arrears, and Mir Jumla, stripped of his titles and offices, was packed off to Lahore. Ultimately in June his titles were restored—at the intercession of Qutb-ul-Mulk and a small jagir of Rs. 3 lakh granted to him. Among the Mughal mercenaries who had made the mistake of entering Mir Jumla's service was Lachin Beg, Bahadur Dil Khan, the notorious *tasma-kash*, who now took up service under Qutb-ul-Mulk.[11]

The episode of Mir Jumla verged on the comical. But differences between the padishah and the wazir persisted. In the beginning of 1717 the emperor had appointed one Inayat Ullah Khan to the diwani of the Khalsa and Tan, another key office of the imperial government. This brought him into conflict with Rattan Chand, and consequently with his patron the wazir, because Rattan Chand believed in farming out the revenue to the amils or collectors from whose bankers he would recover the money in advance. This was anathema to the old school of revenue management which held this to be ruinous to the peasantry and detrimental to the imperial interest. The protection given to certain corrupt officials by Rattan Chand was another cause for disagreement.

It was about this time too that the *jaziya* was revived once more in the face of opposition from the minister. The abolition of the poll tax which was leviable only on the non-Muslim subjects of the padishah was one of the first acts of Farrukhsiyar and was designed to win popularity. That the measure did not have the desired effect was partly owing to the growing indifference of the people to the State, but its reimposition was hardly likely to pass unnoticed. Although theoretically the burden was not excessive it was the source of much avoidable harassment and a blow to the *amour propre* of the well-to-do.

The wazir was extremely indolent and more intent on relaxing in his zenana—which was famous for its beautiful women—and weeks, sometimes months, elapsed before he deigned to attend durbar or visit his office. Till then work would be at a standstill. He promised that he would attend his office in the palace at least once a week. For a while this was observed but soon events came to pass which put an end to this truce.

After the departure of Syed Hussain and Mir Jumla in the beginning of 1715, the city was free from conspiracies for some time. But towards the end of 1717, with the rise of a new royal favourite Muhammad Murad Kashmiri, plots and counterplots again became the order of the day.

Murad was a minor chamberlain but in January 1718 he was appointed superintendent of the *harkaras* and he soon became a close confidant of the emperor, with influence over his mind and, apparently also, his heart.

He undermined and discredited Samsam ud-Daulah insinuating that he was in league with the wazir, which was why all plans and conspiracies had failed in the past. Now fresh plots began to be hatched, and Murad was the prime mover.

Honours were showered on him. From third Mir Tuzak he was moved to the second position and was in addition given the charge of superintendent of the pages or *khawas*. According to Yahya he was at one time promoted daily: on one day his rank was 5,000 *zat*, the next day it was raised to 6,000 and on the third day it was raised to 7,000!

The rain of favours continued. One day he was appointed faujdar of Jammu and allowed to administer his sarkar through a deputy appointed by himself. He was also permitted the privilege of displaying a standard with kettledrums and given the title of Itiqad Khan. Presents and riches were bestowed profusely. A fringed palki, a gold bedstead, and jewels that had belonged to the Emperor Jahangir—not a night passed without his receiving some valuable gift in gold or silver. In the course of little more than a year he became the owner of a hundred elephants![12]

With Murad dominating the emperor the wheels of intrigue started grinding again. Plots and conspiracies were hatched but never executed, for Murad, like the rest of the emperor's favourites, was eloquent in speech but indecisive in action. First Sarbuland Khan, who had succeeded Mir Jumla in Patna was sought to be made the instrument. He was recalled by the emperor and came with 8,000 Mughal troops, hot and eager for action. The emperor held a review in person and everything seemed to be proceeding smoothly. But one day on asking the emperor as to who he thought fit to become wazir once Qutb-ul-Mulk had been removed he received the name of Itiqad Khan in reply. Sarbuland who had been seeing visions of himself as wazir now sat down like a deflated balloon. And that was the end of this conspiracy.

On another occasion it was planned to seize Qutb-ul-Mulk on the occasion of Id prayers. But the plot was leaked and the night before, the wazir filled the entire Idgah with thousands of his followers.

Then Farrukhsiyar summoned Maharaja Ajit Singh, his father-in-law. It was assumed by him and Murad that Ajit Singh would support his son-in-law to the hilt against the wazir. But the chief of the Rathors had no faith in the emperor. He had been forced to give him his daughter and there could be no love lost between them. When Qutb learnt that Ajit was on his way, he got in touch and convinced him about the emperor's fickleness. When he arrived he refused to be drawn into any conspiracy and made it plain that he would not act without the wazir's counsel.

Efforts were then made to win over Nizam-ul-Mulk (Chin Qilich Khan). But this cautious nobleman was in no hurry to commit himself to a rash adventure. He had already suffered and the sarkar of Moradabad was nothing when compared to the six subas of the Deccan. The negotiations fell through but the nizam was in for another rude shock. He was recalled from Moradabad which was then elevated to the rank of a suba and handed over to the royal favourite as another of his absentee charges. So instead of gaining a friend, the emperor had made an enemy in this Mughal amir.

By this time Samsam ud-Daulah had also abandoned the emperor and made his peace with Qutb-ul-Mulk. This became evident on the occasion of the failure of another plot to seize the minister during an audience. Armed men were concealed behind the Diwan-i-Am and were to rush forward and seize him at a signal given by Khan-i-Dauran.

Qutb-ul-Mulk entered the hall leaving his bodyguards outside as was the normal practice. The agreed code word was '*Qul*', but instead of shouting this word Khan-i-Dauran called out '*Qur*' which was the signal for letting in the others who were waiting for audience, and also signified an armed body. So when the nawab called out the word *Qur*, the concealed guards who were supposed to seize the minister did not stir, and instead the minister's own guards rushed in throwing the emperor into confusion.[13]

Then, to cap it all, Mir Jumla decided to come back to Delhi. It appears that he set out on receipt of the emperor's summons but as soon as Qutb-ul-Mulk came to know he protested and the timid Farrukhsiyar immediately cancelled his orders and sent confidential servants to intercept him and turn his back. But Mir Jumla decided to appeal to Qutb-ul-Mulk and travelling incognito went directly to his house on reaching Delhi.

This precipitated the final crisis culminating in the overthrow of Farrukhsiyar and the establishment of the Syed dictatorship.

NOTES

1. The sultan's mother. This was the usual title used in the Ottoman court. Often spelled 'Valide' after the French manner.
2. Tabatabai, *Seir Mutaqherin*, i, pp. 64-6. Irvine, *Later Mughals*, i, pp. 281-4.
3. Tabatabai, i, p. 66.
4. Irvine, i, pp. 297-8.
5. Ibid., i, 298-9.
6. Ibid., i, pp. 301-2.
7. Tabatabai, i, pp. 91-2.
8. Irvine, i, p. 315.
9. Tabatabai, i, p. 91. Lest the description of Banda's execution appear too horrid for words and be construed as being typical of Oriental barbarism, it should be remembered that right up to the end of the eighteenth century in England, common criminals were 'hanged, drawn and quartered', a mode of execution no less horrific.
10. The account of Churaman's rebellion is from Irvine, i, pp. 324-7.
11. Irvine, i, pp. 330-2.
12. Ibid., i, pp. 340-5. Shah Nawaz Khan, *Maathir ul-Umara*, i, pp. 330-2.
13. Irvine, i, pp. 354-5.

CHAPTER 12

Take Warning Ye Who Have Eyes: The Fall of Farrukhsiyar

What reasons Mir Jumla had, if any, for returning to Delhi is unclear. There is nothing to suggest that this was part of a new conspiracy to overthrow the wazir. Probably he was simply desperate to return. He was one of those for whom life outside the charmed circle of the court held no meaning whatsoever. After all Qutb-ul-Mulk had interceded on his behalf in the past and had been instrumental in restoring him to some of his titles and jagirs. If he could be convinced that there was no danger to be feared there was no reason why he should oppose his return to court. He might even help in his further rehabilitation.

But the emperor took the news of his arrival at the house of Qutb-ul-Mulk as a personal affront. It was as if another old friend had defected to the enemy. He sent macebearers to remove him physically from the wazir's house, confiscated his principal residence (known as Asad Khan's haveli), once again stripped him of rank and titles and ordered him to be confined in another of his houses, the one known as Fidai Khan's haveli, the same to which he had fled in 1715 to escape the demands of his mutinous troops.

Qutb-ul-Mulk felt outraged at the violation of the sanctuary of his house by the emperor's minions and taking it, as a visible proof of Farrukhsiyar's continued ill-will he immediately wrote to his brother to come to Delhi.

But Hussain had already decided on going to Delhi as soon as he had come to know of the Idgah plot and had begun to prepare the grounds. The first was the standard excuse of all civil servants seeking a change of station, namely, that the climate did not suit his health. The second was more elaborate and in fact a veiled threat. He informed the emperor that one Muin ud-Din Hussain, reportedly a son of the Shahzada Muhammad Akbar who had fled to Iran in the reign of Aurangzeb, had been captured by Raja Shahu. Shahu in turn had handed him over to him on the understanding that the viceroy would secure the release of his mother and brother who had been state prisoners ever since 1689.

The emperor asked that the prince be sent under escort to Delhi, but the Syed pretended that so distinguished a personage as a prince of the blood could not be escorted by anyone lower in rank than the viceroy himself.[1]

Ominously elaborate arrangements were made by the viceroy for the *istaqbal* of the supposed prince, scarlet tents, a throne and a crown being ordered for him! In the meantime he had also entered into a rather humiliating treaty with Shahu, promising him *chauth* and *sardeshmukhi* for the entire Deccan. Thus vital imperial interests were sacrificed to secure Maratha cooperation. The grandson of the contemptible mountain rat, as Aurangzeb had dubbed Shivaji, was virtually acknowledged as co-sovereign of the Deccan.

A large army which included a force of 12,000 Marathas was raised. The latter were to be paid at the rate of a rupee a day per man, after crossing the Narmada. Most of the Deccan umara accompanied the expedition and the total strength was 30,000 cavalry, besides 10,000 matchlockmen and artillery.[2]

Hussain set out in October. At Burhanpur he was met by Ikhlas Khan who had been sent by the emperor to persuade him to turn back. The emperor had earlier conveyed that if his doctors insisted on a change of air he could post him to Ahmedabad in Gujarat and the offer was repeated. But it was too late now; as far as the Amir-ul-Umara was concerned the die was cast. And the news which Ikhlas Khan imparted to him privately was only calculated to spur him on.[3] So he gave a conventionally proper reply to the emperor's letter, that he did not think he could entrust the prince's charge to anyone else and the Maratha sardars also insisted that he should accompany them in person to secure the release of their Raja's mother and brother. Moreover, he added tongue-in-cheek, there were important matters to be discussed with His Majesty whom he had not met for a long time.

In the meantime a reconciliation of sorts had been effected at Delhi between Abdullah Khan and the emperor. Sarbuland had been totally ruined after his return from Patna. He still had his troops but as he had given up the idea of using them against the wazir he soon found himself embarrassed for funds. The soldiers forced him to disgorge whatever he had towards their arrears and he even had to sell his house. Rendered penniless he sought the help of the wazir who secured for him the suba of Kabul. The emperor too was anxious for a rapprochement, and Maharaja Ajit Singh, who was with the wazir, was given the honorific of Rajeshwar and the government of Gujarat of which Khan-i-Dauran had earlier been an absentee subedar. To his own friend, Raja Jai Singh Sawai, the emperor granted the title of Rajinder Raj Adhiraj. The raja and the minister were also formally reconciled.

Muhammad Amin Khan Chin was subedar of Malwa which lay directly in the path of Hussain's advance. He had no desire to fight him as his force was too weak, and taking advantage of conflicting orders he abandoned his post and set off for Delhi. As for Nizam-ul-Mulk, the wazir was able to secure his rehabilitation by appointing him to Bihar, vacant since Sarbuland's return from Patna.

In the meantime Hussain continued his advance through Rajasthan. While passing through Mewar territory some villages were looted, but after an envoy of the Rana had brought offerings of cash and other presents for the Amir-ul-Umara, strict discipline was enforced. On the other hand when they entered the territories of Jai Singh the troops gave full vent to their usual tendencies for license and plunder and some peasants were carried off as servants.[4]

In February 1719, the Amir-ul-Umara reached Sarai Alavardi Khan near Gurgaon. Here Muhammad Murad and Zafar Khan Turra-i-Baz were awaiting him with a letter from the emperor. But Rattan Chand had already briefed him on the situation in the capital, and their words made no impression. When pressed for an answer he answered brusquely that he would send his reply from the next stage, but if His Majesty turned out all his servants and handed over the keys of the palace to his men, and he was allowed to place his own men in the Qila-i-Mualla, he would act as was necessary.

Two days later he marched through the city with his band playing and pitched his tents on the ridge near the hunting lodge of Firoz Shah. According to the etiquette of the court, no nobleman, however great, could play his music within a mile of the capital. Farrukhsiyar could hear the Syed's kettledrums and trumpets but he chose to overlook the insolence and seemed stricken with fear.

Raja Jai Singh, advised the emperor to place himself at the head of his troops and fall upon the impertinent rebel. He assured him that he and other loyal umara would support him with all their strength and was confident that many of the nobles in the Syed's camp would also return to their proper allegiance once they saw that His Majesty meant business. But it was all to no effect.

But something was still required to precipitate action. Qutb-ul-Mulk tried to break the stalemate by demanding that the emperor dismiss Jai Singh, a known enemy of their family and order him to depart for his country. He also demanded the two offices of the mir atish and superintendent of the diwan khana for his nominees, and permission to take what precautions they considered necessary for their own security. Then, and only then, would he and his brother present themselves before His Majesty, 'ready to carry out his commands as of old'.

At first the emperor tried to play for time but two days later he capitulated and gave in to all their demands. By a note written in the emperor's own hand, Jai Singh and Rao Budh Singh of Bundi were asked to leave for their estates and informed that the following day was particularly auspicious for departures. The eunuch who delivered the note also brought the customary *khillats* of departure, and he let them know that a formal audience would not be necessary! Raging with fury, Jai Singh complied and pitched his tents at Sarai Sahil, outside the city.[5]

This was on 22 February. The next day was fixed for the audience with the Amir-ul-Umara. The Wala Shahis, one of the emperor's household regiments had already evacuated the fort. Qutb-ul-Mulk and Raja Ajit Singh came in the morning and posted their own men everywhere. All the emperor's staff left. Only Muhammad Murad Itiqad Khan, the scandalous favourite, Imtiyaz Khan, comptroller of the household, Zafar Khan and a few others whom the wazir considered to be of no account remained with a few servants and eunuchs.

A few days later, the Amir-ul-Umara was received in audience. He marched through the streets in martial array with the Maratha lancers in the van. It was a stately progress and he did not enter the fort till three in the afternoon. When he, accompanied by the wazir, entered the Diwan-i-Khas, all the attendants were turned out. Only the wazir and Ajit Singh remained. The usual courtesies were observed; the viceroy offered a *nazar* of a hundred gold coins and a equal number of rupees. When he bent over to touch the emperor's feet Farrukhsiyar stopped him and embraced him.

The first question asked by the emperor was about the prince whom the viceroy was supposed to be escorting. Where was he? He was assured that he would be presented as soon the Marathas had received their prince's family members. Whereupon the Maratha hostages were immediately produced. The viceroy then promised that the prince would be handed over the following day. Discussions continued into the night and although some of the points raised, such as the subject of the letters found in Daud Khan's camp were delicate, things did not get out of hand. Extravagant return gifts were made by the emperor, elephants, horses, the jewels he was wearing, and as a final grand gesture, turbans were exchanged. But the Syed accepted only a small part of what was offered and then took leave.

It seemed that an understanding had been reached and things would settle down. But on the evening of the second day when Farrukhsiyar had given orders that he would go out for shikar on the 27th as usual, a message was received from Hussain Ali Khan that he was anxious to have an audience the very next day for handing over the captive prince. The emperor demurred, and desired that the audience be postponed to some other day but the amir was insistent that it could not be put off as that day was particularly auspicious! According to one version the Syeds suspected that the hunt was but a ruse on the part of the monarch to escape from the fort and the clutches of the Syeds.

The arrangements this time were even more stringent. The wazir and Ajit Singh, accompanied by close relatives entered the fort in the morning to reassure themselves that everything was in order. Then in the afternoon came Syed Hussain, as on the previous occasion, accompanied by all his army with the captive prince seated on an elephant, a canopy over his head, and heralds running ahead shouting out his titles. His retinue was more suggestive of a pretender monarch, than that of a captive prince.

But instead of entering, he stopped at the baradari of Shaista Khan, a pavilion which belonged to him and was situated opposite the Lahore Gate of the fort. Meanwhile within, the wazir had already got down to moot discussions with the emperor and Itiqad Khan. Farrukhsiyar repeatedly asked, 'Why doesn't my brother the Amir-ul-Umara bring the supposed prince?', but his plaintive appeals were ignored.[6]

The discussion began on the subject of the agreement agreed on the occasion of the first audience when the Syeds had allowed the emperor to retain Itiqad Khan and some other members of his personal staff as their deputies. This was no longer acceptable, said Abdullah. Itiqad Khan must go entire and, furthermore, be reduced to the mansab he had held in the time of Aurangzeb! This too was conceded. Then the vexed question of the letters written by the emperor and Khan-i-Dauran to the late Daud Khan Panni and Raja Shahu was again raised. Abdullah seemed determined to provoke the emperor. Soon tempers rose. The helpless Itiqad said something which provoked both the emperor and the wazir who turned upon him, abused him roundly, and demanded that he be thrown out. Terror-stricken he fled, got into the first palki he saw, and left as fast as his bearers could run.

The emperor than turned on the wazir. Goaded beyond endurance, he declared, throwing all caution to the wind, 'By God! I won't be my father's son, and shall forfeit all claim to being a descendant from the great Timur if I don't exact vengeance for all your insults and audacity! I shall have your ancestral acres ploughed by asses and mice thrust into the trousers of your women!'[7]

Stung by these words, the wazir also stormed out of the diwan khana.

When the emperor had cooled down he asked Zafar Khan to go and bring him back. Zafar Khan shook his head. It was too late now he told Farrukhsiyar. The emperor must go himself.

But the emperor was now like a deflated balloon. He was seized with terror. He left the diwan khana and sought refuge in the harem. Pathetic appeals were addressed to Raja Ajit Singh through the eunuchs, but the Raja shrugged. What could he do?

The wazir, meanwhile ordered Zafar Khan to quit the qila with the handful of soldiers that constituted his escort. Outside, the city was in an uproar. The night was passed in vigil, and no one slept. The wazir's troops stood ready, tense and alert, while on the other side, the amazonian guard of the seraglio anxiously paced the courts and loggias, ready to protect the craven emperor.

The morning of 28 February began with an unexpected development in the streets outside the fort. Outside no one knew of the goings-on within and the city was rife with rumors. Some even claimed that Raja Ajit Singh had stabbed and killed the wazir. Some of the emperor's friends and relatives like Saadat Khan, his father-in-law, Ghazi ud-Din Khan Khosa, his foster brother, and Aghyr Khan Turk collected what troops they could and set out towards the Qila-i-Mualla. About the same time, quite unconnected with this movement and purely by chance, a clash had occurred between the Marathas and a regiment of household troops called the *kambalposh*[8] under the command of Khan-i-Dauran.

In the crowded streets there was some pushing and jostling as the *kambalposh* forced their way through the Maratha horse. Tension was at breaking point because of the night-long vigil; there was an altercation, swords were drawn, and some of the *kambalposh* shot a few arrows into the Marathas. The Marathas, nerves stretched to breaking point, in an unfamiliar city, and strangers to street-fighting panicked. Seeing their terror, the *kambalposh*, who were all Turks recruited from Central Asia and bitterly resentful of the presence of the Deccanis in what they considered to be their city, fell upon them. They were joined by the unruly elements of the city, and a veritable massacre took place in which about 1,500 Marathas were butchered. The horses of the slain troopers were siezed by the rioters who, on breaking some saddles accidentally, were surprised to find the stuffings full of gold pieces.

Quite separate from this fracas there now ensued some street-fighting around the bazaar known after Sadullah Khan, between Saadat Khan and the other partisans of the emperor and the troops of Muhammad Amin Khan, who was now with the Syeds. Even Itiqad Khan pitched in.[9] Sadat

Khan and his sons withdrew after they were wounded, and others also pulled out after it was confirmed that the wazir was well and a roll of drums and a flourish of trumpets announced to all the world that a new reign had begun. The street-fighting did not last more than an hour.

In the fort, ever since daybreak Abdullah Khan had been sending messengers to persuade the emperor to come forth and take his seat on the throne. Apparently he had not yet decided to replace him; on the other hand, his authorization was needed before his partisans could be arrested. But the craven emperor refused to come out.

Abdullah Khan had sent messages to his brother that since all the offices of the imperial government and the palace were now in the control of their friends and adherents there was no need to dethrone Farrukhsiyar, but Muhammad Amin Khan urged Hussain to think otherwise. Khan-i-Dauran, now with the Syeds, also sent a note urging the viceroy to place some other prince on the throne without delay. Subsequently the Amir sent a message urging his brother to forget the recalcitrant emperor and replace him.

Maharaja Ajit Singh was also pressing for action. Finally, in a hurried conference, it was decided to raise Bidar Dil, son of Bidar Bakht, to the throne, as he was reputed to be the most intelligent of the princes. But when the wazir and Raja Ajit Singh sent their attendants to fetch the prince the women refused to open the doors and started wailing and crying. In vain the emissaries shouted that they had been sent to fetch Bidar Dil to make him emperor, but the women had convinced themselves that the Syeds were about to begin a general massacre of all the salatin prior to assuming the throne themselves, and refused to unbolt.

Ultimately the door was broken in, but Bidar Dil, locked in a closet could not be found. In desperation they turned towards the apartments of the sons of Rafi ush-Shan and from among them they seized Rafi ud-Darjat and dragged him out.

Abdullah and Ajit had been pacing anxiously outside the seraglio so when the prince came they heaved a sigh of relief. Seeing his plain clothes, Qutb-ul-Mulk removed one of his own pearl strings and placed it round the neck of the prince. Then with the wazir holding him by one hand, and Raja Ajit Singh by the other, the prince was led to the throne and requested to take his seat. The wazir leading, all the nobles in turn made their *taslimats* and presented *nazars*, while the musicians in the naubat khana were ordered to announce the new reign.[10]

With a flourish of trumpets and the reverberating boom of the massive kettledrums it was proclaimed to all the world that Rafi ud-Darjat had ascended the throne of the padishahs of Hind.

With the enthronement of Rafi an accomplished fact, casting aside all delicacy, Najm ud-Din Ali Khan, was sent with about 400 men to hunt out Farrukhsiyar. The scene can well be imagined with women and eunuchs running helter-skelter. Some of the Abyssinian and Kalmuck guards resisted but they were killed. Lamentation filled the air. To the inmates it must have seemed that the Day of Judgement had arrived, for never before had the sanctuary of these apartments been so rudely violated.

The room in which the craven Farrukhsiyar was hiding was soon broken in. He came out at last holding a naked sword. His mother, wife, daughters and maidservants, tried to shield him but they were pushed aside. Easily overpowered, he was dragged out with every mark of indignity. His turban was knocked down while his captors taunted and abused him. Thus he was produced before the wazir in torn and disordered clothes, sans turban and in bare feet. It is said that Abdullah Khan himself opened his writing box and took out a needle which he used for applying collyrium. Handing it to one of the men he ordered that the ex-emperor be thrown down and blinded—a command which was obeyed instantly. Thereafter, he was led away to the room above the Tirpoliya, the same where his predecessor had been imprisoned and subsequently strangled.[11]

His imprisonment was needlessly harsh. Often days would pass before he was given water for a bath. An attempt at poisoning brought on diarrhoea and vomitting, and he had to tear off bits of his clothes to wipe himself. The soldiers who guarded him grieved at his miserable plight. Several melancholy verses are attributed to have been composed by him during this period. A few days after his accession Rafi sent a eunuch to enquire after him. Farrukhsiyar invoked a blessing on the eunuch's head and recited the following verse by way of an answer:

> Be not taken in by the garderer's deceit,
> O nightingale,
> Ere this I, too had my nest in this garden.[12]

It is said that inspite of his being blinded he could still see a little, and he continued to hope for a rescue and restoration. He made overtures to his jailors to help him escape, and when those failed, sent plaintive appeals to the Syeds to restore him. Finally the brothers decided that he should die. Suggestions were made to several persons whose families he had harmed that they could kill him. Poison having failed, ultimately professional stranglers had to be sent for. This was on the night of 28 April, two months after his dethronement. Next morning the body was laid outside the diwan-khana for identification. It was remarked that the face had turned black and he had been stabbed in several places. Whether Lachin Beg the *tasma-kash* was involved in this execution is not mentioned. Probably after his earlier services and promotion as Bahadur Dil Khan he had moved on to more dignified duties.

Farrukhsiyar was buried in the crypt of Humayun's tomb and the funeral was well attended. Besides palace functionaries, some mansabdars and eunuchs, thousands of townsmen turned out for the procession. The beggers and fakirs of Delhi deeply mourned his death. The late emperor was highly rewarded for his lavish generosity, and for many days these 'people of God' refused alms from the nobles involved in the Syed coup. Even the ritual feast and the silver and copper pieces which were customarily distributed to the poor on such occasions were declined. Instead, a few days later these people pooled their slender resources and had their own feast, distributing food to passers by.[13]

NOTES

1. Irvine, *Later Mughals*, i, pp. 357-8.
2. Ibid.; Tabatabai, *Seir Mutaqherin*, i, p. 118.
3. Tabatabai, i, pp. 120-5.
4. Ibid., i, pp. 126-7.
5. Irvine, i, p. 376.
6. Ibid., p. 380.
7. Ibid., p. 381. Kamraj, *Ibratnama*, p. 66a. Yoking donkeys to a plough and driving them over the ruins of a captured fort was a well-known practice. Introducing mice in pyjamas was also a popular torture. One still hears of it now and then.
8. So called because of a protective coat of quilting.
9. Irvine, i, pp. 383-5.
10. Tabatabai, i, p. 136. Irvine, i, p. 389.
11. Irvine, i, p. 390. Elliot and Dowson, vii, p. 478.
12. Warid, *Mirat-i-Waridat*, p. 158b.
13. Irvine, i, pp. 393-4. Tabatabai, i, pp. 140-2.

CHAPTER 13

The Syed Dictatorship and Puppets on a String

Coin was struck in Hind, with a thousand blessings,
By the King of Kings on land and sea, Rafi ud-Darjat[1]

With this typical declamatory couplet Rafi ud-Darjat began his reign. In reality this 'King of Kings on land and sea' was a twenty year old opium addict with his lungs far gone, consumed by tuberculosis. In the crisis situation of 28 February after failing to secure Bidar Dil the important thing was to get hold of a prince—just any prince would do—and there was no time to check out details like his health.

As it was, it made little difference. The emperor was a cipher, every detail of his life supervised by his keepers. Within and without the palace, in every hall and at every door, the Syeds posted their own men who kept a watch on all that happened. After a couple of months control was relaxed to the extent that the hereditary doorkeepers and palace servants were allowed to return, but as far as the person of the emperor was concerned the tutelage remained as strict as ever.

It is said that even his meals were served on the bidding of his tutor who was a Barha Syed by the name of Himmat Khan. He scarcely ever ventured beyond the walls of the Qila-i-Mualla. Only three extra-mural excursions are recorded: one being a condolence visit to Qutb-ul-Mulk on the occasion of the death of a daughter, the other being a call at the mansion of Hussain Ali Khan, and the last a shikar excursion to Shakharpur.[2]

But that was not all. Abdullah Khan was a sensualist celebrated for his harem which was filled with beauties from far and near. Taking advantage of his control of the palace he was able to add to their numbers from the harem of the late emperor.[3] The ladies may well have been willing, for the colourless lives of the widows in the bewa khana were tedious to say the least. But worse, the wazir made amorous advances to Begum Inayat Bano, consort of Rafi ud-Darjat himself.

Through Sadr un-Nissa, the superintendent of the harem, he sent messages to the empress but the lady spurned the overtures with cold contempt. However the infatuated minister would not take no for an answer, and continued to urge his suit. Ultimately, the empress cut off her tresses to which he had alluded in his *billets-doux* and sent them to him through Sadr un-Nissa. If he was so infatuated by her tresses, then he may as well have them!

It may well have in the context of the wazir's excessive interest in the ladies of the seraglio that Maharaja Ajit Singh requested that his daughter be allowed to return to her parental home as her husband had now died. This had never been permitted before, and in the case of a former empress it was certainly an insult to the dignity of the Imperial House. Nor did it conform to the normal practice of orthodox Hindus, Rajput or otherwise. A good Hindu wife, never left her husband's house except on a bier and it was considered a disgrace to die elsewhere. But the maharaja insisted, and Bai Inder Kanwar was allowed to leave the Qila-i-Mualla with all her possessions valued at nearly Rs. 1 crore.[4]

What outraged the orthodox clergy even more was the fact that her father performed expensive and complex religious rites to cleanse her on account of her residence in the qila where ritual pollution after the lights of the Hindus was unavoidable. Then she was readmitted to the religion of her ancestors. Now if the very act of her leaving the qila was scandalous, the abandonment of Islam was far worse since apostasy is a capital offence in Islam. But the Syeds needed the support of Ajit Singh and he could not be denied.

Maharaja Ajit was anxious to leave for his home as early as possible because of the unwelcome notice he attracted whenever he ventured in the streets of Delhi. Urchins would follow him calling him all sorts of embarrassing names among which the epithet of *damaad kush*, or killer of one's son-in-law, was the most embarrassing.[5]

The emperor, inspite of his secluded existence both before and after his accession was no idiot. On one occasion when a warrant of appointment was brought for signatures, he recollected that a similar order had been put up a few days earlier. He asked the wazir whether it was the same mahal[6] or another by the same name. The minister conceded that it was the same, but the second candidate was more suitable as he offered more money. The emperor refused to sign stating that the government should be more consistent and orders of appointment should not be countermanded so casually.[7]

He was particular about his dignity and the observance of decorum. Once at a private audience Hussain presumed to take his seat without permission. The emperor, stung by this assumption of equality, calmly extended his feet and asked him to remove his shoes! Inwardly seething, the Amir-ul-Umara complied.[8]

But it was obvious, even to the emperor, that he was a dying man. He told the Syeds that it was his desire to see his elder brother crowned in his lifetime. About the same time in Agra, Nekusiyar, the eldest surviving son of Prince Muhammad Akbar—one of two who had actually been left behind when the father fled to Iran—had raised the standard of revolt in Agra fort where he resided. Abdullah Khan was at first quite open to the idea of replacing Rafi with the new pretender. Besides, while Rafi and his brothers were great-grandchildren of Aurangzeb, Nekusiyar was a grandson and thus had a better claim.

But Syed Hussain in his usual manner took this revolt as a personal affront and would not even consider the suggestion. Finally Rafi's request was accepted and on 4 June Rafi ud-Darjat returned to his old apartments, and his brother was installed two days later. He had reigned exactly three months and four days. Five days later he expired.

One important decision was taken during the reign of this shadowy emperor. The *jaziya* was once again abolished. Abdullah Khan had always been against its reimposition and he was only too happy to accede to the earnest requests of Maharaja Ajit Singh, Rattan Chand and the other non-Muslim umara. Apart from the repeal of this obnoxious tax the administrative changes were minimal. The only significant posting was that of Nizam-ul-Mulk for whom, in the previous reign, he had secured a posting to Bihar, but Nizam-ul-Mulk was reluctant to go, and being an important amir, he had to be humoured. He was adjusted in Malwa which had been vacant since Amin Khan Chin's return to Delhi.

But one loose end remained to be tied up—that of Nekusiyar. He had been born in October 1679, so he was about forty at the time—nearly twice the age of Rafi. Hence the querulous tone of the letter which he addressed to the Syeds and nobles like Muhammad Amin Khan:

> What new born child is this that has been placed on the throne of Hindustan? Never before has anyone thought of passing over an elder for a younger heir. As for the seizure, imprisonment and death of Muhammad Farrukhsiyar, those events had been decreed by the Eternal, let them (i.e. the Syeds) wrapping their head of shame in the skirt of humility, make due submission. No revenge will be taken, but all their mansabs and dignities will be maintained as before.[9]

The revolt was sparked off when Ghairat Khan, the new governor of the province, and Samandar Khan, the new qiladar, arrived to take charge. They were accompanied by Dawar Dad Khan who was sent to take charge of the fort's treasure. But the rumour spread that he had been sent to superintend the blinding of the princes residing within.

On his own Nekusiyar was incapable of inspiring the revolt. The brain was that of Mitter Sen, a brahmin in his service. The latter practised medicine and lent money on interest to the garrison and had thus acquired considerable influence over them. When the Amir-ul-Umara had passed through Agra some months earlier, en route to the Deccan, this wily brahmin had sensed by the gossip among the Syed's officers that sooner or later Farrukhsiyar would be dethroned. Called upon to attend to the old injuries of the Amir he had ventured the suggestion that in that event the claims of his master who was the seniormost prince be kept in mind. The suggestion was however ill-received by the Syed who felt irritated that this man should have so easily divined his innermost thoughts, and he ordered that he should not be admitted to his presence in future.[10]

But now when Samandar Khan sent word that all the officers should come out and wait on him before conducting him into the fort, he was met with a cold rebuff that they did not know any qiladar by the name of Samandar Khan. Shortly after, on 18 May Nekusiyar was escorted from his apartments and placed on the throne, all the men and officers of the garrison presenting congratulatory *nazars*. The incumbent qiladar, Safi Khan, who was 70 years old, had joined just a few months earlier and had no hold on the garrison. He appears to have been a mere spectator carried along by events.

The force with Samandar and Ghairat was very weak, but apart from shelling the governor's mansion which was close to the fort, the garrison did not venture forth. Mitter Sen had established contact with Jai Singh and Nizam-ul-Mulk, but the latter did not respond. Jai Singh advanced only upto Biyana and then paused to see which way the wind was blowing. Chabela Ram who would have liked to join was detained in his own province by a minor disturbance led by a disgruntled zamindar.

Mitter Sen, now transformed into Raja Birbal, had the treasure vaults opened and gold and silver coins to the value of Rs. 1 crore and 8 lakh were drawn and partly distributed among the garrison. Advances were given to unemployed soldiers who flocked to sign up for service under the new emperor. Nekusiyar appeared before the public, standing under a domed chhatri with an attendant holding a royal umbrella over his head while Mitter scattered gold and silver largesse to the crowd below.[11]

Towards the end of June 1719 Hussain Ali Khan set out for Agra. The garrison began to lose heart when neither Chabela Ram nor Jai Singh made any move. Safi Khan the qiladar, never a willing participant, become quite depressed on learning that his family had been placed under arrest in Delhi. On 7 August Asghari, Nekusiyar's younger brother, was apprehended by the encircling army while attempting to escape. A few days later on 12 August the fort surrendered, Safi Khan having been promised a pardon.

Nekusiyar, accompanied by a nephew known as Baba Mughal, was taken on an elephant to the Syed's camp. The two were received respectfully by the Amir-ul-Umara who had prepared a mansad for them while he himself stood respectfully by with folded hands. But Nekusiyar, who had lived all his life in isolation, immured within the walls, was terror-stricken. He stood up and started blubbering, pleading for his life. Hussain was embarrassed at this undignified display of fear by a grown man and did his best to calm him. When his fears had been put to rest an eunuch was sent at his request to allay the fears of his mother and other ladies, and to inform them of the kind reception he and his nephew had received.[12]

Nekusiyar's behaviour is a good instance of the debilitating effect of a life of long confinement. True to his word, the Amir-ul-Umara ensured that no harm came to him. He simply exchanged his apartments in Agra for a somewhat smaller suite in the Salimgarh where he lived another four years, dying in 1723.

As for Mitter Sen who knew well that he would not be forgiven so easily, he tried to kill himself with a dagger. But he was still alive when he was carried to the presence of Hussain who ordered his execution. His head was sent to the wazir.

Then ensured a hunt for the hoards which were reputed to be still buried in secret vaults in the fort. Old retired treasurers and other employees of the tosha khana were traced out and persuaded to search their memories. Eventually substantial treasure was recovered, variously estimated at upto Rs. 3 crore. Much of it was in coined metal buried since the time of Aurangzeb, and it included a jewel studded shawl belonging to Nur Jahan, a sword of Jahangir's and a sheet embroidered with pearls which Shah Jahan had ordered for the tomb of Mumtaz.

It is time to return now to Delhi where on 6 June Rafi ud-Daulah, the middle son of Rafi ush-Shan had succeded his younger brother, Rafi ud-Darjat. He was his senior by only eighteen months, and though his lungs were clear he was addicted to opium, which appears to have been a common habit among the salatin.

Like his brother, his life was monitored closely by the Syeds through his tutor and attendants. He was not allowed to go out anywhere unless one of his keepers was in attendance. He received the title of the Second Shah Jahan and it is as Shah Jahan that he is styled on his coinage. The wit who suggested the title must have had a wry sense of humour.

About this time it was learnt that Shaista Khan, the maternal uncle of the late Farrukhsiyar, was raising troops and planning to escape to Amber from where he hoped to challenge the Syed dictatorship with the help of Raja Jai Singh. The wazir sent troops commanded by Zafar Khan and Nahar Khan Hansawi. His house was stormed and plundered while Shaista himself was taken prisoner.

After this incident the wazir decided to march against Jai Singh, and he took the emperor along with him. They had not gone far when messages were received from Hussain that the raja had been effectively neutralized by a blockading force under Zafar Khan and that he should either turn back or join him at Agra. The wazir decided to push on to Agra as he wanted to be present at the capture of the fort. But as chance would have it, he learnt at Mathura that the fort had already fallen. Nevertheless he decided to continue, lest the entire treasure should fall into the hands of his brother.

It was while encamped at the sarai of Bidyapur near Fatehpur Sikri that another unexpected development took place which forced the wazir to halt. The emperor had been trying to give up his opium habit, but a too rapid withdrawal of the drug brought on an attack of diarrhoea. After a few days, he expired (18 September 1719). He had reigned only four months and sixteen days.

The wazir dispatched his nephew Ghulam Ali Khan and some other nobles to Delhi to bring another prince from the Qila-i-Mualla and his death was concealed until their return. The personal attendants were sworn to silence and each morning the wazir would present himself in the emperor's tent for the daily audience and would come out wearing new robes of honour. The farce went on till the return of Ghulam Ali on 24 September.[13] He brought with him Prince Roshan Akhtar, son of the late Khujista Akhtar (entitled Jahan Shah), the fourth son of Bahadur Shah.

The enthronement was fixed for 28 September and the new emperor took the title of Abdul Fath Nasiruddin Muhammad Shah Badshah Ghazi. He was a handsome and fairly intelligent young man in his eighteenth year, and unlike his two immediate predecessors destined for a long reign of nearly thirty years.

NOTES

1. Irvine, *Later Mughals*, i, p. 418.
2. Ibid., p. 416.
3. Irvine (on the authority of Khushal Chand), i, p. 417. Irvine does not give much credit to the later part of the story as it is remarkably similar to Manucci's story about Rana Dil and Aurangzeb. Elliot and Dowson, vii, p. 481.
4. Elliot and Dowson, vii, p. 483.
5. Tabatabai, *Seir Mutaqherin*, i, p. 138. Irvine, i, p. 408.
6. Mahal, a village or revenue estate.
7. Irvine, i, p. 417.
8. Ibid., p. 417.
9. Ibid., p. 415.
10. Ibid., p. 411.
11. Ibid., p. 412.
12. Ibid., pp. 426-7.
13. Tabatabai, i, p. 145.

CHAPTER 14

The Fall of the Syeds

The year 1719 had seen the installation of three emperors and the proclamation of one pretender. Hence, fully aware of the delicacy of the situation, the emperor's mother Mariam Makani (now Nawab Qudsia), took care not to offend the susceptibilities of the Syeds. When the wazir's messengers came to call her son to the throne, she had given them *khillats* and had similar *khillats* distributed among all the palace officials, as had been the custom on such occasions in earlier times. But when she was told that this had drawn adverse attention in the Syeds' camp she refused to entertain other requests for favour, and on coming to know that many of her late husband's adherents were getting ready to accompany the two to Agra, she sent word that it was her express desire that they should desist.[1]

Initially, things were exactly as they had been during the ephemeral reigns of the two pageant emperors. Muhammad Shah remained virtually a prisoner of the Syeds, every waking hour closely superintended by his tutor, who was the same Himmat Khan. But before long the Turanian nobles would combine to overthrow the Syed dictatorship.

Although the pretensions of Nekusiyar were easily scotched the Syeds still felt insecure. Raja Jai Singh in neighbouring Amber, Chabela Ram in Allahabad, and Nizam-ul-Mulk in Malwa, were all regarded as hostile. This was inspite of the fact that none of them had committed any overt act following the proclamation of Nekusiyar. Except perhaps for Jai Singh who had ostentatiously donned his yellow robes and marched one or two stages towards Agra.

A number of fugitives from that city had also taken refuge in his territories. Preparations were made in the imperial camp to march on Ajmer via Amber, ostensibly to visit the shrine, but in reality to overawe Jai Singh and compel him to submit to the new emperor. But thanks to the mediation of Maharaja Ajit Singh who was still in the imperial camp, this was not necessary.

According to the terms of the settlement drawn up by the Rathor chief, Jai Singh was to be appointed to the faujdari of Sorath in the suba of Gujarat of which he himself was the governor. In addition he was to be given Rs. 20 lakh 'to buy back the city of Amber from the Brahmans'. For his efforts as mediator, and for his loyalty in the revolts of the previous year, Maharaja Ajit Singh was also appointed to the government of Ajmer.[2] Thus the entire country from 60 miles to the south of Delhi, all the way to the Arabian Sea down as far as Surat, was now in the hands of these two Rajputs.

Chabela Ram, governor of the Allahabad suba, who had been a protégé of Azim us-Shan and Farrukhsiyar, would certainly have marched to the assistance of the rebels at Agra had he not been held up by disturbances in his own suba by a zamindar of Kalpi who was encouraged in his defiance by the moral and material support of Muhammad Khan Bangash of Farrukhabad, who was acting at the behest of the Syeds.

An imperial army was also dispatched against him but he suffered a paralytic stroke and died suddenly in November (1719).[3] But matters unfortunately did not end with his death for his nephew Girdhar Bahadur had succeeded him. Abdul Nabi Khan, the imperial commander conveyed to him the wazir's offer of the subedari of Awadh-Faizabad if he would submit. But Girdhar Bahadur did not comply with his wishes.

A stronger army was sent under Haidar Quli Khan and the fort invested. Muhammad Khan Bangash was in touch with Girdhar but the latter lost faith when he learnt that the subedari had been promised to him. Finally he declared that he could only trust Raja Rattan Chand. So the latter was sent to the east, backed by a strong artillery train and additional troops.

The first meeting took place inside the fort which Rattan Chand entered, accompanied by only four officers, including Haidar Quli and Muhammad Khan Bangash. The following day Girdhar returned the visit. In this meeting they began serious negotiations and finally Girdhar agreed to evacuate Allahabad and accept his appointment to Awadh-Faizabad, provided he was reimbursed the expenses which he had incurred as a result of the 'misunderstanding'. The sum agreed was Rs. 30 lakh and it was to be paid out of the Bengal tribute which had been held up at Patna, on account of the operations at Allahabad.[4]

Since the reduction of the fortress would have been a long and protracted affair, it was considered prudent to concede the demand, but it is interesting to observe that here, as in the case of Raja Jai Singh, it is the rebel who is dictating terms and not the imperial government.

On 11 May Girdhar Bahadur marched out with all his treasure and belongings and set off for Awadh while Ahmad, a brother of Muhammad Bangash moved in with 500 men and occupied the fort. Raja Rattan Chand returned to Agra.

But Jai Singh, Chabela Ram or Girdhar Bahadur were small fry compared to Nizam-ul-Mulk, at the time subedar of Malwa. He had been posted there for barely a year, after the revolution which toppled Farrukhsiyar, and he had accepted it only after the Syeds had promised that he would not be transferred again without his consent.

Although he and the Syeds had never actually crossed arms, there was no love lost between them ever since his recall from the viceroyalty of the Deccan in 1714, and replacement by Syed Hussain Ali Khan. Nizam-ul-Mulk and his late father, the blind Ghazi ud-Din Khan had started their careers in the Deccan and both had been favourites of Aurangzeb. Since his departure for Malwa he had not committed any overt act but the Syeds could not feel easy on his account. Reports were received that he was raising troops beyond the ordinary requirements of a suba, and that he favoured officers not conspicuous for their devotion to the Syeds. His cousin Muhammad Amin Khan Chin sent him a confidential letter written in the emperor's own hand and another bearing the seal of the Validah Sultan, complaining of the restraint under which they suffered, and calling upon him to deliver them.

Although this last was not known to the brothers and the nizam was too prudent and cautious to plunge precipitately into so rash an enterprise, the brothers decided to transfer him out. The route to the Deccan passed through Malwa and for the security of the former, they reasoned, they must have a more dependable governor. A firman was issued giving the Amir-ul-Umara the charge of Malwa, in addition to the Deccan, of which he was already absentee governor. The nizam was offered the choice of any one of the subas of Akbarabad, Allahabad, Multan or Burhanpur. This was a clear violation of the understanding under which he had accepted the Malwa posting, and he inferred that his destruction had been decided.

Syed Dilwar Ali Khan was sent with a large force towards Malwa. It was given out that he was being sent to escort the family of the Amir-ul-Umara which had been left behind at Aurangabad when Hussain Ali set out to overthrow Farrukhsiyar, but his real instructions were to seek and destroy the nizam. Simultaneously, instructions were conveyed to Syed Alam Ali Khan, Hussain's deputy in the Deccan, to attack the nizam from the south. Alam Ali Khan also started recruiting troops and both he and the nizam engaged Maratha auxilliaries.

At first Nizam-ul-Mulk set off in a northerly direction but he suddenly doubled back, and crossing the Narmada entered the Deccan. The most formidable fortress in the area was Asirgarh, which he was able to occupy by the simply expedient of offering to pay the garrison its salary which was in arrears, and as chance would have it the mother of Saif ud-Din Ali Khan, a younger half-brother of the wazir who was travelling north to join her son, fell into his hands. But he treated her with courtesy and sent her under escort upto the Narmada, which marked the northern border of his suba.[5]

The first battle, however, was with Dilawar rather than Alam Ali and the location was a village named Ratanpur, about 20 miles from Burhanpur. Dilawar Ali Khan was struck by a bullet in the chest and killed. Another notable casualty was Rao Bhim Singh Hara who had only recently won the throne of Bundi with the help of an imperial army. The date was 19 June 1720. The defeated army broke up and scattered, retreating to the north. The wounded were taken care of by the nizam who offered to enlist them in his army but on their declining he allowed them to proceed northwards, even giving them a small sum to cover their travelling expenses.

The news of the disaster at Ratanpur caused consternation at Agra. A whole army had been lost and the Amir-ul-Umara's family was in peril. At first he was all for rushing to the Deccan and taking on the nizam head-on, but saner counsels prevailed and it was decided to write a conciliatory letter to the nizam.

The emperor expressed surprise at the governor's action in leaving his jurisdiction without leave. What was the cause? What were his apprehensions? Whatever they were, he ought to have brought them to the notice of His Majesty. He also added that the question of conferring the Deccan viceroyalty to him had been, and still was, under consideration. After having assumed charge he should make arrangements for sending the family of the Amir-ul-Umara.

Accompanying it was a letter from Syed Hussain Ali Khan. In this he disavowed any hostile intention on the part of Dilawar. His instructions were simply to bring his family, and if he had exceeded this brief, his action was entirely unauthorized. He also repeated that the emperor had decided to issue a patent conferring on him the Deccan viceroyalty. He offered his congratulations in advance, and adding that Alam Ali would now be escorting his family, requested his assistance and cooperation.

What ought to be the appropriate course of action was hotly debated in the innermost counsels of the Syeds. At one time it was proposed that Hussain Ali should go south with the emperor and take the bull by the horns; at another moment attention would shift to his cousin Muhammad Amin Khan Chin who was considered too dangerous to be left behind. The Amir-ul-Umara was of the view that he should be arrested and put to death but the wazir refused to sanction such precipitate action. The Mughal had committed no transgressions which warranted such extreme action, nor was there any evidence of his being party to a conspiracy and they were bound by solemn oaths to protect him. Muhammad Amin, moreover, aware of the hostile undercurrents, took care to repeatedly and loudly condemn the rebellious attitude of his brother.

It was in the end the wazir who prevailed and Muhammad Amin was not touched. But coming events cast their shadows and Syed Ghulam Hussain reads portents of the violent events in a severe earthquake which shook Agra and Delhi in the month of Ramzan. So severe was the shock that bricks from the cupola of the Jama Masjid were dislodged while the imam was reciting the *khutba* during the Friday prayers. Many houses collapsed and minor tremors continued for the scriptural period of 40 days so that people were convinced that some extraordinary occurence was imminent.[6]

In the Deccan events were moving at their own pace, notwithstanding the conciliatory letters addressed to the nizam. Syed Hussain's family had obtained shelter in the fortress of Daulatabad. Thus, easy on this score, Alam Ali concentrated on destroying Nizam-ul-Mulk. The latter called upon Alam to hand over the charge of the Deccan according to the contents of the imperial farman and the letter of the Amir-ul-Umara, but Alam Ali had his own instructions and no intentions of obliging. But the nizam gave wide publicity to the firman according to which the viceroyalty had been practically conferred upon him and replied unblushingly to the oblique charges levelled in the letter that accompanied the firman.

On 10 August the armies of the nizam and Alam Ali faced each other on the field of Balapur not far from Akola. Like all the Barha Syeds, Alam was a brave man and fought stoutly still the end. It was a strange battle. About seventeen or eighteen senior officers, i.e. those entitled to elephants were killed on Alam's side, while the nizam did not lose a single notable. At Ratanpur it had been a similar story, the army of Dilawar being destroyed and his officers slaughtered in droves, while not a single senior officer fell on the side of the nizam. The latter was nearly fifty when he fought these battles, and his approach was very different from that of hot-headed youths like Alam Ali. He fought not for glory, but only when it was unavoidable, and his object was victory, nor martyrdom. At both these battles he had carefully positioned his troops, taking advantage of the terrain, concealing them wherever possible from the view of the enemy, and depending on surprise rather than elan.

The news of this second disaster which reached Agra on 26 August caused panic. The wazir's hands trembled as he read the letter but the Amir-ul-Umara preserved his equanimity in public but he was even more perturbed, because he did not know that his family was safe in Daulatabad.

It was decided that Hussain should leave immediately with a strong army for the Deccan, taking the emperor with him, while Abdullah would stay behind at the capital. Conditions in the north were also disturbed. The Pathans of Kasur in the Punjab had defied the imperial authority and had been suppressed with difficulty by Abdus Samad Khan. Kashmir was also going through a period of turmoil, a fanatic named Abdul Nabi Muhtavi Khan having incited the Mussalmans to massacre the Hindus. In the reprisals that followed Muhtavi Khan and his two little children were executed by the orders of the deputy governor, which led to another and even bloodier round of massacre, arson and loot. About three thousand people—mostly Mughals, merchants and other transients rather than Hindus—were butchered and 'an infinity of women and children were seized on and carried away as fair booty'. A new deputy had to be sent to restore law and order—'a difficult task, this in a country known for a disposition to turbulency, and for being inhabited by a wicked race of men with whom a man in power must make a shift to live, sometime by yielding and as often by stiffening'.[7]

The preparations for Syed Hussain's expedition were made under a pall of gloom. Inspite of the brave front which he tried to present, it was evident even to the least discerning, that the star of the Syeds was in decline. Their adherents started falling away and found excuses to avoid going to the Deccan. The Amir-ul-Umara had hoped to raise an army one hundred thousand strong, but inspite of his best efforts he could raise little more than half that number. And many of these, like those commanded by Muhammad Amin Khan, were of doubtful value. This Mughal or Turanian chief was forced to join the expedition simply because he was too dangerous to be left behind. Syed Hussain knew that the Turanian would take the first opportunity to desert, and if he managed to retain him till the hour of battle, he would undoubtedly abandon him and join his cousin when most advantageous.

But Amin Khan (now known by his latest title of Itimad ud-Daulah) had no intentions of waiting that long. While to all outward appearances, there existed every sign of amity between him and the Syed, a conspiracy was already afoot. The army started on its march on 6 September and since the deed was done in barely a month's time the conspiracy might well have been hatched at Agra. And all this time the Amir-ul-Umara was addressing Itimad ud-Daulah as 'respected uncle', and was hopeful of winning him over completely to his side. His judgement was no better than Qutb-ul-Mulk's.

Rumours of a conspiracy were rife in the camp. Some of the Syeds' confidants warned against admitting the Turki chiefs to his daily conference with their armed guards, but he scoffed at their fears. When some of them commented adversely on his appointment of Haidar Quli Khan, a Turanian, to the artillery he lost his temper. Haidar Quli Khan was a very capable man, he observed, and had shown his worth at the time of the operations against Girdhar Bahadur. They were jealous merely because the post had been given to a Turk!

Muhammad Amin had established communication with Nawab Qudsia through the superintendent of the harem, Sadr un-Nissa. One Shah Abdul Ghaffur, a faqir from Sindh who was accompanying the army and was in the conspiracy, passed to and fro in a black 'burqa' posing as a female milk vendor.[8] The tacit assent of the Validah Sultan having been obtained, Muhammad Amin dropped oblique hints of the impending event to the emperor as well, in the Turki tongue which they both spoke—but which the Syed, who was Indian, did not.

It seemed that assassination was the only possible way. The Mughal chief made an appeal to his followers, asking for a volunteer ready to risk his life. Should he succeed and survive the attempt the nawab would be in his debt forever. Should he die in the attempt, he could be assured that family and dependents would be well looked after. At first no one spoke but then one Mir Haidar Beg Dughlat stood up and offered himself saying, 'I am a Syed and so is he. If brother kills brother, what does it matter?'[9] This gentleman was descended from an ancient family whose ancestors had been Khans of Kashgar. His ancestor, Mirza Haidar, had been governor of Kashmir under Humayun and was the author of the *Tarikh-i-Rashidi*, a history of the Chughatas and Timurids.

Other conspirators were Haider Quli Khan, who had rightly been suspected by the Syed's well-wishers, and Muhammad Amin Saadat Khan, faujdar of Biyana.

On 7 October the Amir ul-Umara was heard to declare that he could make any man emperor. It was a foolish thing to say and the way he phrased it caused great offence, for he is reported to have said that he only had to indicate his choice by throwing his shoe at the man. This insolent boast was commented upon widely in the camp and the conspirators decided to take advantage of the ill-feeling by striking the very next day.

It was the custom of the Amir to pay his respects to the emperor in the morning, and again in the afternoon on reaching the camp he would escort him to his tent. Accordingly, the next day after the march, Syed Hussain, Muhammad Amin and some other nobles escorted the emperor to his tents. After he had gone in they began to scatter. Syed Hussain had just got into his palki to leave when Muhammad Amin who had previously filled his mouth with fresh blood pretended to vomit blood and sat down complaining of dizziness. Syed Hussain stopped and called for doctors. Then pretending to revive after restoratives had been administered, he indicated that he should be carried into the tent of Haidar Quli which was just outside the gulal-bar.

After he had been carried away there were only one or two persons left around the Amir-ul-Umara. Then Haidar Beg Dughlat advanced—shouting 'Dohai, dohai!', the traditional cry of an aggrieved complainant. In his hand he held a piece of paper and complained loudly that Muhammad Amin, who was also the second bakhshi, was holding back his soldiers' salaries and their plight was desperate. The complaint had just the right degree of verisimilitude as Itimad ud-Daulah was notorious for his tight-fistedness. One of the attendants came forward to take the man's representation but Haidar Beg refused to give it to him. Smiling, the Amir-ul-Umara beckoned him to come forward. Coming close to the palki Haidar Beg handed him his representation which the latter started reading. Then another attendant passed him his hookah from the other side and as he turned towards him to accept the mouth-piece Haidar found his opportunity. Quick as a flash he drew his dagger and plunged it into his breast. The Syed shouted and kicked him back with his feet as the palki bearers dropped their burdern and ran. Haidar recovered sufficiently to catch him by the heels and pull him out of the tumbled palki, and sitting on his chest dispatched him. Thereafter he cut off the head.

Syed Nurullah Khan, a young boy of 15 and a cousin of the Amir drew a pistol and fired at the assassin. Then drawing his sword he dispatched him. Meantime other Mughals slew him in turn.

It took less than a minute. Muhammad Amin, now fully 'recovered', picked up the severed head and throwing it before the entrance to the royal tents, called upon Muhammad Shah to come and assume the command in person. The emperor, who had come out, seemed to have lost his nerve, and whether or not he had been informed of the conspiracy, he now remonstrated. His mother, nervous for his safety, pulled him back into the tent.

By this time some of the Syed's adherents had also recovered and a small group led by Mustapha Khan, bakhshi to Raja Mokham Singh, cut their way past the few Mughals and the canvas qanats, into the royal tents, before they were driven back by Saadat Khan who, casting aside all ceremony, pushed in after them. There was no time to be lost because at the same time anoher small group led by Khwaja Maqbul Ahmed, *nazir* to the Amir-ul-Umara, followed by a water carrier and sweeper, had also made a valiant but fool-hardy attempt to penetrate the royal tents and seize the emperor. The Khwaja was severely wounded and fated to die a few days later.

Saadat Khan found the emperor cowering behind the ample skirts of Sadr un-Nissa, the redoubtable superintendent of the harem.[10] Seizing His Majesty by the arm he dragged him out and placed him on an elephant belonging to Qamr ud-Din Khan, the son of Muhammad Amin Itimad ud-Daulah. Muhammad Amin climbed in behind and they stationed themselves prominently in front of the royal enclosure, the head of the murdered Syed held aloft on a lance.

Runners were sent in all directions bearing urgent messages to the captains of the Turanian amirs asking them to stand firm and be on their guard against any attempt to rally by the partisans of the Syeds. The signal to loot the tents of the Amir-ul-Umara was given and the artillery ordered to limber up and fire to create the desired panic and confusion in the enemy's camp. The fighting and looting lasted about twelve hours. By that time the Syed's camp had been completely stripped of valuables, almost everything being appropriated by the soldiery of the Turanian nobles, Itimad ud-Daulah not deeming it prudent to interfere.

The career of the Amir-ul-Umara, Bakhshi-ul-Mumalik, Syed Hussain Ali Khan was over. Now only the elder brother remained.

There being no reason to continue the journey it was decided to return to the capital to overthrow the wazir. The emperor appointed Muhammad Amin as his new wazir and the other nobles were rewarded or conciliated with exalted mansabs of 6,000 and 7,000. The bodies of Syed Hussain, Ghairat Khan and Nurullah, were laid out in biers and sent for interment in the family vault at Ajmer. Letters were also sent to provincial governors known to be hostile to the Syeds, informing them of the recent events, and asking them to report to the imperial camp.

Raja Jai Singh sent a force of 4,000 men and wrote that he himself would be following soon. Girdhar Bahadur also sent word from Awadh that he was collecting troops and would soon be setting out. Nizam-ul-Mulk, to whom the head of his enemy had also been sent along with the letter, replied that he was on his way.

Abdullah Khan received the news within eighteen hours of the event. He was shaken but revenge was uppermost in his mind. As the emperor was now in the hands of Muhammad Amin his position was definitely weaker so he decided to place another prince on the throne in order to legitimize his actions. But first he wrote a letter to Muhammad Shah, reproaching him for the crime which had been committed in his camp, and while he expressed the conviction that His Majesty had nothing to do with it, he requested him to arrest the persons responsible for the deed. To this the emperor replied that he had no knowledge of the plot, but the assassin had been killed and it was not known if he had any associates. If the wazir had any such information His Majesty would like to be informed. In the typical flowery verbiage used for all formal correspondence in Oriental courts the emperor concluded:

> The extreme loyalty and the clarity of the thoughts of that pillar of the State (i.e. Abdullah Khan) are more evident than the sun itself, and are impressed on my heart. By the aid of God, I, too, will soon reach that place (i.e. Delhi). That Loyal One also proposed to come to the Presence. If it please the Lord Most High, this matter will then be decided in the most perfect and satisfactory manner according to the Holy Law and Justice.[11]

But that pillar of the State, 'the most loyal one', was feverishly raising an army and had already found a compliant prince. Rumours of the military preparations reached the Urdu-i-Mualla. More letters were exchanged, and in his reply the wazir boldly acknowledged his apprehensions for his safety in Muhammad Shah's camp and the measures he had taken:

> If there were safety where your Majesty is, how would it be possible for a lowly thing like me to disobey the exalted order. Guardian of the Realm! Muhammad Ibrahim, too, is of your Majesty's family and kin. Yea, verily, in him I have provided an instrument for my safety. If it please the Most High God, in a short time, attending on his stirrup, we shall be honoured with the felicity of an audience, and the true state of the matter will be laid before you. To say more would be to transgress the rules of politeness.

The stage was set for the final struggle.

Abdullah had sent a letter to Najm ud-Din Ali Khan, another of his brothers, asking him to place a prince immediately on the throne and to begin raising troops. But finding a willing prince was not easy. The messengers first went to the apartments of Jahandar Shah's family. But on learning their purpose the princes shut the gates and refused to open. Then Nekusiyar, only recently arrived from Agra, was approached. But he also declined. He had had his moment of glory and had no desire to repeat the experience. Finally Prince Ibrahim, the last surviving son of Rafi ush-Shan, gave his consent. Both his brothers Rafi ud-Darjat and Rafi ud-Daulah had reigned, however briefly, and he did not wish to be the exception. Thus though Rafi ush-Shan himself had been denied the honour, all three of his sons ascended the throne.

He was placed on the throne on 15 October 1720. As usual coins were struck and the *khutba* read in his name. As in the case of his other two brothers very little is known about him personally, but his age appears to have been about 23 and all three were children of the same mother, Nur un-Nissa.

For raising an army money was required. Much of the spoils of Agra had been grabbed by Syed Hussain and were dispersed among the soldiers of the army now marching to overthrow him. So he dug out all his hoards, seized Raja Rattan Singh's house, had it searched for buried treasure, and drew whatever was available in the treasury. By these means about Rs. 1 crore was raised.

Much of it was disbursed in the next few days by way of advances to the new recruits who were engaged at extraordinarily high rates, Rs. 80 being offered per month to a trooper with one horse and Rs. 150 for a trooper with two. These rates were offered indiscriminately to one and all, no distinction being made between veterans and the scum of the bazaars, which led to much heartburning among his old soldiers. Many of the new recruits just took the advance and never reported. But the response from the Syed homeland was generous, with many of his kinsmen flocking to his call. The situation was grave and Qutb-ul-Mulk knew that there would be no second chance.[12]

He first pitched his camp at the Idgah but because of the large number of desertions he moved further from the city to the village of Bilochpur in Palwal pargana. The battle took place at Hassanpur about 6 miles further on 13 November.

It was a strange battle. On the first day the two opposing armies kept up a desultory cannonade. Many of the raw levies of Abdullah Khan melted away, and at night desertions were wholesale. When morning dawned the wazir found that only his closest relatives, most of them men from Barah, and barely a thousand horsemen were left.

But Qutb-ul-Mulk was not the man to give up without a fight. The battle was joined. Most of the men fled. Najm ud-Din, who was separated from his brother, seeing the howdah of his elephant empty galloped back towards it to find his brother fighting on foot as was the Indian custom when the situation became desperate.

Seeing him Abdullah called out, 'Behold the fickleness of fortune, and the end of dreams of terrestrial glory!' and added a verse of Saadi, appropriate to the occasion. He was bare-headed and wounded. Then Haidar Quli, the mir atish, approached, leading an elephant, and, addressing him respectfully, begged him to give up, for no option remained but to surrender to the emperor. Then with as much dignity as he could muster he took his brother's hand and together they mounted the elephant. Haidar Quli tossed him a shawl to wrap round his head and led his prisoners to the presence of Muhammad Shah.

Thus the wazir got the audience for which he had expressed a desire in his last letter to the emperor. But the circumstances were quite the reverse from what he had hoped for. Itimad ud-Daulah wanted the emperor to entrust him with the prisoner's custody, but Khan-i-Dauran, who realized that the Turki chief would make short work of him, interposed, and at his suggestion, he and Najm ud-Din were allowed to remain in the custody of the mir atish.

Fortunately for the fallen prince no blindings or executions were considered necessary, and Ibrahim was sent back to his quarters in the Salimgarh, a generous allowance of Rs. 40 per day being fixed for him. He lived on for many years, dying in 1746.[13]

Abdullah was kept in reasonable comfort but the Turki chiefs remained uneasy and rumours of plots in which he was supposedly implicated refused to die down. Eventually the emperor gave his consent to his removal by poison, and he died in October 1722. He was buried at the side of his favourite mistress, a singer by the name of Kesar Mahi in a walled garden outside Old Delhi.

Abdullah Khan, was popular and loved by the people of Delhi for his frank and forthright manner, and generosity towards the poor. He was noted for his patronage of scholars and the learned. The cruel treatment of Farrukhsiyar was attributed to the evil influence of Rattan Chand, the wazir himself being neither corrupt nor venal. A Dutch embassy which visited the court of Farrukhsiyar had earlier made the mistake of approaching Khan-i-Dauran, who extracted all he could without giving anything in return. Finally they approached the wazir who, without taking offence at their earlier neglect, took their business in hand and settled it expeditiously without trying to extract anything in return. So much so that the envoy has styled him 'The Good Visier'.

Syed Hussain was less popular though he was undoubtedly more active as compared to the sensual and slothful Abdullah. But his pride and haughtiness bordered on insolence and often crossed the bounds of propriety. Consequently he was disliked both by his peers and the people at large.

A curious story is told about a partisan of the wazir who visited a learned astrologer to consult him about the outcome of the final struggle between him and the Turanian amirs. Without drawing up any horoscope and using only the letters of the words used by the visitor to frame his questions, the astrologer selected the following letters of the alphabet: *Ghain*, *Lam*, *Be*, *Ain*, *Dal*, *Vow*, and *Qaf*; which on being put together formed the Arabic words: '*Ghalab Aduqa*', i.e. 'Thine enemy shall prevail'. On being inverted it signifies, 'Thine end is come'. Read as chronograms, these words give the year of the fall of the Syeds. Rarely has a prediction been more accurate.[14]

NOTES

1. Irvine, *Later Mughals*, ii, pp. 3-4. Tabatabai, *Seir Mutaqherin*, i, p. 146.
2. Irvine, ii, p. 4. In an extravagant gesture Jai Singh had gifted Amber to the brahmans before setting out in his saffron robes 'to fight to the death'. Embarassingly, there was no fighting.
3. Tabatabai, i, p. 147.
4. Ibid., i, p. 150. Irvine, ii, pp. 8-15.
5. Irvine, ii, p. 25. Elliot and Dowson, vii, p. 490.
6. Tabatabai, i, pp. 164-5.
7. Ibid., i, p. 161.
8. Irvine, ii, p. 57.
9. Ibid., ii, p. 57.
10. Ibid., ii, p. 63.
11. Shiv Das, *Munawwar ul-Kalam*, f. 55a. Irvine, ii, p. 73.
12. Elliot and Dowson, vii, p. 509. Tabatabai, i, pp. 186-7.
13. Irvine, ii, p. 94.
14. Tabatabai, i, p. 198.

CHAPTER 15

The Reign of Muhammad Shah Rangila
The Turanian Ascendancy

The fall of the Syed brothers saw the beginning of a period of relative tranquillity. The reign was long and the peace of the marble courts was not disturbed until the invasion of the Persian Shah in 1739. There would be changes in the wazarat. Muhammad Amin Khan Itimad ud-Daulah was fated to die suddenly to be succeeded by Nizam-ul-Mulk who would thereafter be raised to the even more exalted dignity of Asaf Jah. But his was a unique case in the annals of the Qila-i-Mualla. Alone among all the umara who would have been ready to go to any lengths to gain the post, he abandoned it in frustration, after struggling in vain to reform. He was succeeded by Qamr ud-Din, the son of Amin Khan, in 1724 who continued in office till 1748 when he was killed on the field of Manupur, fighting another invader from the north-west.

But if all seemed placid in the marble courts of the Exalted Fort, that could not be said for the rest of India. When the nizam retired from Delhi it was to the Deccan (of which he was also the absentee viceroy) that he went. The court at Delhi as per its usual policy incited a subordinate to challenge him, but after Mubariz ul-Mulk had been crushed, the nizam reigned virtually as a sovereign monarch. The plundering armies of the Marathas were furthering their inroads continuously. Gujarat and Malwa were practically lost, while in Bengal Alivardi Khan was to establish himself, in fact if not in name, as an independent ruler, after the example of Nizam-ul-Mulk.

Thus inspite of the stability of the throne and the continuity in the wazarat this was the reign when the empire broke down and virtually disintegrated.

The emperor entered Delhi on 22 November 1720. This was his first entry as sovereign since his departure the previous September, in response to the summons of Qutb-ul-Mulk. It was made with the usual éclat to the sound of trumpets and kettledrums, with swivels firing blank shot from camels. There were the great *alams*, and the imperial insignia carried aloft on elephants, the umbrella, and the signs of the sun and the fish, and the columns of troops interspersed with slave boys and attendants clad in silks and brocades. The emperor rode a gigantic elephant seated upon a throne ablaze with jewels. He entered Shahjahanabad by the Ajmeri Gate scattering handfuls of gold coins amongst the hordes of mendicants and destitutes.

He was received at the entrance to the private apartments by his mother, the Nawab Qudsia, with a train of princesses and ladies of the highest distinction. The Sultan Validah, holding a large golden tray, filled with gold and silver coins and a variety of gems and jewels, poured the whole as a libation over his head, and she conducted him within after wishing him a long and prosperous reign.[1]

The first durbar was held three days later. Honours and dignities were conferred on the umara. On the appeals of Raja Jai Singh and Girdhar Bahadur the abolition of the *jaziya*—last abolished on the occasion of the installation of Rafi ud-Darjat—was also confirmed.

With this auspicious announcement the reign began. The new wazir also appeared to have turned a new leaf. Ever since his arrival from his native Bokhara Amin Khan had been noted for his pride and haughtiness. He was oppressive and cruel and in order to enlarge his mansion he had forcibly evicted 700 shanty dwellers paying them a pittance for their land.[2] The people had dreaded the day when he would come to power but now they were pleasantly surprised to observe that he treated everyone with kindness and impartiality. He was indulgent towards the other Syeds from Barha and once Abdullah Khan had submitted he did not press matters further.

But unfortunately his days were numbered. He suddenly fell ill, and succumbed to it a week later. He had been wazir for barely three months. The sudden death of a nobleman of high estate was bound to give rise to speculation among a credulous and superstitious people. The partisans of the Syeds interpretted it as divine retribution for the murder of the late Amir-ul-Umara. Others connected it with another incident in which a religious charlatan had been flogged at his instance.[3]

The regime had barely settled when the office of wazir had fallen vacant again. Qamr ud-Din, the son of the deceased, claimed the office but Muhammad Shah was not keen to oblige. The father had proved an even stricter keeper than Abdullah and he had to be content with the grant of his father's title of Itimad ud-Daulah. The emperor's choice fell on Khan-i-Dauran who was now Amir-ul-Umara with the additional office of Paymaster-General. But this glib courtier was unable to carry through his candidature, so in order to counter Qamr ud-Din's pretensions, he suggested that the emperor call Nizam-ul-Mulk.

After the fall of the Syeds the nizam had intended to return to Delhi, but fearing that his return would be misunderstood by his cousin he decided to stay away. But then came the news of Amin's death and the subsequent invitation of the emperor. As viceroy of the Deccan he was independent in all but name and exercised far more power than he would in the faction-ridden court at Delhi, but on the other hand, the wazir's post was still the most prestigious in the empire and its allure irresistible. Perhaps he also hoped to revive the empire and restore it to some semblance of the prestige it had enjoyed in the reign of Aurangzeb, under whom he had started his career.

Even so he took his time. He did not set out until October—more than eight months after Amin's death—and he reached Delhi towards the end of January 1722. During this time Inayat Ullah Khan Kashmiri officiated as wazir.

His difficulties were many. The disappointed aspirant Samsam ud-Daulah did not conceal his hostility. Nor could Qamr ud-Din, inspite of his close relationship, be entirely happy. The nizam had to be particularly careful to avoid offending him. Directly after the audience he called on him to condole on the death of his father, Amin Khan. Haidar Quli, Sarbuland and Burhan ul-Mulk, all saw themselves as potential prime ministers and were waiting to supplant him at the first opportunity.

His first challenge came from Maharaja Ajit Singh Rathor. He had been rewarded by Syed Abdullah for his support at the time of the coup against Farrukhsiyar and the revolts that followed by the grant of Gujarat and Ajmer. Now with the Syeds overthrown, he judged the time appropriate for striking out on his own, and to begin with, he passed an edict banning the slaughter of cows in his two subas and the reading of the *khutba* in the Friday prayers. The Qila-i-Mualla had always been sensitive to the susceptibilities of their non-Muslim subjects who constituted the vast majority, so much so that on the event of the sacrifice of Id ul-Zuha a camel was substituted for the cow. This festival was one of the most celebrated in the Muslim calendar and the emperor himself took part in the ritual sacrifice which was performed in front of the Diwan-i-Am. But substituting camels for kine is one thing, and the general prohibition of cow-slaughter another, and was clearly intended to convey to the inhabitants of those provinces that they were no longer under the rule of the padishahs. And the ban on the *khutba* was a direct challenge to the sovereignty of Muhammad Shah.

It was decided to send Muzaffar Ali Khan to Ajmer and Haidar Quli to Gujarat. As the maharaja was in Ajmer at the time, Haidar Quli's deputy was able to join his post without difficulty but Muzaffar's task was more formidable inspite of the proximity of Ajmer. Various nobles including Haidar Quli, Khan-i-Dauran and Saadat Khan had been offered Ajmer, but aware of the difficulties they had declined. Ajit had a formidable reputation and everyone was aware that the treasury was empty, and much of the outlay on the campaign would have to be borne by the subedar-designate himself.

Muzaffar was, in that respect, an unfortunate choice for he was in no position to finance the expedition. Nonetheless he obtained an order for Rs. 6 lakh on the treasury, out of which Rs. 2 lakh were paid, and on the basis of a promise that the rest would be forthcoming shortly, he opened recruitment. He enlisted about twenty thousand soldiers and advanced as far as Manoharpur near Amber, where with his money exhausted, he halted.

Raja Jai Singh readily submitted. He personally visited all the mosques in Amber and directed them to resume the *azzan*, i.e. the muezzin's call to prayer. The bans on the *khutba* and on the slaughter of kine were also revoked. He reiterated his family's long standing services to the dynasty and his personal loyalty, and produced an agreement reached with the emperor's own father, Jahan Shah, by which the Ajmer suba was to go to him in the event of the prince attaining the throne. With the support of Khan-i-Dauran and Turra-i-Baz he was pardoned.[4]

But things were not going well with the new subedar-designate. Muzaffar had not received any additional assistance and his soldiers mutinied, took to plundering, and the army disintegrated. With the help of an escort sent by Jai Singh he reached Amber, whence disgusted with the treatment he had received, he dispatched his resignation. He returned the robes and sanads of appointment, distributed what remained of his wordly goods among his few remaining soldiers, and donned the robes of a faqir.[5]

Maharaja Ajit Singh, not surprisingly, showed no intention of submitting to the emperor. Instead he sent an army under his son Abhai Singh which plundered Mewat, including the towns of Narnaul, Alwar and Tijara.

All this had transpired before the arrival of Nizam-ul-Mulk. When the maharaja learnt of the latter's appointment he thought it wise to dissemble and submit, for the nizam was known for his firmness and his wazarat was likely to be very different from that of Amin Khan Itimad ul-

Daulah, or of Inayat Ullah Khan Kashimiri. So a month after the appointment of the nizam an emissary arrived at the Qila-i-Mualla to plead the cause of the maharaja.

With bland effrontery the emissary protested his master's loyalty inspite of the many wrongs done to him by the emperor. He had, for instance, been deprived of the governorship of Gujarat as well as Ajmer without legitimate reason. But he bore no resentment on that account. He had not opposed the appointment of Haidar Quli and would have readily relinquished his other charge to Muzaffar, if only that esteemed nawab had reached Ajmer! As for the expedition of his son, it had been misrepresented. He had only gone to pacify the Mewatis who were in rebellion and had given much trouble to the court of Delhi over the centuries.

Since the maharaja had shown an inclination towards peace and apparently did not have any designs beyond Rajasthan the nizam felt it would be wise to accept the protestations at face value. A vague reply was given, expressing satisfaction at his loyalty and glossing over the reasons for depriving him of his charge, and it was confirmed that he would continue at Ajmer, and perhaps later on, he might again be given Gujarat.

But in order to clip his wings, some months later one Nahar Khan was appointed as diwan, leaving Ajit only the executive charge of nazim. This challenge to his authority was not taken lying down by Ajit.

Meanwhile in Gujarat Haidar Quli had been one of the aspirants to the wazarat, so when the nizam was appointed he started intriguing against him, and his income from the surplus revenues of Gujarat fuelled his ambition. The nizam spoke to the emperor about his activities, and, acting on a hint of the latter, Haidar Quli thought it prudent to go to Gujarat and assume the charge of that province in person.

He left Delhi in April 1722, two months after the nizam's assumption of office, and reached Ahmedabad in June. In Gujarat he started amassing money by extorting money from the local magnates and revenue officers. What was much more reprehensible, he started raising a formidable army by hiring foreign mercenaries. Behaving as if he was an independent potentate he dispensed favours and privileges to his favourites without seeking permission from Delhi. Then he sought to settle scores with old enemies who had jagirs in Gujarat by resuming them, but here he was easily checkmated by the wazir who retaliated by resuming his jagirs in Upper India. The last straw was his seizure of a pair of Arab stallions which the faujdar of Surat was conveying to the emperor.

Using all this material the wazir obtained in October the emperor's orders for the recall of the wayward governor and his own appointment to that province. Leaving his son behind as his deputy the nizam set out in November to chastise Haidar Quli and assume the governership of that province.

When the crunch came none of his officers were willing to fight for Haidar Quli. They bluntly informed him that as the suba was now with the nizam he could no longer command their allegiance. His illusions shattered, Haidar feigned madness, gave up eating and fled to neighbouring Mewar, and thence to Rewari where he waited till his friends had interceded and obtained the imperial pardon.[6]

The nizam was aware that, inspite of his rebellion, Haidar Quli, who was an old favourite of the emperor, would be easily forgiven, so he made no effort to pursue him. He spent some time in Ahmedabad and after installing his uncle Hamid as his deputy, turned towards Malwa where he had old scores to settle with Dost Muhammad Khan of Bhopal. This Afghan chief had made the mistake of joining Syed Dilawar Khan when the later set out from the Deccan to oppose Nizam-ul-Mulk in 1720. After his submission, the wazir turned his face towards the capital, reaching Delhi in July 1723.

The emperor had surrounded himself with wasters and was devoted to sensual pleasures. The wazir struggled to make him see the evils arising from the current practice of farming out the revenues to the highest bidder, i.e. *ijara* as against *amani* but there being too many vested interests involved he made little headway. The practise of officers presenting a *peshkash* to the appointing authority had been on the increase since the death of Aurangzeb, and the size of this offering, which was equivalent to the 'first fruits' of the post, could be very large. In practise the *peshkash* was discharged by the bankers of the appointee and the officer assumed his post with a heavy debt. As tenure was uncertain officers were always in a hurry to collect as much money in as short a time as possible, as a premature recall could spell ruin. Time and again in the annals of the later empire we read of amirs like Muzaffar Ali Khan who had been beggared by a sudden turn in the wheel of fortune and reduced to faqirs.

The hostility and intrigues of nobles like Khan-i-Dauran and Qamr ud-Din also irked him. His closest advisers counselled him to depose the emperor and deal with his detractors with the harshness they deserved. Supplanting Muhammad Shah with Prince Ibrahim or anyone else would have been easy enough, as the Syeds had shown, and the nizam was much more shrewd and capable than those 'blockheads' from Barha. Khan-i-

Dauran and Qamr ud-Din were unquestionably his inferiors, and their overthrow would have been no loss to the State. Like his predecessor who bore the same title in the reign of Farrukhsiyar, Khan-i-Dauran was only a carpet knight, a *sher-i-kalin.* A man of smooth words, handsome, and of great natural charm he was a courtier par excellence but had no stomach for a fight. Time and again, he showed his pusillanimity by declining postings where harsh fighting was probable, as in Rajasthan.

But in an age of iron when few of the umara had such scruples, the nizam was an exception. He had secured for himself the Deccan and he was determined to hold fast to that, but he had no desire to sully his 'honour' as a king-maker. He would fight to the death to protect his due, but he could not be another Qutb-ul-Mulk or Syed Hussain. If the emperor did not value his services he would rather resign and retire to the Deccan, and this was what he determined to do.

But in Delhi nothing was that simple. A straightforward resignation with a request for permission to retire to the Deccan would have been the signal for his fall. It would have been interpreted as an admission of defeat and everyone around would close in for the kill. To avoid such a development he had to be more circumspect.

On the pretext of ill-health he applied for leave to visit his jagirs in Sambhal and Moradabad. Leave was granted on 17 December and a few days later he crossed the Ganga. He lingered for some days in the hope of a reconciliation with the emperor but had to abandon all hope when Raja Girdhar Mall who had been advocating his cause suddenly died. On 6 January (1724) the emperor appointed his son Ghazi ud-Din Khan as deputy wazir.

From Moradabad he went to Agra where, learning of a Maratha incursion into Gujarat and Malwa, he left for those provinces as they were in his or his son's charge. Soon news came that the raiders had returned but the nizam continued to press forward until he reached Aurangabad, the headquarters of the viceroyalty, in July 1724, without encountering any opposition.

But his enemies had not been inactive. Even before he had shown his hand the emperor had dispatched a firman to one of his deputy governers Mubariz Khan, who held Hyderabad, appointing him viceroy of the Deccan. This officer was the son-in-law of Inayat Ullah Khan Kashmiri, who had served as a wazir temporarily before the arrival of the nizam. Inayat Ullah enjoyed the emperor's confidence and he had been held in high regard by Aurangzeb. His son-in-law had acquired a reputation for firmness, and despite the fact that *chauth* had been promised to the

Marathas from all the Deccan provinces by treaty, Mubariz Khan refused to pay them anything, and as a result was constantly having to fight their raiding parties. The firman was followed by a letter from his father-in-law advising him to advance with all speed to Aurangabad, which unhappily for him, was intercepted by the nizam who quickened the pace of his march. At the time of the receipt of the firman Mubariz had been engaged in the siege of the fortress of Phulchari near Machhlibandar (Mausalipatnam) and he did not think it necessary to abandon the siege. Only after it had been successfully concluded did he set out northwards. By that time it was too late and the nizam reached his capital unopposed, thus winning half the battle.

Now seeing that Mubariz had lost whatever chance he might have had, the emperor tried to backtrack. A conciliatory letter was addressed to the nizam, in what had now become a standard format, denying the obvious and offering to restore the status quo ante. But a bullet once fired cannot be recalled and Mubariz Khan's army was nearing Aurangabad. Some letters were exchanged between the nizam and Mubariz Khan also, in which the nizam piously exhorted him to refrain from shedding Muslim blood and called upon him to submit. But Mubariz Khan was not inclined to listen, or maybe he was in no position to, since his Afghan allies, the relatives of the late Daud Khan Panni, were all itching for a fight and hoped to avenge the death of their kinsman in the battle of Burhanpur/Pandhar in June 1720, fought between the nizam and Syed Dilawar Ali Khan.

The armies clashed at Shakkar Khera, about 80 miles from Aurangabad on 11 October 1724. It was a hard-fought battle in which about 3,500 soldiers were killed on the side of Mubariz Khan. The nizam was victorious and as usual his losses were far lighter. Mubariz was slain, two of his sons were also killed, besides a brother-in-law and a maternal uncle. Among the dead was also Bahadur Khan Panni—a brother of the late Daud.[7]

With the nizam in firm control the emperor had no choice but to acquiesce. In the compromise that followed, a fresh patent reappointing him to the Deccan was sent while he was deprived of his other charges of Gujarat and Malwa. Gujarat was conferred on Sarbuland who appointed Shujaat Khan as his deputy, while Malwa was given to Girdhar Bahadur.

From this time onwards there was no interference in the affairs of the Deccan by the Qila-i-Mualla. The nizam appointed his subordinate officials and conferred jagirs and titles without reference to the emperor. For all practical purposes he was independent but he refused to proclaim himself as such. Each Friday in the mosques of the Deccan the khutba continued to be read in the name of Muhammad Shah and the coins continued to bear his name.

But if the Deccan finally received the blessings of a resident viceroy who no longer had to keep looking over his shoulder all the time, the unfortunate province of Gujarat was in for a time of troubles. Hamid resented his replacement and engaged Maratha auxilliaries whose ravages soon reduced the fair province to a wasteland. The Maratha *bargirs* had already acquired notoriety for gang-rape and in the town of Sarkhej the upper-caste Hindu gentry preferred to slaughter their women rather than allow them to suffer the indignities they would otherwise have had to undergo. In another village, one populated by Mohammedan Afghans, the women similarly preferred to take recourse to mass suicide. The Marathas made no distinction between Hindu or Mussalman, because Gujarat was not their *desh.*

Sarbuland had nominated Shujaat Khan, a local nobleman, as his deputy and he quickly marched to Ahmedabad and demanded that Hamid evacuate the governor's mansion, known as the Bhadar Mahal. When Hamid demurred and asked for time he commenced firing. Eventually on the intervention of Safdar Khan Babi, an influential nobleman of Afghan origins whose family had been settled in Gujarat for centuries, he evacuated the mansion, but, pleading lack of money and carriage, he camped at Dohad about 10 miles from the city.

Smarting from his humiliation he wrote to his nephew (the nizam) and asked him to send Maratha cavalry to his aid. They came under the command of Kanthaji, one of Raja Shahu's generals, destroying all that lay in their path. Shujaat Khan, who was away from the capital subduing refractory chieftains, hurried back with a small force but was surprised and killed.

Hamid Khan reoccupied the Bhadar Mahal. His Maratha allies had come on the strength of his promise to pay them *chauth* and *sardeshmukhi*. They dispersed, appointing their own officers and set up a parallel administration to receive their share of the revenue. About this time Ibrahim Quli, a brother of the late Shujaat Khan made a daring attempt on the life of Hamid, forcing his way into the Bhadar with forty or fifty followers, but was eventually cornered and killed.

Hamid had informed the court that Shujaat Khan had been killed by the Marathas whom he had subsequently defeated. His courier was first believed and presented with the usual *khillats* as befitted a bearer of good news. But soon the truth reached the qila, and promptly fresh firmans were drafted and dispatched, authorizing another brother of Shujaat, Rustam Ali Khan, to assume the government as Sarbuland's deputy.

Rustam was at that time near Surat pursuing a Maratha raider by the name of Pillaji. On being informed of his appointment he promptly made terms with Pillaji, and engaging him and his troops, headed towards Ahmedabad. Hamid too had not been idle. After summoning Kanthaji's Marathas he also set out to seek his enemy and the two armies met at Aras, about 60 miles from Ahmedabad.

At night Hamid made contact with Pillaji and persuaded him to defect. Rustam Ali was informed but he refused to be perturbed. Victory, he said, depended on the will of God. As it was, the first day's engagement went in favour of Rustam. Hamid was driven from the field and barely escaped with his life. The Marathas, as usual, played no role in the fighting but Kanthaji plundered Hamid's camp and burnt his tents, while Pillaji did the same to Rustam's. But in the days that followed, Rustam was severely handicapped as the Maratha cavalry cut off his supplies and he had difficulty in getting even forage for his horses.

The final battle took place on 21 February when Rustam's force, now severely diminished, was overwhelmed and destroyed. Rustam was killed and his head sent as a present to Hamid while Pillaji cut off a hand and sent it to his home at Songarh as a trophy.[9]

When the news of the first engagement reached Ahmedabad, the canaille rioted, broke into the Bhadar Mahal and sacked it. Hamid started a witch-hunt against Rustam's adherents and dreadful atrocities were committed in the process. Meanwhile the Marathas had spread out into the country to collect their *chauth*. This was a traumatic period in the history of Gujarat. The Marathas treated the country as conquered territory and no woman's honour was safe. Many instances of the mass slaughter of women are recorded. Kanthaji even succeeded in extorting Rs. 5,000 from the English at Cambay. Two sons of the late Shujaat Khan were killed, and only one twelve year old (who was at Surat) survived.

With Shujaat's family finished Sarbuland at last bestirred himself to restore order. Hamid had become very unpopular because of his Maratha auxilliaries, and at the approach of Sarbuland his men began to desert him. The Babi chiefs went over in a body to the subedar and finally realizing that the game was up, Hamid fled with Kanthaji to the Deccan.

Sarbuland entered Ahmedabad and held his first durbar on 11 December 1725. He remained governor till 1730, being replaced in October by Raja Abhai Singh son of the late Ajit Singh of Marwar. He was a strong and vigorous administrator but the province saw little peace in his time. Nearly every year some part of the suba or the other suffered the horrors of invasion, for the Maratha tribute was always in arrears. He had to maintain a large standing army to counter the menace and forced contributions by way of *peshkash* were a heavy burden on the people. In the beginning he had received a monthly subsidy of Rs. 5 lakh a month to pay for the military expenses but this was later stopped on the advice of Khan-i-Dauran.

Because of his heavy expenditure which he had not been able to recoup from the imperial government, Sarbuland was faced with the prospect of utter ruin when he learnt of Abhai Singh's posting. He resolved to resist and drew up his troops in battle order, the clash taking place on the banks of the Sabarmati on 20 October 1730. It was inconclusive but negotiations were opened and on being promised a solatium of Rs. 1 lakh (out of which only Rs. 80,000 were actually paid), Sarbuland handed over charge and marched away.

In Delhi he was harassed by his creditors and he deployed armed men outside his haveli to keep them at bay. Whenever he was called to Court the emperor would send an escort to protect him from assault.[10] He lived in retirement at the capital dying in 1742 at the age of 69.

Girdhar Bahadur had been appointed governor of Malwa about the same time as Sarbuland Khan. This province, being closer to the Maratha heartland, suffered even more from their depredations. In the eastern part, and spilling over into the western part of the suba of Allahabad, Raja Chhattarsal Bundela had established his principality. This hilly tract with deep ravines and dry scrub forests had never before been governed directly by the imperial authorities. The rajas of Orchha were the principal power in the region and they had grown in wealth and power during the reign of Jahangir. After the death of Bir Singh Deo however, his son fell out of favour and the star of Orchha declined, while that of Champat Rai, originally a minor princeling and adherent of the Orchha princes rose. He extended his territories at the expense of the neighbouring zamindars, and usually in contempt of the imperial faujdars, until finally he was brought to bay and slain in 1661. Then his son Chhattarsal, who succeeded to his heritage at the age of twelve, resumed his father's career, sometimes under the imperial banners, and sometimes on his own, until he dominated the western part of the Allahabad suba. He did not hesitate to seek the aid of the Marathas when it suited him, and though Muhammad Khan Bangash whose territories also bordered Malwa inflicted on him a stinging defeat in 1728, it made little difference in the see-saw struggle for supremacy in central India.

Girdhar Bahadur had cherished the desire for a principality of his own in emulation of Nizam-ul-Mulk, but he was opposed by the Rajputs on the one side and the Marathas on the other, and depended entirely on imperial favour for survival. On 29 November 1728 his struggles were finally terminated when he was defeated and killed by a Maratha army led by Chimnaji, a brother of the Peshwa Baji Rao. With him fell his energetic cousin Daya Bahadur, the son of the late Chabela Ram (who had died as subedar of Allahabad in 1719).[11] These two Hindu nobles had died fighting against heavy odds to uphold the empire of the Mughals against their co-religionists.

In the meantime Muhammad Khan Bangash, subedar of Allahabad, after a brilliant campaign against Chhattarsal Bundela, found himself trapped and besieged in the hill fortress of Jaitpur. His pleas for succour went unheeded at the Qila-i-Mualla. Qamr ud-Din could not be bothered, and the Bakhshi Samsam ud-Daulah was delighted at his embarrassment. In vain his wife sent her veil to the great noblemen of the court, pleading for an army to rescue her lord. In vain did her son Qaim plead in person. Eventually the begum pawned her jewels and Qaim Khan collected a large body of Afghans from Farrukhabad and Shahjahanpur, and, with their aid, relieved Jaitpur, rescuing his father in August 1729.[12]

After the death of Girdhar Bahadur, his son Bhawani Ram took over but he was unable to establish himself. The wazir's support was half-hearted, and financial troubles, compounded by the intrigues of Raja Jai Singh who was hand-in-glove with the Marathas, kept Malwa in turmoil. Then he was informed that he had been replaced by Muhammad Khan Bangash. Allahabad was a better and more productive suba (only the Bundela tract was difficult), but palace intrigues would not allow him to remain there, and in desperation he applied for the vacant subedari of Malwa, and his request was accepted.

But Muhammad Khan Bangash was not popular at court and he received very little monetary assistance. And as a further illustration of how divorced from reality the great court umara were, Muhammad Khan was pledged to march against Nizam-ul-Mulk after he had pacified Malwa and driven out the Marathas!

At first the Bangash was remarkably successful and on 14 June 1731, a stinging defeat was inflicted on the Marathas at Sarangpur. But he desperately needed money and no support, material or otherwise, was forthcoming from the capital. He got in touch with the nizam and the two decided to act in concert, which further enraged the carpet knights at the

Qila-i-Mualla and soon he was informed that a new governor was on his way.

The new governor was Raja Jai Singh Sawai of Amber who had never been distinguished as a general. His tenure was brief and inglorious and the Marathas soon expelled him from the province and invaded Hindustan. Negotiations were opened, and the craven Khan-i-Dauran, his patron, thought it advisable to appease the Marathas. In 1735 the Peshwa's mother, Radha Bai had passed through Rajasthan on a pilgrimage to the Ganga as far as Banaras and Gaya. Everywhere she was received with honour and respect as a noble brahmin widow and the mother of an all-conquering son. While she was still on pilgrimage her son also visited Rajasthan. His was a triumphal tour. The Rajput rajas promised tribute and a treaty was discussed with Raja Jai Singh at Dholpur in which the latter offered him the naib-subedari of Malwa in exchange for a pledge by the Deccanis not to invade imperial territory in future—a pledge which was not worth the paper on which it was written. It was in effect, if not in form, the virtual cession of the province to the Marathas. The treaty was never finalized and the Marathas kept raising their demands but it was an indication of the shape of things to come. Within a short time Baji Rao was appointed full-fledged governor of Malwa, no longer a mere deputy.

Half the reign of Muhammad Shah was over. Nadir had not yet invaded India but the effective control of the emperor was now confined to northern India. The Deccan with its six provinces was with Nizam-ul-Mulk and it was beyond the power of any noble to displace him. Malwa had been virtually ceded to the Marathas; and Gujarat, ruined and devastated was practically under their control. *Chauth* and *sardeshmukhi* were levied by them in all these provinces. They were in truth the masters of the south and centre already, and ready to attempt the conquest of the north, reversing the usual course of empire.

NOTES

1. Tabatabai, *Seir Mutaqherin*, i, p. 201.
2. Ibid., i, p. 204.
3. Irvine, *Later Mughals*, ii, p. 104.
4. Ibid., ii, p. 109.
5. Ibid., ii, p. 110. Tabatabai, i, p. 232.
6. Irvine, ii, p. 113.
7. Ibid., ii, p. 148.
8. Ibid., ii, 184.
9. Ibid., ii, p. 182.
10. Ibid., ii, p. 215. Shah Nawaz Khan, *Maathir ul-Umara*, ii, pp. 707-8.
11. Irvine, ii, p. 243.
12. Ibid., ii, p. 241. Tabatabai, i, p. 261.

CHAPTER 16

First Maratha Invasion of Hindostan

The ink had barely dried on the treaty brokered by Raja Jai Singh when the Deccani cavalry debouched from the eroded hills of central India onto the rich plains of Hindostan. They knocked at the very gates of the imperial city, *Dar ul Khalifa Shajahanabad*, pitching their tents at Kalkaji and Talkatora, and for a moment the fate of the empire seemed to hang in the balance. Boats had been drawn up besides the water gate of the fort for the ladies, in case a hurried evacuation became necessary, but fortunately they were not required. The expected assault did not take place and the Marathas hurriedly retreated into Rajasthan; but their daring dash had caused panic in the councils of the chicken-hearted emperor and exposed his conceited courtiers as paper tigers.

It was a mere thirty years since the release of Raja Shahu who had been brought up in the Urdu-i-Mualla of Aurangzeb under the fond supervision of the emperor's maiden sister, Zinat un-Nissa. On his release Shahu's first act was to proceed to the old emperor's grave to offer prayers and feed the poor in his name. So lightly had his imprisonment weighed on his shoulders. Left to himself Shahu (or Shivaji II as he is sometimes called) could never have posed a threat to the empire. Shahu still reigned but the world had changed immeasurably in those thirty years!

After the execution of Zulfiqar in 1713 and the transfer of his deputy Daud, the Marathas resumed their activity, and the Maratha chiefs Chander Sen Jadon and Balaji Vishwanath, agent of Raja Shahu, set out to collect *chauth* and *sardeshmukhi* in the Deccan. But the two fell apart and nothing came of it. Balaji, however, gradually improved his position and was appointed peshwa or prime minister, and when in 1719 the Amir-ul-Umara Syed Hussain Ali Khan turned his attention towards them he found he could make no headway. In the end he agreed to their terms and when he set off to challenge the emperor he took a large body of Maratha horse with him. After the deposition of Farrukhsiyar a formal treaty was signed by which the emperor and his viceroy agreed to pay *chauth* and *sardeshmukhi*. In return Shahu agreed to pay a handsome *peshkash* for the succession to his hereditary lands and accepted the responsibilities of a peer of the empire, viz, to preserve law and order, suppress banditry, and maintain an army for the imperial service.

The Marathas had the advantage of continuity in their leadership. Shahu reigned till 1748 and while he became more and more of a nonentity with the passage of time, the Peshwas were able and vigorous men. Balaji Vishwanath held office till 1720 when he was succeeded by his son Baji Rao, who now launched a well-considered plan to overrun the whole of India and plant the saffron flag of the Marathas on the heights of the Himalayas. On the other hand, within the same time span the Peacock Throne had known six incumbents and as many wazirs.

1720 onwards the Marathas became more aggressive and we have seen how in the third decade Gujarat and Malwa were subjected to invasion nearly every year so that ultimately the imperial administration was paralysed. The Marathas seized whatever they could carry. What they could not, was burnt or destroyed, and large tracts lapsed into waste. The revenue realizations declined, and the accumulating arrears provided a ready excuse for more raids.

On 16 July 1736 a treaty had been discussed at Dholpur between Baji Rao and the emperor's representatives by which the governor of Malwa, Raja Jai Singh Sawai, proposed the peshwa as his deputy, and the Marathas agreed to respect the imperial territories in future. But these hard-headed realists had no respect for treaties. The face-saving compromise reached at Dholpur was recognized as being just that. It was an admission of weakness which it would be foolish not to exploit. And as it happened, the treaty was never ratified by the emperor.

In March 1737 the Maratha horse was again on the rampage in the vicinity of Agra. The Bakhshi Samsam ud-Daulah (Khan-i-Dauran) set out with an army from Delhi while instructions were conveyed to Saadat Khan Burhan ul-Mulk, governor of Awadh, to cooperate with him. Two weeks later, even that pleasure-loving drunkard, the wazir Qamr ud-Din, took the field with another army, closely following the mir bakhshi. The peshwa, Baji Rao, after plundering the country of the Bhadauria Rajputs entered Bundelkhand where Jagat Raj, the son of the late Chhattarsal, offered assistance and shelter. Meanwhile Malhar Holkar and other sardars like Pilaji Jadon and Vittoji Bule crossed the Yamuna and invaded the Doab.[1]

Shikohabad and other towns were plundered or forced to purchase immunity. Looting and burning, the Marathas came within 15 miles of Agra when the vanguard of Saadat Khan, led by his nephew Abul Mansur Khan Safdar Jang, hove into sight. This young man retreated in good order, drawing the Marathas after him until the main body under his uncle's command was within striking distance. Then he closed and the Mughal heavy horse, 50,000 strong, struck with telling effect. The Maratha cavalry with its country-bred ponies and lightly armed troopers could not withstand the shock. They broke and fled, not stopping till they had put the Yamuna behind them. Many were killed or taken prisoner; many more drowned while attempting to cross.

This was on 23 March 1737. On 1 April Khan-i-Dauran and Saadat Khan met at Mathura and while they were dining they were informed that the main Maratha army led by Baji Rao had reached Delhi. Startled by this sudden and unexpected development, the imperialists broke camp and hurried back to the capital.

Malhar Holkar and other fugitives from the broken army had joined the main body commanded by the Peshwa. Coming to know through his agent of the vainglorious and exaggerated account given by Saadat Khan of his victory over Malhar, he decided 'to let the Emperor know the truth, that I was still in Hindustan; and to show him the Marathas at the gates of his capital'.[2]

Six days before Khan-i-Dauran's dinner with Saadat the Peshwa had set off towards the capital passing between the camps of the wazir and the mir bakhshi, without either coming to know of it. Ten stages were covered in two days, and on 9 April he suddenly appeared before the temple of Kalkaji where a fair was being held on the occasion of Ram Navami. After cheerfully looting the crowds of the faithful, the representative of the Hindupad padishahi continued his advance, finally pitching his tents besides the tank of Talkatora on the Delhi Ridge.

When the news of the attack at Kalkaji penetrated the red sandstone walls of the Qila-i-Mualla, there was general disbelief. How could the Marathas have by-passed two—nay three imperial armies? Surely the marauders must be Mewati bandits or Gujjars! But scouts confirmed the reports. There was general consternation. All kinds of ridiculous suggestions were put forward, but ultimately the advice of Saduddin Khan, mir atish, was accepted.

The capital, he reminded them, was by no means denuded of troops. There were 10,000 to 12,000 household cavalry and 20,000 foot soldiers who constituted the ordinary garrison of the qila. Then there were the personal troops some of the nobles present in Delhi—the Turki, Kalmuck and Kirghiz soldiers of Raja Shiv Singh and Raja Ajmeri Singh, who belonged to the Amberi regiment of the bodyguard. Mubariz Khan, superintendent of the mace-bearers, also offered his services.

The troops were placed under the command of Amir Khan, who, though no general, was a brave noble. So leaving about 3,000 soldiers in the fort Amir Khan marched out at night to take up positions opposite Talkatora.

But the carpet knights of Muhammad Shah were eager for battle and sneered disdainfully at the cautious moves of Amir Khan. Chief among them was Mir Hasan Khan Koka, recently elevated as 'Khan Jahan Bahadur Kokaltash Zafar Jang'. He was very ambitious and anxious to justify this title of Zafar Jang which meant 'victorious in war'. Left behind with some household troops to guard the palace-fort he felt he had been intentionally slighted, nay a victim of a conspiracy to prevent him from showing his worth! Loudly berating the emperor for staying back in the qila he marched off without orders to join the main army at Talkatora.

As the Marathas did not show any immediate anxiety to attack, Hassan Khan started getting restive, and finally, after denouncing, Amir Khan and the other senior nobles as cowards he set off with his troops, accompanied by some of the younger swashbucklers like the sons of the late Kokaltash Khan and of the Rajput chiefs, Shiv Singh and Ajmeri Singh.

Leaving their entrenchments, they advanced across the rocky plain. Maratha skirmishers drew them away from the main army by slowly retreating before them. Meanwhile Baji Rao had observed that these were inexperienced riders and when they were about 2 miles from their base he gave the signal to Malhar Holkar and Ranoji Scindia to attack.

These Deccani chiefs made short work of them. According to Baji Rao's report over 600 imperialists were killed and over 2,000 horses and an elephant captured. Only one Maratha officer was reported wounded (two of his fingers being cut off). Presumably some of the ordinary troopers must have fallen also but as usual their numbers were not considered worth mentioning. Raja Shiv Singh came to the rescue and died fighting gallantly. Ajmeri Singh was among the first to flee. Mir Hasan Khan, the Zafar Jang, was overtaken in his flight and unseated by a lance. The Marathas stripped him of his fine clothes and fancy, ornamented weapons, leaving him almost naked. When one of the imperial soldiers approached to assist him, he begged him not to address him by his titles or treat him as a person of distinction, 'Otherwise the Marathas would surely take him prisoner and he would have to pay a fantastic sum by way of ransom'.

The defeat and slaughter of these great 'swells' and their hapless followers created further panic and an all-out attack was expected any time. But it did not materialize and the Marathas furled their tents and disappeared into Rajasthan as suddenly as they had come.

News had reached the Peshwa that the imperial troops led by the wazir and Khan-i-Dauran were coming in hot pursuit. Baji Rao had no wish to engage them in a pitched battle but the two armies ran into each other near Badshahpur. The wazir too was disinclined. It was evening and the troops were tired because of the incessant marching. But Zahir ud-Daulah, the wazir's cousin, had sworn before the emperor that he would track down the Marathas and fight them wherever he came across them, hence he would not let this chance go by without a fight. He charged. The wazir was thus obliged to throw the full weight of his force into the battle. An indecisive engagement took place in which the advantage lay with the imperialists, because, after disengaging, the Marathas abandoned the field and quickened their retreat into Rajasthan.

Even before the scare of April 1737 the emperor had decided to once again call the nizam as he appeared to be the only person capable of saving the empire from the Marathas. Khan-i-Dauran had opposed his return as he could brook no rival close to the throne. Of Qamr ud-Din he was not afraid; he was so immersed in pleasure that he could be no threat to anyone. The cold, calculating nizam was however very different. But after the scare of 1737 even Khan-i-Dauran conceded that the situation was out of control. So letters were sent urging the nizam to return to court. Glittering prospects were held out, and the nizam, once again accepted. Leaving his son Nasir Jang behind he left for the north in April, reaching Hodel in July. Here he was received by the wazir and his eldest son Ghazi ud-Din Khan Firoz Jang whom he had not seen for thirteen years. The subsequent entry to the capital was tumultous. Crowds thronged the road, the rooftops and balconies were packed with cheering onlookers, and his elephant made its way through the throng only at a snail's pace. At the barbican he dismounted and got into his palki, severe in its stark simplicity and plain broadcloth, while the wazir's that followed was covered with rich brocade and carried a golden fringe, the kind used only by the emperor and the highest umara. The nizam was promoted to the rank of 8,000 horse with the title of Asaf Jah—the highest dignity to which a man could aspire—with the office of Vakil-i-Mutlaq, revived once again after a gap of twenty-four years.

But inspite of his undoubted ability Delhi proved once again unlucky for the nizam. His labours as vaqil were destined to be as barren as his earlier efforts as wazir. He, the most loyal of the imperial umara was destined to be remembered in history as the first nizam of Hyderabad, the founder of the Asaf Jahi dynasty of the Deccan, rather than as a prime minister of India.

The treaty of Dholpur which Khan-i-Dauran had signed with the Marathas under the influence of Jai Singh was scrapped. His son Ghazi ud-Din was given charge of both Malwa and Agra, replacing Baji Rao in the former, and Jai Singh in the latter.

After the rains the nizam—or Asaf Jah—set out to chastise the Marathas and pacify Malwa. He had a large army 50,000 strong, with a good artillery train and many Rajputs, recruited from among the troops of Raja Jai Singh and Khan-i-Dauran. Several Bundela chieftains came with their feudal levies. But this heterogenous army was to prove more a hindrance than an advantage.

It had long been suspected at the Qila-i-Mualla that the nizam had a secret understanding with the Marathas by which the latter left his Deccan territories alone, and directed their attentions instead towards Gujarat, Malwa, Rajasthan and Hindostan. By recalling him his enemies hoped to place him in the embarassing position of having to fight his secret allies. The Marathas would, in revenge, turn their attentions towards his territories in the Deccan.

The nizam reached Bhopal in December 1737 where he learnt of the death of Mughani Khan who had been killed resisting the Marathas. He was also informed that Baji Rao was advancing towards him with a large army numbering 80,000. Aware of the disunity prevailing in his heterogenous army and also of the fact that many of the Rajput and Bundela chiefs were in touch with the enemy, the nizam moved with extreme circumspection. He had always been noted for his caution and he never risked battle unless he was certain of the outcome. Seeing his hesitation the Marathas surrounded him from all sides and the nizam found himself trapped in Bhopal. Soon provisions ran out, the grain convoys of the banjaras being unable to penetrate the encircling Maratha cavalry.

The nizam tried to break through but failed. An all-out attack of the Peshwa also crumpled before the fire of the imperial artillery. The peshwa was equally incapable of prolonged operations as he was desperately short of funds; so on 16 January 1738 a convention was signed at Doraha sarai by which the nizam agreed to grant to the Peshwa the whole of Malwa[3] along with Rs. 50 lakh by way of reparations, also from the imperial treasury. Inspite of his efforts he was unable to get any money from the nizam himself. 'I have tried', he observed in a letter to his brother Chimnaji, 'to get something from the Nawab himself, but this I scarcely expected. I recollected his unwillingness to part with money when I entered into an agreement to assist him.' The allusion was to the understanding arrived at between the nizam and the Marathas before the battle of Shakkar Khera in 1724.

The emperor was also pressing the nizam to conclude matters with the Marathas and hurry up north, because a new and much more menacing threat was developing to the north-west, where the Persian, Nadir Shah stood poised to invade India.

Baji Rao tried to take advantage of the departure of the nizam and while north India had yet to recover from the horrors of the Persian invasion he started on a fresh campaign in December 1739. But Nasir Jang, the nizam's second son, defeated him in a pitched battle and forced him to accept a humiliating peace. By this the Marathas surrendered all claims on the Deccan revenues, accepting, in lieu thereof, the two districts of Khargaon and Handia in jagir. The Peshwa was a broken man. He wrote to his brother:

> I am in deep difficulties, heavily in debt, disappointed and ready to take poison. The Raja is surrounded by my enemies and should I at this time go to Satara, they will put their feet on my chest. I should be thankful if I could meet death.

His wish was granted. On his way to take possession of his jagir he was seized by a violent fever, and on 28 April 1740 he expired, without having to face his royal master again.

After having humbled Nizam-ul-Mulk and secured Malwa *de jure*, and Gujarat *de facto*, Baji Rao had died after a humiliating defeat at the hands of the latter's son. The Maratha state was as bankrupt as the Mughal but they also had fewer liabilities. Outside their own *desh* territories in Maharashtra they assumed no responsibility for administration. They claimed *chauth* and *sardeshmukhi* but the burden of collection was that of the imperial administration, like that of the police and justice machinery. No works of public benefit, such as roads, bridges or sarais can be attributed to them during this period. Their hold on the country was marked by ruined towns and stretches of waste where once stood flourishing villages.

But the expenses of the Maratha armies were much less than those of the imperial one. Salaries were much lower, and they were able to live off the land. For them the whole country outside the confines of Maharashtra was enemy territory. And in the wake of their regular armies, and often preceding them, were hordes of marauders who enjoyed their protection.

These were a species of purely predatory cavalry, known as *pindarries*, who existed solely by plunder. The *pindarry* captains attached themselves to particular Maratha sardars, who also did not hesitate to squeeze them for a percentage of their gains. An understanding existed that each *pindarry* chief would give a share of his loot to the chieftain whose protection he enjoyed, but when hard-pressed for money the sardars would squeeze them at gun-point for as much as could be had. Whatever the regular soldier could not carry was removed by them. Cattle, plough-shares, the very beams and doorframes of houses, all was grist to their mill. Even women and children would be driven off and sold into slavery.

A greater curse than these marauders is difficult to imagine, but with all this the Marathas possessed a vigour and energy sadly lacking in the imperial troops. The latter were now fighting to hold what was theirs, while the Marathas were reaching for new worlds to conquer.

NOTES

1. Irvine, *Later Mughals*, ii, p. 287. Tabatabai, *Seir Mutaqherin*, i, p. 285. Sardesai, *A New History of the Marathas*, ii, pp. 152-5.
2. Letter of Baji Rao to his brother Chimnaji (letter 27, *Brahmendra-Swami Charitra*). Quoted by Irvine (ii, p. 288). The subsequent account is based on Irvine who has relied on Ashob and Rustam Ali (*Tarikh-i-Shahadat-i-Farrukhsiyar* and *Tarikh-i-Hindi* respectively).
3. In 1736 at Dholpur Sawai Jai Singh had 'appointed' the peshwa deputy governor. Now in 1738 the nizam is doing the same. The actual firman or rescript was only issued on 4 July 1741 to his successor Balaji Baji Rao.

CHAPTER 17

The Court of the Merry Monarch

Before we take up the subject of Muhammad Shah Rangila a few words by way of a preface would not be out of place. Western writers, especially those of the nineteenth century are loud in their condemnation of the imperial court and its provincial offspring as sinks of iniquity. Sleeman's savage denunciations of Wajid Ali Shah, surrounded by jugglers, acrobats, dancing girls, musicians ('drummers' and 'guitarists') pimps and other assorted parasites is famous. But on the other hand, this prince was also a notable poet, so was Zafar the last of the Mughals, and Shah Alam, Muhammad Shah, and even Farrukhsiyar could turn out striking couplets a talent for which no prince of the house of Hanover or Windsor was ever noted. Elsewhere Sleeman has observed that the average Indian gentleman showed much more culture, finesse and polish than the officers of the Company Bahadur with whom they had to deal with. They were much more courteous and could converse on a much wider range of subjects, such as philosophy, comparative religion and astronomy. The British, on the other hand, had no conversation other than the business in hand. Cultural differences and linguistic shortcomings could account for some of their apparent brusqueness. They had only a working knowledge of Persian and the native languages, and not many could be expected to be conversant with the poetry of Sheikh Saadi or Hafiz; but in general it may be said that the Indian umara were much better educated than the writers and officers, of the East India Company.[1]

The harem which included the private apartments of the emperor, housed beside himself the female members of his family, i.e. his mother, maiden aunts, wives, concubines, slave girls and servants, including singing and dancing girls, and his younger children. The elder princes had independent and spacious apartments within the Qila-i-Mualla and frequently outside as well, but as members of the family they had free access to the harem.

The widows and concubines of former emperors and princes were housed in a neglected portion of the harem known as the *bewa khana* or *suhagpura*, while those who were mothers frequently lived with their sons in the *salatin khana*. Within the harem the servants were either women or eunuchs. The most valuable among the latter were the Africans or Abyssinians who invariably came as slaves.

Apart from the eunuchs whose functions were primarily administrative there was an armed female guard which ensured security within. These were stout muscular women, usually from among the Turki slaves, most often Kalmucks or Uzbegs. The slave woman Raiman, honoured as Rustam-i-Hind by Jahandar, had been a Kalmuck. The outer ring was manned by Rajput soldiers who were considered the most trustworthy, particularly as their religious scruples forbade any kind of physical contact with Muslim women.

At the apex of the harem, its 'First Lady', was usually the mother of the emperor called the Validah Sultan, which in the reign of Muhammad Shah was the Nawab Qudsia. In the absence of a mother—as happened in the case of Bahadur Shah in 1707—this position went usually to the eldest of the padishah's maiden sisters, if any. When Bahadur ascended, only one of his sisters, Zinat un-Nissa was living, and it was she who was honoured with the title of Padishah Begum. She maintained this position until her death in 1721 when she was replaced by Nawab Qudsia. There was resentment at the rule of this old spinster, and Lal Kunwar had ignored her and spoke of her slightingly with all the bitter venom of the bazaar where she had come from, but her reign like her husband's was short. As for Sahiba Niswan, being Farrukhsiyar's mother she occupied an eminent position, but she always deferred to the Padishah Begum, the senior-most female member of the imperial family.

After the First Lady of the harem, be she the emperor's mother, sister or aunt, there was the post of the superintendent. This was an administrative appointment usually held by the wife of one of the nobles, who enjoyed the confidence of the First Lady. One such person was Sadr un-Nissa, wife of Raza Quli Khan Jahandar Shahi. It was again through her that the Wazir Abdullah Khan had pressed his suit for the favours of Begum Inayat Khan, the consort of the Emperor Rafi ud-Darjat.

Below this functionary there was the *nazir* of the harem. He handled the accounts of the haram sarai. It was through him that the allowances were released to the inmates, salaries to servants, purchases made, etc. He was usually an eunuch.

Early in the reign the emperor and his mother fell under the influence of a persuasive and charming young woman known as Koki Jiu. Her real name was Rahim un-Nissa and she was the daughter of Jan Muhammad, a geomancer, a diviner that predicts the future by casting dice on the ground. Even before the enthronement of Roshan Akhtar as Muhammad Shah, Rahim un-Nissa and her father were known in the harem where they had carried on a lively practice. The hundreds of women who lived within were often unlettered and had little besides gossip to occupy themselves; and fortune tellers and vendors plied a thriving trade among them.

When Nawab Qudsia was only one among the many widows living in a small apartment in that part of the harem set aside for the widows and concubines of former emperors, Jan Muhammad had on one occasion correctly foretold the recovery of her son Roshan Akhtar from a minor illness. On another occasion he predicted that he would one day become emperor. Some other minor predictions also turned out correct and the stock of Rahim un-Nissa and her father rose. Because of her charm the daughter was particularly popular and was in high demand for writing and conveying letters of friends, relatives and former lovers in the world outside.

In order to render her access to the palace more easy, Nawab Qudsia gave it out that Rahim un-Nissa and her son had been suckled by the same wet-nurse and were thus foster brother and sister. This was the origin of the appellation of 'Koki-Jiu' or 'Madam Foster Sister'.[2]

When her father's prediction about the accession of Roshan Akhtar was fulfilled Koki Jiu became the closest confidant of the Empress Mother and a potent influence for favours and appointments. Soon even provincial subedars and district faujdars were approaching her and money flowed in. It was said that she shared her income with the emperor.

She had three companions and together they constituted a caucus which controlled much that happened at court. There was Abdul Ghaffur, a fake faqir and a vendor of charms and amulets, a eunuch, Hafiz Khidmatgar Khan, and Zafar Khan Roshan ud-Daulah, also known as Turra i-Baz (falcon-crested) after the plumed turbans affected by him and his followers. He was the only nobleman of name and family among the three.

Shah Abdul Ghaffur claimed to be a Syed but was a weaver by origin. He was reputed to be a sorcerer capable of raising djinns and spirits, in which there may have been an element of truth, for in his chequered life he had spent some years as the disciple of an Aghora tantric who lived in the dry hills beyond the Indus. With the help of a eunuch in the service of Muazzam (later Bahadur Shah) he was able to gain a footing in the latter's camp where he changed his appearance to that of a Muslim faqir and came to be known as Shah Abdul Ghaffur. Gradually his fame spread.

When Koki Jiu arrived the two joined hands. Each praised and promoted the other. He was consulted by the Empress Mother for interpreting dreams and was part of the conspiracy to assassinate Syed Hussain. He had acquired great influence over Itimad ud-Daulah Muhammad Amin Khan Chin and his son the wazir Qamr ud-Din Khan was also kind to him out of regard for his father's memory.

Many offices were showered upon him and he became immensely rich with a daily income of Rs. 5,000 from his offices, and much more by way of bribes. For twelve years he was almost as powerful as Koki. About one-fourth of his income was given to the emperor and the remaining he divided with her. In personal habits, however, he was extremely miserly and continued to affect the beggarly habit of a faqir. But not so his children.

He had a son and a daughter. The son Abdur Rahim, a handsome youth, was debauched and a ruffian, always surrounded by a pack of bravos ready to attack anyone who looked at him disrespectfully. He never thought twice before killing a man—so long as he was poor and defenceless. But if the other side was strong he would turn tail and flee with his bullies. At times he would be seen in full armour, wearing a closed helmet with only his eyes showing, his cronies similarly attired. At times he would dress as a courtesan, with henna on his hand and feet, gold ornaments—and, incongruously, a sword and shield. His *sawarry* would be preceeded by mace bearers and musketeers, with the matches of their muskets lit and ready to fire. At such times woe betide any who chanced to cross his path!

Nautch girls would be called to dance at his *deohri* and he would stand by, wine cup in hand. When sufficiently roused he would attach bells to his own ankles and plunge into the dance! In the India of those times for a man to dance in public was the pits of degradation, but this ludicrous caricature had been elevated to a mansab of 6,000 *zat*.

The third member of this caucus, the eunuch Hafiz Khidmatgar kept a low profile. He had been in the imperial service since the reign of Aurangzeb and had been attached to him. Thus he was efficient and capable but his close association with Koki Jiu and Abdul Ghaffur throw doubt on his intrinsic worth. He appears to have been used by them in their earlier days, and was not quite a full-fledged member of the group.[3]

Roshan ud-Daulah had risen in the reign of Farrukhsiyar on whose accession the title of Zafar Khan was bestowed on him. He showed no great ability but was articulate and a good talker with a supple and calculating mind. As a faujdar in the field he was undistinguished, but in Delhi he acquired a reputation for ostentatious piety. He was a *murid* of Shah Bhik of Thanesar and made handsome additions with gilt domes to the shrines of Bu Ali Shah Qalander. The mosque of Roshan ud-Daulah in Chandni Chowk was built by him, and on the occasion of the Prophet's birthday he was assiduous in his services at the shrine of Qadam Sharif.

All these favourites fell from favour and were disgraced in 1732 or thereabouts. First to go was the eunuch Khidmatgar Khan who was lucky to die a natural death. Because of his association with the caucus, and the offices he had held he was reputed to have secreted a large hoard of treasure and his diwan, Khushal Chand Kayasth was put to the torture to reveal the hiding place.

Khan-i-Dauran was jealous of this caucus and had been plotting its downfall. Koki Jiu's brother gave offence and one of the emperor's consorts, Malika-i-Dauran quarrelled with her. Her money was demanded of her. She submitted tamely and left the palace with the remark that whatever she had was the emperor's.

Then came the fall of Roshan ud-Daulah. The man was the conduit through whom subsidies amounting to several lakh rupees were passed to the governor of Kabul for distribution among the turbulent tribes of the frontier as the price of keeping the passes (the Khyber and others) open. But for several years he had failed to transmit the funds and embezzled the entire amount. This came to the notice of the Amir-ul-Umara who demanded that he make good the difference. The auditors drew up a demand of Rs. 3 crore of which he paid up two, but his influence was finished and he was a broken man thereafter.

An additional cause for his fall was the conduct of his brother Munavvar Khan. He was a boon companion of the emperor but he committed the folly of falling in love with the famous dancing girl Nur Bai and eloped with her. As Nur Bai was a mistress of His Majesty this was a capital folly and it was with difficulty that the emperor was persuaded to spare his life.[4]

Abdul Ghafur also fell foul of the auditors. His conduct gave offence to the emperor and on one occasion he raised his voice and addressed His Majesty disrespectfully. Complaints, inspired by Khan-i-Dauran and Saadat Khan Burhan ul-Mulk, governor of Awadh, were lodged against him. The wazir, who was friendly, advised him to make good the money and submit, but Abdul Ghafur was defiant and abused the wazir. The amount demanded at this stage was Rs. 60 lakh. In a state of intoxication he headed for the palace inspite of the wazir's remonstrances, and insolently protested to the emperor. The latter took umbrage, got up and left, leaving Khan-i-Dauran to sort him out.

The auditors went to work afresh, and now drew up a shortfall of Rs. 3 crore. Bailiffs were sent to seize his goods but he broke down completely, shouting like a lunatic that the emperor was dead, and the qila had crumbled to dust. Eventually more than a crore was realized and he was packed off with his family, including his licentious son and daughter, to confinement in the fort of Rohtas in Bihar.

Thus by the end of 1732 Khan-i-Dauran had destroyed this caucus which had been a formidable power centre. But as far as the well-being of the state was concerned it made little difference. Khan-i-Dauran, Amir Khan and Ishaq Khan, the favourites of the next phase were scarcely more able, and Khan-i-Dauran's action in stopping the subsidy to the trans-Indus tribes was partially responsible for the disaster of 1739. His logic was that since the subsidy had not been paid all these years, it was unnecessary and need not be paid at all, even for the future!

Of the wazir we hear hardly anything. He went after his pleasures in a big way and is said to have had a harem comprising 5,000 women and 1,500 boys.[5]

Historians are reticent in describing the details of the amorous pleasures of Muhammad Shah himself. In contrast to Farrukhsiyar and Jahandar, other notable sensualists, Muhammad Shah was relatively harmless and historians have therefore been kind to him. But his more mundane pleasures have been recorded, such as his love of hunting and his delight in watching the mutual combat of animals—an old Mughal weakness to which even Akbar was addicted. Often extraordinary care and trouble were taken to organize these spectacles.

NOTES

1. Sleeman, *Rambles and Recollections of a District Officer*, ii, pp. 53, 283-4. 'Perhaps there are few communities in the world among whom education is more generally diffused than among Muhammadans in India. He who holds an office worth twenty rupees a month commonly gives his sons an education equal to that of a prime minister.'
2. Irvine, *Later Mughals*, ii, pp. 264-5. Tabatabai, *Seir Mutaqherin*, i, p. 244.
3. Ashob, *Tarikh-i-Shahadat-i-Farrukhsiyar*, p. 66b. Khushal Chand, *Nadir uz Zamani*, pp. 1059b-61b.
4. Irvine, ii, pp. 270-1.
5. Tabatabai, iii, p. 280n.

CHAPTER 18

The Persian Invasion

For two hundred years the Turanian porte had been quiet. After the invasion of Babar no other adventurer had ventured to turn his face towards India. Relations between Persia and India had all along been friendly and but for the crassness of the advisers of Muhammad Shah there was no reason why Nadir should have suddenly decided to invade India.

There had always been some minor sparring on the border and Kandahar had long been a bone of contention, having changed hands many times; but, apart from this, the two empires respected each other's borders and ever since the days of Humayun, they had held each other in affectionate regard. The court language of the padishahs of Hind was Persian rather than Turki, their true mother tongue, and there was a distinctive Persian flavour to their durbar. So that when the Persian dynasty was on the verge of being eclipsed by the Ghilzai Afghans of Kandahar, Nizam-ul-Mulk suggested to his master that the time had come for the descendants of Humayun to repay their debt to the Safavids. Inspite of the decades of war and the spreading cancer of the Marathas, the throne of the Timurids was still apparently secure.

The house of Safi and that of Babar both started on their imperial mission about the same time, but the Persian dynasty had run its course by the time Muhammad Shah ascended the throne. Abbas the Great, who died in 1627 was followed by a succession of weak, cruel and debauched monarchs;[1] and the state survived on the reputation it had acquired rather than its own strength. Shah Hussain, the last of the Safavids, who reigned from 1694 to 1722 was free from vice, but he was a religious bigot, and after a pattern that has now become familiar to the world, he surrendered all power and authority to the Shi'ite priestly class, the Mullas and Ayatullas, and thus lost the support of the intellectuals and the heterodox Sufi philosophers who have always been as much a part of the national fabric as the hysterical flagellants bewailing the tragedy of Karbala.

In 1708 the Ghilzai Afghans under Mir Wais rose against the governor of Kandahar, the strong and assertive Gurgin Khan, and killing him declared their independence. In 1717 he was succeeded by his son Mahmud who commenced the conquest of the Iranian heartland. Isfahan was captured in 1722 and Shah Hussain abdicated. The country dissolved into chaos and Mirza Tahmasp, the son of Shah Hussain, assumed the royal title, and with the support of Nadir Quli, who was to prove himself the greatest general of the age, sought to recover his heritage.

Nadir was the son of Imam Quli, a poor Afsharid Turkman, long settled in Persian Khurasan. He earned his living by making coats and caps of sheepskin, but in the anarchy that followed the Afghan conquest, he found his big opportunity. He took up the life a free-booter and was able to seize much of Khurasan, including the city of Nishapur. He declared his adhesion to the cause of Shah Tahmasp and recruits flocked to his banners. By 1729 the liberation of Iran had been achieved and Shah Tahmasp acknowledged his debt to Nadir by bestowing on him half his kingdom.

In 1732 Tahmasp was deposed, and Abbas, his son of eight months, was proclaimed king with Nadir as regent. In February 1736 the infant died and the Regent assumed the imperial title of *Shahanshah*, mounting the throne as Nadir Shah.

Kandahar was still held by Hussain the younger son of Mir Wais. Nadir felt that unless this centre of Afghan power was reduced it would always remain a threat to Persia. Moreover, as it had been a province of the Persian empire, Nadir who saw himself as the successor of the Safavids, felt it as a point of honour to recover it.

The siege began in March 1737. The walls of the citadel were of great natural strength and it was well-provisioned as Hussain was expecting the Persians. The siege lasted a full year but at last on 12 March 1738 the fort capitulated. The conqueror was merciful, the prisoners were released, and pensions given to the Ghilazi chiefs. Many of the clansmen enlisted under Nadir and the rest were deported to Khurasan, while the Abdali Afghans, who were already there, were moved to the Kandahar region; their sardars being appointed to responsible posts.

By this time relations between Nadir Shah and India had virtually broken down and the former had already determined on war. Within two months of the fall of Kandahar he was at the gates of Kabul. Before embarking on the siege of Kandahar Nadir had sent a message through an ambassador to the court at Delhi, requesting the emperor to instruct Kabul to seal the borders and to turn back any Afghans who might seek refuge from the armies of Nadir. To this the Qila-i-Mualla replied that suitable instructions would be sent, and the military forces at Kabul strengthened. After some time a second envoy, Muhammad Ali Khan arrived, bearing a similar message which was answered in the same casual terms.

But in fact nothing was done, so that when Nadir began his siege operations at Kandahar many fugitives fled northwards. A Persian force pursued the fleeing Ghilzais upto the border of Kabul. The Persians having no instructions to advance further, stopped, but the Afghans meeting no opposition from the Indian side continued their flight. According to the request made by the Persian Shah, a Mughal army should have stopped them, and then pushed them back across the frontier, and their failure to do so could only be interpreted as an unfriendly act.

Nadir now sent a third envoy, one Muhammed Khan Turkman, this time by way of Sind, to demand an explanation from Delhi. His instructions were to insist on an answer and to return to Kandahar within forty days. The arrival of this third ambassador put the emperor's advisers in a quandary. Various drafts were prepared but no reasonable reply seemed possible. In the end it was decided to await the outcome of the siege. After all, the Persian Shah may be forced to raise the siege and retreat into Iran proper, and with the Afghans left in possession there would be no need to reply to Nadir's letter![2]

But the Persian envoy insisted on an answer and the forty days being over he demanded leave to return. But the Qila-i-Mualla would neither give a reply nor would they give him leave to return, and the poor envoy found himself virtually a prisoner. Subsequent messengers sent by Nadir to enquire from the ambassador the reasons for his delay were also detained! To the courtiers of monarch this may have seemed an ingenious solution but it could have hardly appeared so to Nadir, under the shadow of the walls of a defiant Kandahar.

The Mughal authorities in charge of the suba of Kabul were in no position to resist. Its condition was desperate; Nasir Khan's soldiers had not been paid for five years. The Afghan tribes that controlled the Khyber and other passes had likewise failed to receive their subsidies. Nasir Khan the governor, though a brave man, had, unfortunately, been identified as a protege of Roshan ud-Daulah. For years the Kabul subsidy had been misappropriated by his Protector.

Roshan ud-Daulah's peculation being discovered, Khan-i-Dauran had stopped the subsidy altogether, his argument being that since the province had already been able to do without it for so many years it was obviously not required! The Amir-ul-Umara was delighted by the discomfiture of the governor, and did not feel at all obliged to help him out.

The earlier emperors of the Timurid dynasty had always paid great attention to the security of the Afghan border and frequently visited Kabul. But for decades no emperor had ever visited that province and after the subedari of Muazzam Shah Alam (later Bahadur Shah) it had been allowed to become a backwater. And now with the Persian Shah actually in the province it remained a victim of party politics. The defence of the realm, the security of the inhabitants of a frontier province were of no consequence for the emperor and his witty courtiers. Khan-i-Dauran was more intent on the ruin and disgrace of a minor officer whom he had identified as an adherent of a rival and discredited faction.

A deputation of the citizens of Kabul waited on the Amir-ul-Umara, Khan-i-Dauran, to plead for succour. The hapless agent of the governor had also come to urge his master's case. Even though the subsidies to the tribal sardars had been stopped, to keep the turbulent tribes happy, many of their men had been enrolled in the governor's militia, well beyond the normal requirements of an ordinary suba. Kabul was a poor province and even at the best of times its revenues were insufficient to meet the expenses of day to day administration. And now with Ghilzais and their Persian pursuers overrunning the province, the times were apocalyptic.

But Khan-i-Dauran chose to regard the deputation as a contrivance of Nasir Khan's to extract money from the court. He refused to believe that the province was already overrun by the Persians. He scornfully laughed at the deputationists and their fears. Turning towards the subedar's vakil he said, 'I am much too experienced a person to be taken in by such stories that are only concocted to extort money.' Then turning towards the deputation he continued, 'My house is in the plain, and my imagination dwells only on what my eyes have seen; the houses in Kabul are built high and the city is on a hill. Maybe from your rooftops you have caught a glimpse of the Persian host.' Then again turning towards the vakil he added, 'Tell your employer that the Governor of Bengal has been ordered to remit treasure after the monsoon. When that is received, the necessary sum will be sent without delay.'[3]

Such ignorance of the ground situation on the part of Khan-i-Dauran, who was also the bakhshi of the army and responsible for the defence of the realm, is almost unbelievable. In better days the passes and the roads leading into Kabul used to be carefully watched and reports of unusual movements would be sent directly to the emperor. Even the routine communications of the newswriters would be periodically scanned by Aurangzeb. But since the last two decades, because of lack of funds, and to some extent the indolence of the governor, the whole fabric of administration had fallen into disrepair. People could enter and leave without check and there were no newswriters to send their reports as the government did not care to pay them for their labours. The governor himself, realizing the gravity of the situation, had for some time been residing at Peshawar (which fell in the Kabul suba) leaving only a qiladar behind in the Bala Hissar, the citadel of Kabul.

But notwithstanding their weakness the Afghans of Kabul, defended the mountain passes and, for a while, were able to check the advance of the Persians. If at that time a well-appointed army under an experienced leader had been sent to the support of the mountaineers it is more than probable that India might have been saved. But no help was sent to Nasir Khan who prepared to give battle at the head of the Khyber with whatever troops he could muster. In addition he was able to raise a levy of several thousand tribals.

The Persian Shah advanced rapidly by night and on the morning of 14 November 1738, he fell on Nasir Khan's force, taking him by surprise. There are conflicting versions of the battle. Some historians allege that the Pathans of the pass were brought over by Nadir; that Nasir Khan was surprised in bed, and there was no resistance. But there was undoubtedly a stiff fight in which the subedar was wounded and captured.[4]

The situation of Nawab Zakariya Khan governor of Punjab was not much better. Khan-i-Dauran who ruled the roost, was not inclined to strengthen the hands of Zakariya. This was extremely unfortunate for Zakariya was a much more vigorous officer than Nasir, and given proper backing he might well have been able to repel Nadir, or at least discourage him from venturing across the Indus. But instead of strengthening his hands the emperor, on the advice of his favourite, issued orders directing Asaf Jah, Qamr ud-Din and Khan-i-Dauran to prepare for the defence of the empire. A crore of rupees was advanced to each of these umara to raise an army. They pitched their advance tents near the Shalamar Gardens but showed no hurry to begin their advance. Nearly a month was wasted in petty intrigues, each trying to discredit the other.

Meanwhile the Persian Shah had crossed the Indus, and in January 1739 he crossed the Chenab. Zakariya decided to offer battle at the bridge of Shah Daula with his main army, about 20 miles from Lahore, while his vanguard was placed at Eminabad, 10 miles further to the north-west, with the small fort of Kacha Mirza behind them, under Qalandar Khan.

The Persians made short work of Qalandar's force. When the news reached Zakariya that the fort had also fallen, he withdrew from Shah Daula to Lahore. On 10 January the Persians reached the city and an artillery exchange commenced, with minor skirmishes between the two sides. Fighting continued throughout the next day, but realizing that the contest was futile and no help could be expected Zakariya requested negotiations.

The next day Zakariya was conducted to the presence of Nadir who received him kindly, giving him a *khillat* of gold brocade, a jewelled dagger and a horse. But according to the terms, a sum of Rs. 20 lakh was levied on the city—the bulk of which was paid out of the treasury—the remainder being raised by a levy on the wealthier inhabitants. The entire amount was paid in two days and thus the city was spared the horrors of a general sack. Some plundering did take place, however, because this was the first exposure of the Persians to the wealth of a major Indian city. Zakariya was retained as governor, but his son Hayatullah was taken into the Persian service with 500 retainers and kept in the Shah's retinue as a pledge for his father's fidelity.

In Delhi, it was alleged that Lahore had been treacherously surrendered by Zakariya without a fight since the latter was a Khurasani like Nadir himself![5]

Although the three greatest amirs of the empire, Asaf Jah, the wazir and the bakhshi had been ordered to prepare an army against the Persians, in typical Mughal fashion none had been placed in supreme command. Of the three, the only one with any ability and experience of war was Asaf Jah, but because of the emperor's suspicion of all Turanians—inspired by Khan-i-Dauran—he was only one amongst three. The month of December was spent by the three in their camp at Shalamar. It was Ramzan, the Muslim month for fasting, another disincentive for action.

It was only after the news of the crossing of the Indus had reached the court that the imperialists set out on the road to Lahore (10 January 1739). Even then they did not show any great anxiety. After reaching Panipat they halted for nine days to enable the emperor to join them. The latter, feeling that this was a good opportunity to earn some military glory, had at length decided to march at the head of his army. By this time the news had already come of the defeat of Zakariya and the capture of Lahore. It was then decided to make a stand at Karnal against the Persians.

It was hoped that the halt at Karnal would enable Saadat Khan Burhan ul-Mulk to join the imperial forces with his troops. He was supposed to be coming, post haste from Awadh with 30,000 cavalry. Besides, more contingents were expected from Rajasthan. Khan-i-Dauran professed great faith in the Rajputs, and had sent appeals to all the chiefs as well as the Marathas. But times had changed. The empire had lost its sheen. With an emperor like Muhammed Shah and a minister like Qamr ud-Din, nothing else could be expected. No Rajput chief of note answered the call, and the small Maratha contingent that had set out with the imperialists from Delhi slipped away at the first opportunity.

But notwithstanding the poor response of the Rajputs and Marathas which is easy to attribute to a sense of alienation from the dynasty, the following lines from a letter written by the Peshwa Baji Rao to his General Pilaji Jadon are significant:

> I shall march to Northern India by regular stages. The Persian sovereign Tahmasp Quli [*sic*, the sovereign was now Nadir Shah] has come to conquer the world. To help Muhammad Shah I am sending the Malwa force under Malhar Rao Holkar, Ranoji Sindhia, and Pawar. It is a glory to this monarchy (i.e. the Maratha state) to help the Emperor of Delhi at such a time.[6]

It is easy to read too much in occasional revelatory fragments like Raja Jai Singh's letter to Nand Lal Mandaloi when he congratulated him on the success of his manipulations which ended in the defeat of the imperial Subedar Daya Bahadur in these words, 'You have defended our religion in Malwa and crushed the Musalmans, establishing Dharma. You have fulfilled my desire.'[7]

The words are suggestive and Jai Singh was instrumental in ceding Malwa formally to the Marathas six years later, but to suggest that the rise of the Maratha power was part of a general Hindu revanche against foreign invaders belonging to an alien culture and faith would be stretching the truth. There was indeed a grain of truth in it but it is more likely that the letter of Jai Singh's was written in a moment of pique and disenchantment on account of various other reasons. The Qila-i-Mualla had long since ceased to value its mansabdars and umara for their intrinsic worth. We have seen how Jai Singh was frustrated before Thun in 1719 by Qutb ul-Mulk. Long-term interests and objectives were routinely sacrificed for immediate personal gains. The country was fed up with the way of governance, with the incessant violence which permeated the country, the frequent resort to arms by one amir against another, and intrigues of court favourites against popular governors which often ended in war.

There was no revulsion against Mughal rule as such. There was no consciousness of nationality, and nor was India a secular state in the modern sense of term. Even if *jaziya* stood abolished the emperor remained the commander of the faithful, the caliph of Islam in India. There was a gulf between the Muslims and the Hindus but this was nothing new as Hindu society had always been highly divided and fractured. But over the centuries India had got used to Islam and had in a sense assimilated the Muslims as another caste. Social intercourse between castes had always been extremely limited. If there was one well in a village for the caste Hindus and another for the others, the introduction of a third for the Muslims made no qualitative difference. India was large, and Indian society had always cherished and emphasized differences.

The weakening of the ruling Mughal 'caste' only meant more opportunity for the others. It meant more opportunities for the Hindustani Muslims like Khan-i-Dauran, for Rajput chiefs like Ajit Singh, Jai Singh or Chhattarsal Bundela, and for the new rising Kunbi Marathas of the Deccan, and the Jat Sikhs of the Punjab.

The unaccommodating attitudes of Christianity which has always preached the superiority of a narrow and literal creed and waged a bitter and exterminating war in Spain, the Mediterranean and the Near East, had been brought by the English to this country, accustomed to a more Laodician attitude. Coming from a country which was fairly uniform, where one sect constituted the Established Church of which alone the king was the defender, they totally misinterpreted the Indian situation. They saw an analogy between the position of the Mughals in India and that of the English in Ireland, where the Catholic majority was subject to a host of penal laws and actively persecuted. It was true that the Muslim, be he Turk, Persian or Indian, was in many ways in a better position than a non-Muslim Indian, but the horrible inequities among the different castes were far more unfair and cruel. The Marathas were only seeking their own advantage and were certainly not waging any national war of liberation. The peshwa had no compunctions about accepting titles from the emperor, and he would later gladly accept the regency as titular Vakil-i-Mutlaq.

NOTES

1. Malcolm, *History of Persia*, i, p. 379.
2. Tabatabai, *Seir Mutaqherin*, i, p. 303.
3. Ibid., pp. 305-6. Anand Ram Mukhlis, *Chamanistan*, pp. 11-12. Elliot and Dowson, *Posthumous Papers* (2nd rpt.), p. 76.

4. Irvine, ii, p. 330.
5. Ibid., p. 336 (on the authority of Shakir Khan of Panipat).
6. Rajwade, *Marathachi Itihasachen Sadhanen*, vi, no. 130. Quoted by Irvine, p. 336.
7. The authenticity of many of these letters is now considered doubtful. Raghubir Sinh (*Malwa in Transition*) suggests that they may well be nineteenth century forgeries, intended only to enhance the Mandaloi family's claims to past importance.

CHAPTER 19

Debacle at Karnal

The imperial army had decided to wait at Karnal to enable Burhan ul-Mulk to join them. Besides news had already reached that Zakariya had been defeated and Lahore occupied. Nadir was aware of the movements of the Indians and of the approach of Burhan. While he took position near the Indian host a strong force was detached with instructions to advance rapidly to Panipat and cut off Burhan before he could link up with the main army.

But Burhan ul-Mulk did not fit into the usual mould of those who constituted the higher umara of Muhammad Shah. During the Maratha invasion of 1736 his was the only army out of three, led by the highest nobles of the empire, which was able to defeat the Marathas. Now he was advancing by forced marches and was able to outwit Nadir's intercepting column. In five days—a remarkable speed for an Indian army—he covered the 75 miles between Delhi and Karnal, arriving around the midnight of 12-13 February.

The Indians had pitched their camp to the north of Karnal with Ali Mardan Khan's canal on their right and a dense forest on the left. They dug in, throwing up earthworks to protect themselves. Then with a ring of guns behind the earthworks they effectively shut themselves up as in a fort. The Persians pitched their camp in the open space towards Kunjpura, between the canal and the Yamuna, but their highly mobile cavalry effectively cut the Indian supply lines. This decision of the Indians to entrench themselves was to prove as fatal as Azim ush-Shan's in 1712, and that of the Marathas later in 1761 at Panipat.

The Persian Shah had set out from Iran with 80,000 troops.[1] More soldiers had enlisted in Afghanistan, but substantial numbers had to be left behind as garrisons in the forts and other strongholds. Hence the number of effective soldiers left by the time he reached Karnal could not have exceeded 50,000 or 60,000. Their servants and camp followers were much fewer than the Indians' and the total host could not have numbered more than 2,00,000. But all the servants were armed and well-mounted and most could fight to defend their camp.

The strength of the Indian army was estimated at '3,00,000 renowned soldiers' as described by the Persian chroniclers.[2] But more probably the number of effective soldiers did not exceed 75,000, while the total strength of the camp may have been a million! The difficulty in provisioning such a huge force, comprising mostly useless servants, tradesmen and camp-followers can be well-imagined. This gross disproportion between teeth and tail was not only a peculiarity of the imperial Indian armies. Even the Europeans maintained an almost equally lavish scale of servants. During the Maratha wars Lord Lake's camp numbering 3,00,000 souls contained only 30,000 fighting men.

The following morning Burhan ul-Mulk waited on the emperor. The audience was followed by a conference. While it was in progress, news was brought that Persian light horse had driven away 500 camels, part of Saadat Khan's baggage. The latter immediately rose, and picking up his sword which lay before him, requested permission to attack the raiders and rescue his camp followers.

Everyone present, including the emperor, advised him to take it easy. His troops had come only a few hours earlier, after an exhausting stage of 20 miles, and they had been marching for more than a month. They would require a few days rest to recuperate and refit. It would take time for the rest of the army too to organize itself for attack. Already half the day was over, and there was not enough time to risk a clash which might develop into a full-scale battle.

But Saadat Khan was adamant and left to chastize the raiders. While heading for thc spot he told his aides to convey orders to the commanders that they should collect their men, saddle their horses and follow, ready for battle. And he left with his personal escort.

The officers were incredulous. Their general had gone for an audience with the emperor and had not returned; surely there must be a misunderstanding! And since their horses were still suffering from the fatigue of the previous march they were reluctant to saddle and attack so soon. In Indian armies the horse was usually the property of the soldier himself, so he was chary of risking it unnecessarily. Therefore not many responded to the call given by Burhan; only about 4,000 cavalry and 1,000 infantry joined him.

The Qizilbashes retreated at the approach of the Indian cavalry, drawing them away from their camp and luring them towards the Persian. Exhilarated, Saadat continued his pursuit, at the same time sending urgent requests for assistance. Khan-i-Dauran responded. The nizam had been against Saadat's precipitate attack from the start, and had no intention of jumping into the conflict in such an extempore manner, but Khan-i-Dauran, declared that it was not the Indian style to abandon a comrade in this cold-blooded manner, even if he was imprudent.

'Let others do as they please, for my part I must go and support Saadat Khan', he is quoted as saying by Ghulam Hussain, the chronicler of the *Seir*.[3] But according to Anand Ram Mukhlis he left only after some grumbling. Khan-i-Dauran was a great admirer of Rajput chavalry, and he was a true blue Indian, without any claim of descent from Iran or Turan. Although never previously known for valour, his bravado may have been the result of a romantic imagination fired by the prospect of military glory, or merely a reaction to the nizam's cold-blooded rationality. Whatever the reasoning, he rushed into the fight with 8,000 cavalry, neglecting to take any artillery.

Nadir's reactions to this developing battle were quick and decisive. Realizing that the Indian entrenchments were too formidable to be stormed he had been on the look out for just some such indiscretion. He drew up a line of light *shutarnals* in the line of the Indian attackers. When the retreating Persian cavalry approached the ambush they wheeled away to the wings leaving the swivels a free field for fire.

The pursuing Indian cavalry were fighting without plan or strategy, and were unprepared for the deadly fire from the swivels and the counter attack that followed. Saadat Khan's troops were the first to break in the face of that withering fire, leaving only a small band of personal followers around him. Khan-i-Dauran's cavalry resisted a little longer, but eventually they too broke and fled, 'for arrows cannot fight bullets'. Khan-i-Dauran dismounted and continued the fight on foot with the sword.

Eventually, severely wounded, he was evacuated from the field by his personal attendants and bodyguards. When they reached the site of his camp not a tent could be seen. It had virtually disappeared. As Ghulam Hussain remarks drily: 'in consequence of that discipline so conspicuous in the camps of the Emperors of Hindustan, they found nothing of Khan Dauran's encampment'.[4] His own followers had plundered it—with all its treasure, tents, horses and draught cattle—and then dispersed. The entire battle had not lasted four hours, but as soon as the news trickled down that their general had been repulsed and was fleeing, they seized what they could and fled, notwithstanding the fact that the bulk of the imperial army was unscathed and had not even joined the fight!

As for Saadat Khan, he had continued the fight from his elephant for some time after his main army had dispersed. An old leg injury, had prevented him from mounting a horse but he continued to discharge quiver after quiver from his elephant. Then one Qizilbash, a native of Nishapur who had known him from his days in Iran, rode up and in a loud voice boldly addressed him by his name: 'Muhammad Amin! Are you mad? Whom are you fighting? On whom are you relying?' Then with a quick movement he climbed up to the howdah and pressing his dagger on his throat compelled him to surrender. He was surrounded by the Persians and led away to the tent of Nadir.

There was no movement from the nizam's side. His troops stood on the *qui vive*, ready for orders which never came. Muhammad Shah stood by the banks of the canal with his generals and his umara and watched the battle from afar, a mere spectator.

As usual the figures of the casualties vary greatly but Irvine adopting Hanway's figures as the most reliable estimates the Indian casualties at about 17,000, and the Persian losses as only 2,500. Many prominent umara and lesser mansabdars were among the dead. Not only was Khan-i-Dauran killed but one brother and three sons also 'quaffed the cup of martyrdom', to borrow the picturesque phrase so often used in the contemporary chronicles.

Apart from the rashness of Burhan ul-Mulk who had plunged into battle without any tactical plan or strategy, defeat was inevitable for the Indians. Living behind the shelter of their mountain barriers they had felt little need to upgrade their weaponry and military skills. In ordinary times there was little danger of invasion from beyond the frontiers for the centre of the Persian empire—the only other great power—was far removed, and inhospitable and thinly populated territories lay between. As for Central Asia, it had been a power vacuum ever since the break-up of Timur's empire. The petty Khans of Bokhara, Khokand and the like were too weak to contemplate great adventures.

After the sieges of Kandahar in the reign of Shah Jahan there had been no interaction between the Qila-i-Mualla and a first class military power. Babar with his small, mobile force and light artillery had easily dispersed Ibrahim Lodi's cumbrous army, even though it was tenfold his strength, but in the absence of a serious threat thereafter the Mughals had not taken long to succumb to the easy-going ways of the natives. The edge of their swords had been blunted, the accent was on pomp and splendour rather than military competitiveness, and the elephant whose unreliability as an instrument of war had been demonstrated time and again since the invasion of Alexander, now half-forgotten in the mists of antiquity, had again become the standard *sawarry* for general officers.

Iran, on the other hand, marched with the Ottoman empire and that state had, until the seventeenth century, been the premier military power in the Western world. Even after the decline had set in, because of the military pressure from Russia, and the 'Holy Roman Empire of the German Nation', it had of necessity to keep up with the advance of military science in Europe. Since ancient times Iran had been in a state of intermittent warfare with its Western neighbour and so some of the advances had rubbed off on them as well. Their artillery was much lighter and better served than the Indian ordnance which had not advanced perceptibly since the sixteenth century. Impressive and frightening in their massiveness the guns often required hundreds of cattle to move them. They were so ill-served that it was virtually impossible to aim at any particular target and the rate of fire was very slow. Their rockets were more noisy than destructive, and the swivels, mounted on elephants and camels, were used more for firing salutes than as an aggressive and mobile light artillery. The matchlock men were hardly counted as serious soldiers; the effective strength of an army was still reckoned in terms of cavalry, with the troopers relying for the most part on the sword and the bow. The latter, on the other hand, had long disappeared from the European armies, and was on the way out in the armies of Turkey and Persia.

The official historians of the Qila-i-Mualla decried the cowardice of the Persians who refused to engage in individual combat with the sword—relying more on firearms, but they had forgotten that war was not so much as a measure of bravery but a means to an end.

Saadat Khan was graciously received by the Persian Shah who questioned him about the country and the strength of the Indian army to which he gave diplomatic answers, emphasizing the strength of his master and the vast extent of his dominions. As for Khan-i-Dauran, of whom the Shah spoke contemptuously that he knew how to die but not how to fight, he was only one among many equally great.

Then the Shah leaned forward and spoke to him confidentially. 'You are my countryman and we are both of the same religion. Advise me how I can extract a large ransom from your emperor. I would like to return quickly as I have to fight the Sultan of Rum.' Saadat Khan advised him to send for Asaf Jah as he was the foremost among the umara of Muhammad Shah and perhaps the wisest and most sensible of them all.[5]

The nizam was sent for and he came the next day. The emissary had come with a Koran as a pledge of good faith. The emperor was apprehensive lest some treachery be intended and as he was leaving he asked for advice as to what should be done in case Nadir detained him. The nizam replied:

The Quran is between us. If there is treachery, God will answer for it. In that case Your Majesty should retreat to Mandu or some other strong fort, summon Nasir Jang (the Nizam's son) from the Deccan with a strong force and fight the Persians.

The Nizam was a skilled negotiator and he was able to secure easy terms. The Shah would advance no further and would retire to his country from Karnal. An indemnity of only Rs. 50 lakh would be paid by the Indians (according to the *Seir* the figure was Rs. 2 crore), of which Rs. 20 lakh would be paid on the spot, Rs. 10 lakh on reaching Lahore, and the remaining Rs. 20 lakh in two instalments of Rs. 10 lakh at Attock and Kabul. To solemnise the agreement he invited Muhammed Shah to dine with him the following day.

The next day (15 March) Muhammad Shah came to the Persian camp with all his greater umara. On the way they were met by the Persian wazir who had brought a Koran with him to reassure the guests. Outside the royal enclosure they were received by Prince Nasrullah on behalf of his royal father, while Nadir himself greeted them on the threshold of his tent. The dinner was preceeded by a private meeting between the two sovereigns with only the nizam, the wazir, and Muhammed Ishaq present from the Indian side. Muhammed Ishaq so impressed the Shah with his ready and intelligent replies that he declared he ought to be the wazir. The dinner was held in a cordial atmosphere with Nadir at his courteous best.

When the emperor returned to his camp he was informed of the death of Khan-i-Dauran. The nizam pressed the claims of his son Gahzi ud-Din for the resulting vacancy, as a reward for securing such easy terms from the Persians. The emperor agreed, but this immediately provoked a negative reaction. Azimullah, a nephew of the wazir, felt that he had a stronger claim to the post. Besides he was older than Ghazi ud-Din, and, in protest, he set off for the Persian camp, presumably to solicit Nadir's support! It was with difficulty that the nizam and the wazir dissuaded him from the foolish course he had adopted. Then to get over the difficulty, the nizam himself assumed the office.

But while this silenced Azimullah it provoked an unexpected reaction in another quarter. When Burhan ul-Mulk Saadat Khan—who was already in the Persian camp—came to know he was incensed. He felt that his services to the emperor deserved better recognition and there could be no better person than he for the rank of Amir-ul-Umara and the post of paymaster-general. He was the only noble who had won a notable victory against the Marathas in the disastrous campaign of 1736-7, and here again at Karnal he had been the first to strike a blow for his master. (It mattered not that the blow had been deflected and he launched his attack against the advice of all experienced generals!) He seethed with a desire to get even with the nizam and to spite the ungrateful emperor. And, like Azimullah, he too had no scruples in approaching the Persian Shah.

At his next audience with Nadir, Saadat declared that Rs. 50 lakh was but a trifling sum and he could easily have got much more. Why, even he himself could give the Shah that much from his personal hoard! He had been duped by the nizam. That nobleman was a smooth talker; if trapped he could easily squeeze the emperor for far greater sums. With the nizam in the hands of the Shah, the emperor would be helpless and Nadir could reach Delhi without opposition. There Rs. 20 crore could be easily collected by way of 'idemnity'. This was Burhan ul-Mulk's way of getting even with the nizam and the emperor.

It took some time to put the plan into execution. In the meantime, on 18 February, the nizam again met the Shah and the following day the Persian wazir dined with the nizam in his tent. The first instalment of Rs. 20 lakh still remained to be paid and these meetings were arranged in that connection. But inspite of the agreement the Persian cavalry maintained their grip on the Indian camp, denying it access to supplies. The ambulant provisioners of the Indian armies, the nomadic banjaras were unable to get past the marauding Qizilbash horse, and within a few days of the battle of 13 March shortages began to be felt.

When on 22 March the nizam again called on the Shah in response to a summons he felt that something was amiss. Instead of being led directly to the audience he was detained in an ante-chamber. Then a message was sent that the Shah had raised the demand to Rs. 20 crore along with 20,000 troops to serve as auxiliaries. When he was at last brought before the Shah he protested that the new demand was absurd. Shah Jahan with his best efforts had managed to amass a treasure of Rs. 16 crore but it had all been expended in the wars of Aurangzeb and His Majesty was having difficulty even in scraping together Rs. 50 lakh!

But Nadir's mind was made up. He replied curtly that he could not leave the Persian camp until the sum was paid, and suggested that he would like to have another meeting with Muhammad Shah. He asked him to write to him, assuring him that he did not intend any treachery. For two days the nizam resisted but he finally wrote to the emperor relating exactly what had passed and informing him of the new demands raised by Nadir.

The failure of the nizam to return had alarmed the emperor and gave rise to all kinds of speculation. And now that the truth was known there was consternation. Many of the umara were in favour of another trial of arms but Muhammad Shah, who never had much stomach for war to begin with, felt that resistance would be pointless and would only lead to more bloodshed and ruin. So placing his trust in God, on 24 February he left for the Persian camp taking with him only Muhammed Ishaq, some eunuchs and pages (*khawas*) and an escort of 2,000 cavalry.

This time there was no one to receive him and he remained unattended for some time. At night the nizam and Saadat Khan were allowed to meet him and he alone was thereafter conducted to Nadir's tent. He was treated as a prisoner and a guard placed over him.

The next day the imperial family was sent for, and the nizam and Saadat Khan were also instructed to send for theirs. Qamr ud-Din Khan was summoned along with his family. With the emperor a hostage in the hands of the Persians there was no resistance from the Indian side. Nadir now announced that the lesser officers were free to leave the camp and return to Delhi if they so wished.

Great was the panic in the leaderless camp after the departure of Qamr ud-Din, the last senior amir. The lesser umara and mansabdars made their way as best as they could. Not only were the roads rendered dangerous by the roving squadrons of the Qizilbash horse but the peasantry, shocked by the news of the debacle, had risen and were lurking in ambush to strip and loot the unwary soldiers of the broken army. It was the greatest calamity that had befallen the dynasty. For the long-suffering people of Delhi and Upper India it would prove to be the greatest catastrophe since the visitation of Timur in 1398.

The Maratha envoy made his way back to Delhi by a devious route, avoiding the imperial highway. His relief at his safe arrival can be easily sensed in his dispatch to Poona: 'God has saved me from a great danger, and permitted me to escape with honour! The Chaghtai Empire is gone and the Irani Empire has commenced!'[6]

NOTES

1. Irvine, *Later Mughals*, ii, p. 337 (on the authority of Mirza Mahdi's *Jahankusha*).
2. Ibid., p. 338.
3. Tabatabai, *Seir Mutaqherin*, i, p. 309.
4. Ibid., i, p. 310.
5. Irvine, ii, p. 353 (on the authority of Harcharan Das's *Chahar Gulzar-i-Shujai*).
6. Rajwade, *Marathachi Itihasachen Sadhanen*, vi, no. 131.

CHAPTER 20

The Persian on his Throne

The news of the disaster at Karnal caused consternation in Delhi. Every man of wealth and property barricaded his house and hired guards for protection. Robbers and highwaymen had closed the roads leading out from the city, and it was apprehended that the sturdy Jat and Gujjar peasantry might seize the opportunity to plunder the suburbs.

But Haji Fulad Khan, the kotwal, was an energetic man and he succeeded in keeping order. Further on 27 February Saadat Khan arrived in Delhi with 4,000 troops and the *badmashes* were overawed. With him came Tahmasp Khan Jalair as the representative of the Persian Shah and they were charged with the responsibility for making the necessary arrangements for the reception of the Persian ruler and preserving the city and the palaces from lawlessness and plunder. For virtually all the treasures, public and private, in the palaces and homes of the citizens, now belonged to the Persian Shah.

The two nobles carried letters addressed to Lutfullah Khan, the governor. The latter had been digging trenches and talking of resistance, but Saadat soon convinced him that this would be foolish as the emperor was already a captive. In a letter Muhammad Shah ordered him to hand over the keys of the stores and treasury to Tahmasp Khan, whom Nadir had designated as his governor of the Delhi suba.

Acting on the advice of Saadat Khan, Lutfullah handed over the keys to the Persian. When the report of the successful assumption of charge was received at Karnal the march began. At the head was Nadir while the fallen emperor followed at a respectful distance with his nobles. He had 1,000 horsemen for his escort while the Wazir Qamr ud-Din was followed by 10,000 troops. They were all that remained of a force of over 1,00,000 men (including Saadat Khan's 30,000 horse). The rest had dispersed.

The Shah was received at the Shalamar Gardens by Saadat Khan. Lutfullah waited on his master who introduced him to Nadir who expressed his appreciation of his ready compliance with the orders for handing over charge to Tahmasp and ordered that he be given a *khillat* consisting of a dress from his own wardrobe.

On 8 March Muhammad Shah entered the city seated in a palki and proceeded without fanfare to the Qila-i-Mualla. The imperial standards and insignia of sovereignty were not displayed. They had been discreetly put away.

The next day was a Friday and it was the day chosen by Nadir for his triumphal entry. In the Jama Masjid the *khutba* was read in his name and coins were ordered to be struck. Truly, as the Maratha vakil had written, the Chaghtai empire had perished and the Iranian come into being!

He was received at the entrance of the qila by Muhammad Shah. The choicest carpets and golden cloths were spread on the ground for the Persian to walk on. The imperial apartments adjoining the diwan khana—those described as the suite of Shah Jahan—were given to Nadir while Muhammad retired to another suite some distance away further along the wall. At night Nadir sent him food from his table as one might to a prisoner.

The following day was the festival of Id ul-Zuha—one of the most important in the Muslim calendar. Nadir had kept his army outside the city to avoid provoking the citizens and to avert unauthorized looting. Most of his soldiers hailed from Afghanistan and Khurasan and had never seen cities like Delhi and Lahore before.

To enable them to enjoy the spectacle of the city in the midst of a major festival, Nadir permitted his soldiers to enter the city in small groups. But what he had feared was fated to happen. A street brawl between some soldiers and shopkeepers resulted in the Persians being killed.

After seeing the orderly and disciplined behaviour of Nadir's troops the Delhi shopkeepers soon got over their awe and started demanding outrageous sums for purchases, throwing contemptuous and scornful looks at the rough rude soldiers from the Khurasan steppe and the barren hills of Afghanistan. According to another version the shopkeepers were holding back grain. Angered, the Shah ordered the godowns to be opened and fixed the sale price, which was considered unduly low. At one such godown the shopkeepers attacked the Persian *nasaqchis* (military policemen) sent to enforce the order and killed them.

The news of this daring attack spread through the city like wildfire and soon everywhere the Persians were being attacked. At the same time the rumour spread that the Shah had been killed in the qila by one of the amazonian Kalmucks of the harem guard.[1] Since the death of the commander is usually the signal for the disintegration of oriental armies the Delhi mob was even more emboldened.

When towards evening the news of the disturbances was conveyed to Nadir he at first refused to credit it. But when the noise of the rioting penetrated even the palace walls he sent an officer to investigate. The officer had barely stepped outside the gate when he was seized and killed. A second met with the same fate. Nadir had first thought that his men were making baseless allegations against the citizens in the hope that he would order a general sack which would benefit them much more than a systematic realization of the indemnity. But now realizing that the situation was serious he ordered out a thousand musketeers to clear the streets, but their commander also reported that the rioting had spread over a large part of the city and it was impossible for his force to 'pacify' it. Besides, it was too dark and he was unfamiliar with the streets. The Shah then ordered his troops to stand on the defensive for the remainder of the night. The canaille would be sorted out when the sun rose.[2]

At day break, 11 March, Nadir sallied forth, with his generals and a large armed force. He proceeded down Chandni Chowk and climbed up the steps of the mosque of Roshan ud-Daulah where he took stock of the situation.

It was indeed grim. After listening to the reports of his officers and identifying the quarters where the seditionists had been most active, he drew his sword from its scabbard and ordered a general massacre. Not a man or woman, he declared, would be spared and his soldiers would be allowed to avenge the slaughter of their comrades.

With grim ferocity the Persians set to work. But the slaughter was not indiscrimate. Only those wards identified as being the most affected were singled out for chastisement. The killing started at about 9 in the morning and continued till about 2 or 3 in the afternoon. In that span of time at least 20,000 to 40,000 men were slain. The estimates, as is usual on such occasions, very greatly. Some give as low a figure as 8,000 while others like Rustam Ali, the author of the *Tarikh-i-Hindi* estimate the toll at 1,00,000!

In some places the citizens tried to defend themselves, and, as often happens in India on such occasions, many of the women were slaughtered by their own menfolk to save them from the proverbial 'worse than death'—particularly among the more respectable classes. Many of the women saved their honour by jumping into wells. Those who survived were retained by the Persians as their property.

At length, on the directions of Muhammad Shah some of the nobles led by the nizam ventured to approach the Shah to plead consideration. The nizam is said to have offered his own head to placate the Persian's anger. But the innocent, he pleaded, should be spared. Enough blood had been shed already. Moved by an apt couplet recited by the nizam, the Shah softened. Looking at him thoughtfully, after a pause he said, 'I shall pardon them in consideration of thy grey beard'. Then he lifted his sword which was lying on the parapet and sheathed it.

It was the signal to stop. The kotwal's officers were sent with Persian *nasaqchis* to halt the massacre. The discipline was such that compliance was immediate.

In the course of the massacre much of Chandni Chowk, the bazaar of Dariba, the fruit market and the buildings around the Jama Masjid had been burnt. What remained had been looted and dug up systematically for treasure. Heaps of the slaughtered lay everywhere and soon the smell of decomposed flesh became intolerable. At length the kotwal received the Shah's permission to dispose of the dead. The corpses were dragged out, piled in the street and with the help of the timbers of the empty houses, Hindus and Muslims were indiscriminately burnt. The figure of 20,000 dead is the official body count of the kotwal, based on the number of corpses disposed of in these mass cremations but another manuscript gives the figure at 8,000. The latter may be an error on the part of the scribe.[3]

Three nobles, one of them a son-in-law of the wazir, had been identified as having incited the rioters and seditionists on 10 March, and of having led an attack on the stables of Nadir. These men had now shut themselves up in a small fortalice on the outskirts of the city, and the kotwal was charged with bringing them to justice. The men surrendered and were produced before Nadir who ordered their execution.

The granaries were sealed and the Shah refused to permit the sale of provisions to the population. Nor were the people permitted to leave Delhi to procure food elsewhere. Eventually after the intervention of Muhammad Shah they were permitted to go to Ghaziabad to procure the necessities of life. But even this was fraught with danger for the Persian cavalry ranged up to 40 miles from the capital, looting, burning and destroying with complete disregard for life.

And lest it be forgotten, the number of Persians killed in the rioting of 10 March was very considerable. A safe figure would be between 5,000 and 7,000.[4] Again the numbers vary considerably. For example the *Seir* gives the figure of only 700 but this work also gives the Persian casualties at Karnal as 3 dead and 20 injured—a ridiculous figure by any measure. But considering that the strength of Nadir's fighting forces did not exceed 50,000 or 60,000 to being with, his losses were heavy.

Another death occurred on the night of 10 March, a death which almost passed unnoticed amid the horrors of the greater blood-bath which had drowned the city. This was the death of Burhan ul-Mulk Saadat Khan, the man responsible for the visitation in the first place. Some Indian historians have suspected that he was throughout in league with the Persian Shah, and that it was at his prompting that Nadir attacked India in the first place. But this is most improbable. The Shah was indeed his countryman, in the sense that both men hailed from Khurasan, but it was only after his supersession by Nizam-ul-Mulk that he turned against his royal master.

He had felt that he deserved as much credit as the nizam, if not more, for the easy terms of the initial peace by which Nadir undertook to turn back from Karnal with an indemnity of a mere Rs. 50 lakh. But when he saw that all the credit had been taken by the nizam he vowed vengeance.

The Shah had appointed him his vice-regent in India with the office of Vakil-i-Mutlaq but his glory was short-lived. The day after his entry into Delhi, Nadir called both him and the nizam and demanded the idemnity he had promised. And, if that was not forthcoming, he made it plain he would hold them personally responsible and would not hesitate to torture them to extract it. Saadat was so overcome with shame, humiliation, and remorse that as soon as he reached his residence he took poison and died.

But the first act in the dispoliation of the Chaghtai empire had already been performed. The Persian records have recorded it with great delicacy. To quote the narrative of Nadir's own secretary:

> Nadir Shah graciously remarked that the throne of Hindustan would be left to Muhammad Shah, in the terms of the agreement made on the first day, and that the Emperor would enjoy the support and friendship of the Persian monarch, because both were of the same Turkoman stock.
>
> Muhammad Shah bowed low in gratitude and gave profuse thanks to the victor for his generosity. He had received no small favour—it was the gift of a crown added to the gift of life. As a mark of his gratitude, he laid before Nadir Shah the accumulated treasures, stores and rare possessions of the rulers of Delhi as presents to Nadir and offerings for his health. But the gracious sovereign of Persia refused to take any of these things, though the piled up wealth of all the other kings of the world did not amount to a tenth part of a tenth part of this immense hoard. At last he yielded to the importunity of Muhammad Shah and appointed trusty officers to take delivery of the money and other property.[5]

But the extraction and delivery of this vast sum of Rs. 20 crore was not as simple as this delicate narrative suggests. The public treasury of the emperor yielded only Rs. 3 crore. The secret vaults where former emperors had hoarded treasure, for occasions like this, yielded much more but it still fell short of the desired total. A levy was assessed on all the principal nobles and five commissions set up in which sat nobles like the nizam, Sarbuland, the wazir, and Azimullah, to ensure that the burden was shared as fairly as possible, due regard being paid to a person's capacity. About

Rs. 2 crore were assessed on the citizens of Delhi. The same five nobles were entrusted with particular wards of the city and they were charged with listing all the households which gave appearance of being in a capacity to pay, and then assessing the share of each, and finally, what was most difficult, actually enforcing the collection.

This was the most painful part, and in this process many reputations were made and destroyed. Qamr ud-Din Khan, otherwise an incompetent wazir earned the gratitude of the people because he was generous and often came to the rescue of an assessee by paying his share from his own personal hoard. But when his turn came he was hard pressed to find the required cash and the Persian *nasaqchis* humiliated him by forcing him to stand bareheaded in the sun until his household servants made up the required sum. Nearly Rs. 1 crore were realized in cash, besides jewels and elephants. His diwan, Majlis Rai was handed over to Sarbuland Khan who had earned a reputation for heartless ferocity. He put the diwan to torture, and in open durbar cut off his ears. The humiliated man took poison. Many others opted for death.

Saadat Khan Burhan ul-Mulk had taken the easy way out but there was no evading the assessment. His deputy and nephew, Abul Mansur Khan Safdar Jang, was summoned and the full amount—Rs. 2 crore according to the *Seir*—was realized from him. The vakils and agents of distant governors were also put to the rack. The vakil of the governor of Bengal was publicly flogged and felt so humiliated that he took poison along with his entire family.[6]

The historian Anand Ram Mukhlis had to cough up Rs. 5 lakh and is bitter in his denunciations of Sarbuland Khan in whose ward fell his house. Whole families were ruined, the savings of generations dissipated and houses reduced to shambles with their floors dug up. It was the twilight of the Delhi umara.

How much was actually taken? The most conservative estimate, that of Nadir's Persian secretary, the author of the *Jahankusha* gives the figure of Rs. 15 crore in cash besides jewels, clothing, furniture, etc. The jewels were of course worth much more. Frazer gives an estimate of Rs. 70 crore and Mukhlis Rs. 50 crore. The jewels included the fabulous *Takht-i-Taus* or Peacock Throne which cost Shah Jahan Rs. 2 crore to make 'and nine other thrones'. And famous jewels like the priceless Kohinoor. Then there were the animals—300 elephants, 10,000 horses and 10,000 camels. After all, the loot had to be transported over 2,000 miles.

He certainly ended up with much more than he had bargained for. But he left behind a ruined state with an empty treasury, no reserves and an impoverished ruling class. The empire never recovered from the blow. Not content with all this he also took a bride from the imperial house. The princes of the house of Babar claimed descent from two of the greatest conquerors the world has ever known, Chengiz and Timur. While no doubt many an obscure Khan in the oases of Central Asia boasted a like descent, the padishahs of Hind were the only ones who lived in regal splendour. Hence a daughter of this house still had some *cachet*.

On 26 March Nadir's younger son Nasrullah was married to an imperial princess, the daughter of Dawar Bakhsh, grandson of Murad Bakhsh, and thus a great-great granddaughter of Shah Jahan. The celebrations began a week before the ceremony and continued day and night. The Yamuna bank was illuminated with lamps after dusk while combats with elephants, bulls, tigers and deer were held in the day for the entertainment of the marriage guests. It was but a fortnight since the great massacre and the kotwal had just about been able to get the bodies cremated. But the smell of death still lingered over the stricken city.

The soldiers of Nadir were paid out of the gold obtained at Delhi. The officers were lavishly rewarded while the soldiers got 18 months pay, one-third of which was by way of arrears, one-third an advance, and the remaining six months' a bounty. He did not believe in spoiling his soldiers with too much gold, lest they grew soft and luxurious. The camp followers were not forgotten. Each received Rs. 60 by way of salary and Rs. 100 as bounty. But the greatest beneficiaries were the people of Iran itself, who were remitted all taxes for three years.[7]

But easy come easy go. At the end of Nadir's brief reign and the troubles that followed, Iran was, even more than India, a devastated country. And the princess whom Nasrullah carried back with so much pride was destined to end up in the harem of Ahmad Shah Abdali, the founder of Afghanistan.

Summer was approaching and Nadir was anxious to return and resume his wars against the Khans of Tartary and the Sublime Porte. On 1 May he held a grand levee at Delhi to which Muhammad Shah and his nobles were also invited. *Khillats* were distributed, and with his own hand be placed a crown on the head of Muhammad Shah and fastened a jewelled sword to his waist.

The grateful emperor, his kingdom restored bowed in gratitude and declared that as the *Shahanshah* had made him 'a second time master of a throne and a crown' he was offering him all his trans-Indus possessions.

Thus Kabul and Sind, besides Kashmir and Tattah (which lay astride the Indus) were lost to the heirs of Babar. The revenues of certain districts of the northern Punjab amounting to Rs. 20 lakh which were traditionally dedicated to meeting the expenses of the garrison at Kabul would also continue to be remitted to that province though they would remain administratively with the suba of Punjab and part of the empire of Hind.

Then Nadir had an admonitory address read out in which he advised the Indian umara to obey their emperor. It was full of homilies on good government. He also decreed that henceforth the coinage would again bear the name of Muhammad Shah and the *khutba* would be read in his name. Firmans containing the substance of his orders were sent off to Nasir Jang in the Deccan, Raja Shahu and Baji Rao.

On 5 May he started on the homeward journey. He also took with him-like Timur more than 300 years earlier—hundreds of stone-masons, sculptors, carpenters, blacksmiths and the like in the hope of building a city like Shahjahanabad in Iran. The bulk of the captives, who were promised handsome salaries and permission to return after three years, were able to escape on the march.

A large portion of his spoils was plundered on the way by the sturdy Jat peasantry and the Sikhs. The latter, twenty years after the suppression of Banda Bahadur, had taken full advantage of the eclipse of the imperial administration following the Persian invasion.

Zakariya Khan, the governor of the Punjab escorted the Shah upto the river Chenab. Nadir was pleased with his services and at the leave-taking ceremony asked if there was anything he could grant him. To his eternal credit Zakariya asked nothing for himself, only the liberty of the thousands of captives, malc and female, which the Shah and his soldiers were taking with them. And to his credit, the Shah granted him the boon.

The visitation was over at last.

NOTES

1. Tabatabai, *Seir Mutaqherin*, i, p. 315.
2. Irvine, *Later Mughals*, ii, p. 367. Mirza Mahdi, *Jahankusha*, p. 357.
3. Kaul, *Historic Delhi*, p. 355 (quoting Fraser's History of Nadir Shah).
4. Elliot and Dowson, vii, p. 63. Rustam Ali places the figure at 5,000. Karim Khan in his *Bayan-i-Waqiai*, gives 3,000.
5. Irvine, ii, p. 364. *Jahankusha*, 355.
6. Irvine, ii, p. 373.
7. Ibid., ii, p. 374. *Jahankusha*, p. 361.

CHAPTER 21

The Morning After

The invasion of Nadir inevitably invites comparison with that of Timur. But while over three centuries separate the two, there are barely 150 years between the latter and the advent of the Mongols with its sombre backdrop of ruined cities and pyramids of skulls. Timur is said to have massacred a hundred thousand captives outside Delhi merely because they were indiscreet enough to exhibit excitement at the possibility of liberation during an attack by an army of the Delhi sultan. If the contemporary historians are to be believed, almost the entire population of Delhi was massacred or enslaved, 'and for two whole months not a bird moved wing in Delhi'.[1] This pattern of pillage and massacre was repeated in a score of smaller towns in northern India, such as Meerut, Bhatner, Dipalpur, Pak Pattan and so on, where the passage of the all-devouring army was followed by pestilence and famine.

By comparison Nadir's invasion was less brutal. Of course, death and devastation marked the route of the invading army and little that was valuable escaped the marauding Qizilbash horse. But the massacres were never as extensive or as pointless as Timur's. Even the notorious Delhi blood-bath was strictly a punitive reprisal. It was limited to specified wards and the slaughter, by all accounts, did not last more than six to nine hours. In comparison, descriptions of Timur's sack read like those of a typical barbarian onslaught during which the killing and looting went on for days. But this is not to suggest that the world was becoming a kinder place. The sack of Mathura by Ahmad Shah Abdali in 1758, and that of Delhi in 1857 by the *Sahiban-i-Inglishia*, would show that the beast in man was alive and kicking.

The Nadir Shahi invasion, in another sense, had far-reaching effects. Timur looted and massacred and returned home but there was no loss of territory. Nadir, on the other hand, acquired Kashmir, Sind and the Kabul subas, besides levying a permanent charge of Rs. 20 lakh per annum on the revenues of Lahore. The Punjab was never free from the threat of invasion thereafter and each eastward foray of an Afghan army would cause tremors all the way down to Lucknow and Calcutta. Within a couple of decades the Punjab would be lost, annexed to the Durrani kingdom which rose from the wreck of the Afsharid empire. The devastating effects of the Durrani invasions sealed whatever hope there might have been of a recovery for the Chaghtai empire of Hind.

After the nightmare of the Persian invasion one would have expected the emperor to make at least some effort to arrest the slide to disaster, but nothing of this kind happened. A few meeting and discussions were held in the beginning but there was no serious attempt in this direction. If anything, the factional infighting became more bitter than ever. The history of the empire now becomes the account of the factional struggles between these groups of rival umaras—at first divided between the Irani and Turani factions, and in the last phase between individuals.

The two persons most responsible for the catastrophe were Samsam ud-Daulah Khan-i-Dauran and Burhan ul-Mulk Saadat Khan, if we leave out that ageing voluptuary Qamr ud-Din as inconsequential. Khan-i-Dauran had refused to recognize the Persian threat and had starved Nasir Khan and Zakariya of funds so that neither of them was able to offer effective resistence when Nadir launched his attack. Khan-i-Dauran was the leader of the Hindustanis and far more interested in embarassing his colleagues of the opposite faction. Nasir Khan, moreover, had been a protégé of the first Amir Khan against whom Khan-i-Dauran had nursed a personal grouse and, as a result, was even less inclined to bail him out. As for Zakariya, he was a Turk and a close relative of the wazir. The embarassment and disgrace of a colleague belonging to the opposite group took precedence over the defence of the empire.

Saadat Khan was the leader of the Irani faction and, piqued at being passed over for appointment to the post of Amir-ul-Umara, he had incited Nadir Shah to scrap the agreement already reached with the Indian emperor and to march on Delhi. Both Khan-i-Dauran and Saadat Khan were brave men. But inspite of their undoubted bravery both these nobles, one an Indian,[2] and the other a Persian, had betrayed the larger interest of the empire for what they perceived as their own.

One might expect that after all this the Irani party would have been finished, but it was far from the reality. Two of the emperor's favourites, Amir Khan Umdat ul-Mulk (son of the first Amir Khan) and Ishaq Khan, were Persians.

Amir Khan was from a well connected Persian family which had been in the service of the Durbar-i-Mualla for generations. Though brave, he had never shown much talent in administration, but he had a ready and facile wit, with a particular turn for the *bon mot*.

Muhammad Ishaq Khan, entitled Mutman ud-Daulah, originally a companion of Amir Khan, was introduced by the latter to the emperor. Nadir was so impressed with his speech and manners that he declared to Muhammad that he ought to be his wazir. During the tense days that followed the clash at Karnal he and Amir Khan were constantly with the emperor. Because of his intimacy with the latter he was raised to the rank of 6,000 with the post of diwan of the Khalsa and Tan and others became jealous of his rapid promotions. He died early in 1740 and in him the emperor lost a sincere friend and adviser. His son, known by the same name, was destined to succeed him in the emperor's affections and in 1747 was likewise raised to the diwani of the Khalsa. His daughter was married to Shuja ud-Daulah and is famous in history as the Bahu Begum.

Asad Yar Khan, another protégé of Amir Khan, rose to high favour and office with a rank of 6,000 and the title of Asad ud-Daulah in November 1739. He was cultured, affable, and agreeable, never turning a suitor from his door empty-handed. Although Amir Khan eventually broke-off with him, he remained faithful to the end.

Abul Mansur Khan Safdar Jang was the nephew, son-in-law and heir of Burhan ul-Mulk. Already his deputy, he was appointed to the suba of Awadh after his uncle's death and in due course became the champion of the Irani party. His importance lay in his military strength. He maintained a force of 20,000 Qizilbash cavalary which, after the Persian invasion, constituted the best cavalry in the north. He took great care that all the troopers and officers employed should be Mughals, for the most part Turkmans from Khurasan—hence the appellation of Qizilbash[3]—and paid them much more than what was normally paid to Indian soldiers. With Maratha cavalry raiding as far as Bihar, the growing Rohilla power in the Ganga-Yamuna doab, and the general collapse of law and order, he soon came to be recognized as a major player in northern India.

Safdar Jang's career too had been launched by Amir Khan and it was at his behest that the former was appointed Mir Atish in 1744. This gave him an ever-growing influence at the court, as a result of which his appointment as wazir, after the death of Qamr ud-Din, seemed axiomatic.

While the inner caucus of the emperor's friends consisted almost entirely of Persians, outwardly the Turanis remained in firm control. Qamr ud-Din Khan Itimad ud-Daulah remained wazir till his death while Asaf Jah was the Vakil-i-Mutlaq and Amir-ul-Umara with the office of Bakhshi-ul-Mamalik. But Asaf Jah was anxious to return to the Deccan where his son was displaying the usual restlessness and impatience at having to remain, apparently forever, his father's deputy. The nizam, now over

80 years old was till vigorous. At his request the emperor relieved him of the charge of first bakhshi, which was conferred on his son Ghazi ud-Din along which the rank and dignity of Amir-ul-Umara.

Amir Khan had set his heart on becoming the wazir and the emperor also wanted to get rid of Qamr ud-Din. But this was easier said than done. Individually, Qamr ud-Din was a nonentity but as the symbolic head of the Turani faction at the court he could not be wished away that easily. So it was decided to wait till the nizam's departure.

When the nizam marched out on 3 April 1740 and camped at Jaisinghpura, in the suburbs of Delhi, to complete his preparations for the long march, to the Deccan, Amir Khan could not hide his excitement. He began to speak and act as if the insignia had already been conferred on him. Sensing that something was afoot, Qamr ud-Din sought the advice of the nizam, his cousin and acknowledged head of the family. The latter advised that he should quit office and leave with him for the Deccan since, anyway, the prime minister's post was now but a useless honour.

The crisis was precipitated by an act of Amir Khana, when, to meet the financial crisis of the state, he advised the emperor to rigorously enforce the old rules of escheat. About this time Badr ud-Din, one of the wazir's sons, died, leaving behind property worth Rs. 12.5 lakh. Amir Khan called for the rent rolls of his jagirs with a view to opening resumption proceedings. The wazir protested to Amir Khan but the latter replied insolently: 'So long as the shadow of my master rests on my head I am prepared to confront Jibreel (Gabriel) and Michael, what to speak of lords like you and Asaf Jah!'[4]

On receiving this insolent reply the wazir sent in his resignation. He also left his residence and joined his cousin who was still encamped at Jaisinghpura.

The emperor consulted Ishaq Khan and asked him to give his own unbiased view of the matter to which he opined:

> Although Amir Khan is an amir, and the son of an amir, and a brave soldier and administrator, yet he is considered by the nobility and people of Hindustan as light in character and manner, known more for his wit and repartee than for courage and experience. But Asaf Jah and Itimad ud Daulah are highly regarded by all the people and obedience to them is considered a gain and a blessing. In my humble opinion it would be unwise to break with such chiefs in reliance upon men like us.[5]

This was all that the emperor wanted. Somebody from Amir Khan's own inner circle of friends and confidants should tell him that the course he had embarked upon was wrong, so that he could gracefully back out from the confrontation

The next day he told Amir Khan that he had changed his mind and decided to retain Qamr ud-Din as wazir. Amir Khan protested, but the emperor was adamant. Visualizing that the game was up, he went to the nizam's camp to beg forgiveness. Amir Khan presented himself like a malefactor, but he insisted that the real conspirators were Ishaq Khan and the other nobles. The nizam and wazir saw through this charade and the nizam advised him that as serious differences had arisen between him and the wazir, it was not desirable that he should remain at the court and he should retire to Allahabad of which he was the absentee governor.

Amir Khan procrastinated, hoping for the dust to settle, but the nizam also put off his departure until he should be gone. Eventually, seeing that there was no option, Amir Khan left and, finally, on 27 July 1740, the nizam started on his southward march.

Meanwhile, on 18 April 1740, Ishaq Khan died and, at least for some time, the court became free of the Irani influences.

But not for long. At Allahabad Amir Khan discovered Safdar Jang, his neighbour and subedar of the adjoining suba of Awadh, and decided that he was the man of the future. He had proved his military skill during the anti-Maratha operations in Hindustan in 1736 and now, with 20,000 disciplined Qizilbash cavalry, was the most powerful potentate in Upper India. Amir Khan described him in glowing terms to the emperor, suggesting that he was best-suited to be entrusted with the governorship of Bengal, the old milchcow of the empire.

After the death of Murshid Quli Khan, also known as Jafar Khan in 1727, this province had fallen upon troubled times. He had been succeeded in turn by Shuja Khan, his son-in-law, and Sarfaraz Khan, his grandson, and finally, in April 1740, by Alivardi Khan (officially entitled Hisam ud-Daulah Mahabat Jang) who had risen to the viceregal masnad by assassinating Sarfaraz Khan.

Although the surplus revenues of Bengal (which also included Bihar and Orissa) continued to be remitted regularly by the governors, the province was virtually independent and was governed with little interference from Delhi, the office of governor or diwan having become more or less hereditary in the family of Murshid Quli Khan. Since the appointment of the latter as diwan—in the earlier period the governors or nazims, who were distinct from the diwans, were usually princes of the imperial house—no outsider had been appointed, and the Qila-i-Mualla had cheerfully acquiesced in the *fait accompli* and letters of appointment would be sent in the name of whoever was successful in establishing his control in Murshidabad. Moreover, Khan-i-Dauran had been close to Shuja Khan, while Alivardi had old ties with Ishaq.

Amir Khan thought there was an opportunity to upset the apple cart in his master's favour. Alivardi had delayed the submission of his predecessor's property returns for the escheat proceedings. He was also embroiled in struggles with the Marathas who, led by the Bhonsles of Nagpur, had been raiding Bihar and Orissa. Amir Khan saw in this embarassment of Alivardi an opportunity for the emperor to realize the escheated estates of the deceased nobles. Any inflow was welcome to the impoverished imperial treasury and to strengthen the position of Safdar Jang whom he wanted to build up as a counterpoise to the armed strength of the Turani party.

The emperor authorized Safdar Jang to enter Bihar, and, if necessary, Bengal as well, to assist Alivardi in clearing out the Deccani raiders and putting the affairs of that province in order. As a reward for his services he was promised the two imperial forts of Rohtasgarh and Chunar.

Alivardi understood the sinister intent behind this move. Luckily for him, he was able to drive out the Marathas on his own, and he wrote back to Delhi that there was no need for the assistance of Safdar Jang. However, Safdar Jang had already started on his march and entered Bihar, but finding that there was no longer any excuse for remaining there, and having received the emperor's orders directing him to return to his suba, he had to return.

The march of Safdar Jang had accomplished nothing. It was a useless outlay of money and, far from giving any relief, his troops had caused more alarm to those whom they had come to rescue. But Amir Khan wrote such glowing descriptions of the impact of this incursion that the emperor called both Amir Khan and Safdar Jang to the court.

The occasion was a kind of conference to discuss ways and means of tackling the Maratha raids which had become an annual occurence in the eastern provinces. Many Rajput princes were also called. Amir Khan arrived in November 1743 to be followed by Safdar Jang a few days later. The latter made his entry at the head of 10,000 cavalry, splendidly attired, and made a tremendous impact on the emperor and his court.

In June, a few months later, the mir atish, Sad ud-Din Khan expired. The post was important as, besides heading the artillery establishment, this officer was also the military commandant of the Qila-i-Mualla and ultimately responsible for the padishah's security within the fort. Sad ud-Din's son, Hafiz ud-Din, a protégé of the wazir, had already been appointed to his late father's post, but Amir Khan persuaded the emperor to remove him and appoint Safdar Jang. The emperor, who was strongly anti-Turani, was more than willing, and on 11 March orders were issued appointing Safdar Jang as mir atish. The Irani influence again became paramount, the wazir and Amir-ul-Umara being put in the shade.

In 1745, at the instance of Safdar Jang, a campaign was launched against the Rohillas of the Ganga-Yamuna doab. The emperor also took personal interest in arranging the marriage of Safdar Jang's son, Shuja ud-Daulah with the sister of Ishaq Khan II Najm ud-Daulah, celebrated in history as Bahu Begum, and whose name was destined to figure so prominently in the impeachment of Warren Hastings.

The year 1745 also saw the death of another royal favourite, Asad Yar Khan. He had, with the consent of the emperor, raised a body of Mughal cavalry which came to be known as the 'Shamshir Dagh', from the mark of the shamshir or scimitar which was branded on the flanks of its mounts. The division, numbering about 10,000 horse, was raised in 1740 after the withdrawal of Nadir Shah when the emperor was virtually defenceless and without an army. But in due course many of the old soldiers of the household regiments returned, and the additional burden of the Shamshir Dagh (Rs. 30 lakh per annum) seemed too heavy. Meanwhile, Amir Khan who had once been Asad Yar Khan's patron had fallen out with his former protégé. He was jealous of his growing influence and the respect that he commanded, chiefly on account of his disciplined cavalry.

On the pretext of economy, Amir Khan persuaded the emperor to agree to the retrenchment of half of the Shamshir Dagh troops. To further humiliate him, Asad Yar Khan was deprived of Kashmir, which he administered through a deputy, and the province was bestowed upon Safdar Jang. Finally, the Shamshir Dagh was ordered to be disbanded altogether. Its pay was in arrears by nine months. Asad Khan pleaded in vain that at least this sum (amounting to Rs. 22.5 lakh) should be discharged by the imperial exchequer, but Amir Khan laughed it off saying that the troops had not served any purpose. For four and a half years they had been sitting idle; why should they be given any arrears?[6]

When this wisecrack of the nawab came to the knowledge of the soldiers they marched around the palace in riotous demonstration raising angry slogans against him. But Asad Khan at length pacified them by assuring that he would endeavour to pay their arrears from his own pocket. He sold everything, down to his household goods, but it was not enough and creditors harassed him until his death in April 1745.

Amir Khan's day of reckoning was not far off either. His pride and insolence seemed unbounded and he began to see himself as a dictator like Syed Abdullah and Hussain Ali Khan. Once Roz Afzun Khan, the emperor's head eunuch, ventured to object to some words of Amir Khan's as being disrespectful to their common master. This immediately brought forth an explosion from Amir Khan who declared that if that slave was to be permitted to speak to him thus, he would forthwith quit the court and would never enter its precincts again. Amir Khan demanded the removal of Roz Afzun to which the emperor reluctantly agreed. But the emperor was as tired of Amir Khan's overbearing ways as the rest of the court. Not only was the emperor fed up with him but he also suspected his intentions, for Amir Khan had some time earlier committed the serious indiscretion of visiting the shahzadas confined in the Salimgarh.

A suitable person who had long been nursing a grudge against the nawab and was on the look out for just such an opportunity was available. On the prompting of the eunuch this desperado, who was a former employee of Amir Khan, attacked him on his next visit to the court and killed him with a single thrust of a dagger on 25 December 1746.

What follows is worth describing in detail for in the years to come such scenes would be oft repeated. Amir Khan's attendants lifted his corpse and hurried home to his mansion. There his soldiers, whose salary had not been paid for fourteen months, did not allow the body to be removed for burial, until their claims were satisfied. The gates of his mansion were also shut so that the umara who had come to condole found themselves shut in.

The emperor had also sent his bailiffs to attach the property of the deceased by way of escheat. Thcy too were denied entry. The emperor, furious, sent soldiers after them with orders to clear the way by force, but the soldiers demurred. The protesters were only asking for their dues; tomorrow, they might well find themselves in the same plight. By the ancient custom of the country any creditor could hold up a funeral procession until his claim was discharged.

The impasse continued for four days. Ultimately Safdar Jang, taking pity on the fate of his former patron, sent emissaries to assure the soldiers that their master had agreed to stand surety. Only then was the body allowed to be taken for burial. But his relatives and mourners were still not allowed to leave his mansion until the auction of his effects was completed. According to the *Seir* he was found to have accumulated a huge hoard, of which the jewels alone were said to be worth Rs. 50 lakh. These were taken by the emperor at the unfair valuation of Rs. 12 lakh to settle the government's claims for outstanding advances from the treasury.[7]

Amir Khan had no children. Yet he had accumulated this vast board while his soldiers and servants were starving. Indian noblemen habitually kept their soldiers and servants in arrears because this was the best way of ensuring their loyalty. If their pay was up to date, if was felt that they would not have any interest whether their master lived or died!

As for the Rangila Badshah, he continued to amuse himself with his women who were numbered in their thousands. Surely, when his wazir boasted a harem of 4,000 beautiful women and handsome boys, the emperor could not do with less. Some of them, besides being skilled in the arts of love as described in the *Kama Sutra*—being from the families of professional courtesans—were also skilled acrobats and gymnasts who could contort themselves into complex formations to resemble animals like elephants and horses and the sovereign of Hind would then ride them.

But he was no longer his old self. Opuim had enfeebled him. He was emaciated and looked much older than his years. With the gradual failing of his virility an air of melancholy settled on him and he became increasingly fond of the society of pirs and faqirs and would often visit their *khanqahs* and *takkiahs* to hold discourse with them.

Although the emperor was himself a cypher, he was universally loved. Even Asaf Jah, who was an extremely serious person, was never rude or disrespectful towards him. Naturally timid and wavering, the emperor was free from insolence or pride and never behaved in a capricious manner or indulged in wanton cruelty. He rarely gave his consent to the shedding of blood.

So the government stumbled along erratically, presided over by this gentle and affable voluptuory as emperor, with an equally amiable sensualist as prime minister. The state of the empire was beyond repair. No lessons had been learnt from the Persian invasion. It had been dismissed from the consciousness of the men who governed India like a night-mare that was over. But those who learn nothing from their mistakes are destined to repeat them and the reign closed with the intrusion of another foreign conqueror, Ahmad Shah Durrani. His depredations beginning from the year 1748 dominated the reigns of the next two emperors.

NOTES

1. Briggs, *History of the Rise of the Mahommedan Power in India*, i, p. 284.
2. Khan-i-Dauran's ancestors had come from Badakhshan but his Persian was poor and he was one of the pillars of the Hindostani Party. He had a particular weakness for Rajputs.
3. The distinctive headgear of the Qizilbashes was a tall red hat. Qizil means red. 'The Qizilbashes are considered to be the descendants of the captives given to

Shaikh Haidar by Taimerlane; they wore the red caps assumed by those captives as a mark of distinction, and are considered as the best troops of the Persian armies; in Turkish the word has become a word of abuse, specially applied to Persians' (Steingass's *Persian Dictionary*).

4. Sarkar, *Fall of the Mughal Empire*, i, p. 28. Shakir, *Tazkira*, p. 84.
5. Sarkar, i, p. 30. Tabatabai, i, pp. 320-1.
6. Sarkar, i, p. 38. Harcharan Das, *Chahar Gulzar-i-Shujai*, pp. 373a-84a.
7. Tabatabai, iii, p. 244.

CHAPTER 22

Creeping Chaos

Before we come to Ahmad Shah Durrani, it would be desirable to go into a little more detail about the rise of the Rohilla power in north India and the Maratha penetration into Bengal and Rajasthan.

The Rohillas were the latest lot of Afghan settlers who had been moving into the western part of the Ganga Valley from the barren hills of Kabul ever since the beginning of the eighteenth century.

Most of these new entrants settled in the region known as Katehar, i.e. the old Mughal sarkars of Bareilly and Moradabad, with Farrukhabad at the southern extreme.

The Bangash principality was the first to be established as an organized state, and its founder was Muhammad Khan Bangash—the family name being derived from a hilly tract in eastern Afghanistan. His father had come to India during the reign of Aurangzeb and settled in Katehar where Muhammad Khan was born in 1665. He started his career as a free-booter, ocasionally hiring out his band to local zamindars in their local struggles. However, his big chance came in 1712 when he joined Farrukhsiyar while the latter was on his march to seize the sovereignty from Jahandar Shah. After the victory Muhammad Khan was rewarded with a grant of land on which he founded the town of Farrukhabad, which he named after his royal patron. He remained loyal but his power grew by virtue of his own strength and the increasing weakness of the imperial authority. He died in 1743 leaving behind only one legal wife and 2,600 concubines.[1] His eldest son Qaim Khan succeeded him.

Daud Khan, the founder of the Rohilla power in Katehar, on the other hand, had to carve out his future entirely by the strength of his own sword, sometimes in opposition to the imperial authority, and sometimes in connivance with the court factions. He too, like Muhammad Khan, started his life as a bandit, and with the wealth gained was able to collect a number of horsemen and raise a small mud-fort. Soon the local Rajput zamindars started seeking his assistance in their private struggles over land and boundaries. The Mughal faujdar at Bareilly was not seen in high esteem by these local magnates. The northern Terai was held by the raja of Kumaon, who ruled from his capital at Almora in the Himalayas, with Kashipur as his principal outpost in the Terai. Shahjahanpur was the other notable town and its environs were held by the descendents of another Afghan family, settled in the area since the time of Shah Jahan.

In 1825 a local Pathan, Sabir Shah, rebelled against the imperial authority and proclaimed himself the king. Daud, acting as an agent of Devi Chand of Kumaon, was directed to assist Sabir Shah as Devi Chand hoped to gain from the rebellion by adding the southern Terai to his domains. But the imperial forces under Azmat Ullah Khan, the faujdar of Moradabad, moved swiftly to crush the uprising. Before the decisive battle, Daud Khan had arrived at an understanding with the faujdar and refrained from joining the battle which took place at Nagina. Daud was summoned to Almora by Devi Chand where he was tortured and executed for his treachery.[2]

Daud was succeeded by his adopted son Ali Muhammad. He was readily accepted by the followers of Daud who now numbered a good 500 horsemen. He also maintained the newly forged connection with the imperial faujdar and it was about this time that he established his seat at Aonla. His strength grew, and by 1730 he was strong enough to be approached by Muhammad Khan Bangash for help during his campaign against Chhattarsal Bundela.

Through Azmat Ullah, Ali Muhammed was able to secure the patronage of the wazir, Qamr ud-Din, from whom he received further grants. For services rendered in the action against Syed Saif ud-Din Khan (another brother of the famous king-makers), he was enrolled as a regular mansabdar, with the right to kettledrums.

During the invasion of Nadir Shah, like many others, he held back the revenues which brought him into conflict with the authorities. Raja Harnand, the wazir's deputy, determined on a show-down with him. Ali Muhammad wanted to avoid the confrontation but Harnand was just as anxious to force a decision and in a clash that took place on 15 March 1742. Harnand was defeated and killed. All the booty of the imperial camp fell into the hands of Ali Muhammad, alongwith the entire district of Katehar. The wazir considered it prudent to recognize his *de facto* control and after a nominal submission and suitable gifts he was recognized by the wazir as his deputy in Katehar which soon came to be known as Rohilkhand.

By this time the Afghan population had increased because the troubled times that followed the Persian conquest of Kabul had driven many

Afghans to seek their fortunes in India. Among them was Hafiz Rahmat Khan, the son of Shah Alam Khan, Daud's erstwhile master who had incidentally been killed by the latter because he would not stop trying to persuade Daud to return with him to the Afghan hills, which the latter found irksome. Ali Muhammad had been Daud's accomplice in the murder but now he welcomed Hafiz Rahmat who became one of his trusted lieutenants.

The rise of this energetic advanturer along the borders of Awadh made Safdar Jang uncomfortable. The Bangash Afghans were already entrenched along the south-eastern borders of his province and there were many people at the imperial court also who looked upon the rise of the Afghans, so close to Delhi, as a threat to the imperial dynasty.

Under such circumstances the emperor forced his indolent wazir to set out with Safdar Jang against the Rohillas, and he himself joined them. It was notorious that the Rohillas enjoyed the secret support of the wazir and the relations between him and the mir atish (Safdar Jang) were tense. Later when Qaim Khan, the Bangash chief, joined the army, dissensious increased, the Bangash joining hands with the wazir to frustrate the efforts of Salar Jung.

It was the middle of May 1745 when the imperial army reached Bangarh, the Rohilla stronghold, and invested it. It was the height of summer and except for Safdar Jang no one was eager to press the issue to extremes. Ali Muhammad too had no desire to openly defy the imperial authority and the wazir was only too anxious to find a compromise which would leave the power of the Rohilla basically intact while the face of the emperor could be saved by the personal submission of Ali Muhammad. All the nobles were also keen to see an early end to the campaign so that they could return to the comforts of Delhi.

With the wazir to safeguard his interests, Ali Muhammad decided to surrender. He agreed to give up all his property and territory in exchange for the emperor's pardon. On 20 June the emperor started on the journey back with the Rohilla chief a prisoner and his power effectively destroyed. But not for long. Soon the wazir procured for his protégé the post of faujdar of Sirhind.

Many of Ali Muhammad's old companions and followers from Rohilkhand joined him at Sirhind where he was able to prove his worth by rigorously suppressing rebellious zamindars. But his tenure in Sirhind was destined to be short. In 1747 Ahmad Shah Durrani crossed the Indus and invaded the Punjab and was rumoured to be heading for Delhi. Some chroniclers allege that Ali Muhammad abandoned his post and fled to his native Rohilkhand but according to others—and this seems more likely—the emperor was apprehensive of his loyalty in the face of another Afghan army, and it was decided to post him back to Rohilkhand, his former charge.

He did not survive the restoration for long and died of dropsy on 14 September 1748. But the Rohilla state had been firmly re-established. Safdar Jang and his successor, Shuja ud-Daulah, continued their feud with the Rohillas until the latter were finally destroyed with the help of British auxilliaries—but that was still many decades in the future. Before that could come about Safdar Jang would be overthrown and Najib Khan, the Rohilla chief and heir to Ali Muhammad's heritage would become Amir ul-Umara and dictator of Delhi.

Murshid Quli Khan, governor of the triple province of Bengal, Bihar and Orissa was succeeded by his son-in-law Shuja Khan in 1727, who in turn was followed by his son Sarfaraz in 1739. But barely a year later he was overthrown by Alivardi Khan, an ambitious nobleman who had entered the imperial service in Bengal under Murshid Quli Khan.

Sarfaraz was pleasure-loving, indolent and debauched, without any compensating administrative qualities, and Aliwardi had no difficulty in winning support among the provincial bureaucracy. Sarfaraz was killed in a furiously contested engagement at Jharia on 10 April 1740, and soon after, with the help of connections at court, Alivardi was appointed governor of Bengal along with its dependencies of Bihar and Orissa.

Alivardi's term was however a troubled one, for with his accession commenced the Maratha invasions of the eastern suba.

Raghoji Bhonsle, the Maratha chief of Nagpur, after failing to establish his ascendancy at Poona, where the Peshwa had proved too wily for him, now turned his gaze eastwards and started raiding across the thick forests of Berar towards Orissa, Bihar and Bengal. He was helped by the confused state of affairs in those provinces after the usurpation of Alivardi Khan. In Orissa the deputy governor was a brother-in-law of the late Sarfaraz. He refused to accept Alivardi's nominee and drove him out with the help of Maratha auxilliaries in 1741.

There was a full scale invasion of Bengal in 1742 led by Bhaskar Rao, the Bhonsle's minister. There were more invasions to follow in 1743, 1744, 1745, and lastly in 1748. In 1742 there also occured the incursion of Safdar Jang, ostensibly for the purpose of assisting Alivardi Khan in driving out the Deccani bargirs, and in 1745 and 1748 there were Afghan risings in Bihar. In 1745 the Afghan risings were led by Mustafa Khan who hoped to become independent governor of Bihar. In 1748 the cause was Zain ud-Din, Alivardi's nephew and deputy governor at Patna, who sought to enlist the support of the Afghan sardars in a bid to seize Bengal from his uncle. Ultimately, however, he was killed by the Afghans.

Bengal, once the richest province of the empire suffered severely as a result of these Maratha incursions and internal disturbances. The revenue collections declined and the ravages of the Marathas earned them a fearful reputation. Like locusts, their bargirs laid waste whatever lay in their path. They exhibited a particular propensity for gang-rape, so that at their approach men of means would send their women and families away. In 1751 Alivardi Khan concluded a treaty by which he agreed to pay *chauth* amounting to Rs. 12 lakh annually, on condition that they would never set foot in Bengal again. But this did not put an end to the Maratha raids, for the Marathas regarded treaties lightly. Besides, Orissa was lost, the deputy at Cuttack was now a Maratha nominee, and the surplus revenue of that region was used to defray the cost of the occupying Maratha force.

Soon after Nadir Shah's departure Asaf Jah received the news that his son Nasir Jang, had rebelled. After having obtained for his other son, Ghazi ud-Din, recognition from the emperor as his deputy in Delhi, besides the post of Mir Bakhshi with the attached dignity of Amir-ul-Umara, which since the death of Khan-i-Dauran had been vested in himself, he left for Deccan to re-assert his authority.

Learning of his father's advance, Nasir Jang at first sent him a message to return to Delhi and to leave the Deccan in his hands. But the nizam was in no mood to abdicate, just yet, to satisfy the ambition of his impatient son. He offered him a pardon and the suba of Bijapur if he would submit, but this offer was spurned by Nasir Jang. Eventually, a battle took place and Nasir was captured. Later he was pardoned and restored to his former dignities and posted to Bijapur as per the earlier offer.

After dealing with his son, the nizam marched through, Karnataka (which at that time meant Tamil Nadu rather than the modern state of Karnataka) at the head of 80,000 cavalry and 20,000 infantry. Karnataka was in a state of disorder and 'every holder of a pargannah had set himself up as a nawab'.[3] Tiruchirapalli, which had been seized by a Maratha, Murari Rao Ghorpade of Gooty, was recovered, after a long siege, in August 1744. After appointing Anwar ud-Din Khan as the governor, he returned to Hyderabad where he died in 1748 at the age of 78.

His death plunged the Deccan again into civil war as Nasir Jang's pretensions were challenged by his nephew, Muzaffar Jang. Closely linked with this struggle, and very much a part of it, was the first of the Carnatic wars in which the English and the French also played a vital role and which laid the foundations of British rule in south India. In such a melee the Marathas could not but be participants. But the story of that struggle, and the wars that followed, belongs more properly to the annals of Fort St. George rather than those of the Qila-i-Mualla.

In Rajasthan the Rajput princes had withdrawn from Imperial politics and retired to their ancient principalities. Some of the minor princes still served in the imperial armies but the great lords of Amber and Marwar had left the field. Sawai Jai Singh had served for many years as governor of the Agra and Malwa subas—both key provinces—but he had served his master ill.

Jai Singh did very little to defend the empire against the Marathas and one could well allege that he connived at handing over the province to them. After Malwa was finally lost, he retired to his seat and occupied himself with building his new capital of Jaipur, and embellishing his harem, until he died of a 'loathsome' disease.

He succeeded in forcing the chiefs of Shekhawati to acknowledge his overlordship and also in enforcing his will over Bundi. In Shekhawati, the house of Amber had old historical claims, but over Bundi there were none. However, he set about brazenly to establish his ascendancy over the lesser states in his neighbourhood.

The decline of imperial authority had put in peril the independence of the lesser states of Rajasthan. The avenues for preferment having dried up at the Qila-i-Mualla, the great magnates of Mewar, Marwar and Amber now turned upon their weaker neighbours, and indeed their own kinsmen, to establish and expand their spheres of influence. Civil wars broke out in many of the states, and there were disputed successions in nearly every principality.

In 1708, Sawai Jai Singh had married a daughter of Rana Amar Singh of Mewar and it was part of the marriage contract that the children of that union would have precedence over all others in the matter of succession to the *gaddi*. At the same time, a compact was entered into by all three princes of Mewar, Marwar and Amber, that henceforth they would not give their daughters in marriage to the emperors and that the offspring of their daughters would take precedence over their children through other wives. This disturbed the usual rule of primogeniture and the death of Jai Singh was inevitably followed by a struggle between Ishwari Singh, his eldest son, and Madho Singh, son of the Sisodia rani from Mewar.

In Marwar, Maharaja Ajit Singh's murder by his second son Bakht

Singh in 1724 was followed by the accession of Abhai Singh. Abhai Singh had been appointed governor of Gujarat vice Sarbuland Khan in 1729 but the times were troubled and the court of Satara had apportioned Gujarat to the share of two Maratha chiefs, Pilaji Gaikwad and Khande Rao. After losing Gujarat in two years Abhai Singh had retreated to his homeland and attacked his kinsman, the chief of Bikaner. Bakht Singh who was chief of Nagor, an appange of Marwar, was always on the lookout to overthrow his brother Abhai. So he jumped into the fray on the side of his Rathor cousion, the raja of Bikaner. So did Jai Singh of Amber. Marwar remained a troubled state; there was fighting with the Daudputras of Bahawalpur, the Bhattis of Jaisalmer, and increasingly too with Jaipur, as each sought to prove that he was the greatest Rajput of them all.

With the struggle in Rajasthan becoming increasingly bitter and bloody, the Marathas could not be far away. The first Maratha invasion took place in 1734. During the next two years, while the struggle raged for Malwa, Maratha armies regularly swept through the Haraoti and the southern states of Rajasthan. When Baji Rao launched his thrust towards Delhi, it was again through Rajasthan that he retreated.

As early as 1736, Mewar had been drawn into the Maratha sphere of influence and the Maharana had bound himself to pay an annual tribute of Rs. 1.5 Lakh. In 1747, he repudiated the treaty and plunged into the civil war in Jaipur on behalf of his nephew, Madho Singh. But on his own death in 1751, a similar war broke out for the Mewar succession as well, and one of the contenders called the Marathas to his aid.

It was in the 1750s that the Marathas really milked the states of Rajasthan for all they were worth. They did not differentiate between these ancient rulers of Hindu India and the other provinces of the empire. Unlike Akbar, they made no effort to harness their spirit and energy in the cause of establishing a Hindupad padishahi. No Rajput chief was ever associated in their campaigns or given a place of honour in their armies. Apart from Marathwada, their homeland in the Deccan, they made no effort to establish a credible government anywhere. The rest of India was merely one large hunting preserve which they felt they had the right to plunder at will. In their spirit and attitude they were scarcely less predatory than the Mongols of yore.

The civil wars of Rajasthan resulted in horrors that surpassed those of the Qila-i-Mualla. But the story of those gory events is the story of Rajasthan and its princes, the Qila-i-Mualla was not touched by them. If the Rajputs had turned their backs on the emperors of Hind, the latter too did not interfere. It was only in 1750 that Salabat Khan, the subedar of

Ajmer, attempted to intervene in the struggle between Bakht Singh and Ram Singh (the successor of Abhai Singh who had died in 1749). Soon after, Ajmer itself fell in the hands of Marwar. Not until the time of the Amir-ul-Umara Mirza Najaf Khan in the 1770s would an imperial army again venture into that region. For the time being, Rajasthan had withdrawn from the national scene.

NOTES

1. Sarkar, *Fall of the Mughal Empire*, i, p. 47.
2. Bannerjee and Ghose, *A Comprehensive History of India*, ix, p. 141.
3. Orme, *Military Transactions of the British Nation in Indostan*, i, p. 51.

CHAPTER 23

The first Invasion of Ahmad Shah Durrani

After his return from India, Nadir set off to conquer Bokhara and Khiva. Then followed a long contest with the Sublime Porte, fought all along the Ottoman frontier, from Mesopotamia to the Caucasian provinces and eastern Anatolia. During the later part his behavior became increasingly maniacal and he ordered massacres and executions at the slightest provocation. Reverses in Daghestan also shattered his reputation for invincibility and his governors started plucking up courage and revolting.

Nadir became increasingly distrustful of his Qizilbash officers. Ethnic Turks—like himself—from Khurasan they had from the beginning constituted the core of his all-conquering armies, but the Shah felt that they were becoming too presumptuous and over-bearing and suspected that they harboured intentions to supplant him on the throne of Persia. He started placing increasing reliance on a new set of bodyguards composed of Uzbegs and Afghans. Among these was one Ahmad Khan, a trusty and confidential slave whom he raised to the rank of a yassawal and to whom he entrusted his personal treasury.

It was at Kuchan, in the extreme north-east corner of Khurasan that Nadir decided to liquidate all his leading Qizilbash officers who he believed were conspiring against him. Giving orders to summon them for a conference the following day, he planned to have them massacred on arrival by his Afghan and Uzbeg bodyguards.

But the plot was leaked and the intended victims decided to forestall the Shah's coup. But so great was the terror inspired by the World Destroyer, that of the seventy sardars who set out only seventeen reached the Shah's tent, the remaining having lost their nerve and slunk back to their quarters.

But the task was accomplished with ease. Neither Nadir nor his guards were expecting the attack. The latter were easily overpowered and the Shah murdered in his bed. In the confused plundering that followed, Ahmad was able to seize a fair portion of the treasure, and rallying his fellow Afghans, fled towards Kandahar.

The assassination occured on 9 July 1747. In the next few months, Ahmad was able to seize the Afghan provinces of the Afsharid empire and was proclaimed sovereign with the title of Ahmad Shah Dur i-Durran, meaning 'pearl of pearls'—a title conferred on him by his pir, Shah Sabir. In common parlance he came to be known as the Durrani Padishah and his fellow clansmen dropped the old cognomen of Abdali in favour of Durrani.

At the time of the assassination of Nadir, Nasir Khan, subedar of Kabul, was on his way to Persia with a convoy of treasure bearing the revenue of Kabul, Sind and the assigned *mahals* of Punjab. This convoy was intercepted by Ahmad. He offered to retain Nasir as his governor but the offer was conditional on the latter remitting Rs. 5 lakh immediately on his return to Kabul. Nasir Khan was a man of all seasons. He had earlier served as the governor of Muhammad Shah, the Merry Monarch, and had continued in his old office on the request of Nadir. Therefore, serving Ahmad would be no great pain.

On his return, Nasir Khan called a meeting of the notables of Kabul. He himself had no cash. The amount would have to be raised by an impost on the wealthier gentry of the city and the tribal sardars, and it had to be done soon. But the Afghan is loth to part with money, and they promptly declared that it was impossible to raise such a sum.[1] When he reminded them that Ahmad was not likely to take 'no' for an answer, they declared that they would fight. On expressing his doubts they repeated their resolve using the most fearsome oaths. Seeing it was useless, Nasir dismissed the officers of Ahmad Shah who had accompanied him, letting them know that it was impossible for him to fulfil his part of the bargain.[2]

Ahmad hastened with an army to chastise Kabul. At his approach the sardars, who had so readily sworn to resist the Durrani Shah, quietly sneaked away to their homes in the hills. Nasir Khan, knowing fully well that he had not the means to resist, left for Peshawar, leaving his deputy behind, and after fortifying the passes to the plains. Ahmad easily occupied the city and after forcing the passes, advanced towards Peshawar. After resisting for a few days, Nasir Khan retreated into Hazara and thence to Lahore, which he reached in November 1747.

The Punjab was in a parlous state. The government of Muhammad Shah had learnt nothing from past experience and the Punjab border was as neglected as in 1739. The strong hand of Zakariya Khan had been removed by his death in 1745. During his reign law and order had been restored in the Punjab and banditry suppressed with a firm hand. The province was just beginning to recover from the effects of the Persian visitation.

Instead of promptly appointing a successor to the Punjab, politics and indecision intervened to undo much of Zakariya's good work. Zakariya Khan was closely related to the wazir. He was married to his sister, and his elder son, Yahya, was the wazir's son-in-law. At the suggestion of Nadir, the province had been enlarged to include Multan, which had formerly been an independent suba. The wazir now proposed to give Lahore to Yahya and Multan to his second son, Hayatullah, also known as Shah Nawaz Khan. But the emperor was hesitant and kept postponing a decision as he did not relish the prospect of two important provinces becoming hereditary appanages of the powerful Turanian umara. Strange though it may seem, notwithstanding their own Turanian roots, the Chughatas felt more comfortable with their Iranian and native Indian nobles.

Finally, as the emperor seemed unwilling to accept the wazir's proposal, the latter asked for the subedari of these regions for himself. This was, surprisingly, accepted and the wazir in turn appointed one Mir Momin as his deputy in Lahore. But this experiment of an absentee governor in a turbulent frontier province was foredoomed to failure. Malcontents raised their heads. Sikh bands, so long inactive, once more came out into the open, while the raja of Jammu revolted. Mir Momin did not have the influence and resources to meet the deteriorating situation, and finally in January 1746, the wazir persuaded the emperor to replace him by Yahya Khan, but still as his nominal deputy.

Of the three sons of Zakariya, Yahya was the least suited to rule. He was week, indolent and effeminate. Shah Nawaz was avaricious, cruel, and much more vigorous. He was not prepared to accept the imposition of his brother, whose only qualification was that he was the wazir's son-in-law.

Shah Nawaz Khan was the faujdar of the Jalandhar doab and under the influence of Adina Beg Khan, one of his subordinates (who was destined to outlast all of them). He quarelled with Yahya over the division of their late father's property. Then he marched to Lahore, overthrew his brother's government and threw him in prison.

Shah Nawaz's counsellor now advised him to seek the assistance of the Durrani Shah, as the wazir was not likely to forgive him for what he had done to his son-in-law. So a letter was sent to Ahmad Shah, offering him the sovereignty of Lahore and Multan and asking him to come and take possession in person. But Adina Beg was not a simple man. In order to cover himself, he also wrote a secret letter to the wazir, and playing the friendly well-wisher, informed him how his nephew was toying with dangerous ideas and had opened a correspondence with Durrani. The advice of sensible and sober people (such as himself) seemed to have no effect on him, and he begged the wazir to write to him. Maybe that would have some effect.

The wazir immediately wrote to his headstrong nephew a touching and affecting letter recalling their family's long years of loyal service to the padishahs of Hind. Without referring to his usurpation of the masnad, and without making any definite promise, he hinted that if instead of aspiring 'for the doubtful honour of serving Ahmad Abdali, the former Yassawal' he would drive Abdali from India, he might easily be appointed viceroy of Kabul, Tattah and Kashmir besides Lahore and Multan. He, the wazir, would, in that case, exert himself to ensure Shah Nawaz's promotion and advancement in the imperial service.[3]

The letter had the desired effect of reclaiming the wayward nawab from the intended betrayal of his master's interest. But the Durrani Shah had already mobilized and crossed the Indus at the Attock ford. He had been thrilled to receive the letter from Shah Nawaz and jumped at the offer, making the counter-offer to Shah Nawaz of the wazarat of his new state. He, an upstart, only a few months old on the parvenu throne of a brand new nation had just been offered two new provinces, without any inducement or provocation. It was particularly welcome since he had, anyway, intended to conquer India. With imperial ambitions, no less than those of the World Destroyer, he needed resources which only India could provide. Afghanistan might be able to supply the men and horses, but an army marches only if it is paid in gold and silver. And funds on that scale could only be squeezed from India.

After his final eviction from the trans-Indus tract of Hazara, Nasir Khan reached Lahore, unknown and unrecognized, travelling with a very modest entourage. He took up his abode in a mosque like any ordinary person. This was brought to the notice of Shah Nawaz Khan who called on him, and did everything to make his stay comfortable. But Nasir Khan wished to proceed further to Delhi. In the meantime, his family and dependents who had been left behind in Peshawar also joined him and they proceeded to Delhi.[4]

In Delhi too the ex-subedar was received with every mark of consideration by Muhammad Shah. Even though Kabul had since 1739 been annexed to the Persian empire, Nasir Khan had remained in touch with his former masters. He recognized the inherent instability of Nadir's mushroom empire, whose dissolution the troubles of Nadir's later years seemed to presage. So there was every possibility of the Kabul suba reverting in due course to its old allegiance. The court of Delhi thought likewise, and the emperor hoped that Nasir Khan's Afghan connections (his wife and mother were from that nation) would help to reclaim that province for the Delhi empire.[5]

But they were not prepared to exert themselves and the military preparations of the Qila-i-Mualla were, as usual, slow and dilatory. Even when the news was received of the fall of Peshawar and of the presence of Afghan troops near the Attock ford, nothing concrete was done. The imperial tents were pitched at Badli, a day's march from the qila, but the date for actually setting forth was fixed three weeks later, for 14 December 1747. The emperor, worn out by dissipation and opium, was extremely reluctant to leave and there were many among his courtiers who argued that it was beneath his dignity to march in person against the upstart Afghan. But the wazir, who was wiser, counselled that he must accompany the army at least up to some place closer to Lahore, such as Karnal or Panipat, from where the wazir could go ahead with the army to tackle the Afghans. The emperor agreed in principle but still did not fix any date for departure.

On 22 December the news was received that the Afghan Shah had left Peshawar with a large army and was heading for Delhi. But now Muhammad Shah was too ill and he did not even permit Prince Ahmad to accompany the army in his place.

Thus the army did not set out until 12 January 1748. Its commander was the wazir, and the other generals were Safdar Jang and Raja Ishwari Singh of Jaipur. The latter was already sulking because just before setting out he had ventured to request the emperor for the imperial fort of Ranthambor, and been refused.

That very day Lahore was captured by Ahmad Shah. With a small but mobile army of 18,000 men he had swept across the Punjab plains, and on 8 January he stood before the gates of Lahore.

Shah Nawaz had made preparations and pitched his war camp on the plain outside the city. The Shah reminded him of his invitation and promise of assistance but Shah Nawaz gave an evasive reply. About this time Shah Sabir, the Durrani's spiritual pir recollected that he had been born in Lahore and decided to visit it on the pretext of sacred shrines. But Shah Sabir's fame as a magician had preceeded him and the soldiers whispered that he had been sent by Ahmad Shah to render the Indian artillery ineffective by magical charms. The Afghans had no artillery and Shah Nawaz was persuaded to order his arrest and, unknown to him, the pir was put to death.

When the pir failed to return, the Afghans crossed the Ravi on 10 January and the following morning they attacked the Indian army.

It was a hard-fought battle, the Afghans avoiding coming to grips, relying on the musket rather than the sword. They would ride up in close formation, stop and discharge their matchlocks and wheel away, to be followed by another wave. Thus it went on, all through the day. Towards evening there was a lull and the Indians, after their casual approach to war, thinking that the day's fighting was, done began to retire to their tents. It was then that Ahmad launched his troops, in massed charges. The heavy fusillades of musketfire took a severe toll, and the Indian ranks at last gave way.

Shah Nawaz took refuge within the city. Then calling for the Abdali's pir desired that he be sent to the Shah to arrange terms. On being informed that he had in fact been killed, he realized that there was no point in tarrying as the Shah would exact severe revenge for the murder of his murshid, and fled the city taking the Delhi road.

The next day a delegation of the citizens waited on the Afghan conqueror and were able to secure the safety of their city upon promising a ransom of Rs. 30 lakh. Out of this sum, Rs. 22 lakh were paid almost immediately. There was some looting and violence in the suburbs, but the city as a whole was spared the agony of a sack. The Shah had acquired a substantial accretion to his war chest in the form of gold, and the guns of the fort, and was confident of being able to take on Delhi itself.[6]

The imperial army had barely reached Narela (only 16 miles north of Delhi) when it came to know of the fall of Lahore. The generals again halted and a deputation was sent to wait on the emperor and to insist that he send the heir to lead them. The emperor at last consented and Prince Ahmad left Delhi on 31 January 1748 catching up with the army at Sonepat.

With his arrival the army's pace quickened. They crossed Karnal and reached Sirhind on 25 February. It was decided to leave the women and heavier baggage behind in the fort, and push on northwards.

The imperial army had no information regarding the enemy's movements. No scouts had been sent ahead to collect intelligence, or watch the fords. There was a choice between the Ludhiana ford and that at Machhiwara; the former was nearer, but the latter was shallower. Without making any arrangement to watch the crossing at Ludhiana the imperial army set off towards Machhiwara. Meanwhile the Afghans crossed the Sutluj at Ludhiana on 1 March and by a night march swooped down on

Sirhind. After destroying the small garrison of 1,000 odd soldiers, they seized the fort with all its stores, camp followers and women.

The imperial army had marched out of Sirhind three days earlier, on 27 February, and were camping at Bharaoli, 14 miles north of Sirhind, and yet they had no knowledge of the movements of Ahmad Shah. So when one of Safdar Jang's scouts brought the news of the disaster that had befallen their base, there was general incredulity. Another day was wasted to confirm the news, then the imperial army moved back towards Sirhind. The Shah had in the meantime dumped his heavier equipment and baggage in the walled garden of Aam Khas and set out to seek the enemy.

Contact was made at Manupur, about 10 miles north of Sirhind, and the Indian forces began to dig in. To all appearances, they had learnt nothing from their disastrous experience of 1739. Their approach was wholly defensive. As at Karnal, the outer perimeter of the camp was ringed with guns, and trenches were dug and *sangars* built. There was not enough water on the site so several new wells were dug while the roving squadrons of the Afghan cavalry cut off the food supply.

The Afghans kept out of the range of the Indian guns. Apart from camel swivels they had no artillery worth the name; but the Indians, although outnumbering the Afghans—in numbers—at least five to one, still stuck to their defensive tactics. The wazir's strategy was to stay in his entrenchments while inciting the neighbouring zamindars to rise against the invaders and cut off their food supply. But the plan failed; his own supply was cut and the zamindars, far from assisting him would probably have plundered him as readily as the Afghans in the event of an imperial defeat.

The Shah had brought some guns from Lahore and on 9 March, one of them was mounted on a small hillock, and the Afghan fire soon started taking its toll. It was decided therefore to give battle two days later. But on the morning fixed for the battle, while all the army stood awaiting the signal to attack, a cannon ball fell within the qanats enclosing the tents of the wazir and hit the wazir in the tent within. It was a sheer fluke, but the wound was mortal and the wazir knew it. He sent one of his confidential attendants to summon his son, while making sure that the news of his injury did not spread among the troops. The son, Mir Mannu—or Muin ul-Mulk—to give his full title, was a dashing young man in his twenties, and popular with the soldiers. With great presence of mind he swore his father's attendants to secrecy and after consigning his parent's body to a shallow grave within the tent he assumed command after announcing that his father had been suddenly taken ill.

The Afghans followed their usual tactics, riding upto the enemy, then reining in to discharge their muskets, and wheeling away, without coming to grips. This unnerved the Rajputs who were unfamiliar with such tactics. No Rajput contingents had been present on the field of Karnal in 1739, at the time of Nadir Shah's invasion. The news of the wazir's death had also reached them and Raja Ishwari Singh's special counsellor—his barber—urged him to flee while there was time.

Finally the Rajputs broke and fled. Their crack-up imperilled the Indian position. Muin counter-attacked furiously, but it was Safdar Jang who struck the decisive blow that cancelled the effect of Ishwari Singh's flight and turned the table on the Afghan Shah. Using 1,700 matchlockmen firing long *jezails*, he neutralized a force of 700 Afghans firing *shutarnals* from behind hobbled camels. Then the *jezailchis* started pouring their fire into the Durrani cavalry. A chance rocket fired several carts of powder and rockets on the Afghan side killing a number of men. A spark from this explosion then set off the main artillery dump and in this massive blast at least 1,000 Afghans were killed. This shattered the Afghans who broke ranks and fled.[7]

But the Indians did not follow up their victory. This was inspite of their tremendous superiority in numbers. Prince Ahmad ordered Safdar Jang to pursue Abdali across the Sutluj but the latter was not inclined to press his luck further. So the Shah was able to rally his troops at a small mud fort nearby. There was a show of negotiations while his men moved their baggage and treasure and finally one night, unperceived by the Indians, he left for Lahore. When on 16 March 1748, five days after the battle, the imperial forces reached the Durrani camp, they found it deserted. Inspite of the prince's orders to cross the Sutluj, Safdar Jang whiled away the time in pointless marches along the river, ostensibly following the Afghan trail until on 9 April a letter was received from Delhi urging the prince to return post-haste. The same courier conveyed letters appointing Mir Mannu to the two subedaris of Lahore and Multan, and—what was sheer optimism—the orders for Nasir Khan to the old suba of Kabul.

Exact details of the battle were not known at the Qila-i-Mualla. The first news of the capture of Sirhind by the Afghans had filled the emperor with consternation. It was expected that Durrani would now march on Delhi. The emperor's advance tents were pitched at Badli and the big guns of the fort ordered out to block the invader in case he actually approached the city. The emperor was on his deathbed, but the news of the unexpected victory at Manupur cheered him up.

Mir Mannu was ordered to proceed directly to Lahore to assume his office and the emperor's equerries also carried with them the *khillats* which usually accompanied such letters of investiture. So Mir Mannu left the imperial army and proceeded to Lahore while Prince Ahmad hurried back with Safdar Jang to Delhi. At Panipat a confidential emissary brought the news that the emperor had expired.

NOTES

1. Tabatabai, *Seir Mutaqherin*, iii, p. 253.
2. Ibid., p. 253.
3. Ibid., p. 255.
4. Ibid., p. 256.
5. Sarkar, *Fall of the Mughal Empire*, i, p. 212. Tabatabai, iii, pp. 255-6.
6. Sarkar, i, p. 210. Anand Ram Mukhlis, *Tazkira*, pp. 312, 325-32.
7. Ganda Singh, *Ahmad Shah Durrani*, p. 67.

CHAPTER 24

The New Reign

The proclamation of the new reign was delayed by some days out of respect for the late emperor. It was only on the fourth day that the scarlet umbrella was raised over the head of Prince Ahmad, and Safdar Jang presented him with a congratulatory *nazar*. Then he invoked the blessings of the Almighty, prayed for his prosperity and wished him a long reign. The next day they reached the Shalamar. This was one of the emperor's own pleasure gardens and here a grand durbar was held to enable the umara and officials from Delhi to salute their new monarch.[1]

It was only after this that the body of Muhammad Shah was taken for burial to the tomb prepared for him in Nizam ud-Din, close to that of his mother. Thereafter, Ahmad Shah made his formal entry into the capital, carried aloft on a moveable throne—an open palki—known as *takht-i-rawan*.

The new padishah was a young man of twenty-two years but his mother, the former dancing-girl Udham Bai, had been out of favour with Muhammad Shah, hence his education had been sorely neglected. His allowance was niggardly and he was given no opportunity to familiarise himself with affairs of state or military command. The Manupur campaign was the sum of his military experience and he had been brought up entirely in the company of women and eunuchs.

Because of his father's neglect, he had no opportunity to indulge himself in luxury but having come into his own, he found everyone willing and eager to pander to him. He, thereupon, plunged into a life of pleasure, delegating all authority to the eunuch Javid Khan with whom his mother's name was scandalously linked.[2]

The office of the prime minister was offered to Safdar Jang. Out of deference to the nizam, who was still alive, Safdar at first declined the post. But when the news of the nizam's demise at Burhanpur (on 21 May 1748) was received, the appointment was made public and Safdar Jang assumed charge on 20 June.

To the post of mir bakhshi (with the attached dignity of Amir-ul-Umara) was appointed Syed Salabat Khan. He was the son of that Saadat Khan whose daughter, Gauhar un-Nissa, had married Farrukhsiyar. The daughter of this union, Malika-i-Zamani, had been married to Muhammad Shah and was the acknowledge head of the harem. Salabat Khan's own daughter, Sahiba Mahal, was also married to the late emperor and bore him a daughter known as Begum Sahiba. During the Manupur campaign Salabat had been sent as the guardian of Prince Ahmad. The latter called him Nana Baba, or maternal grandfather, because the childless Malika-i-Zamani had brought up Ahmad as her son. Thus Salabat, besides being closely related to the imperial house was also known to the prince.

The second paymastership went to Intizam ud-Daulah, the eldest son of the late wazir Qamr ud-Din, while Nasir Jang, the nizam's impatient second son, was formally appointed governor of the Deccan in April 1749. This was merely a confirmation of the *de facto* position as he was already in possession, and had been his father's deputy for many years. Ghazi ud-Din Khan, the nizam's eldest son, who had acted as his deputy at Delhi was, for the moment, without office.

Allahabad was added to the holdings of Safdar Jang because of its proximity to Awadh, while Ajmer and Agra were conferred on Salabat Khan. No other changes were made among the subedars. Mir Mannu had already been appointed to the two Punjab subas of Lahore and Multan. There was no attempt to disturb the possession of Alivardi Khan, subedar of the east, while central India was already in Maratha hands.

Safdar Jang had shown some military talents in 1738 and 1748, both against the Marathas and Abdali. Thus his appointment might have been expected to impart a certain vigour to the empire which had become nearly moribund under the easy-going Qamr ud-Din, whose governing principle appears to have been to avoid taking any action or decision as long as possible. But unfortunately his wazarat was destined to be an even greater disaster than that of his dissipated predecessor.

While the gangrene of corruption had been spreading in the body politic of the empire, the outer crust of normalcy was preserved. But during the wazarat of Safdar Jang dissolution set in apace and it was impossible to preserve the equanimity, so characteristic of the preceding reign.

Safdar's first problem was that he was a Persian and a Shia, while in India the vast majority of Muslims happened to be Sunnis. This was not, however, the decisive factor for the failure of Safdar Jang. After all, since the earliest days of the dynasty, some of the greatest administrators and wazirs had been Persians. But Ab'ul Mansur Khan Safdar Jang was, unfortunately, a 'new man'. He was the first of his family to migrate to India and his uncle Saadat Khan, Burhan ul-Mulk, whose daughter he espoused, was also a first generation immigrant without roots in the country. On the other hand, the leaders of the Turani umara, like Qamr ud-Din or Nizam-ul-Mulk, though undoubtedly of foreign origin, had been in the country for several generations. Thus, besides being supported by a wide kinship network among the peerage, they had acquired many more adherents by virtue of long association of service. Because of the long hold which Qamr ud-Din's family had enjoyed on the highest offices of the state, they regarded the wazarat as theirs, almost by hereditary right, and they started intriguing against Safdar Jang and the bakhshi, Salabat from the very beginning.

And finally there was the emperor himself. A man of no experience, either in administrative or military matters, indeed of practical life itself. He was totally lacking in firmness of will and was liable to be swayed in his judgement by favourites who enjoyed his confidence but had no responsibility. And chief among these was Javid Khan, one of the palace eunuchs, who owed his power and influence to his control over the mind and body of the emperor's mother.

With her son as emperor Udham Bai was able to play a more active role. She dreamt of emulating Nur Jahan and transacted business in person. Every day the officers would go and sit at her *deohri* and she would discuss official matters from behind a screen through the medium of eunuchs. Files and letters would be passed to her and she would have them read out.

The humble origin of the Empress Mother, the suggestion of the courtesan's *kotha* so evident in her very name, was cloaked under high sounding titles and honorifics. Bai Jiu Sahiba, Nawab Qudsia, Sahiba-uz-Zamani, Sahib Jiu Sahiba, Hazrat and Qibla-i-Alam were her sonorous titles. Nawab Qudsia was, it may be recalled, the style of the late emperor's mother. And as for Qibla-i-Alam—the vault of the Universe, could anything be grander than that? She was given the honorary rank of 50,000 *zat*, while her worthless brother, Man Khan, a vagabond and occasional dancer, was elevated to the rank of 6,000 with the equally sonorous *luqab* of Mutqad-ud-Daulah Bahadur.[3]

Javid Khan, the lover of Udham Bai, was also made a *shesh hazaari* (6,000) and appointed superintendent of the Diwan-i-Khas—a post through which he could control access to the monarch and keep away all those whom he considered undesirable. Other pluralities showered on him were the Intelligence department, the superintendence of the elephant stables (or pilkhana), the confirmation of grants and appointments (Arz-i-

Mukarrar), the estates of the begums and the diwani of the Khalsa and Tan. Soon he was raised to the rank of a *haft hazaari* (7,000) and given the title of Nawab Bahadur along with the most exalted of the heraldic insignia, that of the fish with banners, kettledrums and a fringed palki.[4] And withal the recipient of these unprecedented honours was absolutely illiterate. Well might the high-born grandees at the Qila-i-Mualla have groaned when they discovered that nothing moved at court without the nod of this fifty year old eunuch.

Many an unlettered man has proved a wise sovereign. Akbar the Great and Ranjit Singh, the Lion of the Punjab, are two great names that immediately come to mind, but Javid Khan was not of that class. Nor was there anything in common between him and the famous eunuchs of the sultanate like Malik Kafur, the *hazaar dinari*, Allauddin Khilji's famous general. Like his mistress he was a common man with vulgar tastes and an itching palm. Salabat Khan, the mir bakhshi, refused to kowtow before this eunuch, a mere slave, and was ultimately destroyed by him.

The salaries of even the household guards were in heavy arrears. In protest they staged a scene. They tied up a young ass and a bitch at the palace gate and when the nobles and other courtiers came to attend the durbar, they urged them to pay their respects to the ill-assorted pair thus: 'First bow to these! This is the Nawab Bahadur, and that is Hazrat Qudsia, the Empress-mother!'[5]

Such was the ignominous ridicule to which the Imperial House itself had been reduced.

But Udham Bai had some redeeming qualities. Her love and attachment for her son were real and she was kind and charitable. Moved by the miserable plight of the impoverished salatin, she had regular allowances fixed for the first time for them. Many poor and indigent people living outside the palace were also the grateful beneficiaries of her charity. But the senior wives of the late emperor, the nobly-born Malika-i-Zamani and Sahiba Mahal, were ignominously sent to the widows' house with no special provision for their comfort.[6]

As for the emperor himself, he delegated almost complete authority to Javid Khan and his mother, and immersed himself in debauchery. According to the *Seir*, a garden of 1 *kos* square (i.e. 4 square miles, undoubtedly an exaggeration) was devoted entirely to pleasure. Here the emperor would relax with his harem for days and weeks at a time. Where precisely this garden was located is not mentioned. If it existed at all it certainly must have been somewhere outside the place-fort.[7]

The negligence of administration by the emperor can be judged from the fact that he appointed his son, then three years old, as subedar of the Punjab, and nominated a toddler of one year (the infant son of Muin ul-Mulk) as his deputy in Lahore! *Khillats* of appropriate size were sent to the infant deputy while Prince Mahmud Shah received his appointment in full court in the Diwan-i-Khas. The province of Kashmir was bestowed upon another prince, still younger, Tala Said Shah, also of course as absentee, while an adolescent of fifteen, son of another court favourite was nominated as his deputy.[8] Such fatuous complacence seems incredible when it is recalled that both these subas were on the frontier bordering the dominions of the Durrani Shah who had already made several incursions into Punjab.

During his last years, Ahmad tried to pull himself together and personally attended to business for six hours every morning. But, again, his manner was hardly normal. He would work at his files non-stop, without pause for refreshment. His orders were detailed, but unacquainted as he was with ground realities or even the elements of administration, his ministers coolly ignored them. After the six hours he had allotted for affairs of State he would retire to his harem with strict instructions that he was not to be disturbed, whatever the circumstances.

NOTES

1. Tabatabai, *Seir Mutaqherin*, iii, p. 264.
2. Ibid., pp. 285-6.
3. Ibid., p. 328.
4. Sarkar, *Fall of the Mughal Empire*, i, p. 338.
5. Shakir, *Tazkira*, pp. 34-5. Sarkar, i, p. 336.
6. Sarkar, i, p. 334.
7. *Tarikh-i-Ahmad Shahi*, pp. 13b-14a, 21a, 25a.
8. Sarkar, i, pp. 330-1.

CHAPTER 25

The Ministry of Safdar Jang

The first years of the ministry of Safdar Jang were marked by military operations in Rohilkhand, where the prime minister took the field in person, and in Rajasthan where the mir bakhshi was in command. During the same period Ahmad Shah Durrani made two incursions into the Punjab which Mir Mannu had to face alone, without assistance from Delhi. The Turani party tried to displace the wazir and though they did not succeed in their first attempt in 1751, their principal leaders were appointed to key positions. Now the stage was set for the final struggle which resulted in the overthrow of Safdar Jang.

Safdar Jang assumed charge in June 1748 and within a few months—on 20 November—there was an attempt on his life. While returning from the Idgah, as he approached the high vaulted gateway of the *deohri* of his house (which was the mansion known as Dara Shukoh's), there was a loud report as a rocket and firearms were fired from the terrace of a house in the bazaar. A *jezail*, a matchlock and a rocket had been fired simultaneously from behind a screen. His horse and two or three of his followers, who were riding behind, were killed and he himself had a narrow escape.

The assailant, who must have been a skilled gunner, could not be found inspite of a vigorous search. But it was rumoured that he was in the service of Intizam, the son of the late minister, and it was in his house that he had taken refuge. Apprehending further attempts on his life, Safdar pitched his tents outside the city and stopped attending court. Thus, within a few months, relations between the wazir and emperor had soured and an armed conflict between him and the Turanian nobles seemed imminent.[1]

About the same time Nasir Jang was invited by the emperor to get rid of his prime minister. The avowed purpose of his northward march was to pay his respects to the new emperor, but his real object, as Nasir told his cousin Intizam, was to restore order and make him the wazir. At the same time, he wrote to the wazir about his intended visit and its ostensible purpose, and to put him off his guard, impudently requested the wazir's good offices in securing the subedari of the Deccan for himself. The post was still officially vacant since the death of Asaf Jah in May 1748, though, of course, Nasir Jang was in effective control.

But Safdar Jang was under no illusions about the purpose of Nasir Jang's intended visit. In order to counter any hostile combination of the Turani nobles, he had entered into an alliance with the Marathas and he wrote to the Peshwa and Malhar Holkar, asking them to block the roads to Hindustan. Hingane, the Maratha agent at the Qila-i-Mualla, was shown the letter received from Nasir Jang. Besides requesting the wazir's assistance in securing the sanads of appointment to the Deccan, he had also asked him to join him in punishing the peshwa, Balaji, whom he described as 'a great deceiver'.[2] Hingane warned the wazir that this seemingly frank and forthright request for an alliance for mutual benefit and the preservation of the empire was intended to alienate him from his only true ally. Once isolated, he would be destroyed.

Safdar had come to the same conclusion and was taking measures to meet the threat. More troops were being recruited and others were called from Awadh. Alarmed at these preparations, his opponents lost their nerve and on 7 April 1749 the emperor himself visited his camp and persuaded him to return to the Qila-i-Mualla. As the price of this reconciliation, the wazir extracted from the emperor a firman addressed to Nasir Jang directing him to return to the Deccan. The appointment of Nasir Jang to the subedari of the Deccan also accompanied the firman. The confrontation was thus averted.

With the death of Ali Muhammad Rohilla in September 1748, his heritage was divided among several sardars—mostly fathers-in-law of one or the other of Ali Muhammad's several minor children. Sheikh Qutb ud-Din Khan, grandson of Azmatullah Khan, former faujdar of Katehar-Moradabad, was encouraged by Safdar Jang to make an attempt to recover what Daud and Ali Muhammad had seized from his family. Intizam ud-Daulah was the nominal subeder of this province, and upon being importuned by the hopeful Sheikh he agreed to appoint him as his deputy. Even though the Rohilla state no longer had a single chief, to reckon with the Pathans were determined to resist any attempt by an outsider to establish himself in their region. Hafiz Rahmat Khan, the most formidable of the Rohilla chiefs, warned Sheikh Qutb ud-Din that he would not be allowed to assume charge. However, Sheikh Qutb ud-Din did not heed the warning, and in the battle that ensued he was defeated and killed by Dundi Khan near Dhampur in January 1749.

During those days the wazir was at odds with the emperor, sulking in his tents outside Shahjahanabad. But after the reconciliation in April, Safdar hatched a new plan to subjugate the Rohillas. Qaim Khan was to be the tool this time. He was the son and successor of Muhammad Khan Bangash whose holdings centred around Farrukhabad, south of Rohilkhand. The strategy was to use one Afghan against another. In this way at least one of them would be destroyed.

Ali Muhammad was supposed to have left behind a huge hoard of treasure. With this as allurement, Qaim Khan was persuaded to accept the faujdari of the turbulent district. He sent his agents in advance to negotiate with Hafiz Rahmat at Aonla. The latter was the *de facto* head of the Rohilla confederacy and he refused to acknowledge the authority of anyone else but the emperor.

In November 1749 Qaim Khan set out to avenge the insult to his honour. Near Budaun he met three Syed divines who had been sent by Hafiz Rahmat to again persuade him to turn back. But the parleys failed and a battle took place at Durine, 2 miles away from Budaun, in which Qaim too was killed. But the gallant Rahmat had his body sent with full honours to Farrukhabad.

Apart from the fact that the Rohillas had declined to accept the wazir's nominee, Hafiz Rahmat's attitude was by no means defiant. But they had no desire to have a neighbouring magnate thrust over them as their governor. Safdar Jang's interest was also natural. He wished to strengthen his position in Awadh by having docile clients as neighbours. But what followed was unforgiveable and shall, forever, stand as a blot on the name of Safdar Jang.

Qaim Khan had died fighting for the emperor in the execution of a task assigned to him. But instead of condoling his death, the wazir chose this moment of bereavement to enforce the old law of escheat. Ironically, Qaim had died trying to enforce the same rule of escheat against the heirs of Ali Muhammad. According to the rule, all the property of the late Rohilla chief stood attached by the emperor and it was upto him to allow what he thought proper to the family and dependents of the deceased.

On 29 November the wazir set out for Farrukhabad, a bare 17 days after the death of Qaim. According to some accounts the emperor accompanied him. At first he made the widow of Qaim Khan, Bibi Sahiba, agree to the payment of Rs. 60 lakh by way of escheatment fine, and in return he promised to secure the succession for her son. But a short delay in furnishing the amount was made an excuse to place her under restraint and seize the entire estate; only Farrukhabad and 12 villages, the original grant of Farrukhsiyar, being left for her maintenance.[3]

The coup accomplished the wazir returned to Delhi on 25 May leaving behind his agent, Nawal Rai, with a small force to settle the annexed territory. While the wazir was busy in Farrukhabad, the Durrani Shah had made an incursion into the Punjab with a small army. Muin ul-Mulk had gone to meet him with all the men he could muster. There was no fighting, but in the stand-off Ahmad Shah was able to get the confirmation of his rights to the revenues of the four mahals of Sialkot, Pasrur, Gujrat and Aurangabad—traditionally linked with the Kabul garrison.

But the Bangash Pathans were not so easily crushed. Shortly after the return of Safdar Jang, Bibi Sahiba, assisted by her faithful servant Shitab Rai, escaped and Ahmad, another of the numerous sons of Muhammad Khan, began to incite the people. Soon Nawal Rai found himself hemmed in by rebellious Pathans crying for vengeance against those who had insulted the dignity of their lord's household. Nawal Rai was a good revenue officer but no soldier. The wazir asked him to avoid action and hold on till he arrived with a relieving army. But before he could, Nawal was forced into battle. His little force was overwhelmed, and he himself died fighting on 25 July 1750.

Safdar Jang arrived with a strong army supported by artillery. But Ahmad Khan had strengthened his position by seeking the help of Dhundi Khan and Hafiz Rahmat, the Rohilla chiefs whom his late brother had so recently tried to disposses. The rival armies clashed on 13 September at Ram Chatauni. At first the right and left wings of the imperial army—commanded by Suraj Mall Jat and Ismail Beg Khan—were successful in driving out the Pathan divisions facing them and they followed in pursuit. This was a mistake, and Safdar Jang compounded it by sending more troops and light guns in support of the pursuing forces so that he had no reserves left to back him while the enemy centre was still fighting stubbornly. In the afternoon the imperial army slackened and this was the moment chosen by Ahmad for his final all-out effort. Eventually, the imperial forces broke and fled. The generals on their elephants were easy targets. Safdar's mahout was killed and he himself fainted from a wound in the neck, while Ishaq Khan Najm ud-Daulah, his son's father-in-law, was slain. When Suraj Mall and Ismail Beg returned, they found everything lost and the battle over.[4]

It took the Pathans some time to realize the extent of their victory. By the time they collected their wits and reached the wazir's camp, nothing was left; the camp having been looted by the wazir's own soldiers, camp-followers and the nearby villagers. It was for the first time that an imperial army, led by the wazir himself, had been defeated in a straight battle by a mere jagirdar.

This provided the wazir's enemies an opportunity to raise their heads. The first messages that reached Delhi suggested that the wazir had also been killed. Preparations were made to seize his property in escheat but his wife took steps to defend the mansion. The gates were closed, and cannon mounted to discourage any attempts at forcible entry. When the wazir appeared on 20 September in Delhi proving that he was very much alive the conspirators were shaken and offered lame excuses for their conduct.[5]

Safdar Jang's opponents now started another move to neutralize him. Tutored by Intizam, who hoped to replace him, the emperor forbade the wazir from coming to the court saying that it was a rule of the dynasty that if a wazir turned his back on the field of battle, he must be sent into retirement in order to maintain the prestige of the state.

But the wazir knew how to overcome such situations, Javid Khan was promised a bribe of Rs. 70 lakh, if he could arrange for the emperor to overlook this loss of prestige.[6] The eunuch obliged and two months later the emperor, while returning to the Qila-i-Mualla from an excursion, paused at the *deohri* of the wazir to enquire about his wounds. The latter, apprised beforehand of the emperor's intention, had come out to receive him. Outwardly, the emperor and wazir were again reconciled, and Intizam was obliged to bide his time.

But Safdar was determined to wipe out the stain of Ram Chatauni, and was in correspondence with the Marathas. The bakhshi, Salabat Khan, had been of no assistance at all till date. He was deeply embroiled in Rajput politics, in the struggle between Ram Singh and Bakht Singh in Marwar, and Ishwari Singh and Madho Singh in Jaipur. The Marathas who could never be far from troubled waters were also involved in the dynastic struggles that were tearing the Rajput states apart. Thus they too were unable to respond immediately.

After the battle of Ram Chatauni, Awadh was practically defenceless. The Pathans spread east and west of Farrukhabad, all the way upto Allahabad, and on the other side of the Ganga, up to Lucknow. At Allahabad they attempted to lay siege to the fort in April 1751. But they had no artillery and after some time, on receiving the news of an approaching Maratha force, they were compelled to retreat. But not before they had looted and burnt most of the city. Only two wards of the city were spared, that of Sheikh Afzal Allahabadi and Dariyabad, both inhabited by Pathans.[7]

Mahmud Khan, a son of Ahmad Khan, had been sent with an army across the Ganga. At Bilgram the local Syeds were able to placate the Pathans with a gift of money. Then Lucknow was occupied. Here, Mahmud appointed his own police officers as the wazir's representatives had fled. But the Pathan faujdar proved so oppressive that the sheikhzadas of Lucknow incited the inhabitants to rebel as a result of which the Pathans were driven back across the Ganga.

In Rajasthan, the Amir-ul-Umara Salabat Khan had been directed to support Bakht Singh in his struggle against nephew Ram Singh, the son of the late Maharaja Abhai Singh who had died on 21 June 1749. Salabat was also, incidentally, the absentee subedar of Ajmer and Agra, and both the subas were at the time being ravaged by the Marathas.

Salabat Khan set out towards the end of 1749 passing through Jat territory. His soilders plundered the Jat villages that fell on the way. The Jat Raja, Badan Singh, was an ally of Ishwari Singh who was supporting Raja Ram in the Rathor civil war. After some easy successes Salabat Khan was tempted to turn aside and threaten Bharatpur in the hope of getting some money for his forbearance. The action was totally unwarranted for the Jats were loyal subjects and at peace with the emperor. But Salabat was hoping to profit from his expedition and on the pretext of the seizure by the Jats of a few of his jagir villages in Mewat, he demanded Rs. 1 crore as compensation. Such impudent banditry, resembling the Marathas, ended in fiasco. The mir bakhshi was trapped and forced to conclude a humiliating peace whose curious terms as quoted by the *Seir Mutaqherin* included the protection of pipal trees (*ficus indica*) within the empire.[8]

After this humiliating rebuff Salabat Khan again turned towards Marwar. It is unnecessary to go into the details of the campaign. There was little actual fighting but the hardship suffered under the desert sun was considerable—and Salabat made no money out of the campaign. Bakht Singh was eventually placed on the *gaddi* of Jodhpur. Meanwhile, during a lull in the fighting Ishwari Singh committed suicide at Jaipur and was succeeded by his old rival, Madho Singh. Thanks to the over-bearing attitude of the Marathas, and specially the licentious behaviour of Khande Rao, the son of Malhar Holkar, there was an uprising by the citizens of Jaipur in which over 2,000 Deccanis were slaughtered in the streets of that city. . . but that is another story which does not directly concern the Qila-i-Mualla.

Salabat Khan had been in the field with a large army for nearly 2 years but had nothing to show except debts to the tune of over Rs. 60 lakh. He returned to Delhi in October 1751. Thereafter Rajasthan was virtually abandoned by the Mughals. Ajmer was taken in 1752 by Jodhpur, while

Jaipur siezed Ranthambor fort in 1754. Thereafter the entire region was left to its own fate—more precisely, to the Marathas.

On his return Salabat found himself a ruined man. Neither Agra nor Ajmer—his two provinces—yielded him any revenue and he had to find at least Rs. 60 lakh to pay his debts. As an old noble, whose family had long been in the service of the padishahs of Hind and had close relations with the emperor himself, he scorned to approach Javid Khan who, for a price, could have settled his debts from the Imperial Treasury. Finally, rendered desperate by the importunities of his creditors and soldiers, he tried to make a personal appeal to the emperor.

But Javid Khan controlled the entry to the emperor, and on his instructions the Amir-ul-Umara was stopped. Stung at the insult, the nobleman burst into wild abuse at the imbecile emperor and upstart eunuch. This was what the wily eunuch had been waiting for. He was arrested, stripped of his rank and titles, and his house surrounded by soldiers backed by cannons. On his release, he was forced to sell off all his property to discharge his soldiers' claims and thereafter lived in poverty and seclusion like a fakir. Such was the mutability of fortune in Mughal India. A prince today, a pauper tomorrow![9]

The fall of Salabat Khan occurred in June 1751. His dismissal and disgrace were an opportunity for the Turani party. Javid obtained the appointment of Ghazi ud-Din Khan Firoz Jang (the late Nizam's eldest son and former deputy at Delhi) as Amir-ul-Umara and Bakhshi-ul-Mamalik along with the charge of the suba of Agra, while his cousin cum brother-in-law, Intizam ud-Daulah, was appointed subedar of Ajmer with the dignity of Khan-i-Khanan. Safdar Jang was, at the time, in no position to counter these moves. He himself had been barely rehabilitated after his disastrous defeat at Ram Chatauni and was engaged in a difficult campaign to regain honour and reputation.

He had succeeded in engaging the services of Jayappa Scindia and Malhar Holkar with their respective contingents at the rate of Rs. 25,000 per day for the projected invasion of Rohilkhand. On 11 February he entered his marching tents and a few days later set out, being joined on the way by Holkar and Suraj Mall.

Most of the fighting was done by his auxilliaries, and he himself stayed in the rear, so that in the event of a reverse, the disgrace should be theirs not his. After some time he returned to Delhi leaving the Marathas and Jats to prosecute the campaign on their own.

Shadil Khan, the Bangash governor of Koil, was attacked by 20,000

Maratha cavalry and his small force of 4,000 cavalry and 4,000 infantry was broken and dispersed. The entire area was cleared of the Bangash officers. It was the news of this disaster that had forced Ahmad Khan to raise the siege of Allahabad.

Ahmad hurried back with a much depleted force, most of his mercenaries having deserted him. He took position inside a small mud fort called Fatehgarh, 3 miles east of Farrukhabad, while the Jats, Marathas, and the Mughal soldiers of Safdar Jang massed themselves opposite him, along the Ganga. Then Sadullah Khan, one of the sons of the late Ali Muhammad, came with a force of 12,000 Rohillas to join the Bangash. Skirmishes took place between the two sides and finally, on 17 April 1751, a battle took place at Singirampur in which the Pathans were completely defeated.

The remnants of the Pathan army retreated to the north seeking shelter in the Terai forests. The Marathas spread out, plundering the country. Malhar Holkar is said to have collected over Rs. 2 crore in cash in these operations.

After the rains the Pathans came out of the jungle and pushed the Marathas south across the Ganga. The wazir who had been all this while at Lucknow, hastened to the scene and the Pathans again retreated north to Aonla. Later Aonla too was abandoned and they sought shelter closer to the foothills at Chilkiya, deep in the Terai.

Fever wrought dreadful havoc among both the Marathas and Pathans. Fighting was in low key, limited to minor encounters between small bodies of troops. Khande Rao, the son of Malhar Rao, was captured by Ahmad Khan in one of these forest skirmishes, but he was treated with courtesy by his captor and released shortly afterwards. Malhar was so grateful for his action that he told the wazir that he would not carry the fight to extremes.[10]

Meanwhile in December 1751 the Durrani Shah had again invaded the Punjab. Muin had sent him a sum of Rs. 9 lakh on account of the tribute of the four mahals as soon as he crossed the Indus. The Shah accepted the amount but continued his march. Mannu, therefore, sent his family for safety to the Jammu hills and prepared to resist. The merchants and richer classes of Lahore were alarmed and fled the city.

Mir Mannu confronted the invading Afghans from a strong entrenched position outside the city. Skirmishes took place daily, but as the Afghans were not strong enough to invest the Indian trenches or storm the city, a stalemate developed. After about one and a half months Mannu decided to shift to a new position because the old camp and entrenchments had become insanitary. But while they were doing so, the attention of the Afghans was attracted by the din attendant on such a move which involved thousands of men. The Afghan cavalry immediately mobilized and hurled itself against the multitudes of soldiers and camp followers.

The bulk of the Indian army was routed. Mannu held on; he still had 10,000 men with him and at nightfall he withdrew into the city. The night that followed was dreadful. No one seemed to know who was in charge. Some of the Afghans had also entered the city and together with the demoralized Indian soldiers and the *badmashes* they terrorized the city in an orgy of looting and arson.

When morning dawned (6 March 1752), Muin took what steps he could to secure the city's defences. But he knew that unless reinforcements arrived, he would not be able to hold on for long. Then an emissary arrived from the Shah, suggesting that he should visit the Afghan camp to discuss peace.

Putting on a bold front Muin went to the Afghan camp accompanied by only three attendants and an eunuch. He was received with courtesy by two high ranking Afghan nobles. The story, as related by Tahmasp Khan 'Miskin', goes that the Shah posed the following question: 'What would you have done to me, if I was your prisoner?'

One can imagine the slightly sardonic smile that might have lit the face of the gallant Muin ul-Mulk as he answered with hold effrontery: 'I should have cut your head off and sent it to my master the Emperor'.

The Alexander of the Age then posed the question whose answer could have meant the difference between life and death: 'Now that you have taken so long to submit what should I do to you?'

The defeated governor, playing to perfection the role of Porus, answered, 'If you are a shopkeeper sell me, if you are a butcher kill me, but if you are a padishah then grant me your grace and pardon'.

The Shah was so pleased with his behaviour that he stood up and embraced him and honoured him with the additional *luqab* of Farzand Khan Bahadur, a robe of honour and the very turban that he was wearing. Taking advantage of the good impression he had made on the Shah, Muin successfully pressed for the release of the captives whom the Durrani soldiers had taken into custody during the course of the campaign.[11]

The next day Muin presented the Shah with a few lakh rupees which had been collected from the Lahore gentry on the pretext of hosting a dinner to the Shah and his troops. A treaty was also signed by which the provinces of Lahore and Multan were ceded to the Afghan Shah. Muin remained the governor, only the surplus revenues of the two subas would henceforth be forwarded to Kabul instead of Delhi. He had at first intended to strike coins in his name from Lahore but on Muin's advice he dropped the idea. In Multan, however, large grants of land were made to the Sadozai kinsmen of the Shah, and the province assumed the character of an Afghan colony.

The Shah then sent his envoy, Qalandar Beg, to secure the ratification of the treaty from his namesake in the Qila-i-Mualla. The ambassador reached Delhi on 1 April 1752. The wazir was still away, pursuing what was virtually his private war. The court was in a panic. There was nothing to stop the Afghan Shah should he choose to march on Delhi. He had come 11 years earlier with Nadir Shah and the strengths and weaknesses of the Indian empire were no secrets to him.

So, when Qalandar Beg appeared with a treaty the terrified emperor jumped at the offer. By the treaty, the sovereignty of the Lahore and Multan subas was ceded to the Afghan Shah. To put it differently, since no administrative changes were made, the emperor agreed to remit Rs. 50 lakh per year to Kabul as the equivalent of the surplus revenue of the two subas and recognized the Shah's special interests in the Punjab which became, henceforth, an Afghan sphere of influence. It was a strange peculiarity that Abdali made no attempt to replace the civil and revenue officers in the Punjab by his own men from Kabul or Kandahar. Later on, his son Prince Timur would be appointed viceroy with Jahan Khan as military commander, but they were simply superimposed over the existing structure.

A substantial portion of the surplus revenues of the Deccan, Gujarat, Malwa, and Rajasthan, had been alienated by the way of *chauth*, *sardeshmukhi* or other special agreements to the Marathas. Kashmir and Tattah (Sind), like Kabul—ceded to the Persians since 1739—were held by the Afghan Shah as the successor to the eastern part of the ephemeral Afsharid empire. Now the two Punjab subas had also been lost. Practically all that was left was the Delhi suba and Awadh. Much of Agra was in the hands of the Jats. The Pathans in Rohilkhand, while not originally disloyal, had been thoroughly alienated by the policies of Safdar Jang.

But what was Safdar Jang the triumphant in battle and vanquisher of enemies doing all this while? The emperor had been sending him frantic appeals but the wazir took his own time. Muin ul-Mulk was, after all, one of the Turanian umara, his sworn enemies. As in the case of Nasir Khan and Zakariya Khan in 1739, the wazir thought it would be in his interest if Muin was cut to size. He was calculating for coming to the rescue after the defeat and humiliation of Muin. The emperor's position would be desperate, and by arriving with a large Maratha army in the nick of time, he would appear in the light of saviour of the empire, and thereafter his control over the emperor would be complete. Thus, it was in his interest that Muin ul-Mulk should be defeated by the Afghans.

Just as Amir Khan had earlier reposed great trust and confidence in Rajput valour, Safdar Jang relied on the Marathas. He was already in correspondence with Poona and he had arranged for a defensive treaty with the Peshwa on the following terms:

1. The emperor would pay the Peshwa Rs. 50 lakh, out of which Rs. 30 lakh was just the price of keeping out the Afghan Shah.
2. One fourth (the *chauth*) of the revenues of the two Punjab subas and the revenues of the 4 mahals assigned to the Afghan Shah, would be assigned to the Marathas. In addition, the revenues of Hissar, Sambhal, Moradabad and Budaun were also to be assigned to them. One half of the revenues of these districts would be assigned for the support of the emperor, and one fourth for paying the contingents of the wazir and Javid Khan, the remaining fourth going to the Marathas.
3. The peshwa would be appointed subedar of Ajmer and Agra with the consequent rights and privileges.
4. The Maratha generals were to attend the imperial court like other umaras.

This treaty, if implemented, would have handed over the charge of the entire north-western frontier to the Marathas. Only a part of the Delhi suba and Awadh would have been left outside their grasp, and the Marathas would have become the paramount power in India with the emperor reduced to a ward, as indeed he was, three decades later, when Mahadji Scindia took over as the deputy of the peshwa who had been appointed Vakil-i-Mutlaq.

Whether the move would have been more successful then is a moot point. As the battle of Panipat would show in 1761, the Marathas suffered from the same weakness as the imperial armies when it came to pitched battles and were slower and much less efficient than the Afghans. There was, undoubtedly, no general at the time comparable to Ahmad Shah Durrani on the Indian side. The Maratha genius lay in guerilla tactics, but, in north India, they suffered from the additional disadvantage of operating in, what was virtually, a foreign territory. The people of the Punjab and Delhi subas were much more familiar with Afghans and Mughals than with Deccanis.

But this is all speculation. Safdar Jang's treaty remained a draft. He arrived in Delhi on 25 April, 12 days after the departure of Qalandar Beg with the ratified text of the treaty which had been negotiated between the Durrani Shah and Muin ul-Mulk. The 50,000 Marathas which he brought with him, came too late.

Safdar Jang was received in his tents near the Yamuna by Javid Khan and Safdar informed him of his intention to proceed directly towards Lahore to fight the Afghans. But Javid Khan informed him that it was no longer necessary as a peace treaty had already been signed by which Lahore and Multan had been ceded to the Afghan Shah.

The wazir became furious. He had made commitments to his Maratha generals. How was he to find Rs. 50 lakh for them? When the Marathas found that the wazir's plans had miscarried and the money not forthcoming, they spread out to plunder the country.

The Maratha generals were in urgent need of hard cash not merely to pay their troops—which was not so serious a problem as they could live off the country—but to repay their bankers who had advanced them huge loans to meet the expenses of war. The later part of the Rohilla campaign conducted in the malarial forests of the Terai had been barren of spoils. Therefore Malhar opened negotiations directly with the court to see if there were other services which could be rendered for a price. Developments in Poona and Satara also necessitated an early departure for the Deccan.

Ghazi ud-Din Khan Firoz Jang had been appointed viceroy of the Deccan after his brother's murder in 1751. At one stage he was about to leave to assume charge, but his soldiers being offered a settlement of their arrears at 50 per cent preferred to collect their dues and opt out of his service. Therefore he had to postpone his departure. A few months later he was also appointed mir bakhshi after the disgrace of Salabat Khan, therefore, it was no longer necessary for him to go. His appointment had been recommended by the peshwa, and amazingly, instead of that being considered a disqualification, it was accepted.

It was even more incredible when Ghazi ud-Din proceeded to nominate the peshwa himself as his deputy-subedar in the Deccan! But this was too much for Ghazi ud-Din's officers and younger brothers and they resisted all attempts by Balaji to assert himself. Finally the problem was solved by the appointment of Salabat Jang, one of Ghazi ud-Din's brothers in the Deccan, as deputy.

Now it was the turn of Balaji to resist and obstruct Salabat's authority. The situation in the Deccan was further complicated by a civil war among the Marathas themselves. Raja Shahu had died on 15 December 1749, and as his successor Ramraja was incompetent, a regency was established by the widow Tara Bai, who at the same time tried to rally the Maratha chiefs against the brahmin Peshwas. Salabat Jang, at one stage, even occupied Poona. Malhar Holkar, on the other hand, was a loyal adherent of the peshwa and he suggested, at the instance of Poona, that if Ghazi ud-Din would assume the viceroyalty in person, he would escort him to Aurangabad and relieve the emperor of the liability to pay Rs. 50 lakh which Safdar Jang had promised. They were now ready to settle for Rs. 30 lakh only, which they would recover from Ghazi ud-Din.

At the time of his appointment Ghazi ud-Din had undertaken to pay a preposterous *peshkash* of Rs. 2 crore and 80 lakh, of which only Rs. 15 lakh were actually paid. Now, in order to get rid of Malhar's horsemen, who had stripped the country bare for miles around, and were a constant threat to the capital, the *peshkash* was reduced to a promise of Rs. 60 lakh only of which half was to be paid to Malhar. Then, on 4 May, nine days after the arrival, on payment of a small sum by Javid Khan, Malhar's soldiers left the neighbourhood of Delhi. All the negotiations were held directly between Javid Khan and Malhar without involving the wazir, who was extremely offended on this account. During Safdar's absence his authority had been completely undermined and he resolved to get even with the wily eunuch.

In July 1752, in response to a snub administered by the wazir, Javid Khan instigated Balu Jat—who had earlier been regarded as an adherent of the wazir—to attach and plunder the town of Sikandra. This town was included in the Khalsa lands, the revenues of which were part of the emperor's privy purse, and the insult to the imperial dignity was intended to humiliate the wazir by showing him up as ineffective. Javid himself sent an armed force to chastise the outlaw, but predictably the officer did nothing, and Balu was able to escape by boat. In open court the wazir upbraided Javid and accused him of being hand in glove with the outlaw.

The wazir was determined to purge the palace of the eunuch's malign influence. He summoned Suraj Mall for counsel. The latter was his adherent as well as a relative of Balu. With him came agents of Balu and the raja of Jaipur. Javid was also called for a meeting on 27 August. In the course of discussions, Safdar Jang led the eunuch away to a domed alcove. While the two were carrying on their discussions, a Turkish officer, Muhammed Ali Jarji, rushed in with some soldiers and killed the eunuch, stabbing him repeatedly.

The headless trunk of the murdered eunuch was thrown on the river sands below the fort. The wazir thought he had removed the biggest thorn in his side, but he was not destined to derive any benefit from the assassination. New and much more formidable antagonists now came to the fore. The days of Safdar Jang's wazarat were numbered.

NOTES

1. Sarkar, *Fall of the Mughal Empire*, i, pp. 352-3. *Tarikh-i-Ahmad Shahi*, p. 17b.
2. Sarkar, i, p. 354. Sardesai, *Selections from the Peshwa's Daftar*, ii, p. 13.
3. Sarkar, i, pp. 383-4. Tabatabai, *Seir Mutaqherin*, iii, pp. 289-90.
4. Sarkar, i, pp. 392-7. Tabatabai, iii, pp. 294-8.
5. Tabatabai, iii, pp. 303-4.
6. Ansari, *Tarikh-i-Muzaffari*, p. 49. Sarkar, i, p. 399.
7. Tabatabai, iii, p. 299.
8. Ibid., pp. 314-15.
9. Ibid., pp. 318-19. Sarkar, i, pp. 356-8.
10. Khwaja Abdul Karim Kashmiri, *Bayan-i-Waqiai*, p. 265. Sarkar, i, p. 409 (fn.).
11. Sarkar, i, p. 433. Tabatabai, iii, pp. 326-7.

CHAPTER 26

The Civil War and the Downfall of Safdar Jang

Safdar Jang had expected that his problems would be solved by the removal of Javid Khan. But Javid's murder proved to be a blunder. Javid was only an eunuch and his power did not extend beyond the Qila-i-Mualla. Javid wanted to remain the immediate power in the palace; he was prepared to use the Turani faction to keep the Irani wazir in check but he had no intention of allowing them to grow so powerful that they could threaten him (Javid). But with the death of Javid, an open confrontation started between the wazir and the Turani umara.

The murder of Javid Khan earned for Safdar the enmity of the emperor and, what was much more dangerous, that of his mother, Udham Bai. She had lost her lover and made no attempt to conceal her grief. Putting aside her jewels and finery, she donned the traditional white clothes of a widow in mourning.[1]

For the next seven months the wazir enjoyed absolute power. But he used this period only to aggrandize himself. His son Shuja ud-Daulah, already mir atish, was appointed to a number of other posts and given the charge of the pay-mastership of the ahadis, the office for confirmation of grants and appointments, the mace-bearers and the emperor's stables. Four days after the murder of Javid Khan, one Abu Tarab Khan was appointed qiladar and police superintendent of the Qila-i-Mualla, posts which came under the supervision of the mir atish. Earlier they had been held by Javid Khan, but with the appointment of Abu Tarab, an adherent of Safdar Jang, the fort came under the complete control of the wazir. In January 1753, Shuja was also given the superintendence of the Diwan-i-Khas which enabled him to regulate the entry to the private audiences of the emperor.

Most of the Turkish nobles had already stopped attending court for fear of assassination. After the murder of Javid they had good reason for not attending the court as the wazir prohibited the bearing of arms in court by the nobles.

The emperor noticed that the attendance in the durbar was thin and those who came were mainly the adherents of the wazir. He complained to Shuja that his underlings were arbitrarily refusing entry to his private audiences.

The wazir went as far as posting some women as his agents inside the harem to monitor and censor the communications and correspondence of the Qibla-i-Alam, Udham Bai. The latter felt outraged and threw out the spies. The wazir took umbrage and stopped coming to court. A reconciliation was effected only when the emperor called on the wazir at his mansion accompanied by his mother. The visit took place on 23 September 1752 and the price of this reconciliation was realized on the 28th when Shuja was vested with the various offices listed earlier.

But Udham Bai was not the woman to forget a humiliation easily. She set up a rival court in her *deohri*, sitting behind a latticed screen, listening to petitions and complaints and passing orders. Malcontents had easy access to her and chief among them was Intizam ud-Daulah who had access to her through his mother, Sholapuri Begum, and soon the beginnings of a conspiracy began to take shape. Rumour placed Intizam at the head of the conspiracy, but the real brain was his cousin Shihab ud-Din, entitled Imad ul-Mulk, the fifteen year old son of Ghazi ud-Din Khan Firoz Jang. This precocious teenager, brought up with extreme strictness by a pious and austere father, was to prove the monster of the age.

His father had left in May, escorted by Holkar's troops, to take up his charge as viceroy of the Deccan. But within a few months came the news of his sudden death. His family feared that the emperor would take this as an excuse to seize all their goods and treasure in escheat, egged on by Intizam, with whom relations were not exactly *comme il faut*, as is so often the case between close relatives. To forestall any such move Imad went to the wazir and sat on *dharna*, weeping and wailing. After the loss of his father there was no one to look after him, he lamented. The wazir was now his father, and it was his duty to protect him. 'You are my only defender and guardian now', was his constant refrain. He sat making shameless exhibition of his pretended grief till the wazir, worn out by his persistence, assured him that he would find a father in him. He called his son and the two boys exchanged turbans as a token of the adoption and Imad was introduced to Safdar Jang's principal consort who appeared before him unveiled, since there could be no *purdah* between a mother and a son.[2]

Safdar Jang imagined that by taking the child under his wing he had split the Turani party and after the prescribed period of mourning was over he urged his cause before the emperor and was able to secure for him the succession to his father's estates and titles, including that of Nizam-ul-Mulk and Amir-ul-Umara and the office of mir bakhshi. But little did he know that he was nursing a viper in his bosom and that soon the snake would strike.

However, even Safdar Jang was hardly the emperor's most devoted servant. Some scholars lay the blame for the fall of the Mughal empire to the Persian element in the Mughal umara. According to this school, they lacked commitment to the dynasty which was orthodox sunni and were devoted entirely to the advancement of their own interest. Thus, Safdar Jang had expropriated scores, if not hundreds, of jagirdars holding estates in the provinces of Allahabad and Awadh—either seizing the jagirs for himself or granting them to his followers. He had also persuaded the emperor to give him all the imperial crown lands in these provinces, which had raised a host of enemies against him, all anxious to contribute their mite towards his downfall.

About the same time, in December 1752, the news came that the Durrani Shah had once again crossed the Indus and was heading towards Punjab. Again there was a panic as the imperial army was virtually in dissolution. The unpaid soldiers rioted almost daily in the streets while the household troops, like the Surkh Posh and Wala Shahi squatted on *dharna* to demand their rightful dues. The wazir promised to get a Maratha army for the defence of the empire but fortunately there was no need. Abdali had no intentions of proceeding as far as Delhi. In February 1753 Abdali's envoy came to the capital and left with the usual unsatisfactory and evasive answers. The crisis broke out in March.

For some time the city had been rife with rumours about an impending coup by Intizam. The wazir avoided the court and remained at home. On 17 March there was a fake alarm, the emperor called out the household troops and Shuja ud-Daulah's deputy, Abu Tarab, fled from his post.

Abu Tarab's was a key post and from his residence atop the Delhi Gate of the fort one could exercise complete control over the fort. With his ejectment the coup had been achieved though, at first, the wazir did not realize it. The emperor and the Turani sardars were able to establish their control over the household troops.

The wazir, expecting that the emperor would be looking for a reconciliation, submitted his resignation the following day. Couched in phrases of wounded dignity he expressed his fear that he had lost his monarch's confidence. To continue as wazir would be an imposition on His Majesty and he desired to be relieved of his duties and granted leave to retire to Awadh.

To his surprise and shock, the offer had an immediate response. Though his resignation was not accepted, the emperor permitted him to retire to his subedari. The letter was in the emperor's own handwriting and on 23 March the customary *khillats* of departure were sent by the emperor and Udham Bai to wish him godspeed. But the wazir was in no hurry, even though the emperor, being informed that the wazir was having difficulty collecting the required transport, sent 50 *raths* for his harem![3] There was a plot to inveigle him into the fort on the pretext of talks and have him murdered. But being warned by Malika-i-Zamani, one of emperor's stepmothers who had been shabbily treated by Udham Bai, Safdar Jang was able to avoid the trap.

Imad ul-Mulk, the mir bakhshi, was sent as an emissary to Intizam by Safdar Jang but the mir bakhshi no longer had any use for his former patron. He had secured his late father's titles and property through the wazir and now he had no qualms in ditching him to join Intizam. His late father had left behind about Rs. 70 lakh, and this would prove decisive for purchasing Maratha support.

On 26 March, the wazir left his mansion and moved into tents. His dwelling, had become untenable as it was commanded by the guns of the fort. It was drizzling as he marched out, and as the rose-red walls of the Exalted Fort came into view, he stopped and dismounted. The rain mixed with the tears streaming from his eyes as he turned and bowed in a low salaam towards his invisible master.[4] It was a poignant moment, for though he did not know it, his ministry was over.

At this time his armed strength was formidable but he desisted from a trial remembering the fate of the Syeds. He wrote to the Marathas and reminded Malhar of their old ties, but the Holkar chief wanted to back a winning horse, and the persuasive power of Imad's gold was stronger. From his old allies only Suraj Mall responded, but the fighting worth of the Jats was uncertain. And the longer he waited, the stronger grew his enemies, while day by day his problems multiplied. Having lost control over the emperor's person, following the ejectment of his agents from the fort, his position had become much weaker than he realized.

For some weeks nothing special happened. The court resumed its normal routine. The durbars were well attended but entry was denied to the wazir's agents. There was one notable accession to the strength of Safdar Jang. Rajindra Giri, *mahant* of an order of martial ascetics—the Naga sadhus—and faujdar of Saharanpur, had come to Delhi on the summons of his patron Safdar Jang with his cohort of armed followers. Delhi was partially blockaded and the price of grain and vegetables rose. The emperor protested, but the wazir replied that his quarrel was with Intizam and Imad, and the emperor should tell them to go and fight it out in the open, instead of hiding behind high walls.

There was also an attempt on the lives of both Intizam and Imad. Imad was the brain behind everything. His energy and organizing talent were astonishing. Intizam was no help; basically a coward, he was even more incompetent than his late father. But for Imad, the struggle would undoubtedly have gone in favour of the wazir. It was he who tilted the balance. One handicap of Safdar's was that most of his soldiers, who were central Asian Turks by origin, had their families within the walled city of Shahjahanabad. But with Safdar camping outside the city they had now become hostages in the hands of Imad.

Towards the end of April, Suraj Mall joined Safdar with 15,000 soldiers. Salabat Khan, living in poverty and obscurity also joined the wazir, his old friend, but his value was questionable as he brought with him no money, and his advice was worthless. Following an attack by Rajindra Giri on some of the houses of the Turanian umara, the emperor stripped Shuja ud-Daulah of his offices, appointing Samsam ud-Daulah—son of the Samsam ud-Daulah Khan-i-Dauran who had been killed at Karnal during the Nadir Shahi invasion—on 6 March 1753. The wazir gave permission to the Jats and Rajindra Giri to plunder the suburbs of the capital. Refugees crowded into Shahjahanabad, and the emperor ordered his gardens, and those of the umara, to be opened to accommodate them.

On 13 May, the wazir was formally dismissed and Intizam appointed in his place with his father's title of Itimad ud-Daulah (the third of the family to bear this title, the first being his grand-father Muhammad Amin Khan Chin). Imad ul-Mulk was at the same time invested with the titles of his father and grandfather, Nizam-ul-Mulk and Asaf Jah.

It was now an open war. Safdar Jang, in turn, produced an unknown boy recently purchased by Shuja, gave him out to be a grandson of Kam Bakhsh, and proclaimed him emperor under the title of Akbar Adil Shah! He declared himself his wazir and Salabat Khan his mir bakhshi.[5]

The emperor now sent a general call for help to all his feudatories. His mother acted with vigour and resolution. She produced Rs. 2 crore out of her private hoards and sat in conferences with officers and amirs, planning the next move.

In a calculated move to weaken Safdar, Imad announced a bounty of Rs. 50 with one month's advance pay to any soldier who deserted from Safdar's army. Nearly 23,000 soldiers defected through this move. A new brigade, known as the 'Seen Dagh' was raised out of these defected soldiers and so named because of the Arabic letter Seen (after Safdar Jang) which was branded on their horses' flanks. They were popularly known as the 'Badakhshis' as many of them were descended from Badakhshani migrants. Another factor helping the massive desertions was a conscious attempt to promote anti-Shia feelings, as the bulk of Safdar's soldiers were Turkish Sunnis.

The largest contingent to come in response to the emperor's appeal was that of Najib Khan, the Rohilla chief, who came with 15,000 horse and foot. Antaji Mankeshwar was already there with 4,000 Marathas, and Khande Rao Holkar promised that he would join later on. In addition, contingents came from Sadullah (son of the late Ali Muhammad Rohilla), Bikaner, Kunjpura, Anupnagar, Baluch sarders from the Mewat, Anupnagar and even from Muin ul-Mulk. In all, about 57,000 men came to help the emperor, besides the deserters who constituted the Seen Dagh Risala.[6]

The first offensive move was made by Safdar Jang. But before that, the imperial forces plundered the house belonging to two brothers-in-law of Shuja ud-Daulah which lay close to the fort's walls. The gentlemen were on the side of the emperor notwithstanding their relationship with Safdar's family but their haveli was full of valuables deposited by umara owing allegiance to both sides, who had also sent their women there for safety. The pretext for the attack was that some cannon balls fired from the direction of the mansion had fallen in the fort. They might very well have been fired from Safdar's guns which lay in the same line, but the emperor's supporters, having assembled such a large army, were desperate for funds, and Imad ul-Mulk, with the impatience and impetuousity of youth, was only looking for an excuse to raise money by any means, fair or foul.

This attack was the signal for a general onslaught on the houses of Safdar's adherents living within the city. The men of the Seen Dagh must have counted themselves lucky to have changed sides.

With the imperial forces getting stronger day by day and his own weakening, Safdar decided to attempt an attack on Delhi. First he obtained possession of the Kotla Firoz Shah with the connivance of some Wala Shahi officers who opened the gates to him. Guns were raised to the top of the hillock shaped Kotla from where fire could be directed over the city walls and into the qila itself. The shelling did considerable damage, and the ramparts and bastion opposite the Kotla were breached.

On 5 June 1753 Safdar launched an assault through the breach. Intizam's mansion, located near the city walls, was the scene of fierce fighting. But the imperial forces repulsed the attack and were even able to regain the

Kotla from whose heights they now poured a punishing fire into Safdar's camp, compelling him to retire further away from the city. In this fighting Najib distinguished himself and he and his brother were both wounded.

On 14 June again Safdar attacked the imperial trenches. Safdar Jang himself went forth in this operation while Imad also came foreward to encourage his soldiers. The attack was repulsed and among the casualties was Rajindra Giri, the mahant of the Naga sadhus, who was probably the best officer left with Safdar Jang. The latter was very fond of him and his death affected him so much that he did not have the heart to again lead his troops into the battle. Safdar Jang respected this warrior-monk and had exempted him from the observance of the usual ceremonies. Instead of the usual low *tasleems*, he was permitted to bless the nawab, in keeping with his spiritual position as the head of a monastic order.[7]

With Safdar Jang disheartened by the death of Rajindra Giri, his forces continued to be pushed further south. At the same time desertions increased. By the middle of July, the forces of Safdar Jang were pushed to a position between Badarpur and Faridabad while the imperial forces were stretched in a long line from the Yamuna to Kalkaji and Mehrauli. The fighting was of a desultory nature, marked by skirmishes between small bodies of troops and occasional cannonades.

But, meanwhile, other problems were manifesting themselves. The imperial treasury, never full, was soon exhausted. The funds contributed by Imad and the Empress Mother, and the additional sum raised by melting the silver and golden utensils lying in the royal stores, had also run out, and the soldiers were restless for their pay. Troops would revolt, sit on *dharna*, and *gherao* their officers.

In the beginning of September the Rohilla, Baluch and Gujjar auxiliaries retreated to Barahpula in protest against the non-receipt of pay and started looting villagers and travellers. Even some units of the artillery abandoned their posts. Taking advantage of the discontent, Safdar Jang again pushed forward to recover the lost ground and cut the grain supply. Imad pleaded in vain with the emperor and his mother for money. At the same time tentative peace moves were being made in secret.

Imad was in favour of fighting to the bitter end and he was angry with his elder cousin who seldom ventured outside the fort and also discouraged the emperor from doing so. Imad, on the other hand, repeatedly urged the emperor to come and lead the army in person. His presence would enthuse the troops, and the opposing forces being in no bette shape, a single vigorous push with the padishah leading them could bring the war to a swift conclusion. Otherwise the indecisive warfare could drag on indefinitely until both armies ultimately broke up and dispersed for want of pay.

Intizam was indeed a coward and he had left the entire conduct of the war to the young Imad who pursued it with an obsessive fixation. With the latter's increasing popularity, Intizam felt increasingly insecure. Thus, while Imad had his eyes on the rich province of Awadh for himself, the contemptible Intizam had come round to the view that the preservation of Safdar Jang was essential as a counterweight to the growing power of Imad. He visualized that there would soon be a showdown between him and Imad, and in that event the ex-wazir might prove a valuable ally.

On 29 September there was another fierce battle in which Imad ul-Mulk and Najib Khan finally succeeded in pushing the rebels further south, towards Ballabhgarh.

The peace overtures made through Intizam having failed, the emperor wrote a letter to Madho Singh, maharaja of Jaipur, requesting him to come and mediate between the warring parties. He arrived in October and the negotiations were resumed. But these again were secret and when Imad came to know of them and confronted the emperor, the latter immediately disavowed the moves, denouncing the copies of Safdar's letters which the mir bakhshi had produced as forgeries!

On 25 October 1753, Suraj Mall was produced before the emperor in the garden at Khizrabad where he made his ceremonial submission and was graciously pardoned, with very generous terms. On 5 November, in the same secret hush-hush manner, a peace was finalized with Safdar. An imperial firman, a horse, a robe of honour, an aigrette and other ornaments were sent to him. Imad again protested but the emperor even now denied that he had given him anything, claiming that the robe of honour must have been the one which he had given to Madho Singh![8] Such was the terror that this fifteen year old inspired in the emperor.

But in this furtive and diffident manner peace was ultimately restored. Suraj Mall marched off with his Jats and Safdar Jang was permitted to retire to Awadh which he retained as governor. And Madho Singh, the peace maker, returned to his principality of Jaipur bearing with him the imperial firman granting him Ranthambor, the last important fortress held directly by the Mughals. The acquisition of this fortress had been the ambition of the house of Jaipur for many years and Muhammad Shah had snubbed Ishwari Singh in 1748 by refusing his request. The civil war had completed the process of the establishment of independent provincial dynasties, Awadh being the last of them. These provincial dynasts, nominally still the umara of the court of Delhi, took no interest in imperial politics which became the playground of lesser men fighting for the illusion of power and prestige, though the core had long since dried up. The area actually under the emperor's control had shrunk to the immediate environs of Delhi; Sirhind, Hissar, Narnaul and Aligarh marking roughly the limits of actual control. Beyond lay the territories of the Afghan Shah, the Rohilla and Bangash Pathans, the Jats and the Rajput princes. Among these powers the most formidable were the Rohillas under the leadership of Najib Khan who, since the civil war, had been dignified with the title of Najib-ud-Daulah. Enjoying the support of Ahmad Shah Durrani he would dominate the stage for the next twenty years.

NOTES

1. *Tarikh-i-Ahmad Shahi*, p. 41.
2. Tabatabai, *Seir Mutaqherin*, iii, pp. 329-30. Sarkar, *Fall of the Mughal Empire*, ii, pp. 453-4.
3. Sarkar, i, p. 474.
4. Ibid., p. 468.
5. *Tarikh-i-Ahmad Shahi*, p. 54b. Harcharan Das, *Chahar Gulzar-i-Shujai*, p. 409b.
6. Sarkar, i, pp. 482-5, 492 (fn.).
7. Ibid., pp. 491-2. Tabatabai, iii, p. 333.
8. Sarkar, i, p. 504.

CHAPTER 27

The Rise of Imad ul-Mulk

The civil war had ended with the victors bitterly divided. The old rivalry between the two great Turkish families, so closely related, came into the open. Intizam was apprehensive that Imad would drive him out of the prime ministership, while Imad was furious at being constantly crossed by his elder cousin and cheated of a decisive victory. It was obvious that the wazir, and Amir-ul-Umara would soon part company. The emperor, though as cowardly and pusillanimous as his wazir, lacked cunning. Fearing the power and ruthless logic of the young bakhshi, he followed the advice of the former and, shamelessly but unconvincingly, lied to the latter. His fate became inextricably linked with the wazir.

The immediate problem before the state was of finding money to pay the soldiers. Six months of civil war had left the sorrounding countryside a waste. The crown estates were in the hands of robbers. The peasants and the merchants had been robbed and plundered, often several times over during the year, and the chances of getting revenue from them were bleak. On the other hand, the salaries of the imperial troops had been in arrears for nearly two years before the out-break of the conflict and the arrears including the dues of Rohilla, Maratha and Gujjar auxiliaries, amounted to not less than Rs. 1.5 crore!

The problems appeared insurmountable. Everyday the peace would be disturbed by rioting soldiers. On 16 and 17 November 1753 the bakhshi had been gheraoed by the soldiers of Najib Khan.[1] Confined to his house he, at last, bought them off by assigning them the revenues of some villages in the doab which had once been held by them. Eventually, on 26 November they left for Rohilkhand, plundering the small markets of Patparganj and Shahdara on the way.

Having got rid of them the bakhshi decided to recover those crown estates, to the south of the city, which had been usurped by Balu Jat and other outlaws. He set about it with characteristic energy and soon succeeded in eliminating Balu, the leading malcontent. The latter tried to brazen it out but Aqibat Mahmud, Imad's former tutor and confidential counsellor, was prepared for action. When Balu's hand touched the hilt of his sword threateningly, Aqibat's Badakhshi escort immediately fell upon him and slew him, alongwith his son, diwan and nine others.[2]

Till the middle of January 1754, Imad and Aqibat remained busy, reducing one mud fort after another. Some of the villages had earlier been held by a Gujjar chieftain, so afterwards they were handed over to Fateh Singh Bargujjar, the son of the former proprietor, from whom they had been seized by Suraj Mall the previous year. The reinduction of the Gujjars was intended to deter the Jats from again usurping the villages.

Khande Rao Holkar (Khandoji) had been assisting Imad in this drive. But he was summoned by his father, Malhar Rao, who had begun a serious campaign against the principal stronghold of Suraj Mall, the famous mud fort of Kumbher. Meanwhile, another force of the bakhshi had cleared the trans-Yamuna area of Koil and Jalesar and reestablished the imperial writ in the middle doab.

The arrival of Khandoji's army had been followed by highly undignified efforts of the wazir to win him over to his side. But Khandoji steadfastly refused to be bought. He refused the *khillats* which were sent by the wazir and even returned the 22,000 gold coins which were sent, with the remark that he was not the emperor's servant, therefore why should he send him *khillats*? He had merely been sent by his father Malhar Rao to assist Imad in his campaign against Suraj Mall.

But eventually, to save the face of wazir and emperor, a presentation of sorts was arranged. The date fixed was 26 December, and the place, the Nili Chhatri Garden, besides the Yamuna, to the north of the fort. When Khandoji arrived, the chamberlain who was to conduct him to the presence asked him what *nazar* he proposed to offer to His Majesty? He was required to be told in advance because at the time of the presentation the chobdars were supposed to announce to the court what had been offered.

Khandoji replied bluntly that he was not carrying any money as he had merely come to bathe in the river, and it was only on his arrival that he had learnt that the emperor was also here and desired to meet him! But Aqibat Mahmud, who was also in the plot, somehow managed to manoeuvre the Maratha sardar towards the presence and the court chamberlain fished out 21 gold coins from his own pocket and placing them on a kerchief handed them to Khandoji, who made the required *tasleemats*. The chamberlain meantime announced in a loud voice, 'Khandoji presents a nazar of a hundred mohurs, an elephant, and a horse!'

It was with extreme difficulty and after many lapses of etiquette that Khandoji could be persuaded to leave. Though a brave soldier,

Khandoji was an alcoholic and perpetually in a state of intoxication.[3]

The siege of Kumbher proceeded in the usual lackadaisical manner. The light guns of the Marathas seemed to make no impression on the solid mud walls of the citadel. The Marathas had demanded Rs. 2 crore from Suraj Mall on the flimsy ground that he had collected much more than that during the civil war. The Jat leader offered Rs. 4 lakh to buy them off besides the regular tribute he owed the imperial government, but this was not accepted.

The siege dragged on. The Marathas plundered the surrounding territory, but no impression could be made on the solid adobe walls. A request was made through Imad for heavy guns from the imperial arsenal but, on the advice of the wazir, it was declined on the lame excuse that supplies of powder and shot had been exhausted. However, the real reason was, of course, that Intizam, having failed in his efforts to detach the Marathas from Imad, was determined not to do anything that could strengthen his rival. This was inspite of the fact that the bakhshi was at the time engaged in trying to squeeze the Jat raja to pay off the starving and mutinous soldiers of the emperor who had virtually taken over the city.

Finally Imad dispatched Aqibat with a large force to Delhi to persuade the imbecile emperor to release the guns. The approach of Aqibat filled the emperor and wazir with terror. But no steps were taken to prevent him from entering the city.

The city was virtually in the hands of the soldiers. The wazir and the emperor had shut themselves up, not daring to venture out for fear of being gheraoed by the soldiers. Now the latter were joined by Aqibat's Badakhshis, and the disorders mounted. Merchants' houses and godowns were plundered. Aqibat's Badakhshis made attempts to persuade the stubborn household troops, who garrisoned the Qila-i-Mualla, that they were attempting to secure not only their own dues, but theirs as well. But the Wala Shahi and Surkh Posh remained loyal to their salt and refused to join the Badakhshis.

Meantime Aqibat instituted a reign of terror. Rich men were haled to his presence and squeezed on the pretext that Safdar Jang and his officers had deposited their valuables with them. There were constant disturbances and clashes between soldiers and citizens. Then Aquibat finally left—still without the guns—he left behind a city devastated, as if by an invading army.[4]

The situation was intolerable and could not continue so for long. At last Intizam patched together a plan which promised some possibility of success. It owed its inspiration to Suraj Mall who was in communications with the wazir in what had become the characteristic style of conducting affairs at the Qila-i-Mualla. The imperial government had long ceased to have any long-term objectives or deliberate policy. All the situations which arose, whether as a result of external invasion—like the Durrani presence in Punjab—or from internal turmoil, were viewed solely from the viewpoint of factional interest. Hence, it was perfectly possible for Intizam to consider entering into a conspiracy with the Jat leader in the hope of turning the situation, in which the bakhshi found himself before Kumbher, to his advantage.

The plan was that the wazir should set out with the emperor to some nearby point, like Sikandra, under the pretext of restoring order and settling the recovered territory. Sikandra was within striking distance of Kumbher and if a message was sent to Safdar Jang, the wazir was sure he would gladly come to the assistance of the emperor to crush his former enemy, Imad ul-Mulk. The idea appealed to Intizam who was a keen intriguer and somehow the required carriage and tents were procured and the imperial party set out.

It was a brave attempt to revive the old tradition. The Empress Mother, the Vault of the Universe, Udham Bai, accompanied by other widows of Muhammad Shah, like Malika-i-Zamani and some of the wives and concubines of Ahmad Shah, were part of the excursion. Sikandra was reached without mishap, but the plan fell through mainly on account of Udham Bai's reluctance to join hands with the murderer of her lover Safdar Jang. Even though Intizam had stepped into his shoes—and very likely into her bed as well—he was unable to win her over to his diabolic plan.[5]

This hasty and ill-planned expedition was to result in a disaster which, in its moral effect, was almost as great a catastrophe as the Nadir Shahi invasion.

The arrival of the emperor and wazir was noted by the mir bakhshi. That something was afoot was obvious, but, uncertain as to what was intended, he thought he would throw them off-balance by seizing the initiative. Accordingly, the faithful Aqibat was sent to the emperor's camp to warn that some thousands of disbanded Maratha cavalry, had made their appearance in his neighbourhood and as suddenly disappeared, without it being known where they would show themselves again. Having delivered this cautionary message Aqibat returned. That, thought Imad, would keep the emperor and Intizam in a state of nervous apprehension for some time, and out of any mischief which they may have contemplated.

But Holkar decided, apparently on his own, to scare His Majesty and the wazir and avenge the denial of the guns. Setting off at night towards the imperial encampment, he attacked with a sizeable force while it was still dark. Amazingly, inspite of the warning of Aqibat, no precautions had been taken. Panic-stricken, the emperor together with his mother, the wazir and Samsam ud-Daulah (the mir atish), fled post-haste towards Delhi abandoning everything.[6]

Considerable booty fell into the hands of Malhar, but the most valuable prize which caused the emperor the greatest embarassment was the capture of the ladies of the imperial house. Nothing like this had happened before, and the emperor became the butt of vulgar jokes in the bazaars of Delhi when the full facts of the disaster came to be known.

The emperor left the camp at Sikandra on the night of 25 May 1754 and arrived at the Red Fort on the afternoon of the following day, sneaking in by a small entrance near the Octagonal Tower. Only the royal jewellery was saved, everything else was lost, including nearly 500 guns of various calibres. The expedition had been put together with tremendous effort. Virtually the bottom of the barrel had had to be scraped to clear the arrears of the gunners and the soldiers, for otherwise they would not march. But it was all for nothing, and it had ended in catastrophe.

The wazir and some officers arrived about three hours later. Unconscious of his own inglorious flight the emperor berated them for leaving behind his 'honour', i.e. the queens, princesses and the people of the harem. Samsam ud-Daulah tried to explain that in the darkness it was difficult to keep them together; the Maratha attack had been too sudden.

As a matter of fact Samsam ud-Daulah had fought for about an hour, and his resistance enabled many of the ladies' carts to get away. Roz Afzun Khan, the aged eunuch in charge of their security, tried to defend them, but the carts got separated and some, including those with him, were captured by Aqibat's brother who conducted them to a qazi's house for safety. Malika-i-Zamani fell into the hands of the Marathas and was escorted back to the camp which was now in Holkar's possession. Two daughters of the padishah and two of his wives, Sarfaroz Mahal and Rani Uttam Kumari were also captured. Most of the women who fell into Malhar's hands were treated with honour and respect but many were the unfortunates who were seized by the Maratha cavalry and violated and robbed of the jewels they were carrying on their persons, or the valuables that were kept in their carts and palkis for safety. Some made their way back to Delhi on foot, days later, tired, bedraggled and travel-stained.

On 28 May Imad visited Holkar's camp and even he was horrified at the turn of events. He called on Malika-i-Zamani, and presenting a *nazar* of 5 mohurs broke down and wept, begging her pardon. 'I was helpless in the matter,' he declared. 'The Deccanis do not listen to me, I am like their servant. I have ruined my reputation and cannot show my face.'

The graceful old lady who remembered the Persian visitation of 1739, tried to console him. What was destined had come to pass. Man was powerless before fate. Shihab ud-Din Imad ul-Mulk on the other hand was born in 1739, and could only have heard stories of the events of that dreadful year.

Advance squadrons of the Maratha light horse followed close on the heels of the emperor. On 31 May, he was informed that the Marathas were plundering Jaisinghpura and other suburbs. The previous day Roz Afzun Khan's head clerk had come, bearing letters from Holkar and the aged eunuch. Holkar placed certain demands which the eunuch recommended for immediate acceptance lest worse befall the female captives who were in the Maratha's possession. Ahmad had asked for a day's time to reply but being informed of the depredations of the Marathas in the suburbs he made haste to convey his consent to whatever the Maratha had demanded.

Intizam, safe for the moment behind the high walls of the Qila-i-Mualla, was breathing fire and vengeance, declaring his willingness to fight, even though two days earlier his mutinous troop had gheraoed him, demanding their pay.

On 1 June Aqibat Mahmud called on the emperor and persuaded him to agree to the appointment of Shihab ud-Din Imad ul-Mulk as prime minister in place of the cowardly and incompetent Intizam. Roz Afzun Khan would be superintendent of the Diwan-i-Khas relieving Intizam of both the key offices. Departing, Aqibat swore on a Koran that his master and Malhar would remain faithful and loyal to him.

The next day, Imad came to the court accompanied by Holkar's diwan and his brother Saifullah. A Koran was produced and the emperor asked him to swear that he would be faithful to him and his trust. This the precocious teenager readily and unhesitatingly did, using the most solemn and dreadful oaths. Then the oaths of office were administered and he was vested with the robes and the ceremonial writing case which symbolized the office of the prime minister. Thereafter he went to the adjoining anteroom where he signed some papers to signify his assumption of charge, dismissing the mir atish and other officers.

Mahmud Aqibat was then summoned and sent to the salatin khana to fetch a suitable prince. Muhammad Aziz ud-Daulah, a son of the emperor Jahandar, and grandson of Shah Alam Bahadur Shah, was brought. He was led in procession to the throne in the Diwan-i-Am which had been vacated barely half an hour earlier, and proclaimed emperor as Badshah Alamgir Sani (i.e. the second).

Imad ul-Mulk could swear the most solemn oaths without having the slightest intention of keeping them and suffered absolutely no remorse at having to break them. He had decided early on that the emperor had identified himself too closely with the wazir, and that both must be replaced at the same time.

The new emperor's first act was to order the arrest of his predecessor and Udham Bai. The haram sarai was again violated and they were found hiding among the trees in the garden before the Rang Mahal. A shawl was tossed to the fallen Empress Mother so that she could cover her face. Propriety having been served they were led away and locked up together. The dethroned emperor, nervous, apprehensive, and fearing the worst, asked for water. A soldier picked up a broken earthen pot and poured out a few sips for the fallen king of kings, and they were gratefully accepted.

So far had the mighty fallen.

NOTES

1. Sarkar, *Fall of the Mughal Empire*, i, p. 510.
2. Ibid., pp. 511-12.
3. Ibid., pp. 517-19. *Tarikh-i-Ahmad Shahi*, pp. 99b-100b.
4. Sarkar, i, pp. 526-36. *Tarikh-i-Ahmad Shahi*, pp. 112a-24a. Tabatabai, iii, pp. 335-6.
5. Tabatabai, iii, p. 337.
6. Ibid., pp. 337-8.
7. Sarkar, i, pp. 536-41.

CHAPTER 28

The Reign of Chaos

The new emperor was entirely a creature of Imad and never attempted to assert himself. A sixty-six year old man he had lived a quiet, secluded and decorous life. History was his passion and Aurangzeb his hero, hence the title of Alamgir II. He was old beyond his years. Immersed in his historical studies, he was free from vice and had lived the simple life of a householder with his family. But chance having brought him to the throne, he yielded to the temptations of luxury, and late though it was, set about stocking his harem with young and beautiful women.

The roving eye of this old man chanced to fall on Hazrat Begum, the daughter of the late Muhammad Shah. When in February, 1756, this girl turned her sixteenth year he demanded her hand in marriage from her guardian, Malika-i-Zamani, the most virtuous of Muhammad Shah's widows, who was treated with the reverence usually accorded to saints. 'Resistance is useless', he told her, when she protested at the disparity in years. 'Either consent to give her in marriage, or I shall take her by force.' But the princess was adamant, and declared that she preferred death to such a marriage.'I regard you as my father,' she pleaded, 'and you too should look upon me as another daughter. If you use force I shall kill myself.'

The frustrated suitor punished her by ordering the gates of her quarters to be closed so that she was isolated from the rest of the palace. However there were other princesses in the haram sarai who were less particular and, on 1 September 1758, he married Zinat Afroz Begum. At the time his health was so poor that he was liable to fainting fits.[1]

It was necessary to provide for his large family—14 princes and princesses, including grandsons and grand nephews—in a manner befitting the children of a padishah. Mansabs of up to 30,000 were conferred, but—the emperor was too poor to sanction the allowances that went with such exalted ranks. Most of the crown lands had been usurped by Safdar Jang, others had been alienated or usurped by Rohillas, Jats and half a dozen lesser umara. Imad himself would be requiring some source of revenue to pay off the Seen Dagh. The salt and grain markets close to the capital were the only sure sources of revenue left to the crown, and these were eagerly grabbed by the imperial family.[2]

The problems which confronted Imad may well have daunted a more capable minister. One is taken aback at the audacity of this fifteen year old who had taken on the burden of the chief executive at such a critical juncture. With the country ravaged by six months of civil war, an empty treasury and a hungry, disorderly, and mutinous army, any person, however capable, would have faced a near impossible task.

That Imad was energetic, decisive, and ruthless was evident. He had given ample proof of it during the preceding civil war. But these qualities were not enough for saving and reviving the glory of the empire. The absence of moral scruples may indeed have been an advantage in that brutal age, but his policy was inconsistent and subject to sudden changes. In the beginning he was firmly in the clutch of the Marathas, later he would abandon them and enter on a hopeless campaign against them on the urging of Durrani. At the same time, on several occasions, he gratuitously annoyed and called down the wrath of Aḥmad Shah and his deputy, Najib. He had, in truth, no policy at all. As a scion of the most powerful Turki family in India, he had considered the post of mir bakhshi, and later that of prime minister, as his, virtually by right. He was driven solely by personal ambition and family pride.

The actions of his celebrated grandfather, the first Asaf Jah, had been governed by the sentiment of respect and loyalty to dynasty. Even when it was suggested that he should assume the sovereignty himself, he had declined saying that his family had served the dynasty for decades and he had no wish to sully its record for mere personal ambition. In the absence of any feeling like patriotism, this respect for the lord whose 'salt' they had eaten could be the only meaningful principle governing conduct. But in a person so utterly lacking the moral sensibility, even this had no significance, and we shall see him proceed from one pointless atrocity to another. All the education which his father Ghazi ud-Din had lavished on him, the labours of his tutors, his skill in languages, philosophy, jurispridence, theology and history was of no account. For a fifteen year old his education was remarkable and he could be described as precocious, but he proved to be the very opposite of his father. He was as evil as his puritanical father had been God-fearing. Without any higher vision to guide him, his term as prime minister was utterly barren of results, and he was subjected to indignities which no wazir had suffered before.

The immediate and most pressing problem confronting Imad was finding money to pay the ransom demanded by the Marathas for the release of Malika-i-Zamani and the other ladies. Not only was it a question of the honour of the dethroned Ahmad, but of the imperial house itself. The sum demanded was Rs. 40 lakh, an absurd sum which he could not, by any stretch of imagination, pay in the immediate future. But nonetheless, he and Samsam ud-Daulah offered personal guarantees for the payment which however the Marathas refused to accept.

To complicate the matter, another Maratha officer had arrived on the scene and he happened to be senior to Malhar. This was Raghunath Rao, the younger brother of the peshwa, and he had come after ravaging Rajasthan, dunning the princes for their arrears of *chauth*, collecting what he could at the point of the sword. As for Imad and the emperor, his instructions were to squeeze them as much as possible. Anywhere between Rs. 50 lakh to 75 lakh would be acceptable. The actual bill presented to the wazir was Rs. 82.5 lakh, of which Rs. 40 lakh was to be paid immediately. For the remainder, bankers bills would be acceptable.

Inspite of the impossibility of collecting this enormous sum, Imad set about raising what he could. He had come to power on the strength of Maratha arms. In normal circumstances a sizeable *peshkash* would have been required to be paid to the appointing authority. Imad had offered Rs. 25 lakh on this account, payable not to the emperor, as would have been normally the case, but to the Marathas instead. But this had been rejected as too small; and then Raghunath Rao had presented his preposterous bill.

Imad's first victims were Udham Bai and her family. The accumulated treasures of her brother and her sister were forfeited. But with the best efforts, inspite of interrogating the servants, and after digging up the floors of their houses, only about Rs. 3 lakh were recovered. This was promptly sent to the Marathas.

The next option available was to apply the screw on the rich and wealthy among the citizens of Delhi. This meant in practise the merchants and bankers, as the umara were too powerful to be touched. The wazir posted soldiers in front of their houses but the Delhi bazaars responded by pulling down their shutters, a form of protest common to this day. For several days they remained closed and crowds of people assembled daily below the *jharokha* window to protest against the extortion. The people of Delhi had suffered enough in the past eight months. Aqibat Mahmud Khan, Imad's former tutor and principal factotum, had done his share of squeezing when he had come to request the emperor for the guns. Groups of starving and desperate troopers from the Seen Dagh were still breaking into the houses of respectable people. There was no pretence of maintaining law and order.

Imad was forced to relent. The expedient of levying a poll tax on all the inhabitants of the city was tried out. But this yielded a paltry sum of only Rs. 1 lakh, even though sums of Rs. 10 to 15 were actually levied from each person. But the very poor had been exempted from the levy and the high and mighty were untouched. Intizam ud-Daulah for instance, down but not out, had barricaded himself in his mansion which was guarded by 600 soldiers, with cannon loaded with grape, and ready to counter any attack. So, as usual, the burden of the impost fell on the bankers, merchants and artisans of Delhi. Anyone who was in any way linked to the wazir and could plausibly claim to be 'his' man, was likewise exempt.

Ultimately, about Rs. 9 lakh was paid. The process by which the money was extracted was painful and only after frequent resort to the cudgel could the honest burghers be persuaded to part with their money. Banker's bills were accepted for Rs. 17.5 lakh while the remaining, Rs. 13.5 lakh, were completely uncovered. There was only the word of the emperor that they would be paid on some future date. As for the remaining Rs. 42.5 lakh, its realization was impossible, but to save face, the Marathas were given assignments amounting to this sum on the revenues of Bengal, Bareilly, Bairat, Sambhar, Kora and some other mahals. But these places had long since passed from the control of Delhi. So the bills were dishonoured and, ultimately, more lands in the upper doab had to be alienated to the Marathas.[3]

High though the cost was, the women were at last brought home, and in February 1755 the Marathas returned to the Deccan.

But paying off the Marathas was only part of the problem. The wazir's own soldiers, and the Badakhshi troopers of the Seen Dagh were also in arrears, and as they had been inducted on defection from Safdar Jang's army with an initial bounty and one month's salary, they were extremely unruly. As early as August 1754 Kishan Chand Sood, a senior accounts officer, was abducted by Baqi Beg Khan, one of the Badakhshi captains and tortured for fifteen days before being released on payment of a large ransom.[4]

In June, Imad's haveli was gheraoed by his gunners. They assaulted Aqibat, tore off his clothes, and thrashed him. He was rescued by his master who was able to secure a banker's draft to defray part of the arrears. But about this time a conspiracy was uncovered, the kingpin of which was Aqibat. He had forged a letter bearing the seal of the deposed Ahmad Shah, calling upon Intizam to liberate him with the help of the Rajput princes and reinstate him on the throne. Then Intizam would be his wazir again and they would all live happily ever after.

Aqibat was called for a discussion and then murdered in Imad's presence. Reluctantly, after being pressed by Imad, Alamgir consented to the blinding of the deposed emperor Ahmad and Udham Bai—the first time such an atrocity had been committed on a female member of the Chughata house.[5] As for Intizam, secure within his heavily guarded mansion, his. estates and property were seized and confiscated.

Later, apprehending danger, Intizam fled to the Maratha camp for protection, which, oddly enough, was readily extended, although a few months earlier they had been bitter foes. Eighteenth century Indian history offers innumerable instances in support of the old aphorism that in politics there are no permanent friends or enemies. Some months later Maratha mediation was able to effect a reconciliation between uncle and nephew and Intizam's property was restored.

But the unpaid soldiers continued to disrupt the peace of Delhi. On one occasion the palki of Sholapuri Begum, the wazir's grandmother (Intizam's mother), was turned back by agitating soldiers. After Imad's gunners had been partially satisfied, the other soldiers assaulted their paymaster. On another occasion Diwan Nagar Mall, diwan of the Khalsa was mobbed by the palace servants who had not been paid for three years. He barely escaped with his life.[6]

Then it was the turn of the imperial gunners who went on a chain fast in the Qila-i-Mualla and obstructed the entry of food and grain into the fort. They were fobbed off with one week's salary—the first payment they had received in seven months. In December they again resumed their agitation. This time with the intervention of Najib, arrears amounting to ten months were admitted and paid by the son of the Jagat Seth of Bengal—the Rothschild of north India.

And so it goes on. The anonymous account known as the *Delhi Chronicle* and the official history of the sorry reign, the *Tarikh-i-Alamgir Sani* recount innumerable such instances. On one occasion, the starving soldiers actually stormed the wazir's kitchen and ran off with the food! One can only wonder at their fortitude and patience that they did no worse. Somehow, as is the case today, the ruling umara were able to keep enough security personnel on their side, so that nobody could make a direct attack on the incompetent rulers who were responsible for the mess.

There was actual hunger and misery in the Qila-i-Mualla. The story is narrated that when a bowl of broth from the fort's *langar*—meant for indigent beggars and mendicants—was brought to the heir apparent for ritual tasting, the prince suggested humbly that some of it be sent inside as no food had been cooked for two days in the harem! Demonstrations by hungry soldiers were common occurance, but on one occasion the women of the harem—including princesses—came out in a body, loudly protesting. The gates of the palace had to be closed to prevent them from going out. And there they sat down in the court of the diwan khana, cursing their fate and bewailing their fortune, throwing dust in their hair with their veils cast aside—traditional modes for registering protest by women. It was only after a day and a night had passed in this manner that they could be persuaded to rise and return to their dreary quarters.[7]

The story is also narrated that the emperor, who happened to be in tents at Loni, had called from the palace two of his wives. But the gates of the fort were barred by agitating soldiers with none of the inmates allowed to enter or leave, so these royal ladies left the fort disguised as common maidservants in a *burqa* on foot! Outside they mounted a *bhishti's* bullockcart and travelled thus for some distance, and only when the fear of detection had passed did they enter a more appropriate conveyance.[8]

When the mode of their getaway was explained to the old emperor he was highly amused, and without and slightest feeling of embarassment he narrated the story to his courtiers to impress them with the intelligence of the wretched ladies.

The reader of these dismal annals will ask; surely the wazir must have done something? At least attempted something? That one of the Orient's greatest empires should sink to these depths of degradation in so short a period is almost unimaginable.

A start had to be made with the immediate neighbourhood of Delhi. Much of the Delhi suba had been usurped by rebel chiefs and robber barons. The wazir's Badakhshi soldiers of the Seen Dagh were one of the best troops in the empire, provided they were paid on time and competently led. But in the past one year, ever since they entered the service of Imad, they had been allowed to run amok and given license to live by plundering the honest citizens of Delhi. As a result discipline had broken down, and the higher officers, their paymasters and the wazir himself were almost daily exposed to insult at their hands.

Nevertheless, it was decided to send the Seen Dagh against Qutb Shah, an Afghan who had usurped many villages in Sirhind. He enjoyed the status of a pir among the Rohillas and on the accession of Alamgir II had been given a small grant in the Meerut and Saharanpur districts. But six months later these same villages were transferred to the Marathas to meet their claims which were more pressing. Qutb Shah then crossed the Yamuna and started seizing lands in the Sirhind sarkar.

The Badakhshis proceeded leisurely against Qutb Shah plundering the honest burghers of Panipat which fell on the way. They clashed with Qutb Shah's small force near Karnal. Although the imperial forces numbered nearly 12,000 and Qutb Shah had barely 2,500 fighting men, the latter emerged victorious, the victory being attributed to a freak duststorm. The imperial army fell back on Sonepat while Qutb Shah, emboldened, continued his rampage towards the Sutluj where he ran into Adina Beg Khan, faujdar of the Jalandhar Doab, who defeated him at Ropar on 11 April 1755.

On receiving the news of the defeat of the imperial forces on 11 March, Imad urged the emperor to set out to chastise Qutb Shah. Protesting weakly, the emperor complied but the starving servants refused to accompany him and in the beginning food had to be prepared in the fort and sent out to the camp.

The wazir seemed to have lost his nerve. Hesitantly, he called on Najib Khan Rohilla and Kamgar Khan Baluch for help and both of them advised him to set forth. A military demonstration was essential but he did not set out until 13 April.

The wazir along with the emperor, reached Panipat. Here he summoned the Badakhshi captains, who had disgraced themselves at Karnal, to bring their troops and receive their pay according to their actual numbers. This they did not like as they would not be able to profit from the pay of the dead or missing soldiers and they broke out in open mutiny. On 3 May 1755 about 250 of these mutineers gathered outside the house where the wazir was staying and created a tumult. The latter came out to inquire and was immediately mobbed by the Badakhshis. They dragged him through the bazaar, his clothes were torn, blows were inflicted on his person and he was made to sit down in the dust and listen to the contumely poured on him while others called for their pay and demanded that he send for the money from his house and pay them then and there. After about two hours Hasan Beg extricated him from their clutches and placing him on an elephant sent him to his quarters.

The insult suffered by the wazir was unprecedented. So far the victims of unpaid soldiers had been only his officers like Aqibat Mahmud Khan or Diwan Nagar Mall, but now, for the first time, they had laid hands on the wazir himself. Such insolence could not go unpunished. He collected all his other troops and attacked the Badakhshis who fled leaving their tents and equipment behind them which the wazir allowed his loyal troops to plunder. The victory was followed by the dispatch of a strong contingent to Delhi with directions to hunt out and slay all the officers of the Seen Dagh. Their jagirs were confiscated and their personal property given up to plunder.[9]

Thereafter a much humbled Imad returned to Delhi. That was the end of his campaign against Qutb Shah. The usurper had indeed been defeated, but not by the wazir. It was Adina Beg Khan who trounced him and he was not under the wazir's control at all. The bulk of the Sirhind sarkar, right up to Thanesar, also passed into his control. As far as the emperor was concerned, Adina Beg did agree to a tribute. The destruction of the Seen Dagh had relieved the capital of a discontented and turbulent soldiery, but under Safdar Jang these same soldiers, had been the best cavalry in north India. They had also been Imad's main fighting force who now had no troops left which he could call his own. He was now totally dependent on people like Najib and Kamgar Khan Baluch who were more interested in themselves.

He had also returned just in time to supress another conspiracy in the making. This aimed at making Shuja ud-Daulah wazir with the support of Suraj Mall and Ahmad Khan Bangash.

In December 1755, he set out again for the trans-Yamuna, subdueing the middle doab from where he advanced up to Kunjpura where the local Pathans waited on him respectfully. He proceeded further upto Sirhind for the ostensible purpose of receiving his betrothed Umda Begum, a daughter of the late Mir Mannu who had died in 1753. Adina Begum, who had briefly gained control of Lahore, acting on his directions, also abducted his mother-in-law to be, the Mughlani Begum and sent her to his camp at Sirhind. Imad had been scandalized by stories of the life she had been leading in Lahore and determined to keep her in Delhi where she would be obliged to observe more restraint and decorum. But this act of violence outraged Mughlani and it drew on his head the wrath of Ahmad Shah Durrani who had adopted the Begum as his sister.

He returned from his Punjab expedition with his fiancee Umda and a fuming Mughlani towards the end of June 1756. A fortnight later he set out again with the emperor, to extort some revenue from the trans-Gangetic Rohillas. He advanced only as far as the first stage at Loni when a mutiny broke out in the Qila-i-Mualla. The long suffering Baksari matchlockmen had taken over the fort. They also seized control of the ferry so that the emperor and his court found themselves stranded with only their advance guard, unable to advance or return as the bulk of their troops had still to be mobilized. This ridiculous impasse continued till the middle of September when the projected expedition was finally scuttled and the emperor and Imad quietly slunk back into the fort.[10]

All this while a great storm had been gathering in the north-west, a storm which would soon burst upon the plains of Hindostan. Ahmad Shah Durrani was about to embark on what would be his most formidable expedition to Hindustan.

NOTES

1. *Tarikh-i-Alamgir Sani*, pp. 67, 185-6.
2. Sarkar, *Fall of the Mughal Empire*, ii, p. 3.
3. Ibid., pp. 11-12.
4. Ibid., p. 17.
5. Tabatabai, *Seir Mutaqherin*, iii, p. 339.
6. Sarkar, ii, pp. 15, 16.
7. Ibid., p. 20.
8. *Tarikh-i-Alamgir Sani*, pp. 76b-78a.
9. Tabatabai, iii, pp. 343-7.
10. Sarkar, ii, pp. 26-7. *Tarikh-i-Alamgir Sani*, pp. 75a-9a. Tabatabai, iii, pp. 347-8.

CHAPTER 29

Rivers of Blood
Ahmad Shah in Hindustan

The abduction of Mughlani by Imad had drawn the wrath of the Afghan Shah. Abdali considered the Punjab as his own territory, and the mere advance of the wazir in that direction was enough provocation. But Imad had gone much further and the insult to Durrani's adoptive sister was not likely to go unavenged.

The Punjab had been in turmoil ever since the death of Muin ul-Mulk in November 1753. The death of this dashing young man has remained something of a mystery to this day. There were whispers of poison, the body turned black very soon, and four months later his infant son (and successor) expired, with similar symptoms. The widowed Mughlani however did not waste much time in mourning. The loss of her lord and only son seemed to make but little impact. She plunged into a life of debauchery and pleasure.

Nor was she indifferent to power. Although the deputy governor, Mir Momin Khan, was a capable and experienced civil servant, he found himself powerless in the face of the Begum's interference. The real power center was the Begum's *deohri* where she held her durbar.

It was 'petticoat rule' with a vengeance with her lovers, eunuchs and other favourites contributing their mite. But this could not long endure in Lahore with its turbulent soldiery and the proud captains of the late Muin ul-Mulk who were anguished at the stain on the honour of their late lord. Bhikhari Khan, Muin's favourite and most trusted officer, was the first to rebel. But this uprising failed and he was imprisoned by the Begum.

After Bhikhari's abortive coup came the turn of Kasim Khan, faujdar of Patti, who dreamt of carving out an independent chieftaincy with Sikh help. But his allies let him down and he was ruined.

After the death of the infant subedar Muhammad Amin Khan the court of Delhi nominated Mir Momin Khan. However, he had been unable to assert himself as deputy-governor; as governor he was just a unsuccessful.

Khwaja Mirza Khan, another of Muin's captains, staged a coup and assumed power, the Begum being confined in her sister's house. But Khwaja Mirza was a usurper and after a short while dissidence raised its head and anarchy spread. The Begum, taking advantage of the growing disorder, appealed to her relatives, and finally her maternal uncle, Khwaja Abdullah, set off for Peshawar from where he obtained Afghan troops with whose support he drove out Khwaja Mirza, and installed himself as subedar of Lahore.

The position had not materially changed for Mughlani, for Khwaja Abdullah was by no means inclined to relinquish power to his niece. The termagent fretted and fumed. Bhikhari Khan was taken out of his confinement; she tried to seduce him and incited him against her uncle but Bhikhari Khan did not respond. It was a slight which few women would have forgiven, and the unfortunate Khan was beaten to death by her servants.[1]

It was after this that she appealed to the wazir to come and free her and take his betrothed Umda. But the Begum had exhausted her fund of good luck. Even this miscarried. We have seen how with Adina Beg's ready connivance the Begum, instead of being reinstalled as governor, found herself transported forcibly to Imad's camp, and thence to Delhi.

Mir Momin was again reinstated by Imad ul-Mulk with one of his trusted officers, Syed Jamil ud-Din, as deputy. But as could be anticipated, Mir Momin remained a figurehead and real power rested with the latter. Khwaja Abdullah, the ousted governor, made his way to the Durrani court at Kandahar. He returned with an Afghan contingent, as on the former occasion, and drove out Imad's puppets in October 1756. A wild terror seized the people of Lahore at their approach, for a rumour had spread that Ahmad Shah was following close behind and all the rich men fled the city.

The rumour was not far off the mark. Ahmad Shah was making preparations for a serious invasion. By 23 January 1757 he had reached Delhi.

Ahmad Shah was preceded by an envoy, Qalandar Beg Khan, who presented his credentials to the emperor on 31 October. The wazir was at a loss for a reply to the Afghan Shah, and though he detained the envoy for a month, the envoy left without a satisfactory answer.

Imad realized that nothing could stop the Shah and made desperate efforts to muster an army. He called upon Salabat Khan Zulfiqar Jang, the bakhshi of the last reign, but he was a dying man. Then he approached the Rohilla chief, Najib Khan, undoubtedly the most formidable general in northern India. But the Rohilla himself had outstanding claims against the wazir and hot words were exchanged between the two. On a subsequent visit by Najib to the wazir's camp, the Rohillas looted some shops in the camp bazaar. Discussions were also held with Suraj Mall who advised that the wazir should place himself at the head of all the principal powers of the region, Jats, Rajputs, Rohillas, and the Mughal umara, drive out the Marathas, and then lead them against the Afghans. But Imad had no intention of giving up the Marathas who had been his principal supporters from day one, and Suraj Mall left to prepare his forts for resisting the Afghans.

But this time even the Marathas deserted him. The Deccanis were no less mercenary than Najib's Rohillas and they too required money before setting out. In this situation it was soon every man for himself. Whoever could, got out of the way of the advancing Afghans. Even the wazir sent his family to Rajasthan. The towns of Mathura and Agra were choked with refugees from Delhi. When the Afghans entered Sirhind, it was deserted.

Antaji Mankeshwar's force of 3,000 Marathas, which was paid by the wazir, came up from Gwalior and established themselves on the left bank of the Yamuna. On the wazir's orders they tried to stem the exodus from the capital. Blocking the road they forced the terror-stricken population to turn back but they did not miss the opportunity to demand contributions in cash and jewels as a price for their protection.[2]

Imad did make some last minute efforts to avert the clash. A cousin of the Afghan wazir, Yakub Ali, since long a resident of Delhi was located, created a peer with the rank of 6,000 and sent with an envoy, Agha Raza, to talk for terms on 25 December 1756. Beforc his return, on 9 January, came the news of the Shah's entry into Sirhind. Thereupon, after much pleading, Mughlani was sent in the hope that perhaps she might be able to avert the Shah's wrath. On 14 January, Agha Raza returned and reported that the Shah had demanded an indemnity of Rs. 2 crore and cession of the Sirhind sarkar (besides the Punjab which was already tributary), and the hand of a princess in marriage. He further reported that the Shah was incensed with the wazir. If he did not intend to fight he could have said so. In that case he would not have taken the trouble to come down from Afghanistan. Peace terms could have been settled at Kabul.

Imad was in no position to furnish Rs. 2 crore and in desperation he sent Agha Raza once again to plead with the Shah to lower the price. The military postition remained as desperate as ever. Some guns were placed in position but there were not enough gunners. After their agitation for their arrears, most of them had left. There was a half-hearted attempted to strengthen the defence, but in the absence of troops these were futile gestures. On 11 January the wazir was prevented from entering his own house by soilders clamouring for arrears! A more hopless situation is difficult to imagine.[3]

On 16 January 1757 small troops of Afghan cavalry could be seen from the city walls on both banks of the Yamuna. The few nobles, who still hung around, pleaded with Imad to make a demonstration with what troops he had, lest it be recorded in the pages of history that the Shah was able to enter Delhi unopposed. But Imad seemed paralysed. He was now a very different person from the impetuous boy who had challenged and defeated Safdar Jang in 1753.

On 18 January Agha Raza and Yakub Ali Khan, returning from the Durrani camp for the second time, reported that the Afghan Shah wanted to see Imad. So next morning, before dawn, Imad left accompanied by only four attendants for Badli where Abdali had established his camp.

The Shah kept Imad waiting a full day for audience. And when, at last, he condescended to receive him, he laughed at him contemptuously, pouring scorn on his incompetence. What kind of a minister was he that he could not even field an army to defend his master! Then he pulled him up for not fulfilling his pledge to Mughlani to marry Umda, and for preferring the daughter of a dancing girl. And finally he told him bluntly that his uncle Intizam had offered Rs. 2 crore for the wazarat, but if Imad was prepared to pay Rs. 1 crore, he would let him retain it.

Imad gave what replies he could. The most powerful of the emperor's amirs was Najib Khan and he had refused to come to Imad's aid, demanding ready cash before moving. As for his engagement to marry Umda, he stood by his pledge and would have married her, but for the insistence of Mughlani that he divorce his first wife, to whose family he had earlier given his word. And for the demand of Rs. 1 crore, he was unable to lay his hand on even Rs. 1 lakh! So, then and there, he resigned his post.

Antaji Mankeshwar's small force had had some brushes with the advanced squadrons of Afghan cavalry in which he lost about 100 troopers. But when on 19 January it became known that the wazir had gone to the Afghan camp and failed to return, Antaji's forward position became untenable and on 20 January he retreaded to Faridabad after suffering further losses.

Confusion reigned in Delhi. The roads to the south were jammed with carts as people struggled to escape the approaching doom. On 21 January, some Afghan officers entered the city and asked the kotwal to restore order. That day too, being a Friday, on the initiative of some sycophantic

Indian noblemen, the *khutba* was read in the golden mosque of Roshan ud-Daulah—with its bloody memories of Nadir Shah—in the name of Durrani, as Padishah-i-Hind. It was unprecedented. Alamgir II was still alive and had not been formally deposed, nor had any order or indication been given by the Afghan Shah in this regard. No one objected to it. On hearing the news, Alamgir quietly vacated the imperial apartments and retired to the old rooms he had ocupied before his accession. The keys of the imperial apartments were handed over to an officer of Najib who had by then openly joined the Afghans.

On 26 January, on the invitation of Durrani, Alamgir visited the Shah in full royal state as per his command. Ahmad received his guest at Wazirabad closer to the fort. The usual courtesies were observed, turbans and *khillats* exchanged, and Ahmad seated his guest on the same carpet assuring him that he would remain emperor. There was a ceremonial feast, Intizam was vested with the robes and insignia of wazir, and in the evening Alamgir returned with his court to the qila.

The courtesies observed, it was time to get down to business, for Ahmad was always in a hurry to return before the onset of summer. On 27 January, Ahmad entered Delhi and took up his abode in the imperial apartments of the Qila-i-Mualla. The same day a public durbar was held in the fort. This was also the occasion to make an example to impress the citizens of Delhi. As could be expected there was some looting by the Durrani soldiers, as a consequence of which the bazaars observed a *hartal*. The Shah had the noses of two or three of the looters slit, cut their stomachs open, thrust arrows into their nostrils, and in this manner paraded them in disgrace. This brought peace to Delhi, records the *Delhi Chronicle* with satisfaction.[4]

Thereafter the Afghans got down to 'work'. Each ward of the city was placed in charge of an officer who assessed the ransom from each householder, which was invariably beyond his means to pay. The whip and the bastinado were freely applied. The new wazir, Intizam, white as a sheet and trembling, was shown a whipping triangle and called upon to produce the Rs. 2 crore he had so rashly promised. He replied he had nothing apart from the ring on his finger and the pearls around his neck. Only his mother, Sholapuri Begum, knew where the treasure was buried. When she in turn was threatened with torture she pointed out the room which contained the hoard. After six hours of digging by a hundred men, it was located and Rs. 16 lakh recovered in coin and jewels. The harem was forced and the women stripped and searched for more jewels.

Nor was Imad spared. His servants were flogged and tortured to reveal the hiding places in the mansion. The clout, and lash were freely applied on the palace servants as well.

And so it went on for nearly three weeks, until the Shah betook himself to Mathura. Each night the air was rent with the screams and lamentations of ravished women, and many were those who preferred suicide to the proverbial 'worse then death'. In all these extortions Mughlani played a key role by apprising the Shah of the approximate worth of each noble, and thus suggesting how much could be extracted from him. By virtue of being a woman she could also inform the Shah about the contents of their harems.

It was on her information that the Shah selected Hazrat Begum, a daughter of the deceased Muhammad Shah as his bride, and Alamgir's daughter Gauhar un-Nissa was taken as a bride for Timur, Durrani's son. It was in vain that the old dowagers cried out, 'We shall slay her and then kill ourselves, but we shall not giver her to an Afghan.' As Sarkar records, 'this tender lamb was to be pounced upon by a fierce Afghan of grand-fatherly age whose two ears had been docked and nose was rotting from a leprous carbuncle'.[5]

Before the Shah set out for Mathura, a convoy of treasure was dispatched to Kabul. Again great hardships were faced as the carriage and oxen for the treasure train were requisitioned from Delhi and the sorrounding villages. The value of the treasure taken out is estimated variously between Rs. 3 crore to 12 crore.

The march of Abdali had so far been unopposed. In Punjab, which was already tributary to him, he had first installed Khwaja Abdullah who drove out Syed Jamil ud-Din whom Imad had left in control. Adina Beg, faujdar of Jalandhar and Sirhind, was also Imad's adherent but he was too wily a survivor to risk quixotic gestures against the might of the Afghan Shah. He prudently side-stepped the Afghan army, retreating towards Hissar. Najib Khan was already in correspondence with the Shah and had repulsed all efforts to draw him into an alliance against the invader. Only Antaji Mankeshwar, with his small force of 4,000, had made some show of resistance near Delhi and suffered substantial losses. While falling back towards Faridabad, he had, on 21 February, come across a small Afghan force near Badarpur which was dispersed by him. But this minor success was short-lived. He was soon sorrounded by a much larger Afghan force at Faridabad nine days later and broke through only after suffering heavy losses. For the remainder of the campaign, he stayed out of the way.

Beyond Faridabad lay Jat country held by Suraj Mall, his relatives, and adherents. In 1739 Nadir Shah had stopped at Delhi but Ahmad was tempted because he had been told that Mathura and Agra were teeming with wealthy refugees from Delhi. Suraj Mall's attitude was ambiguous. He was opposed to Imad who had tried to destroy him with Maratha help in 1754. He joined Najib to petition Durrani to remove Imad from Delhi and imprison him in Kandahar, and his ambassadors waited on Durrani to negotiate his tribute. But, as the guardian of Braj, he was determined to protect the sacred shrines at Mathura. But when Antaji Mankeshwar approached him for help he refused. He was not prepared to enter into direct confrontation.

On 22 February, Abdali gave orders to begin the drive towards Mathura. The little fort of Ballabhgarh was taken on the way. Its Jat garrison, headed by Jawahar Singh, Suraj Mall's son, resisted fiercely but the stronghold was stormed and its garrison put to the sword. Eight hundred heads were brought back and a bounty of Rs. 8 was collected on each head. The soldiers were given orders to kill and destroy whatever lay in their path, and to retain all that they seized.

The soldiers set about their grisly labour with zest and enthusiasm. At Chaumuha, 8 miles north of Mathura, the Afghan vanguard led by Sardar Jahan Khan and Najib Khan Rohilla was confronted by Jawahar Singh at the head of 10,000 men. The battle raged for 9 hours and the Jats fought stoutly, determined to defend their temples to the last. But the superior numbers of the Afghans began to tell at last and the Jat line was broken. The casualties of this battle were estimated at 10,000 to 12,000. The Afghans, maddened by their losses, fell on the defenceless town and its helpless population.

It was during the Holi week that this disaster transpired. With the sudden descent of the Afghans, the inhabitants of Braj—the name given to the Mathura region—were destined to play a very different kind of Holi, in which blood was to flow like water. There was virtually a general massacre of the population, and immense booty was acquired. The soldiers brought in strings of mules and horses loaded with plunder and numbers of male and female captives. All night long, and the next day, the rape and slaughter went on. Much of the city was set on fire. While the Afghans passed on after the massacres Najib's Rohillas lingered among the shambles digging for conceded treasure and ferreting out the remaining women who had escaped the notice of Jahan Khan's Afghans.

Abdali himself followed a fortnight later but he wisely avoided the charnel house of Mathura and camped near Mahaban on the other side of the Yamuna. A detachment was sent to plunder Gokul, another temple town in the vicinity. Here again there was fierce resistance by 4,000 militant Naga sadhus who had an *akhara* located there. They died, almost to a man defending the temples of their deity. Vrindaban, another temple town was likewise pillaged.[6]

Jahan Khan pushed on to Agra. Apart from the garrison in the fort there were no troops, and there could be no question of resistance. The leading citizens and bankers received the Afghan general in a body and offered a ransom of Rs. 5 lakh for sparing the city. Jahan Khan's force was small and he accepted the offer, but the money was not immediately forthcoming. So, the troops broke into the city and started looting and killing until they came under the fire of the guns of the citadel. The qiladar, Mirza Saif Ullah Beg, kept his cool and directed his artillery with such telling effect that Jahan Khan hastily accepted Rs. 1 lakh and departed. But what really saved the city was an urgent message from Durrani, urging him to return post haste.

Cholera had broken out in the Shah's camp at Mahaban. Mahaban was downstream of the shambles of Mathura and thousands of corpses had infected the waters of the Yamuna. Most of the wells had also been contaminated and soon the soldiers began to die in hundreds. After dispatching couriers and recalling his troops from Agra and the siege of Jat fortresses, Durrani struck camp and prepared to return to Afghanistan. Moreover, March was ending, the temperature was rising, and the weather becoming more and more uncomfortable.

On 30 March he reached Faridabad, and then marching along the river be halted for three days to the north of the city of Delhi to receive Hazrat Begum and Gauhar un-Nissa who had been married to his son. Along with these princesses went two dowagers Sahiba Mahal and Malika-i-Zamani. There were now quite a number of princesses from the Mughal house in the Afghan's harem. Besides these ladies there was also a great grand-daughter of Aurangzeb, Aiffat un-Nissa, whom Nadir Shah had obtained in 1739 for his son Nasrullah. After the death of that monarch she had, after many vicissitudes, been taken by Ahmad into his harem. Luckier than these princesses were the thousands of captives who were being taken by his soldiers as slaves. On the request of Alamgir II they were released and permitted to return home after the time-honoured tradition set by Zakariya Khan who had obtained a similar release of captives by requesting the Persian Shah in 1739.

The visitation was over but it left the already enfeebled monarchy more debilitated than ever before. Imad was once again wazir. Intizam was found to be of not much use even by Abdali, and within a few weeks of his appointment had been replaced by the heir apparent Ali Gauhar (later Shah Alam II). But Imad was soon reinstated in the Shah's favour by his strenuous exertions in the latter's behalf in operations conducted against the Jat forts, and on his request Alamgir reinstated him as wazir.

While leaving, the Shah had charged Imad with an impossible task. Declaring that it was his sincerest desire to see the Indian monarchy restored to its former glory, he charged the wazir to take with him two princes and lead a campaign against Shuja to recover Awadh, and maybe, if all went well, to reconquer Bihar and Bengal as well. How this could be accomplished by a wazir who had been unable to field even a modest army against him, and especially when the palace and the city had been ruthlessly plundered of every article of value, he left unsaid.

Anyway, the two shahzadas were seen off by Ahmad Shah. One was Hidayat Bakhsh, a son, and the other, Mirza Baba, a nephew and son-in-law of the emperor. A small force of 3,000, stiffened with a few hundred Durrani Afghans under Jangbaz Khan was attached to them with Imad in charge of diplomatic negotiations. They first went to Farrukhabad where they were received with the courtesies appropriate to imperial princes by Ahmad Khan Bangash. Their small force was sufficient enough to drive out the Marathas from their symbolic posts in the Etawah region, where Antaji Mankeshwar had his jagirs. Hafiz Rahmat Khan also joined them but then came the news of the approach of Shuja ud-Daulah with 16,000 men and 400 cannons and swivels. He meant no disrespect to the princes, went his reassuring message, but Imad was his enemy and he must settle with him. However, negotiations were opened and they dragged on inconclusively until the arrival of a strong Maratha army changed the situation materially. The Maratha sardar now became the mediator and imposed a settlement in which Shuja made many promises but the two princes got a bare Rs. 50,000 each. The princes returned empty-handed for whatever money they had received was spent on paying the salaries of their troops. Jangbaz Khan, who had received Rs. 1 lakh only out of the promised five, ravaged and plundered the country and then left for Bareilly to extort whatever he could from Hafiz Rahmat and Shuja's officers.[7]

Imad gained nothing. By this pointless expedition in pursuit of a chimerical objective he had lost whatever credit he had earlier enjoyed with the Marathas. Soon the Jats reoccupied their old outposts, and the Marathas, who had now joined hands with the Jats, became all-powerful in the lower Doab.

NOTES

1. Bhikari Khan signifies, 'the beggar who is a lord', while his other titles signify, 'the Light of the Empire, the Rustam in War'.
2. Sarkar, *Fall of the Mughal Empire*, ii, p. 50. *TALS*, pp. 87a-88a.
3. Sarkar, ii, pp. 50-1.
4. Ganda Singh, *Ahmad Shah Durrani*, p. 164 (on the authority of the *Delhi Chronicle* and *Tazkira-i-Imad*).
5. Sarkar, ii, p. 75 (Orient Longmans, 1991).
6. Rajwade, *Marathachi Itihasachen Sadhanen*, i, p. 63. Sarkar, ii, p. 71.
7. *TALS*, p. 127b. *Indian Antiquary*, p. 69. Sarkar, ii, pp. 77-9.

CHAPTER 30

Towards Panipat

One might have thought that after the blood-bath of Mathura and the devastation wrought by the Durrani army there would be peace for some time. That the local chiefs, shocked by the horrors they had witnessed, would be too numbed to challenge the supremacy of Najib whom the Afghan Shah had designated as his representative in Hindustan. But the Durrani invasion marked only a brief pause in the mindless struggle that had been going on in the Delhi region ever since the incursion of Nadir Shah in 1739. The principal actors, the Marathas, the Jat chief of Braj, the Rohillas under Najib and other chiefs, the wazir and his adherents, and indeed the rude peasantry—Jat, Gujjar, Rajput or Ahir—had been so utterly brutalized that the sufferings of innocents did not matter to them. The mercenary armies had become a scourge. With the towns denuded of wealth and the soldiers' pay in arrears, they lived off the country in every sense of the word, looting the peasant's grain, tearing the silver off his women and driving away his cattle whenever draught animals were required.

Within a few months of the Shah's withdrawal, Suraj Mall had recovered all his territory and even the citadel of Agra dropped into his hands like a ripe orange. The Marathas had again re-established their old thanas or outposts in Etawah and the Doab, and were ready to challenge the ascendancy of Najib Khan.

But where were the Marathas when Abdali's troops were piling up the dead in the streets of Mathura? When their troopers were gathering up the heads of the faithful to claim their bounty of Rs. 5 per head? Why was poor Antaji Mankeshwar left alone to face the invader with his 3,000 horsemen?

Raghunath Rao was not far off. Since February 1757, both he and Malhar Holkar had been in Rajasthan under orders to collect the tribute due from the Rajput princes. The going was tough, the arrears heavy, and the Marathas, were, the most hated people in Rajputana. Two years earlier, Jayappa Scindia in a passionate outburst had threatened that he would collect tribute from the Rathors even if he had to beat them with his shoes. Stung by these insolent words the Rajputs whipped out the khanjars from their cummerbunds and the intemperate Maratha was killed on the spot on 25 July 1755. This happened in the Maratha camp. The Rajputs were in turn attacked and killed with most of their escort.[1]

But the Rathors derived no advantage from the murder of the Maratha general. The normal consequences of such an occurrence in an Indian army would have been its dissolution and plunder by its own soldiers and camp followers. That this did not happen was on account of the presence of mind of Dattaji Scindia, the brother of the deceased, who immediately had Jankoji, Jayappa's young son, proclaimed as his successor and restored order in the camp. The peshwa also sent more troops, and finally in February 1756 the princes of Marwar and Jaipur were forced to submit to a humiliating peace, the famous citadel of Taragarh, at Ajmer, being surrendered to the Marathas, along with its dependent territory.

After this peace the Marathas returned home but, by the end of the year, Malhar and Raghunath Rao were back again. By that time Ahmad Shah Durrani was already in Delhi. At first Raghunath Rao proposed to Malhar that they should march on Delhi to challenge the Afghans, but he soon realized that the task was beyond their capability. The total strength of the scattered Maratha forces in the north did not exceed 16,000. The peshwa, under heavy debt, had not been able to equip the armies properly. Soon, to his exasperation, the peshwa started receiving letters from Raghunath, describing the sufferings of the army on account of lack of money and provisions. As for attacking Durrani, he was by now thoroughly disabused of all his delusions. 'Abdali is strong,' he wrote. 'It requires very great resources to chastise him. Send Dattaji Scindia to me from the Deccan.'[2]

The Maratha forces in the north were in no position to attack Abdali and they were too realistic to make quixotic gestures to defend the temples of their gods. Antaji Mankeshwar was in the imperial service. He had made the necessary gesture which honour demanded and suffered heavily in the process. As for the Braj raja, sheltering behind the high walls of his impregnable forts, he had left his son Jawahar and the Naga sadhus to defend the temples.

Abdali's invasion had achieved nothing decisive. The emperor himself was a shadow and Imad a broken reed. Some Maratha and Jat blood (more of the latter) had indeed been shed, but the main Maratha army in Rajasthan was intact, and Suraj Mall had preserved his main strength and escaped paying all but a nominal offering of a few lakh rupees.

Thus, it was not long before Najib found his supremacy seriously challenged. The emperor was the first to be alienated. Alamgir found Najib overbearing and rude. Imad, whatever, his faults, was at any rate cultured and educated. He was polite and soft-spoken in his dealings with the emperor while Najib treated the latter with the contemptuous indifference one reserves for a puppet. Meanwhile Imad, still the nominal wazir, was able to make up with the Marathas, and the emperor promised to back them both, if he could be rid of Najib.

Raghunath Rao had entered the Delhi region towards the end of July 1757 from Rajasthan. On the way, at Rewari, he had captured Prince Ali Jah, the emperor's second son, who was trying to restore order in that district. By the middle of August, the city of Delhi was invested by the Marathas who were demanding *chauth* from Najib, on the ground that the estates reserved for this purpose since the reign of Muhammad Shah had been usurped by Najib. In the meantime, other Maratha armies under Naro Shankar from Jhansi and Sakharam Bapu from Jaipur were on the move. These generals coerced Suraj Mall into submission and extracted from him a promise of tribute. Agra was occupied. The peshwa had nominated Malhar as his subedar, and he, in turn, appointed Vithal Shivdev as his deputy. The latter made Agra his base, and from there he crossed the Yamuna and occupied much of the Doab upto the Ganga and north-westward, upto Delhi. Imad ul-Mulk also openly joined the Maratha forces facing Delhi at Patparganj.

In the meantime, Najib Khan had abandoned the suburbs and much of the old city, placed a small garrison in the fort and drawn up the artillery on the banks of the Yamuna. A small garrison was also placed in the Old Fort (the Purana Qila).

On 11 August 1757 the Marathas launched their attack. The Purana Qila was easily taken, the houses in Old Delhi looted, and the inhabitants forced to flee. Qutb Shah obtained Najib's permission to attack the haveli of Imad which lay within the city walls, in order to avenge the slaughter of the Pathans in the old city. Permission being given, the house was stormed and looted, the women being stripped and raped by the infuriated Pathans. Finally Saif ud-Din Muhammad Khan, a brother of Aqibat Mahmud, intervened. He pacified Najib and the order was given to stop. After this disgraceful event a reconciliation between Imad and Najib was inconceivable.[3]

Desultory fighting went on for nearly a month. A severe food shortage was felt in the city. The Maratha shelling did some damage to the palace in the Qila-i-Mualla and two bastions near the Delhi Gate were destroyed. Eventually, hopelessly outnumbered, Najib submitted to the inevitable, and on 3 September terms of truce were finalized. A few days later he marched out with all his property and followers, while the wazir re-entered the palace. Ahmad Khan Bangash was appointed the mir bakhshi in place of Najib. Najib's appointees were replaced by those of the Marathas, on the strength of whose arms the wazir had been able to make a comeback. The emperor sent *khillats* to Malhar to make new appointments at his discretion. The persons thus appointed went to pay their respects, dressed in their *khillats*, to Raghunath Rao in his tent. Antaji Mankeshwar was among those so honoured. He was appointed faujdar of the Delhi sarkar; the Maratha triumph seemed complete.

Najib's brief dictatorship was over, but he had marched out with honour, having yielded only to famine. He retired to his estates in Saharanpur from where he kept writing to Durrani, urging him to come back and expel the Deccani unbelievers from Delhi.

The people of Delhi had suffered immensely from this round of civil war following so closely the withdrawal of Abdali. Then, as of now, Delhi was essentially a city of bureaucrats, and most of them were living in great distress as they had ceased to receive any receipts from their jagirs which had been usurped by Rohilla Pathans, Marathas, Jats or other outlaws. The city was rife with incidents of robbery and house-breaking, and many of the sons of the umara and lesser mansabdars had taken to brigandage. The kotwal himself was suspected to be in league and accused of sharing the fruits of their depredations.[4]

Abdali had supposedly come on the urging of Mughlani Begum, to avenge the wrongs done to her be the wazir. She had rendered him invaluable—if rather discreditable—services at Delhi. For these, she had expected to be reinstated as governor at Lahore, but here the Shah, inspite of the fact that he publicly described her as his adopted sister, disappointed her. He left behind his son Timur Shah as viceroy. The Shah offered her substantial estates worth lakhs of rupees, but these she spurned scornfully. It was the subedari she wanted or nothing. The Shah went on his way, inflexible in his own determination to have none but his son in charge of the turbulent province. After this Mughlani fades from the pages of history, destined to die in obscurity and poverty.

Timur was unable to control the Punjab after the departure of his father. The brutal flogging which he inflicted on Baba Badbhag Singh of

Kartarpur, a Sikh leader who had a considerable following, enraged the Sikhs who broke out in open rebellion. He also annoyed Adina Beg, who refused his summons and fled to the hills.

The conquest of the Punjab was one of the objectives of the Marathas. In February 1758, led by Raghunath Rao and Malhar Holkar, they commenced their invasion. The Sikhs and Adina Beg joined them; the Sirhind district was overrun, and on 21 March the city was siezed, the faujdar Abdus Samad, Jangbaz and other Afghan captains being captured. These officers were treated well by Raghunath Rao but the town was given up to plunder and the looting was so thorough that its inhabitants were left with barely the clothes on their backs. This event in the history of that unfortunate city is known as the second sack of Sirhind. In a few years it was destined to be plundered all over again in the third and final sack, after which it remained for a long time abandoned by its inhabitants.

After their easy success at Sirhind, the Marathas advanced further, the Afghans evacuating the Bist Doab and, on 19 April, Lahore as well. The forces of Prince Timur were weak, and the Lahore fort in disrepair; so the viceroy evacuated the Punjab rapidly without risking another engagement. The Deccani cavalry chased them as far as the Indus, but they did not try to cross the river, the traditional border of the Indian world. Nor do they appear to have ever garrisoned the fort of Attock which presumably remained in Durrani hands. But for a few months at least, the whole of Punjab including Multan, was dominated by the Marathas and their Sikh allies.

Meanwhile, another pathetic drama was being enacted in the Delhi region. Ali Gauhar, the heir apparent (who had for a few weeks been raised to the wazarat by Ahmad Shah) had been trying to restore order in the Crown lands near Rewari. His force was small and lived off the country, but he was a prince of the blood and the heir apparent, so some of the local zamindars submitted out of respect. Others, in order to avoid the embarassment of having to fight, got out of the way, or made empty promises which they had no intention of keeping. But at Kanaud, the prince was hemmed in by Jaipur troops and had to flee, abandoning his artillery.

But the prince's greatest enemy was the wazir who could not allow an alternate power centre to grow, particularly when it was centred around the heir apparent. The petty successes of the prince were enough to rouse his jealousy. He forced the emperor to recall the latter and Ali Gauhar—most of whose soldiers had by now deserted him—was forced to come back to Delhi, harassed by the Baluch zamindars who had been emboldened by his recall.

Near the Najafgarh lake, on the outskirts of Delhi, Ali Gauhar was visited by Vithal Shivdev, one of Raghunath Rao's principal officers, whom he won over. The two of them, supported by the Rao's troops, proceeded to Khizrabad and then to Patparganj, where they defeated a small force sent by the wazir. This sent Imad into a panic. Openly accusing the emperor of abetting his son, he placed the other princes in confinement. Intizam was also called to the fort and arrested. Even the mir bakhshi, Ahmad Khan Bangash, his protégé, felt so insecure that he engaged a special bodyguard to protect himself against any stroke directed against himself by his patron!

After plundering the suburbs, the prince established himself in Ali Mardan Khan's mansion while Vithal Shivdev camped with his troops in the adjoining Qudsia Bagh. But eventually, Imad's gold neutralized the latter, and thus assured of his inaction. The wazir tried to storm the mansion on the night of 19 May 1758. The prince resisted but finding the position hopeless, with a hundred followers, cut his way through the besieging force and reached the safety of Vithal's camp. The latter had not deserted the prince, the wazir's gold had only immobilized him for the duration of the attack.

The prince resumed his wanderings, extorting what he could from the villages in the Rewari ilaqa, accompanied by Vithal Shivdev. But the latter was eventually ordered to return by his master Raghunath, and so he took leave of the prince at Dadri on 16 June 1758. In fact he was instructed to bring the prince back with him to Delhi as prisoner, but this the chivalrous Maratha ignored. Instead he left his own son with the prince, together with a small escort, with instructions to accompany the latter wherever he went. The behaviour of this officer presents a refreshing contrast to the sordid venality of the times when every man had his price.

The prince proceeded north to Hissar where an emissary from the raja of Bikaner waited on him. He presented him with a purse of Rs. 10,000 by way of *nazar* from his master but suggested that the prince look elsewhere for asylum. So the prince turned east, crossed the Yamuna and reached Muzaffarnagar in the heart of the Barha country where he was joined by many of the young Syeds, who were always ready for any rash enterprise. With a strengthened escort, he proceeded to Najib's headquarters where he was well received, but Najib declined to go to war against Imad so soon on his account. He, in turn, suggested that he seek the help of Shuja ud-Daulah. The prince arrived at the latter's court at Lucknow where he was received with ceremony on 2 January 1759.[5]

The wazir, in the meanwhile, after many delays set out in pursuit of the prince. To legitimize his actions and to secure himself against the possibility of a *coup d'état* behind his back he forced the emperor to accompany him but they returned to the capital on 22 November without accomplishing anything.[6]

A few weeks later the Marathas, led by Dattaji Scindia, arrived at Najafgarh with orders to re-establish Maratha control over Delhi and the Punjab, crush Najib and collect the arrears of tribute. With him was his nephew Jankoji, Jayappa Scindia's son and heir. Dattaji's position was that of a guardian.

There was the usual shadow fighting. While negotiations were going on for fixing the instalments, the Marathas ravaged the sorrounding countryside in search of provisions. The wazir protested that they were still at peace and the behaviour of the Deccanis was outrageous.

Finally, towards and end of January 1759 an agreement was reached after which the Marathas set off towards the Punjab. Adina Beg Khan, faujdar of Sirhind and Jalandhar, had died the previous September but his son waited on the Marathas at Machhiwara. Here Dattaji was offered some cash by way of tribute. In the meantime a force was sent under Sabaji Patil to Lahore. The Scindias returned to the Delhi region in May.

The Marathas had appointed Mirza Jan Khan as their governor in Lahore after the death of Adina Beg but the latter had not been able to assert himself. But with Sabaji Patil on hand they showed their true colours and incurred a lot of odium on account of their cruelties. Whereupon some of the Qizilbash offices who had entered Maratha service conspired with the Maratha pandits in Lahore and overthrew Mirza Jan and his brother Khwaja Said Khan who were paraded through the streets before being thrown into prison.

Ahmad Shah could not remain a passive spectator to these happenings. He sent an army from Kabul to clear the Deccanis from the province. But the Afghan general met with an unexpected reverse at the hands of Sabaji and had to retreat in utter confusion across the Indus in August 1759.

Back in Delhi, Dattaji was negotiating with Najib Khan. An invasion of Bihar was being planned. It was proposed that if Najib joined the Marathas in this expedition, his territories would be spared. But the wily Pathan was not taken in by the smooth promises of the Marathas. Clashes had already taken place and some villages held by the Rohillas were plundered. Eventually the negotiations were broken off and Najib retired into prepared positions at Shukartal, 16 miles from Muzaffarnagar on the banks of the Ganga, to await the expected Maratha attack.

While the main Maratha army settled down to beseige Shukartal, another army was sent up to seize Najibabad and ravage the home country of the Rohillas. The attack failed. Shuja ud-Daulah sent troops to the succour of the Pathans, and among them were the ferocious Naga sadhus led by Umraogir and Anupgir Gossain. This intervention of Shuja forced Dattaji to come to terms. At the same time, matters in Punjab had taken a complete summersault. After the repulse of Jahan Khan, Abdali himself had taken the field and his formidable army swept everything that lay in its path. The fugitive governor reached Dattaji's camp on 9 November and informed him about the turn of events. The siege of Shukartal had to be lifted and he shifted his camp to the rear leaving a light force to hold the lines. Shuja, now acting as mediator, tried to negotiate a peace between Najib and the Marathas but the attempt failed, and hostilities were resumed.

Dattaji frantically tried to collect his allies. Fast riders were despatched to Rajasthan to ask Malhar Holkar to come up. Ahmad Khan Bangash joined him from Farrukhabad while Suraj Mall sent a force of 5,000. Another envoy was sent to urge the wazir to join the Marathas, and knowing fully well the sorry state of the imperial finances, the emissary was authorized to sanction Rs. 2 lakh to enable the wazir to meet his expenses.

On 16 November, Imad took leave of the emperor to join the Marathas before Shukartal. There he was apprised of the gravity of situation. The entire Punjab had been lost. A few days later, on 23 November, 500 troopers, naked waist upwards, and bereft of baggage, straggled in, the remnants of 6,000 Marathas who had garrisoned Multan, proving beyond doubt, in the words of Govind Billal, that 'a great disaster' had befallen.[7]

Imad hurried back to Delhi and it was followed by a crime. He had the emperor murdered on 29 November 1759, and, the following day, his old rival Intizam was also strangled by his orders. Imad suspected that the emperor had been in correspondence with the Afghan Shah, and had invited him to come and rid him of his wazir and replace him with Intizam.

The old dotard was lured to the ruined old Kotla of Firoz Shah under the pretext of being introduced to a saintly dervish possessed of miraculous powers and reportedly camping there. When the emperor's party arrived at the Kotla in the afternoon, only one eunuch was allowed to enter the chamber which was in one of the bastions of the Kotla, the door of which was guarded by Balabash Khan's Turki troops. All the other members of the retinue, which included one of his sons, were detained outside. Inside the chamber Balabash himself killed the emperor with a dagger, and coming out, seized and disarmed the shahzada and took him back to the Qila-i-Mualla. His soldiers plundered the imperial cortege and the body of Alamgir was thrown on the sand by the riverside below the Kotla. It was given out that he had accidentally slipped and fallen to his death from the walls of the Kotla.[8]

Later, about midnight, Alamgir's corpse was buried in the grim crypt of Humayun's tomb, and the following morning Mohi ul-Millat, the son of Mohi ul-Sunnat, and grandson of Kam Bakhsh, was placed on the throne with the title of Shah Jahan (the third to bear this title). He was a cousin of the late emperor and so, once again, the direct line had been abandoned in favour of a collateral.

Intizam and Lutfullah Beg were strangled in their cells while reciting the *fatiha* and their bodies, weighted with stones, tossed into the nearby Yamuna at night. At the same time, it was given out that they had escaped. Imad ul-Milk's chancellorship was ending, as it had begun, in a bloody sunset, a fitting prologue to the bloodiest battle in Indian history.

Dattaji abandoned his useless seige and marched westward, crossing the Yamuna at Ramra Ghat near Panipat. Here he learnt that Ahmad Shah had crossed Sirhind and was in the vicinity of Chhat-Banur and that his vanguard had occupied Ambala and was advancing rapidly, with a screen of skirmishers, at the rate of 20 to 30 miles a day.

The Maratha vanguard, commanded by Bhoite and reinforced by 1,000 Turki mercenaries of Imad, led by Muhammad Said Khan Qipchaq, met the Afghans in battle near the old battlefield of Taraori. The Afghans were led by one of Durrani's most celebrated captains, Shah Pasand Khan. At first the Afghans fell back with the intention of luring the Marathas into an ambush. Rashly, the Deccanis plunged right into it. Qipchaq's Central Asian troops, most of whom had earlier served under Abdali, recognized the dread banners of the famous commander and prudently turned tail and fled. But the Deccani cavalry was trapped in their deadly fire, broken up and decimated, over 400 being killed. The Afghans cut off the heads to send them to Ahmad as intimations of the victory. By the time Dattaji rode up to the field, the short winter sun was about to set and it was too late to resume the battle.[9]

The next day it was learnt that Ahmad and the main Afghan army had crossed the Yamuna at the Buria ford. Apprehensive of being cut off from his base, Dattaji rushed back to Delhi.

The strength of the invader was increasing day by day with more and more Indian adhesions. Dattaji arranged for the despatch of his officers to the relative safety of Rewari and took position near the Barari Ghat, the shallowest ford near Delhi. Sabaji Scindia was stationed at the crossing for its protection.

However, on 9 January 1760 Najib Khan, who had succeeded in crossing the river unperceived, fell on Sabaji taking him by surprise. In the confused battle that followed, Dattaji was struck by a musket ball and killed. Although Sabaji escaped, almost his entire contingent was destroyed. The Marathas abandoned even their chief's body and Mian Qutb Shah cut off his head and took it as a trophy to show it to Abdali.

The surviving remnants of the Maratha army led by Jankoji Scindia retreated to Rajasthan, stopping briefly at Kot Putli to regroup. It was here, two days later, that they were joined by Malhar Holkar who was marching in the direction of Delhi in answer to Dattaji's call.

Malhar decided to avoid pitched battles and to adopt the old Maratha tactics of guerilla warfare, a mode to which he was well-fitted by long experience. For a time he led the Afghans a merry chase through Mewat and seized Sikandra on 28 February, thoroughly sacking the city. There he paused on learning that a large convoy of treasure was expected from Najib's country and would be crossing the Ganga at Anupshahar. A strong Afghan detachment led by Sardar Jahan Khan, the ablest of the Durrani generals, took them by surprise and in the ensuing clash many senior leaders were killed and Malhar fled in the direction of Agra. Even Malhar's campaign, with modified tactics, had failed. Collecting his shattered forces he retreated into Rajasthan, passing through Bharatpur, where Suraj Mall waited on him.

The usual forms of politeness were observed, robes exchanged and eternal friendship sworn over *bel* leaves and Ganga water. But it was all empty form. The Marathas were hated in the north and a contemporary writer. Badrinath, writes that, 'if only his promise of safety could be relied upon, every one of the rajas would gladly wait on him'.[10] They knew from past experience that Abdali's incursions were of short duration, while after his return to Kabul they would again have to face the wrath of the Deccanis. So, at this stage, most of the potentates of north India preferred to sit on the fence and watch.

NOTES

1. Sarkar, *Fall of the Mughal Empire*, ii, p. 106. *Tarikh-i-Alamgir Sani* (*TALS*), p. 59a.
2. Rajwade, *Marathachi Itihasachen Sadhanen*, i, 52, 53. Sarkar, ii, p. 113 (fn.).
3. Sarkar, ii, p. 86. *TALS*, pp. 130a-5b.
4. *TALS*, p. 148.
5. Sarkar, ii, pp. 95-8. Tabatabai, iii, pp. 365-70.
6. *TALS*, p. 182a-188a. Sarkar, ii, pp. 98-9.
7. Rajwade, *Marathachi Itihasachen Sadhanen*, i, p. 146 (letter of Govind Ballal, 24 November 1759).
8. Sarkar, ii, pp. 125-6.
9. Ibid., p. 128.
10. Ibid., p. 132.

CHAPTER 31

The Panipat Campaign

While the Marathas faced defeat after defeat in Hindustan, the position in the Deccan was quite the opposite. On 3 February 1760 the subedar of the Deccan, Nizam Ali, was encircled at Ausa and forced to capitulate, ceding vast territory to the Deccanis, including the two cities of Bijapur and Burhanpur, each the headquarters of a suba, as well as Asirgarh and Daulatabad, two of the strongest forts in Mughal Deccan. Of the six subas of the Deccan, practically all that was left with the Nizam was the old province of Hyderabad and some portions of Bidar and Bijapur. Even this rump was subject to the payment of *chauth*. A peace treaty was signed on 9 February. Great were the rejoicings that night in the Maratha camp, with illuminations and fireworks. Sounds of revelry reverberated through the night. Nautch-girls cut graceful patterns on the floor, while poets addressed panegyrics to Balaji Baji Rao Peshwa, calling him the Alexander of the Age.

The news of Durrani's invasion of the Punjab had reached Poona on 27 January, but there was ominous silence thereafter, broken finally on 15 February by the news of the death of Dattaji Scindia. It became necessary to send a strong army again to Hindostan to retrieve the Maratha position. The obvious choice to lead it was Raghunath Rao, the peshwa's brother, who had led an earlier invasion of Hindostan. But that campaign had yielded no financial results and some scathing remarks by his nephew, the thirty year old Sadashiv Rao Bhau, the hero of the Deccan campaign, sent Raghunath Rao into a sulk. He declined the offered command. With the peshwa's brother refusing, the choice fell on Sadashiv Rao himself. Lest the young man should get too independent, the peshwa sent along his own son, Vishwas Rao, a boy of seventeen, who was designated joint commander.

The campaign began on 16 March. Thirty thousand troops had been assembled but, as most of these had been on active service in the Deccan, many of the units were undermanned and their equipage required replacement. Powder and shot for the artillery was insufficient, and money, as always, tight. There were problems in giving the men their *nalbandi* advance to enable them to provide for their families during their absence, and equip themselves for the operations.

The Bhau himself was ignorant of the politics and personalities of Hindustan. Even the geography was unknown to him. His principal advisor should have been Malhar Holkar, but he was patronizing to the old warrior. Malhar resented it, and once, exasperated to the limit, was heard to exclaim, 'If God does not teach these Brahmins from Poona a lesson, they will make us wash their underwear!'[1] Clearly all was not well with the army high command.

Malhar, however, did join the Bhau's force, though much later. Hafiz Rahmat Khan had attempted to negotiate a peace between him and the Shah but Malhar was waiting for the arrival of the Bhau and spun out the parleys. In the meantime, Jahan Khan led a strong force through the Doab, sweeping away the Maratha thanas at Shikohabad and Etawah, right up to Bithur. Najib Khan visited Lucknow as an emissary of Abdali's and was further strengthened by Malika-i-Zamani, the widow of Muhammad Shah who had accompanied Hazrat Begum to Kabul after her marriage to Abdali in 1757. She too had been sent by Durrani to persuade Shuja. The Marathas were also counting on the latter, and their vakils reminded him of the old friendship which had existed between them and Safdar Jang.

Shuja would have preferred neutrality. He was easy-going and indolent. He knew that the protestations of friendship of the Marathas could not be relied upon. In 1757 they had demanded the sacred cities of Banaras and Allahabad, and Imad ul-Mulk, his avowed enemy, was possibly their only friend in the north. On the other hand, he was equally apprehensive of Durrani. Though belonging to a Persian family, Shuja was Indian born. He knew that Afghans and other *vilayatis* looked down on such people—in the same manner as, a hundred years later, the English from the 'home country' would look down on country-bred 'Anglo-Indians'. He was, therefore, apprehensive of being snubbed and insulted by the Shah's officers. Najib allayed his fears, declaring,

> What have you to do with the nobles in the Abdali camp? God be my witness that if the Shah himself frowns on Your Highness, I shall immediately tear his eyes out! If I fail, I'm not my father's son! There are one and a half lakh Afghans in India. Consider them your servants. If you had refused any other emissary I would not have complained. But as I have come, putting my faith in your grace, you must listen to me. Do one of two things now: either join Abdali, or here is my dagger and here my neck; cut it with your own hand. If you so desire, I shall give in writing that you should be absolved from the consequences.[2]

Shuja was won over by this eloquence.

The Bhau had hoped to persuade Shuja by quickly crossing into the Doab. With a Maratha army on the borders of Awadh, Poona's persuasive efforts could certainly have had more predictable results. But the Bhau was frustrated by an early monsoon. The Yamuna was unfordable and the flood too high to permit the laying of a boat-bridge. Thus, from 8 June to 13 July he remained stuck. On 18 June he was joined by Malhar Holkar. After consulting with the latter, and Suraj Mall, the Bhau abandoned the idea of the Doab incursion. If they could not cross the Yamuna, neither could the Shah. Instead it might be better to seize Delhi which was held by a weak force.

How had the capital been faring in the meantime? After the murder of Alamgir, the wazir had ransacked the palace, including the haram sarai. About Rs. 50 lakh were taken out; nothing portable was spared. Even the sums set aside as marriage dowers for the princesses were seized. But soon the city became too hot for him as well.

Alamgir had been murdered on 29 November. By 6 January the Maratha baggage train had left for the relative safety of Rajasthan. On 9 January came the news of Dattaji's death at the Barari crossing followed by the flight of the remnant of his army. A few days later even Imad left. On 21 January Durrani visited the shrine at Nizam ud-Din. He installed Yakub Ali Khan, whom we had come across in 1757 at the time of Durrani's first visit, governor of the Delhi suba. He, in turn, appointed his own kotwal, raised a police force and, with a few Durrani soldiers to stiffen it, restored order in the distracted and rudderless city. Abdali did not stay in Delhi but pushed on to the Doab. Meanwhile, life went on, almost as before, in the Qila-i-Mualla, with durbars being held by the faineant emperor who bore the distinguished title of Shah Jahan. Nauroz was celebrated on March 20 in the usual manner with the padishah seated on his throne, receiving the homage of his officers and palace functionaries.[3]

The Marathas attacked Delhi on 22 July. The Durrani contingent was too weak. Entry was easily forced by way of Javed Khan's mosque. The peshwa's troops then assaulted the fort. Most of the Indian soldiers abandoned their posts but the handful of Afghans kept up the defence. At one point, while the garrison was distracted by an assault on the Khizri gate, about a hundred men entered the fort by escalade near the Asad Burj, but instead of proceeding to open one of the main gates they commenced looting. Drawn by the tumult, half a dozen of the Afghans came running to investigate, and with a few shots drove them off. The plunderers panicked and jumped off the walls. A fort which had been practically taken was lost due to sheer indiscipline.

Thereafter the Marathas went for a regular siege. Three guns were mounted on the riverside and the beautiful pavilions of the palace complex, the Rang Mahal, Diwan-i-Khas, Asad Burj, Samman Burj and the haram sarai were damaged in the ensuing cannonade. On 29 July the Bhau himself arrived. Yakub Ali knew that the Shah was in no position to come to his relief and sued for peace. He was allowed to march out on 3 August with his little force.

The acquisition of Delhi was a barren triumph for the cash-starved army of the Bhau. The palace had already been stripped bare by Imad the previous December. The Shah, suffering keenly from the humid heat and anxious to return to Kabul, made overtures of peace through Shuja. At Anupshahar the Shah's horses were dying of disease by the hundred every day and he saw no point in staying in India any longer. But Najib was anxious that the Shah should not leave before the Marathas had been decisively defeated. He even contributed Rs. 2 lakh to the war chest of the Abdali and organized the transport of grain and provisions from his own estates. But Najib need not have worried about premature peace. While the Bhau himself might have been willing to end hostilities, the peshwa's instructions left no room for manoeuvre. On his part Shuja suggested the following terms:

(i) ceding Punjab and Sirhind to the Shah.
(ii) the removal of Shah Jahan III and the installation of Shah Alam as emperor with his eldest son, Jawan Bakht, as deputy in Delhi till such time as the father could return to the Qila-i-Mualla,
(iii) the replacement of Imad by Shuja as wazir.

Imad took umbrage that the proposals were considered at all, and left the Maratha camp in a huff in the company of Suraj Mall. The latter was uneasy about the Marathas' long term plans. His lands lay in their line of advance and he was in no position to resist them unassisted. This is why he had gone along with them. But Jat and Maratha relations were never cordial. The latter had never hesitated to squeeze the Jats whenever they could. Substantial sums were still owed by the raja to the Deccanis, and, though the Bhau was careful not to remind him about these dues, he gave no assurances for the future. Though a certain understanding had developed between Suraj Mall and Malhar, both being realists, it was only too evident that Malhar's counsel was discounted by the Bhau, who considered the old warrior a spent force. Caste susceptibilities also played their part. The Bhau, a high-born Brahmin, looked down on the Jat raja whose origins were humble, and position in the caste heirarchy—like that of Holkar's—modest. Imad ul-Mulk's sensitivities were not of much consequence since the military force at his command was insignificant, but the desertion of Suraj Mall, the only Hindu chieftain who had joined the Marathas, was ominous.

There were strains in the Afghan camp too. Ahmad Khan Bangash, the weakest of the Indian chiefs on that side, sent peace feelers to the Maratha camp. Shuja was also beginning to regret his choice. The Shah, who had gained nothing by this expedition, had hinted to him that a contribution towards his expenses would not be out of place. After all he was reputed to be the richest nobleman in north India. But apart from this gentle pressure the Shah's iron discipline ensured that Shuja should have no real reason for complaint. When some Durrani soldiers rioted and looted shops in his bazaar the Shah immediately rounded up two hundred of the rioters. Their noses were pierced, and strung up like camels in a row, a string passing through their noses, and hands bound, they were led by the nasaqchis to Shuja to be dealt with as he thought fit.[4] What a contrast this was to the disgraceful behaviour of the Maratha auxiliaries brought by Imad in 1754! They were commanded by no less a leader than Malhar Holkar, and they had come as his allies to fight for the emperor against the rebel Safdar Jang. But this did not deter them from plundering Nizam ud-Din and the markets in the suburbs. Imad, shocked had gone up to Malhar and reproached him: 'What is this? Why are your soldiers plundering the city?'

Malhar had coolly replied, 'They are soldiers. They always do so.'[5]

Apart from the initial morale boost the capture of Delhi gave, the Bhau soon discovered that the occupation of the capital provided no strategic advantage. In fact it was the reverse, for it made him responsible for the upkeep of the nominal padishah and his phantom court. The expenses exceeded Rs. 1.5 lakh per month; not only were the salaries of the palace functionaries required to be paid, but the kitchen expenses of the emperor, his wives and concubines and immediate family had also to be provided for. Then there were the hundreds of royal dependents, the widows and concubines of former emperors, and the descendants of former emperors and their families, living in the warren of apartments and courtyards that constituted khawaspura and the salatin khana. In desperation the Bhau cast his eyes upwards at the silver ceiling of the Diwan-i-Khas. About half of it had already been despoiled by Imad on 6 August. Now the Bhau stripped down the remainder and melted it for coin. It yielded Rs. 9 lakh. According to the *Seir* they also siezed 'the gold and silver vessels consecrated to the use of the monument of the sacred foot, and of the mausoleum of Saint Nizam ud-Din; nor did they spare Mahmed-Shah's mausoleum, which they stripped of its incensory, candelabres, lamps and other utensils, all the solid gold . . . all of which were torn . . . and sent to the Mint'.[6]

The newsletters from the Maratha 'conquerors' of Delhi give a woeful picture of their plight. One dated 5 August reads thus, 'There is no money for paying even a week's subsistence in a month; our men and horses are fasting. If we could discover the hiding places in the fort, ten or twenty crores could be secured. But we cannot enter the female apartments of the palace.'[7] The silver ceiling of the Diwan-i-Khas helped to tide over the financial crisis for some time, but by the end of September the position again became desperate. As the river was still too high to permit an expedition into the Doab, it was decided to attack Kunjpura, further upstream and on the same bank. There was no military advantage or logic. The compulsions rose from the penury of the Maratha camp. Kunjpura was said to be a rich town and held out good prospects of plunder, which might temporarily relieve the chronic cash problem. In addition, by cutting the Shah's communications with his base in Afghanistan, he might force him to a fight. Otherwise, further delay might result in the dissolution and dispersal of the Maratha army.

Leaving Naro Shankar in charge at Delhi, the Bhau moved out to the Shalamar gardens where he remained till October. Then on 10 October he sent two officers to the Qila-i-Mualla with instructions to depose Shah Jahan III. Ali Gauhar was proclaimed padishah under the title of Shah Alam II (he had already assumed the title in Bihar on learning of his father's murder), and Jawan Bakht appointed as his deputy in Delhi. As a final sop to Shuja, with the hope that he might thereby be induced to abandon the Shah, the Bhau appointed him wazir in absentia. Having done this, he moved north, reaching Kunjpura on 16 October.

Abdus Samad Khan, the Afghan faujdar of Sirhind, and Mian Qutb Shah faced the Marathas with 2,000 troops outside Kunjpura. This small contingent was no match for the whole mass of the Maratha army which had encircled the town. Its men broke ranks before the withering fire of Ibrahim Gardi's musketeers, who were drilled after the European pattern, and fled towards the town. At first Nejabat Khan refused them entry but when they threatened him with the wrath of Abdali, he opened the gates, and in they rushed. And along with them came the pursuing Marathas who had tasted blood and were enthused at the prospect of an easy victory.

About a thousand Deccanis were killed in the street fighting, but vast booty had fallen into their hands. Abdus Samad Khan was killed, Nejabat died later of his wounds, and Qutb Shah was captured. This was indeed a particularly welcome prize, for it was the latter who had delivered the *coup de grâce* to the fallen Dattaji Scindia at the battle of Barari Ghat and cut off his head. He knew he could expect no mercy and roundly abused the Marathas when brought before the Bhau. Orders were passed for his execution and his and Abdus Samad's heads were paraded as trophies in the Maratha camp, and we can be sure they drew the loudest cheers in the bazaar of the Scindia contingent. Two sons of Nejabat were taken prisoner; they were fated to die at Panipat. A third had escaped and it was he who was destined to continue the line and recover his father's seat.

The booty included Rs. 6.5 lakh, 3,000 horses, besides guns, draught animals and a quantity of wheat so large that the Maratha troops were paid in grain for some time. More booty was recovered during the subsequent week as the houses were dug up for treasure.

The Dussehra festival was celebrated at Kunjpura and the Marathas set off for Kurukshetra, to bathe in its sacred tank. But at Taraori the Bhau learnt that the Shah had crossed the Yamuna at Baghpat and was moving up. He immediately stopped and turned to face him. At Panipat the Afghan vanguard was sighted and the Deccanis pitched their tents in anticipation of the final decisive struggle.

The rivers were still high but at the news of the sack of Kunjpura the Shah bestirred himself. He marched up river in search of a ford, and finally at Baghpat found one. Many lives were lost but by the successful crossing he had turned the tables. Now it was the Bhau's communications that were cut while the Shah had a friendly Rohilkhand behind him, and beyond that lay Awadh, the suba of another ally Shuja ud-Daulah.

The Shah had held a muster a day after Dussehra. His strength was about 40,000 cavalry and 40,000 infantry. Of these, his allies numbered 10,000 horse and 30,000 foot. The estimates of the Maratha army vary greatly from source to source, and the later the account, the greater the numbers. But the most reliable figure, is that of 60,000, 45,000 being cavalry and the remainder infantry.[8] Thus, even in absolute numbers the Afghan host outnumbered the Maratha. And, of course, man to man,horse to horse, the Afghans were superior to the wiry Marathas with their diminutive country-bred ponies. And when one considers their relative discipline, the Marathas stood nowhere in comparison to the Durrani troops. The privations of the coming months would tilt the balance even more decisively against the Deccanis.

Both Durrani and the Bhau were foreigners in Hindustan. But there was a vital difference. In Shuja ud-Daulah and Najib Khan—specially the latter—the Durrani Shah had valuable allies. Besides, there were lesser chiefs like the Bangash nawab, Hafiz Rahmat Khan, and others. The Bhau stood alone with his Maratha sardars and the mercenaries of Ibrahim Khan Gardi. Suraj Mall Jat, the one noteworthy chief who had joined in the beginning, had long since deserted the Bhau. Even that broken reed, Imad ul-Mulk, had gone.

None of the great names from the ancient chivalry of Rajasthan, the Rathors of Jodhpur, the Kachhwahas of Jaipur, the Hara Chauhans from Kotah-Bundi or the Sisodias from Mewar, was present to support the Maratha cause, even though for two decades past Maratha armies had been fighting on behalf of one or the other in their fratricidal wars. The Marathas had not endeared themselves to their clients, and all of them, if not actually praying for an Afghan victory, were at least indifferent to the result. In reality, we had two foreign armies ranged against one other for the mastery of Hindustan. One of them had powerful allies within the country, and, unhappily for them, the Marathas were not the ones so favoured.

The Bhau's financial distress was soon acute. The peshwa had seen him off with a parting gift of barely Rs. 2 lakh. He had inherited a heavy burden of debt and he expected the Bhau to live off the sums collected by Maratha collectors like Govind Ballal Bundele, who were under instructions to remit half their collections to Poona and convey the rest to the Bhau.

Govind Ballal himself was in arrears to the extent of Rs. 25 lakh, and the peshwa expected that the presence of a strong Maratha army in the region would be enough to persuade the recalcitrant debtors to pay up. But the effect was quite the opposite. The Bhau could not afford to alienate the Rajput princes or the Jat raja, for fear that they might join the other side. Therefore, he could not press them for their arrears, and the debtors preferred to sit on the fence and await the outcome of the struggle. Besides, the Maratha districts, particularly in the Doab, were too badly ravaged by the wars to yield their normal revenue. With the Shah himself at Anupshahar or Aligarh in the heart of the Doab for most of this period, it was too much to expect the zemindars to remit their dues to the Maratha agents.

It is estimated that against the estimated expenses of Rs. 72 lakh for the ten month period, the Bhau actually received only 22.5 lakh[9]—including the receipts obtained by coining the silver ceiling of the Diwan-i-Khas and the loot from Kunjpura. Without a single prince to support him, and bankers refusing credit, his distress was extreme.

Apart from the fact that the Shah had resourceful allies in Najib Khan and Shuja, he was nearer to his base in Afghanistan as compared to the Bhau. From Delhi, as the crow flies, Poona is farther than Kabul or Kandahar. Before the final battle in December 1760 the Shah was able to receive a sizeable reinforcement (of 15,000 men, according to the author of the *Shah Alam Namah*) from Kabul while the Bhau had been constantly losing men by attrition in a number of engagements, like the one at Kunjpura, without any accretion to his strength.

One thing neither adversary could be accused of at this stage was overconfidence. At last, face to face at Panipat, each moved with caution and circumspection. Neither was in a hurry to come to grips; both wanted to assess each other's strength before attacking.

The Bhau interpreted the cautious hesitation of the Shah as a sign of timidity, and news of temporary shortage of food in the enemy camp cheered him further. He hunkered down for a long confrontation, entrenched himself, and conveyed instructions to Govind Ballal Bundele in the Doab to cut off the Shah's grain supply from the agriculturally rich Doab. He hoped that famine and starvation would break up the Afghan alliance, and his Indian confederates would desert in the face of the privations that were certain to follow.

But the Maratha armies of the 1760s were very different from those of the time of Shivaji which had kept the emperor tied down for more than twenty years. In course of time, with increasing success and prosperity, their baggage had become as cumbersome as that of the imperial armies, with the generals as luxury-seeking and easy-going. As for mobility, the hardier Afghans, coming from a poorer country with a harsher climate, were certainly at an advantage. The position soon changed for the Marathas. The stocks of grain acquired at Kunjpura were exhausted, Rs. 7 lakh won but a brief reprieve for the cash-starved Deccani army. Govind Ballal was too fat and too old to mount a horse. A mere revenue collector, he was in no position to lead an effective campaign to cut off the flow of grain to the Afghans from the Doab.

Throughout November the Marathas patrolled aggressively and frequent clashes took place. But in December they suffered two serious reverses. On 7 December Balwant Rao Mehendele, one of the Bhau's principal advisers, was killed in a raid against Najib's Rohillas. Not only were the Maratha raiders repulsed, and their guns captured, but the Afghans penetrated the Maratha lines. The raid had commenced in the evening and in the darkness heavy casualties were suffered by both sides. But the loss of Mehendele was a great loss for the Bhau. Ten days later another blow fell which put paid to any hopes which may have been placed on Govind Ballal Bundele's operations in the trans-Yamuna.

With less than 10,000 men, mostly raw recruits, Bundele started from Etawah with the object of ravaging the mahals of Najib in Meerut and Bulandshahr. He fondly imagined that the Doab was denuded of Afghan troops, and was proceeding leisurely, in imagined security, when a body of 5,000 Durrani horse, newly arrived from Afghanistan, fell upon him at Jalalabad, about 10 miles from Ghaziabad. The old Brahmin was actually engaged in his ablutions, prior to preparing his food, when the Durrani cavalry struck. In his half-naked state he mounted a horse but was struck by a bullet and decapitated before his identity could be established. Thereafter, the Durranis had assured supplies while conditions in the Maratha camp steadily deteriorated.

The Afghan patrols grew more aggressive, the Maratha supplies failed, and soon the prospect of famine and starvation seemed very real. Whatever was procured was obtained at exorbitant prices from Panipat. The townsmen, who were mostly Muslims, bitterly resented the Maratha occupation which was the cause of their ruin. Every tree in the town and its environs, including the fruit trees in the orchards, had been cut down either for fuel to feed the campfires, or to strengthen the entrenchments.

Naro Shankar at Delhi was able to send one convoy of treasure with Rs. 1,10,000 on 21 December, but the second attempt to deliver the remainder failed. The riders, each of whom was carrying Rs. 500 on his person, by mistake approached the Afghan camp and only one reached the Bhau's tents to tell the tale of disaster.

The Bhau made one desperate effort to make peace through Shuja, sending him an emissary with a blank piece of paper bearing the impression of his hand in saffron by way of authority. He had given him *carte blanche* to negotiate any terms. The Afghan wazir, Shah Wali Khan, favoured peace for a large indemnity, but Najib Khan would not be cheated of the prospect of a crushing Maratha defeat.

Apart from the scarcity of provisions, the Maratha camp had become extremely insanitary, with the smell of ordure and death omnipresent. The carcasses of dead animals lay in the open, a feast for the vultures and scavenger dogs. Finally on 13 January a number of officers surrounded the Bhau's tent and demanded that they be led to battle. They would rather die sword in hand, they declared, than of starvation or disease in that stinking hell. It was thereupon decided to launch an all-out attack the following morning.

The Marathas rode out the next morning not so much to conquer as to die. The odds were formidable. Not only did the Afghans outnumber the Deccan force, their heavy mailed cavalry, mounted on Khurasani horses, was far superior to the half-starved Deccani mares. In their camel mounted swivels they had a highly versatile field artillery whose mobility cancelled the heavy calibres of the Maratha guns which, once placed in firing position, could not be moved again easily. But the Marathas still had a faint chance, for their decision had been so sudden that the Afghan spies had no prior information, and the surprise of a sudden attack might have carried the day yet. But a simple breakthrough would not have sufficed, for the Bhau was encumbered with a large number of women, and the plunder accumulated in seven months of campaigning. It was essential to destroy the Afghan army. Had the women been left behind in some safe base like Bharatpur or Mathura, there might have been a chance. Unfortunately, the Deccanis had no friends in the north and no stronghold which could be made a safe base.

The formal methods of fighting a general battle in vogue then also precluded surprise. It took an hour or two for an army of this size to move out of its tents and assume battle stations. The noise and tumult and the dust raised by the movement of thousands of men and animals would give the game away. Besides, between the assumption of battle positions and the launching of the attack, there had to be a pause to allow the dust to settle so that the armies could see each other.

Late at night Shuja came to suspect that something was afoot, for the Bhau had unwisely made a last desperate appeal to him to make another attempt to secure peace terms. There would not be another chance, he had written, for 'the waters have now passed over my head'.[9]

Shuja at once warned the Shah, who immediately got up and rode out to inspect the frontline. While he puffed at his hookah in the crisp cold of a winter dawn, he could hear the unmistakable sounds of movement in the opposing camp. And when he heard the clank of chains as the heavy guns were dragged forward into their firing positions, he alerted his generals.

The Marathas had begun their movement an hour before dawn. The sun was up by the time the battle could begin. In the centre, the Bhau was ranged against the Afghan wazir, Shah Wali Khan; on the right wing Malhar Holkar and Jankoji Scindia faced Shuja, while on the left, Ibrahim Khan Gardi faced the par-Rohillas, i.e. the trans-Ganga Rohillas led by chiefs like Hafiz Rahmat Khan, Dhundi Khan and others. Ahmad Bangash was also with them. Najib Khan's troops were ranged with Shuja's, opposite the Holkar and Scindia contingents. There was very little fighting on this flank. The troops of both Holkar and Scindia had suffered many reverses at the hands of the Afghans and had no stomach to face them again. When at last Najib, who was also very cautious, advanced to engage them, they turned and fled.

The battle began with an attack by the sepoys of Gardi against the par-Rohillas, while in the centre the Bhau charged the Afghan centre. There was no movement on the right where each side simply neutralized the other. Attempts had been made to tamper with Ibrahim Khan's loyalty by making an appeal to religion, but the stout condottiere rejected these overtures with the declaration that he held loyalty to one's salt as the highest virtue. Reporting to his commander as the battle was about to begin, he assured him thus, 'Ram! Ram! Your Lordship was irked with me because every month I used to insist on the payment of the dues of my soldiers, even though I knew you were short of funds. This month your treasure train had been looted and we weren't paid. Nevertheless, today you shall see us do our duty.'

With 6,000 men he attacked the par-Rohillas. Heavy casualties were inflicted by the sepoys of Ibrahim Khan (who had received his military education under Bussy in the Deccan), but in the afternoon superior numbers began to tell, and when the Shah threw in fresh reserves, Ibrahim's men began to wilt. By then, in the centre, the Bhau's division was also beginning to break up. However, Ibrahim and his Telinga sepoys had fought with great tenacity, and the loyal Gardi was later to pay for his devotion with his life. Had his infantry column been backed by cavalry, it might have broken the Rohilla battalions, but, unlike the Shah, the Bhau had no reserves to exploit the initial gains.

In the centre, as on the left flank, the Bhau's division achieved some initial success but in the afternoon, when the Indians began to tire, the Shah threw in fresh troops to back up his wazir. About the same time Vishwas Rao was killed by a bullet. When the Bhau was informed he was disheartened; the charge that had been entrusted to him by a weeping mother, whom he had promised to protect with his life, was dead. There was no longer any reason for him to live, and he plunged anew, where the battle was thickest, desperately seeking death.

The Bhau had made no provision for an orderly retreat in the event of defeat and, forsaking his responsibility as the commander-in-chief, made no attempt to extricate his army or what remained of it, when it became clear that the battle was practically over with only a few small groups of Marathas still fighting on the field.

Sadashiv Rao Bhau, however, had still not found death. Three horses had fallen under him and he had been wounded in the leg, pierced by a musket ball and a lance. Now supporting himself with a short spear he was seen limping across the battlefield. Seeing the distinguished figure, still conspicuous by the pearls and jewels which he wore round his neck, five Durrani horsemen rode upto him and demanded that he give himself up or die. But it was not safety that the Bhau was seeking. We can picture him pause, looking his would-be captors in the eye, and, with the cry of a wounded lion brought to bay, striking out with his spear at the Afghan horsemen. And that was how he met his end, fighting until struck down. His head was cut off and taken as a trophy by the Durrani dragoons.

Thus ended the peshwa's dreams of establishing the Maratha ascendancy over all of India.

NOTES

1. Sardesai, *Selections from the Peshwa Daftar*, xxvii, pp. 225, 257. Sarkar, *Fall of the Mughal Empire*, ii, p. 148.
2. Sarkar, ii, p. 162.
3. Ibid., ii, p. 148.
4. Kashiraj, *Indian Historical Quarterly*, 1934-5, p. 8.
5. Sarkar, i, p. 542.
6. Tabatabai, iii, pp. 387-8.
7. Sarkar, ii, p. 155.
8. Ibid., pp. 167-70.
9. Ibid., p. 155.
10. '*Ab az sar guzashta*'; Sarkar, ii, p. 193.

CHAPTER 32

The Aftermath

Panipat is probably the bloodiest battle in the history of modern India. Rarely, if ever, have two armies grappled with such ferocity and determination. The roll of the martyrs of Panipat is long and distinguished. Virtually all the great Maratha families were represented. Vishwas Rao, the young hope of the Maratha nation, led the roll. Then there was the peshwa's younger brother, the Bhau, who only a few months earlier had thrilled the Maratha nation by humbling its old adversary, the Mughal viceroy of the Deccan, Nizam Ali, also known as Asaf Jah II. Another brother, Shamsher Bahadur, was severely wounded and died a few weeks later at Kumbher, in spite of the ministrations of the physicians of the Jat raja. The house of Scindia had already suffered the loss of its chief, Dattaji, a few months earlier at the battle of Barari Ghat. Two others, Tukoji and Jankoji, were claimed by Panipat. Mahadji, who was later to cut so great a figure, was lamed for life, wounded in the knee by an Afghan plunderer who stripped him of his ornaments and left him for dead. Ibrahim Khan Gardi, severely wounded, surrendered to Shuja who concealed him in his tent but the Afghans, on coming to know, demanded and obtained his custody, and then killed him as an apostate to his faith. Santaji Wagh and Antaji Mankeshwar were two other notable casualties. The latter's dispatches are a valuable and accurate source of information right upto the battle. Had he survived we would have had another detailed and accurate eye witness account to supplement that of Kashiraj Pandit, a Deccani Brahmin in the service of Shuja. The only important chiefs who survived the slaughter were Malhar Holkar and Mahadji Scindia. There was scarcely a home in Maharashtra that did not mourn the loss of one of its members. It was a national catastrophe.

About 28,000 bodies were counted on the field of battle. Afterwards, several thousand Marathas who had foolishly tried to hide in the city were massacred by enthusiastic Afghans who were resolved to send as many of the 'infidels' to hell as possible, specially as their bigoted mullas had assured them that they would thereby acquire religious merit. Kashiraj describes the scene thus:

> Every Durrani soldier brought away a hundred or two of prisoners and slew them in the outskirts of their camp, crying out, 'When I started from my country, my mother, father, sister and wife told me to slay so many kaffirs for their sake after we had gained victory in this holy war, so that they may also benefit by the merit of my deeds.' Except for the Shah's own quarters and those of his nobles, every tent had a heap of severed heads before it. One may say that it was verily doomsday for the Maratha people.[1]

Probably 30,000 more died in the pursuit. In India most battles were followed by an immediate plunder of the vanquished camp which usually enabled the shattered remnants of the defeated army to make their get-away. But the iron discipline of Abdali was such that he refused to allow the plunder, and after detaching a small body of his personal slaves and *nasaqchis* to protect the camp he kept up the pursuit for 20 miles, late into the night. As long as the moon remained up, the pursuit was maintained. Thousands were slain on the trail; many others died of their wounds in the wintry January night, or were later butchered by the Jat and the Gujjar peasantry, and Baluch or Mughal grantees who held jagirs in that area. Since 1754 the Maratha armies had crossed and recrossed this tract, looting peasants and landlords alike with insane greed. Payment of the fixed revenue or tribute to one Maratha officer had not saved the villagers from the exactions of another. Appeals for redress, even to their highest generals, had only elicited the chilling reply: 'They are soldiers, they always do it.'[2] Now the Marathas were reaping as they had sown.

Small parties and individuals were robbed and often killed. To larger bodies the peasants refused entry, and offered resistance from behind the walls of their fortified villages and houses. Antaji Mankeshwar, who was marked out as a chief by his rich clothes, was robbed and killed by the Baluch jagirdars of Farrukhnagar. Even women boldly stripped solitary stragglers and many a survivor reached safety clad only in his loin cloth.

At least 60,000 Marathas were thus sent 'to the region of Nothingness'—to borrow the expressive phrase of the author of the *Seir*. This, of course, included many camp followers and other non-combatants, for the total fighting strength of the Bhau's army did not match this figure. For every fighting man there were at least eight non-combatants in those times. In the town of Panipat, among the captives were 22,000 women, many of them 'fair, rose limbed beauties' from the northern hills who have always commanded a premium in the flesh markets of the great cities of the north.

Most of the booty in the Maratha camp was appropriated by the Afghans and very little fell to the share of Najib or Shuja. It was considerable, though not as much as in 1757, and Kashiraj records how every trooper of the Shah brought away ten to twenty camels laden with valuables. 'The captured horses were beyond count; they come like droves of sheep in their thousands.'[3]

It was only in the territory of the Jat raja that the fugitives found safe haven. Suraj Mall received them kindly, fed them, provided medical attention to the wounded and conveyance up to their city of Gwalior. His rani attended to the ladies and was particularly attentive to the Brahmins. A Jesuit, Father Xavier Wendel, who was then in the Jat court, asserts that not a single Maratha could have reached the Deccan if Suraj Mall had willed otherwise. At least 50,000 of the survivors owed their lives to him.

It may be observed that the savage blood-lust of the Afghans was not shared by their Indian allies. Shuja did his best to save as many of the vanquished that surrendered to him. He was unable to protect the gallant Ibrahim Khan Gardi, but at least 400 other officers and 6,000 soldiers owed him their lives, and received monetary assistance from him for the long journey to the Deccan. The bodies of the fallen chiefs were re-covered and cremated with due respect as a result of his exertions. The Afghans had wished to stuff the body of Vishwas Rao with straw to take home as a trophy, but at Shuja's insistence it was handed over to him and saved from that ultimate ignominy.

Malhar Holkar was among the fugitives who brought the news of the disaster to Poona. News of the defeat had reached the Deccan by way of a banker's letter intercepted at Bhilsa on 27 January, only thirteen days after the battle, but it was Malhar Rao Holkar who revealed the full magnitude of the catastrophe.

The early flight of Malhar from the killing field gave rise to some reproaches, but his apologists ascribe his escape to his superior qualities as a leader which enabled him to keep his party together and retreat in good order when he saw that the battle was lost and catastrophe was in the offing. The story is narrated that he had entreated the Bhau to delay the battle, but the latter, impatient of his advice, exclaimed, 'Who wants the advice of a goatherd?',[4] alluding to the general's humble origins. A similar snide remark had lost the Maratha commander the services on this day of the only ally he had acquired in the north, Suraj Mall.

But it is a fact that Malhar's men, like the Scindia contingent, had no stomach left for serious fighting. The unbroken series of reverses had unnerved them. Malhar thought only of saving himself. It did not even occur to him to take along young Jankoji Scindia who was on his immediate left, and, according to Maratha tradition, clung to him as a child to its mother.

Malhar, who was now seventy six, did not long survive the disaster. He left behind no male heir, his son Khande Rao having been killed at the siege of Dig in Bharatpur territory in 1754. Ever since, the management of the Holkar estates had been in the capable hands of the virtuous and celebrated Ahalya Bai, the widow of the young Khande. She had a son but he was mentally incompetent and died in his youth. Ahalya showed her wisdom and discernment by nominating another member of the clan, Tukoji, as the heir to the heritage of Malhar. Tukoji Holkar was older than the young widow but never failed to show her respect.

The Peshwa was already in a decline, slowly dying of a wasting disease, sunk in deep melancholy, rarely speaking to his courtiers, and responding only with grunts and monosyllables. He breathed his last on 23 June 1761. His death inaugurated a tragic period in Maratha history dominated by the evil figure of Raghunath Rao Dada. It was thus that the empire was to have a respite from Maratha raids for some years.

One may say that the effects of Panipat were temporary. After all, in 1772 the Marathas were back in force in Hindostan. Mahadji Scindia was eventually to be appointed Amir-ul-Umara and the deputy of the peshwa, the titular Vakil-i-Mutlaq. On the face of it the Marathas could not have asked for more. They were now the keepers of the emperor, the 'mayors' of the palace and, like Charles Martel, could have reasonably been expected to replace the faineant emperors in due course. But in the decade that lay between, the world was to change immeasurably.

Four years before Panipat, on the field of Plassey in Bengal, the richest province of the empire, the merchants of the East India Company had become the local kingmakers. Siraj ud-Daulah had been replaced by Mir Jafar, who, in turn, would be replaced by Mir Kasim. These foreigners from an obscure island kingdom, which no Indian notable had ever seen, had become a decisive military factor in Bengal politics. And three years afterwards, at the battle of Buxar, they would defeat Shuja ud-Daulah, the titular prime minister and north India's richest potentate, together with the Emperor Shah Alam II, still far from his capital of Delhi. From the reluctant hands of the fallen monarch they wrung the rights to the diwani of Bengal, Bihar and Orissa. In this sprawling viceroyalty, comprising three subas, the Mughals of the old days had been careful to keep the diwani and the nizamat, i.e. the revenue administration and the magisterial functions, in separate hands. It was only after the death of Murshid Quli, the last diwan, that the two offices became concentrated in a single subedar. But now with the treaty of Allahabad, the office of diwan had been vested in an officer of the Company Bahadur, the governor in charge of the factory at Calcutta, who together with his trained sepoys became the real master of Bengal, the nominal nazims with their seat at Murshidabad being steadily reduced to the status of faineants. The same process was to be repeated in the south with the nawab of Arcot, himself a subordinate of the viceroy of the Deccan, Asaf Jah.

All the labours of Najib ud-Daulah, Najaf Khan and Mahadji Scindia were in vain. Theirs were barren and inconsequential victories; the Afghan threat would recede with the decade, but the Indian empire of the Timurids was as dead as a dodo; the predestined rulers of tomorrow were the *Sahiban-i-Inglishia Ali-Shan*. The sword of Robert Clive *Sabit Jang*, former clerk and ensign of the East India Company, would succeed where all these great nobles had failed.

NOTES

1. Sarkar, *Fall of the Mughal Empire*, ii, pp. 210-11 (on the authority of Kashiraj).
2. Ibid., i, p. 542. A memorable quote of Holkar's when the Marathas had come to Delhi at the invitation of Imad ul-Mulk, May 1754.
3. Ibid., i, p. 211.
4. Malcolm, *A Memoir of Central India*, i, p. 153.

CHAPTER 33

The Dictatorship of Najib ud-Daulah

The wazir's post had been offered to Shuja by Ahmad Shah when the two met at Anupshahar. It was their first meeting and Abdali was anxious to bind him to his side, but Shuja declined saying: 'Who is the emperor? If you sit on the imperial throne I shall be ready to serve you, but, as things stand today, you would make me feel ridiculous by giving me the robes of an office without its functions.'[1]

It was the reply of a courtier and did not mean that he had no wish to become wazir. Later, tentative feelers were sent proposing that Shuja be made wazir and Ali Gauhar emperor, but at that time Shuja judged it prudent not to appear too anxious. In a last desperate attempt to win him over the Bhau had deposed the puppet Shah Jahan and proclaimed Shah Alam (Ali Gauhar) padishah with Jawan Bakht, his son and heir, as deputy, and Shuja the wazir. The ghastly Imad ul-Mulk had by then abandoned the Marathas and taken up with Suraj Mall, whom the Bhau had earlier alienated by his arrogance. But it was now too late. Shuja was not in a position to change sides.

After Panipat Ahmad spent three months in Delhi. There was not much to be gleaned from the oft-ravished city. Habash Khan, the Abyssinian kotwal, was stripped of 10,000 gold coins which he had managed to squeeze from Naro Shankar, the Maratha commandant, before the latter fled; and the Queen Mother, Zinat Mahal, presented him with a *nazar* of Rs. 1 lakh. But before long the Shah had to beat a retreat to Afghanistan on account of disorders in his army. His troops had been away from the cool hills of Afghanistan for over a year, and the prospect of another summer in Hindustan was intolerable. So he left hurriedly, setting out from Delhi on 22 March.

Two weeks earlier Shuja had left Ahmad Shah's camp in a huff after a riot between the sunni troops of Abdali and his own shia soldiers. Thus, the Shah left annoyed with both Najib and Shuja. His parting instructions were that Shah Alam should be recognized as emperor, and Imad reappointed wazir, with Najib as the mir bakhshi—a return to the arrangements of 1757. The latter two were piously enjoined to bury the hatchet and work together to restore the empire to some semblance of its former state.

Under the circumstances, this was impossible. A river of blood lay between the two and Imad could never forgive Najib for the outrage against the ladies of his harem in August 1757. However, this time Imad was not on the scene to assume his office. He was away in Bharatpur with the wily Jat raja, from whom he drew his strength.

The Jat leader was at this time undoubtedly the richest potentate in north India with a formidable army. Some losses had been suffered in the defence of Ballabhgarh and Mathura, but the bulk of his troops were safe behind the high walls of his impregnable forts, for Ahmad Shah had no time to undertake long sieges. At the end of the campaign the Shah was in too much of a hurry to press for a heavy tribute. Suraj Mall had scarcely paid anything in 1757 and now in 1761 he escaped again. Nor was there any serious fighting in his domains, which, but for a few mahals in the Doab, lay to the south of the Yamuna. So while the Doab and the Haryana region of Rohtak and Bhiwani had been repeatedly ravaged by the passage of the Durrani armies, Suraj Mall was able to collect his revenue without difficulty from the peasantry of the Braj. Thus, the support of Suraj Mall was not something to be sniffed at.

However, Najib, already in Delhi, was able to forestall Imad. He reminded the Queen Mother of the enmity between Imad and Shah Alam. If he was allowed to come and assume office, he would immediately place some other prince on the throne, and that would be the end of her son's hopes. Thus persuaded, the sensible lady lost no time in sending Najib an invitation to assume office.

So, while Yakub Ali Khan, the Abdali's cousin, was still at Bharatpur where he had gone to convey the Shah's instructions and invest the wazir-designate with the insignia of office, Najib entered Delhi in the company of Prince Jawan Bakht. He assumed the title of Amir-ul-Umara with the office of mir bakhshi as well as the faujdari of Delhi. With his own son, Zabita, appointed as faujdar, and another nominee as qiladar, his control was complete. He also assumed the title of *mukhtar* or regent, but not the more prestigious title of Vakil-i-Mutlaq. What he wanted was the substance of power; others could fight for the empty title of wazir.

When the news of this coup reached Suraj Mall, the Jat raja's determination to support Imad's pretensions also petered out. He had hoped to aggrandize himself if the wazir was of his choice, and also totally dependent upon him, but he shrank from a direct struggle with the battle-hardened veterans of Najib, specially when his protégé had already been upstaged by his rival.

Yakub Ali's mission to Mathura was not limited to investing the wazir-designate. Ahmad Shah was a statesman, and now that Panipat had been fought and the Marathas crushed, there was nothing that he desired more than an amicable settlement. He had instructed his envoy to call on the peshwa himself, convey his regrets for the death of his son and brother, and to request him to let bygones be bygones. But the peshwa's vakil at Delhi, Mahadev Hingane, as well as representatives of Shuja, the par-Rohillas, and Ahmad Khan Bangash—all the forces inimical to Najib—gathered and dissuaded Yakub from proceeding further. There was no point in going to the Deccan, they said. The peshwa was dying, his sanity was affected, and until a successor was appointed nothing could be accomplished by the visit. Yakub Ali thus returned to Delhi, and the other vakils also dispersed. Meanwhile, Suraj Mall had also lost interest in Imad ul-Mulk.

The advantages which might accrue from a pocket wazir were hypothetical, while a more attractive and immediate gain appeared to be at hand. Agra, the second city of the empire, had always been the object of the Jat raja's ambition. He had occupied the city once, in the wake of the Durrani invasion of 1757, and now the moment again seemed opportune. After Yakub's return, he set his armies in motion and blockaded the fort. The news reached Najib who had just assumed his charge at Delhi. At first Najib talked of marching to the relief of Agra, but shrank from renewing hostilities so soon after the blood-letting at Panipat. Thus on 12 June Agra surrendered, the commandant being persuaded by the promise of a hefty bribe. As it happened, Suraj Mall got out of paying even this on the pretext of unaccountable shortages in the imperial stores. The wretched qiladar, thus got nothing! All that the Jat actually gave out were the salaries of the garrison which, as usual, were in arrears. With the fall of this city, the Qila-i-Mualla lost control of all territory to the south of the Yamuna, except for the immediate vicinity of Delhi. Najib judged it prudent to let matters rest this way for the time being, and to concentrate on consolidating himself in Delhi and its environs.

From 1761 to 1772 the Qila-i-Mualla was without a resident sovereign. Jawan Bakht officiated as the absentee sovereign's representative, but all power lay in the hands of Najib ud-Daulah. The north was spared the ravages of the Marathas for most of this period. The first Maratha army to enter Hindostan after Panipat came in 1767. Nor did the Afghan Shah advance beyond the Punjab in this time. Panipat marked the zenith of Afghan power. The destruction of the Maratha army was followed by the annihilation of a large Sikh army the following year in what is commemorated in the Sikh historical tradition by the sombre description of the *wadda ghallughara* or the 'Great Blood-bath'. But the Sikhs were fighting in their homeland, unlike the Marathas at Panipat. They retaliated promptly the following year (1763) and, swooping down on Sirhind, killed the Afghan faujdar, Zain Khan, and cut up his small force. Then ensued the third and final sack of that unfortunate city. Virtually every building was destroyed, the entire population massacred or dispersed, and only blackened ruins remained to remind people that there once existed Sirhind of evil memory. The city was held in such execration that for long the Sikhs considered it inauspicious to even utter its name.

Ahmad Shah visited Punjab again with a large army but realized that matters were beyond repair. Domestic troubles and revolts in other parts of his far-flung empire would now occupy most of his time and 1769 would see the last of him. His successor, Shah Zaman, was to make a weak attempt to recover Punjab in the later years of the century, but by that time the situation in Punjab had undergone a sea-change.

The Afghan withdrawal created further problems for Najib at Delhi for the Sikhs were now free to plunder where they willed, and soon their raids into the Doab and the Delhi region became an annual feature. Most of Najib's estates lay in the Upper Doab, and he suffered the most. His health broke down, and from 1763 onward he was under constant pressure. It was only his iron determination that kept his state from utter dissolution.

Taking Agra had meant a vast accretion of wealth to Suraj Mall a prince who was already reputedly the richest in Hindostan. Unlike Delhi, which had been ravished by Nadir and Abdali, besides being milked dry by the exactions of Imad ul-Mulk, Agra was still a virgin city. Neither the Persian nor the Afghan had entered her walls, and though much of the hoarded treasures had been dissipated in the civil wars of the earlier part of the century, there was still a substantial amount left in the form of gold and silver vessels and valuable furnishings. Besides, there was the formidable imperial artillery, much of which was removed to strengthen the defences of the Jat forts at Bharatpur, Kumbher and Dig.

After taking Agra, Suraj Mall concentrated on extending his hold on Mewat which he hoped to set up as an appanage for his son Jawahar. The old imperial fort of Alwar had fallen into his hands in 1754 but the whole region was infested with bandits who enjoyed the protection of the Baluch zamindars of the area with whom they shared the loot. On the pretext of extirpating these bandits Suraj Mall hoped to extend his authority in the region.

The trail of one notorious freebooter, Sanulba, was traced to the fortalice of Tauru held by Asadullah Khan Baluch. Jawahar led an expedition against him but was compelled to retreat as all the Baluch zamindars led by Musavi Khan of Farrukhnagar mobilized their forces to oppose him. So, the next expedition was against Musavi himself. Ignoring a message from Najib to refrain from molesting the Baluch since he was his protégé, Suraj Mall took the fort in December 1763. Najib was, however, still reluctant to use the military card. Accepting the capture of Farrukhnagar as a fait accompli, he requested the Jat raja to release Musavi and his family 'out of regard for my friendship with you'.[2]

But Suraj Mall was eager for a trial of strength. He replied with a provocative letter accusing Najib of having betrayed his friendship by supporting Musavi Khan. There was now no option left for Najib. Gathering what forces were available—about 15,000 men in all—he set off to meet the advancing army of Suraj Mall.

The clash occurred on 25 December on the Hindon river, 10 miles south of Ghaziabad. Suraj Mall was killed. The precise circumstances of his death remain obscure and the body was never identified, but it seems he was slain in a minor ambush before the battle. It was some time before the news of his death spread, but people would scarcely believe it. During the night, however, the Jat army stole away to the south, confirming the correctness of the news. Suraj Mall's dream of becoming master of Hindustan remained unfulfilled.

Najib did not think it prudent to pursue the Jats, and retired. The vast treasure accumulated by Suraj Mall remained intact. Jawahar was known to be a man of spirit and had bravely defended Mathura against Durrani when greater men had considered discretion the better part of valour. Najib addressed a conciliatory letter to the young prince: 'What was destined has happened to your father. If by fighting you can bring him back to life, then, go ahead by all means. But I have not siezed any of your territory. Why then are you worrying about me? God alone is the giver of victory or defeat.'[3]

But Jawahar's strong sense of honour demanded that the death of his father be avenged, and he made extensive preparations for war. Najib was forestalled from pre-emptive action by a Sikh invasion of the upper Doab. Flushed with victory after the sack of Sirhind, the bearded warriors swarmed across the Yamuna by way of Burhia, looting and burning, and Najib had his hands full containing them.

In November Jawahar set out on his campaign. He had written to the Marathas for help, and 20,000 troops led by Malhar Holkar joined him near Delhi. Some desultory fighting took place near the Purana Qila and the Firoz Shah Kotla, but Najib's troops were well entrenched. So, the Jats fell back across the Yamuna and gave vent to their frustration by looting the *mandis* of Patparganj and Shahdara. Then they again crossed the river, and, after erecting batteries on the riverside, commenced a desultory shelling of the Qila-i-Mualla.

In January 1764, a Sikh force, 12,000 strong, belonging to the 'Budha Dal' appeared near Delhi. Jawahar Singh hastened to hire their services. It was a chastening experience for the proud Jat. The Sikhs acknowledged no man their superior. They were an army of latter-day saints, like the Puritans of yore, and it was almost mandatory for them to invoke the 'True King' or the 'Khalsaji' before taking any decision. When Jawahar's hookah-bearer brought in his master's pipe, he was driven out with abuse, for tobacco was the worst abomination for the followers of this strange new sect. Then the prince was enjoined to stand up respectfully with folded hands while the bearded chieftains solemnly invoked the spirit of the Lord and informed the *Sacha Padishah* that one Jawahar Singh, son of Suraj Mall, had implored the protection of the Khalsaji and had petitioned to be admitted as a disciple of Guru Nanak and Gobind, and craved redress for the killing of his father.[4] To all this mummery Jawahar submitted.

The Jats and Marathas remained on the east bank of the Yamuna while the Sikhs took up positions on the west bank to the north of the city, from where they looted the suburbs and villages. Finally, in February, peace was concluded. Jawahar gained nothing. He had spent Rs. 1 crore and 60 lakh of his treasure, and came to suspect that the Marathas had an understanding with Najib. When news came that Ahmad Shah was on the move once again, the Marathas showed a distinct anxiety to be off as soon as possible. Likewise the Sikhs, who abruptly left for their homes. Imad and Malhar also immediately sent their families into the Middle Doab for safety. No one was prepared to face the Afghan.

Jawahar returned to Mathura. For some time thereafter he was embroiled in domestic problems. He was his father's eldest son but his mother was from an inferior caste. While Suraj Mall had always intended to provide an appanage for him, his designated successor was another son, Nahar Singh, who held Dholpur as an appanage. The latter acquiesced in Jawahar's accession, but soon felt threatened by his elder brother and sought help to safeguard his position in Dholpur.

Most of the old Jat chiefs also resented Jawahar's quick temper and haughty manner. They had been more or less bullied into submission but their natural inclination was towards Nahar. Sensing their resentment, Jawahar promptly had most of them arrested and set himself to raise a new army which would make him independent of the feudal levies of the Jat chiefs. His father's accumulated hoards enabled him to hire Europeans, and he took Rene Madec and Walter Reinhardt alias 'le Sombre', or 'Samru', into his service. Nahar called the Marathas to his aid but Jawahar succeeded in crushing him, and the poor prince, deserted by his allies, took poison and died. This was in 1766.

Suraj Mall was a vassal of the Jaipur rajas and had loyally continued to acknowledge his subordinate relationship, visiting Jaipur personally each year to present his *nazar*. But towards the end he had become suspicious of the Kachhwaha prince, and gave up the annual visits. Since nearly everybody had his eye on the Jat's reputedly fabulous treasure, the suspicion was understandable. So relations between the former vassal and lord were distinctly cool.

After a victorious campaign in Bundelkhand against the Rana of Gohad and the Marathas, culminating in the capture of Kalpi and Jhansi, Jawahar deliberately provoked a breach with Madho Singh of Jaipur by demanding the surrender of the widow and family of the suicide Nahar Singh who had sought asylum in Jaipur. The raja demurred. How could he turn out a defenceless woman? Moreover, the widow was beautiful and Jawahar's propensities in the matter of women were notorious. To make matters worse, Jawahar openly imputed to the Jaipur raja the very same designs which he himself was nursing.[5] This was unforgivable.

On the pretext of a pilgrimage to Pushkar, Jawahar set off with his army through Jaipur territory. At Pushkar he sent word to Bijai Singh of Marwar. The latter came; they sat on the same carpet and together sent an invitation to Madho Singh to join them. The proud Kachhwaha chief, the first of the Rajput feudatories of the empire, declined the invitation and wrote a stinging letter to the Rathor chief, upbraiding him for having degraded himself and his Rathor lineage by treating the Jat as an equal.[6]

Infuriated by the insult, Jawahar collected his army and turned his face homeward, now openly looting the Kachhwaha towns and villages and destroying the crops. By this time Madho Singh had mobilized his clansmen and attacked the Jat army at Maonda on 14 December 1767. The battle was bloody, with heavy losses on both sides, but Jawahar managed to extricate himself and continued his retreat homeward. Madho followed, in spite of his heavy losses, ravaging Jat villages, but on the arrival of 20,000 Sikhs, auxiliaries hired by the Jat raja at the rate of Rs. 7 lakh a month, the Kachhwahas withdrew.

That was the last venture of the restless Jawahar Singh. The following year, in August 1768, he was killed by an unknown soldier while watching an elephant fight.

After the campaign of 1764-5 the Jats had not troubled Najib who had his hands full with the Sikhs. It is not necessary to go into details of the latter's annual excursions. Through his victory at Panipat the Afghan Shah had saved north India from Maratha domination, but if he had hoped to restore law and order, he had utterly failed. Twenty years of anarchy had destroyed all respect for constituted authority. People bowed before superior force because they were familiar with the havoc of war and the reality of suffering. The moment the oppressor's attention was diverted the worm would turn; survival alone mattered. Revenue was collected only at the point of the sword.

If Panipat removed the Maratha threat, it only meant that the Jats had more space to spread their wings. The Sikhs could also raid further, since there was little likelihood of a Maratha incursion. There was only the Durrani monarch, and he too, with uprisings in Khurasan and elsewhere, was tiring of the pointless warfare. This prince, to borrow Cunningham's words 'the very ideal of the Afghan genius, hardy and enterprising, fitted for conquest, yet incapable of empire, seemed but to exist for the sake of losing and recovering provinces'.[7]

After the *wadda ghallughara* of 1762 the Shah had gone to Amritsar where he destroyed the gurdwaras held sacred by the Sikhs. But far from being cowed by this act, the very next year this fledgling nation sacked Sirhind and then swarmed across the Yamuna. Cunningham, who wrote eighty years after the event, has described it in memorable prose: 'Tradition still describes how the Sikhs dispersed as soon as the battle was won, and how riding day and night, each horseman would throw his belt and scabbard, his articles of dress and accountrement, until he was almost naked, into successive villages, to mark them as his. Sirhind itself was totally destroyed, and the feeling still lingers which makes it meritorious to carry away a brick from the place which witnessed the death of the mother and children of Gobind Singh.'[8]

The next five years were bitter years for Abdali. Almost every year he visited the Punjab with his dreaded legions, but for all the effect he had, he may as well have stayed at home. He was ready to confer the subedari of the Punjab on any leader, if only someone would volunteer. But the jealous republicanism of the Sikhs who only acknowledged the mystical sovereignty of the 'Khalsaji' would not permit anyone to accept any office at the hands of the Afghan who had blown up their temples and defiled the sacred tank of Amritsar with the blood of kine in 1762. Only the maverick Ala Singh, the leading sardar among the Cis-Sutluj Sikhs stooped to accept the title of Raja in 1762. His son, Amar Singh, would in turn be dignified with the title of Raja-i-Rajgan in 1767 and the vague sovereignty—or to be more precise, the faujdari—of the Sirhind sarkar.

Najib ud-Daulah waited on the Shah in 1762 and 1764 but he was in no position to render assistance. His own estates in the Doab were being wasted and ravaged by upstarts who had started levying black-mail under the name of 'rakhi' in his own mahals, just like the Marathas earlier. The villages were well marked out as the beat of particular sardars and, unlike in the case of the unprincipled Marathas, these were generally respected. In 1768 Ahmad Shah finally retired, a sick and tired old man with an ulcerous sore on his nose, the wound being inflicted, according to the Sikh tradition, by a stone fragment while he stood at the edge of the 'tank of nectar'—*amrit sarowar*—watching his engineers blow up the Sikh holy of holies—the Hari Mandir Sahib at Amritsar.[9]

All that Najib ud-Daulah can claim, in retrospect, is the preservation of Delhi as the seat of a nominal emperor. He could do little to restore imperial authority with his own mahals being ravaged by the Sikhs. But the Crown lands in the immediate vicinity of the capital, in Rohtak and Bhiwani, and east of the Yamuna, were recovered from usurpers, and the expansion of Jat power, which in 1761 seemed the natural successor to the Maratha, was checked. But the Crown lands were largely appropriated by the regent for his own use who showed no particular anxiety to bring the emperor errant back to the seat of his ancestors. In 1763 Najib paid his respects to the emperor at Sikandarabad, a bare 25 miles from the capital. The emperor was with Shuja ud-Daulah, and Hafiz Rahmat and other trans-Gangetic Rohillas were in attendance. But Shuja, in whose custody the emperor really was at the time, was only interested in exploiting the occasion to seize the territories of the Bangash nawab preparatory to the emperor's march on his capital. The plan failed; the other Rohillas refused to go along with it and left. Najib was incapacitated by fever and on his recovery retired to Najibabad, where he was building his new capital alongwith a strong fort, suitably called Pathargarh (citadel of stone). Shuja left with his royal pawn. The road led to Buxar and the emperor's ignominious semi-confinement in Allahabad fort.

In 1770 a large Maratha army led by Ramachandra Ganesh, including Tukoji Holkar, the successor of Malhar Rao, and Mahadji Scindia, crossed the Chambal into Hindustan, with the avowed object of recovering their old paramountcy as it had existed before Panipat. Some of their mahals were in the hands of the Jats, others were held by Shuja and Najib. Differences arose in the Maratha camp over the policy to be followed. Tukoji pressed the argument of expediency. According to this line of reasoning, Najib was the dominant power and it was easier with his help to isolate the Jat raja. Mahadji was indignant. Three members of his house—Dattaji, Jankoji and Sabaji—had been killed battling against Najib (and the Durrani Shah) and his own lameness was a constant reminder of the disaster of Panipat. 'The blood of three and a half persons of my family is on his head. And Tukoji is proposing to embrace him! I shall write to the Peshwa and seek his orders.'[10] The peshwa too preferred this option, much to Najib's relief, who was thus able to save his estates and the Crown lands from being ravaged by the Deccani locusts. The house of Holkar had an old friendship with Najib. Even in 1764-5, when Malhar had come as an auxiliary of Jawahar Singh, a tacit understanding had existed between him and Najib.

The Marathas crossed the Yamuna after defeating the Jat raja, Nawal Singh, near Mathura where they were joined by Najib. The *mahals* usurped by the Jats were recovered easily enough but then followed the hard part—the negotiations of a suitable tribute from the Jats, the Bangash nawab and the par-Rohillas. The rains intervened, reducing mobility and restricting the Marathas to the discomforts of a camp. All the time, however, the wily regent was at work, silently undermining the Marathas and urging the par-Rohillas to stand firm. His diplomacy proved altogether too subtle and devious for the Decannis. They had come to collect money to reduce the peshwa's debts, but so far they had not been able to secure a penny. Finally, in October, Najib was able to patch up a settlement, and was able to fix the tribute of the Jat raja, bringing the Maratha campaign to an end.

Najib was now a dying man, and placing his son Zabita's hand in that of Tukoji Holkar, he prayed that the latter should be as kind to the son as Malhar had been to the father. Then he returned to Najibabad to die.

In fact, Najib had already retired from public life. For the past two years Zabita had been in charge at Delhi. Najib had come out on this occasion only because he feared that Zabita might not be able to cope with the Maratha challenge. He had written thus to Shah Alam: 'Until this hour I have manifested the firmest devotion and loyalty to the young princes and the Empress in the palace. But I am no longer able to protect them. Let your Majesty advance to your capital and yourself defend your own honour. Your slave frankly represents that he is unequal to the charge in the present situation.'[11] He wrote to the Empress Mother, Zinat Mahal, in the same vein and offered to escort the entire imperial family to Allahabad if she so wished.

He also took steps to secure Zabita's position among the other Rohilla sardars, and on a visit to the Qila-i-Mualla on 18 October was lavishly entertained after a formal durbar where he was presented to Jawan Bakht and Zinat Mahal. This was a farewell dinner, and the prince gave him his own turban as a mark of his high esteem.

At this point it would be convenient to give an account of the subsequent life of Imad ul-Mulk. Ever since the rupture with the Marathas in 1760, he had been living under the protection of Suraj Mall, notwithstanding the fact that the wazir had once been the Jat raja's bitter enemy. The Jat, out of respect for the family, readily granted him asylum. One of Imad's women, the celebrated beauty and poetess Ganna Begum (who Mughlani had insisted in 1757 should be reduced to a maidservant of her daughter Umda, upon the latter's marriage with the wazir), had excited the amorous interest of that notorious Lothario, Jawahar Singh, and it was on that account that Imad eventually abandoned the asylum of the Braj raja and shifted his abode to Mainpuri. In 1770, on the occasion of the Maratha invasion, he turned up uninvited at the negotiations but to no profit to himself. Eventually he retired to Poona and was able to secure a jagir for himself from the Marathas. Imad went on a pilgrimage to Mecca and is known to have spent some time with the English at Surat. He left behind several volumes of poetry in Persian, Arabic and Rakhta.[12] The year of his death is unknown but he is generally supposed to have died about 1800. From the obscurity surrounding his death, it may be surmised that he died in poverty, unwept, unhonoured and unsung. The location of his grave is also not known.

A word too about the Rajputs, the glorious have-beens of Indian history. Every power in north India benefited from the eclipse of the Marathas that followed the debacle at Panipat, except the Rajputs. These heroes of yesterday seemed to have sunk into a drugged stupor from which nothing could rouse them.

Madho Singh, the Kachhwaha chief of Jaipur, did try to weld together a coalition comprising the chiefs of Kotah, Bundi, Karauli, Khichi, and others, but the Marathas led by Malhar Holkar fell upon the Rajput army between Bhatwara and Mangrol on the evening of 28 November 1761. The battle continued into the next day, and if the Maratha account is to be credited, practically the entire Rajput army was annihilated. Malhar, and the Scindia family contingent, which was present, had wiped out at one stroke the disgrace of their panic-stricken flight from Panipat. This decisive victory was sufficient to force the others to submit.

For two years thereafter the Marathas left Rajasthan alone as they were distracted by Shah Alam's operations in eastern Bundelkhand, but in 1764 Holkar returned to settle the Jaipur tribute. Rs. 5 lakh were paid towards the current instalment and bankers' bills accepted for the balance.[13]

The following year a force of 25,000 Sikhs led by Sardar Jassa Singh and three other sardars descended upon Jaipur. They had attacked in concert with Jawahar Singh but Scindia's troops led by Achint Rao Ganesh were close by and quickly responded to Madho Singh's appeal, and the invaders retreated. The Maratha force was paid by the Jaipur prince at the rate of Rs. 5,000 a day, but by the time they arrived the invaders had left. Presents had to be given to the Maratha commanders to persuade them to leave, and considerable damage was done to crops as was the normal Maratha practice.

During this period Mewar remained distracted by civil war, the violent Ari Singh being challenged by a prince named Raj Singh. The Marathas continued to fish in troubled waters, and dues to them kept mounting. Towards the end of July 1769 Mahadji assessed these at Rs. 64 lakh out of which about Rs. 33 lakh were paid, 8 lakh in cash and the remainder in the form of gold, silver and jewels, and orders on tributory chiefs. Disputes over the payment of the balance remained a running sore in Maratha-Mewar relations for many years to come. Substantial tracts of land were alienated or brought under joint management with Maratha agents appointed to receive the payment of the balance.

The fortress of Taragarh at Ajmer and the surrounding dependent territory remained in their undisturbed possession ever since its initial seizure in 1755. The history of Marwar was inglorious and we have seen how Bijai Singh drew upon himself the contempt of Madho Singh when he degraded himself by treating the Jat raja as an equal. Jodhpur was also bound to the Marathas by tribute but it was lucky to be spared the ravages of war.

The ruling Rajput princes of the period had absolutely no vision or ambition beyond the confines of their states. Blood feuds within the ruling families took precedence over external enemies, and as would be expected, the pretensions of their Maratha overlords increase day by day. On the death of Madho Singh, the peshwa impudently demanded a *tika nazar* or succession fee from his successor Pirthi Singh, something to which only the emperors of the Qila-i-Mualla had so far pretended on the basis of being the sovereigns of Hind.[14]

NOTES

1. Rajwade, *Marathanchya Itihasanchi Sadhanen*, i, p. 236.
2. Sarkar, *Fall of the Mughal Empire*, ii, p. 269.
3. Ibid., ii, p. 267.
4. Ibid., p. 277.
5. Ibid., p. 284.
6. Ibid., p. 284.
7. Cunningham, *History of the Sikhs*, p. 91.
8. Ibid., pp. 92-3.
9. Ganda Singh, *Ahmad Shah*, pp. 282, 325-6.
10. Sarkar, ii, p. 246. Abdur Rashid, *An Account of Najibuddaulah*, pp. 129-30.
11. Sarkar, ii, pp. 243-4. *Calendar of Persian Correspondence*, iii, p. 1101.
12. Beale, *Biographical Dictionary*, p. 143.
13. Sarkar, ii, pp. 305-6. Sardesai, *Selections from the Peshwas Daftar*, xxix, pp. 99, 102, 107, 108.
14. Ibid., p. 307. Sardesai, ibid., xxix, p. 248.

CHAPTER 34

The Wanderings of Shah Alam

Where was the Sovereign himself while the regent Najib ud-Daulah was holding the Qila-i-Mualla at Delhi? That Sublime Jewel, the Asylum of the Universe, the Ruler of the World, how was he faring? We met him last in Chapter 32. On the initiative of the Afghan Shah, he had been given Jhajjar as an appanage while two of his younger brothers had been sent on a chimerical project to conquer Awadh and Bihar. Even Shah Alam's pitiful successes achieved in Jhajjar were intolerable to the jealous wazir who forced the pliant Alamgir, the sovereign to repudiate his son's actions, had him proclaimed a rebel, and sent troops against him. The gallant Vittal Shivdev was sufficiently moved to lend him his support but, on the orders of his commander, Raghunath Rao Dada, was obliged to leave him. Even so, the gallant Maratha ordered his son to accompany the prince, wherever he went, with strict orders not to leave him until the prince gave his express permission to do so. Undoubtedly the young Shah Alam could fire men's imaginations and inspire devotion.

With this modest train the heir apparent made his way to Najib who received him respectfully at Miranpur in the middle Doab. But Najib himself had recently been ousted from Delhi by Imad, and was in no position to take up the prince's cause. He spoke to him in general terms and suggested that the person best situated to help was Shuja ud-Daulah as he was the richest amir in northern India. He also hinted that great opportunities lay in Bihar, a traditional appanage of Mughal princes. The province was, moreover, in turmoil after the revolution of the previous year which had toppled Siraj ud-Daulah and placed Mir Jafar on the provincial masnad.

The revolution, of course, was wrought by the battle of Plassey through which the English merchants of the East India Company raised themselves to the position of kingmakers with the new subedar, Mir Jafar, as their puppet. After his elevation, the new governor was forced by his English masters to virtually empty his treasury by giving splendid gifts in cash and jewels to his benefactors. This brought his administration into contempt among the populace and the bureaucracy. As luck would have it, while at Miranpur, the prince received an invitation from Muhammad Quli Khan, subedar of Allahabad, inviting the prince to conquer Bihar, for which undertaking he promised his full support. Muhammad Quli was a cousin of Shuja ud-Daulah and popularly known as Mirza Kuchak.[1]

The prince stayed three months with Najib. In this period he contracted a marriage with a local Syed girl who was dignified with the title of Mubarak Khanum, and in November left for Lucknow. On 7 January he was received by Shuja at Mohan, twelve days march from Lucknow, and offered many costly presents and Rs. 1 lakh by way of *nazar*. But the prince's sojourn in Awadh was brief, and after a few days he resumed his march, arriving at Jhusi, opposite Allahabad, on 23 January. Here Muhammad Quli awaited him.

The province of Allahabad was small and relatively poor, much of the southern portion being hilly and rocky and groaning under the Maratha yoke. Mirza Kuchak was anxious to extend his control over the neighbouring province of Bihar, and in the distracted state of that province he perceived an opportunity. In these ambitions he was encouraged by his cousin Shuja, who was a much shrewder and far more devious person. Shuja assured Kuchak that he would soon be following. Likewise he also assured the prince of his desire to help, without having the slightest intention of doing so. If anything, he had an eye on the two strong forts that lay in his cousin's province, namely, Allahabad and Chunar. He would strike when he felt the moment was right, and this would be the proverbial stab in the back.

The prince did not tarry at Allahabad. Mirza Kuchak was anxious to leave, and after enlisting more soldiers they set off. By 18 March they were at Phulwari at the gates of Patna.

The approach of the prince had thrown the local authorities into confusion. Not since Azim-ush-Shan and Farrukhsiyar had a prince of the Blood visited the eastern provinces, where in spite of the decay of the imperial administration, the imperial name still inspired awe and respect. So while neither Mir Jafar nor the English had any intention of allowing the prince to assume real control, there was the legal aspect to be considered. Bengal and Bihar were provinces of the empire, and there could be no pretext for opposing the prince. The compunctions of the English were particularly strong, because in their own country while the 'Divine Right' of the 'Lord's Anointed' and 'Most Sacred Majesty' were no longer applicable after the revolution of 1688, 'legitimacy' was still a key consideration. Alamgir II was still the legitimate sovereign of India and Shah Alam his acknowledged heir. But happily for the authorities at Murshidabad and Calcutta, the imperial chancellor himself extricated them from their dilemma.

Ghazi-ud-Din Imad ul-Mulk had not been able to stomach the grant of Jhajjar to the prince. Still less was he going to permit the same prince to take over Bihar. On 26 February 1759, as soon as it became clear that the prince was heading towards that province, he issued a proclamation appointing another mirza, Hidayat Bakhsh, subedar of Bihar. Shah Alam was proclaimed a rebel, relieving Mir Jafar and his English allies from any anxieties about the manner in which he ought to be received.

But before the news of this proclamation could reach the east, the ragtag army of the prince and Muhammad Quli Khan had attacked the fort of Patna. The naib nazim, Raja Ram Narayan, had pitched his camp outside Patna on receiving the news of the approach of the prince. Ever since Plassey, his standing with the new government at Murshidabad was shaky and he was quite as ready to submit to the prince as to fight him, depending on the circumstances. And for now the moment seemed to favour the prince. There was no news of an army coming to Ram Narayan's relief from Bengal, and the English merchants at the Patna factory hastily boarded boats and fled eastward, leaving behind a small garrison of Telingas in the factory. The naib nazim had already been suitably impressed by the terrors of the imperial name, and the reputed prowess of the Mughal cavalry. So, when the imperial army attacked, he hastily withdrew into the city, shut the gates and sent feelers for talks.

After an exchange of emissaries a date was fixed for Ram Narayan's audience with the prince. Syed Ghulam Hussain, the author of the *Seir*, has left a detailed account of how the nervous officer with 'lips dried up by fear' was conducted to the imperial presence, and how Midar ud-Daulah, the prince's master of ceremonies, prompted him to make the customary *tasleemats* and thrust forth his hand which was full of gold coins to offer as *nazar*. The usual civilities were observed: *khillats* were presented to Ram Narayan and to two of his officers, but our historian, who was present in the camp, observes that after he had recovered from his audience, Ram Narayan must have reflected in his mind

> on that air of wretchedness and misery that pierced through all the flimsy gaudiness which was intended to disguise the prince's condition, and that of his famished courtiers. The misery of what was styled the Imperial army, struck his sense forcibly; and he repented heartily his coming. It is true that he did not utter a word of all that; but I comprehended very well his sense of it, from his humbled looks, the colour of his complexion and from the whole cast of his features; he wished himself gone and out of the clutches of those famished vultures.[2]

After the audience Ram Narayan returned to the fort but ordered immediate steps for strengthening its defences and ordered his officers to remain vigilant. A demand of Rs. 4 crore had been raised by Mirza Kuchak. Besides, all the guns of the fort were required to be surrendered. The naib nazim did not have anything approaching that sum and gave dilatory replies to the prince's officers, and pretended that he was making efforts to raise the money, while all the time he prayed for a relieving army.

The prince's chief support, Mirza Kuchak, was however behaving as if Patna was already his. He wasted his time in shikar and dissipation, relaxing in the company of dancers and courtesans. Meanwhile, the news of the prince's denunciation as a rebel had reached Murshidabad and Calcutta. The scruples of the English being satisfied, preparations were soon under way for sending an army to the relief of Patna.

There were dissensions in the imperial camp as well. Courtiers and flatterers were to the fore while capable men were sidelined. Mirza Kuchak was empty-headed and a fool. On 3 April arrived the French adventurer, Jean Law, with his company of trained musketeers. After the French factory at Chandernagar had been taken by the English, he and some other officers with their trained sepoys had entered the service of the raja of Chhattarpur in Baghelkhand. Law had now come at the invitation of the prince and Mirza Kuchak. But it was too late. News had already arrived that an army duly stiffened with an English contingent was coming up from Bengal. And on 20 April Mirza Kuchak learnt that his cousin Shuja had seized the fort of Allahabad.

The news came at a particularly unfortunate moment. When Ram Narayan had learnt that a relieving army was on the march, he dropped his mask and unceremoniously turned out the prince's agents. He handed them a letter for their master Muhammad Quli Khan in which he declared insolently, 'I owed you, as to a superior, a visit and a present, and that ceremony I have gone through. But that is all; for I acknowledge no master, but the Nazim of Bengal, and if you are displeased with this message take your parting by all means.'[3]

Enraged by the message, Muhammad Quli decide to attack. Two days later a full scale assault commenced. The imperialists had been strengthened by the arrival of Law and his sepoys. Considerable damage was done to the fort walls, and had Muhammad Quli persisted he may well have taken the city, for Ram Narayan was no great soldier either.

But just then came the news of his cousin's stab in the back, the same cousin who has assured that he would be following to assist in the conquest of Bihar—as soon as he had lodged his family in a strong fort to save them from the wrath of the wazir. And for that purpose the unsuspecting Muhammad Quli had even commanded his qiladar, Mirza Najaf, to regard Shuja's orders as his own.

Kuchak now insisted on disengaging and returning to Allahabad to recover his capital. In vain the others advised him to stay and complete the task at hand. There was little chance of his being able to recover Allahabad but with Patna in his possession his position would be far stronger.

But the distraught Muhammad Quli could not be persuaded. He departed on April 23 for Allahabad where he was defeated and killed by his cousin. The prince lingered slightly longer. Pahalwan Singh, zamindar of Bhojpur, had rallied to his banner but Ram Narayan was able to defeat him. Shah Alam then gave up and left with the remnants of his army for Rewa, while Law fell back on adjoining Chhattarpur.

The rainy season of 1759 was passed at Rewa. Towards the end of October Shah Alam set off again with his little force, and entered the Sahasram district in western Bihar. It was in this district on 21 December, at the village of Gothauli (5 miles from the Sone East Bank Railway Station of today), that he received the tidings of his father's murder at Delhi. Three days later, in the usual rough and ready manner of the Chughatas, a throne was erected on the open plain, the masnad laid out with cushions and pillows, and with Shah Alam seated under a crimson awning, the new reign proclaimed.

Titles and mansabs were granted to the handful of the prince's adherents and Munir ud-Daulah was dispatched to seek the Abdali's help, while another emissary was sent to offer the wazarat to Shuja ud-Daulah. After all, the latter was the richest prince in northern India and alone had the strength and ability to conduct the emperor with appropriate dignity to his capital at Delhi. Najib was also confirmed in the offices which he already held.

Some days were wasted in the celebrations. In the meantime Ram Narayan set about raising more troops. But most of his recruits were raw levies, untried and without battle experience, provided by neighbouring zamindars. Lord Clive, Sabit Jang, had sailed for England on 5 February but had already dispatched two battalions of sepoys under Major Caillaud, backed by 15,000 nawabi troops commanded by Miran, the vicious son of Mir Jaafar.

However, without waiting for the troops from Bengal, Ram Narayan rashly attacked the imperialists at Masumpur on 9 February. Shah Alam's forces had also received an accretion to their strength—in keeping with his elevation in rank. More zamindars and adventurers were ready to lend him their support, now that he was the badshah. Among the most valuable of the new adherents were Kamgar Khan, a zamindar of Narhut-Simai who brought with him a force of 5000 horse. Two other young men, Dilir Khan and Assalat Khan, both brothers commanding a thousand cavalry each, were to render signal service in the coming engagement.

The battle was won by the imperialists, thanks mainly to the skill of Kamgar Khan and the courage of Dilir and Assalat Khan, both of whom were slain. The small British force which was attached to the Patna factory was cut up and two officers, Captains Cochrane and Barwell, perished. Ram Narayan was wounded by a spear thrust of Kamgar and was barely able to retreat into the fort of Patna.

The emperor did not venture to attack the fortified city. Had he done so he might well have taken it, for it contained very few troops. Kamgar now turned to fight the Bengal army which was also close by. The clash took place at Sherpur, and though the imperialists had some success against Miran, who lost his nerve after an arrow knocked out one of his teeth, the British were victorious and the imperialists abandoned the field, though in good order. Kamgar Khan fell back on the fortified town of Bihar Sharif with the emperor.

From Bihar Sharif he made a daring dash aimed at Murshidabad, travelling by forced marches and using unfrequented roads through the jungles, with the emperor in tow. But the move failed for Caillaud followed close on his heels and a small force from Calcutta blocked the road at Mangalkot, 20 miles north of Burdwan. Realizing that the move had failed, he turned back and, returning the same way, appeared before Patna.

Here Law was waiting to join him. Ram Narayan had been in an agony of suspense, for had Law taken into his head to attack the city it would have assuredly fallen, being denuded of troops. With the arrival of the emperor and Kamgar, an attack was launched against the city but luck was against Shah Alam. While the attack was in progress Captain Knox arrived from Bengal with a detachment, having covered 19 stages in 13 days. He had arrived on the opposite bank and hurriedly ferried his force across on boats. Then, after only a night's rest, he attacked the camp of Kamgar Khan in the early morning, taking the general by surprise. The latter fled in the utmost confusion and haste, without turban, clothes, or even the proverbial slippers.

That was the end of the emperor's second attempt at conquering Bihar. Kamgar soon found his position near Patna untenable and fell back on Gaya. Some hope was raised when Khadim Hussain Khan, who had seized the sarkar of Purnea, declared himself in favour of the emperor, and set off with a formidable force of 5,000 horse, 10,000 foot soldiers, and 40 guns in the direction of Patna. Again it was too late. Had he arrived before the relieving force of Captain Knox, he might have tipped the scales in the emperor's favour, but by now the latter was a beaten man and had retired with Kamgar Khan to a safe retreat. Though his strength was formidable, the sepoys of Knox, ably supported by Shitab Rai, defeated him at Hajipur. In the subsequent pursuit, Miran, the depraved son of Mir Jafar, died a spectacular death, being struck by lightning in his tent during a storm. This happened only a few days after the execution of the begums, Ghasiti and Aminah, daughters of the late Alivardi Khan, by drowning. It is said that when their executioner revealed to them that their time had come, and that they should therefore perform the ritual purificatory *wozu* and don clean clothes, the younger of the two ladies raised her hands towards the heavens and implored,

> O! God Almighty, we are both sinners and culprits; but we have committed no sin against Miran. On the contrary he owes to us everything in the world, nor have we seen any better return from him than this unjust order for putting us to death. Sendest Thou Thine lightning to crush his guilty head and to exact from him a full revenge on our own account and that of our children.[4]

After this imprecation they recited the *kalima* in the usual posture of prayer and jumped to their death in the river. This was only one among the many atrocities attributed to the sadistic Miran, but the career of this monster belongs more to the pages of a Bengal history than to that of the Delhi empire.

The battle of Hajipur took place on 16 June. The emperor lingered for two more months in the south where he was joined by Law. Then he retreated westward, reaching the Yamuna near Allahabad in August. Here he waited for the rains to end and the floods to abate. Further west, Ahmad Shah Abdali was similarly sitting out the rains cooped up in his cantonment at Anupshahar in the Doab while Delhi was in the hands of Sadashiv Rao Bhau. Shuja ud-Daulah was in the Afghan camp. He had written to Shah Alam inviting him to join him, and promising his support, but the emperor had replied that he had some unfinished business in Bihar and his honour required that he wind it up before returning.

So, towards the end of October, he set out again to settle that 'unfinished business'. For the third time he entered Bihar but his army was without money, discipline or artillery. It was only the indomitable spirit of Kamgar Khan, typical of the zamindars of Bihar, that kept him going.

Everyone else was by now wholly sick of the adventure and longed for an accommodation with the powers that controlled Bengal and Bihar.

Meanwhile another revolution had taken place in that distracted country, groaning under the twin yokes of the corrupt administration of Mir Jafar and the tutelage of the East India Company. Mir Kasim (Kasim Ali Khan), son-in-law of Mir Jafar, had won the confidence of the English and had convinced them that he would make a much better nazim than the half-mad, opium-sodden pervert, Mir Jafar. Vansittart had proposed at first to make Mir Kasim the deputy nazim while Mir Jafar would continue as the titular governor, but the latter doggedly refused to give his consent to the arrangement so that ultimately there was no option but to remove him altogether and place the son-in-law on the masnad.

Shah Alam, along with Kamgar Khan and Jean Law, was living off the land, forever on the move, subsisting by plunder. He could not stay too long in one place for that would exhaust the local resources and give time to the zamindars to combine against him. His mode of life was thus more befitting a vagrant *pindari* than a sovereign emperor. The end was not far. It came on 15 January 1761 when at Suan, 6 miles west of Bihar Sharif, Colonel Carnac defeated the imperialists.

The emperor followed his general, Kamgar Khan, but Law had tired of the vagrant life and instead of following the retreating imperialists stayed with his guns on the field and surrendered to Carnac who received him with honour and respect. Carnac then sent Raja Shitab Rai to the emperor with offer of peace on generous terms. Kamgar was still full of fight. The emperor first refused the offer and turned away the raja. The latter warned, 'One day His Majesty would of himself seek those very terms which he now refused and would not find them; or if he found any at all, they would fall short of those now proffered and would not redound so much to His Majesty's honour and advantage'.[5] Sure enough, the situation on the ground paved the way for peace. The emperor was persuaded by his followers to send a message recalling Shitab Rai. They persuasively argued, 'Kamgar Khan was a zamindar and to be endlessly fighting, and flying again, was nothing but the trade he had been bred to, but such a vagrant life is beneath the dignity of an emperor and is disgraceful to his name.'

When Shitab Rai received the note recalling him, he showed it to Carnac, who told him to repair again to the imperial camp and convey that Colonel Carnac would be coming to pay his respects near Gaya. This was done in style. Carnac rode out to meet the emperor as the latter advanced in battle array. Approaching the imperial elephant he dismounted, and placing his cap under his arm he proceeded on foot. The emperor indicated that he should mount his horse again. Thus they proceeded to the camp site, the Colonel leading by the length of an arrow's shot.

The imperial tent was pitched in a garden close to the town. Here the emperor dismounted and took his seat on the throne. Carnac, his officers and Ram Narayan, paid their respects, by the presentation of *nazars*, while dancing girls and musicians presented a royal entertainment. The emperor in turn gave return gifts, *khillats* and the like. Later, the Colonel was received in a private audience when *paan* was offered, and *attar* or rose-water sprinkled, and the usual small talk exchanged.

A few days later the armies reached Patna where more ceremonies were held. Shah Alam was shown the English factory, a durbar was held in its premises, and here Mir Kasim was introduced to the royal presence. He made the customary *tasleemats* and tendered a *nazar* of 1,001 gold pieces along with a number of trays of costly brocades and jewels. The emperor in turn honoured him with a *khillat* of six pieces with a chaplet of pearls and a circlet for the turban, together with a jewelled aigrette decorated with black eagle feathers.

The English were eager to please the emperor and sought his favour to legitimize their proceedings in Bengal. Mir Kasim also needed the imperial confirmation of the high office to which he had been called some months earlier by the grace of the Company Bahadur. In the private audience which followed the public presentation, he also agreed to the payment of the surplus revenues of Bengal which amounted to the considerable sum of Rs. 24 lakh per annum—a tribute which had been discontinued since the days of Alivardi Khan. Highly gratified with this offer, and the purse of Rs. 1,800 which was being given to him every day during his stay in the English camp, the emperor readily agreed to ratify all the actions of the English and confirm the accession of Mir Kasim to the nizamat.[6]

By this time Panipat had been fought and the Abdali had returned to Afghanistan. Shuja wrote again to Shah Alam and offered to escort him to Delhi. So, on 12 April, the emperor set off, the English escorting him up to the border of Bihar. On 19 June Shuja received him at Sarai Syed Razi and they continued their march upto 23 July when they went into cantonments at Jajmau near Kanpur. The rains had commenced and it was decided to wait till they were over before proceeding further. Shuja, moreover, as it turned out, was in no hurry to get to Delhi. With the emperor in his hands, he saw many possibilities opening before him, and he determined to make the most of them.

After the debacle at Panipat the Marathas were everywhere on the defensive. Shuja thought it was a good opportunity for easy pickings in the hills and ravines of Bundelkhand. So in November 1761 he set off with the emperor, crossing the river opposite Kalpi, a Maratha outpost. Kalpi surrendered, and thereafter Jhansi was taken while the Bundela chiefs of Orchha and Datia submitted and agreed to give tribute to the emperor. Mahoba, however, resisted successfully. Then the rains intervened again and the summer monsoon of 1762 was also passed in the Kanpur district.

Early in 1763 Shuja set out for the middle Doab and summoned the Rohilla and Bangash chiefs to the imperial camp at Sikandarbad for escorting the emperor jointly to Delhi. We have already seen that the move failed because of Shuja's designs against the Bangash nawab of Farrukhabad. The latter, rightly suspicious, had stayed away but Najib and the other Rohillas protested vigorously against any attempt to resume his estates. A sectarian riot also broke out between Shuja's shia soldiers and the sunni Pathans in Najib's army, and the congress at Sikandarabad dispersed hurriedly without anything being decided. Shuja left for the east with the emperor, abandoning for the moment the plans for setting him up in the Qila-i-Mualla.

The rainy season was passed at Allahabad.

Allahabad and much of the old suba that went by that name was now in the hands of Shuja, having been treacherously seized by him from Mirza Kuchak (Muhammad Quli Khan) while the latter was engaged in the vain enterprise of effecting the conquest of Bihar. Shuja too had designs on that rich province and in 1764 another revolution would offer the wazir an opportunity to interfere in its affairs.

It is axiomatic that a kingmaker and his puppet cannot long remain on friendly terms. The English had by now masterminded two revolutions in Bengal, and on each occasion the members of the Company's Council at Calcutta had benefited immensely, receiving princely gifts in cash and jewels from their beneficiaries, Mir Jafar in the first instance and Mir Kasim in the second. So inflated were the English by a sense of their own importance that they openly boasted of their ability to auction the viceroyalty at intervals. The fantastic fortunes made during this period had roused the avarice of the servants of the Company to such an extent that the evil of private trade among officers of the Company spread throughout the province, and the exemption from duties which had been granted to the Company was mercilessly exploited by its servants to cover their private trade. They readily gave their permits or 'dastaks' for a consideration to the Indian merchants and the nawab-nazim saw a steep fall in his revenue from tolls and customs.

Mir Kasim was not the kind of person to take it lying down. He was determined to be master in his own house and, appalled by his empty treasury, strove vigorously to suppress abuses and put the English merchants in their place. He was emboldened in this policy by the advice and backing of Gurgin Khan, an Armenian in his service who showed a certain skill in the military sciences, specially the handling of artillery.

But the servants of the East India Company could not brook attempts of the nazim to curb their malpractices, and, as for the members of the Council, they were always ready to listen to proposals to topple the viceroy and replace him with a creature of their choice, so that they could share in the general distribution of largesse which accompanied such revolutions.

Driven to desperation, Mir Kasim delivered what was in one sense a master-stroke. He abolished *all* tolls and customs on riverine traffic, thus negating the advantages which the English enjoyed in their private capacity over Indian merchants and traders. Although this made no difference to his revenues, the English merchants were infuriated because with their higher overheads and lavish mode of life they could never compete with the Indians on a level field.[7]

It is not necessary here to go into the details of the third and final revolution, the discussions of Mr. Amyatt with Mir Kasim, the English attempt to seize the citadel of Patna, their failure, the death of Mr. Amyatt and the subsequent restoration of Mir Jafar who was now an old man of 72, and a leper to boot. These events belong to the realm of Bengal history, and that of British India, and are only too well known. It is sufficient to observe that this putsch was very different from the earlier two which had been almost bloodless, though the result was the same. In December 1763 Mir Kasim was finally, and decisively, defeated and expelled from 'British territory'.

Apart from these results, the period is notable for two events; viz., the massacre of the English prisoners (about 150 in all) at Patna by the European mercenary Walter Reinhardt, better known in India as Samru (supposedly from 'le sombre' on account of his swarthy complexion); and the emergence of Mirza Najaf who was to play so important a role in the later part of the reign. This cold-blooded massacre was no doubt ordered by Mir Kasim who had so far held on to his prisoners—taken at the capture of the English factory at Patna—in the hope of using them as a bargaining counter during negotiations. But the death or murder of Amyatt had so infuriated the members of the Council that they pushed on, regardless of the threat of Mir Kasim to kill his hostages. This massacre is far better authenticated than the rather doubtful 'Black Hole' incident but it never became half as notorious. One wonders whether the reason is that the perpetrator in this case happened to be a European, and the facts do not conform to the conventional image of 'oriental barbarism'.

Mirza Najaf, who was later to be appointed Amir-ul-Umara and Bakhshi-ul-Mumalik, was the son of the Sadr us-Sadr of Iran and closely related through his mother with the royal Safavid house, and to Mirza Mohsin, the brother of Safdar Jang. After his arrival in India he had entered the service of the latter and thereafter served his son Muhammad Quli, the unfortunate Mirza Kuchak. On the death of the latter, and apprehensive of the hatred which Shuja nursed for all the relatives and adherents of the deceased, he had, after some vicissitudes, entered the service of Mir Kasim as a commander of Mughal horse. He distinguished himself in the campaign by his professional ability and strongly opposed Mir Kasim's decision to take shelter in Shuja's territory. But it was of no avail. The nawab had no stomach for further fighting.

In February 1764 he arrived with the remnants of his army at the pageant court of Shah Alam at Allahabad. He was well received by Shuja. Mir Kasim had managed to bring away a good deal of his treasure, and many of the covered carts and palkis, which were supposed to be conveying the women of his harem, actually contained bags of coin, jewels and other valuables. By paying Rs. 10 lakh and Rs. 17 lakh to the emperor and Shuja respectively,[8] he was able to purchase their support in a war for his reinstatement in Bengal. Shuja undertook to subsidize his expenses from the day he crossed the Ganga into Bihar at the rate of Rs. 11 lakh per month for the duration of the campaign.[9]

But the army of the wazir was a huge disorderly mass, utterly lacking in discipline and resembling more a rabble of highwaymen. The officers of Mir Kasim, who were familiar with the European mode of warfare and had seen how a few hundred well trained sepoys with two or three well served field guns could easily put to flight a traditional Indian army, ventured to advise the wazir that it would be better if he left his baggage behind at Banaras and advanced with a body of hand-picked men.

But the wazir was so full of himself because he had had the honour of fighting by the side of Ahmad Shah that he was impervious to reason, and cut short all advice with the cutting reply, 'Do not trouble yourself about that: You shall fight as I bid you'.[10] And so they advanced into Bihar 'with an army as numerous as the ants and locusts', wasting the country, plundering the peasantry, driving away their cattle, and firing villages.

The English at first fell back. Shuja attempted to lay siege to Patna with his huge host but was repulsed and forced to retreat towards the south. With the onset of the rains there was a pause in the fighting, and some half-hearted parleys began. There were dissensions in the wazir's camp; Mir Kasim fell out of favour and was insulted and humiliated by the wazir who also encouraged his officers to embarrass and humiliate him. Shuja even had the former viceroy arrested. Shah Alam was also humiliated by the wazir, who showed no consideration towards his courtiers so that the poor emperor regretted his decision to throw in his lot with Shuja.[11]

After the cessation of the rains the armies again prepared for war, and finally on 23 October Hector Munro delivered a crushing defeat to the wazir at Buxar. According to Ghulam Hussain Khan, about 5,000 men were killed and twice as many trapped and drowned in the shallows. For years afterwards their bones kept turning up on the river banks. Mir Kasim had been set at liberty by the wazir before the battle and given a lame elephant as a mount on which he managed to make his getaway. Samru, the Alsatian mercenary who was wanted by the English for the Patna massacre, also withdrew in time with the bulk of his sepoys and guns. The behaviour of the bulk of the wazir's troops was typical of the old Indian armies which were bereft of discipline. As soon as it became evident that the battle was going against the imperialists, the Mughal cavalry of the wazir turned on their own troops and, commenced to loot them![12]

Shuja ud-Daulah had also escaped, but the tired and disillusioned emperor, who had discovered too late that he was virtually a prisoner of his wazir, readily surrendered to the English who received him courteously.

Mirza Najaf Khan who had been campaigning in the hills of Baghelkhand on behalf of the wazir returned after the battle. There was no love lost between him and Shuja; he knew from experience how treacherous the former was, and had warned his master, Mir Kasim, against linking his future with Shuja's. Now he offered his services to the English, who welcomed him as they were deficient in cavalry and Mirza Najaf had acquired a reputation as a commander of horse. He had proved his usefulness before the fortress of Allahabad, of which he had been the commander for many years and with which he was intimately acquainted. Guided by the Mirza's knowledge, the English concentrated their fire on a weak stretch of the wall and the commandant hastened to surrender.

During this time Shuja had succeeded in raising another army with which he advanced against the English. The final battle was fought at Kora on 30 May 1765. Shuja was decisively beaten and the whole of Awadh lay prostrate at the feet of the victors.

In the meantime the fortress of Chunar had also fallen and the aged leper Mir Jafar had died. His dreaded affliction was, oddly enough, appropriate to the man for his reputation, to this day, is that of a moral leper. Of all the princes and umara who have nonchalantly made deals with the invader down the centuries, his name (together with Raja Jai Chand's) remains a byword for perfidy and betrayal, the epitome of all that is wrong with our ruling elites.

Robert Clive, Sabit Jang, now recognized at home as well, and ennobled as Baron Clive of Plassey, landed at Calcutta on the day the battle of Kora was fought and won. He had no role in it, the third and most hard fought of the three Bihar campaigns. But in winning the peace he was to play a decisive role.

After Buxar, the English had promised Shah Alam that Awadh would be restored to him, but now that Shuja had at last been brought to the negotiating table after the disaster at Kora, the English went back on their word. It was decided to reinstate Shuja, but the province of Allahabad, including the district of Kora, was separated and made over to the emperor with the fort of Allahabad as his residence and an assured revenue of Rs. 28 lakh per annum. The Bengal tribute amounting to Rs. 26 lakh was again assured to him but a stipulation was made that Rs. 2 lakh out of this would be paid to Mirza Najaf in recognition of his services in the late campaign. An English force was stationed in the citadel for the emperor's protection.

As for Shuja, the rest of his dominions, excluding the fort of Chunar, were restored to him subject to the payment of an indemnity of Rs. 50 lakh. Of this Rs. 25 lakh was to be paid immediately while the remaining half would be paid by assignments on future revenues. Raja Balwant Singh of Banaras, with his estates comprising the districts of Banaras and Ghazipur, was also placed under British protection though he remained legally subordinate to Shuja. Lastly, and this was the greatest achievement of Clive, he persuaded the reluctant emperor to grant to the East India Company the diwani rights to the province of Bengal.

In the larger provinces of the empire, specially when they happened to be 'viceroyalties' comprising two or more subas, the nazim and diwan were usually two distinct entities, the nazim being the magisterial authority while the diwan was the superintendent of finances in charge of the revenue administration. For instance, Azim ush-Shan had been nazim while Murshid Quli Khan was the diwan. Both were appointed by the emperor, were independent of each other, and were intended to be a check on the other. Only where the two offices were combined were the officers concerned properly subedars. With the appointment of the Company itself as the diwan, the English had entered the active politics of the empire, and became part and parcel of the imperial system.

Also, with the death of Mir Jafar, and the appointment of his son Majm ud-Daulah as successor, the British control over the triple province of Bengal, Bihar and Orissa was rendered absolute. Clive, and later Warren Hastings, became the real governors of Bengal, while the nawab-nazims of Murshidabad were reduced to pageants like the nawabs of Arcot in the South.

And finally, to patch up matters between the emperor and Shuja, the latter was reappointed wazir. In his annoyance, after Buxar, Shah Alam had ordered his removal and replacement by his son Asaf ud-Daulah, but under British pressure status quo ante was restored. However, the title was now little more than an empty honorific. Neither Shuja nor his successors would ever exercise its functions from Delhi. The real rulers of India were the English governors of Bengal, soon to be dignified as Governors-General of India. It was this realization that was behind Syed Ghulam Hussain's sense of loss when he observed bitterly, while speaking of the treaties of Allahabad,

> Thus a business of such a magnitude . . . which at any other time would have required the sending of wise ambassadors and able negotiators as well as a deal of parley and conference with the Company and the King of England, and much negotiation and contention with the ministers, was done and finished in less time than would have been taken up for the sale of a jackass, or of a beast of burden, or of a head of cattle.[13]

There were patriots, of a kind, even in the eighteenth century in India, though the entity whose degradation occasioned this lament was not Bharat Mata or the Hindustan of today but the Daulat-i-Mughlia, the Mughal imperial state.

NOTES

1. Kuchak signifies little, hence the 'little' or 'younger mirza'.
2. Tabatabai, *Seir Mutaqherin*, ii, p. 303.
3. Ibid., p. 307.
4. Ibid., pp. 365-71.
5. Ibid., p. 403.
6. Ibid., p. 408. Sarkar, *Fall of the Mughal Empire*, ii, p. 323.
7. Tabatabai, ii, pp. 468-70 (fn.).
8. Bannerjee and Ghose, *A Comprehensive History of India*, ix, p. 694.

9. Tabatabai, ii, p. 524.
10. Ibid., p. 528.
11. Ibid., pp. 538-52. Barnett, *North India Between Empires*, p. 64.
12. Barnett, ibid., p. 65. Tabatabai, ii, p. 564.
13. Tabatabai, iii, p. 9.

CHAPTER 35

The Gilded Exile

With the treaties of Allahabad, concluded in August 1765, we enter a quiet period in the stormy life of Shah Alam. Things were bad enough in the west with the Sikhs ravaging the Doab and the Haryana region right up to the walls of Delhi, but here in the fort of Allahabad, overlooking the sacred Triveni where the Ganga, Yamuna and the mythical Saraswati meet, all seemed peaceful.

The emperor enjoyed for the first time a regular and assured income which was more than sufficient for his needs. Here, there was no danger from Sikhs, Jats or Marathas. The turbulent Pathans of Rohilkhand were also several hundred miles to the west and the red-coated sepoys of the East India Company ensured that the even tenor of life was undisturbed in the court of the 'Emperor of the World'. The days ran into weeks, and the weeks into months, and so on, from year to year.

To Shah Alam, in his old age, those six years in Allahabad must have seemed a Golden Age that did not last long enough. The seven years which preceded it were years of storm and stress; he had been constantly on the move, always short of money, and never quite out of danger. In 1772 he was back in Delhi in the palace of his ancestors but fearful nightmares lay ahead.

The security of Allahabad would appear golden only in retrospect. All the trappings of a court existed, regular durbars were held on fixed days, and business of State transacted. The administration of Kora and Allahabad required some attention. Festivals like the various Ids, the Nauroz, and Holi were celebrated. But nothing could make the emperor forget that he was not really master of his house, not even within the walls of Allahabad fort.

The attitude of the English hardly helped. Colonel Smith who commanded the English garrison, made no bones about the fact that he considered himself the superior authority. 'His office was only that of an agent near the emperor's person,' laments the author of the *Seir*, 'but in fact he was his master and Lord to all intents and purposes'. One day the Colonel's sleep was disturbed by the noise of the imperial kettle drums in the naubat khana. So he dispatched soldiers to throw the musicians, their drums and instruments from the terrace to the ground. The bandsmen ran away but their drums and pipes were smashed.[1] This was a gross insult to the imperial dignity for the naubat with its kettle drums was one of the several attributes of sovereignty; as much part of the furniture of royalty as the 'shamsi' banners, the yak-tail fly whisks, *mahi* and *maratib*, silver maces, and the very throne itself. But Colonel Smith (later promoted brigadier general) appears to have been a particularly odious sort of person. When the emperor recommended the taking back into favour of a person who had incurred the wrath of this Englishman, the latter remarked to the emperor's emissary who happened to be one of the emperor's uncles, 'Do you know, Sir, who is the master here? It is I, because I am the strongest.'

On another occasion the same officer confined one of the emperor's servants to a punishment cell because he had failed to salute him. The emperor interceded on his behalf, assuring the colonel that the man would not give any reason for offence in future. Smith had the man taken out of his dungeon and, in the emperor's presence, gave him a hundred lashes with a leather strap saying, 'See how I punish those who say they do not know me'.[2]

Several Europeans like the Comte de Modave, Gentil and the Swiss engineer Major Polier have mentioned the over-bearing behaviour of this anglo-saxon. But even if the behaviour of Smith had not been odious, it was natural for Shah Alam to chafe against his confinement to a provincial backwater, however well his creature comforts may have been looked after. But for a few relatives, most of his family was in the Qila-i-Mualla. With a nonfunctional wazir at Lucknow, several hundred miles away, and the de facto chancellor, the Amir-ul-Umara, Najib ud-Daulah, exercising authority from Delhi through his own son, Mirza Jawan Bakht, as his deputy, Shah Alam was a nullity at Allahabad.

He repeatedly asked the English to escort him to Delhi but the English, who were loathe to lose such a valuable 'guest', kept putting him off. One year it was the war with Haidar Ali which had drained Bengal of troops, the other it was the rainy season, and so on.

Munir ud-Daulah was an English agent and, as per the instructions of his principals, strove to convince the emperor that it would be folly to leave the security of Allahabad and venture forth on the long and dangerous road to Delhi. But man does not live by bread alone, and Shah Alam was more than a man. Himself an emperor, and descended from a long line of reigning princes, 14 of whom had sat on the throne of Hind, not counting the ones that intervened between Babar and Timur or Genghiz, Shah Alam found it intolerable that he should now submit to being cooped up in this gilded prison while Najib ud-Daulah ruled from Delhi. Eventually what really clinched the matter was the resignation of Najib, occasioned by his deteriorating health.

After Najib's retirement to his capital of Najibabad, his son Zabita Khan took over in the Qila-i-Mualla. Soon disturbing stories of strange goings-on reached the emperor. A eunuch sent by the Queen Mother arrived at Allahabad. This was the usual method of conveying delicate messages relating to the harem. What this confidential message may have been is not certain, but perhaps Major Polier's note about a piece of palace gossip, written years later in 1778, may shed some light on the developments:

> It was whispered that Zabita Khan while he was all powerful in Delhi and in the fortress after Najib ud-Daulah's death, had presumed to enter the royal seraglio to have connection with some of the ladies immured within. The King's own sister, Khair un-Nisa, was of the number.[3]

Indeed, to give an ironic twist to Najib's letter of resignation, it was now up to Shah Alam to defend his own honour.[4]

By 1768 the Afghan threat had receded and it seemed unlikely that Abdali would ever return to India. About the same time the Jat power was also broken, and, but for the Sikhs, the road seemed clear for Shah Alam's return to the capital. At one time, in January 1768, even Sardar Jassa Singh Ahluwalia, then the most important of the Sikh chiefs, wrote to the emperor inviting him to come to Delhi, assuring him that the whole empire would be again restored to him.[5]

But the English avoided giving the required assistance, and Shah Alam realized that as far as they were concerned the rains would never cease,[6] and that they had no intention of assisting him to reach his capital. Shuja ud-Daulah was also unresponsive. For all practical purposes he too was an English agent, and unwilling or unable to assist the emperor in a course that ran counter to the English interest. So, the emperor turned to the Marathas who in 1768 had returned to Hindustan, as we have seen earlier, as auxilliaries for the Jat raja, and later, had allied themselves to Najib ud-Daulah.

The news of Najib's death in October 1770 forced the emperor to take a definite initiative. Zabita Khan was young and inexperienced, having lived so far in his father's shadow. The reports about his transgressions in the haram sarai of the Qila-i-Mualla had not yet reached the emperor but his ability to stand up to the Sikh raiders was uncertain. Any delay could mean the loss of the imperial capital. This could have dangerous consequences for Shah Alam, for the Sikhs might be tempted to raise any of the scores of beggarly princelings living in the salatin khana to the throne.

Towards the end of December 1770, the emperor sent Saif-ud-Din Khan to open talks with the Marathas who were then operating in the middle Doab. This was the same force which was led by Ramachandra Ganesh and Visaji Krishna, with Tukoji Holkar and Mahadji Scindia as the principal generals. It was the first attempt by the Marathas to assert themselves in Hindostan after Panipat. The object was to recover their old *mahals* in the Doab seized during their eclipse by the Jats, Rohillas and Bangash Pathans, and to collect their arrears of tribute. But we have seen how the decision to seek the alliance of Najib—against the furious protest of Mahadji—and the diplomacy of the latter, had frustrated the Maratha objectives. Finally, after a face-saving peace with Raja Nawal Singh, the Jat raja, the dying Najib sought to return to Najibabad. This was in October 1770. Najib died on the way, at Hapur, on 31 October. Thereafter, the Marathas spread out, ravaging the districts of Etawah, Shikohabad and Kanauj, held either by the Ahmad Khan Bangash, or the two Rohillas, Dhundi Khan and Hafiz Rahmat.

Both Zabita and Ahmad were vying for the favour of the Marathas in order to obtain their recommendation for appointment to the vacant post of Bakhshi-ul-Mumalik. Visaji demanded a fee of Rs. 25 lakh. Normally such a *peshkash* would have been demanded by the emperor, but in the changed circumstances the Marathas were in a position to demand a *peshkash* merely for putting in a kind word to His Majesty. The imperial umara knew that the bakhshi could only be a Maratha nominee. The Holkars had old links with Najib Khan and Tukoji Holkar secretly promised Zabita that he would obtain for him his father's post without the payment of any *peshkash*. Had not the dying regent placed his son's hand in Tukoji's, with the earnest prayer that he should be as kind to the son, as Malhar had been to the father?

So far Ramachandra Ganesh and Tukoji Holkar had been the determining factors, but their failure to realize any of the Maratha objectives had discredited them in the eyes of the peshwa and henceforth Visaji Krishna and Mahadji Scindia were to take charge.

The Marathas decided to take Delhi which at the time was quite defenceless. Saif ud-Din Muhammad Khan, Shah Alam's envoy, arrived in the city on 7 Feb. 1771, and two days later the Marathas attacked. The Asad Burj of the fort was destroyed by their artillery and the qiladar,

Kasim Ali, opened negotiations. The next day the Marathas entered the city. The garrison, which was composed of Zabita Khan's men, was expelled, and Scindia posted his own men in their place. Five thousand Marathas occupied the city.

Mahadji Scindia had already assured the emperor of his willingness to escort the latter if his expenses were paid. It was in response to this letter that Saif ud-Din had been sent. Now with the fort, and the city, firmly in their hands the Marathas opened negotiations with Saif ud-Din and Jawan Bakht.

The price agreed was Rs. 40 lakh, in addition to the district of Meerut, and some mahals near Delhi, besides Kora-Jahanabad and Kara-Manikpur. On the payment of the first instalment of Rs. 10 lakh, the Qila-i-Mualla would be handed over to the emperor's agent, and, on arrival at Delhi, *mahals* worth Rs. 15 lakh would be assigned to the Marathas with the balance to be cleared in seven months. Interestingly, the Marathas also stipulated that half the *nazar* and *peshkash* paid by the new appointees to the emperor would be made over to them!

The draft of the agreement was sent to Allahabad and duly ratified by Shah Alam. The move caused consternation among some of the courtiers who were reluctant to give up the comforts of Allahabad for the uncertainties of Delhi. Shuja also happened to visit Allahabad and the craven courtiers hoped that he would persuade the emperor to change his mind, but Shuja was only too pleased to learn that his assistance was not required as escort. So, he readily contributed Rs. 12 lakh in cash to the emperor along with the tentage, carriage and other necessities of the long march.[7]

The English warned Shah Alam that he was throwing away the substance to grasp a shadow, and sacrificing his solid and substantial interests to the vain and idle gratification of residing in the imperial palace. They also advised him against placing too much reliance on the Marathas. But the emperor was now determined and on 13 April, the auspicious first of *Baisakh*, he set out from the fort and pitched his camp at Sarai Alamchand, 20 miles to the west where he halted for nineteen days.

Although the English had declined to sanction the emperor's departure, they allowed a small contingent commanded by General Sir Robert Barker, to escort him as far as Bithur (in the district of Kanpur) where he took leave of the emperor on 28 June. Munir ud-Daulah, who had always opposed the emperor's determination to return to Delhi, also took his leave here and returned with the English. Shuja accompanied the imperial cortege upto Jajmau, one march short of the town of Kanpur, where he crossed the river into his own dominions. Clearly, the wazir had no desire to be a working wazir. Content with the empty dignity of the title, he had no intention of abandoning the security of Lucknow and Faizabad for the doubtful glories of an imperial career at Delhi.

At Farrukhabad, where Nawab Ahmad Khan Bangash had died on 17 April, the emperor rashly demanded the escheat of his property. The indignant Pathans rallied round the young heir of their lord and prepared to resist. The emperor then appealed to Scindia for help who promptly came with a large army. On learning of the Marathas' approach, Fakhr ud-Daulah, the late nawab's bakhshi, opened talks and agreed to pay Rs. 6 lakh by way of *peshkash* for the recognition of the succession of Muzaffar Jang, the late nawab's son.

By this time the rains had set in. So, after settling this matter, the emperor pitched camp at Nabiganj, 19 miles south-west of Farrukhabad, to sit out the monsoon.

The first instalment having been paid, the fort had been handed over to Saif ud-Din Khan, the emperor's agent, by the Marathas on 2 August. At Nabiganj it seems there was some unpleasantness when Anant Rao, another emissary from Poona, waited on the emperor and tried to extract further concessions from him. But everything was smoothed over. On 15 November Saif ud-Din and other officers from Delhi waited on the emperor, and three days later Mahadji, Visaji and the other Maratha officers paid their respects. Shortly afterwards the march was resumed. At Gharoli, 4.5 miles south-east of Shahdara, Shah Alam was received by the Queen Mother, his heir apparent, and other members of the family. On 6 January, which also happened to be the feast of Id ul-Fitr, he rode into the capital and entered the Qila-i-Mualla. We can imagine the celebrations in the streets of Delhi as the people jostled and climbed on to rooftops and filled the balconies to catch a glimpse of their lord, so long absent from the seat of his fathers. The very hour of his entry into the city has been noted;[8] doubtless it must have been fixed by the court astrologers, but the limits of astrology would become painfully apparent as the reign unfolded itself. But on that crisp January morning, as the 'Emperor of the World' entered into his own amid the delirious acclamations of his people, and, as the children and the beggars rushed to pick up the scattered largesse, all must have seemed bright and rosy.

The Afghan Shah had died in Afghanistan and the threat from that direction had vanished. The Jat state had also been humbled by the Marathas, and Najib Khan was dead. Only the Sikhs remained. Surely with the support of the Marathas, the empire could be resuscitated to some semblance of its former glory? Time would show how vain was the hope.

NOTES

1. Tabatabai, *Seir Mutaqherin*, iii, p. 10. Sarkar, *Fall of the Mughal Empire*, ii, pp. 328-9.
2. Sarkar, ibid., ii, p. 329, quoting Joseph Gentil.
3. Polier, *Shah Alam II and his Court*, pp. 23-4.
4. See Chapter 33, note 11.
5. *Calendar of Persian Correspondence*, ii, p. 849.
6. Ibid., ii, p. 660.
7. Sarkar, ii, pp. 330-1.
8. Ibid., p. 331.

CHAPTER 36

Mirza Najaf: The First Phase

Thus began the second phase of Shah Alam's reign. With his years of wandering behind him, he had great hopes for the future, and certainly every intention of ruling. But his options were limited. With an empty treas-ury, an army whose pay was already in arrears, and a palace and capital which had been repeatedly looted, the odds were stacked against him. In spite of the energy he displayed in his early years, he was a weak man, easily dominated by others. Though in this period he was by no means a puppet, his reign can be conveniently divided into phases, after its domi-nating personalities.

Mirza Najaf was not yet the dominating figure, but whatever was achieved during these early years was largely because of the exertions of this Persian nobleman. He was the brother of the wife of Mirza Mohsin, the younger brother of Safdar Jang, and it was at the latter's request that he was released from the dungeon where Nadir Shah had cast him. On arrival in India, shortly after his release, he took service under his sister's step-son, the luckless Muhammad Quli or Mirza Kuchak as he was affectionately known. After the collapse of his master's plans he entered the service of Mir Kasim who had just been overthrown by the English and replaced by Mir Jafar. He distinguished himself in the service of his new employer and attracted the notice of the English who extended him tempting offers to join their service.

Join he eventually did, but only after Buxar when it had become clear that the cause of his master was irretrievably lost. We have seen how he rendered valuable service to his new masters at Allahabad, so much so that at the time of the treaty of Allahabad, the English persuaded the fallen emperor to take Mirza Najaf into his service, and Rs. 2 lakh out of the Bengal tribute was explicitly assigned to him. English influence again secured for him the faujdari of Kora, but palace intrigue led to his dismissal from that post. For about a year thereafter Najaf was unemployed. But with Shah Alam's decision to return to Delhi, he again attracted the emperor's notice and was given Rs. 50,000 to equip his contingent for the march.

The task which Shah Alam faced was daunting. Money was the first imperative, for the balance of the sum promised to the Marathas still had to be paid. His nominal wazir was an absentee, and the next most important man, the Amir-ul-Umara, who held the vital office of Bakhshi-ul-Mumalik, was also absent and defiant.

On the death of Najib (31 Oct. 1770), the emperor had sent an emissary to Zabita, offering his condolences, and expressing his desire to invest him with the patents to the offices held by his late father, including the title of Amir-ul-Umara and the bakhshiship. The emperor also asked Zabita to come to Allahabad and escort him back to Delhi 'where the throne would belong to the emperor and the control of the empire to Zabita Khan'[1]—as in the time of his father. At the same time he was called upon to offer the customary *peshkash* and succession fees and render the accounts of the Crown lands, which had been so long in his father's charge.

These were normal processes instituted on the death of a nobleman holding offices and fiefs from the Crown. But Shah Alam had already, in anticipation, offered Zabita the offices and fiefs held by his father. If the accounts had been properly kept, Zabita would have had nothing to fear, but even during Najib's lifetime it was believed that the Amir-ul-Umara was paying into the treasury only a fraction of the actual collections, the rest of the money being diverted to strengthen his interests in Rohilkhand. Zabita, contemptuous of his sovereign's weakness, and with an inflated sense of his own wealth and power, expected the investiture as a matter of course, but on the subject of accounts and *peshkash* he was evasive, and dismissed Shah Alam's envoy.

It was essential for the emperor's prestige that the insolence of this overgrown vassal be curbed. Already, on his way to Delhi, Shah Alam had tasted some success, against the Bangash chief in a similar affair.

Zabita was the only notable person from whom some money could be extracted to pay the Maratha dues. But aware of the strength of the Rohilla state, the emperor gave Zabita another chance to mend his ways. The Rohilla was once again invited to come and make his ritual *tasleemats* like a loyal umara at the next general durbar fixed for celebrating the emperor's return to Delhi. All the other nobles came, or they sent their vakils, and paid their respects, offering the customary *nazar* and receiving in turn robes of honour. But Zabita stayed away.

Now there was no alternative left. Military preparations were made and soon the army set out against Zabita, the emperor himself accompanying it. Husam ud-Di- (now ennobled as Husam ud-Daulah) was at this time the emperor's principal man of business, the substitute prime minister, while Mirza Najaf was his only general. Of course the

Marathas were present in force with the imperial army, and constituted its main strength, for it was partly on account of their dues that the campaign was being commenced. Besides, the emperor had engaged to divide with them, equally, all the spoils which should accrue in the joint operations.

Zabita entrenched himself in the old strong point of Shukartal, while soldiers were deployed to watch and guard the other fords on the river. The families of all Rohilla chiefs, and their treasures, were shut up in Pathargarh, near Najibabad, with a small garrison. Zabita hoped to repeat the success of his father against Dattaji Scindia in 1759 by using the same strategy.

The imperialists spread out along the river, concentrating on points opposite the Rohilla entrenchments, but by cleverly concealing their movements surprised the Afghans by crossing at Chandi Ghat just below Hardwar. During this river crossing Najaf Khan distinguished himself. He inflicted heavy casualties on the enemy by opening up with his camel swivels from a sand-bank in the middle of the river.

The heads of the fallen Rohilla chiefs were sent to the emperor, who was about 10 miles in the rear, along with the captured officers. The news of the victory electrified the camp and when Najaf Khan presented himself, the emperor stretched out his beard with both hands towards him and exclaimed, 'You have saved my honour!'[2]

The news of the successful crossing and the heavy losses at Chandi Ghat filled the Rohillas with trepidation. Zabita appealed to his brother-in-law, Faizullah Khan, who was camping with 4,000 men near Shukartal, but the latter, panic-stricken, fled into the Terai jungles. The position at Shukartal had become untenable, as it could now be turned from the rear. It was now Zabita's turn to be struck with terror. He mounted an elephant and fled with only 40 men into the darkness of the night.

The leaderless Rohilla camp at once disintegrated when the flight of their leader became known in the morning. It was every man for himself, and the Jats and Gujjars living in the vicinity plundered the Rohilla camp. When the Marathas arrived at the devastated camp, all they could secure were a few pieces of artillery which were too heavy to be carried away.

The Maratha light horse overran the Doab villages. The Rohillas, unnerved by this first serious reverse suffered at Maratha hands since Panipat, retreated into the jungles. Pathargarh was besieged. After twenty days the garrison sued for terms. They were allowed to march out, but the Marathas stationed themselves at the exit and stripped each person of whatever valuables be was carrying. In desperation the people threw their gold and jewels into the flooded moat. The riff-raff in the camp robbed them of even the clothes on their back, and some ladies were dragged away, but Najaf sent soldiers to recover them and they were escorted to safety.[3]

The surrender of the fort was followed by the usual treasure hunt, with the floors being dug up in search of valuables. The moat was also drained and the gold and jewels that had been thrown into its waters were recovered. And, as might be expected, when the victors took stock of their gains, they fell apart. Half of the booty was to go to the emperor, one quarter was to be set aside for the peshwa, and the remainder was to be divided among the Maratha sardars, but it seems that much of the booty was appropriated by the Maratha soldiers and their sardars, the emperor and the peshwa being deprived of their shares. A derisory sum of Rs. 2 lakh, in cash, was promised by Scindia to Shah Alam, while only three large cannons, 2 *jizails* and 7 *zamburaks* were shown in the official list.

There was further unpleasantness over the disposal of Zabita's jagirs. Saharanpur was given to Fakhr ud-Din Khan, a son of the late wazir Qamr ud-Din Khan (killed at Manupur in 1748), while Karnal and Anupshahar were given to Mahadji Scindia who undertook to bring Shuja ud-Daulah to the emperor and make him perform his duties. But the effort failed. Shuja merely sent his turban to Scindia who sent his headgear, the Maratha *pagoti*, in exchange, as a token of brotherhood and good-will.[4]

Zabita retreated further east into Awadh where he was received respectfully by Shuja on account of the close friendship which had subsisted between Najib and Safdar Jang. With Shuja's mediation, a peace was arrived at between Zabita and Visaji Krishna. Zabita promised an indemnity of Rs. 40 lakh and upon this promise, backed by the doubtful surety of Shuja, his estates were to be restored. Mahadji Scindia was furious, and the emperor refused to be a party to the deal. Then Tukoji Holkar and Visaji urged the emperor to march on Allahabad which, after the emperor's departure, had been resumed by the English in violation of the treaty of Allahabad. The Bengal tribute had also fallen due, but Shah Alam refused to undertake this hopeless expedition. Najaf Khan, who was anyway an English agent, also advised against it. Mahadji Scindia concurred.

Thereafter the imperialists and the Marathas returned to Delhi, plundering the towns and villages on the way. The rainy season of 1772 was spent in the capital. The expedition had been successful but the financial results were disappointing, and it had ended with the allies in disarray.

After the rains the imperialists set out against the Jats. Some mud forts were taken, but peace was soon made with the Jat raja agreeing to a cash payment to the Marathas. It was during this campaign that Najaf Khan persuaded Rene Madec to leave the Jat service for imperial employment. The two were acquainted with each other from Bengal days. Madec had first been in the service of the English but had joined Mir Kasim before Mirza Najaf's arrival at Undhua Nala. After Buxar, like Mirza Najaf, he had sought service in central India. Mirza Najaf later joined the English, and ultimately Shah Alam, but Rene ended up in Bharatpur where he helped modernise the army of Jawahar Singh, and fought in his campaign against Najib ud-Daulah and Jaipur. Now on the persuasion of Najaf, and the advice of Chevalier, the French governor of Chandernagar, he switched sides and joined the emperor. The French were working according to a well thought out political plan, and French mercenaries were always susceptible to patriotic appeals and remarkably amenable to directions from representatives of the French Crown, whether at Chandernagar or Pondicherry.

Madec entered Delhi on 15 Nov. 1772 and the ceremonies and honours which he received quite turned the head of the rough Breton sailor. He was granted a mansab of 6,000 *zat* and *sowar*, about the same which Clive had secured for himself through Mir Jafar, and the grandiloquent title of Nawab Shams ud-Daulah Bahadur Qaim Jung. Madec's transfer of allegiance was effected at some personal cost, for he had to abandon his property and the goods in his house at Bharatpur.

Besides this accretion to the imperial strength, Shah Alam commissioned Mirza Najaf to raise more troops and assigned to him the revenues of some of the districts near Delhi for the purpose. His experience in Rohilkhand had shaken his faith in his Maratha allies. The task which confronted the emperor was virtually a fresh conquest of the empire. This was not possible without a strong and efficient army squarely under his control, and there could be no better person than Mirza Najaf for raising this force.

The Mirza had learnt much from his days with the English. He had observed how a few hundred trained sepoys could prevail over traditional armies ten times their number, and also recognized that artillery and musketry would henceforth rule the battlefield. He raised a brigade of 7,000 men including a strong body of foreign or 'Mughal' horse, his particular passion.

It was not a moment too soon. Najaf had scarcely had time to drill the new force when it became clear that the Marathas had turned against him. They had by then taken up the cause of Zabita and the Jats, and when the emperor refused to give concessions to their protégé, they turned against him. The underlying reason was, of course, money. The emperor had undertaken to pay Rs. 40 lakh to the Marathas for escorting him to Delhi but had paid only Rs. 10 lakh so far. The Jats and Rohillas, on the other hand, were in a better position to pay and seemed better prospects. The peshwa's burden of debt was as oppressive as ever, and the operations in Rohilkhand and Bharatpur had brought little by way of money. In the second half of the eighteenth century, apart from strategic aims and policy, money was often the most important consideration in military manoeuvres.

The Marathas moved against the emperor and on 21 November came within 8 miles of the capital, all set for battle. Mahadji had dissociated himself from them. He was strongly opposed to their espousal of the cause of Zabita, the hereditary enemy of his house, and had left Visaji Krishna in high dudgeon. Rene Madec had reached Delhi a week earlier. Najaf's newly raised battalions would soon be put to the test.

After some preliminary skirmishing the battle took place on 17 December near the Purana Qila. The Mirza's new battalions could not stand up to the veteran Maratha force. They were clumsy in their manoeuvres, and either fired too quickly or were too slow to reload. The emperor timidly stayed in the rear. Had he come forward and shown himself to his troops, his presence might have enthused them. Only Madec's brigade stood firm. It formed a tight square with three guns and maintained a steady fire, keeping the Maratha horse at bay, and inflicting heavy casualties. But Husam ud-Daulah, the emperor's first minister, did nothing to protect his camp and was openly accused of firing blank shots from his guns in a pretence of fighting. This courtier was more intent on letting down Najaf, of whom he was extremely jealous, but when the battle was over the emperor did nothing to punish him.

Rene Madec's sepoys had saved the imperialists from disaster but the emperor had no stomach for further fighting, and two days later peace negotiations were opened. The Maratha demands were exorbitant and there were secret talks between the emperor and Visaji's diwan, but finally the emperor capitulated.

On 26 December a farcical scene was enacted for the benefit of imperial 'face'. Visaji Krishna, Tukoji Holkar, and Zabita were presented before the emperor in the diwan khana, with their hands bound like defeated rebels craving forgiveness. *Nazars* were offered and the emperor 'forgave' them, ordering their wrists to be unbound. Robes of honour were distributed and Zabita was pronounced mir bakhshi, and all his paternal estates in Rohilkhand, Saharanpur and Meerut were restored. Thus, all the gains of the previous campaign were wiped out. Worse was to follow as Kora and Allahabad were ceded to the Marathas. After the departure of the emperor these had been seized by Shuja, the fort being held by the English in his name. On 2 January the emperor issued another order dismissing the battalions of the valiant Madec and Najaf. Hussam ud-Daulah was uneasy. He knew that once the Marathas left, Najaf would have his revenge. So, on the minister's pressing, the Marathas now insisted that the Mirza be expelled from Delhi.

The craven Shah Alam obliged, but the Mirza defied the order, put his house in a state of defence, and declaring that he was now a private citizen, and therefore not obliged to quit the city, prepared to resist. However, after a few days of disorder, he agreed to enter the Maratha service and left with them on a subsidy of Rs. 3,000 per diem for himself and his contingent.[5]

The Marathas were planning an incursion into the Doab with the object of taking Allahabad and Kora, as per the terms of their treaty with Shah Alam, and also to collect their dues from the Rohilla chiefs. But they wanted to achieve this without fighting, for with the departure of Scindia their strength had been considerably depleted, and another contingent had to be sent to Bundelkhand. Thus, Visaji Krishna and Tukoji Holkar did not have more than 30,000 soldiers between them. With them went Zabita Khan, Mirza Najaf, and Rene Madec, each with a small contingent. Tukoji was hoping that a quick advance on Faizabad, which was an open city, would force Shuja to come to terms, but Visaji was less certain. He knew that Zabita had an understanding with Shuja, and both the Mirza and Rene were in correspondence with the wazir, and if it came to fighting they could not be depended on.

Shuja sent frantic appeals for troops to the English to counter this Maratha threat to Allahabad. The English had no intention of letting these districts slip from their hands—since Awadh had already become a virtual English protectorate. An English brigade, composed of Indian sepoys and British infantry under Colonel Champion, set off westward in response to Shuja's call.

That Visaji was only interested in extracting an indemnity from Shuja, and not in serious fighting, soon became evident. Instead of proceeding down river towards Allahabad, the Marathas massed threateningly at Ram Ghat on the west bank of the Ganga not far from Bulandshahr in the middle Doab. Shuja had joined Colonel Champion near Kanpur, and together they proceeded up the country, camping opposite Farrukhabad where they were joined by more British troops led by General Barker, the commander-in-chief of the Bengal army. On 19 March their combined forces reached Sahaswan, 20 miles short of Ram Ghat.

That very day the Marathas crossed the river which was equivalent to a declaration of war, the river being at this point the boundary. Shuja and the English moved up and some confused fighting took place, with the Marathas crossing and re-crossing the river several times. A Maratha raiding party also seized the opportunity to make a dash up to Sambhal and plunder that town.

The simmering differences between Tukoji and Visaji now became an open rupture. Each blamed the other for their failure to achieve anything in the past three years. In the face of English determination, they retreated. At Etawah they buried the heavy guns seized at Pathargarh while their lighter booty was sent to the Deccan by way of Kalpi. The campaign had been directed as much against the par-Rohillas as against Shuja. An agreement was reached by which the latter accepted bonds from Hafiz Rahmat and the Bangash nawab for Rs. 20 lakh and gave them to the Marathas a year earlier in discharge of the promised indemnity of Rs. 40 lakh.

On 5 May Mirza Najaf was dismissed by the Marathas with *khillats*, jewels, Rs. 26,000 in cash, and a land grant. Thereafter they themselves left for the south after calling on General Barker at Anupshahar. It would be years before they returned again to Hindostan. Internal troubles following the murder of the Peshwa Narayan Rao on 30 August 1773, and war in the Deccan, would keep them busy. Not until Mahadji Scindia's campaign of 1782 would they again become a factor in north India.

Mirza Najaf returned to Delhi and was received with honour by the emperor and reinstated in his former offices. He again set about raising an army worthy of an emperor. Rene Madec was recalled, and over the next two years he engaged other European freelancers like Major Polier, the Comte de Modave, and eventually Walter Reinhardt, 'le Sombre' himself. Husam ud-Daulah, the deputy wazir, was dismissed, disgraced and imprisoned, while Abdul Ahad Khan was appointed in his place on the advice of Mirza Najaf.

The reason for this bouleversement was not merely the departure of the Maratha patrons of Husam ud-Daulah, but sober consideration of policy. The English had suspended the payment of the Bengal tribute since 1770. That year the pretext had been famine. The famine was severe and the letters of that period speak of people dying in the streets and distressed parents offering their children for sale in the streets of Calcutta. But three years had passed since then and the tribute remained outstanding. Of all his nobles, Mirza Najaf was the only one who knew the English well, and Shah Alam felt that he was the most suitable person for negotiating with them. Moreover, since Rs. 2 lakh out of the tribute of Rs. 24 lakh was the Mirza's own pension, he had a personal interest in the issue and could be expected to pursue the matter with zeal. Secondly, the emperor needed an army, and, apart from the Mirza, there was no other person in his court with military talents. Husam ud-Daulah was a mere courtier, at best a diplomat, but certainly no general. Abdul Ahad Khan, the choice of Mirza Najaf, was happily in accord with the emperor. The man was a Kashmiri, and like all his race had a silver tongue with polished manners, grace and charm. He had held a position of trust under Najib ud-Daulah. Thereafter he had attached himself to Zabita Khan, but after the fall of Pathargarh he sought and obtained the emperor's pardon. For some time he hung about the court without employment, but soon attracted the notice of the emperor and of Najaf, whose confidence he won, and whom he swore to serve faithfully.

Mirza Najaf knew that he himself, a Persian and a shia, would not be acceptable. He had no party on whose support he could bank. His relative, Shuja, had tried to have him killed. And, unlike Najib, he did not have the backing of a powerful patron like Abdali. He could only hope to find and support candidates who would be loyal to him. But Abdul Ahad Khan proved a poor choice and gave him no end of trouble, forever intriguing and trying to poison the emperor against him. However, for the present, Abdul Ahad was the man of the hour. Elevated to the ranks of a daulah, with the titles of Majd ud-Daulah Bahram Jang, he was the deputy or stop-gap prime minister.

Besides the European officers who held independent jagirs, and drilled and paid their own batallions, Mirza Najaf had a number of able and devoted lieutenants in Najaf Quli Khan, Afrasiyab Khan and Muhammed Beg Hamadani. The first two were so close to him that they were regarded as his adopted sons. Then there were other Turki officers, formerly captains of the Mughal Horse, including the Afghan, Mullah Rahimdad Khan, and that strange man from the Caucasus, Tahmasp Khan 'Miskin', the memoirist.

Najaf was able once again to raise a formidable army of 20,000 men. It was undoubtedly the best army in northern India; if only it could be paid. The history of the 'Seen Dagh' risala was a painful reminder of what could happen to even a good army when the flow of money dwindled. The imperial armies were all mercenary armies, radically different from the Maratha and Sikh armies, which at a pinch could live off the country, content with what they could squeeze from the merchants and townsmen. For the imperial armies, however, all of India was the empire; Awadh,

Punjab, Braj, and Rajasthan were not enemy territory; at worst they were lost territories which ought to be recovered. It was only in extreme cases of outright rebellion, as at the time of the rising of Banda Bahadur, that the imperialists resorted to wholesale massacre.

The Jat prince was the most convenient target for the new model army raised by Mirza Najaf. Ever since the death of Suraj Mall, that state had been in decline, but its treasury had not been exhausted, and it remained a most alluring attraction for the cash-starved emperor.

In September 1773 a Jat contingent operating from Aligarh ravaged the imperial territory from Sikandra to Ghaziabad. Mirza Najaf immediately sent a strong cavalry detachment to push them back. At Dankaur a battle took place where the Jats were defeated. Volley followed volley, delivered with deadly effect by Najaf's musketeers. The remnants of the Jat force hastily evacuated the Doab and crossed the Yamuna.

In the meanwhile, on 24 September, the main imperialist force led by Mirza Najaf had begun its advance from Mehrauli. Maidangarh, a small fort close to Mehrauli, was first stormed. Then they proceeded by way of Badarpur and Ballabhgarh where Ajit Singh and Hira Singh, the dispossessed heirs of the founder of Ballabhgarh, Balu Jat, waited on Najaf and offered help if he would restore to them their patrimony. Leaving the fort of Ballabhgarh alone for the moment, the Mughal force continued its advance towards Palwal and into Mewat, the Jats retreating without offering any resistance. So great was their panic that, at Bachari, a Jat force fled at the sight of a moving dust cloud which turned out to be an ephemeral whirlwind![6]

The decisive battle took place near Barsana. It lasted four hours and the Jats fought well, but at the critical moment Nawal Singh, the Jat chief, lost his nerve and fled. Considerable booty fell to the imperialists. After taking the fortress of Kotwan the Mirza turned towards Agra. An army was reported to be marching from Awadh towards this city. Nawal, in desperation, had offered Shuja the city as a bait for his support; thus for Najaf it was essential to occupy it before Shuja arrived. He did so with relative ease but, as he lacked cannon, the citadel held out. He then appealed to Shuja in the name of their common master the emperor. Shuja had no intention of fighting the imperialists, for he was, after all, the wazir and had only hoped to occupy the city and seize the proffered fort; and then, with his commission secured beforehand, broker a peace between the two parties. He sent Major Polier and the eunuch Basant Ali Khan to Najaf's help. In a few days Polier's well directed guns were able to make an impression on the wall, and the garrison sued for peace. On 18 February 1774 the fort was occupied by the imperialists.

Shuja then invited the Mirza to join him in an expedition against the par-Rohillas. The latter met Shuja, on 27 February, who pressed him to also persuade the emperor to come. This would give the expedition the imperial blessings. Najaf agreed and the emperor actually set out, but was compelled to turn back on account of the illness of the heir-apparent. Thus, by the time Najaf joined Shuja the fighting was over, and the emperor gained nothing from this Rohilla war.

A strong English force led by Colonel Champion ensured the triumph of the nawab-wazir. The Rohilla chiefs of the Aonla branch, the descendents of Ali Muhammad, were effectively crushed, and Zabita Khan's trans-Gangetic possessions, including Najibabad and Pathargarh, were coolly annexed. Practically all that was left was Saharanpur, and a few years hence he would suffer yet further loss and humiliation. Ultimately, whatever he held would be by the grace of the emperor and Mirza Najaf. The Rohilla threat was practically over.

After Agra the imperialists took Ballabhgarh and Farrukhnagar from the Jats. The latter fell on 6 May. It was about this time that Sombre abandoned the Jat service for the imperial under Mirza Najaf.[7]

Abdul Ahad had already started his intrigues against the Mirza. He recalled how Najib Khan, as bakhshi, had seized all the Crown lands. This Persian adventurer could reduce the emperor to the same level of helplessness to which Imad had reduced Alamgir II. And who knew, being a shia, he might eventually ally himself with his co-sectarian Shuja? With the latter's immense wealth, it was suggested, he would be in an unassailable position. Thus, Abdul Ahad persuaded the emperor to give Zabita the actual control of military affairs, which his appointment as mir bakhshi entitled him to. Zabita came to Delhi and was presented to the emperor on 9 October 1773, but soon retired to Saharanpur leaving his son behind as deputy. He realized he was in no position to match the Persian Mirza.

For the remaining part of 1774 and till April 1775, Mirza Najaf remained in Delhi in order to re-establish his position in court. Shah Alam had many grouses against him—fomented by Abdul Ahad. The Mirza had been granting jagirs and offices by using the wazir's seal which Shuja had given him when they had met during the recent campaign. Thus there were virtually two deputy wazirs at the same time! On one occasion the Mirza was refused entry to the durbar at the instance of Abdul Ahad, as a consequence of which Najaf sulked at home for two months. Zabita was again brought to court in November 1774 but again his visit proved futile.

Then the Mirza fell ill in the beginning of 1775 and was for several months confined to bed. Fortunately for the emperor, his campaigns in Braj, the pacification of the Delhi districts, and the destruction of the par-Rohillas, had resulted in a lull in the crazy anarchy. About this time the Comte de Modave also joined the imperial service.

In 1775 the imperialists again invaded the Jat territories. Mirza Najaf was incapacitated by illness but Najaf Quli and Afrasiyab took the field; the former invading Mewat while Afrasiyab crossed into the Doab. The parganas of Sadabad and Jewar were occupied and the fort of Ramgarh taken after a three-month seige, while in Mewat Mullah Rahimdad stormed the fort of Kama belonging to the Jaipur raja. The town was spared the horrors of a sack by paying Rs. 25 lakh raised by its traders and bankers.

The Jaipur prince bestirred himself and hired a few thousand Maratha horse that were in the area for collecting revenue, and allying himself with the Jats focussed all his efforts on recovering Kama. Mirza Najaf also set out from Delhi and, recalling his troops from the Doab, crossed the Yamuna. An encounter took place at Barsana following which the Jats retreated into the nearby fortress of Dig which the imperialists beseiged. In the meantime, Sombre's diplomacy succeeded in making peace with Jaipur who marched away on condition of Kama being restored. This angered Rahimdad who had been promised Kama, and in disgust he crossed over to the Jats with his Rohillas.

Then the rains began. Mullah Rahimdad attacked Bani, the jagir of Rene Madec who rushed to its defence, but was defeated with heavy loss about 16 miles from Fatehpur Sikri. He retreated to Agra to refit and recoup his losses.

Nawal Singh, the Jat raja, died on 11 August 1775 in Dig while his brother Ranjit was at Kumbher. His absence, and the confusion and disarray arising from the death, enabled Rahimdad to gain control of the fort and stage a coup. Placing the infant Kesri Singh on the throne, he proclaimed himself regent. Ranjit hurried back and, collecting all his troops, attacked Rahimdad's camp which lay outside the city. The city was seething with resentment against the Rohillas. The Afghans behaved with their customary arrogance and, during their brief ascendancy, many women were molested. Thus, while Ranjit was attacking the Rohilla camp outside, there was an uprising within the city resulting in the almost complete destruction of the Rohilla force. The Mullah fled to Delhi where he was welcomed by Abdul Ahad who sent him to seize the Hansi-Hissar districts which were held by Najaf's deputies. But on the way he clashed with the Sikhs under Raja Amar Singh of Patiala, and the eternal malcontent finally got his just desserts at Gohana (30 December 1775). Amar Singh had come at the request of Mirza Najaf to counter Abdul Ahad and Rahimdad.

The siege of Dig continued from November 1775 till the end of April 1776. Attempts at escalade failed, and it was ultimately starvation that led to its fall. On the night of 29 April Ranjit fled from the fort with the remnants of his troops to Kumbher, cutting his way through Himmat Bahadur's Naga troops. The imperialists rushed in, and the miserable town was sacked for three days. The powder magazines caught fire and many were killed in the explosions. Three dowager ranis committed suicide to escape violation.[8]

It took Najaf three days to bring his rioting troops to order. Apart from cannon and other weapons of war, very little booty fell to the share of the emperor. Some buried treasure was unearthed, roughly valued at Rs. 6 lakh, but this was too little to discharge the claims of the soldiers who still clamoured for their arrears. His generals, Najaf Quli and Afrasiyab pressed him to give up Agra to plunder and thus satisfy the troops, but he angrily rejected the cynical proposal.

The breaking of the monsoon meant a suspension of military operations. This period was spent in camp at Agra. In early October Najaf entered the Doab, where he occupied himself with suppressing refractory zamindars, collecting revenue and taking forts, the most important of which was Mursan. In February 1777 the Mirza had to leave in response to an urgent summons from the emperor.

We have seen how Abdul Ahad Khan had tried to use Zabita as a cat's paw in his intrigues against Najaf. But Zabita soon realized that he was in no position to challenge the Mirza and returned to his estates in Saharanpur. He had already lost much. The other Rohilla chiefs had been crushed by Shuja, and his own trans-Gangetic holdings, including Najibabad and the fort of Pathargarh, had been annexed by the latter. Now all he held was Saharanpur and some scattered estates in the Doab. He was mir bakhshi only in name and without any authority, which was exercised exclusively by Mirza Najaf. As an ordinary mansabdar he was obliged to pay tribute and he had no wish to imperil his position any further.

But his failure to play Abdul Ahad's game earned him the enmity of the intriguing Kashmiri. Unfortunately for him, his revenues were in arrears. In fact, he had made no payments whatever. Using this, Abdul Ahad sent his brother Abdul Kasim Khan against Zabita in 1776. Abdul Kasim had gone most reluctantly; he had a presentiment that he would not return. As he had feared, on 4 March 1776 at Amirnagar, he was defeated and killed by Zabita who had called the Sikhs to his aid.

Zabita sent back the body of Abdul Kasim Khan with a letter offering his condolences and regrets. He presented himself at the Qila-i-Mualla before the emperor and was duly forgiven and allowed to return. Correspondence continued between him and the court to persuade him to pay up his arrears of tribute, but this the Rohilla steadily refused to do. Eventually, the emperor determined on war.

On the Mirza's return from the Jat country, an expedition was fitted out for dispatch to the Rohilla's territory. Lutafat Ali, the Awadh general, tried to effect a compromise at the imperial camp at Loni but nothing came of it. Najaf began his march on Ghausgarh, the principal stronghold of Zabita, the emperor following close behind. On 17 May the emperor issued a proclamation by which Zabita was stripped of his titular dignities which were now formally conferred on Mirza Najaf. But Abdul Ahad, doggedly determined to cross the Mirza, had himself nominated as second bakhshi, the post vacated by the Mirza!

Ghausgarh is located on the banks of the Mrishni rivulet near the border of modern Saharanpur and Muzaffarnagar districts. The country is broken, with swamps and hillocks and a number of Afghan villages. Initial attempts to force the Afghan positions were repulsed and, amid much recrimination between Abdul Ahad and the Mirza, the imperialists finally hunkered down for a prolonged siege. Towards the end of August fresh reinforcements were brought by Afrasiyab, and finally on 14 September the outer defences were forced after furious fighting. Zabita Khan galloped away with his Sikh allies while his son Ghulam Qadir was taken prisoner. The garrison then opened parleys and on 23 September capitulated. The entire family of Zabita fell into the hands of the victors. The last important Rohilla chief had been finally crushed.

The captives were sent to Agra fort while Zabita fled with his Sikh allies across the Yamuna. He lived with them for several months near Karnal, absolutely penniless and totally dependent. But his friends looked after him, and so impressed was he by their sincerity that he actually consented to be baptized into the Sikh faith and assumed the name of Dharam Singh![9] The remainder of 1777 passed peacefully but in 1778 the Amir-ul-Umara was deeply involved in siege operations before Alwar, and Abdul Ahad's intrigues only stiffened the Rajput resistance. Taking advantage of his involvement, the Sikhs crossed the Yamuna and spread all over the Doab, ravaging and looting, right up to Sikandra and Khurja. Najaf Quli was besieged in Ghausgarh, but soon he was relieved by Afrasiyab. At his approach the Sikhs lifted the siege and fled to their homes across the river with the imperialists at their heels.

Sardar Gajpat Singh, who held Karnal and was Zabita's protector, favoured peace. So too did Daulat Singh, the chief of Malaudh, but Bhag Singh of Thanesar remained defiant. However, after the imperialists had taken the fortified village of Baragaon, where the Sikh sardars had kept most of their baggage, the latter came round to peace.

They gave their word that they would not shelter the emperor's enemies, and would not raid the mahals of the Amir-ul-Umara. Zabita agreed to return with the imperial generals and throw himself at the emperor's feet. Najaf promised to intercede on his behalf with the emperor and secure favourable terms for him.

The promise made by the Amir-ul-Umara was faithfully kept. Zabita was pardoned. His family, and all the property seized at Ghausgarh, were released. Even Ghausgarh, and seven mahals in Saharanpur, were returned. So grateful was the Rohilla that he offered his daughter in marriage to the Mirza. By this generous treatment of a fallen foe, Mirza Najaf won a devoted adherent to counteract the intrigues of the shifty Abdul Ahad who would soon dig his grave.

During the Ghausgarh campaign of 1777 the Jats had again become active. In alliance with the restless chief of Macheri, and with the help of Maratha auxilliaries, Ranjit tried to recover Dig. The attempt failed but the Jats plundered the town of Farah, 15 miles north-west of Agra, and slew the Mughal collector stationed there.

In November, as soon as Ghausgarh had been taken, the Amir-ul-Umara turned towards Agra. The mud fort of Sonkh between Mathura and Kumbher was stormed and terrible punishment meted out to its garrison, which was massacred, the women and children being sold into slavery. The terrorized Jats hastily submitted, Kumbher did not resist and Ranjit Singh and his stepmother Rani Kishori fled to Bharatpur. In two months they were brought to their knees and the rani personally waited on the Amir-ul-Umara to beg for mercy. As in the case of the house of Najib ud-Daulah, the state founded by Suraj Mall was on the verge of extinction.

Again Mirza Najaf showed that he preferred to conciliate rather than destroy an enemy. He restored Bharatpur to Ranjit with lands yielding a revenue of Rs. 7 lakh, and to Rani Kishori he released the fort of Kumbher as a personal gift. Once again by his moderation Mirza Najaf had made a friend out of an enemy.

But operations against Macheri continued. Lachhmangarh fort was besieged by the imperialists. The Macheri chief sued for peace. About this time Raja Pirthi Singh, the feeble prince of Jaipur, also died. The fertile mind of Abdul Ahad saw in this event another opportunity to try to embarrass Najaf. He suggested to the emperor that he could now collect a succession fee from the successor, besides an indemnity from his feudatory, the Naruka of Macheri, if he negotiated directly. Envoys from Macheri and Jaipur arrived in Delhi and the imperial marching tents were pitched at Talkatora as the emperor, under pressure from his favourite, made preparations for going to Rajasthan in person.

But Mirza Najaf had no intention of letting the Kashmiri ruin his negotiations. After Abdul Ahad refused to react to an appeal made by him, he ordered Najaf Quli and Afrasiyab to march on Delhi with their armies and overawe the timid emperor into dismissing the Jaipur and Macheri envoys. The officers chosen were good, and the emperor immediately climbed down and did as advised while Abdul Ahad was discredited. The Amir-ul-Umara then quickly pushed through a deal with the Macheri raja, who agreed to pay an indemnity of Rs. 33 lakh, of which Rs. 3 lakh was paid in cash and a security given for the first instalment.

Rs. 3 lakh paid by the Naruka were a loan from the Jaipur treasury, and now a dispute arose between Macheri and Jaipur for its repayment. The Jaipur diwan called for Mirza Najaf's assistance. There was some further fighting and matters dragged on. Ultimately Shah Alam did set out with Abdul Ahad Khan for Jaipur. At the village of Aminpur the coronation ceremony of Raja Sawai Pratap Singh took place on 19 February 1779 with Shah Alam himself applying the *rajtilak* on his forehead. A *peshkash* of Rs. 2 lakh was given to the emperor and a tribute of Rs. 20 lakh agreed upon. As for the Macheri raja, Mirza Najaf had been able to get only Rs. 2 lakh from him, and he again revolted. While the emperor returned to Delhi, Mirza Najaf resumed operations against Macheri.

While Najaf remained entangled in Mewat, in an apparently endless struggle to wear down the Naruka of Macheri, Abdul Ahad was about to embark on his crowning folly which would lead to his disgrace and final downfall. Najaf Khan Zulfiqar ud-Daulah would soon reach the apogee of glory with his appointment as Vakil i-Mutlaq, but all to no avail. The Mirza, notwithstanding all his other qualities, showed an astonishing lack of administrative ability. Circumstances such as the famine of 1782, the terrible 'chalisa' long preserved in the people's memories, his own fatal disease, and a rapid moral collapse, combined to ensure that ultimately he had nothing to show for these three years.

NOTES

1. Ghulam Ali, *Muqaddamah-i-Shah Alam Namah*, ii, pp. 266, 283. Munna Lal, *Tarikh-i-Shah Alam*, pp. 121-3.
2. Ghulam Ali, ibid., pp. 284-96. Munna Lal, pp. 125-7. Sarkar, *Fall of the Mughal Empire*, iii, p. 32.
3. Miskin, *Tahmasp Namah*, pp. 281-3. Sarkar, iii, p. 32.
4. Ghulam Ali, pp. 297-8.
5. Miskin, pp. 285-6. Munna Lal, pp. 141-4.
6. *Poona Akhbarat*, A42.
7. *Calendar of Persian Correspondence*, iv, p. 1184.
8. Modave, *Journal du Voyage du Bengale a Delhi*, pp. 298-9. Sarkar, iii, p. 75.
9. Miskin, pp. 336-8. Bihari Lal, *Life of Najibuddaulah*, *Indian Historical Quarterly*, 1935.

CHAPTER 37

The Fall of Abdul Ahad Majd ud-Daulah

Abdul Ahad Majd ud-Daulah was intensely jealous of Mirza Najaf, once his patron. Whatever he was he owed to Najaf's initial recommendation, but the wily Kashmiri was the perfect example of the proverbial ingratitude of man. He just could not resist biting the hand that had fed him.

Recognizing his own inadequacy in the military field, he first tried to raise Zabita as a counterpoise to the Mirza. But the latter was now a devoted adherent of the Amir-ul-Umara. The Jat raja, another old malcontent, had also been converted by the Mirza into a grateful dependent. The Rao Raja of Macheri was proving more intractable, but while he tied down the Mirza in Mewat, Abdul Ahad needed more powerful backers in Delhi. In the Sikhs, who were by now a regular part of the Doab scene, plundering upto Delhi and beyond, he saw the possibility of such an ally.

In 1778 he had held parleys with some Sikh chiefs, camping near the Shalamar Bagh, and procured for Malhi Khan, brother of Zabita, who was still with the Sikhs, the title of Najib ud-Daulah II. He called on the sardars and gave them *khillats* in the emperor's name while those rustic chiefs celebrated the martial festival of Dussehra by demolishing a mosque on the site of the present gurdwara of Bangla Sahib, where the seventh and eighth gurus had stayed when summoned to Delhi by Aurangzeb! The impotent government could do nothing to chastise them.[1]

Abdul Ahad had his son-in-law, Syed Ali, appointed faujdar of Sonepat, a district dominated by Sikh chieftains, with the intention of weakening the hold of Mirza Najaf's collectors. After the emperor's return from Jaipur Ahad sent for the sardars of the Karnal region and tried to prevail on the emperor to receive them, but the latter declined as that would have been contrary to Najaf's policy. But Abdul Ahad allowed himself to be deluded that he could re-establish imperial control over the entire Cis-Sutluj. His delusions were strengthened by an envoy sent by Raja Amar Singh of Patiala, to seek imperial support.

The minister tried to bully the emperor into accompanying the planned expedition but Shah Alam pleaded ill-health and the summer heat.

Finally, one of the shahzadas, Farkhunda Bakht, was deputed to represent him.

The march began on 3 June. On the way the Amir-ul-Umara's agents were expelled and replaced by the nominees of Abdul Ahad. At Karnal, Gajpat Singh of Jind was waiting and soon became his confidential adviser with respect to Sikh affairs. Unfortunately for Ahad the Patiala raja, to whose call he was marching, was at odds with most of the lesser chiefs in his camp. This roused the suspicions of the former. Gajpat Singh was an agent of Amar Singh, and while recommending the sardars to Abdul Ahad he also sought to provoke their suspicions of the emperor's minister.

On Gajpat's advice, Abdul Ahad placed all the sardars (including Gajpat) under restraint. That was the only way, he explained, to extract money from Bhai Desu Singh of Kaithal. This move at once angered and alienated them. In his negotiations Ahad was wavering and indecisive. The Patiala diwan waited on him with drafts for Rs. 5 lakh, but the minister, who had exaggerated ideas of his own importance, insisted on the raja's personal appearance, which Amar Singh was determined to avoid.

The minister determined on an advance against Amar Singh and moved up to Ghuram, 22 km. south-east of Patiala. A deputation of sardars was sent to persuade the raja to come and make his submission. He at first agreed, then changed his mind. So, on 7 October, the imperialists attacked. The raja retreated and shut himself in his fort. Then mutiny broke out. Abdul Ahad had been in the field for four months and had run out of money. Scarcely anything could be squeezed from the Sikhs; there was ill-feeling between his Afghan and Turki troops, and the Sikh auxiliaries were clamouring for their pay. The approach of a strong force of trans-Sutluj Sikhs led by Tara Singh tempted many to desert. Raja Amar Singh's gold did the rest.

On 14 October Abdul Ahad began his retreat. Some chiefs like Bhag Singh of Thanesar remained loyal and fought bravely. The minister thus succeeded in keeping the army together and a debacle was prevented. Actually, it was the presence of Prince Farkhunda Bakht that saved the army. Respect for the imperial name still survived, even among the independent and turbulent Sikhs, and the pursuers contented themselves with loot and shrank from extremes against the emperor's son. If Abdul Ahad had been alone he would not have returned alive.[2]

The emperor and the court had been frantic with worry on account of the prince, and Shah Alam had sent an urgent message to Mirza Najaf (who was still in Mewat) to return to Delhi. So, when Abdul Ahad arrived in Delhi on 5 November, he found himself in deep disgrace. But with his silver tongue he was soon able to insinuate himself again in the emperor's favour. Reminding him of the Syed brothers and Imad ul-Mulk, he persuaded Shah Alam to write to Najaf, countermanding his earlier order to return to Delhi.

But it was too late. Najaf received the second message when he was only two marches from the capital. Ignoring it, he continued his advance and on 12 November camped at the tank of Kishan Das in the southern suburbs. It was upto Abdul Ahad now to conciliate his former patron.

Two days later Mirza Najaf was to be presented to the emperor. Gracious and affable as ever, Abdul Ahad, accompanied by Prince Akbar, advanced to Najaf's camp to conduct him to the emperor. But in the meantime many of Najaf's soldiers led by Afrasiyab managed to infiltrate the fort. The red-uniformed guards known as the Surkh Posh or the Lal Paltan were under orders not to provoke a clash, so Najaf's soldiers simply pushed their way in. When they showed reluctance in abandoning their posts Afrasiyab gave an undertaking that their dues would be duly discharged by his master, the Mirza. Reassured they readily yielded, thus, when Najaf entered the fort, sitting behind the prince on the latter's elephant, the outer works of the fort were already in the hands of his men. One is reminded of the coup of Syed Hussain Ali Khan.

After the durbar Abdul Ahad walked with Mirza Najaf through the audience halls to see him off. They were walking hand in hand, outwardly reconciled, but soon the minister noticed that they were surrounded by the bakhshi's soldiers and from their looks, he could tell, mischief was intended. Lutafat Khan, the Awadh envoy, who was his friend, had also sensed that something was afoot. He had rushed after them as soon as the presentation was over. He interposed himself between the general and Abdul Ahad, and snatching the latter's hand from the bakhshi's, he held it in a protective gesture. Afrasiyab urged the general not to let the opportunity slip; the viper was in their power; he had only to give the order and they would sieze him and bundle him out of the Qila-i-Mualla.

But Najaf refused to give the command. He would not violate the sanctity of the imperial residence. No violence could be used against any of the emperor's nobles without his express consent. Ordering Afrasiyab to remain on guard with his men inside the fort, he retired to the Sunehri Masjid of Roshan ud-Daulah to await events.

All day long, and the next day, emissaries continued to come and go between the emperor and his bakhshi, between the fort and the masjid. At night the city was in tumult as law and order threatened to break down, and honest citizens barricaded themselves in their homes, as at the time of the Syed coup d'etat. The emperor made dramatic gestures; he donned armour and, taking a bow and quiver, set out to drive Afrasiyab and his men from the fort. But before he had taken five steps his courage evaporated, and he gave heed to his timid advisers who cautioned against such dramatics lest Afrasiyab and his men fail in showing Majesty its due respect.

Finally, on the fifteenth, the gold of Mirza Najaf began to take effect. Abdul Ahad's adherents began to desert him; and when even Lutafat Ali and Mir Syed Ali defected, he knew the game was up and sent word to the bakhshi that he was ready to submit. The latter swore on the Koran to protect his life and property. Thus reassured, the minister took leave of his royal master and left, escorted by Afrasiyab for the camp of Mirza Najaf.

The next day, on 16 November, Mirza Najaf was again received by Shah Alam. A handsome *nazar* of Rs. 2 lakh in cash, besides some trays of jewels, costly *khillats* and five horses soon conciliated him to the needy emperor who bestowed on him the highest post in the empire, that of Vakil-i-Mutlaq. The other posts held by Abdul Ahad, the command of the artillery, the second paymastership, and the diwani of the crown lands were bestowed on the three princes, with Mirza Najaf as their deputy. At last the duality in the imperial government was at an end, and unified control restored. Najaf was now supreme and at the height of his power.

But ironically, the great days of Mirza Najaf were also over. His regency lasted only two years and four months. Though he no longer had Abdul Ahad to contend with, the period was barren of results. His victory over Zabita, the destruction of the Jat power, all belong to the first phase. The second phase found him confined to Delhi due to ill-health and the compulsions of court duties. It was also witness to a moral disintegration so spectacular as to be almost incredible. Nothing in Najaf's previous career had prepared us for such a rapid descent. Instead of the clean-living soldier interested only in recruiting the best *vilayati* officers, drilling his troops and casting better and better guns, we see a shameless voluptuory picknicking by moonlight on the Yamuna banks with his harem women, procastinating, eternally procrastinating. One cannot help wondering what had happened to that cool cavalry commander who first came to our notice at Undhua Nala? The man who captured the fortresses of Allahabad, Pathargarh and Ghausgarh, not to mention fabled Kumbher.

On achieving supreme power, Najaf found to his dismay that the situation was hopeless and beyond repair. The treasury was empty, his troops were dunning him for pay, and the terrible 'chalisa' famine aggravated matters so that no revenue was forthcoming. The regent found himself unable to pay even the emperor's monthly expenses. Accustomed to the life of the camp, and the open air, the general sickened and wilted in the unhealthy atmosphere of the court and the city.

There is considerable evidence to suggest that Delhi at this time was also unusually pestilential. The chronicles of the time frequently speak of illness and premature death, even in the imperial family. Probably the water was infected, the old irrigation system laid by that other Persian genius, Ali Mardan, had fallen into disrepair, and was choked at many places. As for Mirza Najaf, consumption was destroying his lungs and would inevitably take his life. But for the moment all seemed bright and every prospect rosy. Tahmasp Khan rhapsodised:

> There was general happiness at the capital. Marriage and rejoicing were seen in every house; buying and selling went on in all the quarters of the city; houses were built or purchased. All this through the gracious and competent administration of Mirza Najaf Khan. All the chiefs, Turani, Irani and Hindustani were happy, prosperous and exalted.[3]

NOTES

1. Sarkar, *Fall of the Mughal Empire*, iii, p. 105.
2. Ibid., p. 110 (fn.).
3. Ibid., p. 115. Miskin, *Tahmasp Nama*, p. 344.

CHAPTER 38

Mirza Najaf Khan: The Second Phase

The moral collapse of Mirza Najaf Khan is a puzzle for the historian. His pleasing manners, and his moderation and openness had won him friends and admirers in all quarters. And he knew the science of war as no other contemporary. But suddenly, having reached the pinnacle, he seemed to have lost the magic touch, and everything seemed to go to pieces.

Some of the reasons have been enumerated above, namely, the financial crisis and famine of 1782, preceded by years of drought which had dried up the revenues. But there were others, besides fate and the weather. Mirza Najaf lacked administrative ability. We have seen how he parcelled out the Crown lands among his lieutenants—Afrasiyab, Najaf Quli, and Hamadani—posting them in the territories assigned to them, so that they became territorial magnates. Once the controlling hand weakened, they became as intractable as zamindars, and getting money out of them was as difficult as extracting tribute from the Raja of Jaipur or the Rao Raja of Macheri.

Amazingly too, in spite of his high descent and family connections, his formal education had been fearfully neglected. He had the grace and courtesy natural to the manor born, but as far as letters went, he was illiterate. And unlike the great Akbar or Ranjit, the Lion of the Punjab, he was unable to identify suitable instruments who could attend to the details of administration on his behalf.

Najaf had hitherto led the simple life of a soldier. Abstemious and clean in his morals, he did not even touch liquor. But now under the guidance of Lutafat, once a general in Shuja's service, he immersed himself in the pleasures characteristic of a decadent nawab of the later empire. Lutafat, in spite of being a eunuch, had 'married' a dancing woman. With this well-matched couple to light the way, the regent plunged into debauchery. Business was abandoned to his Kashmiri diwans and the regent spent most of his time in the company of Lutafat, nautch girls and singers.[1]

Lutafat's wife became his mistress, the queen of his harem, and she introduced to him other women who revealed to the declining regent the infinite variety of the perfumed garden. From a general of distinction, he had sunk to the level of a libertine, a Muhammad Shah Rangila or Wajid Ali Shah, but without the latter's cultured aestheticism.

Afrasiyab controlled Najaf's domestic finances. The emperor's privy purse, the allowances of the princes, the princesses, the begums and salatin, fell into arrears. On one occasion, the princesses protested that they would join hands and jump into the Yamuna to end their lives of humiliation. The shopkeepers of Delhi stopped their credit, and Shah Alam, 'emperor of the world', moaned that the humiliation was insufferable. With characteristic hyperbole, he declared to Maulvi Ataullah that he had no second coat left in his wardrobe.[2] The regent himself seemed to be oblivious to the surrounding decay. He immersed himself in a delirious frenzy of pleasure in the arms of his bewitching hetaera, while Lutafat, her mutilated master, and Afrasiyab helped themselves to the coffers of the degraded Mughal state.

Abdul Ahad's expedition against Patiala had exhausted the treasury and it was imperative that the money be somehow recouped. The basic expenses of the emperor's private establishment amounted to nearly Rs. 1.5 lakh per month. Another Rs. 3 lakh were required to pay the new, thirty thousand strong, army. Mirza Najaf's last campaign had ended in the submission of the Macheri and Jaipur chiefs, but in order to realize the promised tribute military pressure was still required.

Najaf had left behind Himmat Bahadur Gosain to realize the second instalment of the indemnity, but even after a year in Jaipur the latter had been unable to realize the money. Raja Pratap Singh was a fifteen year old imbecile and there was not a single sensible person in the government. Khushhali Ram Bohra, the faithful old diwan, had been ousted by his own deputy, Daulat Ram Haldia, and thrown into prison on trumped up charges. Haldia would shortly be replaced by a tailor named Roda Ram, and finally by an elephant driver, who, according to the English historian Todd, 'played the Mazarin to the Chundawat Rani-dowager who was the Regent'.[3] To such depths of ignominy had the house of Mirza Raja Jai Singh sunk in the last quarter of the eighteenth century.

Najaf decided to send another army to enforce payment. The task had been rendered easier by Najaf Quli's capture of Kanud, or Mahendragarh as it is now known, in March 1780. The raja of Kanud, Balwant Singh, had encroached on some villages in the Hansi region falling in the charge of Najaf Quli. After a gruesome and treacherous massacre in which fell the raja's son and thirty of his leading nobles, Kanud was taken, clearing the road to Jaipur.

The regent was unable to head the expedition in person, both on account of his duties at court and ill-health. But the arrival of a well-known general at Delhi seemed a heaven-sent opportunity. This general was another of the several talented eunuch generals of the court of Awadh, Mahbub Ali Khan.

Shuja ud-Daulah had died and was succeeded by Asaf ud-Daulah in 1775. Asaf was even more spoilt than his father and his administration was capricious. In disgust, Mahbub Ali Khan, a distinguished soldier who had fought on the English side at Ram Ghat at the time of the last Maratha incursion, resigned and left with the avowed intention of making the pilgrimage to Mecca.

He arrived in Delhi with his dependents and 600 soldiers on his way to the coast. The regent, who always had an eye for good commanders, prevailed upon him to postpone the pilgrimage and pressed him to raise an army to march against Jaipur. He confessed he had no money to offer him, but authorized him to raise the troops on his own account and pay them afterwards out of the spoils of the campaign. Unfortunately for Mahbub, he allowed himself to be persuaded.

Two armies were to march on Jaipur, Mahbub's proceeding by the direct route through Mewat, while another under Murtaza Khan Bahraich would advance by the northern route through Shekhawati. In May Mahbub set out, accompanied by the turncoat Daulat Ram Haldia. By 20 October he had arrived at the gates of Jaipur after plundering the towns and forts that fell on the way.

Khushhali Ram Bohra had been given back his position as diwan by Raja Pratap Singh, but the talks with Mahbub broke down as the latter did not trust him. The imperialists spread all over the state as they were living off the land and could not stay too long at one place. Of the 34 parganas of Jaipur, 32 were in their hands. Practically all that remained with the ruler was the city of Jaipur.

But Jaipur would not submit. The Raja shut himself up in the fort which was practically impregnable. Disappointed, Najaf took the negotiations out of Mahbub's hands and again entrusted them to Himmat Bahadur, then sulking at his jagir near Vrindaban. The latter was promptly approached and bribed by emissaries of Jaipur who appealed in the name of their common religion to save their raja.

In spite of the earnest efforts of Himmat Bahadur to discharge his double commission, mutually acceptable terms could not be settled. Meanwhile the position of Mahbub became more and more difficult. His soldiers deserted in droves. In desperation he pulled his army back to Dig in February and proceeded to the capital to beg for money from the regent in person. But all he could get was Rs. 10,000, a ludicrous sum in view of the lakhs he had already spent from his own purse, and the lakhs he was still owed. His house was surrounded by agitating soldiers and ultimately whatever personal effects he had were plundered by them. Finally on 22 June he took leave from Najaf and resumed his pilgrimage to Mecca, now in the patched garments of a fakir.[4]

A good general had been ruined and a fine army destroyed. Perhaps Najaf also felt that his own end was high, and at the leave taking ceremony he told Mahbub, 'Wait for me at my sister's place at Agra, I shall also be coming with you.'

Murtaza Khan Bahraich, the commander of the northern army, had also returned to Delhi in March burdened by debts. He owed his troops Rs. 1,80,000 but the Mirza could give him only a bill for Rs. 20,000, payable ten days hence, and promised the balance at the rate of Rs. 20,000 a month out of the Jaipur tribute—if and when realized. Then, in April, he was dispatched to the Doab against the Sikhs.

The debacle suffered by Abdul Ahad in October 1779 was followed by an invasion of the upper Doab by the exultant Sikhs. There was no one to oppose them and it was only in January 1780 that Mirza Muhammad Shafi, the regent's grand nephew, was sent with an army of 10,000 and a strong battery of artillery. Zabita Khan joined him later in October. After chastising recalcitrant zamindars in the Doab, they crossed the Yamuna at Kunjpura in November, entering the home ground of the Cis-Sutluj chiefs, who were as usual absorbed in their own internecine struggles. Amar Singh of Patiala was ranged against the Kaithal chief, while the Jind and Ladwa sardars were pitted against Bhag Singh of Thanesar. Gajpat Singh of Jind and three other chiefs waited on the imperialists at Kunjpura, but Shafi seized them in the hope of squeezing money out of them, a rash and ill-thought act which angered Zabita who had long been an ally and protégé of these sardars. He dissociated himself from his action and marched off with his army to Delhi leaving the Mirza to face the music alone.

But Shafi was not Abdul Ahad. He defeated a strong Sikh force near Saharanpur and among the slain was Sahib Singh Khunda. At Indri again he routed another body of the Sikhs, and then again at Ladwa, but soon the usual shortage of cash was felt. He had won battles in the field but had failed to collect money, and as usual there was none to be expected from Delhi. Now, after months of campaigning, even his supplies of powder and shot had run out.

Finally, in July, peace was made with the intervention of Zabita. Gajpat was released, given a robe of honour and the title of 'Maharaja' on 12 June 1781, and his tribute was fixed at Rs. 6 lakh per annum. The regent abandoned all ambitions of recovering territory from them. Gajpat agreed not to raid the imperial territory and to serve the emperor when called, against pay. At the same time the right of the Sikh chiefs to *rakhi* (protection money, comparable to the Maratha *chauth*) at the rate of 2 *annas* to the rupee, i.e. one eighth, was conceded right upto Delhi and in the upper Doab.[5] Just as the Mughals ultimately conceded the Maratha claims in the Deccan, so here too in the north, the empire had succumbed to the Sikh demands.

Meanwhile how were the lords of the Deccan faring? Years had passed since a Maratha army had been seen in Upper India. The 'locust-like Maratha myriads', seemed to have receded forever. The death of Peshwa Madho Rao in 1772 had been the signal for civil war. The uncle of the deceased, the notorious Raghoba, i.e. Raghunath Rao Dada, had staked his claim to the masnad of the peshwas and, with the help of the English, sought to achieve it. Thus began a series of wars which could only have one end: the increased strength of the English 'auxilliaries' and the progressive enfeeblement of the Maratha state which at one time had seemed a likely candidate for the sovereignty of Hind.

The English had already swallowed Bengal with its dependencies of Bihar and Orissa. The nawab of Awadh was their puppet, like the nawab of Arcot in the south. Together with the Arcot Carnatic, they had seized the entire Andhra coastline or the 'Northern Sarkars' as these districts were known. They were in the process of swallowing up Mysore; and with the onset of Raghoba's war they were well on their way to establishing a firm grip on the west coast. Salsette and Bassein had been ceded to them at the outset, and after a false start, by 1781, they were sweeping towards a resounding victory. Bassein was captured. Goddard swept through Malwa. The fort of Gwalior, considered impregnable, was taken by surprise, almost single-handed, without loss of life! 'How could you lose such a fort!' Mirza Najaf snorted at the Maratha ambassador who had been trying desperately to forge an alliance with the emperor. The negotiations for the alliance have been described by the historian Jadunath Sarkar as 'a case of one drowning man clutching the neck of a still more helpless swimmer in the expectation that both would be saved thereby'.[6]

The reason for the emperor's dissatisfaction with the English gentlemen of the Company Bahadur was, of course, the vexed question of the Bengal tribute, in arrears since 1770. This tribute of Rs. 26 lakh had been an integral part of the treaty, which conferred on the English the diwani of the eastern province, but since the departure of Lord Clive, Sabit Jang Bahadur, they had been finding excuses not to pay. First it was the famine, then the expense of the war with Haidar Ali. After the emperor's departure from Allahabad, the English pretended that since he had left against their advice, they were justified in withholding the tribute. Warren Hastings, or Jaladat Jang Umdat ul-Mulk, to give him his Indian titles, continued to protest his loyalty and readiness to please His Majesty, but not a pie of the tribute was tendered. He wrote soothingly that the matter had been taken up with the directors in London but little did poor Shah Alam know that he had recommended discontinuing the tribute altogether.

Though Jaladat Jang never denied the padishah's claims, the latter had given up all hope and that was why he toyed with the idea of a link-up with the Marathas against the English. Fortunately, nothing came of it. Najaf Khan was too perceptive to fail to see its futility, specially in the wake of British successes in Central India in 1780-1. Popham captured Gwalior fort on 3 August 1780, and Camac defeated Mahadji Scindia at Sipri on 16 February 1781. On 13 October the latter came to terms.

On 2 May 1781 the emperor designated Prince Akbar Shah as his heir with great pomp and ceremony. Only four months afterward, Farkhunda Bakht, a much loved shahzada, died. He had been a scholar. The same night his infant daughter passed away. As could be expected, people read portents of coming disasters in these untimely deaths in the imperial family. On 11 June there was a fearful duststorm of unusual violence followed by an earthquake, and, to cap it all, a meteor fell near Jhajjar.[7] By then it was also clear that the regent was on his death-bed. He lingered for some months more until 6 April 1782 when he breathed his last.

The last two years of the regent's rule had been disastrous but his death was universally lamented. Crowds of people, rich and poor, joined the funeral procession, for the man was loved, as a kind and humane nobleman at a time when cruelty, rapacity, and unscrupulousness were the rule. In a crumbling world the Persian Mirza stood as a fine contrast to the men that followed. As a soldier and general, he stood head and shoulders above his peers. Had he half as much skill in administrative matters as in military affairs, his achievements would have been far more substantial. All the enemies (save the Sikhs) who had been nibbling at the imperial carcase for the past two decades—the Jat, the Rohilla and the Jaipur raja—had been humbled, but the Mirza came to grief on the hard rock of finance.

NOTES

1. Sarkar, *Fall of the Mughal Empire*, iii, p. 118. British Museum, Or. 25020, 25021 (Claude Martin's newsletters).
2. Sarkar, iii, p. 121. British Museum, Or. 25020, 92a.
3. Tod, *Annals and Antiquities of Rajasthan*, ii, pp. 301-2. Sarkar is not so sure; op. cit., iii, p. 200 (fn.).
4. Sarkar, iii, p. 128. Khairuddin, *Ibrat Namah*, ii, p. 23.
5. Sarkar, iii, p. 133.
6. Ibid., p. 135.
7. Ibid., p. 137. Munna Lal, *Tarikh-i-Shah Alam*, p. 233.

CHAPTER 39

Night Falls over the City After Mirza Najaf

The death of Mirza Najaf left a vacuum in the Qila-i-Mualla. There was no obvious candidate for his post. After the death of Shuja, the wazarat had been conferred on his son, Asaf ud-Daulah who was even less fit to hold that office. Like his father, he too had no inclination to leave the pleasures of Lucknow for the perils of Delhi.

Abdul Ahad Majd ud-Daulah was too old, and, notwithstanding the emperor's fondness for him, there was no possibility of his winning the support of the turbulent captains of Mirza Najaf who commanded the few trained soldiers then available. And power, then no less than today, flowed ultimately from the barrel of a gun. Himmat Bahadur had urged the emperor to take over the command himself, but Shah Alam had become so used to having his decisions made by others that this was unthinkable.

The choice was thus limited to the officers of the late regent: Afrasiyab, Najaf Quli, Hamadani and Mirza Shafi. The last, as the closest male relative of the late regent—he was a great-nephew—could have been a natural successor, but he was considered too young and did not enjoy the necessary prestige among the soldiers. The regent himself had died early. He was only forty-five, and had no son. He left behind three daughters and his widowed sister.

Afrasiyab was the regent's personal slave. The son of a Hindu grocer, and Muslim by conversion, he had enjoyed his master's confidence, and was supposed to control all his finances. The dying regent had recommended him to the emperor and he enjoyed the support of Najaf's sister, Begum Khadija Sultan, which was a strong factor in his favour. Of the others, Najaf Quli was a *bon vivant*, addicted to wine women and opium, naturally indolent but occasionally rousing himself to bursts of reckless activity. Muhammad Beg Hamadani was the most cunning, and enjoyed the support of the *vilayati* soldiery from Khurasan and Central Asia, but he was a sunni and scorned by the shi'ite supporters of Begum Khadija and other members of the family.

Thus, at the time of Najaf's death everything seemed to favour Afrasiyab. The emperor himself needed money—as always—and hoped to turn this opportunity to some advantage to himself. Out of consideration for the regent's family, and out of his special regard for the begum, he dared not apply the principle of escheat, though Najaf's personal wealth was estimated at Rs. 30 lakh, but he was ready to offer the office to the highest bidder. In short, the regency was up for sale.

Under this criterion Afrasiyab enjoyed an advantage over the others as he had been the manager of Najaf's finances and was reputed to have salted away a small fortune. He rashly offered the emperor a *peshkash* of Rs. 5 lakh for the office—a mere pittance considering the dignity on offer—but the Mughal umara had fallen so low that there was no one who could improve on it. And, ultimately, even Afrasiyab failed to raise the full amount.

On 11 April he was invested with the offices of Amir-ul-Umara and mir bakhshi along with the regency, but with the inferior title of Mukhtar rather than Vakil-i-Mutlaq. Of the promised fee of Rs. 5 lakh, he could scrape up only Rs. 1,87,000. With this he entered upon his short and troubled term.[1]

Afrasiyab soon realized that the problems he faced were insurmountable. Ranjit Singh, the Jat raja of Bharatpur, was on the move again and had recovered some of his lost territory. Muhammad Beg Hamadani, in charge at Agra, found himself hard pressed and sent urgent calls for help, suggesting that Afrasiyab should come with the emperor in person. But the expense of taking the emperor along was too much for Afrasiyab's slender means. Thus it was decided to send Prince Jawan Bakht instead. Accordingly, tents were pitched and the prince moved out of the palace. But there were further problems, for the troops had to be provided with the *nalbandi* advance so that their families could survive in their absence.

Afrasiyab just did not have the money. His cash reserves were exhausted. In desperation he called his officers to Delhi with their troops so that the *mahals* assigned to them could be adjusted to match their actual strength. This provoked a strong reaction and the malcontents gathered around Begum Khadija and Mirza Shafi, then at Karnal.

Finding that the expected march on Agra was not likely to materialize, the disgusted Shah Alam recalled the prince from his marching tents. Afrasiyab also realized that he had lost the favour of the begum. So he left her house and moved into Abdul Ahad's which had been confiscated.

Along with him went the old noble who had been living as a personal prisoner of Mirza Najaf in the latter's mansion. Afrasiyab hoped to use him to advantage in the coming trial of strength.

Mirza Shafi was now adopted by the virago begum as her champion. Patching up a truce with the Sikhs, Shafi set off for Delhi. In desperation Afrasiyab tried to ingratiate himself with the emperor. Under pressure he withdrew his troops from the Qila-i-Mualla, leaving the emperor's own bodyguard, the Lal Paltan, in charge. Rightly suspecting that Shah Alam was also in touch with Mirza Shafi, he proposed that Abdul Ahad be restored as regent while he himself remained the bakhshi. The emperor immediately showed interest but persuading Ahad took longer. The old man had no illusions. He was penniless and knew only too well that in the sadly fractured world of 1782 the emperor's favour could not take him far.

In the meantime Shafi had arrived in Delhi. He had come without orders and his position was highly irregular, but in his characteristic vacillating manner the emperor decided to talk to him as well. He hoped, in a confused sort of way, that with this division among the inheritors of Mirza Najaf, he might be able to play an independent role, and on 14 July Shafi was received in audience.

Begum Khadija had already greeted him as her son and promised him her late brother's eldest daughter in marriage although she was only eleven years old. Hamadani too declared himself in favour of Shafi. Patching up a truce with the Jat raja, he crossed the Yamuna to plunder Afrasiyab's jagirs in the middle Doab. Najaf Quli set off from the Jaipur border also with the intention of joining him, but at Gurgaon he was intercepted by the frantic Afrasiyab who begged him to stay by his side. He consented. Thus on one side were Afrasiyab, Najaf Quli, Lutafat and Abdul Ahad; on the other, Mirza Shafi, Begum Khadija and the soldiers of the absent Hamadani.

The citizens were terrified. At any moment the soldiers of the two rival camps could clash in the streets of Delhi. On both sides the soldiers were hungry and eager for plunder. They had not been paid for months and people shuddered as they recalled the civil war between Safdar Jang and Imad ul-Mulk. The only saving grace was that there were no Maratha troops on either side this time. So, the looting would be limited.

It continued thus for some time. Finally, on the strength of a promise of Rs. 5 lakh, the emperor agreed to appoint Mirza Shafi to the vacant post of mir bakhshi on the next auspicious day, which was identified as 10 August, the first day of the holy month of Ramzan. This was a crushing blow to Afrasiyab but he pleaded with the emperor to appoint Abdul Ahad as regent. The latter had at last given his reluctant consent, and the emperor, only too happy to get back his old favourite, restored to him all his old offices the very next day.

Shafi fumed. With Abdul Ahad's restoration the position remained deadlocked. On 21 August, following an altercation between Jamal Khan from Afrasiyab's army, and Pauli, a German officer of Shafi's, tension again mounted. The streets were barricaded and guns trundled out, but on the emperor's intervention Afrasiyab was persuaded to retire to his estates in the middle Doab which was being ravaged by Hamadani. He went leaving Najaf Quli behind. The armed confrontation in the capital continued but the tension was less as Najaf Quli was a relaxed gentleman, more intent on pleasure than fighting. He left the house of Abdul Ahad and moved into the haveli of Safdar Jang, which was closer to the fort, where he continued with his carousing. The outcome was predictable.

On the night of 10 September, which happened to be the feast of Id ul-Fitr, on Shafi's orders the mansions of both Abdul Ahad and Safdar Jang were surrounded with troops and artillery. When the guns commenced their fire, Najaf Quli was lying senseless, having passed out after a night of revelry. There was only a small guard at his mansion with five cannon, but when he recovered he resisted bravely for he was not wanting in ordinary courage.

Muhammad Shafi had parked himself on the steps of the Jama Masjid, and from that vantage point he directed the attack. Abdul Ahad was in no position to offer effective defence. In order to preserve his harem from violation he promptly surrendered and was sent to the house of Qamr ud-Din to be confined. As for Najaf Quli, he kept fighting until the death of Jalal Khan Afghan, his bravest officer, who was killed charging the enemy. Then he surrendered to Begum Khadija.

Shafi was now on top. By defying the emperor he had removed the hurdles in his path, but this coup was only a temporary pause. The position remained fluid. Mirza Shafi now tried to make up with Shah Alam. He and Begum Khadija sent appropriately worded letters to His Majesty and on 15 September he was received in audience and reappointed to the regency as well, with the additional titles of Nasir ud-Daulah, Zulfiqar Jang, and the subedari of Agra. But Shah Alam was not quite happy, as the Mirza had been no more successful than Afrasiyab in paying the price promised to secure his post. Many of the Crown lands attached to the emperor's privy purse also remained with him. Hence a new plot was hatched with the emperor's blessings.

Shafi's financial problems were driving him to desperation. In early

October there was a mutiny among his troops and they mounted a cannon with its muzzle pointing threateningly at the *deohri* of his haveli. It was with difficulty that they were persuaded to lift the *dharna* and remove the guns. In the meantime Lutafat Ali, who had attached himself directly to the emperor after the fall of Afrasiyab, succeeded in seducing the mercenary Pauli to the emperor's side. On 9 October Shafi asked Shah Alam for money and was coldly refused. His Majesty moreover could not resist the temptation to reiterate his long list of grievances and the regent's many and repeated defaults. Shafi lost his temper, hot words were exchanged, and their relations became more strained than ever.

On 16 October the emperor struck.[2] In the early hours of the morning sepoys surrounded the house occupied by Mirza Shafi. Shah Alam himself rode out and blessed his troops at the Jama Masjid. As resistance would have meant a direct challenge to the emperor, the Mirza fled to Agra, leaving his house and property to be plundered. But Begum Khadija's house was not touched though the emperor was just as incensed with her.

At Agra Shafi secured the adhesion of Muhammad Beg Hamadani by making profuse promises. Other adherents also gathered, and on 6 November they turned towards Delhi. Their rapid advance frightened the emperor but Lutafat forced Shah Alam to accompany him to meet the advancing column. At Barahpullah, the envoys of Muhammad Shafi waited on His Majesty and protested their unswerving loyalty. Shah Alam was, however, determined to be rid of Shafi and entrusted the matter to one of his confidential slaves, Muhammad Yakub Khan, nick-named Kallu Khawas.

This slave hatched an elaborate plot by which he promised Muhammad Beg Hamadani the regency if he would abandon Shafi. The wily Mughal agreed and a date was fixed for his meeting with Lutafat, representing the imperial interest.

But Hamadani revealed the plot to Shafi, and when on 17 November he rode to his rendezvous with Lutafat he turned the tables on Lutafat by giving his soldiers the signal to arrest the imperial detachment while he was shaking hands with Lutafat. The conspirators were nonplussed. Only Pauli attempted to resist and was wounded. The imperial camp was paralysed. Hamadani followed up this success by sending a strong detachment to Delhi which was in an uproar. There Shafi's brother Zain ul-Abdin had already siezed the house and property of Lutafat Ali and Muhammad Yakub.

Lutafat and Pauli had really been acting on behalf of Afrasiyab. Now the game was definitely up. Shafi and Hamadani again wrote the usual florid letters to the emperor protesting eternal loyalty, and explaining their late conduct as forced by circumstances. The emperor sent his eldest son to convey his pardon, and on 24 November they were formally presented to him. All this took place in the camp at Barahpullah. Then the emperor returned to the fort, accompanied by Muhammad Shafi and others. As he changed into a palki in the courtyard of the Diwan-i-Am, Muhammad Shafi, Hamadani, Abdul Ahad and Afrasiyab picked up the poles of the chair and raised it to their shoulders in a gesture of humility and loyalty. It was thanks to these hypocrisies that the charade was kept going so long.

The next day Lutafat Khan was blinded by passing a needle through his eyes. The European Pauli protested and declared he would rather die than suffer the barbarous mutilation. In deference to his sentiments, he was spared the horror but hacked to pieces. Kallu Khawas was luckier. Thanks to the emperor, he was able to offer a large bribe. Since money was desperately needed, his offer was accepted.

Everything seemed fine but the basic problem remained intractable. Mirza Shafi lacked money, and without funds his position could not be stabilized. He had failed to meet his commitments to Shah Alam, and had entered into new ones with Hamadani. Worse, he had quarelled with him. He had returned to power with Hamadani's support; a quarrel with him could only end in disaster.

Hamadani's troops had looted the houses of innocent citizens. This had revolted Shafi and he upbraided him for his soldiers' indiscipline. Further, most of the loot siezed in the plunder of the camp of Lutafat and Pauli had been seized by Hamadani. This he had steadfastly declined to surrender. Relations between the allies became so cool that for months they did not speak.

Taking with him Prince Suleiman Shukoh and Begum Khadija, Shafi left on 22 December for Agra in order to pacify that disturbed suba, and to curb the Jat raja who had had a free hand ever since the revolution that toppled Afrasiyab. About the same time there was a Sikh incursion. Famine was raging in the Punjab, as elsewhere, and the hungry horsemen of the Punjab plains had come to plunder the rich marts ringing Delhi. After plundering the *mandis* they retired.

Meanwhile the stage was being set for a showdown between the Mirza and Hamadani. The latter had now raised new demands, asking for more jagirs, half the property and artillery of Mirza Najaf, and the transfer in his favour of all the imperial claims against Jaipur. Hamadani also won over Ranjit Singh, the Jat raja, by proposing mild terms, and started enlisting soldiers. Because of his formidable reputation, the unemployed mercenaries flocked to his banner. He seemed bent on carving an independent principality for himself. It was on account of these fears that the regent had left for Agra, taking the shahzada with him.

Hamadani appeared before Shafi at Agra and they were outwardly reconciled. Hamadani then set off for Jaipur where his army was operating.

But the reconciliation was a sham. Shafi wrote to the Jaipur raja asking him not to pay any of the tribute to Hamadani and, ignoring the settlement already concluded between Ranjit and Hamadani, recommenced operations against the Jats. At the same time, Shafi opened negotiations with Mahadji, whose prestige was at its height, specially after he had brokered a peace between the Peshwa and the English.[3]

With Himmat Bahadur as go-between, Mahadji Scindia agreed to meet Shafi, provided he came with the shahzada and the begum as a pledge of good faith. Scindia was at the time engaged in the siege of Gwalior which the English had handed over to the rana of Gohad. On 27 June 1783, Scindia visited the imperial camp and called on Shafi. Three days later he paid his respects to the prince and the begum. Several days thus passed, turbans were exchanged, and Scindia promised that he would visit Delhi after the rains, by which time he expected the operations against Gohad to be concluded.

Hamadani realized that these negotiations were meant to strengthen Shafi's hands in order to crush him. So he broke into open rebellion. Shafi took counsel with Afrasiyab about how to go about taming the contentious Turkman, but the wily Afrasiyab was in league with Hamadani to whom he conveyed all that transpired in the regent's camp. Together then they conspired to turn the tables on the Mirza and to destroy him.

Mirza Muhammad Shafi was too simple for the byzantine world of prevailing politics. In September, Hamadani sent word that he wished to submit, but first he would like a personal meeting with the regent. Friends warned Shafi that the Turkman was not sincere, but when a man's time draws near the best advice has no effect. The meeting was fixed for 23 September.

On the appointed day, as the Mirza was mounting his horse his turban accidentally fell to the ground. His attendants murmured. The incident was too ominous to be ignored but the regent called for an elephant and left amid much shaking of heads.

When Shafi neared the place fixed for the meeting, it was pointed out to him that Hamadani had brought a much larger escort than had been agreed, but the Mirza pushed on nonetheless.

Arriving at the appointed spot, he stood in his howdah to greet

Hamadani. The latter rose likewise. The elephants came alongside and Hamadani leaned forward and took Shafi's hands in his after the formal salaam. But the Turkman's grip was like a vice. His nephew Ismail, who was on another elephant, also moved closer, and jumping from his mount, dagger in hand, stabbed the immobilized regent. Muhammad Amin Khan, a relative of the Mirza, who was sitting behind him in the howdah, grappled with the assassin and they all rolled down to the ground.

In all, three were killed, the Mirza and two of his attendants who had tried to defend him. When the news spread there was a brief cannonade, but the shaken imperialists soon retreated, the treacherous Afrasiyab being the first to fly.

The Maratha vakil in the Mirza's camp summed up the position in a terse communication to Poona: 'Muhammad Shafi is dead. All Hindostan is lying bare. No sword is left for fighting.'[4]

The emperor was again without a keeper. The position was complicated by the presence of the English mission under Major James Browne in the imperial camp at Agra. Browne had been sent by Warren Hastings, Jaladat Jang, on a rather vague mission which had caused considerable unease at Delhi. The emperor feared that the English wanted to reduce him to the position of a ward, as they had done with Shuja.[5] He also now feared that, taking advantage of the vacuum created by the death of Mirza Shafi, Major Browne, might with the support of Afrasiyab, proclaim Mirza Suleiman Shukoh emperor with Afrasiyab as regent, and then combining forces with Hamadani, march on Delhi and depose him! It was necessary to preempt any such action.

Though Afrasiyab's complicity was suspected in the murder of Shafi, the emperor hastened to appoint him as the successor, and urgent messages were sent asking him to return to Delhi. Zain ul-Abdin did make an offer to purchase the regency for Rs. 3 lakh but his offer was ignored. In the meantime Afrasiyab had rallied the demoralized imperial camp. He made theatrical demonstrations of grief and vowed vengeance, all calculated to restore his credibility with Khadija Begum. Thereafter, on the quiet, he arranged for Hamadani's withdrawal to his jagirs near Dholpur, secretly promised to obtain for him the emperor's pardon, and authorized him to claim and take the entire Jaipur tribute—as Hamadani had demanded from Mirza Shafi.

It took Afrasiyab some time to reach Delhi as he had to secure Agra and place his agents in key positions in place of Mirza Shafi's. He reached Delhi on 14 December together with the prince and Abdul Ahad, the old favourite of Shah Alam. Besides his old titles of Majd ud-Daulah and Bahram Jang, more honorifics were showered on Abdul Ahad, such as Sharf-ud-Daulah, Umdat ul-Mulk, Madar ul-Mulk, Abdul Majid Khan Bahadur and Fateh Jang. If only by dressing out a man with the right titles one could produce the Man of Destiny!

Afrasiyab started out by imprisoning some of the late Mirza Najaf's officers and attaching their property. Some of the jagirs of Zain ul-Abdin, the brother of Mirza Shafi were transferred to his own son-in-law Qutb ud-Din, in the process creating another malcontent.

There was another Sikh incursion about this time led by Bhag Singh of Thanesar and Baghel Singh of Chalundi. The Sikhs poured into the Doab in search of loot, food and fodder. Zabita tried to resist but was defeated near Ghausgarh. The Sikhs then pushed further south into Meerut where they were joined by the discontented and recently dispossessed Zain ul-Abdin.

Within a week of his arrival in Delhi Afrasiyab set out for Meerut, again taking the prince with him, much as a modern regiment might take its pet mascot. Zain ul-Abdin was conciliated, the decision regarding his Meerut jagirs being left to the emperor's arbitration. The Sikhs retreated. They were not out for conquest but merely looking for subsistence in a parched famine-stricken land. There was little serious fighting. Afrasiyab returned with his army, arriving in Delhi on 28 January.

It did not take long for Afrasiyab's relations with the emperor to sour a second time. His financial position had by no means improved between his first and second term, and he was in no better position to pay the succession fee, or even the monthly subsistence for the imperial household.

Afrasiyab proposed an expedition against Jaipur to enforce the payment of the promised tribute. He wanted Shah Alam to accompany him but could not pay for the expenses of the emperor's train, and the latter, more intent on embarassing his umara and highlighting their failings than accomplishing anything, had no intention of helping out. He also wanted to be assured that his regent could make proper arrangements for the maintenance of the rest of the imperial family and its dependents during his absence. Thus, the plan fizzled out.

Major Browne had effected a conciliation between the Jat raja and the late Shafi over the question of the town and fortress of Biyana, for which the raja undertook to pay Rs. 90,000 which sum was actually deposited with the major. But Afrasiyab refused to confirm the agreement. He demanded more. So the deal fell through.

About this time—14 April 1784—occurred the curious flight of Mirza Jawan Bakht. Nothing illustrates so well the vacuity of life in the Qila-i-Mualla as this incident. Twenty-five years earlier, his father, the young Shah Alam, had also fled Delhi, but the circumstances on that occasion were entirely different. For his part Jawan Bakht had simply got tired of a pointless existence. During the long years of his father's exile he had deputized for him in the Qila-i-Mualla. The real master, of course, was Najib and he merely a puppet. One might have hoped that things would change with the return of the absent master, but they had not. Life seemed to have got set in a standard format. The padishah reigned, his wazir—or rather the deputy, for the real wazir was an absentee—ruled. And latterly it seemed these substitute wazirs seemed to be having difficulty in governing what remained of the empire of Delhi. Indeed, words like empire, padishah or emperor sound embarrassingly pretentious for the shrunken realm of Badshah Shah Alam.

The prince has been described as a young man of spirit, and his objective in fleeing to British territory appears to have been to seek the help of the foreigners to rid Shah Alam of Afrasiyab and enable him to govern effectively with British support. Warren Hastings was at first tempted to intervene but the certainty of opposition from his Council at Calcutta restrained him. Eventually the incident turned out to be of no consequence, merely an indication of the emptiness of life in the Exalted Fort, the so-called Refuge of all the World, and of the naivete of the prince. Until his meeting with Major Browne—who had at last been received by Shah Alam on 5 February—Jawan Bakht had not met any officer of the East India Company. In the course of that audience, the prince is reported to have observed,

> that not having been with the Shah at Allahabad [he] had only heard of the loyalty of the English, but. . . in future he doubted not that he should see the Effects of it, since they had made professions to that purport and were a Nation famous for Veracity.[6]

The English wanted to send the prince back in proper state with an English escort, but Mahadji Scindia was opposed. He eventually did return in 1787 but not before Ghulam Qadir had blinded his father. He was thus again entrusted with the role of his father's deputy, but failing to receive the necessary support he left, and died at Banaras on 1 June 1788. It was his younger brother who was ultimately destined to sit on their father's throne.

Abdul Ahad's hand was suspected to be behind an attempt to murder

Afrasiyab. This finally led to the fall of that over-clever minister. Afrasiyab had him arrested and confined in Aligarh. The emperor looked on helplessly, powerless to help Ahad. Now, though it was the height of summer, Afrasiyab hustled the emperor into accompanying him on an expedition to Agra for the purpose of crushing Hamadani.

Hamadani was his erstwhile friend who had done the dirty work which had enabled Afrasiyab to return to power. He had promised to procure for Hamadani the emperor's pardon, but now he was marching against this old friend. Outraged by this treachery, Hamadani revolted and started plundering the countryside. When Shah Alam arrived at Agra, he did not even care to pay his respects. Afrasiyab was never regarded as much of a general and he knew that Hamadani would be a hard nut to crack. So he sought the assistance of Mahadji Scindia.

The latter was not in the imperial service and expected to be paid for his aid. He pushed ahead, occupied Hamadani's jagirs and some other mahals but declined to hand them over to Afrasiyab until his huge army was compensated. Himmat Bahadur confessed that there was little likelihood of getting any money out of Afrasiyab. So the Maratha chief held on to his gains. Eventually, however, a reconciliation was effected and the Maratha decided to effect a junction with the imperialists at Rupbas. All this took time. Afrasiyab and Shah Alam had left Delhi towards the end of June. Thereafter the monsoons set in and it was not until October that they could return.

Hamadani had antagonized all the neighbouring potentates and Mahadji Scindia's diplomacy now wove them into an intricate net to isolate him. The latter had tried to buy off Scindia, offering him Agra and all the territory to the south, if he remained neutral. But Scindia was not after mere territory. He was playing for higher stakes. Steadily the noose was tightened around Hamadani. The Maratha moved his divisions to close all the escape routes and Hamadani's supplies were cut.

It was decided to engage the rebel in battle on the 3 or 4 November. But Afrasiyab's fate was to be decided before the battle. There were other men besides Hamadani gunning for him.

Mirza Shafi had been murdered by Muhammad Beg Hamadani. Afrasiyab was also implicated in the plot. But the former had made himself much more odious to Shafi's family through subsequent actions. First there was the move to appropriate for his son-in-law the jagirs of Zain ul-Abdin. A compromise had been effected on that issue, but the subsequent demand was impertinent and insulting. Afrasiyab asked for the hand of Mirza Najaf's daughter Fatima, who had earlier been affianced to Mirza Shafi.

Afrasiyab had entered the household of Mirza Najaf as a slave. He was by birth a Hindu, and the son of a mere grocer. That he should have dared to ask for the hand of his master's daughter in whose veins ran the sacred blood of the Martyr Ali and the imperial Safavids of Iran was intolerable. The Persians had always been conscious of their race and India in the late eighteenth century was very different from the India of the thirteenth century when one Turkish Sultan after another gave his daughter and his throne to his favourite mameluke.

Zain ul-Abdin was—after Begum Khadija, of course—the eldest of the late Mirza's family. It was upto him to avenge the insult. He had been directly behind the murder attempt which failed in March—the same which led to the arrest and confinement of Abdul Ahad—and he was ready once again for a fresh attempt. With the Maratha army close at hand, he felt the chance was opportune.

On 2 November 1784, early in the morning, Afrasiyab rode out to reconnoitre the positions occupied by Hamadani's army, and while returning dropped in at Himmat Bahadur's tent where he played a game of chess. After about an hour he left for his own tent. Here he dismissed all his officers who were in attendance. All left but four, including Zain ul-Abdin. Then one man came forward with an application. As the bakhshi was reading the application the applicant pulled out his dagger and stabbed him in the chest. At once there was a tumult. The assassin was cut down by servants, but the deed was done. Afrasiyab tottered a few steps and fell down, bleeding profusely. Seeing that the bakhshi was finished, Zain ul-Abdin left the tent, mounted a horse and galloped towards the Maratha lines.[7]

It was early afternoon when he arrived at Scindia's tent. The general was taking his siesta and had to be roused and informed that there was an officer from the imperial camp bringing dreadful news, and that the man sought sanctuary as he was innocent of the outrage but feared that he would be suspected of complicity.

The news was sensational. Scindia refused to receive Zain and ordered him to be kept under guard. In a few hours the news was confirmed. Meanwhile he took steps to prevent a surprise attack by Hamadani or a general plundering of the now leaderless camp by the soldiers and camp followers themselves.

The news of the audacious assault spread panic in the imperial camp. The first worry of the soldiers was for their pay. With their employer dead, who would undertake to pay their salaries? Some attempt was made, therefore, to conceal the death, it being given out at first that the general had been wounded. But such news cannot be kept secret for long and Scindia undertook to take up the soldiers' case with the emperor lest they mutiny and disperse. By a judicious disbursement of some money from his own resources, he won over the contingents of Himmat Bahadur and Raja Narayan Das, and the damage was contained.

Hamadani also tried to exploit the situation. His agents tried to seduce the imperialist soldiers. He sent an emissary to the Maratha general pleading for peace but Scindia demanded the surrender of all his guns, elephants, horses and camels, after which he could leave with his family for whichever place he wanted. Hamadani refused; he would rather die fighting than surrender on such humiliating terms.

So on 7 November Scindia tightened the noose and the cannonade began. He possessed overwhelming superiority in artillery and relied on the pulverizing effect of his fire to annihilate Hamadani whose soldiers, tired and hungry, had little fight left in them. They had already consumed the bulk of the animals in their camp and, as the Maratha grapeshot started cutting them down, they deserted and surrendered in droves. Finally, three days later, Muhammad Beg admitted defeat and surrendered. All his guns and property were seized and he was taken into the service of Scindia under conditions which left him incapable of mischief.

As for Zain ul-Abdin, his guilt was established and he was confined in Gwalior fort by Scindia till his death.

Of the four successors to the heritage of Mirza Najaf, Afrasiyab Khan and Mirza Shafi were dead, while Hamadani's power had been destroyed. Najaf Quli alone survived, but he was dissipating himself in drink and debauchery. Moreover, unlike the others, he had never been in the race to become the emperor's keeper. Thanks to Zain ul-Abdin, the road was at last wide open for Mahadji Scindia. As Brown observed, 'from Gujerat to Jumboo, and from Aittock to Rohilcund, there is no power but Scindia and the Seiks, everything else is but a Name.'[8]

NOTES

1. Ghulam Ali, *Muqaddamah-i-Shah Alam Namah*, iii, pp. 152-4. Sarkar, *Fall of the Mughal Empire*, iii, p. 146.
2. Ghulam Ali, ibid., pp. 161-5. Munna Lal, *Tarikh-i-Shah Alam*, pp. 256-62.
3. Munna Lal, ibid., p. 272.
4. Parasnis, *Dilli-yethil Marathyanchin Raj-Karenen* (*DY*), i, p. 91.
5. Bhargava, *Browne Correspondence*, letter 49, p. 104.
6. Ibid., letter 58, p. 119.
7. Ibid., letters 109, 110, 115; pp. 215-16, 221. Sarkar, iii, pp. 167-70.
8. Bhargava, letter 114, p. 223.

CHAPTER 40

The Regency of Mahadji Scindia

Mahadji had acted not a moment too soon. In the bare week that interved between the assassination of Afrasiyab and the destruction of Hamadani, the anti-Maratha party made desperate attempts to find an alternative. One suggestion was to call Hamadani. Himmat Bahadur and Narayan Das—Afrasiyab's diwan—on the other hand proposed that Afrasiyab's son, a child of three, be made the nominal regent with the two of them wielding real power. And then there was another wife of Afrasiyab, an imperious Afghan lady who had no son of her own, but was willing to adopt a suitable infant and rule through him! Besides, there was also a party in favour of Zain ul-Abdin. The politics of the Durbar-i-Mualla had reached the level of the absurd![1]

The emperor himself had set his heart on his old favourite, Abdul Ahad, at the time confined in Aligarh. He had been an English agent and Major Browne strongly supported his candidature. Accordingly he was sent for.

Agra lay between Aligarh and the imperial camp and Abdul Ahad made the mistake of halting and calling on his old friend, Raja Daya Ram. The news reached Shuja Dil Khan, the qiladar of Agra fort, who happened to be the father of Afrasiyab's Afghan begum, and thus an interested party. Even though Abdul Ahad was proceeding to the Urdu-i-Mualla on an imperial summons, Shuja Dil Khan arrested him and made him his prisoner!

When the news reached Shah Alam, he was furious, and declaring that Mahadji was his only loyal subject, appealed to him to come to his rescue. Scindia, flattered, requested His Majesty to advance to Fatehpur Sikri where he sent baggage animals and carts with a suitable escort to bring him to his camp, which was at Khanua where the Rajput chivalry, led by Maharana Sanga, had been routed in 1526 by Babar.

On 14 November Scindia's presentation took place. It was a date specially chosen for its auspicious connotation, being the first of Muharram. The usual ceremonies were performed. The emperor, all graciousness, out of consideration for the Maratha's lameness, asked him to sit down on the carpet with him. As was the custom, at the first meeting only polite civilities were exchanged, but in the days that followed, the details of how Scindia could be associated with the imperial government were fully discussed.

It had long been Scindia's ambition to take the emperor under his protection and govern the empire in his name. In 1772 he seemed to have nearly achieved this goal when he occupied Delhi and escorted Shah Alam home from Allahabad. But the troubles that broke out in the Maratha heartland after the death of Peshwa Madhav Rao forced him to withdraw, and he was unable to return to Hindostan for the next eleven years. The opportunity had presented itself again, but he knew that the problems that he would now have to face were far greater. The fragmented Indian polity, the increasing recalcitrance of local chiefs and the imperial umara, the severity of the late famine, and the uncertainty of support from Poona, had made the burden of the regency so much more onerous. The financial problems were the most serious. Not only was the emperor bankrupt but Mahadji Scindia, after months of campaigning in Bundelkhand, and the long drawn out siege of Gwalior, was very nearly in the same position and owed his troops nearly Rs. 80 lakh.

But he agreed to be regent. His own proposal was that his master, the peshwa, should be the titular Vakil-i-Mutlaq while he would exercise authority as his deputy, but the emperor felt this would not be workable as the peshwa was too remote. He, thus, insisted on granting the office directly to Scindia. The peshwa was instead appointed the emperor's deputy—*naib-i-munaib*[2]—with the inferior office of mir bakhshi, again with Scindia as his deputy for the latter office. The assumption by Scindia of the office of vakil would give rise to suspicions in Poona, which Nana Fadnavis fully exploited to create problems for Mahadji later.

The special durbar for investing Scindia with the robes and insignia of office was held on 2 December after which the new regent moved to Dig with the emperor. The fort of Dig was held by an agent of the murdered Afrasiyab who readily submitted, but thereafter Scindia ran into difficulties. The fort of Agra was held by Shuja Dil Khan, father of Afrasiyab's Afghan wife, who refused submission. It soon became evident that Scindia would have to fight every inch of the way to establish his authority. Afrasiyab and Muhammad Shafi, on the other hand, had not experienced any such difficulty after the initial coup, but Mahadji was a Maratha and a rank outsider to the Delhi-based umara. He was not even a Muslim, and his elevation to the highest rank and office seemed to these proud nobles, whose ancestors had come from Iran or Turan, the ultimate subversion of the ascendancy of Islam in Hindostan.

For two months Shuja Dil held out, but as the imperial guns began to have effect, his detachments started deserting as Scindia (himself owing nearly Rs. 1 crore to his troops!) had promised them service and their arrears. Finally, on 27 March, he capitulated and surrendered on being promised a suitable jagir.

The regent did his best to conciliate the family of the late Afrasiyab. His infant son, the three-year old Khadim Hussain Khan, was on Shuja Dil's request dignified with the resounding titles of Hussain ud-Daulah, Khadim Hussain Khan, Ghalib Jang and Ashraf ud-Daulah II, the latter being his late father's title, besides a jagir of Rs. 4 lakh per annum. In return Scindia expected the family to play fair and surrender the imperial property which had been in their charge, some of it since the days of Mirza Najaf's dictatorship.

That they had no such intention became plain when Scindia sent a force to take possession of the fort of Aligarh where the bulk of Afrasiyab's treasure was supposedly hidden. The qiladar, Jahangir Khan, refused to submit and the imperialists settled down to a long siege.

The emperor had, in the meantime, proceeded to Delhi while the regent established his field headquarters at Mathura, conveniently close to his base in central India. But as the siege dragged on, and winter drew near, Scindia became alarmed. In October he took the emperor with him and marched in person against Aligarh. Eventually, in November, the fort surrendered, but Scindia was shocked to discover that the reputed treasure, rumoured to be worth Rs. 1 crore, had disappeared. Only Rs. 40,000 were produced. Evidently, the qiladar had, in the course of the siege, successfully smuggled out most of it.[3]

This was highly embarrassing, specially as the emperor himself was present. At the time of the capture of Pathargarh in 1772 the bulk of the treasure had been plundered by the Marathas and very little could be recovered. This time too Scindia feared his enemies would accuse him of the same, though nothing of the sort had happened. Convinced that the treasure had either been smuggled out or concealed, the regent ordered searches, and interrogations began. Female slaves were sent to search the ladies of Afrasiyab's harem. In the course of these some of the Crown jewels were recovered, besides interesting letters which showed that Jahangir Khan had been encouraged in his resistance among theirs by Himmat Bahadur Gossain, members of Afrasiyab's family, and also the nawab-wazir Asaf ud-Daulah. Appeals for succour had been made to Lucknow and to the English at Anupshahar. General Cummings, who commanded the brigade at the latter station, even made a hostile demonstration which drew a strong protest from Scindia. Thereafter, many of the late regent's officers were imprisoned and their estates seized, while Scindia swore that all Hindostanis, Hindu or Muslim, were equally faithless and could not be relied upon.

While Scindia was still engaged in reducing Agra, he had dispatched Ambaji Ingle to take possession of Delhi and appointed him faujdar of the capital. Najaf Quli, the sole survivor of Mirza Najaf's generals, readily accepted the new situation and did not resist, but the turbulent Gujjars who inhabited the surrounding countryside, had to be suppressed with an iron hand. The Delhi Gujjars had always shown a marked recalcitrant propensity, and during the years of anarchy that followed the death of Mirza Najaf, had become increasingly bold. Ambaji struck with a ruthlessness that would have done credit to an Abdali or a Najib. Four Gujjar villages were sacked and their male population slaughtered, several hundred being publicly executed in the city to set an example, and shock the rest into quiescence.[4]

Some Sikh sardars of the Panipat district also called on Ambaji, and an understanding was reached on the vexed subject of *rakhi*. Two of them accompanied Ambaji to Mathura where they met Scindia who ratified the agreement initialled by his general.

Throughout most of 1785 another Maratha army, commanded by Khandoji Ingle (Ambaji's brother) and Hamadani, had been operating in Khichiwara, where the Khichi Chauhans of Raghogarh, a small principality created in the reign of Akbar, had encroached upon some Maratha villages. The state was ultimately extinguished, the raja, Balwant Singh, being detained in Gwalior while the rest of his family was kept at Bhilsa. One of his sons, Jai Singh, however, remained at large and carried on a prolonged resistance, rendering the Deccan road unsafe.

After the discovery of the perfidious correspondence between Jahangir Khan, Narayan Dass and Himmat Bahadur, Scindia ordered the arrest of Narayan in January 1786. He shrank at first from striking at Himmat, who was a Brahmin, and called upon him and his brother to surrender their jagirs which were worth Rs. 20 lakh a year. He also undertook to take their soldiers into his service, and allotted small jagirs in Vrindaban and Jhansi for their maintenance.

But the two brothers were not inclined to part with their command. They had been born and bred to war, and their adoptive father, Rajinder Giri, had seen service under Safdar Jang more than thirty years earlier. First Umrao Gir revolted and soon, in March 1786, he was joined by Himmat Bahadur. The two threatened to throw the Doab once again into turmoil, and for a time the fate of the Maratha garrison at Aligarh hung in the balance. But with the dispatch of additional forces under Ambaji Ingle, the rebellion was broken and the two Gossains took refuge in Awadh. But when Mahadji suffered his reverse at Lalsot in the subsequent Jaipur campaign, they again took the field and invaded the Doab.

During 1785-6, another Maratha army under Apa Khande Rao, Mahadji's governor at Gwalior, had been operating in eastern Bundelkhand, trying to exploit the ever-smouldering warfare among the descendents of Chhattrasal Bundela. At first there were some successes, but eventually he got bogged down, his funds ran out and his soldiers mutinied. It was with difficulty that he extricated himself. The troops had been deployed for nineteen months in difficult country, and at the end he had nothing to show except a massive debt.

But Mahadji's biggest challenge was the reduction of Jaipur. The military reputation of Mirza Najaf had foundered before its stout walls which had also defied Mahbub Ali Khan. Ironically, Sawai Pratap Singh, its ruler of the day, was one of the most contemptible princes to sit on the *gaddi* of the Kachhwahas of Jaipur-Amber. During his minority his mother, the Chundawatni rani, was the nominal regent and the diwanship, for the most part, alternated between two persons, Khushhali Ram Bohra and Daulat Ram Haldia. But real power was concentrated in persons as variegated as a tailor, a Brahmin who looked after the raja's supply of *Gangajal*, and an elephant driver!

Even after the raja had attained his majority, his habits were odd. He was fond of dancing, and, in the privacy of the zenana, would don the dress of a female dancer and try the steps with anklet bells! His companions were low characters, in whose company he indulged in wild pranks reminiscent of Shakespeare's young Prince Hal. He was a transvestite, and, disgusted by his vices, the proud Rajput nobles forsook his court for their country seats.[5]

A state governed by such a prince should have been an easy walk-over for any aggressor, but the capital of the Kachhwahas was blessed with stout walls and a near impregnable fort. By the simple expedient of abandoning the defence of his country and hiding behind his walls, he had frustrated the army which Najaf had sent against him, and he would adopt the same simple 'strategy' against Scindia.

After the capture of Aligarh, Mahadji turned to Jaipur. Taking the emperor with him he marched upto Dig where he camped for a month, and then moved on to Lalsot, closer to Jaipur. The Rao Raja of Macheri, Pratap Singh 'the Naruka', had been sent by Scindia a month in advance to open negotiations. He returned to Lalsot accompanied by the agents of the Jaipur prince, Khushhali Ram Bohra and Balaji Mahant, the latter being the spiritual guru of the late Raja Madho Singh. At the first meeting the mahant was received with extraordinary honours, or rather it was Scindia who went to meet him. The mahant, who was dressed in the usual garb of Brahminical sanctity, remained seated as Mahadji entered the tent, but he graciously stretched out his foot for the regent to kiss. The Maratha chief was not lacking in manners. Taking the foot in his hand he reverentially rubbed his forehead against the sacred toes of the sadhu![6]

But despite this abasement the negotiations failed. The Jaipur envoys did make an offer, but they wanted the release of the mahals occupied by the Naruka on behalf of the emperor, and a deduction for the damage caused by the military manoeuvres, and of course the arrears would be cleared slowly by annual instalments. But the Naruka who had no inclination to release the mahals, urged the regent to press for more, saying the sum offered was too small and below his dignity to accept.

The Jaipur agents offered Rs. 10 lakh in full and final settlement while Scindia, egged on by the Macheri raja, insisted that his dues were Rs. 3 crore and 40 lakh! Khushhali Ram protested, 'We don't have that many pebbles, how can we produce so many rupees!' But eventually after much negotiation the dues were reduced to Rs. 63 lakh. It was decided that Rs. 11 lakh would be paid within six months and, of the remaining Rs. 52 lakh, Rs. 20 lakh would be met by the cession of land, and the rest was to be raised from the feudatories of Jaipur.[7]

Of this large sum Rs. 3 lakh was paid immediately, and the remaining Rs. 8 lakh raised by squeezing Roda Ram, the tailor, and other rich men of the city. The first instalment having been discharged by the end of May 1786, Mahadji returned with Shah Alam, leaving behind the Rao Raja of Macheri, Najaf Quli and Rayaji Patil to collect the second.

The remainder of the year was passed in Delhi with the regent struggling with financial problems. The famine was still not over and it was impossible to collect the revenue.

The emperor's subsistence money, which the regent was bound to pay, was in arrears by five months, and Scindia was driven almost to desperation. But this did not prevent him from spending vast sums on religious ceremonies and feeding Brahmins at Vrindaban in his efforts to beget a son. And, of course, the Jaipur durbar failed to pay the second instalment. Neither Najaf Quli nor the Macheri raja were conspicuous for their energy, and the force with them—a contingent of 5,000 Maratha horse—was not strong enough to intimidate Jaipur. From December 1786 onwards the Rajputs became more impudent and aggressive.

In January 1787 Khushhali Ram Bohra, who favoured a soft line towards the Marathas, was dismissed and replaced by Daulat Ram Haldia, who advocated a more aggressive policy. Relations between the durbar and the regent were further strained on account of the rejection of Scindia's proposal for the marriage of his little daughter to the young raja. Obviously the Kachhwahas did not consider the proposed alliance good enough for their young chief. In comparison with the Kachhwahas, the Scindias were upstarts and their pretensions to Kshatriya status were scornfully dismissed by the lords of Rajputana.

In March 1787, after careful deliberation, the regent again took the field against Jaipur. As on the former occasion, he proceeded via Dig where the agents of the Jaipur court awaited him. Rayaji Patil and Rana Khan Bhai—another of his most loyal and trusted generals—counselled moderation, but again, as before, the Rao Raja and the dismissed Khushhali Ram Bohra fed his vanity by urging him to insist on an unrealistically high figure. The Rao Raja apprehended that if the regent failed in securing adequate money from Jaipur, he might turn on him and force him to relinquish his encroachments on imperial crown lands. As for Bohra, he was burning to avenge himself against Haldia who had seized all his property after his dismissal. Scindia appears to have lost his judgement and allowed himself to be persuaded into a crazy scheme to depose Raja Pratap Singh and replace him with the infant Man Singh, a posthumous son of the late Raja Pirthi Singh. According to the strict application of the rule of primogeniture, Man Singh should have succeeded his father, but since his mother would then have become the regent—and that would not have suited the Chundawat widow of Madho Singh—the infant's claims were brushed aside and he lived out his life in exile.

The talks failed. The Rajputs were insincere. The negotiations were only a ploy to enable the feudal levies of the Jaipur court to be mobilized. About 20,000 soldiers were thus collected and a contingent of Rathor horse was sent by his ally, the raja of Marwar. Some of the 'Mughal' (i.e. Turki) captains in Scindia's service were also bought over by the Rajputs, the most notable being Muhammad Beg Hamadani, who crossed over on 25 May and was engaged by the Jaipur raja at Rs. 3,000 a day, and given the responsibility of organizing the defence.[8]

The defection of Muhammad Beg immediately put Scindia on the defensive. His old distrust of 'Hindostanis' was confirmed, and fearing that in the event of a battle his northern troops would most probably turn against him, his efforts were directed at avoiding a pitched battle at all cost. He, therefore, hunkered down at Lalsot and decided to wait for reinforcements before offering battle. He had sent urgent calls to Ambaji Ingle and Khande Rao, the latter still besieging hill-forts in Bundelkhand.

At the same time the Rajputs were also relying more on intimidation, and were equally anxious to avoid action. They knew only too well that their feudal levies, armed mainly with sword and lance, were no match for the trained battalions of de Boigne and other European mercenaries. Their artillery was also hopelessly obsolete.

Khande Rao arrived with 10,000 veterans from Bundelkhand on 26 June. Besides the usual Maratha horse, the force included two of de Boigne's sepoy battalions and 2,000 fighting Naga sadhus. Now feeling more confident, Mahadji moved up his divisions to come to grips with the enemy, but it would be a month before the final battle took place.

For the next few weeks minor skirmishing continued between patrols of the opposing hosts. On 16 July the little daughter of Mahadji died after a short illness. The fond father was plunged in grief and for a few days was oblivious to the world. At first Scindia fixed the 21 July as the date for the battle, but later changed it as the astrologers felt the date was inauspicious.

On 23 July the little fort of Bidakha, which lay on the Morel river and blocked the line of advance, was attacked and forced to surrender. Although this action at Bidakha took place virtually under the nose of the main Rajput army, there was only a token demonstration in support of the stronghold. But the situation was getting more and more untenable even for Scindia. Food was short, the soldiers mutinous, and the situation ominously reminiscent of Panipat. Scindia ultimately decided on battle and distributed Rs. 5 lakh among his troops to infuse some cheer into them. About the time a taunting challenge was also received from Sawai Pratap Singh, which the regent accepted, and 26 July was again fixed as the date of the battle. The engagement which ensued is generally known as the battle of Lalsot, even though Lalsot was 14 miles away and, as Sarkar points out, it should be called the battle of Tunga, being fought between the villages of Bidakha and Tunga.

At the puja, the night before, Scindia had the *prasad* distributed among his generals. He slept for only two hours. The imperialists began their advance early in the morning. At about nine the cannonade began. The Rajput guns were heavier and inflicted more damage on account of their greater calibre and range. After about two hours the shelling stopped, and the Rathor cavalry, intoxicated with opium, and frenziedly shouting its battle cry of '*Han*! *Han*!', charged the imperialists at full gallop. The imperialist line trembled under the shock of this charge, and even gave way at some points, but the Marathas held on, and when their artillery had moved up they repulsed the Rajputs.

Early in the battle Muhammad Beg Hamadani was killed by a rebounding cannon ball which tore up his side. With their general killed, the Mughal troops in the Rajput camp did not stir thereafter. There were some cavalry sorties in the remaining part of the day but in general both sides stood on the defensive, the imperialists coming to know of Hamadani's death too late to exploit it.

Thus night fell. It was a drawn battle though both sides claimed a victory. But Scindia certainly derived no advantage. His position remained as before. In fact it became more desperate than ever, as his mutinous soldiery could no longer be kept in check. They clamoured for their dues, and when on 30 July news came that a large convoy of grain had been intercepted by enemy scouts, the sepoys rose and gheraoed their officers, insisting on payment. Scindia tried to resist but the contagion spread and other battalions and divisions followed suit. Then Scindia desperately tried to placate them, and even offered them his wives' jewellery, which was scornfully rejected, the soldiers insisting on cash. Eventually some of the units accepted part payment, but a body of 7,000 'Hindostani' and some 'Mughal' troops refused to be placated and marched off with their artillery towards the Rajput camp, where they were welcomed by Ismail Beg—nephew of the late Hamadani—and others who had defected earlier.[9]

On 1 August Scindia began his retreat. It was an orderly withdrawal and nothing illustrates better his genius than this successful extrication of a frustrated and mutinous army through hostile territory. There was no panic and he succeeded in keeping the soldiers together, marching them in close formation, held tight together, while simultaneously fighting off the exultant Rajputs who were always on his flanks.

He first headed for Dig as his family was there. After sending them off to his stronghold of Gwalior under a strong escort, with all the heavier artillery and stores, he again turned to face the enemy.

NOTES

1. Bhargava, *Browne Correspondence*, letter 113, pp. 220-1. Sarkar, *Fall of the Mughal Empire*, iii, pp. 175-8.
2. Parasnis, *Dilli-yethil Marathyanchin Raj-Karenen*, i, pp. 106, 133.
3. Sarkar, iii, pp. 185-6. Parasnis, i, p. 141.
4. Sarkar, iii, p. 187.

5. Tod, *Annals and Antiquities of Rajasthan*, ii, pp. 301-3.
6. Sarkar, iii, p. 206.
7. Ibid., p. 207. Khairuddin, *Ibrat Nama*, ii, p. 155.
8. Parasnis, i, pp. 220, 221.
9. Sarkar iii, p. 230.

CHAPTER 41

Ghulam Qadir: His Rise and Fall

The battle of Tunga took place on 26 July 1787, and on 1 August the regent commenced his retreat. He reached Dig ten days later, but in those few days the reverse he had suffered was magnified by rumour into a debacle, and its news spread all over the country. Malcontents immediately raised their heads, and before the month was out Scindia's imperial master had been overawed into replacing him with a daring usurper.

Ghulam Qadir Khan was Zabita Khan's son. The father had reconciled himself to his condition and loyally supported Najaf, regarding him as the saviour of his family. Najibabad and Pathargarh had been lost to Shuja ud-Daulah and after the imperial campaign of Ghausgarh the family had lost all its possessions. But the magnanimous Najaf had restored to the Rohilla his old jagir of Saharanpur, thus earning his everlasting gratitude.

Ghulam Qadir was however different from his father. He had probably suffered personal indignities in the brief captivity that he had undergone, for which he nursed an abiding grudge against the imperial house. A Pathan will have his revenge, and as soon as the news of Scindia's difficulties before Lalsot reached him, Ghulam Qadir saw his chance. He thought of himself as an avenging angel; *Kahar-i-Khuda*, or God's own scourge was the honorific he arrogated to himself and the revenge he took was savage.[1] At no time in the history of the dynasty had the denizens of the Qila-i-Mualla been handled with such cruel disdain. Not even at the hands of Abdali or Nadir, nor even Imad ul-Mulk, had they suffered the indignities and barbaric treatment meted out by this Rohilla. Veritably, for them, it was the day of judgement.

Mahadji Scindia had summoned Ambaji Ingle to his assistance after the defection of Muhammad Beg Hamadani. The withdrawal of the Maratha troops encouraged Ghulam Qadir to drive out the Maratha collectors from the Doab, and when the news of Scindia's retreat became known, the Rohilla thought his hour had struck. He swore that he would supplant the Maratha interloper and become the dictator of the Delhi empire, like his father and grandfather before him.

Scindia was represented in Delhi at the time by his son-in-law, Ladoji Deshmukh Sithole and Shah Nizam ud-Din, a fakir of distinguished descent. Neither was a soldier. After Ambaji's departure there was with the emperor only the fort garrison, whose men had become more accustomed to sitting around than fighting. Moreover the Rohilla had also a secret ally in the harem nazir, the eunuch Mansur Ali Khan. The latter claimed to have saved the life of Ghulam Qadir at the time of the capture of Ghausgarh by throwing his shawl over the young boy in a protective gesture.[2] Mansur also bitterly resented the Maratha ascendancy. Most of the palace officials were, in fact, opposed to Scindia. There were others too, nursing a hatred and bitterness as consuming and malignant as the Rohilla's, and they were members of the imperial family itself. The dreary cells of the salatin khana, housed many princes who had as good a right to the throne as Shah Alam, and who only lived in the hope of one day seeing him humbled.

Imad ul-Mulk had placed Alamgir II on the throne after murdering Ahmad Shah in 1762. Alamgir represented a rival line, and, were primogeniture and legitimacy as strictly regarded in the orient as in the west, he and his descendents could well be regarded as usurpers. Though this was not the sole consideration, it was natural that the descendents of the ousted line should nurse a sense of grievance, specially since their vacuous lives afforded them few distractions. Shah Alam had put aside a sizable private fortune during his exile in the east when the Bengal tribute and the surplus revenues of Allahabad, Kora and Kura yielded him a substantial income. But he was so miserly that even in times of need he was loath to open his purse strings, insisting always that it was the function of the regent to look after him and his family. Thus at times the salatin did not even get their usual wretched fare. They would then raise such a deafening clamour that it penetrated even to the diwan khanas, much like the 'howls of ravenous beasts in a neglected zoo', as Jadunath Sarkar puts it.[3]

Yet nothing may have possibly happened but for the unslaked fires smouldering in the breasts of two ageing harpies, the Begums Malika-i-Zamani and Sahiba Mahal, Muhammad Shah's widows who lived in ample comfort in mansions outside the fort. They were relatively rich, had ample private fortunes of their own, and Malika-i-Zamani sent word to the avenging Rohilla that she was ready to pay him Rs. 12 lakh as the price of restoring the throne of Hind to her grandson, Bidar Bakht.[4] With these two women eager to pour their vials of hate into the witches' cauldron, the stage was set for the consequent tragedy and its attendant horrors.

On 21 August the Rohilla reached Baghpat, not far from Delhi with his army and sent a message to the emperor demanding an interview. Sithole and Shah Nizam ud-Din were in a quandry. If they had simply decided to sit out the siege, nothing may have happened. The forces of the Rohilla were weak, and the Yamuna in flood. It would have been easy to defend the line of the river, and the fort was well provisioned.

But Shah Nizam ud-Din decided to play the soldier. He sent a small force of raw levies across the river where there was already a small Maratha force under Madho Rao Phalke. These raw recruits were driven back into the river. Phalke tried to come to their rescue, but his force was weak, and he shut himself up in the fortalice of Shahdara, surrendering a few days later.

This brief encounter occurred in full view of the public. The failure of the pitiful imperial sally was the signal for the canaille of Delhi to riot and plunder the bazaars. The emperor, thereupon, sent his confidential slave at night to open talks with the Rohilla. Ladoji Deshmukh and Shah Nizam ud-Din fled, taking what money and valuables they could carry, but the mob looted twenty of their camels. The emperor confiscated Shah Nizam ud-Din's house and arrested his brother.[5]

Three days later Ghulam Qadir crossed the Yamuna and, occupying the mansion vacated by Shah Nizam ud-Din, established his control over the city. His emissaries opened negotiations with the Qila-i-Mualla.

On 5 September he was received in audience by the emperor in the Diwani-i-Khas. The Rohilla was drunk, and it was with blood-shot eyes, and a breath that reeked of liquor, that he swaggered into the audience chamber. The chamberlains whispered to the emperor that Ghulam Qadir was unfit for any office of state, but the terrified sovereign replied that it could not be helped.[6]

At any rate, Zabita's son was vested with the offices held by his late father, namely, that of Bakhshi-ul-Mumalik with its attached title of Amir-ul-Umara, and the additional honorific of Raushan-ud-Daulah Bahadur.

But the Rohilla was not in undisputed control. There was the disciplined brigade of Begum Samru—to whom had passed the command after the death of her husband, Walter Reinhardt (le 'Sombre' or 'Samru'). The doughty old lady refused to take orders from the Rohilla, and since there was already bad blood between the two (Ghulam Qadir having designs on her jagir of Sardhana), the new bakhshi thought it prudent to leave Delhi to aggrandize himself in the Doab. On this occasion Sardar Bhanga Singh of Thanesar also distinguished himself in the emperor's defence, joining hands with Begum Samru to man the walls of the fort and the outer defences.

A month later Ghulam Qadir was back and started shelling the fort from the far side of the Yamuna. Not much damage could have been caused by such a distant cannonade, but on 30 October several large shells fell in the courtyard of the Diwan-i-Am, killing a child. The terrified emperor dashed off an appeal to Scindia who dispatched Ambaji Ingle to bring the emperor to his camp. Ambaji was received in audience on 14 November, but by then Shah Alam had changed his mind. He was too overawed by the Rohilla, and reports about Scindia were not re-assuring. Wrongly concluding that Scindia was finished, he refused to quit the palace and the baffled Ambaji had to return without him. At the same time, the harem nazir, Mansur Ali Khan, was able to obtain an order from the wretched emperor forbidding Scindia from approaching Delhi!

How was Mahadji faring in meantime? He had been able to reach Dig more or less unmolested, the Kachhwahas being glad to see him out of their territory. Thereafter, Sawai Pratap Singh turned towards Macheri in an effort to recover the *mahals* in the latter's possession.

The Mughal and Hindustani troops who had deserted Scindia to join the Rajputs had not got much from their deal. Muhammad Beg Hamadani had been killed at Tunga, and the mantle of their leadership had fallen on his nephew, the equally bold and energetic Ismail Beg. The Jaipur raja had not cared to clear the arrears of the troops and had no inclination to help them carve out estates for themselves. So they abandoned him and set off on their own for Agra where the Maratha governor, Lakhwa Dada, came out to meet Ismail. But Dadas' disgruntled Hindostani troops treacherously opened the city gates, and Agra was occupied by Ismail Beg. This was a severe blow to Scindia but the fort held, and it successfully defied Ismail for nine months. Eventually, it was relieved by Scindia himself.

The capture of the city by Ismail Beg was followed by the usual squeezing of its richer inhabitants. The houses of Naubat Rai (Scindia's manager) and Narayan Das were plundered and dug up for buried treasure. With the money thus gained, Beg was enabled to recruit more soldiers.[7]

Scindia dispatched Ingle to Jaipur to make a diversion which failed to accomplish anything. Then Ingle was sent to Delhi to bring the emperor, which expedition too proved infructuous. Thereafter, Scindia moved to Rewari where he decided to await the reinforcements for which he had sent urgent letters to Poona.

In the meantime, Ajmer fort, which was earlier with the Marathas, was taken by Bijai Singh of Jodhpur, almost without a blow being struck in its defence. The qiladar, Sher Khan, and his family, took poison, the former out of shame and the latter to escape dishonour.[8]

In December the shahzada, Mirza Jawan Bakht, arrived on the scene, hoping to profit from the fluid situation. Shah Alam had written to him for help, but his arrival made no difference to the military situation as he came without troops, and on his arrival, on 8 December, immediately started intriguing against his father! Shah Alam was alarmed and hastily dispatched him to Agra where Ismail Beg was already in possession. After revolting against Mahadji he was not prepared to subordinate himself to the prince. Besides the irascible behaviour of the prince was not suited to winning friends. It did not take long for him to quarrel with Ismail. He left in disgust, crossing into the Doab in the hope of meeting with a more gracious reception from Ghulam Qadir.

But if Ismail Beg had been brusque, Ghulam Qadir went one step further and tried to kidnap the prince! Disgusted, the prince returned by way of Farrukhabad to Awadh territory in February.

Just before the prince's arrival at Agra, Scindia had tried to recover the city, but the attempt failed. Ismail Beg, who was in every way a fitting successor to his uncle's heritage, drove off the Marathas with well-directed volleys of musketry. During the diversion created by the battle, Lakhwa Dada was able to make a sally and take in provisions. Mahadji tried to rally his men at Dholpur but Ismail pursued him and a second battle was fought on 20 December. Mahadji had to admit defeat and was forced to retreat east of the Chambal.

Ghulam Qadir had also been active in the Doab. He captured Khurja, and laid siege to Mursan and the fortress of Aligarh. Even the easy-going Najaf Quli had bestirred himself and seized Gokulgarh. By the end of the year 1787 Scindia's star seemed on the wane.

But in three months the situation changed and Mahadji was able to resume the offensive once again. The change in fortune was not on account of the arrival of troops from the Deccan. The Poona court had indeed responded to his appeals, their consternation notwithstanding. They could not understand why Mahadji, after striking a gold-mine by becoming master of Delhi, and considering the vast territory which he nominally controlled, should still be short of funds. Tukoji Holkar and Ali Bahadur—the latter the son of Shamsher Bahadur, an illegitimate son of the Peshwa Baji Rao I, were detailed to go to Scindia's relief, but they took nearly a year to reach their destination, and were just in time to join the hunt for Ghulam Qadir. Neither of the two had been particularly keen. Memories of Panipat haunted the court of Poona. On that occasion another large Maratha army had left the Deccan at the call of another Scindia, only to feed the dogs and vultures on the plain of Panipat. Many at Poona felt premonitions of another catastrophe. Moreover, the houses of Holkar and Scindia had always been rivals, and Tukoji was to prove more of a hindrance than a help. As for Ali Bahadur, he was a young man in the making, under the tutelage of Nana Fadnavis, who wrote him long and detailed letters, often with contradictory instructions. So Mahadji owed nothing to Poona and everything to his own officers.

They raised a loan of Rs. 13 lakh on their personal securities for his use. Rana Khan Bhai and other senior officers pawned their own silver dinner services, and Scindia brought out his own stocks from his palace in Ujjain. The Macheri raja furnished about Rs. 7 lakh, Rs. 1 lakh being his personal contribution and the remainder being raised by loans from bankers. Even Nana Fadnavis arranged Rs. 5 lakh from the Poona bankers for Scindia's use. Besides, his officers had also started bringing in the revenue collections.[9]

Instead of immediately rushing back to the theatre of war in Hindostan, Scindia first suppressed malcontents in Malwa and Bundelkhand. The Khichiwara was reconquered, and then, recognizing the impossibility of a permanent occupation, he released the Khichi raja and restored him to his throne. The rajas of Narwar, Datia and Karauli, who had encroached upon Maratha possessions, were forced to surrender their gains while bandits from Mewar, who had been raiding Ujjain, were put down.

More troops were raised and some of the arrears paid, priority, being given to his Deccani troops, as the loyalty of the Hindostanis was now suspect. In April he took the field and sent his army across the Chambal. Ismail Beg called Ghulam Qadir to his aid. For two months the fighting continued in the Braj where the Jat raja had remained loyal to Scindia. Kumbher fort was taken jointly by Ismail Beg and Ghulam Qadir, but an attack to capture Dig by escalade failed, the rebels suffering heavy losses in the attempt. Himmat Bahadur was taken prisoner and a Maratha army sent across the Yamuna to harry Ghulam Qadir's holdings in the Doab.

The rising waters of the Yamuna and the anxiety of Ghulam Qadir to protect his Doab possessions, led to a split between the allies. Ghulam Qadir abandoned Ismail and crossed over to the Doab with his army on 15 June.

Two days later the Marathas fell on Ismail who was camping at Bagh Dara in the suburbs of Agra. Ismail fought bravely, showing great personal courage, but the superior discipline of the sepoys of Boigne and Lesteneau carried the day. Samru with his four batallions of 'Telingas' deserted Ismail and crossed over to Rana Khan Bhai, who had bought them the night before the battle. The final crushing blow, however, was delivered by the Maratha cavalry which, by a wide flanking detour, fell on the Mughal general's rear, spreading panic among his hard-pressed troops who at last broke and fled towards the river. Ismail, badly wounded, tried to court a soldier's death by charging alone into the masses of Jat and Maratha horse, but his nephew seized his horse's bridle and forced him to turn back.

The defeated general paused only to pick up his favourite mistress whom he placed before him on his own steed. Then, following the fleeing remnants of his shattered army, he plunged into the river. He made it across to safety, but his favourite was swept away and drowned.[10]

In March Shah Alam was out on an expedition on his own. Sawai Pratap Singh of Jaipur had sought his help in crushing Najaf Quli's growing strength, centred on the fortress of Kanud (modern Narnaul). He hoped to arrive at an understanding with his sovereign without the mediation of Scindia. The Marathas had claims against him dating back to the civil wars of the 1750s and the 1760s. By settling with the emperor directly he hoped to strengthen his position against the Marathas, as and when they were in a position to assert their claims. The emperor, on the other hand, looked forward to the possibility of collecting some tribute and handsome *nazars*. Besides, Shah Alam found Najaf Quli obnoxious, and the prospect of cutting him to size was an attractive one.

Himmat Bahadur Gossain, truly a man for all seasons, was the go-between in the talks between the emperor and Sawai Pratap Singh. The talks were held at Bharawas, 6 miles south of Rewari. But nothing was accomplished. Shah Alam kept insisting that the arrears of the tribute be cleared while the raja protested that the country had been so devastated by Mahadji's last invasion that the revenues were not easy to collect. Eventually, Pratap took his leave after presenting his sovereign bankers' bills for the piffling sum of Rs. 25,000.[11]

Then His Majesty turned his attention to Najaf Quli. This bon vivant had not bothered to call on his sovereign, let alone surrender his encroachments. Instead he impudently claimed all the offices and estates of Mirza Najaf as his last surviving 'adoptive son'!

With desertions on the rise, and dissolution threatening, the emperor decided to attack Najaf Quli and moved closer to Gokulgarh beneath whose walls the latter was camping. At night, while the imperial officers were deep in revelry, a surprise attack was delivered by Najaf Quli as a result of which the emperor had to quit his own tents and take refuge in the square of Begum Samru's sepoys.

Eventually it was the Begum who saved the emperor's face. She persuaded Najaf Quli to appear in audience, bare-headed, with his hands tied with a silken scarf, like a penitent rebel. Shah Alam received him graciously and ordered his hands to be freed. *Khillats* were handed out as usual, and the emperor, in a show of magnanimity, 'restored' to him his estates and jagirs which he was in any case holding. The charade over, Shah Alam returned to Delhi with as much dignity as he could muster.[12]

After his crushing defeat in the battle of Bagh Dara, Ismail Beg crossed the Yamuna and appeared in the camp of Ghulam Qadir in the garden known as Bagh Nur Afshan. But the Marathas had already brought their artillery up to the river and commenced shelling the Rohilla camp. So Ismail Beg decided to flee to Delhi but the emperor ordered the gates of the Qila-i-Mualla to be closed and refused him audience. Then Ismail Beg once again returned to Ghulam Qadir who had moved to Aligarh which surrendered to him on 17 February.

Here the two confederates replenished their stores and left for Delhi by way of Ghaziabad, Patparganj and Shahdara, which were rich market towns affording ample opportunities for loot and plunder. They had mutually decided to divide the lands and property that fell in their hands in the proportion of two shares for the Rohilla against one for Ismail.

After learning of the annihilitation of Ismail Beg's army at Bagh Dara, the emperor sent robes of honour to congratulate Scindia on his triumph, and invited him to come to Delhi. The nazir, Mansur Ali Khan, and others of the Rohilla's party, were terrified and apprehensive of the wrath of Scindia. But Mahadji was unable to follow up his success with an immediate advance on the capital.

Before abandoning his campsite at Bagh Nur Afshan Ghulam Qadir had destroyed all the boats he could lay his hands on to impede Scindia's crossing. The river waters, swollen by the melting snows, were also fast rising. So, abandoning the idea of crossing into the Doab, Scindia moved up to Mathura and paused to link up with Ranjit Singh, the Jat raja. So far the Maratha had won just a single battle, and he was not one to rush forward without consolidating his gains. His long suffering troops also grounded their arms in protest against his failure to pay them. It took time to persuade them to resume their duties against part payment. This delay gave Ghulam Qadir the opportunity to seize Delhi.

In response to Shah Alam's call Scindia sent a small force of 2,000 horse under Ranoji Scindia on 8 July. Three days later Ranoji reached Barahpulla and was received in audience but Ghulam had also reached Shahdara and was looking for a suitable ford. Unfortunately Ranoji's force was much too weak to defend the city. Begum Samru's brigade was not in Delhi where there was only Himmat Bahadur, detested on account of the extortions of his troops. The 'Mughal' troops were all disaffected and throroughly unreliable as their subsequent behaviour would show. The only loyal troops were the Surkh Posh, also called the Lal Paltan, the emperor's personal bodyguard, but they were too few.

On 14 July the Rohilla force crossed the river at Barari Ghat, north of the fort. The 'Mughal' troops commanded by Ismail also promptly crossed over and joined the Rohillas. Himmat Bahadur and Ranoji Scindia retreated in the face of the enemy's overwhelming strength and fell back on Faridabad while the Rohillas occupied the city.

Even so, the tragedy that followed need not have occurred if the emperor had simply decided to shut himself in, leaving famine to complete the dissolution of the Rohilla's rag-tag force. The troops within the fort were loyal and capable of holding out for several months.

But no man can rise above his destiny. Ghulam Qadir had his agents within the Qila-i-Mualla. On 15 July the eunuch Mansur Ali Khan persuaded Shah Alam to receive the Rohilla, who was now officially his regent and mir bakhshi. Accordingly, Ghulam Qadir entered with his troops while the loyal musketeers of the Lal Paltan looked on helplessly. The nightmare was about to begin.

The Rohilla swore that he had become regent to save the empire from the clutches of the idol worshipping Marathas. But to do so, he needed funds, and it was the duty of the padishah, as the Commander of the Faithful, to provide the wherewithal for this 'jehad'. The hapless emperor handed him the keys to the stores and tosha khana, and said he was free to help himself to what there was.

So far the forms of propriety were being observed. Shah Alam was requested to provide one of the princes to lead the army as the royal presence would inspire the soldiers. A memorandum of understanding was drawn up and Sital Dass, Treasurer of the Household, read out its clauses to His Majesty. According to it, the command of the citadel and its garrison was to be delivered to the nominees of the Rohilla. In return for the confidence reposed in him, the Rohilla swore to defend the person and interests of the padishah against all opposition.

The emperor asked Sital Dass to express his opinion. The faithful servant stated frankly that no reliance could be placed on the word of the regent, and declared that if His Majesty permitted, he himself would slay the Rohilla. The Surkh Posh were prepared to die for their sovereign, and they could readily expel the Rohillas from the qila.[13] But fear had paralysed the doomed monarch. He instructed Sital Dass to convey to the Rohilla his consent to the terms laid down in the memorandum.

The consent obtained, the Rohilla called in more troops. Shortly, the whole of the exalted fort came under his control. The soldiers who were hungry and had not been paid for a long time started plundering the palace. The emperor came out of his private apartments and asked his regent to bring them to order, but the regent insolently demanded more money to satisfy them. Humiliated, Shah Alam withdrew.

The next morning the emperor was deposed. Malika-i-Zamani had promised the regent Rs. 12 lakh if he placed her grandson, Bidar Bakht, on the throne, and now the moment seemed opportune. Shah Alam had failed to come up with the money demanded for fitting out the expedition against the Marathas, and the Rohilla had thus got a fig-leaf of an excuse for replacing him.

In the morning hours Ghulam Qadir entered the room in which the emperor was seated, surrounded by some of his sons. The regent was accompanied by armed soldiers who brusquely ordered the princes to withdraw. Then the Rohilla picked up the sword and buckler which were placed on a cushion beside the emperor's masnad as a symbol of his authority and, handing them over to an attendant, commanded the sovereign to descend from his seat, as his reign was over.

The stunned monarch declared that he preferred death to such an indignity. The regent gripped his swordhilt, but the nazir interposed and begged His Majesty to comply with the Rohilla's command.

At the same time officers and attendants were sent with soldiers to the salatin khana to bring Bidar Bakht. The bewildered prince was placed on the throne and hailed as 'Jahan Shah'. The usual congratulatory *nazars* were offered by the smiling traitors, while another squad escorted the dethroned emperor and his 19 sons to the salatin khana.[14]

The new emperor sanctioned Rs. 36 lakh drawn on the provincial revenues to equip the army. But it was only a paper order for the treasury was empty, and no revenues could be expected in the immediate future, considering the devastation wrought by war and famine. If Ghulam Qadir was to get any money he would have to extort it from the hapless residents of the Qila-i-Mualla.

The regent threatened the emperor that if the money was not forthcoming he could be replaced just as easily as he had been elevated to the throne. Meanwhile Ghulam Qadir's soldiers had already started looting the palace. The screws were tightened on the harem ladies to compel them to disgorge their jewels. The were denied food and drink, and several young girls died of thirst. The lash, and even more gruesome tortures were applied to the servants and slave-girls to extract information about the hiding places.

The triumph of the two dowagers, Malika-i-Zamani and Sahiba Mahal, was short lived. Ghulam Qadir now demanded the price for the enthronement of their grandson. The old ladies protested that he had already realized much more from the plunder of the palace, but the Rohilla laughed. What he was taking from the palace rightfully belonged to him, he maintained. He was only recovering what had been plundered by Shah Alam from Ghausgarh. The old ladies were subjected to insults, the veils torn from their faces, and they were exposed to the public gaze from the balcony of the octagonal tower while the floors of their mansions were dug up in search of hoarded treasures.[15] For these high-born ladies who had never unveiled their faces outside their private apartments, this was the ultimate degradation. The people shuddered with horror. The hour of judgement had verily struck.

The palace rang with the cries and wails of violated women. Like an obsessed maniac, the Rohilla tried to trace out all the spoils of Ghausgarh, and great was his joy when some artillery pieces were identified as having been brought from that stronghold.

Shah Alam was dragged out from his cell for interrogation. The regent jeered at him, passed his arm round his neck with insolent familiarity and, blowing tobacco smoke on his face, pressed him to reveal his secret hiding places. Bitterly the old man protested, 'Whatever I had you have taken. Do you think I have hidden something in my stomach?'

With brutal humour the Rohilla replied, 'Maybe, we shall have to tear open your belly too'.[16]

A few days later, on 10 August, the old man was again hauled out. In a fit of rage the Rohilla threatened to tear out his eyes.

'What?', the terrified old man is recorded to have cried out, 'Will you tear out these eyes which for 60 years past have been assiduously employed in reading the sacred Quran?'

Notwithstanding this bathetic appeal, the Rohilla threw him down and, sitting on Shah Alam's chest drew his dagger and gouged out his eyes. Then he called for the court painter and ordered him to draw the scene exactly as he had seen it so that it could be commemorated for posterity. Then, getting up, the Rohilla walked away with a parting kick at the bleeding old man.

For two days no one was allowed to approach Shah Alam, and servants were cut down while trying to give him water, to deter others from trying to relieve his agony.

The turn of the faithless nazir came next even though he had been the Rohilla's most active partisan within the palace. A demand of Rs. 7 lakh was assessed on him. When he protested he was beaten, and threatened that his face would be rubbed in excrement if he failed to reveal the place where he had concealed his treasures.

Kings had been dethroned and blinded many a time in the blood soaked annals of the throne of Delhi. Torture had been applied before now to extract treasure, but the wholesale violation of all decencies with regard to women was unprecedented. Even at the worst of times the sanctuary of the sergalio was by and large respected. When searches were required to be conducted, female slaves would be sent, or other pressures applied, but now empresses and aged dowagers had had their veils torn from their faces and brazenly exposed in public.

Among them were ladies like Sahiba Mahal who had been so bashful in her days as empress that she would blush with confusion even if a male child happened to cross her path. But now the monstrous Rohilla would each night, in the course of his drunken revels send for princesses to attend on him. They would be stripped and passed from one drunken brute to another, with lewd jokes about their intimate anatomy.

Estimates of the treasure extracted vary. Ghulam Qadir's wife claimed that the value of all the booty was Rs. 25 crore, but according to a more sober estimate the actual cash was only about Rs. 15 lakh. The jewels, and furnishings were worth much more, but for most of these items there was no market, and their value was only hypothetical. The oft-plundered palace of the Indian Caesars had little left to offer.

Ismail Beg was Ghulam Qadir's confederate, and according to the terms of their understanding all their gains were to be shared in the ratio of 2:1, the two parts being the Rohilla's. But the Rohilla and the Mughal soon fell out. As Ghulam Qadir showed no intention of sharing the booty, Ismail dissociated himself from the regent and moved his camp away. He thus had no hand in any of the atrocities committed in the fort. A state of armed neutrality existed between the two, and the Afghan and Turki soldiers would often come to blows in the streets. On such occasions the Rohillas usually came off worst as the Delhi mob would side with the Turks.

Not satisfied with the loot from the qila, the Rohilla ordered the gilt covering on the smaller cupolas of the Jama Masjid to be removed. But after one *chhatri* had been stripped, Maniyar Singh, the fort commandant, cautioned him from proceeding further, lest the people of Delhi rise in protest against the descration of their shrine.[17]

August onward flying columns of Maratha cavalry had started harassing grain convoy headed for Delhi, affecting the food supply of the city. By the end of September, Rana Khan Bhai followed by Jiva Dada Bakhshi at last reached Delhi with a sizeable force and occupied it on 2 October. Begum Samru and Ismail Beg at once joined them. The Rohillas crowded inside the fort. The Marathas dug trenches and a desultory cannonade began.

Ghulam Qadir now started sending out his looted treasure and baggage to Ghausgarh, but much of it was plundered on the way by Sikhs, Marathas and Gujjars. The Rohilla made several sallies into the Doab against the Maratha light horse but would return to the fort at night. The floggings and the torture continued as he endeavoured to squeeze the last possible rupee out of the princes in the benighted fort. Even his puppet Bidar Bakht was not spared.

On 10 October, on the eve of Muharram, a powder magazine in the fort exploded accidentally. With fiendish humour the Rohilla remarked, 'Even the Fort refuses to keep me now.' The next morning he packed up the remaining loot and fled with his troops, crossing the river by boats in the early hours, unnoticed by the besieging Maratha force.

Later in the day, while Rana Khan Bhai was holding his daily conference, his attention was drawn to the fact that the walls of the fort were deserted. At once scouts were sent to reconnoitre. As they approached, some prisoners, whose cells opened on the riverside, shouted out that the Rohillas had left and the fort was deserted. A man was sent in by throwing a rope over the walls, and the gates opened. The long night was over.

Cooked food was sent into the qila in huge quantities to relieve the hunger of the inhabitants. Barbers and physicians were sent to administer to their needs. Maniyar Singh had given shelter to many of the women from the seraglio. They were now restored to their families.

Very little news about the horrific happenings within had leaked out. One of Bidar Bakht's wives had died of shock. Two dowager-empresses perished of thirst and starvation, and the body of one was allowed to be removed only when the stench became unbearable. In all, 21 members of the imperial house had perished during the occupation.

On 16 October Rana Khan Bhai and the other sardars waited on the sightless monarch, now restored to his blood-spattered throne. The next day happened to be a Friday and the *khutba* was once again read in his name. The reign of Bidar Bakht was thus over.

Ali Bahadur had also just arrived with the first of the reinforcements for which Scindia had been pleading for. He and Rana Bhai were immediately dispatched in pursuit of the fleeing Rohillas. Ghulam Qadir had taken shelter in Meerut which was closely invested. He tried to negotiate his freedom by using the captive princes as a gambit, but the talks failed. Frustrated in his attempt he ordered their massacre, but Maniyar Singh (who had been forced to accompany him) prevented this last infamy though the Rohilla threatened him with a drawn sword.

On 17 December Ghulam slipped out of the fort after dark with 500 horsemen while Maniyar Singh distracted the besiegers in the Suraj Kund suburb. Ghulam Qadir was trying to head for Ghausgarh but a Maratha patrol under Jiva Dada attacked him. In the pursuit that followed Ghulam was separated from his companions. His horse stumbled and was lamed, but the Rohilla continued the flight on foot.

When morning broke he found himself in front of the village of Bamnauli near Shamli. Here he sought shelter in the house of a Brahmin and offered him money if he would procure him a pony and a guide for Ghausgarh. The Brahmin either recognized him, or otherwise guessed his identity. Instead of complying he sent word to Ali Bahadur who was camping nearby, and a party of Marathas arrived and took the Rohilla prisoner.

The Rohilla's troops surrendered soon after. The nazir and Maniyar Singh were taken prisoner but the soldiers, who numbered 3,000, were allowed to go free after being disarmed. The princes, including Bidar Bakht, were sent to Delhi. Scindia kept the Rohilla with himself, hoping to learn from him the whereabouts of his treasure, for very little of value had been recovered from Meerut.

But the Rohilla would not reveal his secret.[18] Meanwhile, the blind Shah Alam was getting restless at Delhi. Why was his regent delaying revenge for the atrocities committed against his master? The emperor wrote to Scindia saying if he did not immediately send the Rohilla's eyes to him, he would abdicate his throne, don the robes of a fakir, and leave for Mecca.

So, on 3 March Scindia ordered the emperor's secretary, Mir Ghalib Ali and physician, Hakim Ajmal, to remove Ghulam Qadir's eyes, and cut off his nose and ears. These were placed in a casket and sent to the sightless emperor in the Exalted Fort the 'refuge of all the world'. When the casket reached the emperor, he is said to have lifted the cover and felt the contents with his own hands to make sure that justice had been done, and that an eye had indeed been taken for an eye.[19]

The mutilated Ghulam Qadir was led out to a place near his camp, 12 miles from Mathura, where, after more torture, his hands and feet were amputated (the prescribed punishment for robbery), and finally his head was cut off, and the body strung up by the legs from a tall tree.

What happened thereafter is not known. There is no record of the monster's grave nor even of the place of burial. The chronicler, Khairuddin, writes that as the soul of the Rohilla belonged to the Devil, the body too was taken by him. Apparently, the headless corpse was sent to Delhi and exhibited in a public place. The tale is told of a black dog, with white rings round its eyes, that sat below the suspended corpse, lapping up the blood and fluids dripping from the neck. Though the dog was repeatedly driven away, it returned again and again to its horrid meal. On the third day, both dog and body had disappeared, never to be seen again![20] Thus ends the most horrible chapter in the tragic annals of the Qila-i-Mualla.

NOTES

1. Khairuddin, *Ibrat Nama*, iii, p. 154.
2. Parasnis, *Dilli-yethil-Marathyanchin Raj-Karenen*, i, p. 232.
3. Sarkar, *Fall of the Mughal Empire*, iii, p. 267.
4. Ibid., p. 268.
5. Parasnis, i, p. 227.
6. Ibid., p. 228.
7. Ibid., p. 286.
8. Sardesai, *Historical Papers of the Scindias of Gwalior*, i, p. 120.
9. Sarkar, iii, p. 241.
10. Ibid., iii, p. 253.
11. Parasnis, i, pp. 262, 274, 279.
12. Ibid., p. 274.
13. Francklin, *The History of Shah Alam*, p. 180.
14. Sarkar, iii, p. 269.
15. Ibid., p. 271.
16. Ibid., p. 270.
17. Khairuddin, iii, p. 158.
18. The treasure was never found but Festing (*Strangers within the Gates*, p. 170) mentions that 'the Crown Jewels of Delhi were hidden in the lining of the saddle upon which Ghulam rode in his flight. They were never seen again; but a French officer in Scindia's army having suddenly returned to his native land about this time, evidently with a large fortune, it was always believed that he had the luck to capture Ghulam's horse.' Keene repeats this story in *India under the Free Lances*, but again without identifying the officer. Desmond Young has identified him as Lestineau (*Fountain of the Elephants*, p. 93).
19. Khairuddin, iii, p. 296.
20. Sarkar, iii, p. 280.

CHAPTER 42

After Ghulam Qadir
The Dictatorship of Mahadji Scindia

Ghulam Qadir had been dispatched; so too the villainous nazir and the hapless Bidar Bakht, but Mahadji was still beset with difficulties. He owed his soldiers two and a half years' pay, and had to put up with all kinds of insults. Himmat Bahadur and Ismail Beg were thoroughly discontented, and looking for an opportunity to embarrass him. Ali Bahadur and Tukoji Holkar, who had been sent to assist him, were no help at all. They had come too late to contribute to the success of the campaign (Tukoji Holkar was in fact still dawdling in Rajasthan) and instead of adding to his strength were proving to be obstacles.

Almost immediately after the execution of Ghulam Qadir Mahadji Scindia fell ill. According to popular belief, his illness, which manifested itself through painful and loathesome eruptions all over the body, was the result of the curse of the late Rohilla's mother. For six months, from March to August 1789, Mahadji remained bed-ridden in Mathura. The physicians could not diagnose the disease and black magic was suspected. A search discovered soon enough a witch in neighbouring Vrindaban who confessed that she had been put up by Himmat Bahadur Gossain to practise the infernal rites.

The Gossain's arrest was ordered but he took, shelter in the tents of Ali Bahadur which flew the peshwa's standard. Scindia demanded his surrender. Ali replied that he had not given him shelter and that the regent was welcome to send troops and take him out. But when Mahadji's soldiers went to seize him, Ali Bahadur's troops resisted. They declared that as the miscreant had sought sanctuary under the *zari patka* of the peshwa, he could only be handed over by the Peshwa's express orders. Ali Bahadur did not attempt to interfere and Scindia lost face. It became evident to all that in spite of Mahadji's exertions and victories, and his being the regent of the empire, Ali Bahadur, who displayed the *zari patka*, was Scindia's superior. An armed conflict seemed imminent but, at the last moment,

Scindia's good sense prevailed and face was saved. On 6 February 1790 Mahadji visited Ali Bahadur's tent where the Gossain was presented to him. Mahadji gave him a *khillat* and declared that he had forgiven him his transgressions.[1]

Tukoji chose this occasion to embarrass Scindia. He hurried up from Rajasthan and demanded an equal share of all the lands held by Mahadji, as per the terms of the original grant of the Poona durbar which divided the northern territories between the two houses. He conveniently forgot that both generals were meant to contribute equally to the cost of conquering and administering these territories, and Holkar's contribution to the recent campaign was virtually nil. Instead, he had ganged up with Ali Bahadur to embarrass Mahadji, and it was only the latter's good sense that had averted war.

In August Mahadji packed off Ali Bahadur to Bundelkhand, and even gave him money to remove himself. Ali took Himmat Bahadur with him. The two were ultimately able to carve out a chieftaincy with its headquarters at Banda where Ali Bahadur and his descendants reigned as nawabs until that state was extinguished by the British in 1858 on account of the last nawab's alleged participation in the mutiny.

Ismail Beg had been dispatched earlier, in October 1788, to Kanud against Najaf Quli whose estates had been assigned to him. But Kanud was a strong fort, and after a few months Beg turned towards Shekhawati while maintaining a loose blockade of Kanud. About this time, his cousin Najaf Ali Khan, the son of the late Muhammad Beg Hamadani, who was living in Jaipur, joined Najaf Quli and attacked Ismail Beg. The latter easily defeated him and chased him into Kanud fort, while he occupied the walled town.

In the latter part of 1789 Beg became disenchanted with Scindia. To get over his financial crisis, Scindia had demanded from his officers one-third of their jagir income. This was bitterly resented. Ismail's ambition was to found a chieftaincy for himself, and he had his eye on the fort of Kishengarh. Mahadji Scindia first gave his reluctant consent to the idea. But it soon became clear that Mahadji had no intention of helping Beg attain his heart's desire. So, in November, Beg abandoned the siege of Kanud, and after a few months entered the service of Jaipur, the only power in the region that could pay his starving troops. He seemed to have struck a good deal. Not only Jaipur, but Jodhpur too, undertook to subsidize him. The latter offered to pay Rs. 7 lakh while Jaipur promised Rs. 5 lakh, of which Rs. 2 lakh was to be paid immediately to enable him to refit for war.

Scindia was at this time passing through an acute depression, mainly on account of his ailment, and the failure of Nana Fadnavis to support him against Himmat Bahadur. Disgusted with the indifference of the Poona court he sent in his resignation. 'I have laboured for ten years, and this is the fruit of it!' he complained. 'It is impossible for me to remain here after what has happened.' But the unstable situation in Hindostan prevented him from leaving for the Deccan to lay his case before his master.

To prepare himself for war he asked de Boigne to raise more battalions. The latter, however, demanded money for the purpose. With none forthcoming, he left for Lucknow in disgust. It needs noting that in spite of his financial difficulties Scindia was never really down and out. In spite of occasional dramatic gestures like placing his wives' jewellery before his generals and declaring that it was the sum total of his property, he never thought twice before spending thousands of rupees on expensive religious rites and the mass feeding of Brahmins in the hope of begetting a son. At all times he carried with him at least Rs. 50 lakh in cash and jewels, but he regarded this as his private hoard and nothing could tempt him to draw from it. Similar was the case with most of the Indian umara, particularly Marathas. Thus, while private treasure chests continued to grow, their estates and ryots went to rack and ruin.[2]

De Boigne's jagirs were well administered and carefully supervised, yielding several times the revenue of a comparable estate in Maratha hands where the administration was entirely in the hands of corrupt Brahmin officials to whom peculation was second nature. There was absolutely no supervision and the chiefs themselves were incapable of going through the accounts. Thus, while the sepoys of de Boigne's camp were always punctually paid from the income of their general's jagirs, the salaries of the traditional *fauj* of Indian generals were even in the best of times, heavily in arrears.

About this time Scindia's army—as well as the armies of most Indian princes—could be divided into two distinct divisions, the European-trained and officered *paltan* or *campoo* and the native *fauj*, the old-style Maratha light horse whose main armament was the sword and lance. The battles were won mainly by the *campoo*, the *fauj* playing the role of onlookers during the battle and plunderers and pursuers thereafter. De Boigne's brigades were to raise Mahadji to pre-eminence in northern India, but in due course the limitations of the *campoo* system would become painfully apparent.

By October 1789, Scindia had recovered fully and sent urgent messages to de Boigne to return. The Savoyard obliged and soon set about expanding his three battalions to a brigade of ten. Men were enlisted, uniforms procured, and a foundry and arsenal established. The fresh troops had put in only about five months training when operations commenced in May 1790 against the Rajputs.

Mahadji himself remained at Mathura. Gopal Bhau was commander-in-chief, the other generals being de Boigne, Jiva Dada and Ambaji Ingle. Holkar contributed a contingent of 4,000 soldiers while Ali Bahadur sent another 1,000. With Ismail in the Rajput camp, Najaf Quli had allied himself to the imperialists and sent a small force, as did the Macheri raja, Pratap Singh Naruka.

The first clash took place at Patan on 22 May. It was inconclusive. A sharp reproof from Scindia forced Gopal Bhau to stake everything on a pitched battle. This came about on 20 June. It was extremely hot. Neither side seemed anxious to come to grips. The battle developed gradually into a number of separate struggles. At first pindaris drove away some of the cattle from the Rajput camp; they were pursued by Rajput cavalry who were in turn driven back by Maratha light horse. The Mughal horse of Ismail Beg replied by driving back the Marathas. The wild Rathor horse recklessly charged some light horse sent by Gopal Bhau and followed them in close pursuit. The Marathas lured them within range of de Boigne's guns, which opened up with murderous effect. This eventually led to the disintegration of the entire Rajput front. The Rajputs were pursued relentlessly throughout the night and the next day, many more being butchered in the pursuit.

Patan surrendered the following day. Considerable booty, including 105 guns, fell into the hands of the imperialists. Jaipur was effectively destroyed as a military power and it did not raise its head again for the next ten years.

But Jodhpur still remained, and its prince feverishly set about mobilizing all his resources to meet the challenge which lay ahead. Ismail's army had also been shattered and he too needed to refit. Jaipur was intimidated into quiescence. In August Ajmer was besieged, and in September the imperialists reached Merta, the gateway to Marwar.

Ismail Beg had not yet arrived on the scene and de Boigne determined to fight before his arrival. Beg was the only professional general on the Rajput side with any knowledge of modern warfare, the rest of the army consisting of feudal levies whose arms were hopelessly antiquated. It would be three or four days before Ismail's troops reached Merta, and de Boigne decided to attack early in the morning on 10 September.

De Boigne's battalions advanced in the early hours, taking the Naga monks opposite them completely by surprise. The latter were still about their morning ablutions when the sepoys opened fire. But in his haste to seize their rich camp, Captain Rohan, who commanded one of the flanks of the *campoo*, moved too far out. The Rathor cavalry, now fully awake, saw in the dangerous gap an opportunity which they were quick to exploit.

Down they poured like a torrent, gathering speed as they approached the imperialists, shouting their blood-curdling battle cry of 'Han! Han!' Rohan and his column were badly cut up, but after the Rathor flood had passed the remnants struggled back to the centre where stood de Boigne. The latter now coolly reformed his battalions into squares which the Rathor horsemen could not ride down. Their steady volleys reinforced by artillery fire, cut deep swathes in the Rajput ranks, and finally the baffled Rathors turned back.

But this was not the end. A final charge was launched by 3,000 picked warriors dressed out in yellow robes—the *kesari risala*—who were sworn to fight to the death in the old Rajput tradition.

'It is impossible for me to describe the feats of bravery performed by the zard-kaprawalas or forlorn hope of the enemy', wrote an English eyewitness, probably an officer of de Boigne whose dispatches were printed in the Calcutta papers. 'I have seen after the line was broken, fifteen or twenty men only return to charge one thousand infantry, and advance within ten or fifteen paces of our line before they were all shot.'[3]

The Rajput rout was complete and their losses appalling. Many of their chiefs were slain. There was scarcely a noble family in Marwar that did not lose one or two of its members.

After Merta, Raja Bijai Singh was forced to sue for terms and Ajmer was handed over to the imperialists in March 1791.

The Marathas were now supreme. There was no other power in the north capable of opposing them, save perhaps the Sikhs, and they had been left in undisturbed possession of the Punjab, the Marathas having finally abandoned their old dream of making the Indus the limit of their empire. As for the Sikhs, they were going through that period of internecine warfare which would end with the establishment of Ranjit Singh's primacy north of the Sutluj, while the Cis-Sutluj chiefs were doomed to become British satellites two decades later.

This would be an appropriate point for narrating the subsequent career of that doughty but unlucky general, Mirza Ismail Beg.

Now in the service of Marwar, he was sent to collect tribute from its outlying tributaries of Sirohi, Palanpur and Radhanpur. With him went a Jodhpur minister, Shiv Chand Singhvi, and a Rathor contingent. His approach spread terror. The Gaikwad expressed apprehensions at his approach, for his territory lay close by. In order to avoid him, Ismail turned towards Kutch. Besides collecting the legitimate tribute he was plundering on his own account to feed his hungry soldiers who had not received pay for many months. But he was forced to return to Jodhpur when news was received of the assassination of Khub Chand Singhvi, the prime minister of Jodhpur, who was the brother of Shiv Chand Singhvi who commanded the Rathor contingent accompanying him.

When he returned to Jodhpur in September 1791, Ismail was faced with a gloomy prospect. His army had shrunk to 4,000 and there was no hope of ever recovering his dues, either from Jodhpur or Jaipur. His father, Munim Beg, had been forced to surrender his fort of Gokulgarh in July 1791 to the imperialists and was now a prisoner in Agra fort. Najaf Quli Khan had also died on 23 August.

At this juncture Ismail Beg received an invitation from Najaf Quli's junior widow, then besieged in Kanud by Khande Rao. The spirited lady offered him everything, her fort, her army, supplies, and finally, herself, if he felt so inclined. Greatly cheered by this invitation, he proceeded first to Jaipur where some months were wasted in trying to obtain money from that government. In this time more of his men deserted. When he reached Kanud, his unpaid Badakhshis defected to Khande Rao as the latter had promised to pay their arrears. Ismail found himself left with barely 400 soldiers. But he was successful in occupying an outlying fortalice called Madhogarh.

But the lady had meantime changed her mind and forbade him from trying to enter the main fort. Her officers had convinced her that Ismail would seize all her wealth and reduce her to the level of his servants, for he was harsh and greedy.

In early March the senior widow, who was the main spirit behind the defence, was killed, being struck by a cannon ball while playing *chaupar* on the terrace with one of her hand-maidens. About the same time also, in Madhogarh, died Ismail Beg's aged mother, Khanum Begum. The death of his mother in the cramped confines of the little fortalice was taken as a sign by the men, that Ismail's end was near and they felt disheartened. At once defections began. Officers of the garrison, led by Madari Khan Mewati and Gulab Singh, opened negotiations with the Marathas.

Much time was lost because Khande Rao insisted that Madari Khan should hand over Ismail Beg. The emperor insisted on this as he was anxious to have his revenge on this erstwhile confederate of Ghulam Qadir, but Madari Khan resisted. In the meantime Khande Rao had been reinforced by a detachment commanded by Colonel Perron.

Mirza Ismail, in a clever move, came out of the fort on 15 April and surrendering to Colonel Perron sought his protection. The news was at once sent to de Boigne, and four days later he came in person. Ismail, his family, and servants, were sent under escort to Agra, while the property he left behind was sold and its value subsequently remitted to him.

When in February 1794 news reached Delhi of Mahadji Scindia's death in Poona, the blind emperor immediately sent directions to the qiladar to put Ismail to death. The qiladar, who was a Maratha, had no scruples in obeying the imperial orders. He first turned out de Boigne's guard which had been posted by the general for the prisoner's security. A few days later Ismail Beg was executed.

In this period one of de Boigne's gains had been a bride for himself. The younger widow of Najaf Quli, who had first proposed marriage to Ismail, had offered her foster daughter's hand to the general. The girl, Moti Begum, had been trained in singing and dancing and was readily accepted by the general who settled three villages near Palwal for the mother's support out of his own jagir. The lady had also enjoined on him to protect the Mirza, which commitment the general faithfully carried out until the confusion following the news of Scindia's death which, as detailed earlier, at last enabled the blind Shah Alam to have his belated revenge.

In February 1792 Mahadji left for the Deccan at last. He was determined to argue his case at Poona, and obtain redress for his grievances against the Holkars, and obtain some of the money which he felt was his due.

It is curious that throughout this period not once did Mahadji think it necessary to visit Delhi. He does not appear to have even called on the emperor to condole with him the terrible sufferings he had undergone during the Rohilla occupation. His headquarters remained throughout at Mathura and he was represented only by his agents like Shah Nizam ud-Din and others at the Qila-i-Mualla. Although fully in control, he was almost as much of an absentee as the nominal wazir.

By the usual norms of oriental monarchies a blind man was disqualified to hold the throne. By the old precedents of the Timurid house also, it was considered sufficient to blind a deposed monarch to effectively debar him from attempting a come-back. That no such objection was raised against the reinstatement of Shah Alam is the best indication that the occupant of the Peacock Throne had been reduced to a pageant king. That he was also blind, was, if anything, a blessing, for he would now be so much less of a nuisance, being unaware of the decay that surrounded him. Unfortunately, everything was crumbling at the same time.

At the end of the eighteenth century India was an exhausted country, apparently incapable of producing men of mettle. A Haidar Ali and a Tipu Sultan in Mysore, or a Ranjit Singh in the Punjab, were exceptions to the general rule. Indeed, they too proved incapable of founding lasting dynasties. Everything was rotten: the ruling class, the princes and umara, and their petty accountants, *serishtadars* and *karkhoons*, all had been corrupted to the core.

If Scindia was bankrupt, his master, the peshwa, even more so. But that did not prevent the latter's keeper, Nana Fadnavis, from accumulating a vast private hoard. This was now the general rule, particularly in the Maratha principalities. Wealth was accumulated on private account while the public treasuries were invariably empty.

As if Scindia's task was not difficult enough to begin with, Nana Fadnavis had hobbled him with Malhar Holkar II. With the prudent Mahadji removed from the scene, the Holkar-Scindia rivalry flared up into open war. This rivalry between the two great houses also prevented the Marathas from reaping the full benefit of their decisive victories over the two leading Rajput states of the north. The Rajputs played one chief against the other and resiled from their commitments.

It is not necessary to go into the details of the Holkar-Scindia rivalry which belongs more to the sphere of Maratha history than to that of the empire. It is enough to know that in the earlier period, as long as the great Malhar Rao was alive, the Holkar house was the senior partner; after his death it was the turn of Mahadji Scindia. The policies advocated by both were diametrically opposed. Malhar, for instance, had regarded Najib Khan as his adopted son, while Mahadji, who had lost so many members of his family in the Panipat campaign pursued him and the Rohillas in the spirit of a vendetta. Holkar was against the Jat raja, while Scindia was for. Whatever approach Scindia adopted, Tukoji and his son Malhar II were bound to oppose. The position was aggravated by the absurd policy of the court of Poona. Instead of clearly demarcating the territorial responsibilities of the two chiefs in Rajasthan and Hindostan, the two chiefs—and sometimes the Puar chief of Dhar as well—were asked to collect specified per-centages of the tribute from each of the various princes. The result of such a division was that if Malhar was the first to tackle a chief he might succeed in collecting his specified 30 or 40 per cent while Scindia who followed him would almost certainly be unable to get what he was meant to collect on account of the ravaged state of the country. This inevitably created friction between the collectors.

In August 1790 Mahadji had obtained a fresh order from the emperor appointing the peshwa as the Vakil-i-Mutlaq with himself as his deputy. This was done to assuage ruffled feelings in Poona where eyebrows had been raised on the earlier occasion in 1784 when the emperor had insisted on appointing Scindia directly as the vakil and the peshwa had been honoured with the purely honorary title of Naib-i-Munaib and the inferior office of mir bakhshi. As was the practise, a shamiana known as farmanbari was erected in the Scindia camp for receiving the imperial patents, and all the officers duly informed. The etiquette required to be observed was that of the imperial court; attendance was mandatory, but Holkar did not come.

He merely sent his diwan. This was a pointed snub to the regent, but Mahadji swallowed the calculated insult. However, if Mahadji overlooked these pinpricks and confined his complaints and fulminations to his letters to Nana, his lieutenants were less tolerant. The first clash took place at Suranli on 8 October 1792. It was a minor squabble over the Macheri tribute. Holkar's advance tents, some artillery pieces, and kettledrums were captured by Gopal Bhau and Jiva Dada. Thereafter better sense prevailed and a compromise was reached.

But the news of this fracas inflamed tempers at Indore, and Ahalya Bai resolved not to swallow the insult to the Holkar house. She opened her coffers for the recruitment of troops and allowed the rash and intemperate Malhar Rao, Tukoji's son, to proceed to Rajasthan.

No attempt was made to restrain the young fire-eater by the court of Poona. A Scindia defeat would not have been altogether unwelcome to Nana Fadnavis. Mahadji had been pressing his claims a little too aggressively for Nana's comfort, and the latter would have liked nothing better than to see Scindia humbled. The young Peshwa was impressionable and the Chitpavan Machiavelli was afraid that the Patil Baba, as Mahadji was called, might establish his own control over the peshwa. Infact, he had felt so uneasy when he come to know of Scindia's determination to come to Poona that he had gone to the extent of requesting the English for their sepoy battalions just released from the war against Tipu Sultan. He dreaded Mahadji's approach just as Farrukhsiyar had cringed at the thought of the return of Syed Hussain Ali Khan in 1719.

When Scindia came to know of this he was furious. For twelve years he had been campaigning in the north for the greater glory of the Maratha state. For twelve long years he had been denied leave to return to his native land. He had absolutely no hostile intention. All he sought was an opportunity to meet the peshwa, put his case before him, and explain to him the true situation in Hindostan of which the courtiers at Poona seemed totally ignorant.

When Malhar Rao, reached Tukoji's camp, Prashar Dada, Tukoji's diwan, had finalized the terms of the proposed settlement with Gopal Bhau and other Scindia generals, and submitted the draft to Tukoji for his approval. Malhar was furious. He cried out before his father:

> We have been maintaining an army costing lakhs of rupees for the last eight months in order to recover our lost prestige in Hindostan. By making peace you have destroyed even the little prestige that was left to us. You remain here with your peace. I shall not listen to anyone but shall fight one battle.[4]

So war it was going to be. The peace treaty was scrapped and Gopal Bhau and de Boigne moved up their troops to meet the Holkar challenge. On 29 May they struck at Panchilas, the battle opening with a well-directed cannonade from Scindia's guns on the massed troops of Holkar. Now was Malhar's opportunity to demonstrate his superior military skill by leading his massed cavalry—'the myriads of Maratha light house'—in their classical charges. Bapu Rao Holkar and Prashar Dada, who had more experience of north Indian warfare sceptically remained aloof.

Malhar led his 'myriads' in a wide flanking detour striking the Scindia camp in the rear. Instead of finding the usual confused medley of camp followers, baggage animals and non-combatants, they found themselves facing a disciplined line of sepoys armed with muskets, bayonets and light guns. The charge ground to a halt, and the horses milled around helplessly while Scindia's artillery tore great gaps in the Holkar ranks. When Lakhwa Dada came up with the Scindia horse to deliver the coup de grace Malhar's much vaunted 'myriads' broke and fled.

Three days later the two armies again faced each other near the town of Lakheri. The ground was broken with thickly wooded hills and ravines. After a quick reconnaissance, de Boigne decided on an immediate attack. While clearing the pass which was held by Holkar's ferocious Naga and Bairagi soldiers, a stray bullet, fired off some of Scindia's ammunition tumbrils. The resulting confusion encouraged the Holkar cavalry to launch their attack, but as they emerged from the woods into the open plain they were met by a withering fire. As their charge was blunted, de Boigne launched his splendidly mounted cavalry against them. Shaken, the Holkar horse broke and scattered.

But the fight continued between de Boigne's *campoo* and Dudrenec's sepoys in Holkar's employ. Dudrenec suffered greatly from thirst, but he hung on grimly, heavily outnumbered. It was a question of honour for him; it was the first time Dudrenec's newly raised battalions had been put to test against de Boigne's battle-tempered veterans.

The rest of Holkar's army had already been broken and scattered, and no one came to the rescue of the gallant Frenchman. As for Malhar, the braggart whose empty boasting had led to the scrapping of a reasonable peace treaty, he was found dead drunk by the side of a water tank where he had probably stopped to cool himself. He was recognized and picked up by some of Tukoji's cavalry as they rode by.

Dudrenec's *paltan* met its doom with stoic courage. His force was practically annihilated. All his European officers were either killed or wounded and he himself escaped death by falling down wounded in a heap of the slain.

The battle of Lakheri left Scindia's forces supreme in northern India. The prestige of the Holkars was shattered. Gopal Bhau now rapidly marched on Jaipur and exacted tribute amounting to Rs. 70 lakh from Sawai Pratap Singh.

A defeated and broken Tukoji Holkar wound his lonely way to his capital of Indore. On his way he gave vent to his spleen by sacking defenceless Ujjain, the seat of Scindia.

But while his northern field army had made Mahadji supreme in Hindostan, Rajasthan and Malwa, at the byzantine court of Poona he was much less successful. Afraid that the victor of Lakheri might now feel encouraged to strike at the devious ministers of Poona, Nana at last agreed to recognize Scindia's financial claims. Mahadji had claimed Rs. 7 crore. Of this vast amount, Rs. 5 crore was finally accepted by Nana. Of course, the payment of this astronomical sum was out of the question. Instead, Mahadji was allowed a free hand in the administration of his northern territories, with full right to the enjoyment of the tribute until his claims had been met.[5]

Unfortunately, the Patil Baba did not live long to enjoy the fruits of this settlement. Time was running out, not only for him or the Holkars, but indeed for the Maratha state as well as for the rump of its old self, the Delhi empire. In little more than a decade, the sun would have set on them all.

NOTES

1. Sarkar, *Fall of the Mughal Empire*, iv, p. 8-11.
2. Broughton, *Letters from a Maratha Camp*, p. 106.
3. Sarkar, iv, p. 29.
4. Ibid., p. 73.
5. Sardesai, *A New History of the Marathas*, iii, p. 252.

CHAPTER 43

War and Strife in the Maratha Heartland

Mahadji had raised the Maratha power to its pinnacle in northern India. The humiliation of Panipat had at last been wiped out. A treaty with Timur Shah fixed the Sutluj as the border between the Marathas and the Afghans. Both Shah Alam and the Maharana of Mewar were his wards; Jodhpur and Jaipur had been beaten, while Malwa and Bundelkhand were equally under his domination. After Lakheri, Scindia was paramount in the vast tract stretching from the Ganga to the Narmada.

The peshwa was now the protector of the holy places of Mathura and Vrindaban, the most sacred of the Vaishnava pilgrimages. This was one of the several conditions laid down by Scindia in 1784 when he was offered the regency after the murder of Afrasiyab, but the formal patents bestowing this district on the Marathas could not be drawn up until all the other imperial grantees in that district had been accommodated elsewhere. What rebounded even more to the regent's credit was an imperial edict forbidding the slaughter of kine throughout the empire.

But it was an unstable achievement. Too much depended on the life of one man, and on the court of Poona, where his achievement was never properly appreciated. The only concern of Nana Fadnavis, the Machiavellian manipulator of that court was the preservation of his own power. The long minority of the posthumous peshwa Madho Rao II had enabled Nana to become the supreme authority at Poona, and after more than twenty years in full command he was loathe to let go.

The young peshwa was twenty years old when Mahadji came like a breath of fresh air from the plains of Hindostan to the byzantine atmosphere of the Shaniwar Wara of Poona.[1] He had had no opportunity to mix with people of his own rank. All the time surrounded by sycophants and flunkeys, Nana had made sure that he had no opportunity to broaden his mind by observation and education. During the third Mysore war which ended in 1792, the English had repeatedly suggested that he should accompany the Maratha field forces so as to acquire some experience of war, but Nana would not permit it. Nor was he allowed to visit Bombay, where exposure to a foreign culture might have been educative. Nizam Ali, the viceroy of the Deccan, several times expressed a desire to meet the young peshwa but each time he was rebuffed. Nana pretended that he was acting in the best interest of the young man, the danger of assassination by the agents of the imprisoned Baji Rao being ever present; but in truth he had no desire that the young peshwa should develop into an independent, clear thinking prince, capable of acting on his own. The boy's mother who lived in seclusion at Nasik, on the banks of the sacred Godavari, once gave Nana a sharp reproof on the manner in which he was bringing up the prince: 'He is always surrounded by small men, clerks and servants. He is not allowed to see outsiders freely and acquire experience. How can you expect him then to acquire wisdom?'[2]

In fact, the peshwa lived in a gilded cage no less than the blind Mughal in the Qila-i-Mualla. With the coming of Mahadji Scindia the door was opened a little, but with the death of the Patil Baba, Nana Fadnavis slammed it once again.

In the weeks preceding his death, which was caused by a fall from a balcony, the young peshwa was observed to be depressed and gloomy, so much so that the fall was rumoured to be a suicide. It came shortly after the discovery by Nana of a secret exchange of letters between Baji Rao and Madho Rao. The former had requested a meeting with the peshwa to which the latter had joyfully replied that he would soon arrange a visit. But the letter was intercepted. When Nana confronted the young ruler, the latter was embarassed. The minister lectured him on the dangers inherent in such a correspondence and went so far as to punish Balwant Rao, the guardian of the confined princes, who had been the go-between in this affair. The story goes that Madho Rao felt so humiliated by the whole affair that he decided to end his life. It had given him little pleasure, and the prospect seemed unendurably dreary. This sudden and untimely death was to set in motion a chain of events that would result in the ultimate destruction of the Maratha state.

The subsequent death of Mahadji was to prove almost as disastrous for the house of Scindia. Mahadji had begat no son of his body, but before his death his wife had, with his approval, adopted the young Daulat Rao after the usual Hindu custom. Daulat Rao was his nephew by blood, the son of his cousin Anand Rao. The act of adoption had been performed only a few months before his death which was sudden, following a recurring fever. His age was sixty-seven, and his heir-designate was only fourteen. It was the long minority of Madho Rao coupled with the baneful influence of Nana Fadnavis that debilitated and ultimately destroyed the peshwas. It was the youthful immaturity of Daulat Rao, combined with the evil influence of the much more depraved Sharza Rao Ghatge, his father-in-law, that wrecked the heritage of Mahadji, and brought the Raj of the Company Bahadur to Delhi and Poona, after more than half a century of strife and confusion. No man symbolized the agony of the age better than the blind old emperor in the Qila-i-Mualla who had seen it all happen, from the terror of the Nadir Shahi occupation, to the horrors perpetrated by Ghulam Qadir.

The house of Holkar was a major actor in this final act of the painfully extended drama. Ever since the death of the great Malhar Rao I in 1768, the guardian angel of his house had been his saintly daughter-in-law, Ahalya Bai, the widow of his only son Khande Rao. After her death in 1795, the fortunes of the house slid rapidly downhill. Tukoji Holkar, the military and executive head of the family, enfeebled by drink, followed her to the grave two years later, in August 1797. His son Malhar Rao II, who had already by his rash intervention in Rajasthan in 1793 invited the disaster of Lakheri, died a month later at the hands of assassins sent by Daulat Rao.

There was family strife within each of these princely houses. Daulat Rao, under the influence of the vicious Sharza Rao, alienated many of Mahadji's officers, and stopped the allowances of his widows, whereupon the ladies appealed to their late lord's officers. What followed is known as the 'Widows War'. In the Holkar house it was first Jaswant Rao ranged against his elder brother, the mentally deficient Kashi Rao, in the interest of the infant of Malhar Rao II. Later it became a struggle for survival against Daulat Rao Scindia, and eventually, after the execution of his brother Vittoji, against Baji Rao II as well.

As if this were not enough, the picture was confused further by the attempt of the Chhatrapatis of Satara and Kolhapur to throw off the yoke of the peshwas and become their own masters. Oddly enough, though the lord of Satara was undoubtedly the legal head of the Maratha state, and the peshwa only his servant, contemporary Maratha historians refer to this attempt to reassert their authority as a 'rebellion'; just as the British in 1857 insisted on calling Bahadur Shah II a 'rebel' against the 'paramount' power, even though the former was the legal sovereign of India. But fortunately for the Chhatrapatis, their 'rebellion' did not have the same tragic consequences. While the Maratha wars ended with the abolition of the office of peshwa, the two princely houses of Satara and Kolhapur survived and the latter was still in existence in 1969 when Indira Gandhi, then prime minister, abolished the princely order (Satara having lapsed during the term of Lord Dalhousie).

During this confused period the main scene of the fighting was Malwa, the upper Deccan, and to some extent Rajputana. Delhi was now a backwater. The relevance of this period was slight to the padishah in the Qila-i-Mualla. But for the Maratha civil wars Baji Rao would not have been driven to take refuge with the English at Bassein and to seek their help to return to Poona. The wars that followed, the occupation of Delhi, and of the Maratha territories of Upper India, and the subordination of the peshwa and the great Maratha chiefs in 'subsidary alliances' constituted the first phase. The destruction of the peshwaship, and further annexations, completed the second.

There was first the struggle for succession in Poona itself. Madho Rao died on 27 October 1795, but it was not until 26 November, the following year, that Baji Rao ascended the masnad. Madho Rao had died issueless. Next in the line of succession were the three sons of Raghunath Rao Dada, Amrit Rao, Baji Rao and Chimnaji Appa. The first, undoubtedly the fittest, was only an adopted son, and Chimnaji was but 11 years old. But Nana Fadnavis had checkmated Raghunath Rao Dada (also known as Raghoba) and kept him and his sons in prison. The last thing he wanted was to see any of them made peshwa for they would be certain to take their revenge against the old Machiavelli.

All kinds of expedients were proposed. It was suggested that Yashodha Bai, the senior widow of Madho Rao, should adopt some boy, and various youngsters were brought forward for the purpose. But the claims of the legitimate heirs could not be brushed aside. Ultimately, it was decided, as a compromise, that she should adopt Chimnaji Appa. The boy had to be practically forced into a *palki* on 12 May and brought under escort to the Shaniwar Palace where, on 25 May, the fifteen year old widow was forced to adopt the twelve year old boy. A week later, on 2 June, Chimnaji was invested with the *khillats* of his office which had been ordered from the Chhatrapati of Satara, in a state durbar.[3]

Nana was an astute intriguer, but it was Daulat Rao Scindia who commanded the biggest battalions and it was difficult for Nana to maintain his power. Scindia desperately needed money to pay his bloated army and had his eye on Nana's fabulous hoards.

Eventually, after many tortuous manoeuvrings and intrigues, Nana transferred his allegiance to Baji Rao. The assent of Scindia was also obtained through Sharza Rao Ghatge. Even Nizam Ali, the Mughal viceroy, and his minister Mushir-ul-Mulk were involved in the plot. On 26 November 1796, Chimnaji was deposed and Baji Rao installed. The Nizam was rewarded by the annulment of the indemnity due from him after his defeat in the battle of Kharda on 11 March 1795.

The next phase begins with the death of Tukoji Holkar on 15 August 1797. The austere Ahalya had died two years earlier. According to the scheme envisaged by the two, the Holkar heritage was to be divided between Kashi Rao and Malhar Rao II, the two legitimate sons of Tukoji, with the dimwitted cripple, Kashi Rao, as titular head while the fire-eating Malhar filled the role played by Tukoji, i.e. of military commander and de facto leader. But even before Tukoji breathed his last, it became evident that it was not a practical solution and Tukoji died a disappointed man, full of dark forebodings.

Kashi Rao sought the help of Daulat Rao Scindia while Malhar courted Nana. Their half-brothers, Jaswant Rao and Vittoji (sons of Tukoji, through a concubine), rallied to Malhar's support. This triumvirate was, however, no match for the ruthless Daulat Rao. While they were still plotting, Scindia struck the first blow.

On 14 September, just a month after Tukoji's death, Daulat Rao, acting under the advice of Ghatge, sent a small force to seize Malhar. The brothers were forewarned and, with the few hundred soldiers they had with them, stood on alert, waiting for the blow. But nothing happened. Then, just as dawn was breaking and Malhar had changed to secure a little rest, the blow fell. Malhar was taken completely by surprise. There was no time to organize a defence and he was felled by a chance bullet in the forehead, dying instantly.

Jaswant and Vittoji were able to escape but the camp and family of Malhar were captured. Among them was Jijibai, Malhar's widow who was several months pregnant. In due course, she gave birth to a son, named Khande Rao, for whose rights Jaswant would wage a bitter struggle against Scindia and, ultimately also, the Peshwa.

Jaswant Rao first took refuge in Nagpur, but Raghoji Bhonsle, who held that city, in order to curry favour with Scindia, arrested and confined him. However, he escaped within six months, was apprehended a second time, and then escaped again. From there he proceeded, a fugitive, to Khandesh and thence to Dhar, where he was able to perform signal service to the ruler, Anand Rao Puar. But he did not stop here long. Accepting a modest sum from the prince, he moved on, plundering the Scindia villages.

Meanwhile, another revolution had taken place at Poona. On 31 December 1797 Nana Fadnavis was arrested by Filose, an officer of Scindia, and thrown into prison, all his property being confiscated. Now began a reign of terror as Sharza Rao and Scindia set about the unpleasant business of extorting money from the Poona sardars. The first to be targetted were naturally the partisans of Nana. Their houses were searched and dug up for buried treasure. The sardars were flogged and tortured in a bid to make them reveal their secret hiding places, and great was the suffering inflicted upon the people. After the sardars, it was the turn of the bankers and merchants.

These atrocities were perpetrated with the consent of Baji Rao who had offered Scindia Rs. 1 crore to be rid of Nana. Nana, in turn, had offered Scindia a sizeable sum to quit Poona, but obviously his offer was not as attractive as Baji Rao's.

Ghatge occupied the mansion of Nana himself and on 26 February, while the extortions were still going on, celebrated the marriage of his daughter, Baiza Bai, with Daulat Rao Scindia amid scenes of unprecedented splendour. By this marriage the bonds between him and Daulat Rao were strengthened even further. In his extortions Ghatge was assisted by Baloji Kanjar, a flunkey of the peshwa, whose name is indicative of the special services rendered by him to his vicious master.[4]

The widows of the late Mahadji were also victims of Sharza and Daulat Rao's lust for gold. The allowances of the ladies, who were three in number, Lakshmi Bai, Yamuna Bai and Bhagirathi Bai, had been stopped by their adopted son. They protested to the peshwa and demanded that independent provision be made for their maintenance, commensurate with the services of their late husband to the Maratha commonwealth. While Bhagirathi Bai was close to Daulat Rao (he was reputedly her lover), the other two were living in comparative poverty and neglect in Ujjain. The ladies, who were popular with the officers of Scindia, dashed off letters appealing for support, to which Sharza and Scindia reacted by arresting and confining their most ardent followers. The ladies set off for Poona, but on the way were intercepted by Ghatge. The ladies refused to see him. Sharza then forcibly entered their tents in a towering rage, abused and assaulted them, laying into them with a whip.[5]

The outrage had its inevitable consequences. Muzaffar Khan, one of Scindia's officers, declared in favour of the ladies. Amrit Rao, the peshwa's brother, also joined them and a full scale war broke out. The ladies, in particular Lakshmi Bai, pressed forward with vigour and on 8 June attacked Daulat Rao Scindia's camp, the doughty Lakshmi Bai leading her forces on an elephant.

The attack was repulsed, and Scindia followed up with an attack of his own on the ladies' camp at Khirkee near Poona. Amrit Rao was decisively beaten and the ladies moved south towards Kolhapur where the Chhatrapatis were sympathetic. Daulat Rao was now eager for peace and opened negotiations. The war had had its repercussions in the north where

Lakhwa Dada had also declared himself in favour of Mahadji's widows. Daulat Rao realized that if the matter was not settled soon, it might result in a full blown civil war which could endanger his position in Upper India. He had made too many enemies and now requested Baji Rao to mediate. But the ladies were adamant. They wanted nothing less than the arrest of Ghatge which Scindia was not yet ready to concede. Instead, he released Nana and begged him to take over the government and intervene in the matter. Meanwhile, more officers, including some of the European mercenaries, deserted Scindia.

Ultimately, Scindia realized that his father-in-law had become a liability. An incident in which Ghatge's men attacked and wounded some of Filose's sepoys provided the excuse for Ghatge's arrest. Filose seized Ghatge and some of his men, and paraded them in the camp bazaar, bound with ropes, the sepoys prodding and pushing them with their musket butts, and loudly abusing them. The widows had been amply avenged, and a temporary settlement was reached bringing the war to an end in August 1798.[6]

While the Maratha state was going through these convulsions, momentous events were happening in the rest of India. Richard Wellesley, Earl of Mornington, had arrived in India as the new Governor-General of the East India Company. His ambitions were imperial and he was determined to make the English the paramount power in India. His brother Arthur, the future Duke of Wellington, had preceded him to India by two years. Then still a colonel, who had seen but limited action in Flanders in 1794, he was to learn the art of war in the Deccan, and, even more than Eton, the field of Assaye was the forge where the future victor of Waterloo was tempered.

For the Indians of the eighteenth century there seemed little difference between the French and the English. Both wore hats, dressed alike, and spoke equally unintelligible tongues. The Indians of the period possessed only a very hazy idea of the geography of what lay beyond their own realm. But Lord Wellesley chose to see in every French mercenary employed in an Indian court an agent of Bonaparte. At Aden he was shown a poster, which the governor of Mauritius had caused to be published in the island colony, calling for volunteers for service under Tipu Sultan of Mysore. This convinced Wellesley that there existed a grand conspiracy to establish French hegemony in India.

When he arrived in India he observed that the Frenchman, Francois Raymond, had already established himself in Hyderabad, which in his eyes was well on its way to becoming a French protectorate. The

Governor-General determined to pressurize the Nizam to dismiss his French officers and accept a 'subsidiary' alliance on the lines of Awadh, that is, the Nizam should accept a British military force, to be cantoned in his dominions for his protection for which he would be charged. He was facilitated in attaining this objective by the chance death of Raymond on 25 March 1798, shortly before his own arrival in India. When pressed, the Nizam reluctantly accepted the English proposals and all the French officers were dismissed. They were replaced in due course by British officers. The Nizam's dominions were now a British protectorate.

Then pressure was brought to bear on the peshwa to join the English in a fresh war against Tipu. But there was no man in Poona capable of taking a decision. Thus, the matter was allowed to hang fire until news arrived that the war was already over and Tipu slain, fighting, sword in hand, in the breach at Seringapatnam.

The swiftness with which the war was concluded left the Marathas dumb-founded. Now Wellesley renewed the pressure on Baji Rạo to accept a subsidiary alliance, relinquish the Maratha claims against the new ruler of the now shrunken state of Mysore, and accept a subordinate position vis-a-vis the British. Baji Rao did not accept these humiliating conditions, but no preparations were made to meet the developing threat.

There was some vague talk of attacking the Nizam, but it soon evaporated when the British made it known that they would support the Nizam to the hilt. Intrigues were set afoot to win over the newly restored Wadiyar raja of Mysore and set him up against the English, but these were easily scotched by Arthur Wellesley, the Governor-General's brother, who was now Resident at Mysore. Nana Fadnavis, though nominally at the helm, concerned himself only with affairs of secondary importance such as the war with the Scindia widows, the two Chhatrapatis and Amrit Rao. He was quite clearly a spent force.

The widows' war had again flared up and the alliance between the ladies and the Chhatrapati of Kolhapur was cemented by the marriage of a daughter of Scindia to the Chhatrapati. Throughout the latter part of 1799 the war raged, and the Chhatrapati of Satara also jumped into the fray in the hope of taking advantage of the confusion to effect a political revolution to his advantage vis-a-vis the peshwa. In March 1800 Nana died. With the only experienced minister removed from the scene, both Baji Rao and Scindia committed one atrocity after another against officers and courtiers whose loyalty was suspect, or whom they disliked. On 31 May two officers were blown from guns for having supported the ladies. On 8 July some others had their noses and ears sliced off and were paraded through the camp before being executed. One Narayan Rao Bakhshi was, with devilish ingenuity, blown up with rockets that had been tied to his body.[7]

Towards the end of the year 1800 the war between Jaswant Rao Holkar and Scindia also picked up. The widows had moved up into Malwa where they made contact with Jaswant Rao and Lakhwa Dada. Jaswant was, however, an uncertain ally and on 1 November, seduced by the offer of Rs. 5 lakh from Ambaji Ingle, actually attacked the Bais and looted their camp, the two ladies barely escaping with their lives to join Lakhwa Dada. Ujjain was occupied by Jaswant and the usual spoliation and extortion began, with the mansions of the rich being dug up to yield their buried hoards. Though Jaswant had abandoned the cause of the Bais, he continued to plunder Scindia's territories.

On 3 May 1801 Lakhwa Dada was brought to bay at Seondha by Perron's *campoo*. It was a hopeless contest. Recognizing his inferiority, Lakhwa had adopted Kazakhi tactics as against pitched battles. His soldiers were disgruntled for want of money and were deserting in large numbers. In the battle that ensued, the Dhar raja (who had joined Lakhwa) was mortally wounded. Lakhwa was hurt in the hand; the wound refusing to heal, he too died nine months later in Mewar where he had sought asylum. The widows took refuge in Datia.

Within two months of the battle of Seondha war again broke out. This time the combatants were Jaswant and Scindia. The latter had opened negotiations with Jaswant but the talks foundered when Jaswant demanded the release of Khande Rao, Malhar's infant son, and the restoration of all the Holkar villages. With negotiations broken off, Jaswant resumed his plundering forays with renewed vigour. Trampled fields, and plundered and smoking villages marked the passage of his predatory armies. It was a time of indescribable suffering for the people of Malwa.

As for Daulat Rao, he took his time to reach the theatre of war. Leaving Poona on 5 December he moved up in easy stages, wasting nearly four months in shikar and merry-making near Burhanpur. In the meantime, to strengthen his army in the north, he despatched reinforcements in small detachments which Holkar's cavalry was able to intercept and destroy one by one. The first such victory was at Newri on 25 June 1801 where Jaswant Rao's cavalry overwhelmed and cut up MacIntyre's infantry battalions with 500 supporting horse. MacIntyre himself was taken prisoner along with many other officers. On 4 July, however, at Satwas, Brownning put up a stout defence and repulsed the Holkar cavalry with heavy loss. But the victory was nullified by the capture of Ujjain only 13 days later.

Scindia's local commander was Hessing. He put up a stout defence, fighting with desperate courage, but at last his force was overpowered, the *campoo* cut up and broken, Hessing himself barely escaping with his life. The unfortunate city now underwent a second sack. It is recorded that the Brahmins were singled out for special attention, but women were surprisingly spared the usual horrors of rape and abduction.

Then came the turn of Indore which was Holkar's own capital. On 14 October he was forced to defend the city in a pitched battle against superior forces led by Ghatge. At first the Holkar horse seemed likely to carry everything before it but poor Michel Filose, whose battalions were overrun, was so overcome by the filthy abuse that Ghatge hurled at him that he cut his own throat. Holkar was routed, all his artillery and equipment falling into Ghatge's hands. The sack of Ujjain was repaid by the city of Indore which was now systematically plundered.

Now Jaswant Rao Holkar took up the life of a roving plunderer, more a pindarri than a sardar. For a short while he and Kashi Rao were reconciled but they soon fell apart again. Meanwhile, Vittoji was independently plundering and wasting the Poona countryside in the name of Amrit Rao. In April 1801 he was captured by Bapu Gokhale and produced before Baji Rao.

The latter, in a fit of anger, had him flogged 200 lashes, then tying him to the feet of an elephant had him dragged about the courtyard until he died, crushed under the pachyderm's feet. Baji Rao and his favourite pimp, Baloji Kanjar, watched with glee from the terrace above. The body was then exhibited in the streets before being cremated.[8] Vittoji's wife and son were imprisoned.

This savage execution which took place on 16 April 1801 filled everyone with horror. Although Vittoji was a ruffian, and little better then a robber, most people felt that as a scion of the Holkars he deserved a less humiliating end. When the news of Vittoji's cruel death reached Jaswant, he swore he would take his revenge against Baji Rao. The war now moved southwards.

By July 1802 Holkar's predatory horse was ravaging the environs of Ahmadnagar. Then it moved on to plunder Nasik. The Scindias' palaces at Jambgaon and Shrigonda were razed to the ground. Famine raged in the Deccan. The movement of grain was impossible because of the marauding armies, and Holkar's cavalry survived only on account of its mobility. The Poona countryside lay in desolation.

Jaswant had not switched entirely to guerilla warfare. In spite of the vicissitudes of fortune, he was still able to retain some of his European mercenaries, and the battalions of officers like Hardinge, Armstrong and Vickers formed the hard core of his army. Their military strength was no match for the might of Perron's *campoo*, but the peshwa's personal troops were wretched in comparison and unable to face Jaswant in the field.

By large promises and small advances Baji Rao was able to collect a few thousand cavalry and infantry and sent them ahead to bar the advance of More, the Holkar general, with the *zari patka* of the peshwa. It was hoped that the respect which was generally accorded to the standard of the peshwa would intimidate the avenging, armies of Holkar. Among the generals commanding the peshwa's rabble was, characteristically enough, Baloji Kanjar!

But the peshwa's prestige was not comparable to that of the Chughata emperors whose mere approach could at one time quell a rebel or a recalcitrant governor into submission. Moreover, it was only the *zari patka* that had been sent forth, the cowardly Baji Rao had not the courage to confront the rebels himself. As anyone could have forseen, More refused to be intimidated by the banners, and the rabble commanded by the pimp and Purandare were easily dispersed. Only Maloji Ghorpade stood by to defend the standard with his personal contingent which held the ground for about an hour. The 'battle' ended when the gallant Ghorpade fell down from his horse after it was pierced by a lance.

Ghorpade had been wounded five times. More had his wounds attended to and sent him back free to Poona, placing a palki at his disposal. The captured *patka* was also returned later by Holkar with the proud declaration, 'We are all one, equal servants of the same master, and no rebels.' Scindia was following hard on his heels and pitched his camp close by a few days later.

Holkar sent another message to the peshwa demanding that his dispute with Scindia be settled and emissaries be sent on the peshwa's behalf to negotiate a settlement between them. He also warned that if the agents did not arrive, he would not waste time in further talk but fight it out with Scindia, and the peshwa must not interfere in that event. 'You must remember I am as loyal a servant of yours as Scindia', he warned. 'My dispute is with him alone and I am prepared to settle it in my own way. You are playing into his hands and ruining the State. The English are at the door. You have only to act the master, let me act the servant.'

This blunt message was delivered to the peshwa on 23 October. But Baji Rao did not send his diwan. Instead, he sent two inferior officers whom Holkar refused to see. Early on the morning of 25 October Baji Rao tried to flee but Baloji Kanjar had him forcibly removed to Scindia's camp.

The battle opened later with a cannonade from the Scindia guns. The day, incidentally, happened to be Diwali, the festival of lights which celebrates the victorious return of Sri Ramchandra of Ayodhya after his triumph over the demon king, Ravana. But there would be no celebratory illuminations in the city and palaces of Poona that night.

Perron's crack troops were not present on the field with Scindia's forces. He had remained with the northern army, the military governor of Delhi and Hindostan. The trained sepoys that faced Holkar were of very inferior mettle. Due to the xenophobic hatred which Perron nursed against the English, most of his Anglo-Saxon officers had left his service, many among them entering the employ of Holkar.

Holkar showed restraint. He had instructed his gunners to wait until the twenty-fifth cannon shot before replying. Both in numbers and artillery Holkar's army was superior to Scindia's. Even the cavalry, stiffened with Amir Khan's Pathans, was superior. The battle was hard-fought but its issue was decided by the flight of the craven peshwa who had been watching from a safe distance. Thereafter the Poona contingent and the Scindia cavalry bolted. The sepoys fought well and three of the four European officers were killed. Only Honore was able to get away with the colours of his battalion to Wanowri but he was forced to surrender a few days later. In all Scindia lost about 5,000 men with all the guns, tents and baggage, while Holkar's losses were about 1,600. Colonel Hardinge was killed and Vickers wounded.

The Scindia infantry consisted mainly of north Indian Muslims and Rajputs. For the Deccanis they were foreigners (*pardesis*) and in their hour of misfortune no helping hand was raised to save them. The Maratha peasantry and the rabble of Poona fell on them and mercilessly robbed them, the wounded being left to die untended in the streets.[9]

The citizens of Poona awaited with dread the avenger's blow but Jaswant Rao kept his troops in rein and the city was spared the horrors of a general sack. Holkar stopped his army outside the city and proclaimed that if any of his soldiers entered the city or robbed the citizens of even a single cowrie, he would be disemboweled. At critical moments, Holkar was always able to enforce discipline on his otherwise desperate and licentious troops.

Of course this did not mean that Poona would be spared the usual fate of the vanquished. Only that Holkar's soldiers would not be permitted to plunder indiscriminately. The rich and noble would be selectively squeezed so that all the treasure and cash went to Holkar's war chest.

The most momentous consequence of this battle, which is known as the battle of Hadapur, was that the peshwa fled to British territory. The final act of the Chitpavan tragedy was about to be played.

NOTES

1. The wards of the city of Poona were called 'waras' and weekly markets were held on different days of the week in each wara. In the quarter where the Peshwa's palace was located the market day was Saturday.
2. Sardesai, *A New History of the Marathas*, iii, p. 283.
3. Ibid., p. 317.
4. Sardesai, pp. 335-7. A kanjar is a pimp. There is also a tribe in Malwa bearing this name. Their women are prostitutes by tradition, while the men-folk pimp for them.
5. Sardesai, p. 338.
6. Sardesai, p. 340.
7. Sardesai, p. 356.
8. Sardesai, pp. 366-7. Sarkar, *Fall of the Mughal Empire*, iv, pp. 161-2. Malcolm, *A Memoir of Central India*, i, p. 197 (fn.).
9. Sarkar, iii, pp. 175-6.

CHAPTER 44

Maratha Twilight

The peshwa sought refuge in British territory. A British vessel, the *Hercules*, took him to the island fortress of Suvarn Durg, and thence to Bombay, where he was received by the English governor. After a few days sojourn, during which he was royally wined and dined, he proceeded to the English factory at Bassein where negotiations began.

Jaswant Rao Holkar had always maintained that his quarrel was with Scindia and that he was the peshwa's loyal servant. Consistent with that role, he sent urgent messages to him not to conclude any treaty without consulting the other sardars and implored him to return to his capital. Before the peshwa entered British territory, Holkar could well have seized him, but he hesitated to use force against the chief executive of the Maratha State.

At first, the English resident, Colonel Close, also advised the peshwa to return, but this would have been contrary to Lord Wellesley's imperial designs. Fortunately for the resident, the peshwa was too frightened to go back. The Governor-Generals's policy was controversial; there was opposition from many quarters, including his own brother, Arthur. To cap it all, this aggresive forward policy was totally unauthorized. But for the present the great proconsul was in full control and he supervised each move in the carefully orchestrated plan.

When Baji Rao failed to return, the Maratha sardars turned to Amrit Rao who, living in retirement on his jagir of Rs. 7 lakh per annum, was by no means over-eager to unseat his undeniably incompetent brother. However, he allowed the Maratha chiefs to use his son Vinayak Rao, and the robes and insignia of peshwaship were procured from the Chhatrapati of Satara in the name of the latter.

But the legality of this revolution was doubtful. To clinch the issue a formal adoption by Yashodha Bai, the widow of Madho Rao Narayan, was required. But the lady was securely held in the fort of Raigarh and the qiladar refused to surrender her. At first all the chiefs were united, and had set their mutual differences aside, but Sharza Rao Ghatge cast his baleful influence on Daulat Rao Scindia, who dissociated himself from the others and wrote to Baji Rao not to return, saying the sardars would assuredly crush Holkar in due course.

It was among these vacillations that the British hammered out the treaty of Bassein which the wretched peshwa signed on 31 December 1802. According to its clauses, a force of 6,000 British troops would be stationed in his territory, and for their maintenance mahals yielding Rs. 26 lakh per annum would be set aside. But what really bound the peshwa hand and foot was the stipulation that in the case of disputes with chiefs, who also had relations of this nature with the British, the peshwa would accept British arbitration. He also bound himself not to engage in hostilities with any other state without prior consultation with the British. Then there were the usual provisions for extending mutual military assistance whenever necessary.[1]

Thus, after the conclusion of this treaty the peshwa's state became a protectorate, incapable of conducting an independent foreign policy. The English had already concluded similar treaties with the Gaikwad of Baroda earlier in the year and with the viceroy of the Deccan, i.e. the Nizam. With the extension of the subsidiary alliance system over Baroda and Poona, the peshwa lost control even of his relations with his own feudatories.

After the battle of Hadapur the Holkar army constituted the most important segment of the Maratha forces. But Jaswant Rao no longer had any regular revenues as the bulk of the Holkar estates were in the possession of Scindia, and he needed Rs. 1 crore to pay his troops. Inevitably, the money had to be extorted from the Poona gentry. The usual oppressive and coercive methods were employed, Amir Khan's Pathans being the principal instruments. For weeks and months the process went on, the floors of houses were dug up, the furniture and silver vessels carted away, and rich respectable men beaten and starved into revealing their secret hiding places. These methods yielded about Rs. 50 lakh, only about half the required sum.

The British had engaged to restore Baji Rao to the peshwa's masnad at Poona. The task was entrusted to young Arthur Wellesley who set about the task with quiet efficiency. A public proclamation announcing that the English were entering the Maratha country as friends, and calling for the cooperation of all officials and zamindars, was issued. Holkar was assured that the English did not mean to interfere with his possessions and persuaded to leave Poona, which he did on 25 February, after receiving *khillats* of dismissal from the wives of both Baji Rao and Amrit Rao.

On 20 April Arthur Wellesley entered Poona, and on 13 May came Baji Rao II himself. The regime of Amrit Rao (or to be more precise, his son Vinayak Rao) had collapsed after barely four months without a shot being fired in its defence.

Now Wellesley set about dividing the Maratha camp. Amrit Rao was undoubtedly the most able member of the peshwa's family, but he had no army and no resources as his jagir had been resumed by Baji Rao's orders issued from Bombay. But now Wellesley, ignoring Baji Rao's protests, secured for Amrit Rao a jagir worth Rs. 8 lakh i.e. more than his previous, and moreover, guaranteed by the British. By this act, the British converted Amrit Rao into a grateful friend who would render good service in the future.[2]

The attitude of Baji Rao towards the English was, in truth, ambiguous. He resented no less than the other Maratha chiefs the loss of his independence, which was implicit in the terms of the treaty of Bassein, but he was too weak a person to take any steps on his own. He was always hoping that something would turn up which would enable him to shake off his shackles. But the English were not the sort to leave things to chance. Even when Wellesley's policy was reversed, his successors made sure that British prestige was not affected.

Baji Rao considered Holkar and Amrit Rao as his worst enemies, and had hoped to use British support to destroy the power of the former and humiliate the latter. But his designs against Amrit Rao had been frustrated by the generous treatment extended by Colonel Wellesley, and a tacit understanding between the former and Holkar. Daulat Rao Scindia was regarded by Baji Rao as a friend, but the English had always viewed Scindia with suspicion. De Boigne's well trained *campoo*, now led by the anti-English General Perron, and largely officered by Frenchmen, was regarded by the Wellesleys as a French army, the destruction of which was of as much concern to them in India, as was that of Bonaparte's in Europe. Equating the two was ridiculous but it sealed forever Daulat Rao's dreams of an imperial hegemony.

By a series of clever diplomatic moves it was made to appear that Scindia and Bhonsle of Nagpur were the real threat to peace in the Deccan. The proximity of their armies to the border of the Nizam's dominions, which were a British protectorate, provided the excuse for war. A bewildered Baji Rao watched helplessly in shocked disbelief when his 'protectors' moved against his best friend.

In August 1803 the operations began with a march by the English against Aurangabad, a Scindia possession, which was seized. Some minor battles followed, culminating in the final decisive battle of Assaye fought on 24 September 1803.

Assaye was a major and well-contested battle in which the English suffered heavy casualties, namely 663 Europeans and over 1,700 Indians. Scindia's general, Gopal Rao Bhau, the hero of Lakheri, put up a bold front and some of the battalions retired in good order. But the Marathas were unable to rally again. They fell back on Burhanpur but the pursuing English easily captured the town. The great fortress of Asirgarh capitulated on its garrison being offered their arrears, amounting to Rs. 7 lakh, by the English.[3]

On 25 November the Bhonsle army was defeated at Adgaum. A month later the great fortress of Gawilgarh, was taken. At the same time operations were also directed against the Bhonsle possessions in the east, while from September onwards Lord Lake, who commanded the Company' Bengal army, had been pressing vigorously against Scindia's northern army.

The fighting ended in December 1803, the treaty of Devgaon being signed on 17 December with Bhonsle, while the treaty of Sirji-Anjangaon concluded the war with Scindia. But Lord Lake's campaign had knocked the Deccanis out of Hindostan and brought the *Sahiban-i-Inglishia* at long last to Delhi. Lord Lake had become the keeper of the blind emperor, and his northern campaign is therefore of vital importance to the history of the Qila-i-Mualla.

As the great Mahadji was succeeded by the inferior Daulat Rao, so the great de Boigne was followed by the lesser Perron. Boigne was a member of the Savoyard gentry, a man of breeding and education, while Perron, a weaver's son, could scarcely write a few sentences of decent French. But like Boigne, he was a careful administrator; diligent, energetic and indefatigable, who carefully husbanded his resources, rigorously supervised his estates, carefully going over the accounts and salting away a huge private fortune. It was in 1798 that Ambaji Ingle, Lakhwa Dada's successor, raised him to the position that Boigne had held and conferred on him the rank of general. On Daulat Rao Scindia's recommendation Shah Alam raised him to the rank of an umara of 7,000 with the *alkab* of Nasir ul-Mulk, Intizam ud-Daulah, Bahadur and Muzaffar Jang.

In 1802, after Lakhwa Dada's dismissal following his triumph at Malpura, Perron became the supreme commander of the Maratha forces in the north. In return for a *peshkash* of Rs. 15 lakh to his insolvent master, he obtained possession of the seven most important forts in Hindostan.

Now, at the peak of his power, he became aware of the precarious nature of his master's dominion, and began to make arrangements for a safe getaway in the event of the destruction of the Scindian state.

What followed was a disgraceful story of treachery and betrayal. Onwards 1802 Perron was busy making arrangements to convert his property into cash and to deposit it with English banks, and negotiating with the Company's agents at Lucknow for favourable terms. While he obviously had no confidence in his ability to fight the English, he did nothing to caution Daulat Rao. De Boigne, on the other hand, had always advised Mahadji not to spoil his relations with the Company, and the latter had always laid great store by his advice. But Perron continued to publicly boast of his preparations and his eagerness to fight.

Although he had ample notice of the British intentions, he made no effort to strengthen the garrison of Aligarh which was the key to the Doab. In fact he sent two battalions to Agra, virtually denuding the Doab of troops. This was no surprise since he was in secret communication with Lord Lake who had been given carte blanche by the Governor-General to settle terms with Perron on his surrender. But Lake wished to first defeat him in the field, because he felt the moral effect of such a victory over the hitherto invincible campoo would have a shattering effect on the rest of Scindia's army.

In contrast to Perron, Lake was a seasoned general, well experienced in European warfare. His military apprenticeship had begun in the Prussian army with no less a mentor than Fredrick the Great. He had made the frontier station of Kanpur his headquarters and had set about preparing for the offensive against the Marathas in a business-like way. His officers regarded him with affection; he frequently joined them at table and at shikar, and his relations with them were free and informal. His soldiers were equally devoted to him on account of his good humour and soldierly qualities. With his Prussian background he also maintained perfect discipline. In short, there could be no comparison between him and Perron.

The garrison of Aligarh consisted of scarcely 2,000 second-rate troops under the command of an aged Frenchman, Colonel Pedron. Lord Lake's march was unopposed. Perron made a show of resistance with a small force at the foot of the fort, but fled westward at the first cannonade without fighting! The flight had a shattering effect on the Marathas. European officers began to desert their units to avail themselves of the bounty which had been announced by Lord Wellesley.

This 'action' took place on 29 August 1803. Lake now tried to negotiate the surrender of the fort. Pedron was only too willing to oblige, but the sepoys, who were largely Rajputs and Rohilla Pathans, refused to stain their honour through such a pusillanimous surrender. They placed their colonel in confinement and determined to resist. However, in the early hours of 4 September, the outer walls were scaled and the fort fell after a brief resistance.

Perron's problem was how to escape from his army. After his flight from Aligarh he had halted at Mathura with his family. At first he toyed with the idea of bringing the emperor to Mathura and obtaining a treaty from him, which would make him a ward of the French instead of the Marathas, but when his emissary arrived at Delhi, Bourquin, the commander at Delhi, refused to recognize his authority. Bourquin had his own plans. Scindia's ramshackle state was crumbling and his European mercenaries were all busy making their own arrangements to get away with their loot.

Perron then pretended to go to Delhi to crush Bourquin's revolt. He crossed the river with his bodyguard and a small force of cavalry. The main army was to cross the next morning, but after the crossing he paid Rs. 5,000 to his men to keep the boats with them instead of returning them to the other side to enable the army to make the crossing. During the night he made a forced march of 30 miles to Sasni, from where he contacted the English. On 8 September, accompanied by his family and some officers, he entered British territory.[4]

Lord lake hurried on to Delhi, arriving at Patparganj on the other side of the river on 11 September. Bourquin had first tried to take possession of the fort. He called upon the qiladar, Drugeon, to surrender, but the latter refused and Bourquin brought up his guns and started shelling.

This was on 9 September. The terrified emperor sent a message to Lake to hurry up and save him. But Bourquin was then forced by his Indian officers to resist and fight the English.

Following the precedent set by Perron, Bourquin and his European colleagues made no attempt to fight. As soon as the battle began, they galloped across to the English lines and surrendered. But their troops, led by their Indian officers, among whom Sarwar Khan was the foremost, fought on until they were cut up by the British fire and pushed into the river.

The progress of the battle was being anxiously watched from the walls of the Qila-i-Mualla. As soon as the outcome was known, the emperor sent one of his nobles to congratulate Lord Lake and to ask him to rescue the emperor from the Marathas and to take him under his protection. Lake crossed over to the city and was received in audience by the blind monarch on 16 September 1803. The Maratha imperium had come to an end.

Agra fell on 18 October. Here again the Indians arrested and imprisoned their European officers who were disinclined to fight. The British batteries soon breached the walls and the fort surrendered on 18 October. Considerable treasure, amounting to Rs. 28 lakh was found, and Lord Lake distributed it as prize money among the troops which greatly annoyed the Governor-General.[5]

When the news of Perron's disgraceful conduct at Aligarh reached the ears of Daulat Rao Scindia, he ordered the Frenchman's dismissal. Thirteen select battalions of the original brigades trained by de Boigne were already on their way to the north to maintain the Scindia power. Orders appointing the Chevalier Dudrenec as the military commander, and Ambaji Ingle as the governor-designate for Delhi and Hindostan were dispatched.

The army had set out from the Deccan on 17 July, but its progress was slow because of the monsoon. It reached the Agra district in the beginning of October, well after the loss of Aligarh and Delhi. Recognizing the military situation to be irretrievable, the Chevalier, following the disgraceful precedents set by Perron, Bourquin and others, promptly surrendered to the English, along with some other European officers.

The command of the army now devolved on the shoulders of Ambaji who was joined at this time by Sarwar Khan, the gallant Rohilla who had forced Bourquin to fight and after the battle of Patparganj escaped from the field with two battalions intact. After vainly trying to persuade the Jat raja of Bharatpur to join them, the Marathas retreated into the broken country of Mewat where they were joined by some minor chiefs. It was a fairly formidable force that assembled. It could have recovered Delhi, but Ambaji was more intent on carving out a principality for himself out of the wreckage of the Scindia state than in re-establishing the fortunes of his master. He, therefore, preferred to use his army to plunder the villages of the rajas of Bharatpur, Macheri and Jaipur, pushing these states more firmly into the arms of the British.

Agra fell on 18 October. Lord Lake was now ready to deal with Ambaji. He tracked down the Maratha army in the hills of Alwar. The two armies were brought face to face on 1 November at the village of Laswari (or Naswari) in the territory of the Macheri raja. Interestingly, this 'Maratha' army consisted almost entirely of 'Hindostanis'. The artillery and infantry consisted mainly of Pathans, Mughals, Rajputs and Brahmins, i.e. its composition was almost the same as that of Lord Lake's 'Bengal' army. But for a force of Deccani light horse numbering about 1,200 men—who abandoned the field without a blow—it was one north Indian army fighting another. The Marathas were averse to enlisting as infantry, their light horse was obsolescent, while the best infantry was recruited from among the 'Purbias' of Awadh and Bihar, with 'Mughals' and Rohillas from the Doab. These were to constitute the principal 'martial' races of Upper India, until the 'Mutiny' of 1857 led to a switch in favour of Punjabis.

The first part of the battle was inconclusive. Lake was unable to break the Maratha lines and had to pull back his cavalry. The Maratha gunners had displayed considerable skill and courage, but Ambaji was unable to utilize the lull that followed to resume the offensive. In fact, he tried to negotiate a peaceful withdrawal by surrendering his artillery, but his gunners indignantly refused.[6]

In the lull, Sarwar Khan tightened his defences and brought up more troops, as the afternoon battle raged around the village of Malpur. The fighting was desperate, and the *campoo* proved its defensive capability, but the initiative remained throughout with the English. After fierce hand-to-hand fighting, the broken remnants of the *campoo* at last surrendered and the fighting died down. The victors were as exhausted as the vanquished, and the setting sun lit up the field covered with the bodies of men and horses. The groans of the wounded, and the explosions of ammunition wagons, with the burning village of Malpur at the centre, marked an appropriately apocalyptic finale to the great struggle in the north.

The battle of Laswari in the north, and Assaye and Adgaum in the Deccan, knocked Scindia and Bhonsle out of the war. The Nagpur raja's far-flung holdings in Orissa had also been attacked by the English and Cuttack, Puri and Balasore had been taken in September-October. Using Baroda (which was already in subsidiary alliance with the British since March 1803) as a base, Scindia's holdings in Gujarat were also conquered.

On 17 December peace was made with Bhonsle. Cuttack and the Orissa coast were ceded to the English, and western Berar was ceded to the Nizam. Bhonsle was to leave the Maratha confederacy and agreed to respect the treaties concluded by the British with his feudatories, and not to entertain any enemy of the English in his service.

On 30 December 1803 Scindia bowed to the inevitable and appended his signature to the treaty of Sirji-Anjangaon. By it he agreed to surrender all the Maratha possessions in the Doab, the Agra and Delhi districts, besides Broach and some districts in Gujarat, parts of Bundelkhand and parts of the Godavari tracts and the fort of Ahmadnagar to the English. He relinquished all his claims on the peshwa, the Gaikwad and the Nizam, and agreed to recognize the independence of all those of his feudatories with whom the English had concluded treaties. And, of course, he was not to entertain in his employ any Frenchman, American, or a national of any other country which the English may choose to consider as their enemy.

Amrit Rao was persuaded to leave the Deccan and to take up residence in the holy city of Benares, both for the sake of his own safety (from the vengeful Baji Rao) and to keep him out of Maratha politics. Although the Maratha confederacy had been destroyed, the treaties were moderate, keeping in view the completeness of the British triumph. The great Maratha chieftaincies had been preserved—though diminished in extent—and removed from the control of the peshwa.

Daulat Rao Scindia's position was pitiable. He had aspired to be the virtual ruler of India by controlling the emperor, on the one hand, and the peshwa on the other. His army had been shattered and he was left with a huge burden of debt. His old hereditary enemy Jaswant Rao Holkar, was still plagueing him. At length, exasperated by the plundering activities of Holkar, Scindia was driven to beg the English for a subsidiary force. On 27 February 1804 he signed the supplementary treaty of Burhanpur.

Jaswant Rao Holkar had kept out of the struggle. The English would deal with him now. During the war he had plundered Ujjain, and extorted tribute from Aurangabad and Jaipur, though the latter had entered into relations with the English and accepted a subsidiary force. For the moment the English swallowed the insult, but it was obvious that having settled with Scindia and Bhonsle, the English would not tolerate such impertinence from Jaswant. In January 1804, Lord Lake communicated these sentiments to him on the instructions of the Governor-General. In return Holkar sent two agents to the General's camp with a letter in which he demanded the recognition of his traditional claims to *chauth* on Indian chiefs, and the return of the old Holkar possessions in the Doab and Bundelkhand. In return he was prepared to enter into an alliance with the English on the same terms as Scindia.

The first two demands were considered unreasonable. Lord Lake sent for the Holkar agents asking them to present only such proposals as were reasonable, whereupon in February Holkar wrote to him in threatening tones:

> countries of many hundred *kos* will be overrun. You shall not have leisure to breathe for a moment, and, calamities shall fall on many lacks of human beings by a continued war, in which my army will overwhelm like the waves of the sea.[7]

To back up his threats Holkar left for Pushkar, ostensibly on pilgrimage, but his army plundered that town and Ajmer, which fell on the way. Then he turned towards Jaipur against whom he had claims exceeding

Rs. 1 crore, and started plundering. This was intolerable, and in April the English commenced operations against this untamed Maratha, a throwback to the days of Shivaji and Shambhaji, and the last of a dying breed.

With the other sardars of the old confederacy, Scindia, Bhonsle and the Gaikwad, beaten, this was a last bold strike for Maratha independence. The activities of Holkar's agents in the courts of Poona and Ujjain ensured that the English received no assistance from their new found 'subsidiary' allies.

Lord Lake advanced against Holkar preceded by a force under Colonel Monson, while Colonel Murray was ordered to march from Gujarat into Malwa. Holkar retreated southwards from Jaipur. Monson's instructions were not to go beyond the Aravalli passes near Bundi and Lakheri, while the commander-in-chief decided to sit out the hot season and the rains in the cantonments at Kanpur. But Monson rashly continued his pursuit through the Mukundara pass, 30 miles south of Kotah, and then tried to attack Holkar as he was crossing the Chambal. But he was too late and found that the enemy had succeeded in fording the river. Murray was supposed to be nearby but at this moment he received a message from him that he had decided to return. Feeling that he alone was too weak to tackle Holkar, Monson decided to retreat to the Mukundara pass. At this point Holkar suddenly became aware of the proximity of the English force and decided to attack. Badly mauled, Monson retreated after spiking and abandoning his heavy guns. The raja of Kotah, terrorized by Holkar's hosts, did not lift a finger to help, and the retreat proved a nightmare. The forest Bhils joined the Marathas in robbing stragglers and plundering the routed army. The monsoon rains added to its plight. It was a thoroughly demoralized force, broken in spirit as well as substance, that at last stumbled into Agra at the end of August. It was the greatest disaster which had befallen a British army in India. The myth of British invincibility lay shattered and Jaswant Rao Holkar's stock rose to dizzy heights. All Hindostan shuddered in anticipation of the calamities he had boastfully threatened in his declaration of war.

But the bubble was burst soon enough. Lord Lake hurried from Kanpur to save Delhi, the loss of which would have had a terrible moral effect. Meanwhile Holkar had taken Mathura, and on 8 October 1804 fell upon Delhi. But after about a week he was forced to abandon the siege as Lake had come dangerously close. Holkar moved up north and then crossed into the Doab, heading towards the Awadh frontier.

At Farukhabad on the Ganga, he came face-to-face with Lord Lake and was completely defeated. His broken forces now trailed back westward across the Doab, re-crossed the Yamuna and sieged Dig, which was promptly besieged by the English.

Ranjit Singh, the Jat raja, openly espoused the cause of Holkar, and the Jat nation rallied enthusiastically to his support. But the siege of Dig did not last long. On 13 December, the fort was taken by storm with fearful loss on both sides. The fugitive princes then took refuge in Bharatpur whose fort, with its massive walls, was much more formidable.

Lord Lake arrived before the fort on 19 December. Four rash attempts were made to storm it, but these failed with heavy loss to the besieging force. Lord Lake's impetuous nature would not allow him to wait until a practicable breach had been effected. But the English hung on grimly, declining to abandon the siege.

Ranjit Singh thought it was an opportune time to obtain peace on easy terms. He sent his vakils to the general's camp and signed a separate peace, by promising an indemnity of Rs. 20 lakh, payable in instalments over a number of years. No territory was ceded, but Holkar was once more a fugitive.

He headed with his army, 60,000 strong, towards Scindia who was camping at Sabalgarh where a huge Maratha congress had been called to deliberate the means to combat the growing encroachments on Maratha liberties. Sharza Rao Ghatge was once again predominant in the councils of Scindia. Now Jaswant Rao Holkar had arrived with his incendiary exhortations. The Chhatrapati of Satara was represented by his brother, Chhatar Singh. It was an attempt to revive the old confederacy, but at the last moment Scindia drew back.

Lord Wellesley was recalled three months after the lifting of the siege of Bharatpur and succeeded by Lord Cornwallis who was sent out once again with explicit instructions to reverse the aggresive policies of his predecessor. The Company's prime interest in India was commercial, not imperial, and Pitt who had just cobbled together the Third Coalition of which England was the principal financer, was not anxious to enter into deep and entangling commitments in distant India. For England, engaged in a life and death struggle with the Napoleonic empire on the European continent, the annexations and subsidiary alliances forged by the Earl of Mornington, were distinctly disturbing. But Cornwallis was a man already marked by death. On his way up country he breathed his last at Ghazipur on 5 October 1805. His place was filled *pro tem* by Sir George Barlow, the senior member of the Governor-General's Council.

The first step taken by Barlow, was to call Scindia to order. The latter had placed his English Agent, Jenkins, under restraint on account of a rash and undiplomatic outburst at the time of the congress at Sabalgarh. His release was demanded, and effected on 13 September by Scindia, who was also obliged to keep away from the incendiary Holkar. A fresh treaty, that of Mustafapur, was also forced on him on 21 November. A special clause stipulated that Sharza Rao Ghatge would never again be admitted to his councils. As part of the new policy, the English also gave up their recent alliances with the Rajputs princes of Mewar, Marwar, Kota and others in Malwa and Mewat, and undertook not to interfere with Scindia's tributaries.

Holkar proceeded to Ajmer where he endeavoured to persuade the raja of Jodhpur, but failing to persuade the Rathor to join him in his enterprise, he entered the Punjab. First he stopped at Patiala where he met many of the Cis-Sutluj chiefs, and then proceeded to Amritsar to meet Ranjit Singh, the Lion of the Punjab.

The youthful Ranjit was only 25 but had started early at the game of empire-building. Slowly over the past 10 years, by a combination of wile and force, he had established his hegemony over the anarchic trans-Sutluj Punjab. Things had just begun to settle down, and he had not the slightest wish to see his state once again become the cockpit for contending armies. The British were encamped close by on the other side of the Beas. It is reported that in order to form his own judgement of the prowess of the feringhees, he visited their camp incognito, wandered about their tents, and saw their disciplined and uniformed sepoys and their well-served artillery and galloper guns. No army like this had ever entered the Punjab before, and not all the hundred thousand spears of the Marathas, the bombast of Holkar, or of his own fire-eating sardars could tempt him to embark on such a risky adventure as fighting the English.[8]

Instead, he played the role of a peace-maker. A vague treaty was concluded with the English by which he disavowed any intention of supporting Holkar. Jaswant himself was persuaded to make peace, and on 24 December 1805 the treaty of Rajghat was concluded. By this he relinquished all claims to territory north and west of the Chambal, while his possessions to the south and west of the river, and in the Narmada valley, were restored.

This was the end of the Anglo-Holkar war. But the troubles of Jaswant Rao were not yet over. He had to down-size his bloated army and pay off his retrenched soldiers, but these problems and his domestic griefs, and subsequent madness, belong more to the pages of the Holkar family chronicles rather than to the annals of the badshahs of the Qila-i-Mualla. There would be yet another Maratha war which would finally extinquish the peshwaship, but no Maratha would again disturb the environs of Delhi.

The Pax Brittannica had been established and the 'Golden Calm' would not be disturbed in the north for the next half-century, until another annexationist Governor-General, and the greased cartridges of the new Lee-Enfield rifle, led to the great explosion known as the 'Ghadar' or the 'Great Mutiny', which a later generation, in the first flush of nationalist fervour, would claim as the 'First War of Independence'.

NOTES

1. Sardesai, *A History of the Marathas*, iii, p. 384.
2. Ibid., pp. 390-2.
3. Ibid., p. 411.
4. Sarkar, *Fall of the Mughal Empire*, iv, p. 241. Fraser, *Military Memoir of Lt. Col. Skinner*, i, pp. 272-4.
5. Sarkar, ibid., iv, p. 247.
6. Ibid., p. 253.
7. Mill, *History of British India*, vi, p. 465. Malcolm, *A Memoir of Central India*, i, p. 237. Sardesai, iii, p. 424.
8. Cunningham, *History of the Sikhs*, p. 116.

CHAPTER 45

The Blind Padishah in the Qila-i-Mualla

Ever since Mahadji Scindia left for the Deccan in 1792 Delhi had become a back-water. There was no great amir, Vakil-i-Mutlaq, Wazir-ul-Mumalik or an Amir-ul-Umara to lend grace to the durbar of Shah Alam. With the emperor incapacitated by his blindness, the need for personal attendance was not felt. Daulat Rao Scindia, in fact, does not appear to have visited Delhi at all! Gopal Bhau, Lakhwa Dada, Ambaji Ingle or General Perron, were considered sufficient to represent the regent's authority.

But how was the emperor faring? How did he pass his time in those marble halls and courts? After Ghulam Qadir had been hunted down, there was relative peace in Delhi. Adventurers and robber barons might plunder the environs of the imperial city but the city itself not disturbed. For some years the vague fear of an Afghan invasion still persisted. Each winter when Timur or Shah Zaman descended to the milder climes of Peshwar to get away from icy Kabul, it was enought to send tremors through the Punjab and Hindostan. Shah Zaman's visits to Lahore in 1796 and 1798 sent a wave of panic throughout the north, but these were false alarms. It soon became evident that the offensive capability of the Durranis had been blunted by their own internecine struggles.

The state of the blind emperor had not improved with the coming of peace to the city of Delhi and its immediate environs. Handicapped as he was, it had become the easier to ignore him. Scindia had appointed as his keeper one Shah Nizam ud-Din, a person of illustrious and saintly pedigree. The family traced its origins to Baghdad and had migrated to Burhanpur in the middle of the seventeenth century and thence to Delhi, where a modest *khanqah* was established near the Agra gate. The Shah had acquired a reputation for piety and was addressed by his disciples as '*Khuda Numa*' or the Revealer of God. He is also described as the 'cowrie faqir', because in his feigned contempt for earthly goods the hazrat professed to accept only alms of the lowest denomination, i.e. a cowrie shell. As soon as the 'cowrie faqir' was nominated subedar of Delhi, his humble *khanqah* began to expand, growing in magnificence and encroaching upon an imperial garden, until it was as big and as grand as the mansion of the greatest of the Delhi umara.

Scindia appointed him to this office for want of someone better. Anand Rao Narsi, his first choice had given offence to the emperor by his public ridicule of His Majesty during a drunken frolic at the time of the Holi festival in March 1786. His successor, Ladoji Deshmukh Sithole, was Mahadji's son-in-law but he had proved incompetent, and a coward, at the time of the coup by Ghulam Qadir. Hence, after the suppression of the rebel Rohilla, Scindia selected Shah Nizam ud-Din for the post. The emperor had a weakness for saints and faqirs and the Shah already enjoyed access to him. There could be no better person than him, reasoned Mahadji, for the appointment of a Maratha would have been odious to the Mussalmans of Delhi. Besides the Shah had married his son to the daughter of Scindia's spiritual mentor, Shah Mansur of Bir.

But Shah Nizam ud-Din was a hypocrite as far as his pretensions to spiritual matters went. He kept the emperor starved of funds, shamelessly pocketing much of the money allocated by Scindia for meeting the expenses of the imperial household. According to one correspondent, an officer of de Boigne, he furnished the old monarch with, 'two *seers* of *pilau* and eight *seers* of meat'. This, with two loaves of bread, had to suffice for five persons, the emperor himself, his physician, Prince Akbar Shah, a little favourite daughter, and one from amongst his 200 begums. The rest of the imperial household, without distinction between slave or princess, had to make do with 2 *seers* of barley flour for every three persons![1] Doubtless the account was exaggerated, but de Boigne confirmed in a letter that the bulk of the revenues of Rs. 7 lakh per annum, which had been set aside for the privy purse, was pocketed by the 'cowrie faqir' who also distributed considerable sums to the Maratha sardars for their continued support to maintain him in office.

What made the burden of this hypocritical Shah more galling was his rough speech and insulting manners, which made the princes gnash their teeth with suppressed fury and reduced the emperor to tears. One day he went too far, and on 6 October 1799 Prince Akhtar and some of the other shahzadas cornered him in the palace and soundly thrashed him. After this he had to go.

De Boigne had left the country shortly after the death of Mahadji, on account of failing health and inability to adjust to the manners of the spoilt and youthful Daulat Rao. After the fall of Shah Nizam ud-Din, General Perron himself assumed charge as subedar though the military command of the fort remained with others like the brothers Hira Singh and Ajit

Singh, Khande Rao, Hari Kumar, Bhawani Singh and others, Bourquin being the last of them all.

The miserable state of affairs in the qila was worsened by the miserly character of the emperor himself. Notwithstanding that the bulk of his privy purse was being appropriated by the 'cowry faqir' and the Maratha sardars, the blind old emperor could never desist from the urge to keep on adding to his own private hoard. The result was beggarliness, starvation and clamorous outbursts in the Qila-i-Mualla which never ceased till the coming of the British. Some of the shahzadas received only a rupee per day as subsistence allowance, others two, three or five. Even this miserable allowance was frequently in arrears, often for months.

But neither the vicissitudes of fortune nor the loss of his eyesight succeeded in cooling the flames of passion. Right up to the end of his days, Shah Alam continued to add new beauties to his harem. The Comte de Modave has spoken of 500 women, and that was in 1775. The number may have been an exaggeration, all may not have been wives or concubines, but certainly their number ran into hundreds. In 1775 the same French nobleman mentions that the emperor had 27 living male children, and there were in all 80 shahzadas in the fort—the others being the sons of former emperors. Elsewhere, Major Polier, the Swiss engineer, speaks of the emperor's 'nearly 70 children male and female, besides grand children'. When in 1804 Lord Wellesley took over the responsibility for the imperial household, he had to provide for 45 surviving children, male and female, besides grand children.

We have seen how the heir apparent, Jahandar Shah (Jawan Bakht), tiring of the vacuous life of the court—and perhaps encouraged by English intrigue—had fled to Awadh and then tried to negotiate a separate appanage for himself where he might have had a free field of action, just as Shah Alam had tried in his appanage of Rewari, created by the orders of the Abdali in 1758. But Shah Alam had treated the flight of the frustrated prince as a rebellion.

During the eclipse of Mahadji's power following the retreat from Lalsot, Jahandar Shah had attempted to attain his object with the help of Mirza Ismail Beg, but he annoyed that proud and somewhat hot-headed general with his haughty manners and superior airs, and eventually had to beat a hasty retreat to Awadh. His rigid insistence on the observation of the forms and etiquette due to a prince of the imperial house—which meant, among other things, that he took precedence over the nawab-wazir of Awadh and even the governor-general—soon lost him all support.[2] After his flight Shah Alam had cut him off from the succession, and the next son, Akbar, became the heir-presumptive, but the former's death in 1788 soon settled one potential point of discord.

Blindness was normally considered a disqualification for a monarch, and after the blinding of Shah Alam and the removal of the puppet, Bidar Bakht, Akbar had looked forward to being placed on the throne. This came to the notice of the jealous father whose love for this son now turned to hatred. At once the emperor sounded the court of Poona about superseding Akbar in favour of a younger son.

During this period several princes escaped from their prison, the Exalted Fort, in the vague hope of improving their lot. The first was Mirzai who descended from a daughter of Farrukhsiyar. He escaped in November 1789. A few months later, in April 1790, Ahsan Bakht slipped away while following the funeral procession of Piyari, one of the emperor's begums. One Sikander Shukoh escaped in January 1796. Similarly, two of the sons of Jawan Bakht also abandoned their father's house and took to a life of wandering. These were Shagufta Bakht and Muzaffar Bakht, nicknamed Mirza Haji and Mirza Juma. The latter's cause was taken up by the former wazir, Imad ul-Mulk who toured the Maratha courts from 1789-95 with Mirza Juma in tow. He hoped to ride back to power and influence by clinging to the prince's coat tails. Nothing came of it, but Imad was able to secure a jagir for himself at Kalpi from the Poona durbar. As for Mirza Juma himself, he died in Poona in genteel poverty.[3]

These flights from the Exalted Fort occasioned much flutter and excitement but led to nothing. Even before Lord Lake's victory at Patparganj, northern India had started settling down. With the British now firmly ensconced in Awadh and Rohilkhand, the Doab under their direct administration, and Perron commanding the 'Maratha' forces in the Delhi region, there was little chance of malcontents exploiting these frustrated princes.

The Jat state of Bharatpur had been laid low way back in the 1770s by the great Mirza Najaf Khan, and had survived only by his grace. The Rohillas had been crushed by Shuja ud-Daulah with the help of British troops, and all that survived was the rump state of Rampur. By the beginning of the nineteenth century the Sikhs had ceased raiding across the Yamuna. As for the Bangash nawabs of Farrukhabad, Muzaffar Hussain Khan, the son of Ahmad Khan, had voluntarily ceded his territory to the British in 1802 and accepted a pension of Rs. 1,08,000 in return. About the same time the English acquired the 'north-western provinces' or the Doab territories, from Awadh, in 'final' settlement of their astronomical financial claims against the nawab-wazir.

In the Deccan there would be one more final Maratha War, to be followed up by the 'Pindarri war', which was a mopping up operation, but in the north the old days of rapine and plunder were well-nigh gone. The grip of the English ferringhees of the Company Bahadur was hardening. Pax Britannica was about to be imposed on the whole of India.

NOTES

1. Sarkar, *Fall of the Mughal Empire*, iv, p. 185.
2. Francklin, *The History of Shah Aulum*, pp. 159-67. Valentia, *Voyages and Travels*, i, pp. 72, 111.
3. The jagir of Imad ul-Mulk survived into modern times as the state of Baoni. Though tiny in size and comprising only 52 villages it was recognized as a princely state whose ruler was entitled to a salute of 5 guns.

CHAPTER 46

The Dawn of a New Age

When Shah Alam conveyed his congratulations to Lord Lake after the battle of Patparganj he had no idea that something revolutionary had occurred. As far as he was concerned, he had just changed one keeper for another. Instead of General Perron, he would now have Lord Lake. In the usual Mughal fashion, titles and honorifics, the insignia of the mahi and maratib, mansabs, kettledrums et al. were showered on the victorious general who now became Ali Jah, Rafi Rayah Samsam ud-Daulah, Astya ul-Mulk, Khan i-Dauran Bahadur, Sipah-i-Salar, Fateh Jang.

European writers assume that Shah Alam welcomed the British as liberators who had rescued him from the ignominous thralldom of the Marathas. It was true that Shah Nizam ud-Din, Scindia's local agent in Delhi who controlled the administration of the Qila-i-Mualla for much of the period, shamelessly misappropriated the bulk of the funds which passed through his hands. He was also frequently rude and discourteous, and the old emperor may have often wished that someone would rid him of this grasping divine. It was true also that the emperor had been in secret communication with Lord Lake before the battle of Delhi, but too much should not be read into this. It was in keeping with the traditional pattern of imperial diplomacy which always aimed at ensuring that, whatever the outcome, the emperor should not be embarrassed. It was like an insurance policy. If the English won, the emperor would be able to deal with them with confidence because of his secret correspondence. If it were the Marathas that came out on top, so much the better; Scindia was his regent and Perron his sword-arm, and he had never wavered in his public support for them. In his helpless condition Shah Alam could at best make a choice between two necessary evils.

The English were not unknown to him. He had spent nine years under the protection of the English Crown at Allahabad. Though his revenues had been ample, and material requirements looked after, he had little reason to feel grateful to them. They had made no attempt to fulfil their commitment to escort him back to Delhi, and instead did their best to dissuade him from returning to his capital. That English officers could be as boorish as the worst of the Afghan or Maratha sardars with whom he had to put up at Delhi, had also been learnt from bitter experience. Such men were not always callow captains or lieutenants come fresh from England; at times they could be as high ranking as Brigadier Smith. As Spear remarks, if he had been in a position to choose, he probably would have chosen the French as his keepers, a people conspicuous for their courtesy and natural amiability. But he was not in such a position, nor did the French have an army of their own. General Perron, like de Boigne before him, was only Scindia's agent.

Unlike earlier occasions there was no treaty between the emperor and his latest keeper. In fact Lake was under Wellesley's express orders not to conclude any treaty.[1] The Governor-General had come to India with a clear imperial design, and having destroyed Tipu in the south and dragooned the Nizam and the Maratha chiefs into signing 'subsidiary alliances' he did not see the need to act as the agent of the emperor. An intensely practical people, a nation of shopkeepers as Napoleon described them, the English did not recognize power without substance.

In India, however, symbols had a powerful hold on the imagination of the masses. For decades the padishah in the Qila-i-Mualla had been bereft of real power. He had no army of his own. Yet the proudest and the greatest chiefs continued to seek from him the ratification of their accession to their provincial masnads. As late as 1803, the Nizam's ambassadors had waited on the blind old man to obtain the sanads of appointment and 6,000 gold *mohurs* were presented by way of *nazar* for the coveted letters patent and the tawdry *khillats* that legitimized naked power. On seven occasions in the year, the agents of all the great princes of India, rajas, maharajas, and nawabs, who were in permanent 'attendance on the Royal stirrup', would pay their respects by offering compliments and *nazars* to their overlord, the emperor of India. The failure of the British to appreciate the power exerted on the Indian imagination by this faineant emperor was in large measure responsible for the mutiny that book place a half century later.

But while Wellesley was determined not to play the submissive umara, he was prepared to be generous in the financial arrangements for the maintenance of the imperial family. Scindia had allocated the sum of Rs. 13 lakh in 1789 for the imperial household, but this sum had dwindled to less than half until the emperor's personal allowance was barely Rs. 17,000 per month with another Rs. 30,000 for the rest, which included the princes, the salatin, the widows and discarded concubines, as well as the palace guards, slaves and other employees. The English raised the emperor's personal allowance to Rs. 60,000 per month and the whole grant to Rs. 11.5 lakh per year. But the amount was not final, and the prospect of an increase in the allocation in the event of an improvement in the general prosperity and an increase in the revenues, was not ruled out.

The increase in the personal allowance of the emperor was substantial, and was more than sufficient for his modest needs. The thrifty Shah Alam was, in fact, able to save a substantial portion. On his death in 1806 he was found to have hoarded Rs. 5 lakh.

But the velvet glove barely concealed the steely determination of Lord Wellesley to cut down the pretensions of the court which claimed to be 'the Refuge of all the World'. While enjoining Lake to show His Majesty every demonstration of reverence, respect and attention, he was urged to persuade him and the heir-apparent to take up residence at Monghyr in Bihar. The Governor-General calculated that once the imperial family had been removed from Delhi, it would rapidly lose its mystique, but Shah Alam was too shrewd to fall into the trap. This had, in fact, been his main reason for abandoning the comforts of Allahabad in 1771. He knew only too well that once cut off from Delhi, he would be just one among numerous pensionary princes.

Notwithstanding the enhancement in his allowance Shah Alam clung pertinaciously to the historical pretensions of monarchy. Soon conflicts arose, the first following immediately upon the occupation of Delhi. Drugeon, the French commandant, had deposited his personal fortune, amounting to some Rs. 5.5 lakh, with the imperial treasurer for safe-keeping in the hope of recovering it at some future date. Lord Lake insisted on seizing it, while the emperor claimed it as his own. But Shah Alam was in no position to resist the will of his 'liberator'. He now offered the money as a donation to the army. Lord Lake was obtuse enough to accept it, but when Wellesley came to know of the affair he ordered his general to return it. Imperial diplomacy had won the first round.[2]

The administration of the Delhi province was reorganized under the direct supervision of the resident, but two accountants or *mutassadis* sat in the *kutcherry* and checked the accounts on behalf of the emperor. A revenue and a criminal court was also set up; the latter administering the *shariat*, but all sentences of death or mutilation were subject to imperial confirmation.

But within the Qila, the old order prevailed. The emperor was sovereign within its walls. Here at least his will was law and the members of the imperial family, including the salatin, enjoyed diplomatic immunity in the city. The etiquette of the Chughata Court remained in force. The resident dismounted like any other person at the naqqar khana from whence he continued on foot past the Lal Purdah to the presence, where he stood respectfully like other umara in the durbar.

The first resident was Lt. General Sir David Ochterloney, a gentleman of the old school who had adopted the mode of life of an oriental umara, complete with hookah, oriental robes and a *bibi ghar*, well stocked with dusky beauties. Deeply imbued with a sense of deference to the imperial house, he created no problems. His successor, Seton, was even more courteous. The British seemed anxious to avoid pain or embarrassment to the aged ruler who was obviously in decline. With his death three years later on 19 November 1806, it was no longer necessary to adhere to niceties, and imperial sensitivities could be ignored. Moreover, British rule was now firmly established. The career of Jaswant Rao Holkar, the stormy petrel of the Maratha confederacy, had come to a close, and the Pax Britannica prevailed throughout the length and breadth of the Deccan and Hindostan.

Akbar II, though by no means a young man, had all his faculties intact. His requirements were consequently greater. In 1809 Wellesley accordingly raised his allowance to Rs. 12 lakh, but the increase was too slight to satisfy Akbar. In 1827 he again reopened the question with a Paper of Requests. The negotiations culminated with the emperor deciding to send an ambassador to the Court of St. James to plead his case before the British monarch. Rammohun Roy, the Bengali reformer, had been planning a visit to Britain on his own, and readily agreed to be Akbar's ambassador. He set out in 1830, the emperor having ennobled him with the title of 'Raja' as befitted an imperial ambassador.

When informed about his intention, the Governor-General asked the resident to convey to His Majesty the government's 'astonishment' and 'displeasure' at the unfounded accusations advanced against the Company. The attitude of the Calcutta government was discourteous and obstructive. Roy's title was not recognized but they stopped short of physically preventing him from boarding a ship for England. On a previous occasion, when the emperor had, bypassing the resident, dispatched an ambassador, Raja Babu Pran Krishen, to Calcutta with instructions to proceed to England, if necessary, the latter had been publicly insulted and deprived of his credentials, his letters being returned to the resident.

So, Raja Rammohun Roy proceeded to London where he was a lion for a season. Charles Grant, president of the Board of Control, was favourably impressed with him and the memorial, but the Court of Directors ignored him. King William IV received him and readily accepted his credentials on the recommendation of Charles Grant, but in the end nothing came of the mission. The raja presented two options to the Company: either the emperor should be allowed to take over the direct administration of the assigned territory and bear its cost out of the gross receipts; or, if that was not agreeable, he was willing to compound all his claims for a final settlement of Rs. 30 lakh per annum, thus, implicitly, accepting the pensionary status.

The Company offered Rs. 15 lakh but this was at first refused as being too paltry. Later, the emperor accepted it. However, when it became clear that the English intended the increase to be distributed for the benefit of the princes and salatin and he himself would not gain directly, he declined the offer. Meanwhile, the ambassador had died, to be followed four years later by Akbar himself. When talks on the subject were resumed with his successor, Bahadur Shah, the latter declined to surrender his other claims in return for the paltry increase, and the matter was allowed to drop. It thus remained unsettled at the outbreak of the mutiny, each side sticking to its stand, the British merely admitting to 'a complimentary recognition of a nominal sovereignty' while the emperor insisted on his recognition as the legal sovereign of India.

But apart from the question of the allowance, there were other causes of friction between the two sides. The first was the vexed question of the succession. We have seen how in his time Shah Alam had sought to set aside the natural claims of his eldest son Mirza Muhammed Jawan Bakht (Jahandar Shah) in favour of Akbar, and later had sought to set aside Akbar in favour of a yet younger son, but the British had refused to give the stamp of approval to his tentative moves. The problem of the first, Jahandar, was solved by his death, and the pretensions of Jahandar's first born, Mirza Khanim Bakht, who according to European custom would have been the next in line, were ignored on the ground that Muslim law did not recognize the rights of the son of a predeceased son to his grandfather's inheritance. The claims of the next son, Mirza Izzat Bakhsh, were not pressed very strongly, and Akbar succeeded quietly without fuss. Now Akbar in turn sought to set aside his eldest son, Mirza Abul Zafar (Siraj ud-Din), in favour of a younger prince, Jahangir, the son of his reigning favourite Mumtaz Mahal.

The British refused to countenance his proposals. The emperor urged the ancient usage of the imperial house, which gave the incumbent monarch the right to nominate his successor. If any other claimant felt he had a better right, there was always the ultimate arbitration of arms. But in view of the debilitated state of the monarchy, which did not permit any of the princes to raise or maintain an army, the will of the British would be decisive. The British saw that conceding the emperor's request could be interpreted as conceding his claims to real sovereignty. On the other hand, a pensionary monarch could not dispute the will of the protecting power. The English were determined to rub in the lesson.

Akbar Shah, and his ladies, were equally determined to stress the recognition of the emperor's rights. The emperor's mother, Qudsia Begum, and two of his consorts, Mumtaz Mahal and Daulat un-Nissa Begum, participated in the discussions with the resident. Seated behind a curtain, they did most of the talking, with the emperor occassionally interjecting a sentence or phrase to emphasise a point.[3] But it was to no avail. There followed the disastrous embassy of Raja Babu Pran Krishen and a desperate attempt to canvass support at the court of the nawab-wazir at Lucknow. But the *Sahiban-i-Inglishia* remained unmoved.

There was a comical attempt to present them with a fait accompli by conferring on the favoured son the insignia of the *aftabgir*, a heraldic device traditionally associated with the heir-apparent. But it fell flat. The English coolly ignored it, and the resident snubbed the emperor by failing to attend the durbar held on the occasion.

Then followed the even more farcical episode of the *khillats* which was intended by Akbar to be a demonstration to the Indian world of the true nature of the relationship subsisting between the emperor of India—whose palace was the refuge of all the world—and the English, whose chief executive in India was his 'most favoured son'. But this too misfired badly.

It was decided to hold a second enthronement at Agra. Shah Haji was sent to Calcutta with *khillats* to be presented to the governor-general on the occasion. At first Lord Minto agreed to accept the robes in private as a token of his personal regard for His Majesty, but Shah Haji spoilt it by announcing in public the purpose of his embassy and by making it known that similar *khillats* would be sent to all the princes of India, who were, after all, nothing but the umara of the Chughata empire. In short, it was to be a demonstration by a phantom monarch of his fancied power. Something like an *ashwamedha* or horse-sacrifice by a Chakravarti raja, with the difference that in the instant case the fancied power, was, in fact, only a courtesy extended to the descendant of a fallen but illustrious house; a mere 'complimentary recognition of a nominal sovereignty'. As could have been foreseen, Lord Minto refused to receive Shah Haji.

The question now arose as to the etiquette to be observed in the event of a meeting between the emperor and the governor-general. Since the latter, or his representative, the resident, refused to take up the mantle of the regency which had been borne by the Scindias (or their master, the peshwa), and chose to consider the treaty of Allahabad, by which the Company was the diwan of Bengal, as being of only academic interest, there could be no question of his crossing the Lal Purdah on foot, performing the triple *tasleemats* of the *korneesh*, and standing in audience like the other umara. The current view, as propounded by the triumphant Wellesley, and Lord Minto, was that they were at least the equals of the emperor who had been restored 'to a state of dignity and tranquility, under the power of the British Crown'. In actual fact they felt themselves to be his superiors, by virtue of being his protectors and preferred to be regarded as overlords rather than mere ministers. The mystique of the imperial house, and its near fabulous descent from two of the greatest conquerors the world has ever known, was quite lost on the new generation of the Company's officers. The world had changed much between 1765 and 1803. England's self-esteem was growing. Bonaparte's Egyptian adventure had ended in disaster, thanks to Horatio Nelson who had made Britannia supreme on the high seas. Pitt the Younger had taken up the challenge to cut an enthusiastic and expansionist France down to size and was bankrolling the coalitions aimed at restoring the old balance of power. For such men the Indian descendants of Timur and Genghiz Khan were no more than historical curiosa.

The very fact that Delhi was now in British possession contributed to the deglamourization of the Mughal monarchy. At the time of Browne's embassy, travelling to Delhi and being presented at court was itself a romantic experience. For the change in attitude, one has only to compare the despatches of Browne with Henry Edward Fane's account (as a young ADC to the commander-in-chief) of a presentation at court in the year 1837.

The tone is throughout contemptuous and sneering. Fane had, for instance, looked forward to the presentation 'with disgust' as he did not like the general 'so lowering himself as to stand in the presence of a dirty, miserable old dog like this man'. He sneeringly scoffs at the Qila-i-Mualla as a 'ruinous mass of mud and dirt', and as for His Majesty's sepoys, they were the most ridiculous he had ever encountered in his travels, besides whom, 'Hogarth's representation of the March to Finchley, would be in comparison splendid.' As for the ceremony itself, it deserves to be described in detail as it is so eminently revelatory of the attitudes of the younger generation of Englishmen:

After each had been presented and paid his money, which his majesty took special care not to lose, we were severally led away to receive the Kelat, or robe of honour—a farce which the government still keep up, in spite of its marvellous absurdity. The general was robed in the king's presence, but we of the small fry marched into another room, to be made such figures as never were seen, even at Greenwich fair. Each of us had first a piece of rag tied round our cocked hats, by way of turban; after which a robe of spangled white muslin was thrust over epaulettes, sword, and all, over which again they treated each of us to a jacket of cloth of silver. In this tomfool's dress we were again trotted across the court, obliged (which was the most difficult performance of the whole) to keep from laughing, and again to be presented to the king and be bedizened with a parcel of glass jewels and trumpery, to the value of two gold mohurs; for which civility the company treated the king to another gold mohur from each. . . .

This ceremony being concluded, we were again made to salaam, and in the dress we had received were trotted out to the gate of our elephants, and again went through the town; I for one, feeling more ashamed to myself than had done for many a long year. . . .

Altogether the ceremony is very ridiculous; but still it is hard to deny to the fallen descendant of Timour the little deference and authority which is still left to him.[4]

In contrast, Major James Browne dwells in detail on the *khillat* bestowed on him, how it was 'one of the most honourable degree' and how 'His Majesty's personal behaviour was to the greatest Degree Cheerful and condescending'. He had, in view of the envoy's weakness (he was recovering from a fever), 'with, the greatest humanity and condescention' exempted him from 'near one half of the tuslimates or ceremonial Obeisances' prescribed by the etiquette of the court.[5]

How the mighty had fallen! In the space of half a century His Sublime Majesty, the Asylum of the Universe, had been reduced to the ridiculous. Familiarity had bred contempt. And to think that Fane's emperor, the last of his line, was a gentleman of culture and sensibility, and a composer of tolerable verse! No prince of the house of Hanover, or any of its subsequent *avatars* to the present day, can claim such distinction.

But if the commander-in-chief and lesser mortals like the resident were still obliged to tender *nazars* and undergo the indignity of being decked out in a 'tomfool's dress', the governor-general had exempted himself. When Lord Hastings proceeded up country at the time of the Gorkha war in 1817, the emperor insisted that he should appear as a subject and present the usual *nazars*. But Hastings refused to meet him except on a footing of equality. As a result, the meeting did not take place. When Lord

Amherst visited the imperial city in 1826, however, Akbar II relented and agreed to meet him on the terms he had earlier refused Lord Hastings. The minutiae of the ceremonial was laid down by Charles Metcalfe and designed to acknowledge Akbar's superior status without any admission of vassalage on the part of the Governor-General. While the Governor-General's entourage left their elephants and horses at the naqqar khana gate and proceeded thence on foot, the Governor-General was carried in a palki up to the steps of the Diwan-i-Khas. Here he was received by the emperor who led him upto the throne. Lord Amherst was given a chair at right angles to the throne while all the other members of his entourage remained standing. No *nazars* were presented by the governor-general, though members of the party were required to do so. The emperor gave his guest a string of pearls as a token gift and then led him to the private apartments. On Akbar's return visit to the residency, the same procedure was followed, the present being given now by Lord Amherst.[6]

Akbar had hoped to be rewarded for this submission to the British stipulations, but he got nothing. Hence, when in 1831 Bentinck came, he refused to meet him. His snubbing of Lord Hastings in 1817 had, to his mind, resulted in his being punished by the proclamation of the nawab-wazir as an independent ruler. But by abasing himself before Lord Amherst he gained nothing. It was after this that he determined to send an embassy to London.

The proclamation of Ghazi ud-Din Haidar on 9 October 1819 as an 'independent' ruler or Badshah was an unnecessary and gratuitous insult to the occupant of the Qila-i-Mualla. From a titular and purely nominal Wazir-ul-Mumalik, he was transformed into a purely nominal king. His sonorous, freshly assumed, titles of Abul Muzaffar, Muiz ud-Din, Shah i-Zaman, Ghazi ud-Din Haidar, Padishah i-Awadh, could not conceal the fact that he was king merely by the grace of the East India Company. The intention was only to humiliate Akbar II who was so far legally the unchallenged sovereign of the whole of India.

Further insults to the imperial dignity were to follow. Although the governor-general's *nazars* had been discontinued, the lesser dignitaries still had to go through the ceremony, not because the emperor happened to be their liege-lord, but merely in acknowledgement of his royal status. Thus it was explained. But while these antique customs might have fascinated orientalists of the old school, they went against the spirit of the times. Francis Hawkins, who was acting resident in 1829, grumbled at the unnecessary expense. As many as, 643 gold *mohurs* had been spent on this account by the resident and his assistants over the previous year, he pointed out. But the authorities at Calcutta snubbed him by replying briefly that they did not wish to make any change in the existing practice. In due course, however, the official opinion at Calcutta also changed.

With the enunciation of the new policy towards the emperor (now referred to as the king of Delhi), the regular payment of the annual *nazars* by the governor-general were stopped. At the same time, without any explanation, the three annual *nazars* tendered by the commander-in-chief also ceased, but the resulting financial loss to the emperor was made up by a corresponding increase in the allowance. Also the commander-in-chief continued to proffer *nazars* on the occasion of complimentary visits to the court. The regular presentation of *nazars* was limited only to the resident, his deputy and the commandant of the palace guard. But Lord Ellenborough abolished even this lingering token. The emperor took umbrage, and in protest did not celebrate the anniversary of his accession that year.

The matter was brought to the notice of the Court of Directors in England. For once they took the emperor's side and gently admonished the governor-general 'that such changes should not be made in the lifetime of the monarch in deference to the feelings of the House of Timur, and that if the king should remonstrate on the subject, the former practice should be conceded to him for his life'.

The 'king' had indeed remonstrated but the directions of the directors were not acted upon by the government at Calcutta, the receipt of the letter being kept a secret. Eventually Bahadur Shah who has succeeded Akbar II in 1837 got wind of it took up the matter again, but between the governor-general at Calcutta and the lieutenant-governor of the North-Western Provinces it was ensured that the practice was not restored. The emperor had willy-nilly to accept an increase of Rs. 833 per month in his allowance as compensation.

The final repudiation of the emperor's claims on the Company was not long in coming. Bahadur Shah was over 60 when he ascended the throne in 1837 and the question of the succession was ever present. Ellenborough had forbidden the resident from initiating any steps for the formal recognition of a successor, but this was going too fast in the eyes of his more cautious but equally ruthless successor, Lord Dalhousie.

The emperor's eldest son and heir-presumptive, Mirza Dara Bakht, died in 1849 at the age of fifty-seven. The English, ready to believe the worst, suspected poison administered at the instance of Zinat Mahal. Bahadur Shah pressed for the recognition of Mirza Jawan Bakht, the son of his favourite consort, Zinat Mahal. Mirza Fakhr ud-Din was, however, the eldest after the deceased Dara Bakht. Moreover he was respected by everyone. Eventually a pact between the Mirza and the English was arrived at; Fakhr ud-Din would be recognized as the successor, provided Bahadur Shah agreed to meet the governor-general on terms of absolute equality, and the family vacated the fort and moved to their palace at Mehrauli. But, in 1856, the worthy Mirza died suddenly, and the question of the succession was once again left open.

Again Bahadur Shah pressed the case of Jawan Bakht, but Dalhousie was now less inclined to be generous. Moreover, the next in seniority, Mirza Kowesh, was dull and unispiring. The English now decided that on the death of Bahadur Shah, Mirza Kowesh would be recognized as head of the family on the same terms as agreed with Mirza Fakhr ud-Din, that is, the Qila-i-Mualla would be evacuated, and the family would take up its permanent residence in its country-house at Mehrauli. Also, instead of the imperial title of padishah he would only be entitled to the style of 'Shahzada'. His monthly allowance would be only Rs. 15,000 and an investigation would be carried out to identify and enumerate the specific members of the family who would be considered privileged to have a right to pensions. The intention was, thus clear. The imperial house was to be extinguished.

This was not announced. Nor was it ever communicated by letter either to the old emperor or to the heir-presumptive. It remained a conscious decision recorded on file, but inevitably there were leaks. The sphinx-like silence on the subject could only lead to speculation and rumours. There had been consternation in the Qila-i-Mualla when the contents of Mirza Fakhr ud-Din's pact with the English slowly came to their knowledge. The silence of the Council at Calcutta on the subject, after the death of Mirza Fakhr ud-Din, could bode no good.[7]

There were other straws in the wind. In 1835 the Company struck a new set of rupees which bore on the obverse the portrait of William IV. In 1840 this was replaced by the profile of the young Victoria. There was no mention of the padishah in the Qila-i-Mualla. The Company had been minting its own coins bearing the mint names of Surat, Arcot, Murshidabad and Farrukhabad for some decades, and these carried the name of Shah Alam and the standard Mughal legend. But now it was evident that a critical transformation was in process.

The sands of time were running out fast for the last sovereigns of the blood of Genghiz and Timur.

NOTES

1. Majumdar, J.K., *Raja Rammohun Roy and the Last of the Mughals*, pp. 1, 2 (dispatch from the Governor-General to Lord Lake, 27 July, 1803).
2. Spear, *A History of Delhi under the Later Mughals*, p. 36.
3. Ibid., p. 45.
4. Fane, *Five Years in India*, i, pp. 139-42.
5. Bhargava, *Browne Correspondence*, letter 58, pp. 118-19.
6. Spear, pp. 45-6.
7. Ibid., pp. 58-9.

CHAPTER 47

The Golden Calm (1806-1857)

Apart from the 'shadow fighting' between the emperor and the resident, these were years of peace. The cantonment was established to the north on the slopes of the Delhi Ridge, and there grew a small European colony to the north of Kashmiri Gate in the quarter known by the evocative name of Khyber pass. Delhi had not known such an extended period of peace since the reign of Aurangzeb, but this proved to be the proverbial calm before the storm.

The early residents maintained great state and lived like the great Mughal umara. Bishop Heber once ran into Ochterlony on tour in Rajasthan and has given a delightful picture of him 'wrapped up in shawls, kincob, fur and a Mughal fur hat'. He was in a coach and four and there were 'a considerable number of led horses, elephants, palanquins and covered carriages', not to mention an escort of two companies of infantry and a troop of regular cavalry besides 40 or 50 irregulars. 'The whole procession was what might pass in Europe for that of an eastern prince travelling.'[1] While camping, his own and his daughters' private tents were fenced in and surrounded by *qanats* of red canvas—evocative of the *gulal bar* which marked off the imperial enclosure when the emperor was on the move.

All these gentlemen—including the Metcalfe brothers, Charles and Thomas—maintained Indian households with bibi-ghars and were perfectly at home in Persian and Hindostani. Ochterlony, for instance, had thirteen wives and William Fraser six or seven.[2] When Heber met Sir David, the latter had been away from England for 54 years; he had neither friend nor relation in the home country, and had been 'for many years habituated to eastern habits and parade, and who can wonder that he clings to the only country in the world where he can feel himself at home?'

The Residency was an important centre of social life. Here people of all grades could meet and mingle with an informality which was not possible in the imperial court. Members of the imperial family, seths and bankers, rubbed shoulders with European officers and Anglo-Indian gentlemen. Indian chiefs, nawabs and rajas, and courtiers of the Qila-i-Mualla would be guests at the entertainments which were of the traditional type. There was none of the awkwardness and artificiality of the bridge parties of the late Raj period so well described by E.M. Forster in *A Passage to India*. There was no attempt to replicate English garden parties or formal dinner-balls. Liquor flowed freely. In the background could be heard the gentle gurgle of the water-pipe or hookah, while the nautch girls danced to Persian or Hindostani songs.

Even in more European surroundings Indian princes and nobles mixed with an ease and lack of self-consciousness which was not possible in post-Mutiny India. Emily Eden (sister of Lord Auckland) played chess with Dost Muhammad (deposed amir of Kabul) in Calcutta, and encouraged Kunwar Pertab Singh, Maharaja Ranjit Singh's grandson, to practise his English with her in Punjab.[3]

There was entertaining in Indian households as well. Hindu Rao, a brother of Byza Bai, the consort of Daulat Rao Scindia, came to Delhi as the latter's vakil in 1832. He was a bon vivant noted for his lavish parties. The raja of Kishengarh was another, and it was while returning from one such entertainment at the latter's house that the resident (William Fraser) was killed in 1835.

The sultan of Turkey had by this time begun to wear European style uniforms. So had the king of Awadh begun to copy the sartorial style of his English masters. The lords of the Qila-i-Mualla, however, were far too conscious of their dignity to cast off their traditional robes for the uniforms of the feringhees but some of the younger princes had adopted the European mode. Mirza Babar, the younger son of Akbar II, wore pseudo-European uniforms and drove round Delhi in a coach and six. In the courtyard of the Rang Mahal, behind the Diwan-i-Am, he built a European villa for himself, complete with Corinthian columns.[4] But European liquor had a much wider and far more appreciative following.

Scotch whisky had not yet become the standard drink of John Bull. Beer and molasses rum were the staple for the common soldiers, but officers and gentlemen drank wines such as bordeaux, madeira and port, besides, of course, champagne. Mirza Jahangir, one of the sons of Akbar II, was dedicated to cherry brandy. Sleeman, who knew him well, quotes him as saying, 'This is really the only liquor that you Englishmen have worth drinking, and its only fault is that it makes one drunk too soon.'[5] He would drink steadily, limiting himself to one big glass to an hour, to prolong the pleasure while relays of dancing girls and musicians tried to keep him entertained. He had been a spirited lad and, like Shakespeare's Prince Hal, had surrounded himself with a roistering set with whom he swaggered about town provoking many an affray. Seton complained to the king and urged him to restrain the prince. Angered, the Mirza fired upon Seton's escort one day as the latter was leaving the fort after an audience. This was going too far, and the emperor was forced to banish him to Allahabad. After some time he was allowed to return, but because of repeated attempts to poison the heir-apparent, and other misdemeanours, Mirza Jahangir was again ordered to return to Allahabad where he died in 1821, at the early age of 31.

There was little in this age for the princes to do, besides carousing or composing poetry. The pathetic helplessness of the emperor and the insensitivity of the English is well illustrated by the incident involving the arrest and trial of Ghalib.

The new morality of the Victorian age was reflected in a law against gambling. Ghalib was fond of playing *chausar* with stakes, and his house had once been raided by the kotwal's minions in 1841. He had been let off with a fine of Rs. 100. In 1847 there was another raid in which Ghalib was again caught red-handed, but this time he did not get away so lightly. The kotwal, Faiz Hasan Khan, was inimical to Ghalib, and insisted on bringing him to trial. The emperor tried to intervene through the resident, but he was told that the matter was sub-judice and must be allowed to run its course.

The poet-laureate was sentenced to six months hard labour with a fine of Rs. 200. The magistrate was new and did not know Ghalib, but the sessions judge was known to him socially. However, he behaved like a stranger in court, refused to recognize him, and mechanically confirmed the sentence. The rigidity of the British legal system chilled Ghalib, and the snub administered to the emperor left the latter humiliated. The insensitivity of the English was surprising, considering that even in England gambling was common among the upper-classes, and playing among friends in a gentleman's home could by no means be equated with 'running a gaming-house'.

The poet was released after three months and was spared the hard labour. The fine was paid by friends, but the humiliation rankled long in his breast. His abortive appointment to the Delhi College as a professor is another interesting episode which underlines the alien character of the new regime and the sharp break with the mores and attitudes of the *ancien regime*.

The Delhi College had been established in the old *madrassa* of Ghazi ud-Din Khan near Ajmeri Gate. In 1842 Ghalib was offered a professorship in Persian at this college but the procedures of the new regime required him to appear before the secretary, Mr. Thompson, for an interview. The poet, whose financial condition was always precarious, left for the interview in his palki in keeping with his social status.

Alighting from the palki, he waited at the steps below the verandah that ran in front of Thompson's office. As per the accepted etiquette between the old gentry and the officers of the Company's Raj, Ghalib was expecting to be received by the secretary in the verandah. After all, he was being honoured by the grant of a post! But Thompson viewed him in the light of an applicant, and did not feel obliged to observe the usual norms on this occasion. In fact, according to his lights, it may even have seemed improper to do so! After waiting in vain, Ghalib returned to his house, puzzled, hurt and humiliated.[6]

A sensational event of those years was the trial and execution of Nawab Shams ud-Din of Firozpur-Jhirka for the murder of William Fraser. It is curious that in contrast to their compunctions vis-a-vis reigning princes in later years, the English did not hesitate to arrest and try the nawab as a common criminal. Perhaps their confidence stemmed from their consciousness of the fact that Shams ud-Din was their creation. His father, Ahmad Bakhsh, had been a vakil of the Alwar raja in attendance on Lord Lake during his memorable campaign. He had been rewarded for his services with the pargana of Loharu by the raja, and that of Firozpur by Lord Lake. Disputes arose between Shams ud-Din and his younger brothers which inevitably came up before the resident for adjudication. The decision went against Shams ud-Din. Fraser had known him since his childhood, and was not happy with him on account of his dissipated life. The Englishman refused to see the nawab when the latter called on him. Seething with rage and humiliation, Shams ud-Din resolved on revenge and plotted his murder.

Notwithstanding the fact that his guilt was proven the nawab acquired a certain posthumous fame as a *shahid* or martyr. The people were shocked at the mode of his execution which was by hanging on the common gallows. Just as the sword or the axe were the customary mode in old Europe, in India the great and mighty were usually blown off from guns when the intention was to make an impression. The superstitious whispered that the body of the martyr swung towards Mecca in its final agony. For many years, thereafter, pilgrims continued to visit the tomb which was erected in the dargah of Qutab Sahib at Mehrauli. Lamps used to be lit while the tomb of the unfortunate Fraser, located in St. James Church, was destroyed during the mutiny. His monument had been singled out for desecration because there were tombs of other Europeans which were left untouched.

There was another angle to this murder. Nawab Shams ud-Din may have be dissipated but Fraser was also a bon vivant with a well-stocked bibi-ghar. The nawab suspected that he was carrying on an intrigue with his sister, for on one occasion he enquired about her health by name! This was a solecism according to oriental etiquette, an unpardonable slur on his family's honour.[7]

But for these interludes, life was peaceful and sedate. The 'new learning' being unveiled in the Delhi College was very exciting, particularly that of science. Some of the brightest students embraced Christianity. Notable among them were Prof. Ramchander and Dr. Chaman Lal. But this did not inhibit the emperor from admitting Dr. Chaman Lal to his service. In the benign atmosphere of Delhi any kind of fanaticism seemed out of place. One of the remarkable features of Delhi in this period was the complete absence of tension between the Hindus and Muslims. The composite culture of the city was bound by the Urdu language which counted both Hindus as well as Muslims among its afficionados. Even Hindu poets opened their poetic publications with the conventional *Bismillah* ('in the name of Allah, the merciful and compassionate').[8]

Cock-fighting was a popular sport. Kite-flying was another passion, and Ghalib was often forced by the emperor to keep him company on the Yamuna terrace of the fort watching the kites duel in the sky above. Not only the plebians, the umara also rejoiced in this sport. So strong was its attraction that poor Bidar Bakht, raised to the masnad from the depressing confines of the salatin khana could not resist its temptations. Indeed, it cost him his throne! Ghulam Qadir had been so disgusted by the infantilism displayed by this retarded product of the salatin quarters, that on being told that His Majesty had taken himself to the bazaar to buy kites when the Rohilla had been planning to take him to the Jama Masjid, the former promptly ordered his deposition and proclaimed the installation of Mirza Akbar.[9]

There was also pigeon flying, essentially an aristocrat's pastime, for pigeons cost money and afficionados took pride in possessing rare and fancy birds. They were flown in the afternoons, and as in kite-flying the effort was to confuse and capture as many of the rival's pigeons as possible. In the ceremonial processions of the emperor on occasions like the two Ids, and the anniversary of the accession, one of the elephants would also carry the imperial pigeon-house on its back!

These processions were loved by the common people of Delhi. First would came the elephants bearing the imperial banners—the 'alams' and 'nishans'—great big flags of green and gold emblazoned with the sun and stars. These would be followed by *shutarnals* which would fire off blank charges every now and then. Then came other elephants bearing the imperial insignia like the umbrella, the *aftabgir*, or the sun symbol, and the *maratib* and the imperial pigeon house.

The royal palki—a highly ornate fringed palki—would be carried aloft empty, preceded and followed by led horses, gaily caparisoned in crimson and scarlet, and soldiers, including the ahadis or 'gentlemen troopers', and the famous Surkh Posh or Lal Paltan in their crimson silk uniform. Then would appear the emperor himself, seated in an open howdah, followed by the heir-apparent and the other princes and the resident, the man who really ruled Delhi, and the commandant of the fort. Behind them would come the imperial band with the great big *naqqaras* or kettle-drums, the ladies of the *seraglio*, in curtained howdahs, led by the favourite consort and followed by the Empress Mother, if she happened to be living. The lesser consorts would be borne on bullock-drawn raths. Then there would be more troops, mounted and on foot, including the troops of the Company Bahadur. Whole crowds of people, including palace *chobdars*, and servants bearing silver sticks and maces, would be part of the procession, besides all kinds of ordinary people such as pedlars, snake-charmers and others who trailed along, adding to the colour and the general carnival atmosphere.

There was another side of Delhi as well, embodied in its night life which catered to every taste and vice. The *Muraqqa-i-Dehli* written by Salar Jang in 1739, shortly after Nadir Shah's visitation, describes the city hundred years before the Golden Calm. The city had suffered much in the decades that followed, and many of the gentle and service class had dispersed to other courts where life was more secure, like Lucknow, Jaipur and Alwar. Lahore too, now in the firm grip of the Lion of the Punjab, was a much more attractive city. No doubt many of Delhi's glittering hetaerae and others, who catered to the pleasures of the umara and the wealthy classes, had moved to these cities, but many still remained. And with the onset of the Golden Calm, life recovered much of the old gaiety.

Some of the fairs like that held on the anniversary of Khuld Manzil (Farrukhsiyar) were frankly worldly and sensual, catering to particular tastes. Farrukhsiyar was bisexual and crowds of 'beardless boys' would be out looking for partners and clients around his dargah. Many a visit to a dargah or a takkiah would be a carefully contrived cover for a rendezvous with a lover.

Kasalpura and Nagal were two quarters dedicated to Aphrodite. They were virtually enormous brothels. Nagal was supposed to have a saint's tomb, on the pretext of visiting which women went on the seventh of each month, decked in all their finery, having fixed appointments with friends and acquaintances beforehand, and 'none came back disappointed'. In Kasalpura there was singing and dancing in every house while women solicited in the street below.[10]

But what was remarkable in this period was the amazing flowering of Urdu poetry. Mir Taqi Mir, Momin Khan Momin, Dard, Zauq and—last but not least—Mirza Ghalib, Delhi had not seen such a constellation of brilliant poets all together at one time in any preceding age, and presiding over them all was the imperial Bahadur Shah 'Zafar', the poet-king, of no mean merit himself.

A love of literature and the arts had been the most endearing quality of the Gurgani dynasty from its earliest days. Amir Timur, the great world-conqueror himself, is said to have written an autobiography. Babur's memoirs are a classic in the genre and can rival Roussean's *Confessions* and Gandhi's *Experiments with Truth* in their frankness. Even the alcoholic Jahangir has left behind the *Tuzuk-i-Jahangiri*, a loose, rambling but extremely entertaining autobiography. A daughter of Babar, Gulbadan, had written a chronicle of her brother's troubled reign entitled the *Humayun Nama*. Babar and Humayun were bibliophiles, and the latter is recorded as having died from a fall from his library steps in what is now known as the Old Fort. Humayun was also fascinated by Persian miniature painting. When he returned to India with a Persian army, he brought with him a number of the finest miniaturists from the schools of Iran, to found the Mughal school of painting which flowered during the reign of his brilliant son, Akbar the Great.

Even the ladies of the house were well educated, and many could turn a polished verse or ghazal. Jahanara Begum, Nur Jahan, and Mumtaz are said to have written verse, but the first diwan or collection to have survived as a whole is the *Diwan-i-Makhfi*. 'Makhfi' was the pen name of Zeb un-Nissa, daughter of the stern Aurangzeb. Aurangzeb had lifted the ban on the marriage of princesses of the imperial house, but Zebun-Nissa did not marry of her own accord. Many romantic stories have been woven round this princess who was said to be extremely beautiful, but the *takhallus* chosen by her was peculiarly apt. 'Makhfi' means 'the hidden one' and 'Makhfi' remained immured to the privacy of the ladies' quarters, accessible only to the immediate males of her family and the palace eunuchs.

The last three emperors of the great house were poets. The *takhallus* of Shah Alam was 'Aftab' meaning sunshine. He left behind a collection known as the *Diwani-i-Aftab*. The verses are in both Persian and Urdu, which in the subsequent reigns was to overshadow the classical tongue of Sheikh Saadi and Hafiz. Akbar II composed verse under the name of 'Shua', while Bahadur Shah II adopted the ironical *nom de plume* of 'Zafar', the 'victorious'. His heir-apparent, Mirza Fakhruddin, composed poems under the name of 'Ramz'. The celebrated Mirza Ghalib was his *ustad*, as 'Zauq' was that of the emperor and had been of his late father 'Shua'! After Zauq's death, Ghalib stepped into his shoes and was also appointed the court poet.

There was more than just a whiff of the unreality of Axel's castle over the Qila-i-Mualla and the aesthetes who would gather round the imperial masnad for an evening of poetry. For the emperor and his family, life seemed to have no significance beyond these indulgences. The emperor, nominally a sovereign, exercised no power or executive authority beyond the palace walls, and all that lived within were little more than his extended family and servants. The princes and salatin were now allowed to take up residence outside, but no service opportunities under the state were open to them as they were considered to be disaffected. Theirs' was indeed a death in life, and verily the words of Axel could have been those of Bahadur Shah himself: 'As for living, we can leave that to our servants.'

The consciousness of belonging to a dying world, and the complete absence of a future, tinges with melancholy the poetry of the time. As the poet of the age, Mirza Ghalib wrote, '*When nothing was, God was. God would still be, if nothing had been; Being born, I was damned; What loss would it have been had I not been?*'[11]

By the time Bahadur Shah came to the throne poetry was in full bloom. Its foundations had been laid during the long reign of Shah Alam. Hatim, Mazhar, Dard and Sauda were the great poets of that age. Insha and Nasikh lived on into the reigns of Akbar II while the notable poets of the twilight years were Zauq, Momin and the great Ghalib. Of them, only Ghalib continued beyond the cataclysm of the Mutiny. There was, of course, also 'Zafar' who lingered on for some years in his dreary exile in Burma. Akbar Allahabadi was the next great poet. But born in 1846 he was the poet of the new age which merged with the modernity of the twentieth century. The race of the house of Timur was but a distant memory, but the historical bouleversement is occasionally touched upon ironically in his verses.

The reign of the Quran is over
and the days of world-wide trade;
We subsist now as landlords on rents
Or for clerical jobs are paid.[12]

The court was but a shadow of its old self. Lord Ellenborough had heaped insults on the emperor and the imperial family. The silver throne which was kept in the Diwan-i-Khas had been removed by his orders and locked in an under-ground cellar in 1844. The Diwan-i-Am had also been closed and the holding of public durbars actually forbidden. The practice of granting *khillats* was discouraged.

As if this was not enough, the new rulers ordered that 'the British officers were not bound to show respect to the king's cavalcade it they incidentally crossed it on the way'. Hitherto, the old traditional forms of respect had been shown to the emperor and the princes whenever they appeared in public. People riding on horseback would at once dismount and salute the cavalcade. But now, by the governor-general's order, British officers were no longer required to do so.

The court had acquired European style horse-carriages and, when he appeared in public, Bahadur Shah's carriage would be drawn by as many as sixteen horses, while the empress used eight. These were considered too grand and ostentatious, and the English ridiculed him. The imperial band which preceded them on ceremonial occasions was also subjected to the same ridicule.[13] William Fraser, on returning from a durbar at the palace, handed over the robes with which he had been honoured to the first beggar he met outside the Delhi Gate.[14] The highest officers of the Company were now cavalier in their disregard of even the rituals of external respect. The matter was reported to Calcutta, and the resident was pulled up, but the incident is a sad pointer to the loss of mystique of the imperial house.

Contacts between His Majesty and British officials were necessarily of a formal nature, and after Seton and Ochterlony often chillingly so. The empress also received callers, and if they happened to be women the meetings could be more relaxed in the privacy of the *seraglio*. These visitors could be of all kinds. It would seem that even the wives of junior English officers and sergeants would occasionally call on the empress or other princesses and dowagers.[15]

We are grateful to Mrs. Mir Hassan Ali for a particularly detailed and sympathetic description of a visit to the empress in the reign of Akbar II. The lady was an English woman married to a young man who was a product of the new learning, and whose father had been in the service of Mian Almas Ali, the famous eunuch and revenue farmer of Awadh. She writes:

I was conducted to the Queens' *mahul* (place for females) where his majesty and the queen were awaiting my arrival. I found on my entrance the king seated in the open air in an armchair enjoying his hookah; the Queen's *musned* was on the ground, close by the side of her venerable husband. . . . After having left my shoes at the entrance and advanced towards them, my salaams were tendered, and then the usual offering of nuzzar, first to the King and then to the Queen, who invited me to a seat on her carpet—an honour I knew how to appreciate from my acquaintance with the etiquette observed on such occasions.

The whole period of my visit was occupied in very interesting conversation; eager inquiries were made respecting England, the Government, the manners of the court, the habits of the people, my own family affairs, my husband's views in travelling, and his adventures in England, my own satisfaction as regarded climate, and the people with whom I was so immediately connected by marriage;—the conversation, indeed, never flagged for an instant, for the condescending courtesy of their majesties encouraged me to add to their entertainment, by details which seemed to interest and delight them greatly.

On taking leave his Majesty very cordially shook me by the hand, and the Queen embraced me with Warmth. Both appeared, and expressed themselves, highly gratified with the visit of an English lady who could explain herself in their language without embarassment, or the assistance of an interpreter, and who was the more interesting to them from the circumstance of being the wife of a Syaad. I was grieved to be obliged to accept the Queens' parting present of an embroidered scarf, because I knew her means were exceedingly limited compared with the demands upon her bounty; but I could not refuse that which was intended to do me honour at the risk of wounding those feelings I so greatly respected. A small ring, of trifling value, was then placed by the Queen on my finger, as she remarked, to remind me of the giver.

The King's countenance, dignified by age, possesses traces of extreme beauty; he is much fairer than Asiatics usually are; his features are still fine, his hair silvery white; intelligence beams upon his brow; his conversation gentle and refined and his condescending manner hardly to be surpassed by the most refined gentleman of Europe. I am told by those who have been long intimate with his habits in private, that he leads a life of strict piety and temperance, equal to that of a *durweish* of his faith, whom he imitates in expending his income on others without indulging in a single luxury on himself.

The Queen's manners are very amiable and condescending; she is reported to be as highly gifted with intellectual endowments as I can affirm with genuine politeness.[16]

The allusion to the king as a 'durweish' deserves some explanation.

Akbar II and Bahadur Shah were both deeply influenced by Sufi mysticism. And, as the emperor was, among his other titles, '*Zill-i-Subhani*', or the shadow of God, it seemed but a natural next step to becoming a murshid, and inducting disciples or murids in the manner of pirzadas or sajda nashins of various shrines like the dargah at Nizamuddin. Even soldiers and officers of the Company's troops became his murids in this manner. The British, however, saw in this a conspiracy to seduce the soldiers from their loyalty, and prohibited the practice.[17]

Percival Spear, has described the imperial court as a marble pavilion built over a vast cesspool. The stink of the cesspool should not blind us to the beauty of the pavilion, while the dazzling marble should not blind us to the corruption and decay beneath it. There was much that was rotten in the Qila-i-Mualla and what passed as the imperial system, and the genuine piety and virtues of the poet-kings cannot hide the fact that they had nothing to offer. Micawber-like, they were vaguely always hoping for something to turn up which they could exploit to their advantage. The chance presented itself when the mutineers from Meerut took over the city and the palace. Trusting only to fate and chance, they themselves had no programme or plans.

None of the princes showed any awareness of the changing world. 'Azfari' was one of the salatin who escaped the prison-house that was the Qila-i-Mualla in 1789, and spent much of his life visiting the courts of princely India. He was well educated in the classical languages, besides having a knowledge of medicine, astrology and prosody, and wrote Urdu, Arabic and Persian verses. But his diary indicates only commonplace sentiments and his preoccupation with etiquette. Though himself penniless, and dependent entirely on the bounty of his hosts, his principal obsession appears to have been to ensure that his reception and treatment was such as became an imperial prince. And amazingly, none of his hosts, including potentates like the Nizam of Hyderabad, and the princes of Jaipur and Jodhpur, appear to have failed in the required courtesies. They all seemed to agree that his very presence under their roof did them honour.[18] Form was everything.

Other currents did, however, exist. One such was represented by Syed Ahmad 'Barelvi', or the 'Shahid', as he is also called. In a sense he was a revivalist, preaching a return to the fundamentals of Islam. He was not yet a republican. He was all the time in search of a prince, and died as a mujahid or holy warrior waging a quixotic jehad on the Afghan frontier against the Sikhs who were now masters of the Punjab.

Another Syed Ahmad, who was destined to become a Knight Commander of the Star of India was more modern in his outlook. The Aligarh

College, the nucleus of the later University at Aligarh, was to be his great achievement. But the activities of such men, 'modern' though they may have been in their outlook, would lead to an increase in communal tensions between Muslims and non-Muslims. The imperial household had by then become quite secular in its outlook. Even the Muslim rite of circumcision had long been discontinued. To avoid giving offence to Hindus, camels were sacrificed in the Qila-i-Mualla on the occasion of the Id. We have already remarked on the nonchalance with which the emperor accepted Dr. Chaman Lal into his service, notwithstanding the furore which his conversion to Christianity had caused in the Indian community.

This attitude appears to have been universal among Muslim potentates. An interesting anecdote is narrated of Haidar Ali of Mysore. A celebrated pirzada once complained to him that some Hindus of Seringapatnam had beaten up his followers—who had themselves attacked a Hindu procession—and demanded redress from him as he was the head of a Muslim government. But Haidar turned on him and snapped, 'Who told you this was a Muslim government?'[19]

One need not belabour the point. It is enough to observe that popular festivals like Holi, Dussehra and Diwali were observed by the Mughal court as well, besides, of course, the usual festivals of the Muslim calendar. In India, Islam had acquired many peculiar overtones unknown in 'Iran and Ajam'.

NOTES

1. Heber, *Journey through the Upper Provinces of India*, ii, pp. 392, 362-3.
2. Philip Woodruffe, *Men Who Ruled India*, i, p. 237. Varma, *Ghalib*, p. 64.
3. Emily Eden, *Up the Country*, p. 210.
4. Spear, *A History of Delhi under the Later Mughals*, pp. 64-5.
5. Sleeman, *Rambles and Recollections*, ii, p. 269.
6. Varma, *Ghalib*, pp. 127, 128.
7. Dalrymple, *City of Djinns*, pp. 109, 145.
8. Andrews, *Zaka-Ullah of Delhi*, pp. 15-16.
9. British Museum, *Additional Manuscripts*, *MSS 29, 171*, pp. 319-20. Jonathan Scott to Warren Hastings.
10. Dargah Quli Khan, *Muraqqa-e-Dehli*, pp. 50-1.
11. Translated by Pavan K. Varma; from *Ghalib*.
12. Quotation taken from M. Mujeeb's *The Indian Muslims*, p. 477.
13. Fane, *Five years in India*, i, pp. 137-8.
14. Ibid., i, p. 142.
15. Kaye and Malleson, *History of the Indian Mutiny*, ii, p. 25 (footnote). Evidence of Mrs. Fleming, wife of an English sergeant who visited Zinat Mahal.

16. Mrs. Meer Hassan Ali, *Observations on the Mussulmans of India*, pp. 290-2.
17. K. Yadav, *Delhi in 1857*, pp. 387, 410-12. Arguments of the Judge Advocate General and the examination of Hakim Ahsan Ullah.
18. Mujeeb, *The Indian Muslims*, pp. 503-5.
19. Ibid., p. 419. Quoted from *A Facsimile Reprint of the History of Haider Khan Bahadur and his son Tippoo Sultan by MMDLT*, Bangabashi Office, Calcutta, 1908, p. 17.

CHAPTER 48

The Ghadar: Reaping the Whirlwind

The published literature on the Mutiny is voluminous. It is enough to observe that the English conquest had been almost too easy, and that the foundations of the Company's power rested on a mercenary army. Sooner or later there was bound to be a reaction.

That India is not a nation and probably never can be one in the European sense is an oft-asserted truism. It is also correct that innumerable races and conquerors have entered or invaded this country at various times and made it their home. In the not too distant past, the ancestor of Bahadur Shah II had also descended from the Afghan hills and made himself master of Hind. But by the seventeenth century the dynasty had struck roots deep into the soil so that even when the military power of the padishah had vanished, there was no attempt by anyone to set him aside and proclaim a new dispensation. The assimilative power in Indian civilization was tremendous, but the new English conquerors had certain peculiarities which worked against their assimilation into India.

The British empire, unlike all preceding systems; was a colonial complex in which the colonies existed for the benefit of British merchants, and provided a field where younger sons of the landed gentry might be enabled to make their fortunes. The prosperity of the native Indian was a consideration that did not exist.

With the conclusion of the Maratha wars, peace had at last come to a country ravaged by more than a century of war, misrule and anarchy. Order was at last restored, brigandage put down, and the bourgeoisie of the towns and the peasants in the countryside, could now go to bed with a sense of security. People returned to the depopulated towns, and the peasants to their deserted villages; agriculture and commerce revived, but prosperity still remained a distant dream. What was most galling of all, the former ruling classes found the doors of preferment and service closed, except in the lowest ranks.

In India's pre-industrial society, great honour and prestige were attached to service, in particular, the service of the state. For Kayasths and Khatris,

Brahmans and Rajputs, this was their bread and butter, and indeed for Muslims as well, specially among those claiming ashraf or gentle status. But now, in the annexed territories, all the higher offices of state were reserved for the younger sons of English squires and clergymen. The army of the Company remained dependent on its mercenary sepoys recruited from among the 'martial' communities of India. As compared to the old Indian armies, the troops of the Company were paid on time—only at the time of Lord Lake's wars did salaries fall into arrears. The higher ranks were as in other spheres, closed to Indians. In the 'irregular horse', or sillahdar cavalry, there was still scope for advancement, but even these were being gradually brought in line with the regular regiments of the presidency armies. After a lifetime of service, no soldier, however capable, could aspire to a salary of more than Rs. 60 or 70 a month.

In contrast, in the old Indian armies, merit was the sole criterion, and every *sowar* or rider could be said to carry a marshal's baton in his saddlebags. The great Haidar Ali of Mysore and Najib ud-Daulah had started as ordinary soldiers. Such careers were not possible in the British armies of the presidencies, where sons and grandsons of former generals and high-placed umara enlisted as common troopers, and retired as jamadars or subedars, and were required to take orders from callow captains and lieutenants, one half or even one third their age. As a result, no self-respecting scion of an ashraf family enlisted if he could help it.

Similarly, in the civil administration, only the lower grade revenue offices, and the lowest rungs of the magistracy, were open to the sons of the Indian gentry. The final emasculation of a proud ruling class would be seen in the later part of the century when the sons of the aristocracy and descendants of mediatized princes were happy to be honoured with the office of 'honorary magistrate' or 'honorary sub-registrar', even though the magistrate would seldom be given more than 'second class' powers, and the sub-registrar merely registered deeds and documents which a lowly naib-tahsildar might do in the normal course of his duties. If a son of a high-born India managed to graduate from one of the colleges set up under the new English-oriented university system, he might be nominated as a tahsildar or to the subordinate civil service of the province, where the farthest an Indian might aspire was the office of a district collector towards the fag-end of his career.

The old peerage of the fading empire with its titles and grades of so many hundreds or thousands of zat or sowar, was replaced by new titles like Khan Bahadur, Rao Sahib and the like. These were purely decorative honorifics given to rich gentlemen who possessed the means to support these dignities, and were usually awarded for services of a political nature. The idea of a titled aristocracy, divorced from functional office, was novel to India, and did little to enhance the prestige of either the recipients or the givers.

In general, the acquisition of fresh territory by the British raj would mean an immediate loss of employment by the old ruling classes, and a general levelling of society. Nor did it signify any increase in prosperity for the peasant in the long run. The new revenue demands were in cash rather than kind, and based on good years rather than average. In time of drought or famine, the peasants would be driven to the wall. The revenue system was much more rigid than in the old 'native states', which were also encouraged to 'reform' their administration according to the norms established in the directly-governed British provinces.

Another reason for general dissatisfaction with British rule was the administration of justice. In India this had always been a simple and very direct affair. The honorific of the 'Just King' was highly respected, and stories of the justice of Vikramaditya, Jahangir or Naushirwan, were part of oriental folklore. Even kings and emperors would set apart one day in the week, when they would listen to the suits of the aggrieved, and administer justice in person. It was regarded as a sacred duty, and there was no question of court fees which had transformed the exercise of this duty in European countries into a source of profit for the government. In view of the Indian tradition, the highly formalized court procedure introduced by the British with pleaders and perjured witnesses to tender 'evidence' left the people dazed and bewildered.

Thus, while large areas of India had, indeed, been areas of darkness before the advent of the British, the raj was by no means an unmixed blessing.

There was a world of difference between the Company's officers of the old school, like Ochterlony and Seton, and the newer, younger lot. Several factors were responsible. One was the arrival of the 'memsahib' following the shortening of the voyage of India. In the old days the ships went round the Cape of Good Hope, a long and tedious journey of five or six months. But with the end of the Napoleonic wars, and the opening up of Egypt, the journey time was cut by more than half. After crossing the Channel one could travel by stage-coach (and later by railway) to Marseilles, from where one could board a ship for Alexandria. From Alexandria it was a short journey overland to the Gulf of Suez from where one boarded another ship for the last lap of the voyage to India.

With the shortening of the travel-time, more and more women started venturing east where they tried to restructure Anglo-Indian society after the standards of English suburbia. In the old days, there were few European women and the officers of the Company rarely went 'home' on leave. Usually they returned only on superannuation or when compelled by ill-health. In India they lived like the Indian umara, and took to wife Indian ladies who were sometimes ladies of quality. From them they learnt the language and the customs of the people, and acquired a much more sympathetic understanding of the complexities of the Indian world.

With the coming of the white 'mem', things changed. The bibi-ghars were shut down, concubinage went into the closet, and the 'mem' laid down the law in her house. The onset of every cold season in India brought a number of unmarried English maidens—the 'fishing fleet'—who would come visiting relatives in India in the hope of hooking a husband. With them came a host of new interests, and the regiment became a bore.

What made the situation dangerous, from the point of view of governance, was that the best officers were being sent on deputation to civil appointments to administer the newly annexed territories, leaving young and inexperienced officers behind who looked down on the sepoys as 'blackies'. Apart from the fact that their knowledge of Indian languages was atrocious, they treated the Indian officers with barely concealed contempt. Chairs were seldom offered, and the easy intercourse between Indian and British officers became a thing of the past.[1] The latter were thus unaware of the real feelings of their men, and the gossip of the barracks did not reach their ears.

Mutinies had occurred before in the Company's army, as they are apt to in armies all over the world, and they had been tackled and suppressed with the ferocity peculiar to European armies, the ring-leaders being frequently blown from guns or strung up from gallows in full view of regiments assembled on parade to watch the edifying scene. But such ferocious retribution was unknown in the old Indian armies where officers were frequently mobbed for arrears, and soldiers had often grounded arms and squatted in *dharna* to voice their grievances. The awful retribution dealt out by the British to their mutinous comrades angered the Indian sepoys and the native officers who did not always appreciate the logic of the British officers.

There was a fundamental difference between the social position of 'Tommy Atkins' and the Indian soldier. In Britain, the soldiers of the line came from the dregs of society and had to be dragooned into enlisting. No self-respecting man ever enlisted voluntarily; recruiting sergeants often had to ply their victims with drink before they could be induced into signing the contract for service with the colours. English soldiers were usually running away from something: their past, financial bankruptcy, a broken marriage, a criminal charge, and so on.

In contrast, the profession of arms had always been an honourable one in India. A capable soldier could hope to rise to the highest ranks, and favour and fortune awaited the intrepid. But in England a soldier was often written off by his family. He was marked as a ne'er-do-well, and his parents and brothers were usually indifferent to his fate thereafter. The severity of the British military penal code may, thus, have been appropriate to deal with the brutalized semi-criminal British other ranks, but was singularly inappropriate for handling their Indian counterparts. The Indian soldier, however poor he may have been, regarded himself as a gentleman, and that was how the rest of society looked at him.

Of late the British had had to contend with increasing resistance in their Indian wars. Victory was not easily obtained in the Punjab, the Gorkha war with Nepal had been a drawn affair, and the debacle of the first Afghan war had shaken the prestige of the red-coats. It was evident that the English were not invincible and, were further proof needed, rumours of the disasters of the Crimean war reached India to further depress the *iqbal* of the sublime English lords. Maulvi Azimullah, the envoy, of Nana Sahib, the Maratha pensionary at Bithur, had visited the Crimean theatre and brought back authentic first-hand information of the wretched manner in which that war was being prosecuted.[2]

An increase in religiosity and evangelical fervour in many Englishmen was probably the most dangerous development. The story of the English officer who forcibly marched his men into a Colombo church with the laudable but imprudent determination to show them the Light of the True Faith became current all over India,[3] and innovations in uniforms, orders suppressing the wearing of caste-marks on the forehead, or of ear-rings—and even beards—were interpreted as attempts to interfere with the faith of both Hindus and Mussalmans. Even the suppression of abominable practices like sati and female infanticide gave rise to further suspicions in the Indian mind.

While evangelist enthusiasm may have stoked the fears of the ordinary sepoy, and, indeed, of the man in the street, in the same manner as Aurangzeb's sunni bigotry is alleged to have created a chasm between the Mughal badshahat and its non-Muslim subjects, what really fanned the fears of Indian princes was the annexationist zeal of Lord Dalhousie. Annexation as a result of the fortunes of war was something the Indian mind could readily understand, but the extinction of a protected state as a result of the application of abstract principles, foreign to Indian law and custom, shook the faith of the Indian dynasts in their 'protectors'.

With the annexation of the Punjab after the Sikh wars, the British frontier had reached the uttermost limits of the traditional border of India. Both banks of the Indus were controlled by the English and an English puppet had pushed the frontier still further to the snowy hights of Karakorum and High Tartary. Whatever the legality of the points which would be raised much later by its mediatized prince, Maharaja Duleep Singh, the Punjab had at least been conquered by the sword. It was an argument that the princes understood. But what had poor Satara done to deserve extinction in 1848? Its prince had failed to produce an 'heir of the body'. They might have argued; so what? Hindu custom recognized sons of various kinds; on innumerable occassions in the past princes had taken recourse to adoption to perpetuate their dynasties. Heirs could be adopted even after the death of their adoptive fathers by their widows. Even the detested Aurangzeb had not dared propound a working notion as monstrous as the 'Doctrine of Lapse'.

The maharajas of Satara were the direct descendants of the great Shivaji, the titular sovereigns of the Maratha nation, and though long superseded in political power by their mayors of the palace, their name still fired the imagination of the people. A more sympathetic mind with longer exposure to India may have recoiled from the application of the Doctrine of Lapse to this petty state, long since shorn of its ancient glories but still venerated as a sort of relic. But not so Dalhousie. The claims of the adoptive prince were rejected and the state annexed in April 1848. Toward the end of 1853 the Bhonsle state of Berar suffered a similar fate. Though nominally a feudatory of the Chhatrapatis of Satara, its territories were spread across the forested tribal belt of central India, reaching almost up to the Bay of Bengal, and was therefore a much more tempting prize than modest Satara. To make things simpler for the acquisitive Dalhousie, Raghoji Bhonsle, too embarassed to make a public confession of his inability to beget a child, had failed even to adopt a successor. The minor chieftaincy of Jhansi, located in Bundelkhand, was another sovereignty that fell victim to the governor-general's insatiable appetite. None of Gangadhar Rao's two immediate predecessors had been able to beget an heir of the body, but previous governors-general had recognized the succession of the next of kin, an uncle—even though he was a leper—and, thereafter the uncle's brother. Gangadhar Rao had adopted an infant, but the claims of the latter, which were urged by the adoptive mother, described as a 'lady bearing a high character, and much respected by everyone at Jhansi', were rejected. Jhansi passed under the control of the Company, and Lord Dalhousie smugly observed that 'its incorporation with the British territories will be greatly for the benefit of the people of Jhansi which a reference to the results of experience will suffice to show'.[4] The English had much to learn.

In the case of Satara and Nagpur the governor-general met with strong opposition. The governor of Bombay, Sir George Clerk, and Sir John Low, member of the Supreme Council, had argued against annexation, but to no avail. Other minor states like Sambhalpur in Orissa, Jaitpur in Bundelkhand, and Tanjore in south India were extinguished almost without a murmur. Even pageant princes, already mediatized and incapable of exercising executive power, were not spared. The foundations of the British power in south India had been laid in concert with the nawab of the Carnatic who had his seat at Arcot. By the time Lord Dalhousie came on the scene, the Arcot durbar had become as much of a pageant as that of the nawab-nazims of Murshidabad. He had never given any ground for complaint, but the governor-general did not let sentimental regard for the old alliance stand in the way of the logical resumption of what little territory and dignity were left to that house, when in 1854 the last nawab died without 'heirs of the body'. The titular dignities of the family were abolished by the application of the Doctrine of Lapse, in spite of the vehement protests of the head of the house. The grant of pensions to the members of the house—as in the similar case of Tanjore—was considered a poor substitute for the lustre of their extinguished dignities.

The extinction of the title of the nawab of Arcot is but a footnote in history. The extinction of the titular dignity of the peshwa was, however fraught with greater and weightier consequences. Since 1819, the deposed peshwa, Baji Rao, had been living on the banks of the sacred Ganga at Bithur. Though shorn of his old territorial holdings in the Maratha heartland, he maintained a make-believe court. Baji Rao had been granted a pension of Rs. 8 lakh per annum and on occasion had come forward to the assistance of the English. For instance, on the occasion of the disastrous Afghan war he had come forward with a loan of Rs. 5 lakh, and at the time of the Sikh war had offered to raise and maintain a force of 1,000 horse and foot. In short, he maintained good relations with the English, and gave them no reason to suspect his fidelity.[5]

But he too was denied the blessings of an heir of the body. He had, therefore, adopted a boy from among his kinsmen, named Dhondo Pant 'Nana', and had moved the British government, seeking recognition of his right to succeed to his title and pensions. The prayer was not granted, but the matter was not closed either. It was left to be decided as and when the contingency should arise.

That happened on 28 January 1851 when, at the age of 77, the peshwa finally closed his eyes. The British commissioner at Bithur supported the claims of Dhondo Pant, but as Malleson observed, 'Empty titular dignities are dangerous possessions, and it may be, after all, only mistaken kindness to perpetuate them when the substance of royalty is gone'. The conclusion was a foregone one with Dalhousie in command. It was observed that the late peshwa had left behind a sizeable private fortune, amounting to Rs. 16 lakh in government securities, Rs. 10 lakh in jewels, and a considerable sum in gold coins and other valuables, which was deemed sufficient to maintain the diminished state of Dhondo Pant. After all, the Nana had never been a peshwa. There followed the usual protests. Azimullah Khan left with a memorial to plead his cause in London where he met the envoy of the unhappy, dispossessed, Chhatrapati of Satara who was pleading a similar case. Like Rango Bapuji, and, indeed, Raja Rammohun Roy and others, his efforts drew a blank. The ensuing resentment and bitterness would soon find ample scope for revenge in the bloody events that were to follow.

There still remained the puppet state of Awadh. Raised to the rank of kings by the grace of the East India Company, the English could not have asked for more docile clients than the rulers of Awadh. Never had they dared to raise their heads in defiance. The chains that bound them must no doubt have been irksome, but they made no attempt to shake them off.

The subsidiary alliance which the English had forced on the nawab-wazir had introduced a vicious system of dual government in the province. While the military direction and external relations came to be vested largely with the British, the internal administration remained with the nawab-wazir. But secure on their masnad with British troops to protect them, the nawabs neglected the onerous responsibilities of government and allowed the country to go to rack and ruin.

> Disorder of every kind ran riot over the whole length and breadth of the land. Never were the evils of misrule more horribly apparent; never were the vices of an indolent and rapacious Government productive of a greater sum of misery. The extravagance and profligacy of the Court were written in hideous characters on the desolated face of the country. It was left to the Nawab's Government to collect the revenue; it was wrung from the people at the point of the bayonet. . . . The expenses of the royal household were enormous. Hundreds of richly caparisoned and voracious elephants ate up the wealth of whole districts, or carried it in glittering apparel on their backs. A multitudinous throng of unserviceable

attendants; bands of dancing girls; flocks of parasites; costly feasts and ceremonies; folly and pomp and profligacy of every conceivable description, drained the coffers of the State. A vicious and extravagant Government soon beget a poor and suffering people; a poor and suffering people, in turn perpetuate the curse of a bankrupt Government. The process of retaliation is sure. To support the lavish expenditure of the Court the mass of the people were persecuted and outraged. Bands of armed mercenaries were let loose upon the *ryots* in support of the rapacity of Amils or Revenue-farmers, whose appearance was a terror to the people. Under such a system of cruelty and extortion, the country soon became a desert, and the Government then learnt by hard experience that the prosperity of the people is the only true source of wealth. The lesson was thrown away. . . .[6]

Thus moralises Sir John Kaye. Sleeman in his *Account of a Tour* dilates on the atrocities committed in the countryside by the taluqdars and the amils, and waxes eloquent on the waste and corruption prevailing at court. The Awadh monarchy had become a byword for degenerate and decadent royalty.

Yet it was not always so. Mainoddin observes that, at the beginning of his reign, Wajid Ali Shah took great interest in the drill and training of his army, but he was soon warned that his martial interest was causing eyebrows to be raised at the Residency, and that it would be wiser to take up other interests.[7]

But no matter how degenerate, the kings and the nawabs were faithful allies. Collectively, they paid as much as Rs. 76 lakh to the English to defray the cost of the subsidiary force in their territories. In 1801, the Doab districts of the nawab-wazir, yielding nearly Rs. 1 crore, had been ceded to the Company in lieu of the subsidy. These constituted the best parts of Awadh, and were under the administration of that remarkable enunch, Mian Almas Ali Khan. The Doab districts were now reorganized to constitute the North-Western Provinces of Agra. Whenever the governor-general's treasury was empty, the king of could be relied on to fork out a loan without demur. At the end of the Nepal war he had obliged the English by purchasing for the sum of Rs. 10 lakh the forested and malarial districts of the Terai which the Nepalese had ceded to them.

This was in the time of Lord Hastings, the Earl of Moira, who had earlier raised Ghazi ud-Din Haider to royal rank for the sum of Rs. 2 crore. Still earlier, Warren Hastings had applied the screws on the begums of Awadh and extorted from them a forced loan amounting to Rs. 76 lakh. This act of heartless brutality was to constitute one of the principal charges laid against Warren Hastings at the time of his impeachment, but atrocious as the act, no doubt, was, it would not have been possible without the cooperation of Asaf ud-Daulah, who assisted in the spoliation of his own step-mother and grandmother. Nasir ud-Din Haider, the second king of Awadh, the one who gloried in the titles of 'the Just Sultan, the Naushirwan of the Age', may have been the worst of them all in the eyes of Kaye, but when pressed for a loan he readily obliged. In spite of its gross maladministration and near bankruptcy, Awadh was a milch cow which the English squeezed without remorse.

Many of the Company's more thoughtful servants readily conceded that they themselves were largely responsible for the mess that was Awadh. Proposals for reform were often mooted, but nothing happened on the ground, and the state seemed to be drifting towards disaster. It was suggested that the only option was annexation, or what would amount to virtually the same thing-the assumption by the British of the responsibility of the entire administration. Colonel Sleeman's tour report was a damning indictment of the government of Awadh, but he too advised against annexation.

Ultimately, however, with Dalhousie at the helm of affairs, the annexationists won. Awadh was taken over a bare three weeks before the governor-general demitted office. It was left to his successor to reap the bitter harvest.

Men like Sleeman were opposed to mindlessly annexing more territory, because they felt that by so extending their territorial control they were becoming increasingly dependent on their sepoy army. It was impossible to hold the country with a purely European army, and it was apprehended by these far-seeing officers that a situation could arise when their mercenaries might turn against them. It was preferable to keep the Indian princes as their allies, tied to them by mutual self-interest, rather than assuming charge directly.

With the annexation of the state, the Company's sepoys discovered that they had also lost their priveleged status. The bulk of the Bengal army was recruited in Awadh, and these soldiers had the right to demand the resident's intervention in their behalf in the domestic problems of their families vis a vis the Awadh administration. Sleeman has given many instances of how this privileged was mercilessly abused to browbeat the king's administration, for the resident was a demi-god whom no officer dared to offend. As the affair of Wazir Ali had showed, his pen had the power to make and unmake the ruler of Awadh.

The newer and younger officers lacked sympathy for India and had little respect for its civilization and customs. Other currents were in the air. The spirit of Utilitarianism, the crude philosophy of the Industrial Age, had little use for the trappings of Indian feudalism. The cession of the Doab districts had been followed by revenue settlements which were hostile to the claims of jagirdars and taluqdars, who were viewed as parasites. Unlike the case of the Permanent Settlement of Lord Cornwallis in Bengal, where the English had sought to create a class of revenue contractors in the mould of landlords after the English pattern, in the North Western Provinces the tendency was the reverse: to eliminate the taluqdars and engage for the payment of the revenue directly with the village communities themselves.

Taluqdars, inamdars, *madad* and *mash* jagirdars, were all required to submit proof of their claims. Written proof was demanded from a class, largely illiterate, which had always placed greater reliance on the edge of their sword, and the fact of possession, than on documents to substantiate their claims. As a result, thousands of petty right-holders, whose families had received their grants for services rendered, were dispossessed. Great estates like the Mainpuri raj were reduced drastically, the latter from 200 villages to a mere 43.[8] The result was turmoil, and it was years before things settled down. The same process had now started in Awadh.

In short, within a few decades of the establishment of the Pax Brittannica, India was seething with the spirit of revolt. Dispossessed princes were plotting revenge; those that still retained their thrones were apprehensive and fearful. The native army, on which the Company's rule depended, could see no future for a man of honour in the Company's service. They grumbled that the *sipahis* of the Nizam and the Maratha chiefs were better off then the Company's subedars and jamadars. If they rode horses or ponies purchased from their savings, the English officer frowned on them as upstarts.[9] And what was worse, the myth of British invincibility had been shaken. The English, out of touch with the mood of the masses, and even their own soldiers, were unaware that they were perched on a volcano that was ready to erupt.

The days of Sir William Jones, or James Prinsep, were over. The Englishman of the age of Victoria looked down on the ignorant native and treated him with withering contempt. Orientalism was out of fashion. Even a distinguished historian like Sir John Kaye could write of the Qila-i-Mualla only as 'that gigantic Palace which had so long been the home of manifold abominations'. The royal family itself is described as 'that great evil of rotting royalty which had so long polluted the atmosphere of

Delhi'. And 'Heaven alone could take account' of their 'tremendous catalogue of iniquities'.[10] To top it all, there were the whispered rumours that the cartridges of the new Enfield rifle were encased in paper greased with the fat of cows and pigs—offensive equally to Hindus and Muslims. The prescribed drill for loading the new rifle required the end of the cartridge to be bitten off by the soldiers, an act which would effectively pollute them. The whole purpose, according to the rumour, was that the polluted sepoys should be left with no option but to embrace the Christian faith!

That something was in the air could be felt. Mysterious fires would break out in cantonments. There was the phenomenon of chapaties being passed from village to village as a forerunner of some news or mysterious orders to come. Wandering faqirs and sadhus of both faiths spread the belief that the English rule was fated to last but a hundred years, and that the English century was approaching its end with the coming centenary of Plassey (1757).

That the Nana was intriguing with the Indian officers from his seat at Bithur has now been established. His agents would send monetary gifts on certain occasions among the regiments stationed at Kanpur. And so would the emperor from the Qila-i-Mualla. How far this could be interpreted as a conscious design to tamper with the loyalty of the troops is debatable. After all, even today it is customary for the rich but powerless to give presents to those who wield power, on festive occasions like Diwali. And the farsighted do not neglect the humbler hangers-on of the high and mighty.

The evidence suggests that the Nana was probably the main spirit behind the rebellion. He had hitherto led a quiet and secluded life, rarely venturing beyond the limits of his estate of Bithur, but between January and April 1857 he visited Kalpi, Delhi and Lucknow, where he called on the notables on 'business'.[11] The nature of the business would soon become apparent.

NOTES

1. Kaye and Malleson, *History of the Indian Mutiny*, i, p. 187 (fn.).
2. Russel, Sir William Howard, *My Diary in India*, i, p. 167.
3. Kaye and Malleson, i, p. 170.
4. Ibid., i, p. 66.
5. Ibid., i, pp. 71-2.
6. Ibid., i, pp. 82-3.
7. Metcalfe, *Two Native Narratives of the Mutiny in Delhi*, p. 32, the narrative being that of Muinuddin's *Kodang-i-Ghadar*.

8. Metcalfe, Thomas R., *Land, Landlords and the British Raj*, pp. 82, 96. Kaye and Malleson, i, pp. 113-22.
9. Kaye and Malleson, i, p. 161.
10. Ibid., ii, p. 7.
11. Ibid., i, pp. 422-6, 454.

CHAPTER 49

The Rebellion in Delhi

Hints of the coming storm first manifested themselves in Bengal, close to the seat of the Company's raj, in the cantonments of Barrackpur and Berhampur. The obnoxious cartridges were the apparent cause of the disaffection. There were mysterious incidents of incendiarism, but little violence, except for the incident of Mangal Pandey when a sepoy, apparently intoxicated with *bhang*, attacked an officer at Barrackpur. But the situation was tactfully handled; two regiments—the 19th Native Infantry and the 34th—were ultimately disbanded, and Mangal Pandey and a native officer were sentenced by a court-martial, and hanged. The first manifestation was in February and the hangings took place in April 1857. Thereafter, on 7 May there was trouble in Lucknow, but the first big explosion took place in Meerut on 10 May. This had immediate repercussions in Delhi.

On 24 April, Lieutenant Colonel Carmichael Smith of the 3rd Light Cavalry, on receipt of the new instructions for the rifle drill which substituted manual tearing of the tip of the cartridge by the use of teeth, ordered a parade to demonstrate the new drill. But, acting in concert, 85 men of the regiment refused to accept the cartridges. The Colonel lectured them, but the men were adamant. This was mutiny and they were promptly placed under arrest. A court of enquiry was followed by a court-martial, and all 85 were sentenced to 10 years rigorous imprisonment.

On 9 May the sentence was carried out; the convicted prisoners being stripped of their uniforms in a punishment parade, with their comrades witnessing the painful scene. Fetters were fitted about their ankles by blacksmiths, and they were marched off to their makeshift jail, guarded by troopers from their own regiment.

The British officers heaved a sigh of relief that the parade had passed off peacefully, but the sepoys were excited and the atmosphere surcharged. When in the evening the sepoys left their barracks to relax in the bazaar, the shopkeepers jeered at them and the prostitutes taunted them. They could not be men if they could watch unmoved while the blacksmiths hammered the fetters round their comrades' ankles. Apparently, one 'Miss Dolly', an English widow and outcaste from her own community, who ran a 'refreshment' place much favoured by sepoys, played a key role in thus provoking the soldiers. She would later be hanged by the authorities for her role in this drama—one of the rare cases of an English woman being executed.[1]

The English slept, but the night was filled with strange terrors for the Indian troops, and rumours were rife that the English were preparing to fall upon the 3rd Cavalry and massacre or disarm them. The sepoys knew what had befallen the 19th and 34th Regiments at Barrackpur, and their terror was heightened by their knowledge that Meerut was the largest up-country cantonment with a formidable concentration of British troops.

It was the Sabbath of 10 May and the English went about oblivious of the tension. It was at vespers that the storm broke. Mrs. Rotton, wife of one of the chaplains, was warned by her Indian maid not to venture forth as she was about to leave for church with her husband[2]. Several other families were warned by loyal domestics.

The troopers of the 3rd Cavalry broke into the jail and freed their manacled comrades. Some officers tried to recall their sepoys to their duty, but the latter were too worked up. Several officers were killed, their bungalows burnt, and families butchered. Besides the 3rd Cavalry, only two other infantry batallions were involved, and had General Wilson, the station commander, taken energetic steps, the trouble might have been contained. Meerut was by no means overrun, but the British were too dazed to react. The general bivouacked with the brigade on the parade ground while the mutineers galloped away towards Delhi. There was no pursuit, but the mutineers were as panic-stricken as the English. They did not draw rein until they reached Delhi about eight the next morning.

Some years before, the British had laid the telegraph connecting Calcutta with Delhi, and it was not long before the news of the events at Meerut reached all important centres of British authority. The news reached Delhi well before the mutineers, in the early hours of the morning of 11 May. But before steps could be taken to secure the river, the Indian troopers had crossed the Yamuna by the boat-bridge and approached the Mussamman Burj where they called for the emperor.

'*Badshah, dohai hai, dohai*!' They shouted the traditional chant for attracting the attention of the sovereign. There was a doorway below the arches of the octagonal tower which had been closed just in time to prevent the troopers from forcing entry. Captain Douglas, commandant of the palace guard, wanted the door to be opened so that he could go down to talk to the soldiers, but he was restrained by Bahadur Shah and Hakim Ahsanullah as they felt it was hardly safe to venture forth among these desperate men. So Captain Douglas spoke to them from the *jharokha* window. But he might as well have spoken to the wind. The *sowars* were in no mood to listen, least of all to an Englishman.

Thereafter, the mutineers managed to enter the city by the Calcutta Gate. Raising the war-cry of '*Din*! *Din*' they passed through the bazaars. Fraser, the commissioner, and Hutchinson, deputy commissioner, were out trying to calm the garrison. They were joined by Douglas, but had to retreat to the fort which they entered by way of the Lahore Gate. Douglas was injured as he jumped into the ditch beside the gate for cover, and had to be carried in by his attendants. The pursuing sepoys—*sowars* from Meerut—pushed in after them, the fort garrison showing no inclination to oppose them. Douglas was carried into his quarters above the Lahore Gate. Fraser tried to address the excited soldiers in the courtyard, sword in hand, but was cut down. Then the soldiers rushed up to Douglas's apartment where they slew the captain, together with Hutchinson who was already injured. Along with them were massacred some guests of Douglas, including two young women. Having tasted blood, the sepoys rushed deeper into the palace, through the jalau khana and the diwan khana, right up to the Diwan-i-Khas.

The emperor had refused to show himself to the mutineers at the *jharokha* but now the men had forced their way in and murdered the resident and the fort commandant, and were loudly and tumultously demanding an audience, shooting off their carbines and pistols in the air. For fear of greater violence, the emperor came out and, seating himself on a chair, addressed them severely, calling upon their officers to explain their sudden and rude irruption. Their leaders stepped forward and explained how they were being compelled to bite the greased cartridges which would render both Hindus and Muslims outcaste because the grease was composed of the fat of cows and pigs. Therefore, rather than suffer the indignity, they had risen in revolt, slain their officers and come to claim his protection, as he was their badshah.

The emperor replied: 'I did not send for you; you have acted very wickedly.' But the troopers crowded round the monarch and pressed him to bless them. 'Unless you join us, we are dead men and we must in that case do what we can for ourselves.'

The emperor still tried to prevaricate. 'Hear me brothers!' he replied. 'Who says I am a king? I am just a retired faqir. Why have you come here? I have neither treasure nor an army. I can only mediate between you and the English. The resident is coming to see me. Let me hear what he has to say.'[3]

But the resident was already dead and the mutineers would not be put off. There was a threatening undertone to their implorings. So the emperor yielded, and one by one the men came forward, and the emperor blessed each by placing his hand on his head. After this he retired.

Meanwhile, the city had been plunged into turmoil. The palace guards and the city garrison did not take long to fraternise with the sepoys from Meerut, and as is usual in such a situation they were joined by the city underworld. All European establishments were plundered and many of the civilians slaughtered. The old magazine, located in the heart of the city, was attacked. There were only nine Englishmen to guard this arsenal. The native sepoys of the guard, instead of attacking their English officers, slipped out to join the attackers. Lieutenant Willoughby, who was the senior officer among the nine, had a powder train laid, and after a brief resistance, set fire to it. Soon a great explosion, followed by billowing smoke rising high into the air, announced to all that the magazine had been fired. The explosion shook even the palace windows, and many scores of people were killed. Of the nine valiant British officers, four survived the explosion but the gallantry was pointless, for the bulk of the powder—3,000 barrels—had been earlier removed to another location 3 miles away. This was guarded by sepoys of the 35th Batallion who repulsed an attempt by the English to seize it. The old arsenal set fire to by Willoughby is supposed to have contained only about 50 barrels of powder, besides some ordnance pieces.

The cantonment was located on the Delhi Ridge, north-west of the city, near the present university. Because of the distance from the city, and lack of information, the Indian sepoys did not make any overt move. The English hoped that troops would come from Meerut, but as the day dragged on, hope evaporated, and they made arrangements for escape. It was a disorganized flight, each man on his own with Brigadier Graves, the station commander, making no effort to organize a proper withdrawal. He was a shattered man. It is said that an attempt was made to collect the troops who were skulking about the lines, and the assembly sounded, but only one sepoy fell in! Then the brigadier also mounted his horse and turned his face towards Karnal. Fortunately, there was no attempt to hinder the British departure. But it was a long and arduous journey that lay ahead for most of them, along infrequented roads and paths. Some made it to Meerut; others headed for Karnal or Agra. Many were robbed and killed on the way, some by sepoys, others by common robbers and dacoits.

But many others also received succour from ordinary villagers.

By nightfall there were no British troops left in Delhi. The Company's raj had vanished almost without a fight, the achievement of half a century wiped out.

The following day, 12 May 1857, a durbar was held in the Qila-i-Mualla to mark the revolution. It was the first durbar since 1842, when, under Lord Ellenborough's orders, the silver throne, which used to be kept in the Diwan-i-Khas, had been removed and locked up in a cellar.

The throne was now taken out and the true reign of Zille Subhani, Khalifat-ur Rahmani, Faragh-i-Khandan-i-Aali-shan-i-Gorgani, Chiragh-i-Dudman-i-najdat, Nishan-i-Sahib qarani, Sirajuddin Muhammed Bahadur Shah Ghazi, Shah-in-Shah-i-Hind, now commenced.

The officers of the army and the courtiers presented their *nazars* and declared their allegiance. Titles and offices were conferred as per the norm on such occasions in the past. Mirza Mughal, the eldest shahzada, was appointed commander-in-chief (or *sipah-salar*), and four other sons were appointed colonels. Sweets were ordered to be distributed to the army, and senior officers were sanctioned large sums to equip their men for the coming struggle.

Administrative measures were taken to restore law and order in the city. Later in the day the emperor himself rode in state through the bazaars on an elephant, with his favourite son Jawan Bakht seated behind him in the howdah. A government of sorts was established, the highest organ of which was a court of administration or a council of state, comprising ten members, six being from the army. The chief executive, i.e. the equivalent of the wazir, was designated as Sahib-i-Alam, and it appears that this office was exercised by Mirza Mughal, the titular commander-in-chief.

Since the life of the revolutionary government was brief, with the British regaining control within four months, it is difficult to make a fair appraisal of its achievements, but it was far from being a piece of *opera bouffe*. Serious work had to be done, and was attempted with some degree of success. The aged emperor showed an energy and activity much beyond what could be expected of a man of more than 80. Courts had to be set up, the police administration revamped, and the old kotwal, who was suspected of being a spy, removed. Later, however, Mirza Mughal was overshadowed by Bakht Khan, who, after his arrival, was appointed the executive commander on account of his military experience.

But it was not easy to control the sepoys. On the pretext of searching for Englishmen they would break into private houses and plunder them.

Some, perhaps, were imbued with patriotic sentiments, but most were plain mutineers and their behaviour no different from that of other soldiers in a like position in other times, like the Badakhshi mercenaries of Imad ul-Mulk or the Jat auxiliaries of Safdar Jang. The situation was aggravated by the comparative poverty of the emperor.

Regular pay could have restored discipline in the rag-tag army, but this the emperor could not assure. It must have been a trying period for the people of Delhi who had just lived through the Golden Calm. But the excesses of the imperial army were nothing in comparison with the horrors the city would experience when the English returned.

On 16 May took place the notorious massacre in the fort. This was the first test of the imperial authority. Unfortunately, it was found wanting. A group of 49 Europeans, almost all—barring four or five—women and children, had been brought into the palace from Daryaganj. The mutineers and the palace rabble wanted to kill them. Unfortunately, many of the princes and salatin—among them Mirza Mughal—enthusiastically supported them. The emperor and Mirza Ilahi Bakhsh—of whom more later—did their best to protect the British group, but found themselves powerless. Finding that no one was prepared to listen to him, the emperor—like Pontius Pilate—washed his hands of them and left, leaving the mob to do its worst. The British group were all brought out and slaughtered in the tank before the jalau khana.

The emperor repeatedly urged the sepoy officers to attack and destroy the English at Meerut, but while these heroes were lions in the safety of Delhi, their hearts quailed at the prospect of fighting the English in the open. Mirza Mughal had no experience of military matters, and no pretensions to generalship. He made excuses that his force was too weak and lacking in equipment, and suggested that it be suitably stiffened by sending the great lords of the new court, namely, the petty chiefs of Jhajjar, Loharu, Dadri and Ballabhgarh—with the army.

These 'great' chiefs, however, held back. Probably at this early stage they did not wish to compromise themselves further. The emperor had sent missives to all the princes and chiefs of Upper India and Rajasthan, the rajas of Patiala and Jind, the petty nawabs of Dujana, Pataudi, Jhajjar and Loharu, and the rajas of Jaipur, Alwar, and Kota-Bundi. Except for the minor chiefs in the immediate vicinity, none of the greater princes responded. In fact, the emperor had received information that the Jind and Patiala rajas were actively cooperating with the British in preventing the mutineers in the Punjab from reaching Delhi.

So far the Bengal army had consisted almost entirely of Hindostanis recruited from the North-Western Provinces, Awadh and Bihar. The induction of Sikhs into the British army had commenced and many regiments already had companies of Sikhs, but it had been noticed that the Sikhs, in spite of the recent conquest of their kingdom, were not inclined to make common cause with the Hindostanis. Attempts to tamper with their loyalty were rebuffed. Often they were the channel through which the English officers were warned of the seditions afoot.

Thus, the situation in Punjab was very different from that obtaining in the territories to the south. Mutiny was crushed with an iron hand in the incipient stages and fugitives were pursued relentlessly. Regimental officers were given plenary powers of life and death, and drum-head court-martials condemned and hanged mutineers—or those suspected of being so—with exuberant severity. At Peshawar forty sepoys were blown from guns. The original number of the condemned was 120 but by the intervention of the 'humane' John Lawrence, the chief commissioner of the Punjab, the number actually executed was reduced to this 'modest' figure. Fredrick Cooper, deputy commissioner of Amritsar, whose name deserves to rank with Nana Sahib's—the most reviled of all the rebel leaders—slaughtered 500 unarmed men in cold blood, according to his own statement, by way of a terrible retribution for the murder of two Englishmen by a soldier of the 29th Native Infantry who ran amok in the lines at Lahore.[4] Earlier at Lahore, 3,800 Indian troops had been disarmed in the face of loaded guns stuffed to the muzzles with grape.

Otherwise decent god-fearing Victorians were seized by a horrifying religious frenzy. All that bloodshed gave them a feeling of exaltation. Cooper saw in the ease with which he performed his bloody task the 'manifest and wondrous interposition of Almighty God in the cause of Christianity'. Robert Montgomery, a Punjab civilian and a fervent evangelist, was convinced that it was 'The Lord our God' who 'saved the Indian empire to England' and 'England to India'.

It was gallows rule, but in this manner, the Punjab was held firmly by John Lawrence. The commander-in-chief, General Anson, was at Simla when the news of the Meerut outbreak reached him. Soon plans were afoot to organize a 'moveable column' and a siege train for the recapture of Delhi. In the midst of these exertions, in the furnace-like heat of the Punjab plains, Anson was carried off by the cholera on 25 May. Meanwhile the British at Meerut had also mobilized and moved up to the river Hindon.

Mirza Mughal, having shown his disinclination to move against the English, was replaced by the youngest shahzada, Abu Bakr, a mere teenager. Perhaps it would have been better if the emperor had gone himself, observes Mahdi Hussain, but the last of the Mughals was not given to making grand gestures.

So Abu Bakr left with three batallions on 25 May. An artillery engagement took place five days later. The young prince watched the exchange from a rooftop. A shell falling close by so unnerved him that, covered with dust, he rode away in panic, the rest of the troops following his unedifying example. Alas, there was no experienced general to act as his *ataliq* in the actual command.

On their return, notwithstanding the boasts of the immature prince, the truth was soon known, and, stung by the gibes of the populace, the sepoys again went forth to give battle. The resulting clash is known as the battle of Ghaziuddin Nagar. But again the result was the same. That the conduct of the 'national' army was not uniformly disgraceful is however borne out by Kaye's narrative of an event in the first day's fighting:

> Our own loss would have been small, but for the explosion of an ammunition wagon; not by an accident of warfare, but by an act of resolute and sacrificial courage on the part of one of the mutineers. A sepoy of the 11th Regiment deliberately discharged his musket into the midst of the combustibles just as a party of the Rifles, under Captain Andrews, were gallantly seizing the gun to which the cart belonged. The explosion cost the man his life; but Andrews and some of his followers were killed by it, and others were carried wounded from the scene. It taught us that among the mutineers were some brave and desperate men, who were ready to court instant death for the sake of the national cause.[5]

On 7 June the Meerut contingent crossed the Yamuna at Baghpat and marched into Alipur where the first elements of the troops from the Punjab under the command of General Barnard had arrived, and the next day contact was made with the imperialists at Badli ki sarai.

Sensible at last to the gathering threat, the imperial army had taken up positions on the Ridge to defend Delhi. On 3 June the emperor had been persuaded to proclaim a jehad, and brisk preparations were made for an offensive.

The battle began with an artillery duel and the superiority of the imperial artillery soon made itself felt. The English had come a long way and had only light guns, whereas the imperialists had the fort cannons and the arsenal to draw upon. Badli, their forward post, was a strong defensive position, the fortified sarai and the numerous walled gardens, the country houses of the nobility, providing good cover.

As the imperial ordnance threatened to silence the English guns and was decimating the waiting infantry, a general attack was launched. The imperialists fought well but the English advance, which was supported by cavalry, succeeded in clearing Badli and much of the Ridge upto the house of Hindu Rao.

The English had expected an easy victory. Even the governor-general seemed to have believed that all that was required was that the army should reach Delhi and the mutineers would either surrender or flee. What encouraged them in this fatuous belief was the track record. It was not in the Delhi tradition to fight to the last. A formal siege and investment of the city had never been necessary in the past. Muhammad Ghori had won Delhi on the field of Taraori, 100 miles to the north of the city; Nadir Shah had confronted the Indian army at Karnal, just a little further south, while three famous battles fought at Panipat 60 miles from Delhi had decided the fate of the capital on different occasions.

The imperial forces had been worsted at the battles of the Hindon and Ghaziuddin Nagar, and again now at Badli ki sarai, but it was evident that no easy walkover could be expected. The mutineers had every intention to fight, but the absence of a general of any brilliance on either side created a stalemate. Neither Wilson nor Barnard were noted for dash or imagination. It was decided to wait till the siege train had arrived and the 'Army of Retribution', as Kaye calls it, was strong enough to take the city by storm.

Throughout June the two armies continued to grapple with each other in small actions around particular strongpoints. Fighting raged for several days around Bara Hindu Rao and on Idgah hill, while 23 June, the centenary of Plassey, was marked by particularly sharp fighting in the Sabzi Mandi, Delhi's wholesale vegetable market. Major Reid, the local officer in command, paid tribute to the stubborn fight put up by the imperialists: 'No men could have fought better. They charged the Rifles, the Guides, and my own men again and again; and at one time I thought I must have lost the day.'[6] But, as usual, it ended with victory for the English and the imperialists abandoned the Sabzi Mandi. The centenary of Plassey had come and gone and the British position on the Ridge of Delhi was more secure than ever.

The month of July opened with some accretion of strength to the national cause. The regiments at Nasirabad and Nimach had mutinied and found their way to Delhi. But more important was the arrival of one Muhammad Bakhsh, entitled Bakhtawar Khan, more commonly referred to as Bakht Khan.

Bakht Khan was a former subedar of artillery in the Company's service. His family appears to have been from Sultanpur in eastern Awadh, but by origin he was a Rohilla Pathan, descended from the notorious Ghulam Qadir. On his mother's side he was distantly related to the former ruling house of Awadh. He had played a leading part in the mutiny at Nimach, and from there had proceeded to Bareilly where he helped instal Khan Bahadur Khan, a grandson of the last Rohilla ruler, Hafiz Rahmat, as faujdar under the nominal sovereignty of Bahadur Shah. Then, with a contingent composed partly of mutineers and other adventurers, he proceeded to Delhi.[7]

He was the most talented among the imperial officers. The British too paid him grudging tribute, and Bahadur Shah nominated Bakht Khan commander-in-chief. This immediately brought him in conflict with Mirza Mughal, the nominal supreme commander. Several times the emperor had to intervene to reconcile the sulking prince with the general.

Bakht Khan was able to instill some semblance of discipline among the imperial troops. The emperor had been deeply hurt by their disrespectful conduct and in a long letter complained bitterly how the soldiers would freely ride in and out of the palace, even entering the court of the Diwan-i-Am on horseback, in violation of long established etiquette. They would lounge about improperly dressed, and many would appear in durbar without a turban! Bakht Khan cleared the courts of these *loafers*; regular drill and parades were held, and the troops were removed from the crowded *mohallas* of the city to the open ground outside the walls. This immediately brought relief to the city and the looting stopped.

On the military side, the British received some setbacks. General Barnard was also carried off by cholera, which was endemic in the British camp, on 5 July, and his successor proceeded on sick-leave 12 days later, to be succeded by the colourless and uninspiring Wilson. The British force was still quite small although some more reinforcements had been received from the Punjab, but the imperial army was incapable of taking the offensive. The emperor did occasionally encourage his soldiers and officers. On one occasion when some heads of Englishmen killed in the fighting at Sabzi Mandi were brought in as trophies, the soldiers who brought them were rewarded Rs. 100 each.

Small actions continued throughout July and August, but the next major engagement occurred on 25 August and is known as the battle of Najafgarh. By that time the situation had changed dramatically. John Nicholson, who had been placed in command of the 'moveable column' and had distinguished himself by disarming restive battalions and ruthlessly hanging mutineers (or those suspected of harbouring mutinous sentiments), had been ordered to proceed to Delhi. In the meantime, the long awaited siege-train with its siege guns and other engines, powder and shot, was also wending its way towards Delhi. Nicholson arrived at the Delhi Ridge on 7 August in advance of his column, covering the 130 miles that lay between Ambala and Delhi in thirty hours, travelling by post horses.

Within hours of his arrival he was inspecting the British lines and studying the enemy positions. At night when this man of blood, with his forbidding red beard, sat down to dinner, a chill fell over what was usually a very convivial gathering.

The forward movement of the 'Army of Retribution' had been reinforced by the approaching column from the Punjab. The imperial army was composed of the Bareilly brigade, directly under Bakht Khan, and the Nimach Brigade, commanded by Sardara Singh. But Sardara Singh, ignoring Bakht Khan's advice, pitched his camp too far ahead on the other side of the canal. A bridge over the canal was destroyed and Bakht Khan was unable to come to his aid and the Nimach Brigade was destroyed.

This battle was the ultimate test of Bakht Khan's military genius. His name 'Bakht' signifies lucky but, as Zaka-ullah was to observe sarcastically, Bakht was anything but that, and ought to have been named Kambakht Khan, or the 'Luckless Lord'. The Nimach Brigade was practically annihilated and 13 guns were lost. Its chief, Sardara Singh, was to later accuse Bakht of having willed his destruction by failing to come to his aid, and the emperor, disappointed and angered at the outcome, told Bakht not to show his face in court again. Other allegations were also levelled against him that he had been pocketing the money which should have been paid to the troops. Thus, this man who had so far been the white hope of the imperial army came under a cloud.

A few days later Nicholson's column reached the Ridge to be followed by the siege train from Ferozepur. The balance was now definitely tilted against the Indians. The British, led by the daring Nicholson, had determined to risk everything on an attempt to storm the city.

It was decided to launch the attack on some point along the city wall from the Water Bastion to the Kabul Gate. Four batteries were set up, and on 7 September the cannonade began.

On the evening of 13 September scouts reported that a breach had been effected near the Kashmir Bastion. It was therefore decided to attack the following morning. The attack was delayed because some more shelling was necessary to sweep away the repairs effected by the Indian during the night, and the sun was high by the time the storming parties rushed forward under heavy covering fire. A small party of engineers managed to blow up the Kashmiri Gate. Considerable drama attended this famous event.

The powder party led by Lieutenant Home succeeded in placing the bags unmolested, but, before they had finished, heavy firing broke out from the open wicket and the loopholed gates. A sergeant was killed and a havaldar was wounded, but the rest of the party dropped to safety into a ditch. Lieutenant Saalkeld, leading the firing party, was hit but as he collapsed he handed the slow torch to Corporal Burgess who succeeded in lighting the fuse, though mortally wounded. The explosion killed and wounded many of the defenders, and the assault parties soon established a foothold.

General Nicholson was with one of the columns that was to assault the Kabul Gate. The British flag had been hoisted on the gate but progress beyond was held up by heavy fire down a narrow street. Impatient as always, Nicholson sprang forward calling on the Fusiliers to follow him, and was instantly shot through the chest. He lingered for some days and had the satisfaction of knowing before dying that the citadel had been taken. He died as he had lived, and his name was to become a legend in the hagiology of the 'Mutiny'.

Once the British troops had established a foothold there was a lull in the fighting. Large stocks of wine and liquor were found in the warehouses along the wall near the Kashmiri Gate. These were broken into, and there followed a drunken orgy as a result of which many of the attackers were out of control for several days.[8] Had the defenders been able to rally and deliver a counter-attack, they would certainly have succeeded in throwing them back, but the evil star of Bakht Khan had sealed the fate of the city and its defenders.

The liquor stocks had to be destroyed before the army could resume its advance on 19 September. During the street fighting five days earlier, the civilian population had come forward to defend their city, and armed with mere swords and *lathis* fought alongside the sepoys, and at certain points even managed to drive back the English, at least for a time. Zaheer Dehlavi, an eye-witness, reports seeing heaps of bodies along the road from the Jama Masjid to the kotwali. On 14 September the English had managed to reach the Jama Masjid, but then were forced to fall back.

During those five days the weaker spirits among the imperial army had started fleeing as did many of the civil population. Thus, when the British, advance was resumed the resistance was weak. On 20 September the Lahore Gate of the fort was blown in, and the troops followed the storming party, all eager to be there for the capture of the aged emperor.

But the Exalted Fort was empty. There was only one soldier at the gate who was promptly bayonetted. The few soldiers and attendants found in the precincts were likewise dispatched and the conquerors left free to wander through the deserted halls and courts, and gaze at the marvels and curiosities within.[9]

General Wilson took up residence in the Qila-i-Mualla. On 21 September a salute was fired announcing the victory. Resistance had ended and the civilians were desperate to leave the city as the victors celebrated their triumph in an orgy of massacre and plunder.

The palace had been evacuated by the imperial family on 19 September. In the evening General Bakht Khan called on His Majesty and tried to persuade him to leave with him for Rohilkhand, but the latter declined. He had never liked Bakht Khan and his familiar republican manners, and was now resigned to his fate. At 82 he was too old to take up the life of a fugitive.

Bakht Khan left that night and with him went the remnants of the imperial army. The imperial family had taken refuge in Humayun's mausoleum which was something of a family tomb as scores of their forbears lay buried in its crypt. The emperor lingered awhile, practically alone, but left before dawn for the shrine of Sheikh Nizam ud-Din Auliya. Here he sat down beside the saint's tomb and wept his heart out. Shah Ghulam Hassan, the custodian with whom he was on familiar terms as a brother sufi, tried to comfort him. It was a sombre meeting. He handed over to the pir a sacred relic, two sacred hairs from the beard of the Prophet, which had been in the possession of his house since the days of Timur. Then he asked for something to eat, 'It is more than a day since I have had a meal!' he sighed.

After a light repast he took leave of his friend and rejoined his family which was bivouacking in Arab ki Sarai which adjoined the garden of Humayun's tomb. Begum Zinat Mahal was already in touch with the English through Mirza Ilahi Bakhsh, a member of the imperial family who was reputed to be pro-British, for the purpose of securing a safe-conduct and guarantee for the emperor's life. The Mirza's emissaries were able to contact Captain Hodson who commanded a regiment of irregular cavalry. The Captain obtained permission from General Wilson, and about noon (21 September) Mirza Ilahi Bakhsh conveyed the news that the guarantee had been obtained, and that Maulvi Rajab Ali had come with Captain Hodson and 25 Sikh *sowars* to escort the emperor back to the fort.

The safe-conduct was in the name of the emperor, Begum Zinat Mahal, Mirza Jawan Bakht, and Hakim Ahsanullah. The Maulvi made a low *salaam* outside the gates of the sarai and presented a *nazar* to His Majesty. He reassured the old man, and after some time Captain Hodson met them on the road. The Captain coldly doffed his hat to the emperor and the party continued on their way. At the Lahore Gate of the qila, the emperor was separated from the rest of the party and taken to General Wilson while the rest were led to their quarters in Begum Samru's haveli.

The emperor's life was guaranteed because it was appreciated that he could have left with the retreating troops of General Bakht Khan, and the English were in no position to pursue the fugitives. With his arrest, one figure round which men might rally had been eliminated, and there is no doubt that Bahadur Shah was certainly the most important of the several supposed leaders of the struggle. But the English were most unhappy. Most would have liked to see him swing on the gallows. Even so sober a man as Sir John Lawrence wrote, 'It is a great pity that the old rascal was not shot directly he was seen—I would not have taken him prisoner.'[10]

General Wilson's explanation was called for offering the guarantee. He tried to pass on the blame to the commissioner, Charles Saunders, who indignantly denied it. Nor was Hodson's attitude any different. From his subsequent action there appears no doubt that he too would have loved to put a bullet through 'the old rascal'. But Hodson had been corrupted by Zinat Mahal's gold.

He had come to know that there were several princes in the complex of tombs and gardens that surrounded the great mausoleum of Humayun. He hurried back the next day looking for more game.

Three princes were persuaded to give themselves up unconditionally. These were Mirza Mughal, Abu Bakr and Khair Sultan—the last a nephew of Bahadur Shah's. Placed in a *rath* drawn by bullocks, they were taken towards the city. A small crowd of onlookers followed the escort. The *rath* was stopped near a ruined gateway on what is now called Bahadur Shah Zafar Marg and the princes were forced to get down and strip to their shorts. Then they were ordered to climb back on to the *rath* where they were shot personally by Hodson. The event is commemorated by the name given to the gateway which is known to this day as the *khooni darwaza* or the 'bloody gateway'. No one in all that crowd which was following lifted a finger to rescue them. The Sikh sowars of Hodson's Horse were probably extremely impressed by their sahib's daring. Then the semi-naked bodies were taken to the city via the Delhi Gate and thrown before the kotwali. They were displayed for some time and, after the vultures and dogs had had their peck, unceremoniously tossed into the Yamuna. This happened the day following the emperor's surrender.

There were many more such examples of 'retributive justice' in the days to come. According to Zaheer Dehlawi, 30 princes—sons, sons-in-law and grandsons of the emperor—were arrested and beheaded outside the Delhi Gate, their severed heads being sent later to the emperor. These were evidently different from the 26 salatin executed by the order of the Delhi Special Commissioner for Rebellion.

The race of Timur and Genghiz was being extinguished, appropriately enough, in a bloodbath, without precedent in the recorded history of India.

NOTES

1. Taylor, *Chronicles of the Mutiny*, pp. 21-4.
2. Rotton, *The Chaplain's Narrative of the Siege of Delhi*, pp. 2-3.
3. Mahdi Hussain, *Bahadur Shah II*, pp. 164-9.
4. Cooper, *Crisis in the Punjab*, pp. 83-90. Cave-Browne, *The Punjab and Delhi in 1857*, ii, pp. 87-90 (fn.).
5. Kaye and Malleson, *History of the Indian Mutiny*, ii, p. 138.
6. Forrest, *History of the Indian Mutiny*, i, p. 94.
7. Spear, *A History of Delhi under the Later Mughals*, pp. 213-14.
8. Kaye and Malleson, iv, p. 41. Cave-Browne, *The Punjab and Delhi in 1857*, ii, pp. 161-2 (including fn. on p. 162). Griffiths, *The Siege of Delhi*, pp. 174-5.
9. Mahdi Hussain, pp. xxviii-xxix, 280-1.
10. *Saunders Papers*, John Lawrence to Saunders, 24 October 1857.

CHAPTER 50

Retribution

The emperor, Zinat Mahal and Jawan Bakht were prisoners in the fort. Three of the princes had already been killed by Hodson, and the victorious British, along with their Indian auxilliaries, were busy administering their brand of retributive justice as the hapless inhabitants scurried about for shelter.

While the emperor cowered in his cell with his consort and their son, the conquerors celebrated their victory with champagne in the marble halls of the palace. The Sunday following, Divine service was held in the Diwan-i-Khas. Doubtless, the altar must have been erected on the marble platform where the emperor's throne used to be set up in former times.

For about a week the troops indulged in indiscriminate slaughter. No distinction was made between Hindu or Muslim. What is surprising is that women and children were seldom harmed, and there was little of the wholesale rape which usually accompanies the storming of a city. How many thousands were killed shall never be known because there were no native chroniclers and, as for the English, their official historians sententiously observed that 'justice was done'. But the number certainly ran into thousands, and enthusiasts continued to kill 'rebels' at random for a long time, whenever they felt the urge. As late as December we find John Lawrence enquiring, 'Is private plundering still allowed? Do officers still go about shooting natives?'[1] Indeed the servants of European soldiers went about their tasks in utmost trepidation, never knowing when some bloody-minded Tommy Atkins, unfamiliar with their faces, might decide to despatch them to hell before they had a chance to identify themselves.

Occasionally we get a hint of what happened. Mrs Dunbar Muter, wife of a colonel, has given a striking picture of Delhi as it looked in October, a month after its fall:

A short street led into the Chandnee Chowk, a more melancholy picture still, than any I had seen. When last I looked on this fine street, not many months before, it presented a gay and joyous sight. Broad as it is, it was scarcely broad enough for the throng that filled it. Elephants and camels, horses and carriages, decked with the finery of the East, crowded the way; now it was silent and empty. The contents of the shops lay strewn in the street, or huddled in a confused mass on the floors. The sneaking figure of some prowling thief, a lean, half-famished dog, or one of the many cats—the sole inhabitants of Delhi—were all that moved. The painful effect of this solitude was even more depressing than even the ruin. Where were the people of Delhi? The tender children, the delicate women, the old and infirm, all were gone, swept away by the fatal crimes of others!

Those who know war, not from books, but from experience of its realities, shrink from it with horror; and a war like this, without quarter and without mercy is the worst affliction that can overtake a land. No city desolated by a plague ever wore the appearance of Delhi at that time, or became the solitude it then was.

Before many months elapsed nearly every great city in the immense Central Provinces of India was stormed or occupied by our armies and the loss of life, the destruction of property, the cruel sufferings, will never be known to the world unless a second Macaulay wholly devotes himself to the task.

Right in the centre of the Chandnee Chowk a hideous erection of wood was the city's newest and only uninjured structure—and this was the gallows. Hundreds perished on that platform, and among them were rajahs and nawabs who had themselves, and their fathers before them, ruled in the territory around. I trust that no innocent men died there, victims to the fierce hatred the massacres had excited.

A war like this, however, acts with the fellest injustice, and were the number of blameless persons who were sacrificed truly estimated, the British public would be horrified at the result. . . .[2]

The imperial army led by Bakht Khan had evacuated Delhi on 19 September, thus all the people killed subsequently were civilians. Some blood-letting was to be expected after all, keeping in view the intensity of the passions roused. For a time the British had their backs to the wall, and the very survival of the raj had seemed doubtful. The massacre of women and children by the Indians, though the total number of victims did not exceed a few hundred, had raised passions to fever pitch. Women were one of the totems of the Victorian world. To wantonly kill a woman was like killing a goddess, and rape was so much worse. Fortunately during this savage war, the Indians appeared to draw a line there. In Kanpur and Delhi, women were simply killed; the most careful investigations could not unearth instances of European women being violated.

But the forced evacuation of the city was unprecedented. Practically the entire population was driven out and no civilian was permitted to enter without a pass. With the city emptied, the British could now set about the task of digging out the concealed treasures. There was no consideration of how the people were to live outside their homes. Each went where he could. Those who had relatives in nearby towns or villages took refuge with them. Others sought shelter in the ruins and tombs of the abandoned sites of the cities that constituted Old Delhi. As they streamed out of the gates, the soldiers searched them and went through their miserable bundles to make sure that they carried nothing of value, for everything within the city was now the lawful prize of the victors.

The English seemed to be aiming at the utter destruction of the city. No other conqueror had displayed such callous indifference to the people's sufferings. Even the Durrani and the Persian Shah had merely demanded a certain definite sum by way of ransom. When this could not be raised they extorted it, beginning with the umara and bankers. The English, in contrast, laid claim to the entire wealth of the city. There was no general massacre after the manner of Timur or Nadir, but by their conduct the English amply demonstrated that they could not care less what happened to the people.

Some city quarters, and select individuals, were spared the travails of the general expulsion. The doctors' quarter in Ballimaran, which housed the family home of the royal physicians, was one such. These *hakims* counted the Sikh chiefs, who were fighting on the side of the English, among their patrons. Thus, as soon as the city was taken, Patiala troops were sent to protect Ballimaran from looters. Many of their neighbours were able to benefit from this immunity by depositing valuables with the *hakims*. Other notables who were identified as loyal or pro-British also received guards to protect their houses from pillage.

The bankers and rich merchants of Katra Nil—the richest quarter—were also able to purchase immunity. Mirza Asadullah Khan Ghalib was one of the individuals other than the *hakims* who stayed on in Ballimaran. But Zakaullah Khan's family were not so lucky. They were expelled and lived for several months in a ruined tomb in Nizamuddin.[3] Refugees like them were the prey of robbers, for with the collapse of organized administration human predators had taken over.

In the meantime the systematic plunder of the empty city commenced. Prize Agents had been elected by soldiers, and placed in charge of different sectors of the city to bring in the booty. But the evacuation of the city had made the task much more difficult. The English soldiers had little idea where the people had buried their valuables.

At first the horses, carriages and furniture—all those items that could not be concealed—were siezed. But the soldiers did not know where to look for the gold and silver. The *badmashes* of the city, i.e. the professional thieves and robbers, many of them Gujjars from Chandrawal and other villages nearby, knew by long experience where such valuables were usually concealed. So, while the soldiers blundered about blindly in the day time, the *badmashes* would sneak into the city after dark and work diligently in the dead of night. The greater part of the buried treasure was probably removed by them!

The Afghan levies raised by Nicholson, his 'Multani Horse', and the Sikhs, were also adept at smelling out treasure, but their plundering was on their own account.[4]

In due course the English did acquire some expertise and were able to unearth a fair amount of treasure. The more valuable articles were displayed in a tent pitched on the flat roof of a house overlooking the Diwan-i-Khas. As can be imagined, there was considerable leakage, and important valuables were often annexed by the finders, human nature being what it is. The servants of the English officers gorged themselves on the leavings, and Mrs Muter recalled how her husband's bearer and become absolutely useless:

> The bearer had been of great service during the Mutiny, but of late had been found impossible to move; he had taken up his residence in a room at the foot of our entrance steps, and he feared to leave the spot, where he kept watch over his plunder. The cares of riches were now embarassing him, and the robber dreaded being robbed. Having a wholesome fear of the prize agents, he did not appear in kincobs and satins till his return to Meerut, but then he turned out in princely costume. Grandeur such as his could not be expected to work so he passed away like a comet. . . .[5]

Even Mrs. Saunders, the commissioner's wife was sending home silver vases and gold-embroidered shawls 'given to us by the Prize Agents'. How much was actually looted will never be known. The old chronicles have recorded the approximate value of the plunder taken out by Nadir Shah and Ahmad Shah, but the English have drawn a discreet veil over their loot. As it was, the distribution of the official 'Prize' was soon wrapped in controversy and there was even litigation between the army and the Indian government. The sum made available for distribution was fairly modest—only Rs. 34,61,213, and the soldiers expressed openly their conviction that some tampering had taken place.[6] This was divided among the troops at the rate of one share per soldier, with Indians getting only a half share. The rates for officers were much higher. In addition, six months *batta*—or active service allowance—was allowed.

In January 1858 the Hindus of Delhi were permitted to return to their homes, or what remained of them, for the Prize Agents had left the city a ruin. After the army had done its worst, to native contractors had been auctioned, street by street, the right to look for whatever treasure might still be lying undiscovered. These vultures removed whatever was marketable, including beams and door-frames! British officers and soldiers were also allowed to buy 'tickets' and dig among the ruins. Some were lucky.

The resettlement of the city was slow, and proceeded by fits and starts. The residents had to buy 'tickets' to return to their homes. There was also the local police to propitiate. It was not until November 1859—*more than two years after the original expulsion*—that general permission to return was granted! So callous were the British that the refugees squatting outside the walls were not permitted even to raise temporary shelters. Orders were issued to demolish all such constructions.

Within the city walls also, apart from the ruin caused by plunderers and prize agents, a lot of regular demolition had been going on. Now that the palace had been cleared of the imperial family, it was decided to house the Delhi garrison inside it. To guard against a future rising, it was felt necessary to secure a clear field of fire around the fort so that guns could play freely on the attackers. It was ordered that all dwellings up to a distance of 448 yards from the walls should be demolished. All the bazaars and dwellings between the Jama Masjid and the fort were pulled down, including the Akbarabadi mosque, the *khanqqah* of Dar ul-Baqa, the Urdu, Khas and Kharam Bazaars. The only structure to be spared was the beautiful mosque of Javed Khan. It stood close to the fort walls, not far from Delhi Gate, and had been erected by the famous eunuch, lover of the Empress Mother, Begum Qudsia, whose murder in 1752 had been the ruin of Safdar Jang.

It was seriously suggested that the entire city and the fort be razed to the ground, but the idea was dropped on account of the expense it would have entailed. As it was, much of the palace complex in the fort was demolished. Only the most important structures were suffered to remain. No effort was made to document what was being destroyed, and only a small sketch by an engineer enables us to reconstruct the qila as it existed before the fall of the city.

The Fatehpuri mosque was sold to a Hindu banker, and the Zinat-ul-Masjid in Daryaganj was converted into a bakery. It continued to be used as such until 1875. The Lahore and Delhi Gates of the fort were renamed as the Victoria and Alexandra Gates respectively. The Jama Masjid, like the other important mosques, was occupied by the army, and it was seriously debated whether it should be demolished or sold for rubble or converted into barracks! Eventually it was decided not to proceed to extremes, and five years later it was handed back to the Muslims for worship. The Fatehpuri mosque, however, had to wait till the Delhi Durbar of 1876 when Queen Victoria was proclaimed Kaiser-i-Hind. In order to placate the Muslims, Seth Chuna Mall, who had purchased the basement, was bought out by the English and the mosque handed over to the Muslims in its entirety.[7]

It is curious that while the memory of the sack of Somnath, the destruction of the Vishwanath Temple (Banaras) or of the Ramjanambhoomi Temple of Ayodhya, is deeply imprinted on the Hindu psyche, this persecution of the Islamic faith by the English is totally forgotten. And the story of Delhi was repeated at Lucknow with English troops quartered in the imambaras, with every effort which ingenuity could devise being made to rub in the lessons of defeat to the Indian Mussalman. The retreat into a shell was a natural consequence, and the conscious effort to curry favour with the conqueror later in the century, a natural and understandable reaction of a broken people.

It is also curious that notwithstanding Nana Sahib and Rani Lakshmi Bai of Jhansi, the mutiny was regarded as basically a Mussalman conspiracy. This is even more strange when one realizes that the Bengal army, which fired the powder-train that led to the uprising, and the Awadh taluqdars and peasants, who supported the cause of the 'Begums', were overwhelmingly Hindu in composition. But the Christian obsession with Islam is an old one, and the occidental mind slots the Muslim much more readily in an adversarial role than the Hindu. Thus, it was easier for a Seth Chuna Mall to pass off as a loyalist than for a Mirza Ghalib.

Then there were the trials. In a sense these were precursors to the Nuremburg trials, for the accused were tried in most cases on charges of murdering, or of abetting the murder of English civilians, besides the general charge of rebellion. The nawab of Jhajjar, while replying to the accusation that he had failed to come to the aid of the British with his force, declared with startling justice:

> It was England who had armed and trained the ruffians who had brought the calamity on the land; and it was not fair to expect him to compel that obedience in his followers which the rulers of the country and his judges had failed in compelling among their own.[8]

The charges against the nawab were that though a troop of the Jhajjar Horse was attached to the resident, it did nothing to assist the British on the fatal day of 11 May, and that there was no response to the demand of the deputy commissioner of Gurgaon. Indeed, when the nawab's troops did come, it was not to give succour but to join the looters. Further, when Thomas Metcalfe, while escaping from Delhi, applied for assistance, he was turned away from the nawab's gate, his horse being seized and replaced with a miserable country pony. No proof of complicity in the murder of British subjects was furnished. Nor was such proof forthcoming in the case of the raja of Ballabhgarh. On the contrary, there was evidence that many English fugitives were assisted to make their getaway through his territories. But it was undeniable that the raja's troops had fought with the imperial armies and that he had contributed to the imperial war-chest. The British argued that if he could not resist the pressures of the mutineers, or of the Delhi court, it was his duty to flee from his territories and join the British at Agra!

The special tribunals set up to try the 'rebel' leaders were in no mood to be understanding or merciful. The death sentence was passed, and the nawab of Jhajjar, the raja of Ballabhgarh, and the nawab of Farrukhnagar were duly hanged on the common gallows in Chandni Chowk, the sentence being carried out in a manner that none could say, in Ghalib's ironical phrase, 'that blood had been spilt'.[9]

The nawab of Dadri and the nawab of Ranian (in the Sirsa district) had been hanged separately by the orders of the judicial commissioner. Major Marsden, the commissioner of Sirsa, had recommended the nawab of Ranian for mercy, but that stern evangelist, Robert Montgomery, was not so easily moved. Although it was not proved that the nawab had been guilty of any murder himself, the town of Sirsa had been plundered and 'a number of lives are known to have been sacrificed, of which there is no record'. The judicial commissioner therefore, considered it imperative to make examples of such men as the nawab. 'The leaders must feel,' he wrote, 'that vengeance will assuredly overtake them. Mercy in this instance would be weakness, and would encourage others to rebel hereafter.'[10]

Thus the nawab of Ranian, Noor Samand Khan, was hanged along with 132 others. In all the Special Commission tried by summary procedure 3,306 persons of whom 2,025 were convicted. Of these, according to the *Delhi Gazetteer*, 392 were hanged and 57 sentenced to life imprisonment. The figures are suspect; obviously they do not tell the whole story, for in another letter 4,011 convictions are mentioned. Apparently several thousands were executed by summary courts martial shortly after the capture of the city. Five or six persons were hanged daily. People would visit the kotwali chabutra, or platform, to watch the show, just as they thronged the Place de la Revolution during the Terror in Paris. For months the gallows stood ready, and the match remained lighted alongside the cannons, for the mode of execution would occasionally be varied by blowing off the condemned from guns. The *Delhi Gazetteer*, for instance, records the case of a village which had surrendered a servant of Sir John Metcalfe to the mutineers, paying for its 'crime' by the execution of 21 of its notables.

And many more died of starvation and cold in the ruins of Old Delhi. 'Numbers of people are daily dying of starvation and want of shelter', wrote Mrs Saunders to a friend. The poet Ghalib wrote to a correspondent, 'Had you been here, you would have seen the Begums of the Qila walking about, their faces like the full moon, clothes dirty, trouser legs torn and shoes worn out.'[11]

But the vengeance of 'the angry lions' was not yet sated. The property of all 'rebel' Muslims was declared forfeit and no proof was considered necessary. It was up to the affected party to prove his innocence before he could return to his home. In spite of the general pardon issued in November 1858, Muslims were readmitted into the city only in January 1859, but their houses were still under orders of attachment, and many prominent Muslims were still under house-arrest. A 'pass' was still required till August 1859. For two years the major part of the population of a great city had been forced to live like animals, without shelter, in the open, or in ruined tombs and hovels.

The venom spewed forth by the Anglo-Indian press was incredible. For instance, it was seriously proposed that the city walls and the fort be pulled down or blown up, the city burnt to the ground, and the entire Mohammedan population transported to Australia! Occasionally, however, a voice of protest could be heard. A letter dated 4 January 1858 in the *Mofussilite* describes in these words the captivity of the aged emperor.

It is not true that Mohammed Shah is treated as a king. He lives in a little room with no other furniture but a charpoy (folding bed), and is daily exposed to the insults of the soldiers and officers, though the Commissioner of the district, Mr. Saunders, makes a point of treating the dethroned monarch with the politeness of a gentleman. Rude visitors take a mean pride in forcing the old man to rise and salute them on their entrance. It is even said that recently one of them laid hold of him by the beard. And not only this, the begum and the Royal Princesses have come to share the prisoner's captivity, and find themselves exposed to the eyes of strangers, who enter the rooms of the captive whenever it suits them; such familiarity would be considered a gross insult even by a woman of the lowest caste. The soldier who furnished me with these details tells me that he has often entered the room of the ex-Emperor, even when the embroidered slippers placed at the door announced the presence of the the women. At the sight of him the unfortunate Sultanas, in a state of bewilderment, turned their faces to the wall, and remained stiff and motionless as stone statues.

The emperor's trial opened on 27 January 1858 and concluded on 9 March. On account of the guarantee of life given at the time of the surrender, it was more in the nature of an inquiry. Nevertheless, a court-martial of five officers, none of whom held even the rank of a lieutenant-colonel, was constituted to go into the four charges, that he aided and abetted his son Mirza Mughal in rebelling, that being a subject of the British government he proclaimed himself sovereign of India, and waged war against the government, and that he was responsible for the massacre of 49 Europeans, mostly women and children, on 16 May, within the palace precincts.

The emperor's defence was the weak one of *force majeure*, that it was not possible for him to resist the mutineers. He and his advisers were still too demoralized to adopt the obvious legal plea that he was still the *de jure* sovereign of India, and it was not possible for the English to put him on trial. Not until 60 years later did a British scholar first put forward the legal argument that it was in fact the Company which had rebelled against the emperor![12]

In view of the prevailing mood, the conclusion of the military commission was predictable. Bahadur Shah was found guilty and sentenced to death, but on account of the guarantee, the sentence was commuted to transportation for life.

After the trial, the emperor had to endure his peep-show prison for some months more. Lord Roberts, then a young officer in the victorious army was one of the less insensitive visitors. 'I went with many others the next day to see the king,' he narrates. 'The old man looked most wretched and as he evidently disliked intensely being stared at by Europeans, I quickly took my departure.'[13]

In October Bahadur Shah left under the escort of Lieutenant Ommanney for Calcutta en route to Rangoon. The party consisted of Bahadur Shah himself, Zinat Mahal, Mirza Jawan Bakht (her son), Nawab Shah Zamani Begum, the wife of Jawan Bakht, with her sister and mother, Taj Mahal Begum, another wife of the emperor, Mirza Shah Abbas, another son, and his mother, Mubarak Nissa, a harem woman; four other harem women, five male and eleven female attendants. In all, they were 29, but at Allahabd 14 of the party expressed a desire to return to Delhi. These included Taj Mahal Begum and the mother and sister of Nawab Shah Zamani Begum, the wife of Jawan Bakht. The others were servants and attendants. Their wish was granted.

Later, 13 salatin who, though imprisoned for life and detained for some time in Agra jail, were also allowed to proceed to Rangoon where they were kept under surveillance with a monthly allowance of Rs. 10 per head for subsistence.

The trial of Bahadur Shah was a needless humiliation of the fallen monarch. There were many Englishmen who felt that his treatment did not redound to the credit of England. Mrs Muter remarks how on his way to the court room—which, incidentally, was the Diwan-i-Khas—the king could not have failed to notice two cleverly executed outlines in chalk on the wall of the recess which, in the days of his prosperity, the guard nearest his person had occupied. Both were so strikingly like the emperor's sharp aquiline face and attenuated form, that the words written beneath were unnecessary to convey to anyone who had seen him the meaning of the drawings: 'The King of Delhi as he is', was the caption of the first; the other represented Bahadur Shah hanging from a gibbet, and beneath it was written: 'The King of Delhi as he ought to be'. The tribunal addressed Bahadur Shah as *tum*, the common Hindostani 'thee' employed for those of rank lower than oneself.[14]

Siraj ud-Din Muhammad Bahadur Shah II died in Rangoon on 7 November 1862. With his death the Gurgani dynasty came to an end. The scores of salatin and princesses, their children, wives and dependents, who survived the holocaust disappeared into the anonymity of the *katras* and *koochas* (lanes and by-lanes) of Delhi like Motia Khan and Mori Gate. Some were reduced to manual labour, those who were lucky eked out a living as school teachers or craftsmen, while others were reduced to actual fakiri, or begging.

Mirza Ilahi Bakhsh survived as a gentleman of note. This prince, also known as Mirza Hidayat Afza, had played a crucial role in arranging the surrender of the emperor and his family to Captain Hodson. The great-great-grandson of Azim ush-Shan (the son of Shah Alam, Bahadur Shah I), he was also the father-in-law of Mirza Fakhr ud-Din, the eldest son of Bahadur Shah II. He was pro-British and remained in touch with the British army on the Ridge during the siege, and rendered them valuable service. Hereditary pensions aggregating Rs. 22,830 per annum were granted to him and his family. A small jagir comprising two villages in Rohtak was also gifted to him in perpetuity, and handsome compensation exceeding Rs. 1 lakh was awarded as compensation for property lost during 'the siege'.

He was accorded the leading place on the list of 'Provincial Darbaris' or courtiers, of the Delhi district, and recognized as the representative of the old royal house. Though the role played by him was analogous to that of the Duke of Orleans vis-a-vis the legitimate line, he was able to secure small pensions for forty princes and sixty females of the imperial house who were in indigent circumstances.[15]

Another prince, by the name of Firoz Shah, played a much more spirited role. His precise relationship with the emperor is uncertain, but Beale describes him as a son of Bahadur Shah. Some have thought he was a nephew, while from the wording of the Azamgarh proclamation issued in his name, Mahdi Hussain concludes that he was a grandson. At the time of the outbreak in 1857, Mirza Firoz was on a pilgrimage to Mecca. On his return he could very well have bided his time in Poona or Bombay until the storm blew over, but without any compulsion and entirely of his own volition he plunged into the struggle. Delhi had fallen, but undaunted, he headed towards Gwalior where he joined the Maratha partisan leader, Tantia Tope, and played an active part in the operations in central and eastern India. Tantia was eventually captured and hanged, but the prince managed to escape. There was a prize of Rs. 10,000 on his head, but he was never caught.

Nothing is known about the manner of his death. It was reported in 1864 that he had been seen in the Sironj jungles. He was reported from Kandahar in Afghanistan the following year, and the next year from Bokhara. Intelligence was received about his appearance at Samarkand and later at Istanbul. Some Arabs who visited Hyderabad in 1866 reported that he was in Arabia, living on the charity of rich merchants. Later, he was reported to have died in Mecca in 1877. It is also speculated that he escaped to Nepal like Begum Hazrat Mahal and many others, including probably also the Nana Sahib.[16]

Of all the princes of the Qila-i-Mualla, who rose to prominence in this first war for Indian independence, his is the most attractive figure. Here, one would have thought, we have all the ingredients of mystery and romance, the seed of a legend, potentially as powerful as that of Subhas Chandra Bose. But unlike the latter, poor Firoz is practically unknown today. Unknown, unhonoured and unsung.

NOTES

1. *Saunders Papers*, iii, 1, John Lawrence to Saunders (British Museum).
2. Mrs Dunbar Muter, *My Recollections of the Sepoy Revolt*, pp. 131-3.
3. C.F. Andrews, *Zaka Ullah of Delhi*, p. 74.
4. Wilberforce, *An Unrecorded Chapter of the Indian Mutiny*, p. 217.
5. Mrs Muter, p. 155.
6. Griffiths, *A Narrative of the Siege of Delhi*, pp. 237-8.
7. Spear, *A History of Delhi under the Later Mughals*, pp. 220-1.
8. Mrs Muter, pp. 145-6.
9. Ghalib, *Dastanbuy* (translated by K.A. Faruqi), p. 58.
10. Cave-Browne, *The Punjab and Delhi in 1857*, ii, pp. 235-6.
11. Ghalib, p. 19. Letter to Tufta, April 1861. Quoted by Faruqi in his preface to Dastanbuy.
12. Buckler, 'The Political Theory of the Indian Mutiny', *Transactions of the Royal Historical Society*, 4th Series, pp. 71 ff.
13. Roberts, *Forty one years in India*, i, p. 249.
14. Mrs Muter, p. 151. 'Tum' is the equivalent of the familiar 'thou', never used in polite conversation.
15. Griffin and Massy, *Chiefs and Families of Note in the Punjab*, i (1909 edn.), pp. 5-7.
16. S.N. Chanda, *1857: Some Untold Stories*, pp. 57-65. Beale, p. 138. Mahdi Hussain, *Bahadur Shah II*, pp. lxx-lx.

Glossary

Ahadi	A gentleman trooper. The ahadis were one of the household regiments.
Akbar	Victorious.
Alam	World, Universe; also a flag or banner.
Alamgir	World conqueror.
Ali shan	Sublime splendour.
Alqab	Titles, honorifics; sing, *luqab*.
Amil	A revenue collector.
Amir	A nobleman.
Arbab-i-tarab	Professional artistes, entertainers.
Asaf	Name of the minister of Solomon; hence signifying wisdom.
Ashraf	The gentle class.
Asharfi	A gold coin.
Asp	Horse.
Ataliq	Tutor, guide.
Aurangzeb	Ornament of the throne.
Azam	Superior.
Azim	Great, supreme.
Badmash	Bad character, who lives by crime.
Badshah	Ruler, emperor.
Bagh	Garden.
Bai	Suffix added to the names of Hindu ladies signifying respect; also associated with superior courtesans.
Bakhshi	Paymaster of a military body.
Bairagi	Order of Vaishnava sadhus.
Banda	Slave, servant.
Bania	A trading caste.
Bargir	Maratha cavalryman.
Begum	Honorific suffixed to a gentlewoman; also wife.
Bhishti	Water carrier.
Bibi, bibi ghar	Honorific attached to a gentlewoman, the latter signified the harem of an European gentleman.

Chaghtai	Descended from Chaghtai Khan, son of Chingiz Khan.
Chauth	A quarter.
Chela	Disciple, follower.
Chhatri	A cupola with open sides, also umbrella.
Chobdar	Mace-bearer, minor dignitary in a great man's house.
Chughata	Same as *Chaghtai*.
Dagh	Mark.
Dara	Darius in the English-speaking world.
Daulah	State, empire; a grade of the peerage.
Deccan, Deccani	Anglicisation of South, signifies peninsular India; a native of the Deccan, a Maratha.
Deohri	Main entrance to a house, opening on to a courtyard.
Desh	The Maratha homeland.
Dharna	A sit-down protest.
Din	The Faith.
Diwan	A collection of verse, an audience, a controller of finances.
Diwan khana	Audience chamber.
Diwan-i-Am	Hall of Public Audience.
Diwan-i-Khas	Hall of Private Audience.
Do	Two.
Fidwi	Faithful, equivalent of 'yours faithfully'.
Firoz	Victorious.
Faujdar	Administrator of a sarkar (i.e. district).
Gaddi	Cushion, signifying throne.
Gajnal	An elephant mounted swivel gun.
Garh	Stronghold, fort. Usually used as a suffix.
Ghazi	A warrior of the Faith.
Ghee	Clarified butter.
Gherao	To surround; a form of protest in which the person gheraoed is not allowed to move and is denied access to refreshment.
Gurgani	Another name for the Mughal house. Originally applied to all Chengezid families.
Haft	Seven.
Hakim	Doctor.
Haram sarai	Harem quarter.

Hasht	Eight.
Haveli	A large house, a nobleman's mansion.
Hazaar	Thousand.
Howdah	Seat carried on an elephant.
Huma	A mythical bird; a person blessed by it becomes a king.
Iqbal	Prestige, respect.
Istiqbal	Reception arrangements.
Jahan	The world.
Jalau khana	Place of splendour.
Jamadar	An inferior army officer.
Jang	War, battle.
Jat	An agriculturist tribe.
Jharokha	A window surrounded by a pierced screen.
Jezail	A matchlock of heavy bore usually requiring a rest.
Kahar-i-Khuda	Scourge of God.
Kalawant	A musician.
Kalima	The Muslim profession of faith.
Kalin	Carpet.
Kambalposh	Blanket clad.
Kanjar	A pimp; a tribe whose traditional occupation is prostitution.
Kastantuniya	An Arabic version for Constantinople.
Katar	A kind of Indian dagger.
Khaima	Tent.
Khana	House.
Khillat	Dress given on ceremonial occasions.
Khatri	A superior caste, usually educated, and often in government service.
Khalsa	Pure, Crown land, The Sikh Commonwealth.
Khanjar	Another kind of dagger.
Khanqah	Seat of a pir or saint, with an attached seminary.
Khwaja	An honorific prefixed to an eunuch.
Khawas	A confidential servant, a page; often a slave.
Kornish	A low bow made before royalty.
Langar	A free kitchen.
Luqab	A title; singular of alqab.
Madad-i-mash	A small subsistence grant.
Mahal	A revenue estate; also a palace.

Mahout	Elephant driver.
Maidan	Open field.
Malika	Queen.
Mansabdar	Rankholder; an officer.
Marusthal	Region of death; desert.
Masnad	A throne.
Memsahib	A lady; usually used for European women.
Mian	An honorific prefixed to eunuchs in great households.
Mirza	Prince, of noble blood; also at times an educated man.
Mohur	A gold coin.
Mualla	Exalted.
Mukhtar	Attorney.
Mulk	Country, state.
Murid	Disciple of a pir.
Murshid	Pir, a spiritual guide.
Mussamman	Octagonal.
Naga	An order of Shaivite sadhus, character military.
Naib	Deputy.
Nalbandi	A sum given to soldiers at the start of a campaign to enable them to make provision for their families.
Naggara	A massive kettledrum.
Nasaqchi	A military policeman.
Naubat	A band, a privilege of royalty and high nobility.
Nauroz	The Persian new year's day.
Nawab	Title of nobility, literally plural of *naib*.
Nazar	A ceremonial offering made by an inferior to a superior.
Nazim	A governor.
Nazir	A minor functionary, accountant.
Nikkah	The Muslim marriage ceremony.
Nizam	Administration.
Nusrat	Illustrious.
Omrah	Nobility, umara (more usual spelling).
Padishah	Emperor; also *Patishah*.
Palki	Palanquin.
Panah	Refuge.
Panj	Five.

Purdah	Curtain, veil.
Qanat	Canvas screen.
Qila	Fort.
Qizilbash	Turkish tribe from Khurassan; noted for their distinctive red hats.
Qutb	Fixed point, the Pole Star is the Qutbi Tara.
Rafi ur-Darjat	Bestower of honours.
Rafi ush-Shan	Bestower of splendour.
Rakhi	Protection, protection money.
Rissala	Regiment of cavalry.
Sabit	Proven.
Sahiban-i-Inglishia	The sublime English lords; an expression current in the last century.
Salatin	Plural of sultan; used for descendants of former emperors.
Sanad	Certificate, letters-patent.
Sani	Second.
Sarkar	Administrative unit, below a suba; a district; also government.
Saropa	A *khillat*; lit., head to foot.
Seer	A unit of weight.
Seh	Three.
Senapati	Army commander.
Shah, shahzada	King, prince.
Shahid	Martyr.
Shamshir	Scimitar.
Shaniwar	Saturday; Saturn's day.
Shesh	Six.
Shutar, shutarnal	Camel, camel borne swivel gun.
Sillahdar	Term used for a type of 'irregular' cavalry.
Sipahsalar	Persian equiv. of senapati, lit., commander of soldiers.
Singh	Lion; commonly suffixed to the names of Sikhs and Rajputs.
Tabla	A small percussion instrument used in chamber music.
Taj	Crown.
Takht, takhtposhi	Throne, enthronement.
Takkiah	Lit., pillow. Abode of a pir.
Tanpura	A string instrument.

Tara	Star.
Tasbih, tasbih khana	Rosary, chapel.
Tasleemat	Low bow accompanied with a salaam, as in a kornish.
Tasma	Leather thong or lace, the Turkish bowstring.
Tattoo	Mule.
Taus	Peacock.
Turan	Turkestan.
Umara	Nobility, pl. of amir.
Urdu	Military camp.
Urs	A gathering in honour of a pir marked by the singing of devotional songs.
Vakil, Vakil-i-Mutlaq	Attorney, representative; regent.
Validah	Mother.
Vilayat, vilayati	Lit., equiv. to a suba in the Ottoman empire; a foreign land, a foreigner.
Wara	A Maratha nobleman's house; equiv. to a haveli.
Wazarat	Office of Prime Minister.
Wazir	Prime Minister, *vizier*.
Yessawal	An armed mace-bearer.
Zamana	The age, the times.
Zamburak	A swivel gun.
Zari patka	Golden flag; emblem of the Peshwa.
Zulfiqar	The name of the sword of Ali the martyr. A coveted title among the Shi'ite umara.

Bibliography

CONTEMPORARY SOURCES

Abdul Karim Khan Kashmiri, *Bayan-i-Waqai*, MS, Khalsa College Library, Amritsar.

Abul Fazl, *Ain-i-Akbari* (3 vols), translated by Blochmann, 1938-48; rpt., Low Price Pub., Delhi.

Ali, Mrs. Meer Hassan, *Observations on the Mussalmans of India*, London, 1917; rpt., Deep Pub., Delhi, 1975.

Anon., *Tarikh-i-Ahmad Shahi*, MS, British Library (formerly India Office Library), London.

Anon., *Delhi Chronicle*, MS, British Library, London.

Anon., *Tarikh-i-Alamgir Sani*, MS, British Library, London.

Ansari, Muhammad Ali Khan, *Tarikh-i-Muzaffari*, MS, Oriental Public Library, Patna.

Ashob, *Tarikh-i-Shahadat-i-Farrukhsiyar*, MS, British Library, London.

Bihari Lal, *Ahwal-i-Nawab Najib ud-Daulah wa Ali Muhammad wa Donde Khan*, MS, Khalsa College Library, Amritsar.

Briggs, John, *Rise of the Muhammadan Power in India* (4 vols), a translation of Ferishta's *Gulshan-i-Ibrahimi*, London, 1829, rpt., Low Price Pub., Delhi, 1990.

Broughton, T.D., *Letters from a Maratha Camp*, Constable, London, 1892.

Browne, James (translator), *Ahwal-i-Jang-i-Bhau wa Ahmad Shah Durrani dar karzar-i-Sadashiv Bhau wa ahmad shah Abdali* by Kashiraj Pandit; Asiatic Researches, vol. III. Some portions translated by Sarkar appeared in *Indian Historical Quarterly*, June 1934.

Bhargava, K.D. (ed), *The Browne Correspondence*, National Archives, Delhi, 1960.

Calendar of Persian Correspondence, National Archives, Delhi. Volumes I, VI, VII, VIII, IX, X, XI, edited by various scholars have been published between 1911 and 1970. Volumes II-V still remain unpublished.

Cave-Browne, J., *The Punjab and Delhi in 1857* (2 vols), Blackwood, London, 1861; rpt., Punjab Languages Dept, Patiala, 1970.

Cooper, F., *Crisis in the Punjab,* London, 1858; rpt., Sameer Prakashan, Chandigarh, 1977.

Cunningham, J.D., *History of the Sikhs,* John Murray, London, 1849; rpt., S. Chand, Delhi, 1966.

Danishmand Khan, *Bahadur Shah Nama*, MS, British Library, London.

Dargah Quli Khan, *Muraqqa-i-Dehli*, translated by Chander Shekhar and S.M. Chinoy, Deputy Pub., Delhi 1989.

Delhi Residency and Agency Records, MS, Punjab State Archives, Patiala.

Eden, Emily, *Up the Country* (2 vols), London, 1866; rpt., Virago, London, 1983.

Elliot, H.M. and J. Dowson, *The History of India as told by its own Historians* (7 vols), London, 1867-77; rpt., Low Price Pub., Delhi, 1990.

Fane, Sir H., *Five Years in India* (2 vols); rpt., Punjab Languages Dept, Patiala, 1970.

Forrest, G.W., *History of the Indian Mutiny* (3 vols), William Blackwood, Edinburgh, 1904.

Francklin, W., *History of the Reign of Shah Aulum*, London, 1794; rpt., Classical Pub., Delhi, 1979.

Fraser, James, *The History of Nadir Shah*, London, 1742.

Ghalib, Mirza, *Dastanbuy*, tranlated by K.A. Faruqi, Asia Pub., Bombay, 1970.

Ghulam Ali, *Muqqadamah-i-Shah Alam Namah*, Calcutta, 1912-14.

Griffiths, C.J., *A Narrative of the Siege of Delhi*, John Murray, London, 1910.

Hanway, Jonas, *An Historical account of the British Trade over the Caspian . . . with the particular History of the great Usurper Nadir Kouli* (4 vols), London, 1753.

Harcharan Das, *Chahar Gulzar-i-Shujai*, MS, British Library, London; Khalsa College Library, Amritsar.

Heber, Bishop Reginald, *Narrative of a Journey*, J. Murray, London, 1828; rpt., Low Price Pub., Delhi, 1993.

Iradat Khan, *Tarikh-i-Iradat Khan*, translated by Jonathan Scott and printed as vol. II of his *History of the Dekhan.*

Kamraj, *Ibratnama*, MS, India Office Library, London.

Kamwar Khan, *Tazkirat us-Salatin Chughataiya*, MS, Aligarh Muslim University Library, Aligarh.

Kaye, John and G.B. Malleson, *History of the Indian Mutiny* (6 vols), W.H. Allen, London, 1888-9.

Khafi Khan, *Muntakhab ul-Lubab* (2 vols), Bibliotheca India, Calcutta, 1874.

Khairuddin, Muhammad, *Ibrat Nama*, MS, Oriental Public Library, Patna, and Khalsa College Library, Amritsar.

Khare, G.H. (ed.), *Hingane Daftar* (2 vols), Bharat Itihas Samshodhak Mandal, Poona, 1945.

Khushal Chand, *Tarikh-i-Muhammad Shahi*, MS, British Library, London.

Madec, Rene, *Memoire*, MS, British Library, London.

Malcolm, John, *History of Persia* (2 vols), London, 1815.

———, *A Memoir of Central India* (2 vols), Parbury, Allen & Co., London, 1832.

Majumdar, J.K. (ed), *Raja Rammohun Roy and the Last of the Mughals*, rpt., Anmol, Delhi, 1987.

Malleson, G.B., *The Mutiny of the Bengal Army* (2 vols), London, 1857-8.

Manucci, Niccolo, *Storio do Mogor* (4 vols), tr. W. Irvine, John Murray, London, 1907-8; rpt., Low Price Pub., 1990.

Metcalfe, C.T. (ed), *Two Native Narratives of the Mutiny in Delhi*, Constable, London, 1898; rpt., Seema, Delhi, 1974.

Mills, James and H.H. Wilson, *History of British India* (10 vols), James Madden, London, 1848.

Mirza Mahdi, *Tarikh-i-Jahankusha-i-Nadiri*, Bombay, 1849.

Miskin, Tahmasp Khan, *Tahmasp Nama*, abridged and translated by Setu Madhava Rao, Popular Prakashan, Bombay, 1967.

———, *Tahmasp Namah*, MS, British Library, London; rotograph of same in Khalsa College Library, Amritsar.

Muhammad Qasim Aurangabadi, *Ahwal ul-Khawaqin*, MS, British Library, London.

Mukhlis, Anandram, *Tazkirah*, MS, Aligarh Muslim University Library, Aligarh.

Munna Lal, *Tarikh-i-Shah Alam*, MS, Oriental Public Library, Patna.

Mustajib Khan, *Gulistan-i-Rahmat*, MS, Khalsa College Library, Amritsar; translated by C. Elliot, Oriental Translation Fund, London, 1831.

Muter, Mrs Dunbar, *My Recollections of the Sepoy Revolt*, London, 1911.

Orme, Robert, *Military Transactions of the British Nation in Indostan* (3 vols), Wingrave, London, 1803.

Parks, Fanny, *Wanderings of a Pilgrim* (2 vols), Pelham Richardson, London, 1850.

Polier, *Shah Alam II and his Court*, S.C. Sarkar, Calcutta, 1947.

Parasnis, D.B. (ed), *Dilli-yethil-Marathyanchin Raj-Karenen* (2 vols), Itihas Sangraha, Bombay, 1913.

———, *Brahmendra Swami Charitra*, Itihas Sangraha, Bombay, 1903.

Rajwade et al. (eds), *Marathachi Itihasachen Sadhanen* (21 vols), Govt. Central Press, Bombay.

Roberts, Lord, *Forty-One Years in India* (2 vols), Bentley & Sons, London, 1897.

Rotton, J.E.W., *The Chaplain's Narrative of the Siege of Delhi*, London, 1858.

Russel, W.H., *My Diary in India* (2 vols), London, 1860.

Rustam Ali Shahabadi, *Tarikh-i-Hindi*, MS, British Library, London.

Santokh Singh, *Sri Gurpratap Suraj*, Bhai Vir Singh Sahitya Sadan, Delhi, 1965.

Sardesai, G.S. (ed), *Selections from the Peshwa Daftar* (45 vols), Govt. Central Press, Bombay.

———, *Historical Papers of the Sindhias of Gwalior*, Satara Historical Society, Satara.

Sarkar, Jadunath (ed), *Mahadji Sindhia & North Indian Affairs* (Poona Residency Correspondence), Govt. Central Press, Bombay, 1936.

Sarkar, Jadunath (translator), *Life of Najibuddaulah* by Bihari Lal, *Indian Historical Quarterly*, 1935.

———, *Journal du Voyage du Bengale a Dehly* by Comte de Modave, *Bengal Past and Present*, 1936.

Saunder's Papers, European Manuscripts; India Office Records, British Library, London.

Shah Nawaz Khan and Muhammad Haiyy, *Maathir ul-Umara* (3 vols); translated by Beveridge and Beni Prashad, Janaki Prakashan, Delhi.

Shakir Khan, *Tazkira-i-Shakir Khan*, MS, British Library, London.

Shiv Das, *Munawwar ul-Kalam, Halat-i-Sultanat-i-Farrukhsiyar wa Muhammad Shah*, MS, British Library, London; Central Public Library, Patiala.

Sleeman, W.H., *Rambles and Recollections of an Indian Official* (2 vols), Hatchard, London, 1844; rpt., AES, Delhi, 1995.

Tabatabai, Seid Ghulam Hussain Khan, *The Seir Mutaqherin* (4 vols), translated by Raymond ('Haji Mustapha'), 1789; rpt., Low Price Pub., Delhi, 1990.

Tod, *Annals and Antiquities of Rajasthan* (2 vols), Smith, Elder and Co., London, 1829-32; rpt., KMN Pub., Delhi, 1971.

Valentia, George, Viscount, *Voyages and Travels* (4 vols), London, 1811; rpt., AES, Delhi, 1994.

Valentyn, F., *Oud en Niew Oost-Indien*; Dordrecht and Amsterdam, 1724-6.

Warid, *Mirat-i-Waridat*, MS, Khalsa College Library, Amritsar.

Warren Hastings Correspondence (with Jonathan Scott), Additional Manuscripts; British Library, London.

Wilberforce, R.G., *An Unrecorded Chapter of the Mutiny*, John Murray, London, 1894; rpt., Academic Press, Gurgaon, 1976.

Yadav, K.C. (ed), *Delhi in 1857: The Trial of Bahadur Shah* (3 vols), Academic Press, Gurgaon, 1980.

Yahya Khan, *Tazkirat ul-Mulk*, MS, British Library, London; rotograph in AMU, Aligarh.

LATER WORKS

Andrews, C.F., *Zaka Ullah of Delhi*, W. Heffer and Sons, Cambridge, 1928.

Bannerjee, A.C. and D.K. Ghose (eds), *A Comprehensive History of India*, vol. IX, People's Publishing, Delhi, 1978.

Barnett, Richard B., *North India between Empires*, Manohar, Delhi, 1987.

Beale, T.W., *An Oriental Dictionary*, London, 1894; rpt., Manohar, Delhi, 1971.

Dalrymple, William, *City of Djinns*, Flamingo, London, 1993.

Edwardes and H.L.O. Garret, *Mughal Rule in India*, S. Chand, Delhi, 1956.

Festing, Gabrielle, *Strangers Within the Gates*, William Blackwood, Edinburgh, 1914.

Ganda Singh, *Ahmad Shah Durrani*, Asia Pub., Bombay, 1959.

———, *Banda Singh Bahadur*, Amritsar, 1935.

Grey, C. and H.L.O. Garret, *European Adventurers in Northern India*, Lahore, 1929; rpt., Punjab Languages Dept, Patiala, 1970.

Griffin, L.H. and C.F. Massy, *Chiefs and Families of Note of the Punjab* (2 vols), Civil & Military Gazette Press, Lahore, 1909.

Gupta, H.R., *A History of the Sikhs* (3 vols), Minerva Book Shop, Simla, 1952.

Hamilton, W., *East India Gazetteer* (2 vols), London, 1828; rpt., Low Price Pub., Delhi, 1993.

Hansen, Waldemar, *The Peacock Throne*, Motilal Banarsidas, Delhi, 1981.

Hibbert, Christopher, *The Great Mutiny*, Allen Lane, London, 1978.

Hussain, Mahdi, *Bahadur Shah II*, MN Pub., Delhi, 1987.

Irvine, William, *Later Mughals* (2 vols), Calcutta, 1922; rpt., Oriental, Delhi, 1971.

Kaul, H.K., *Historical Delhi*, OUP, Delhi, 1985.

Keene, H.G., *Fall of the Mughal Empire*, London, 1876.

———, *India under the Free Lances*, Brown, Langham, London, 1907.

Khurshidul Islam and Ralph Russel, *Three Mughal Poets*, OUP, Delhi, 1994.

Lockhart, *Nadir Shah*, Luzac & Co., London, 1938.

Mujeeb, M., *The Indian Muslims*, George Allen & Unwin, London, 1967.

Muni Lal, *Mini Mughals*, Konark, Delhi, 1989.

Natwar Singh, *Maharaja Suraj Mall*, BI Pub., Delhi, 1981.

Nigam, N.K., *Delhi in 1857*, S. Chand, Delhi, 1957.

Qureshi, I.H., *The Administration of the Mughal Empire*, Low Price Pub., Delhi, 1990.

Raghubir Sinh, *Malwa in Transition*, Bombay, 1936.

Sardesai, G.S. (ed), *Historical Papers of the Sindhias of Gwalior* (2 vols), Satara Historical Society, Satara, 1934.

Sardesai, G.S., *A New History of the Marathas* (3 vols), Phoenix Pub., Bombay, 1946-8.

Sarkar, Sir Jadunath, *History of Aurangzeb* (5 vols), Longmans, London, 1912-24.

———, *Fall of the Mughal Empire* (4 vols), M.C. Sarkar, Calcutta, 1932-50; rpt., Orient Longmans, Delhi, 1991. References to volume I are from the 1932 edition; references from later volumes are from the 1991 edition.

Sen, Surendranath, *Eighteen Fifty-Seven*, Publications Div., Delhi, 1957.

Spear, Percival, *A History of Delhi under the Later Mughals*, Low Price Pub., Delhi, 1990; earlier appeared as *Twilight of the Mughals*, OUP, Cambridge, 1951.

Taylor, P.J.O., *Chronicles of the Mutiny*, Indus, Delhi, 1992.

Varma, Pavan, *Ghalib*, Penguin, Delhi, 1989.

Woodruff, Philip, *Men Who Ruled India* (2 vols), Jonathan Cape, London, 1953.

Index